CONSTITUTIONAL LAW FOR POLICE

Third Edition

By

JOHN C. KLOTTER, B.A., J.D.
PROFESSOR AND DEAN
SCHOOL OF POLICE ADMINISTRATION, UNIVERSITY OF LOUISVILLE

AND

JACQUELINE R. KANOVITZ, B.A., J.D.
PROFESSOR OF LAW, UNIVERSITY OF LOUISVILLE

 anderson publishing co./cincinnati

Publisher's Staff Editor
Carol Niehaus

PREFACE

The year 1789 has tremendous historical significance for most Americans. From grammar school forward, we are taught that 1789 was the year in which our Constitution was *finally completed* and assumed its position as the supreme law of the land. Few bother to question the truth of their learning. This historical association is correct only in a limited sense. Certainly the foundations of our government were laid in this year. But the words which emerged from the Philadelphia Convention, and which form the text of what we conveniently and through force of habit refer to as "the Constitution of the United States," were never designed to interpret themselves. In the separation of powers, this task was delegated to the courts. The meaning which the courts attach to the constitutional language, particularly the Supreme Court, is as much a part of the "Constitution" as the ink contained within the four corners of the original document. In the broadest sense, the "United States Constitution" is still not completed nor will it be so long as the Republic stands.

In 1969, Chief Justice Earl Warren retired from the Supreme Court bench, ending a career that spanned sixteen years. The Warren Court era was a period unprecedented in American history in its concern for individual rights, particularly in the area of criminal justice. There are few educated Americans who have not heard of *Mapp* v. *Ohio*,[1] *Miranda* v. *Arizona*,[2] and at least a half-dozen other major milestones in constitutional history dating from the Warren Court era. The Supreme Court under Chief Justice Earl Warren dedicated itself assiduously to the task of "reforming" the criminal justice system. For many Americans, however, and particularly for those engaged in law enforcement professions, the Warren Court's crusade for the rights of the criminally accused reflected an ivory tower philosophy, far removed from the arena of life's practical experience.

With Mr. Chief Justice Warren's retirement and the departure from the bench of several other stalwarts from his era, the Supreme Court today has taken on a new complexion. We are now witnessing a period of constitutional consolida-

[1] 367 U.S. 643, 6 L.Ed.(2d) 1081, 81 S.Ct. 1684 (1961).
[2] 384 U.S. 436, 16 L.Ed(2d) 694, 86 S.Ct. 1602 (1966).

tion and, in some instances, retrenchment. Can we look to the Burger Court to roll the criminal justice scene back to the pre-Warren era? The answer is: "not likely." Opposing the force in favor of discarding old rules and doctrines which, tested by experience, are unsatisfactory, is the interest in stability and orderly legal development. Justice Cardozo once remarked, concerning the nature of the judicial process, that "the labor of judges would be increased almost to a breaking point if every past decision could be reopened in every case, and one could not lay one's own course of bricks on the secure foundation of the courses laid by others who had gone on before him." [3]

Responsible jurists do not lightly overturn the work of their predecessors. The compelling force of precedent is particularly strong in constitutional litigation. The American public would properly lose all respect both for the Constitution and the Supreme Court, should the Court announce that the Constitution means one thing today and something entirely different tomorrow. If a major constitutional upheaval is unlikely, what, then, can we expect from the Burger Court in the criminal justice field?

During the past five years, there have been some significant changes, but the changes have come about in large measure through a gradual erosion process—distinguishing past cases or confining them to their facts—rather than forthrightly overruling them. We can expect this trend to continue.

When our first edition was published a decade ago, we pledged to keep our book current through periodic supplements and frequent new editions. In no area of law enforcement is the most current information more critical. We will continue to fulfill this pledge.

Where this book is used as a text, it is strongly recommended that the student be required to brief the cases in Part II as well as any additional cases which the instructor decides are of current importance. The law is constantly changing and the necessity of keeping up-to-date can be accomplished only by a reading of the latest pronouncement.

Louisville, Kentucky   John C. Klotter

August, 1977   Jacqueline R. Kanovitz

---

[3] B. Cardozo, THE NATURE OF THE JUDICIAL PROCESS 149 (1921).

PREFACE TO FIRST EDITION

> Decency, security, and liberty alike demand that governmental officials shall be subjected to the same rules of conduct that are commands to the citizen. In a government of laws, existence of the government will be imperiled if it fails to observe the law scrupulously. Our government is the potent, the omnipresent teacher. For good or for ill, it teaches the whole people by its example. Crime is contagious. If the government becomes a lawbreaker, it breeds contempt for the law; it invites every man to become a law unto himself; it invites anarchy. To declare that in the administration of the criminal law the end justifies the means—to declare that the government may commit crimes in order to secure the conviction of a private criminal— would bring terrible retribution. Against that pernicious doctrine this court should resolutely set its face.

This philosophy, that government agents should be subjected to certain restrictions in enforcing laws was summarized by Supreme Court Justice Louis D. Brandeis in the case of *Olmstead* v. *United States.*[1]

Today, more than ever before, those who have been entrusted with the challenging but rewarding responsibility of protecting life and property must thoroughly understand the principles of state and federal constitutions and the duties which flow from their application.

The constitutions of the original thirteen states were written during a period in history when the people were keenly aware of their rights and of the possibility that a strong government might deprive them of these rights. The Constitution of the United States, which was written only a few years after the Declaration of Independence, was framed by men who had lived during a period of strict control and later during a period of too little control. As a result it was the intention of these dedicated men that the new government established under the United States Constitution protect both the rights of the individual and the rights of society.

One abiding principle which has endured since the adop-

[1] 277 U.S. 438, 72 L.Ed. 944, 48 S.Ct 564 (1928).

v

tion of the Constitution and the Bill of Rights is that which recognizes the dignity and worth of the individual human being. Even those who have violated the codes of civilized human behavior are entitled to certain minimum protections.

While maintaining a system which assures adequate respect for the rights and dignity of those charged with crime is a fundamental goal of our society, it is certainly not the only goal. Those who do not violate the law, the great majority, the producers, also have rights. They have the right to use the streets of this nation free from the fear of bodily harm, the right to protection from the rapist, the thief, and even from automobile drivers who operate their vehicles without regard for the lives and safety of others. And perhaps most of all society has the right to establish reasonable procedures to solve the crime problems. There are some who feel that the Supreme Court has erred too much on the side of the lawbreaker and has made the task of enforcement impossible. It is not the purpose of this book either to praise or condemn the Court for its record in recent years. In an area of enforcement where certainty is vital, it is more important that the dictates of the law be understood than that consensus be reached as to the wisdom or necessity of an announced rule.

In preparing this book the authors have emphasized the provisions of the Constitution which directly relate to the powers of both federal and state law enforcement officers and prosecutors and limitations on these officers. Inasmuch as the constitutional provisions draw their meaning from judicial interpretation, selected cases have been included along with the textual analysis.

The synthesis of constitutional decisions is not a mechanical process. Inescapably some degree of interpretation is involved. The authors have not always agreed on the interpretations to be given the court decisions nor on the extent to which these court rulings should be projected. They consider this diversity in views prevents a "one-sided" interpretation of the law and provides a stimulus which should be utilized by the instructor where the book is employed as a text. While there has been a great deal of consultation and mutual interchange of ideas, in the interest of intellectual integrity, the

authors have documented the chapters for which each assumes
primary responsibility.

Chapter 1 of Part I deals with the development of the
Federal Constitution and the history of the Bill of Rights. The
remaining chapters in Part I discuss in depth the substantive
content of the first eight Amendments and corresponding state
provisions with emphasis on recent court interpretations and
trends. These are of primary concern to police agencies and
prosecutors.

In Part II of the book leading decisions handed down by
the Supreme Court have been included in order to give the
reader an understanding not only of what the law says but
of the processes used by the Court in reaching its conclusions.
The cases are included in Part II rather than immediately
following the related discussions because many of them have
broader application than the subject matter of any one chapter. The decisions should be studied carefully by the student
or reader in order to develop a richer understanding of the
policies and reasons underlying the rules which have been
devised by the courts.

The book is prepared primarily for those who are engaged
in the immense task of enforcing the criminal laws of the
fifty states and of the United States. No effort has been made
to use the local laws of any particular jurisdiction. Therefore,
it is necessary and even imperative that the student familiar-
ize himself with the constitutional, statutory and decisional
law of his own state.

The trend has been toward an ever increasing uniformity
in state and federal laws in the area of criminal procedure.
This is attributable in part to the voluntary adoption of uniform standards by state legislators and judges, but mostly
to the force of Supreme Court interpretation. Insofar as there
are differences between local laws and the rules announced
by the Supreme Court, it bears repeated mention that the
Federal Constitution as construed by the highest tribunal in
the land takes precedence over any conflicting state constitutional or statutory provisions. In other words, the Federal
Constitution establishes the minimum protection which the
states can and must afford to their citizens. Beyond this, how-

ever, the states are at liberty to formulate stricter requirements by legislative action or court decision.

Where this book is used as a text it is strongly recommended that the student be required to brief the cases in Part II as well as any additional cases which the instructor feels are of current importance. The law is constantly changing and the necessity of keeping up-to-date can be accomplished only by a reading of the latest pronouncements.

We express our sincere gratitude to Professor David A. McCandless, Director of the Southern Police Institute; to Professor Lawrence W. Knowles, Professor of Constitutional Law at the University of Louisville Law School; and to Mrs. Pearl W. Von Allmen, Librarian, University of Louisville Law School for their valuable assistance in preparing the manuscript.

Louisville, Kentucky   John C. Klotter
October, 1967   Jacqueline R. Kanovitz

CONTENTS

PART I:

AN ANALYSIS OF CONSTITUTIONAL PROVISIONS AND COURT DECISIONS

Chapter 1: HISTORY AND GENERAL APPLICATION OF THE CONSTITUTIONAL PROVISIONS

Chapter 2: SPEECH, PRESS AND ASSEMBLY

Chapter 3: AUTHORITY TO DETAIN AND ARREST

Chapter 4: SEARCH AND SEIZURE

Chapter 5: WIRETAPPING AND EAVESDROPPING

I. WIRETAPPING HISTORY

Chapter 6: INTERROGATIONS AND CONFESSIONS

Chapter 7: SELF-INCRIMINATION AND RELATED ISSUES

Chapter 8: ASSISTANCE OF COUNSEL

Chapter 9: DOUBLE JEOPARDY

Chapter 10: THE RIGHT TO A FAIR TRIAL AND HUMANE PUNISHMENT

Chapter 11: CIVIL RIGHTS AND CIVIL RIGHTS LEGISLATION

PART II:

JUDICIAL DECISIONS RELATING TO PART I

PART III:

APPENDIX

Chapter 1

HISTORY AND GENERAL APPLICATION OF THE CONSTITUTIONAL PROVISIONS*

We the People of the United States, in Order to form a more perfect Union, establish Justice, insure domestic Tranquility, provide for the common defence, promote the general Welfare, and secure the Blessings of Liberty to ourselves and our Posterity, do ordain and establish this Constitution for the United States of America.

PREAMBLE TO THE UNITED STATES CONSTITUTION

§ 1.1 Foundations of American constitutional government

The men who met in Philadelphia in 1787 had ample precedent for the establishment of a written constitution. Americans had been living under colonial charters for over a hundred years. When ties with England were severed in 1776, the Continental Congress had issued a resolution recom-

* by John C. Klotter

1

mending that the thirteen colonies adopt constitutions in preparation for statehood. New Hampshire was first to respond to the call on January 5, 1776.[1] By 1779, all thirteen of the former colonies had framed local constitutions. These early documents drew heavily from the colonial institutions of government and from English political traditions. Nearly all of the original state constitutions provided for bicameral legislatures which would be responsible for selecting the governor. This pattern closely resembled the English parliamentary system.

§ 1.2 —Early steps toward national unity

The federal union, consummated by the adoption of the Constitution in 1788–89, was not the first attempt at alliance between the colonies. As early as 1643, an alliance called the New England Confederacy had been formed between the four colonies of Massachusetts, New Plymouth, Connecticut and New Haven for their mutual defense against the Dutch and the Indians. Because the colonists were reluctant from the outset to confer sovereign powers on a central government, the delegation was a gradual process.

The Revolutionary War provided the first real impetus for unity. Coordination of the war effort required something more than thirteen independent nations fighting separately for a common goal. When the First Continental Congress assembled in Philadelphia in 1774, all of the colonies except Georgia sent delegates.[2] Americans, however, were not yet ready to give their irrevocable and permanent allegiance to a new central governing body. They were throwing off the yoke of an oppressive monarch and were jealous of their independence. Consequently, the powers given to the Continental Congress were only those that were strictly necessary for the immediate purpose of winning the war. The states retained their sovereignty and the Continental Congress functioned purely in a representative capacity as the agent of the several states.

---

[1] Eriksson, American Constitutional History, ch. 7 (1933).

[2] Evans, Cases on Constitutional Law, ch. 1 (1933).

§ 1.3   Articles of Confederation

It soon became apparent that a stronger central government was necessary in order to carry on the war and conduct the common affairs of the nation. A committee was appointed in 1776 to study the problem and to draw up articles of union. This committee wrote the Articles of Confederation which were adopted and became effective in March, 1781. While the Articles of Confederation set up a national government, its powers over domestic affairs were so limited that the new government was doomed to fail even before its short career was launched. Fearing a strong central government, the states refused to give the newly formed Congress the vital powers to levy taxes, regulate commerce or enforce its laws.[3] The Union established under the Articles of Confederation was nothing more than a loosely joined league of sovereign and independent states. The chief function of the national government was to represent the league of states in foreign affairs. It possessed no authority to pass laws affecting private citizens at home.

After the War of Independence was won and the colonists obtained the liberty they were struggling for, they found that the government, which they had so hastily set up, was not workable. The period immediately following the war was one of too little political control rather than too much. Fortunately, the leaders of this period were capable men who were able to work out a solution to the problem without further bloodshed, or without a dictatorship, which often follows a revolution.

§ 1.4   Drafting the Constitution of the United States

In February of 1787, the Congress, established under the Articles of Confederation, adopted a resolution recommending the calling of a convention to revise the Articles of Confederation. On May 25, 1787, the delegates assembled in Philadelphia and made George Washington their unanimous choice for president. Fifty-five delegates, representing all of the states except Rhode Island, attended during the session, which lasted nearly four months.

---

[3] Eriksson, *supra* note 1.

The most immediate question to be decided by the convention was whether the Articles of Confederation could be salvaged or whether the delegates should begin anew. It was James Madison's proposal to incorporate the best feature of the Articles of Confederation—its provision for the *separation of power* into three branches of government—into the new Constitution. After much debate and compromise on such issues as the amount and kind of power that should be granted to the central government, the basis for representation in the national Congress, and the relation of the nation to the states, the convention submitted a finished document which bore very little resemblance to the instrument which they had been called upon to "revise." The new Constitution conferred a vast range of new powers on all branches of the central government and provided for corresponding limitations on the powers of the states.

This draft of a constitution proposed to give to the three million people and their descendants the framework for a legal and political system which would insure freedom and independence. Never before had a people been given such an opportunity for individual and collective development.

§ 1.5   —Ratification by the states

Although much effort went into preparing the proposed Constitution, the important task still remained. When the Congress called for a convention in February, 1787, the members did not anticipate drafting a new constitution; however, when the draft was submitted, the Congress neither approved nor disapproved it but, instead, passed it on to the state legislatures. After much debate, the state legislatures submitted the document to state conventions (as recommended by the Constitutional Convention) with a proviso that if nine states ratified this new Constitution, it would supersede the Articles of Confederation.

Many people bitterly opposed the adoption of the Constitution, while others argued that only by adopting it could the states work together toward a common goal. James Madison, Alexander Hamilton and John Jay undertook the task of selling the new Constitution to the people. In their famous *The*

Federalist papers, the authors urged the need for a strong national government to provide for political stability and national security. Their opponents argued that (1) the taxing powers of Congress were too great, (2) the Constitution lacked procedural safeguards which would insure an impartial trial, (3) the Constitution contained no Bill of Rights, and (4) excessive power was concentrated in the central government, with the result that the individual states would be swallowed up and lose their sovereignty.

On September 28, 1787, the Constitution was submitted to the people by way of state conventions, but it did not receive the necessary nine-state ratification until June 21, 1788, when New Hampshire ratified it. This was sufficient to make the Constitution operative for those nine states. However, the advocates of the Constitution were aware that in order to have a workable government, the states of New York and Virginia —neither of which had ratified the Constitution—must be included in the new Union. Finally, on June 25, 1788, by a margin of ten votes in a convention of 168 members, Virginia (number ten) ratified the Constitution over the objection of such delegates as George Mason and Patrick Henry. On July 2, 1788, the president of the Confederation of Congress announced that the new instrument of government had been duly ratified. New York (eleven) ratified the Constitution on July 26, 1788.

It is interesting to note that North Carolina (twelve) did not ratify the Constitution until November 21, 1789; nor did Rhode Island (thirteen) until May 29, 1790.[4] These two states existed as sovereign states outside of the Union for many months. One of the events that encouraged them to become a part of the United States was the passage by Congress of a tariff on foreign imports including those imported from North Carolina and Rhode Island.

[4] The dates that the individual states ratified the Constitution are as follows: Delaware—December 7, 1787; Pennsylvania—December 11, 1787; New Jersey—December 18, 1787; Georgia—January 2, 1788; Connecticut—January 9, 1788; Massachusetts February 6, 1788; Maryland—April 26, 1788; South Carolina—May 23, 1788; New Hampshire—June 21, 1788; Virginia—June 25, 1788; New York—July 26, 1788; North Carolina —November 21, 1789; Rhode Island— May 29, 1790.

On September 13, 1788, after the two additional states of New York and Virginia had ratified the Constitution, the Continental Congress, which was meeting irregularly, passed a resolution to put the new Constitution into operation. The first Wednesday of January, 1789, was set as the date for choosing presidential electors, the first Wednesday of February for the meeting of electors, and the first Wednesday of March for the opening session of the new Congress. Because of several delays, Congress was late in assembling, and it was not until April 30, 1789, that George Washington was inaugurated as the first president of the United States.[5] Thus, within a period of twenty-five years, two major victories had occurred—the War of Independence was won and a firm and stable government was established for the thirteen states.

§ 1.6   Structure of the Constitution

The United States Constitution as drafted was a relatively brief document and was not expected to cover every point that might arise in the future. The original document is divided into seven parts or articles.[6]

ARTICLE I. The first article of the Constitution sets out the structure and functions of Congress. It provides that the legislative powers of the United States shall be vested in Congress, which shall consist of two chambers—the Senate and the House of Representatives. Sections 2 through 7 of this article provide for the number of representatives in each chamber, the qualifications for membership, the methods of selecting such members, the procedures to be followed in enacting legislation, and the manner of impeachment. Section 8 outlines the powers of Congress in domestic and foreign affairs; sections 9 and 10 deal with specific limitations on the powers of Congress and the states.

ARTICLE II. The second article sets up the executive branch of government. It provides that the executive powers of the

---

[5] THE CONSTITUTION OF THE UNITED STATES OF AMERICA, ANALYSIS AND INTERPRETATION, U.S. Government Printing Office, 1964.

[6] The Constitution is reprinted in Part III of this book. It should be studied carefully for a more complete understanding of its contents.

United States shall be vested in the president. The remainder of this article deals with the qualifications of the president and vice president, the manner of election, the oath of office, the method and grounds for removal, and the powers and duties of the chief executive.

ARTICLE III. The third article vests the judicial power of the United States in the Supreme Court and in such inferior courts as Congress should see fit to establish. It defines in general terms the scope of the judicial power and outlines those cases in which the Supreme Court is to have original and appellate jurisdiction. The third article also contains a definition of treason and the requirements for a conviction.

ARTICLE IV. The fourth article spells out some of the duties which the states owe to each other, including the duties of extending full faith and credit to the laws of sister states, of granting equal privileges and immunities to citizens of other states, and of interstate extradition. This article also contains provisions for the admission of new states, grants Congress plenary power to govern territorial possessions of the United States, and assures each state a republican form of government. Finally, it guarantees the states protection against external invasion, as well as federal assistance in quelling internal violence and uprising.

ARTICLE V. The fifth article defines two procedures for amending the Constitution. First, it may be amended when two-thirds of both Houses shall propose amendments and these proposed amendments are ratified by the state legislatures of three-fourths of the states or by state conventions in three-fourths of the states. Second, the Constitution may be amended when, by the application of the legislatures of two-thirds of the states, Congress shall call a convention for proposing amendments which shall be valid when ratified by the legislatures of three-fourths of the states or, by conventions in three-fourths of the states.

ARTICLE VI. The sixth article contains the "supremacy" clause which provides that the Constitution, laws and treaties of the United States shall be the supreme law of the land and that state judges are to be bound by it regardless of what their state constitutions and laws provide to the contrary. It also provides that all legislative, executive and judicial officers, both of the United States and of the several states, must take an oath of office to support the Constitution.

ARTICLE VII. The seventh article is of historic importance only. This article provides that the Constitution shall become effective when ratified by nine states and shall be operative for those states which ratify it.

The first three divisions of the Constitution are commonly referred to as the *"separation of powers"* articles because they separate the essential powers of the national government into three coordinate branches—legislative, executive and judicial. One of the reasons why this great document has proven workable for almost two hundred years is that the governmental powers have been diversified so that too much power is not given to any one branch of government. The division of power among the three branches of government has, at least up to the present time, prevented the development of an autocracy which might result in a dictatorship.

§ 1.7   Nature of the federal union

In order to appreciate the nature and problems of the state-federal government in the United States, it is necessary to review the history of the American colonists' relationships with England and the events which led to the Constitution. For many years prior to the Declaration of Independence in 1776, a controversy existed regarding the sovereign powers of the colonies. The individuals who drafted the Declaration did not recognize the parliament of Great Britain as having any sovereign authority over the states.[7]

After the Declaration of Independence, sovereignty resided in each of the several states. Each state had its own constitution and each functioned as an autonomous local unit. Even under the Articles of Confederation, the states retained their sov-

[7] Bennett, AMERICAN THEORIES OF FEDERALISM, University of Alabama Press, 1963.

ereignty. As a necessary condition to formulation of a federal union, however, the new states yielded a portion of their sovereign powers to the planned national or federal government which was created by the Constitution.

There was no precedent for the dual (state-federal) system of government which the Americans established in 1789. Consequently, it remained for the subsequent course of history to define and re-define the precise nature of the federal union and the relationship between the nation and the states. The original understanding was that the federal government was to be one of enumerated or delegated powers, and that all powers not expressly delegated to it were reserved to the states. In other words, the federal government was said to possess only such powers as were expressly granted to it by the states. Those powers not delegated remained in the states, where they originally resided, or were retained by the people. Once a state had joined the Union and had ceded a portion of its sovereignty, the relationship would be permanent.[8] The Civil War put to the test whether a state could disassociate itself by its own voluntary act of secession. The indestructible nature of the federal union was reaffirmed on the battlefields.

§ 1.8 Powers granted to the federal government

The enumerated powers granted to the federal government are found primarily in article I, section 8 of the Constitution. Although the powers are stated specifically and succinctly in these clauses, their interpretation has been a matter of debate for almost two centuries. The remainder of this section will be devoted to a discussion of those powers, with emphasis on those which are most important in the criminal justice process.

a. *The power to lay and collect taxes, duties, imposts and excises, and the power to provide for the common defense and general welfare.*

The power to tax is essential to the existence of a strong government. Without a source of revenue, no government can survive. One of the chief shortcomings of the government

[8] Texas v. White, 74 US(7 Wall) 700, 19 LEd 227 (1868).

established under the Articles of Confederation was the lack of independent financial powers.

The power to tax is also the power to regulate. Therefore, within limitations as determined by the courts, Congress, under the taxing power, may regulate an activity indirectly by taxation if Congress has the power under the Constitution to regulate that activity directly. For example, the Supreme Court has upheld a tax on coal producers, even though the tax was designed for penalty and control purposes rather than for revenue purposes, on the theory that under the "commerce" clause, Congress may regulate the production and distribution of coal.[9]

Using the power to tax, Congress has regulated narcotics dealers by imposing a special tax upon such dealers and has regulated the distribution of firearms by placing a tax on dealers in firearms. Such taxes have been upheld as having a reasonable relation to revenue raising.[10]

b. The authority to borrow money on the credit of the United States.

In the event that taxes are inadequate, the power to borrow money provides a second important source of funds to meet the operating expenses of the federal government. Relying in part on this clause, the United States Supreme Court has approved the authority of Congress to issue Treasury notes and to make them legal tender for satisfaction of debts.[11]

c. The power to regulate interstate and foreign commerce.

Through Supreme Court interpretation, the power to regulate interstate and foreign commerce has become the most singularly potent of all the specifically enumerated powers. Any activity, interstate or purely local in character, is potentially within the reach of the regulatory powers of Congress if it has an appreciable effect upon the flow of interstate commerce, regardless of whether the effect is direct or indirect.

[9] Sunshine Anthracite Coal Co. v. Adkins, 310 US 381, 84 LEd 1263, 60 SCt 907 (1940).

[10] United States v. Doremus, 249 US 86, 63 LEd 493, 39 SCt 214 (1919)

and Sonzinsky v. United States, 300 US 506, 81 LEd 772, 57 SCt 554 (1937).

[11] Knox v. Lee, 79 US(12 Wall) 457, 20 LEd 287 (1871).

Exercising this power, Congress has prescribed safety standards in transportation and industry, labor legislation, crop restriction programs, anti-trust laws, and even civil rights legislation, such as the 1964 Public Accommodations Law.[12] There is a whole body of federal criminal statutes built around the commerce powers, including the Mann Act, making it a federal offense to transport women across state lines for an immoral purpose; the National Motor Vehicle Theft Act, making it an offense to transport stolen vehicles in interstate commerce; and the Federal Kidnapping Act, imposing penalties for kidnapping an individual and carrying him across state lines. The authority granted to the United States under this "commerce" clause, used in conjunction with the "necessary and proper" clause (article I, section 8, clause 18) serves as the basis for the establishment of federal law enforcement agencies such as the Federal Bureau of Investigation.

This power to regulate commerce not only vests vast powers in the federal government, but also, with the possible exception of the "due process" clause, is the most important limitation imposed by the Constitution on the exercise of state power. The distribution of power by national and state governments is predicated to a great extent upon the implications of the commerce clause. Under the police power, the state may regulate matters of local concern; however, if the state laws, even under the police power, are deemed to impede substantially the free flow of commerce from state to state, these may be declared invalid under the authority of the commerce clause of the Constitution.[13] For example, if a state trespass law is applied in such a way as to come in conflict with the Civil Rights Act (based in part on the commerce clause), the trespass law cannot stand.[14]

d. *The right to establish rules of naturalization and laws relating to bankruptcies.*

Based on this clause, Congress has enacted the Immigration and Nationality Act. The states have no authority whatsoever

[12] Heart of Atlanta Motel, Inc. v. United States, 379 US 241, 13 LEd (2d) 258, 85 SCt 348 (1964).
[13] California v. Thompson, 313 US 109, 85 LEd 1219, 61 SCt 930 (1941).
[14] Hamm v. City of Rock Hill, 379 US 306, 13 LEd(2d) 300, 85 SCt 384 (1964).

regarding naturalization, as this is the exclusive power of Congress.

Under this authority, Congress has enacted uniform laws on the subject of bankruptcies. States may enact laws relating to payments of debts, but any state law which is in conflict with the national bankruptcy laws enacted under this provision is invalid.[15]

e. *The authority to coin money, to regulate the value thereof, and to fix the standards of weights and measures.*

Congress has the exclusive authority to regulate every aspect of currency. Congress also has the power to designate the medium of exchange, to forbid defacement, melting, or exportation of money, and to establish agencies to enforce these laws.

f. *The power to provide for the punishment of counterfeiting the securities and current coin of the United States.*

Relying on this provision and the "necessary and proper" clause, Congress has established a federal agency to enforce the counterfeiting laws. The Supreme Court has sustained federal statutes penalizing the importation or circulation of counterfeit coins.[16]

g. *The authority to establish post offices and post roads.*

This provision gives Congress the authority to enact legislation regarding theft from the mails and to establish federal agencies to enforce these laws. While states have the authority to regulate the use of vehicles that carry mail, such as mail trains, the Supreme Court has held that the state cannot punish a person for operating a mail truck on its highways without procuring a driver's license from state authorities.[17]

h. *The jurisdiction to secure to authors and inventors the exclusive right to their respective writings and discoveries.*

This clause is the foundation upon which the national

---

[15] International Shoe Co. v. Pinkus, 278 US 261, 73 LEd 316, 49 SCt 108 (1929).

[16] Baender v. Barnett, 255 US 224, 65 LEd 597, 41 SCt 271 (1921).

[17] Johnson v. Maryland, 254 US 51, 65 LEd 126, 41 SCt 16 (1920).

patent and copyright laws are based. The history of this provision traces back to the English statute of 1710 which procured to authors of books the right of publishing them for designated periods. A state may not pass a law which conflicts with federal laws based upon this clause.[18] However, a state may prescribe reasonable regulations to protect its citizens from fraud.

i. The prerogative of establishing judicial tribunals inferior to the Supreme Court.

Under the authority of this provision, Congress has established inferior federal courts. The Judiciary Act of 1789 provided for thirteen district courts, which were to have four sessions annually, and three circuit courts. Consistent with the provisions of this act, Congress has established the federal circuit courts, the federal district courts, the court of claims, the court of customs and appeals, and various tax courts. Not only may Congress establish courts, it may vest in these courts nonjudicial functions as well as judicial functions and can limit the powers of the courts established.[19]

j. The rights to make and enforce laws related to piracies and felonies committed on the high seas and offenses against the laws of nations.

Congress has the power to define crimes that may be committed on United States vessels while on the high seas. An act punishing "the crime of piracy as defined by the laws of nations" was held to be an appropriate exercise of the constitutional authority to define and punish the offense.[20]

k. The power and responsibility for declaring war and making rules concerning captures on land and water.

This provision gives Congress the power to declare war. In addition, it has been interpreted to vest in Congress the authority to regulate rents during wartime and to establish

[18] Wheaton v. Peters, 33 US(8 Pet) 591, 8 LEd 1055 (1834).
[19] Lurk v. United States, 370 US 530, 8 LEd(2d) 671, 82 SCt 1459 (1962).
[20] United States v. Brigmalekabhel, 43 US(2 How) 210, 11 LEd 239 (1844).

other extensive wartime controls on the use of economic resources.[21]

l. The responsibility to raise and support armies.

Under this clause, Congress alone can raise and provide for the support of armies. Also under this authority, Congress may establish laws for the drafting of citizens to serve in the armed forces and may even suppress "houses of ill fame" in the vicinity of the places where forces are stationed.[22]

m. The power to provide and maintain a navy.

This provision, as the preceding one, was inserted for the purpose of designating Congress as the department of government which should exercise these powers. Generally, the court interpretations concerning the power to raise and support armies also apply to the navy.

n. The authority to make rules for the government and regulation of the land and naval forces.

This provision gives Congress the authority to establish the Code of Military Justice and to designate rules relating to trials by court-martial.

o. Power to provide for calling forth the militia to execute the laws of the Union, suppress insurrection, and repel invasions.

Based on this power Congress has enacted laws delegating to the president the authority to call forth the militia. Not only is this authority granted in the event of rebellion, but the militia may also be called to carry out the orders of the Supreme Court.

p. Limited authority to organize, arm, discipline and train the militia.

This provision was interpreted as giving the Congress power to bring the militia under the control of the national government. In 1916, Congress reorganized the National Guard and

[21] United States v. Central Eureka Mining Co., 357 US 155, 2 LEd(2d) 1228, 78 SCt 1097 (1958).

[22] McKinley v. United States, 249 US 397, 63 LEd 668, 39 SCt 324 (1919).

authorized the president in emergencies to draft into military service members of the National Guard who thereupon should "stand discharged from the militia."

q. *The exercise of exclusive legislative control over the seat of government in Washington and other federal installations.*

Since Congress possesses legislative power over the District of Columbia, it may enact legislative provisions for the government of that District. Congress also has jurisdiction over certain lands within the states which have been ceded to the United States.

r. *The power to make all laws necessary and proper for carrying into execution all of the above specifically enumerated powers.*

This final broad grant of power has provided the necessary flexibility to enable the Constitution to be a living instrument and to endure for almost 200 years. By virtue of this "necessary and proper" clause, Congress can adopt measures for carrying out the enumerated powers appropriate to the times.

Although the powers granted to Congress were stated in the Constitution, the question arose early and still remains regarding the scope of this power. For example, in 1819 a controversy arose as to whether Congress had the power to charter a national bank. There was certainly no authorization for this within the powers specifically written in the Constitution. Nevertheless, Mr. Chief Justice Marshall in the celebrated case of *M'Culloch* v. *Maryland* [23] affirmed the power to exist and declared:

> Let the end be legitimate, let it be within the scope of the Constitution, and all means which are appropriate, which are plainly adapted to that end, which are not prohibited, but consist within the letter and spirit of the Constitution, are constitutional.

This broad interpretation of the necessary and proper clause has remained and has formed the basis of the implied powers

[23] 17 US(4 Wheat) 316, 4 LEd 579 (1819). See case in Part II of this book.

doctrine. Since the New Deal era the trend has been toward an even greater expansion of federal powers.

§ 1.9   Limitations on state powers

The powers granted to the federal government and discussed in the previous section are enumerated in the Constitution in positive terms. To further define the state-federal relationship, express limitations were placed on the states. Among the powers which the Constitution *prohibits* the states from exercising are the following: [24]

a. To enter into treaties, alliances, or confederations.

The power to make treaties lies exclusively in the hands of the federal government; states may not make treaties with other countries. Nor may states, once they have given powers to the federal government, withdraw from that government and bind themselves by confederations with other states or countries.

b. To coin money, emit bills of credit, or to make anything other than gold or silver coin legal tender in payment of debts.

As Congress has the authority to coin money, it would be confusing if the states had similar powers. Therefore, the Supreme Court declared that a law in Missouri authorizing the issuance of interest-bearing certificates was banned by this provision. [25]

c. To pass a bill of attainder.

A bill of attainder is a legislative act which inflicts punishment without trial. A Missouri statute which required persons to take an oath stating they had never given aid to the Confederacy was held invalid under this section as being a "bill of attainder." [26]

d. To enact ex post facto laws.

Ex post facto means "after the fact" and as used in the

---

[24] USConst art I, §10.
[25] Byrne v. Missouri, 33 US(8 Pet) 40, 8 LEd 859 (1834).

[26] Cummings v. Missouri, 71 US(4 Wall) 277, 18 LEd 356 (1867).

Constitution signifies a law which (a) makes an act, innocent when committed, a crime, (b) stipulates a greater punishment than was attached to the crime when it was committed, or (c) alters the situation of the accused to his disadvantage.

e. *To lay imposts or duties on imports or exports without the consent of Congress.*

This restriction is a necessary concomitant of the exclusive power of Congress to regulate interstate commerce.

f. *To keep troops or ships of war in times of peace.*

This provision was intended to prevent the states from embroiling the nation in a war by their unilateral acts. The declaration of war as well as the conduct of the war are in the exclusive control of the federal government.

In addition to these explicit limitations, certain other restrictions on state governmental powers are implied from the nature of the federal union. The proposition that a state may not tax a federal agency is an example of such an implied limitation. Finally, there are those limitations which have been applied indirectly to the states by means of the "due process" clause of the Fourteenth Amendment. More will be said about these latter restrictions in future sections.

§ 1.10   Powers retained by the states

While the Constitution of the United States enumerates the powers granted to the federal government by the Constitution and limits the powers of the states, it is quite clear that the states, in granting specific powers to the federal government, intended to retain most of their inherent powers. Despite the broad interpretations of the powers granted to the federal government, the states assumed the major responsibility for government for the first eighty years after the adoption of the Constitution. Since the Civil War, and especially in the twentieth century, there has existed some tension between the states and the national government as more centralization has threatened the sovereignty of the individual states. The likelihood of this situation had been anticipated much earlier, and an attempt was made in 1791 to remove all doubt by the adoption of the Tenth Amendment. This amendment states that the powers not delegated to the United States by the Constitution, nor prohibited by it to the states, are reserved to the states respectively, or to the people.

It is interesting to note that some ten years after the adoption of the Constitution, the Kentucky and Virginia legislatures adopted resolutions concerning the rights retained by the states. In the Kentucky resolution, adopted on November 19, 1798, it was resolved: [27]

> That the several states composing the United States of America are not united on the principle of unlimited submission to their general government; but that, by compact, under the style and title of the Constitution for the United States, and of amendments thereto, they constitute a general government for special purposes, delegate to that government certain definite powers, reserving, each state to itself, the residuary mass of rights to their own self-government; and that whenever the general government assumes undelegated powers, its acts are unauthoritative, void, and of no force.

Notwithstanding such resolutions, powers assumed by the federal government have been extended and powers remaining in the states have diminished. However, the primary responsibility for the protection of the health, welfare and morals of the people remains with the state.

The courts have agreed that the *police power* of the state is inherent in the government of the state and that this is a power which the state did not surrender by becoming a member of the Union.[28] The police power of the state comprehends all those general laws and internal regulations necessary to secure the peace, good order, health and prosperity of the people, and the regulation and protection of property rights. In the case of the *District of Columbia* v. *Brooke* [29] the Court stated this is one of the most essential of powers, at times the most insistent, and always one of the least limitable of the powers of government. Under this power, the states have passed laws defining crimes, regulating traffic, and providing for criminal procedural rules.

---

[27] Eriksson, *supra* note 1, at 455.
[28] Jacobson v. Massachusetts, 197 US 11, 49 LEd 643, 25 SCt 358 (1904).

[29] 214 US 138, 53 LEd 941, 29 SCt 560 (1909).

Strictly speaking, the federal government has no police power. However, Congress may exercise a similar power as incident to powers expressly conferred upon it by the Constitution.[30] Therefore, the validity of any statute so enacted depends on whether it directly relates to one of the powers delegated to the federal government.

§ 1.11   The Bill of Rights

During the battle over ratification of the Constitution, the anti-Federalists in the thirteen states strongly objected to the fact that the Constitution did not contain a bill of rights.[31] Although the Federalists argued that such a bill was unnecessary inasmuch as the powers granted to Congress were expressed powers and therefore had no need of limitation, many of the states refused to accept the Constitution without a promise that a bill of rights would be added. In Massachusetts, for example, the Federalists agreed to a list of nine proposed amendments in order to secure the ratification of the Constitution in that state. These amendments were not made a condition of ratification but were submitted as recommendations to be acted on after the new government should become operative. All of the states which ratified after Massachusetts followed this example and submitted recommended amendments to the Constitution.

Partly because seven of the thirteen original states which finally ratified the Constitution proposed amendments concerning the Bill of Rights, James Madison, during the first session of Congress, introduced twenty amendments which he had formulated after a careful study of the over two hundred amendments suggested by the ratifying conventions. After much discussion, the number was reduced to twelve and, of these, ten were ratified by three-fourths of the states and became the first ten amendments to the Constitution. These amendments are known as our Bill of Rights. This Bill of Rights was not intended to establish any novel principles of government but simply to embody certain guarantees and im-

---

[30] United States v. DeWitt, 76 US (9 Wall) 41, 19 LEd 593 (1869).

[31] Eriksson, *supra* note 1, at 220.

munities which the colonists had inherited from their English ancestors and which had from time immemorial been subject to certain well recognized exceptions arising from the necessities of the case.

At the time of its adoption, the Bill of Rights was intended to operate as a restriction only upon the national government. At this point in history, the states had given some of their sovereign powers to a strong central government and the people wished to insure that this strong government would not abridge those individual rights stated in the first ten amendments. The first ten amendments—more strictly speaking the first eight amendments—do not themselves restrict the states in any respect.

The amendments which made some of the provisions of the Bill of Rights applicable to the states will be discussed in a later section. The restrictions placed upon the federal government by the Bill of Rights are discussed here briefly. Much of the remaining part of this book will be devoted to a careful analysis of the individual protections afforded by the Bill of Rights and the manner in which these are applied.

The specific provisions of the Bill of Rights lay down only a broad framework; they would mean little without court interpretation. Here each of the ten amendments that make up the Bill of Rights are briefly explained.[32] As most of these amendments—the first, fourth, fifth, sixth and eighth—are discussed thoroughly in the chapters that follow, no cases will be cited in reference to these sections. Those that are not discussed in future chapters are more fully explained here.

• 1 The First Amendment prohibits Congress from making any law concerning the establishment of religion or prohibiting the free exercise thereof or abridging the freedom of speech or of the press or the right of the people peaceably to assemble and to petition the government for redress of grievances.

• 2 The Second Amendment provides that "a well regulated Militia, being necessary to the security of a free State, the

---

[32] The specific provisions of the Bill of Rights (first Ten Amendments) are reprinted in Part III of this book.

right of the people to keep and bear Arms, shall not be infringed." Early cases interpreted this provision to mean only that *Congress* may not infringe upon the right of the citizens to bear arms. Therefore, a state statute prohibiting regulation of the use of firearms was considered constitutional. There is a difference of opinion as to whether this right to bear arms, as protected by the Second Amendment, is related to a well-regulated militia. In deciding whether the National Firearms Act violates this provision, the U.S. Supreme Court answered that in the absence of evidence tending to show that possession or use of a shotgun having a barrel of less than 18 inches in length has some reasonable relationship to the preservation or efficiency of a well-regulated militia, a law prohibiting transportation of unregistered shotguns in interstate commerce is not unconstitutional.[33]

• 3 The Third Amendment provides, "No Soldier shall, in time of peace, be quartered in any house without the consent of the Owner, nor in time of war, but in a manner to be prescribed by law." This amendment was included because the people remembered the outrages occasioned by the thrusting of armed troops into their homes by the British.

• 4 Because the homes of the people had been invaded indiscriminately by the British prior to the revolution, the Bill of Rights, in which the Fourth Amendment was inserted, provided generally against "unreasonable searches and seizures." This amendment has been carefully interpreted by the courts. One chapter in this book will be devoted to detention and arrest and another to search and seizure.

• 5 The Fifth Amendment enumerates safeguards for persons accused of crime. It provides (a) that the government shall not require a person to be held to answer for a capital or otherwise infamous crime unless on a presentment or indictment of a grand jury; (b) that no person shall be subject for the same offense to be twice put in jeopardy of life or limb; (c) that no person shall be compelled in any criminal case to be witness

[33] United States v. Miller, 307 US 174, 83 LEd 1206, 59 SCt 816 (1939).

against himself; (d) that no person shall be deprived of life, liberty, or property without due process of law; and (e) that no person shall be deprived of his property for public use without just compensation.

• 6 The Sixth Amendment assures that in criminal prosecutions the accused shall enjoy the right to a speedy and public trial by an impartial jury of the state and district wherein the crime shall have been committed; the right to be informed of the nature and cause of the accusation; the right to be confronted with the witness against him; the right to have compulsory process for attaining witnesses in his favor; and the right to have the assistance of counsel for his defense.

• 7 The Seventh Amendment is included primarily as a safeguard of property rights. It provides that "In Suits at common law where the value in controversy shall exceed twenty dollars, the right of trial by jury shall be preserved, and no fact tried by a jury, shall be otherwise reexamined in any Court of the United States, than according to the rules of the common law." Although it has been held that this amendment is not a limitation on the states and does not affect litigation in the state courts, each state has provisions in its constitution to secure generally the right to trial by jury in common law actions.

• 8 The Eighth Amendment restricts both the legislative and judicial branches of government and guarantees certain rights to the individual. This amendment guarantees that excessive bail shall not be required, excessive fines shall not be imposed, and unusual punishment shall not be inflicted. These rights were guaranteed under the unwritten English constitution and those who ratified the Constitution felt that they should be added specifically to the Bill of Rights.

• 9 The Ninth Amendment states, "The enumeration in the Constitution, of certain rights, shall not be construed to deny or disparage others retained by the people." This means only that, even though some of the rights of the people are not specifically mentioned in the Constitution and Bill of Rights, these rights will be retained by the people.

• 10 The Tenth Amendment states, "The powers not delegated to the United States by the Constitution, nor prohibited by it to the States, are reserved to the States respectively, or to the people."

§ 1.12 "Due process of law"—provisions and definitions

When the first Congress established by the Constitution convened, hundreds of amendments to the Constitution were considered by that body. Among these was the proposal that an amendment be adopted providing that "no person shall be deprived of life, liberty, or property, without due process of law." The amendments, which were ratified in 1791 and became known as the Bill of Rights, included this provision which was tucked away as part of the Fifth Amendment to the Constitution.

The first step in comprehending the application of the "due process" provision of the Constitution is to recognize that this provision as it appears in the Fifth Amendment is a restraint upon the federal government only. This provision was adopted in 1791 because there was a fear of a strong central government and it was inserted at the insistence of the representatives of the various states.

It was not until 1868 that a federal Constitutional provision concerning due process became applicable to the states. In that year the Fourteenth Amendment was ratified. Part of that amendment was:

> Nor shall any *State* deprive any person of life, liberty, or property, without due process of law. (Emphasis added.)

This latter provision specifically applies to states and not to the federal government. Therefore, if a due process violation is claimed in a state case, the applicable due process provision is the Fourteenth Amendment clause and not the Fifth.

From the time of adoption, efforts have been made to define these clauses. No phrase has been the subject of greater controversy than the provision that no person shall "be deprived of life, liberty, or property, without due process of law." One reason for the confusion is the Supreme Court of the United

States has consistently declined to give a comprehensive definition. This is intentional because such a definition would limit the Court in future cases which could involve situations not presently anticipated. State courts, too, have refused to be pinned down to a specific and exact definition of due process.

Even though the courts have refused to give a specific definition, piecemeal definitions can be gleaned from the cases. For example, in the case of *Twining* v. *New Jersey* [34] the Court held:

> What is due process of law may be ascertained by an examination of those settled usages and modes of proceedings existing in the common law and statute law of England before the emigration of our ancestors, and shown not to have been unsuited to their civil and political condition by having been acted on by them after the settlement of this country.

In the case of *Murray* v. *Hoboken Land and Improvement Company*, [35] the Supreme Court made this statement:

> The Constitution contains no description of those processes which it was intended to allow or forbid. It does not even declare what principles are to be applied to ascertain whether it be due process. It is manifest that it was not left to the legislative power to enact any process which might be devised. The article is a restraint on the legislative as well as on the executive and judicial powers of the government, and cannot be so construed as to leave congress free to make any process "due process of law," by its mere will.

In his dissenting opinion in the case of *In re Winship*, [36] Justice Black stated that the four words—*due process of law*—have been the center of substantial legal debate over the years. He explained, however, that the words lose some of their ambiguity when viewed in the light of history. In the opinion he makes this oft-quoted comment:

> "Due process of law" was originally used as a shorthand expression for governmental proceedings according to the "law of the land" as it existed at the time of those proceedings. Both

---

[34] 211 US 78, 53 LEd 97, 29 SCt 14 (1908).

[35] 59 US(18 How) 272, 15 LEd 372 (1856).

[36] 397 US 358, 25 LEd(2d) 368, 90 SCt 1068 (1970). This case should be studied for a comprehensive discussion of the history of the due process clause.

phrases are derived from the laws of England and have traditionally been regarded as meaning the same thing.

In arguing his view that some members of the Court had unjustifiably used the due process clause as a means of expanding the power of the Supreme Court, Mr. Justice Black continued with these words:

> In my view both Mr. Justice Curtis and Mr. Justice Moody gave "due process of law" an unjustifiably broad interpretation. For me the only correct meaning of that phrase is that our government must proceed according to the "law of the land"—that is, according to the written constitutional and statutory provisions as interpreted by court decisions. The Due Process Clause, in both the Fifth and Fourteenth Amendments, in and of itself does not add to these provisions, but in effect states that our governments are governments of laws and constitutionally bound to act only according to law.

Although the Supreme Court has said that it would be difficult, if not impossible, to frame a definition which would be accurate, complete and appropriate under all circumstances,[37] it can be safely stated that the provisions have been broadly interpreted. Because of this broad interpretation many state cases have reached the Supreme Court of the United States, especially during the last two decades. Reference will be made to some of the cases in subsequent chapters.

§ 1.13 General scope of the Fourteenth Amendment due process clause

It is important to note that when the Fourteenth Amendment was written and ratified it did not embrace those specific rights which are enumerated in the Bill of Rights. For example, it did not say that "the accused shall have the assistance of counsel for his defense." Soon after the Fourteenth Amendment was ratified, the Supreme Court faced the difficult task of determining whether the due process clause of the Fourteenth Amendment protected those individual rights against the state

[37] Louisville Gas & Electric Co. v. Coleman, 277 US 32, 72 LEd 770, 48 SCt 423 (1928).

in the same manner that the Bill of Rights protected them against the federal government. Was, for example, the search and seizure provision of the Fourth Amendment made applicable to the states by the Fourteenth Amendment due process clause? This doctrine, later to be referred to as the "shorthand" doctrine was considered in the case of *Hurtado* v. *California*.[38]

In the *Hurtado* case the defendant was charged with murder upon information filed by the district attorney. He was later tried by a jury, convicted, and sentenced to be hanged. The defendant appealed to the United States Supreme Court on the ground that the due process clause of the Fourteenth Amendment had been violated, as he had been held to answer for the crime upon information and without presentment or indictment by a grand jury. The defendant argued that the express provision of the Fifth Amendment requiring "presentment or indictment of a grand jury" was made applicable to the states by the due process clause of the Fourteenth Amendment. In denying this claim in the *Hurtado* case, the Court stated:

> If in the adoption of that amendment [Fourteenth Amendment] it had been part of its purpose to perpetuate the institution of the grand jury in all states, it would have embodied, as did the Fifth Amendment, express declarations to that effect.

Notwithstanding this statement in the *Hurtado* case, the argument persisted that as the Bill of Rights enumerated fundamental rights, they should be guaranteed against state infringement through the Fourteenth Amendment due process clause. Although some of the judges of the Supreme Court and the various state and lower federal courts argued that those protections enumerated in the first eight amendments should be made applicable to the states by way of the Fourteenth Amendment, the majority of the judges found it difficult to read this into the Fourteenth Amendment.

As late as 1947 the Supreme Court, by a five to four decision, refused to give such broad meaning to the due process clause of the Fourteenth Amendment. In the case of *Adamson* v.

[38] 110 US 516, 28 LEd 232, 4 SCt 111 (1884).

California,[39] the defendant was convicted of murder in the first degree in the Superior Court of California. In accordance with the provisions of the California Penal Code, a district attorney for the state commented upon the failure of the defendant to testify at the trial. Defendant appealed the case under the Fourteenth Amendment due process clause arguing that this penal code or this action under the code violated the federal Constitution.

The majority in *Adamson* agreed that such comment would infringe upon defendant's privilege against self-incrimination protected by the Fifth Amendment if this were a trial in a court of the United States, but refused to make this standard applicable to the states, saying:

> It is settled law that the clause of the Fifth Amendment, protecting a person against being compelled to be a witness against himself, is not made effective by the Fourteenth Amendment as a protection against state action on the ground that freedom from testimonial compulsion is a right of national citizenship, or because it is a personal privilege for immunity secured by the Federal Constitution as one of the rights of man that are listed in the Bill of Rights.

The majority went on to explain that the due process clause of the Fourteenth Amendment does not draw all of the rights of the federal Bill of Rights under its protection. Mr. Justice Frankfurter, concurring with the majority in discussing the history of this theory, made this additional statement:

> Of all these judges, only one, who may respectfully be called an eccentric exception, ever indicated the belief that the Fourteenth Amendment was a shorthand summary of the first eight Amendments theretofore limiting only the Federal Government, and that due process incorporated those eight Amendments as restrictions upon the powers of the States.

Notwithstanding the strong words by the majority in the *Adamson* case, Mr. Justice Black, perhaps indicating some of the reasoning of the courts which were to make future decisions, made this comment:

[39] 332 US 46, 91 LEd 1903, 67 SCt 1672 (1947).

In my judgment history conclusively demonstrates that the language of the first section of the Fourteenth Amendment, taken as a whole, was thought by those responsible for its submission to the people, and by those who opposed its submission, sufficiently explicit to guarantee that thereafter no state could deprive its citizens of the privileges and protections of the Bill of Rights.

A broad interpretation of the due process clause of the Fourteenth Amendment vests great powers in the United States Supreme Court and conversely limits the powers of the state courts. Many of the state court justices resent this and have felt impelled to voice disagreement with what the Utah Supreme Court considers the almost unbelievable "arrogation of power by and to the federal government." [40] Expressing doubt that the Fourteenth Amendment was properly adopted in the first place, the majority of the Utah Supreme Court argued that even if the Fourteenth Amendment were adopted properly, there is nothing in the language to justify the application of the rights of the first ten amendments to the states by way of the Fourteenth Amendment. After commenting that the Fourteenth Amendment has been used to distort and nullify in some measure the purposes of the first ten amendments, the majority of the Utah court continues:

> The foregoing is said in awareness of the proliferations that have occurred on the first ten amendments, and particularly by the use of the Fourteenth Amendment, to extend and engraft upon the sovereign states, limitations intended only for the federal government. This has resulted in a constant and seemingly endless process of arrogating to the federal government more and more of the powers, not only not granted to it, but expressly forbidden to it, and in disparagement of the powers properly belonging to the sovereign states and the people. This development is a clear vindication of the forebodings of the founding fathers and their fears of centralization of power.

§ 1.14   Federalization of specific protections via the due process clause

In the early decisions of the Supreme Court the judges reasoned that certain rights, such as free speech, were so fundamental that they must be protected against abuse by state

[40] State v. Phillips, 540 P(2d) 936 (Ut 1975).

officials. These judges, in applying the "fundamental rights" theory, justified making these rights applicable to the states by way of the Fourteenth Amendment due process clause on the basis that they were so fundamental that a state, in violating these rights, failed to comply with the demands of the Fourteenth Amendment. The reasoning was that they were made applicable to the states not merely because they were a part of the Bill of Rights but because they were fundamental rights that the citizens of the United States were entitled to have protected, against state or federal action. Although the shadow of the "fundamental rights" rationale remains, the courts apparently no longer rely on this reasoning in making those rights which are enumerated in the first amendments applicable to the states.

Because the federal courts were slow to make the specific provisions of the Bill of Rights applicable to the states, one set of standards was applied in federal courts and a separate set of standards applied when the federal courts were reviewing state court decisions. Gradually the reluctance on the part of the Supreme Court and other federal courts to apply federal standards in state cases faded. A brief discussion of the federalization of the specific provisions of the Bill of Rights will help demonstrate the rapid acceleration of this process.

Because freedom of speech and the other rights protected by the First Amendment are clearly fundamental, they were made applicable to the states by the Fourteenth at an early date. After some confusing decisions, all doubt was removed in 1925 when the Supreme Court in the case of *Gitlow* v. *New York* [41] expressed the opinion:

> For present purposes we may and do assume that freedom of speech and of the press—which are protected by the First Amendment from abridgement by Congress—are among the fundamental personal rights and liberties protected by the Due Process Clause of the Fourteenth Amendment from impairment by the states. We do not regard the incidental statement in *Prudential Insurance Company* v. *Cheek*, 259 U.S. 530 [66 LEd 1044, 42 SCt 516], that the Fourteenth Amendment imposes no restrictions on the states concerning freedom of speech, as determinative of this question.

[41] 268 US 652, 69 LEd 1138, 45 SCt 625 (1925).

Although the "shorthand" rationale gradually became more palatable to the judges sitting on the Supreme Court,[42] it was not until the 1960's that this doctrine, if not adopted in principle, was widely applied. In a landmark decision in 1961,[43] the Supreme Court of the United States made it clear that the protections of the Fourth Amendment would be applicable to the states and that the federal courts would establish minimum standards in determining the legality of searches and seizures. In 1963 the "right to counsel" protection of the Sixth Amendment was made applicable to the states.[44] Having opened the door, the courts found little difficulty in 1965 in including the "self-incrimination" protection of the Fifth Amendment as one of the rights which would apply to state agents.[45]

Continuing this trend, the United States Supreme Court in 1968 rejected what it called dicta in prior decisions and held that the Fourteenth Amendment guaranteed a right to a jury trial in all criminal cases which—were they to be tried in a federal court—would come within the Sixth Amendment's guarantee.[46] In the *Duncan* case, the Court acknowledged that the protections of the Bill of Rights were being made applicable to the states by the Fourteenth, commenting:

> In resolving conflicting claims concerning the meaning of this specious language (the Fourteenth Amendment) the Court has looked increasingly to the Bill of Rights for guidance; many of the rights guaranteed by the first eight amendments to the Constitution have been held to be protected against state action by the Due Process Clause of the Fourteenth Amendment.

Even here the acceptance of this reasoning was not unanimous, however. Justice Harlan viewed the decision as an uneasy and illogical compromise, commenting:

> I believe I am correct in saying that every member of the Court for at least the last 135 years has agreed that our founders did not consider the requirements of the Bill of Rights so fundamental that they should operate directly against the states.

---

[42] Powell v. Alabama, 287 US 45, 77 LEd 158, 53 SCt 55 (1932).

[43] Mapp v. Ohio, 367 US 643, 6 LEd(2d) 1081, 81 SCt 1684 (1961).

[44] Gideon v. Wainwright, 372 US 335, 9 LEd(2d) 799, 83 SCt 792 (1963).

[45] Malloy v. Hogan, 378 US 1, 12 LEd(2d) 653, 84 SCt 1489 (1964).

[46] Duncan v. Louisiana, 391 US 145, 20 LEd(2d) 491, 88 SCt 1444 (1968).

Apparently disregarding Justice Harlan's views, the Supreme Court near the end of the sixties reversed previous specific decisions and added the "double jeopardy" protection of the Fifth Amendment to those made applicable to the states by the Fourteenth Amendment.[47] The Court stated that "on the merits we hold that the double jeopardy clause of the Fifth Amendment is applicable to the states through the Fourteenth."

There are still a few of the protections of the Bill of Rights which have not been specifically made applicable to the states by the Fourteenth. For example, the protections of the Second and Third Amendments and the grand jury provisions of the Fifth Amendment have not yet been brought completely under the "due process" umbrella. There is little likelihood that the protections of the Third Amendment will be brought before the Supreme Court, but it will be interesting to see how that court handles the grand jury provisions of the Fifth Amendment if brought before the court in a proper case.[48]

As there are so few rights of the first ten amendments that have not been made applicable to the states by the Fourteenth Amendment due process clause, there is a valid argument for abandoning the past confusing and contradictory rationale and admitting that the Fourteenth Amendment, by implication, makes those rights applicable to the states. Until this is judicially recognized, the piecemeal method of determining what specific provisions of the Bill of Rights are enforceable against state action will continue.

§ 1.15 Effects of broadening the scope of the Fourteenth Amendment due process clause

With the broadening in scope of the due process clause of the Fourteenth Amendment, the powers of the Supreme Court and other federal courts have been enlarged. Where state officials previously looked primarily to the state court cases to determine standards in protecting the individual rights, they must now look as well to the Supreme Court decisions. For example, only a few years ago the states were free to formulate

[47] Benton v. Maryland, 395 US 784, 23 LEd(2d) 707, 89 SCt 2056 (1969).

[48] These provisions of the Constitution will be discussed more thoroughly in future chapters.

their own policies in multiple prosecution situations, as the double jeopardy provision of the Bill of Rights did not super-impose the whole body of federal double jeopardy law upon the states. Since the decision in the *Benton* case [49] in 1969, however, federal cases must be examined to determine the federal standards in double jeopardy situations.

As indicated in the previous paragraph the states may require more strict standards by interpreting the state constitution to impose conditions not required by the federal courts. An interesting case decided in 1975, however, mandates that the states, in requiring stricter standards, must do so by way of their own state constitutional provisions and not by way of the federal constitutional provisions. [50]

In the *Hass* case, the Supreme Court held that a state may not impose greater restrictions than the federal courts as a matter of federal constitutional law when the Supreme Court specifically refrains from imposing them. For example, if the United States Supreme Court finds that the Fifth Amendment self-incrimination provision does not prohibit the use of statements for impeachment purposes when made without the *Miranda* [51] warnings, the *state* cannot then interpret the self-incrimination protection of the Federal Constitution as prohibiting the use of such confessions for impeachment purposes. By way of its *own* self-incrimination provision, the state may so limit the use of the confession, but it may not refer to the Fifth Amendment self-incrimination provision for that purpose.

Because both federal and state courts may by court interpretation of constitutional provisions limit police action, state officials must be familiar not only with the state statutes and court decisions but with federal laws and especially federal court decisions which to a great extent determine police procedures.

§ 1.16   Adjudication of constitutional questions

When studying cases, especially federal cases, which limit

[49] Benton v. Maryland, 395 US 784, 23 LEd(2d) 707, 89 SCt 2056 (1969).

[50] Oregon v. Hass, 420 US 714, 43 LEd(2d) 570, 95 SCt 1215 (1975). See case in Part II.

[51] Miranda v. Arizona, 384 US 436, 16 LEd(2d) 694, 86 SCt 1602 (1966).

police procedures while investigating crimes, some criminal justice personnel and lay people are confused by the judicial process. For example, in the *Mapp* case [52]—fully discussed later in the book—the police were acting under a state law and following procedures established by the Supreme Court of the State of Ohio. But when the decision declaring the evidence inadmissible was handed down, it was done so by the Supreme Court of the United States. How does a question involving the enforcement of a state statute by state officers ever get to the United States Supreme Court?

In article III of the Constitution, the Supreme Court is given original jurisdiction in all cases affecting ambassadors, other public ministers and consuls, and those in which a state shall be a party. That article also provides that the Supreme Court shall have appellate jurisdiction over cases and controversies arising under the Constitution, the laws of the United States, treaties, etc., subject to regulation by Congress. The Constitution does not expressly provide for the power of the Supreme Court to determine the constitutionality of acts of Congress or state statutes. Neither does this article provide for the power of the Supreme Court to review decisions of the state courts.

Other provisions of the Constitution which have been interpreted to give additional powers to the Supreme Court are the amendments and the supremacy clause (article VI, section 2) which provides that the Constitution and those acts of Congress made in pursuance thereof shall be the supreme law of the land. Probably the most far-reaching provision and the one that has given the Supreme Court and other federal courts the authority to act in "police power" cases is the Fourteenth Amendment. Had it not been for the Fourteenth Amendment due process clause and the Fourteenth Amendment equal protection clause, the Supreme Court could not have reviewed state decisions relating to search and seizure, self-incrimination, right to counsel, and other Bill of Rights protections. Had it not been for the Fourteenth Amendment, the Supreme Court could not have demanded that state officers abide by the requirements of the *Miranda* case.

[52] Mapp v. Ohio, 367 US 643, 6 LEd(2d) 1081, 81 SCt 1684 (1961).

To better understand the process, the reader should look for the review procedure followed in each case. If the case is a federal case, i.e., the person is charged with violating a federal statute, he will be tried first in the federal district court. He may then appeal to the federal circuit court of appeals and, finally, to the United States Supreme Court.

If he is accused of violating a state statute, the procedure is generally as follows (although the states differ as to the procedure followed and the designation of courts). In a felony case, after a preliminary hearing in a lower court, the trial is in a felony court, often called a circuit court. If convicted, the defendant may appeal to a state court of appeals and to the supreme court of the state. Then, on constitutional questions, he may appeal directly to the Supreme Court of the United States.

Neither the supreme court of the state nor the Supreme Court of the United States is required to hear all cases and to do so would be impossible. The United States Code (28 U.S.C. § 1257) provides some guidelines as to which cases will be reviewed by the United States Supreme Court. In essence, a review is granted only when there is a substantial federal question involved.

In addition to review by appeal, state cases reach the federal courts by way of the *writ of habeas corpus*. This was used very sparingly in earlier cases but in the last twenty years has been used more frequently, especially in reviewing constitutional claims. The Code, at 28 U.S.C. § 2241, provides that persons convicted of crimes in state courts may seek review by habeas corpus proceedings in federal courts on the issue of whether they were afforded their fair, full, constitutional rights and safeguards in the state proceedings. As an example, in the case of *Gideon* v. *Wainwright*,[53] Gideon sought habeas corpus re-

---

[53] 372 US 335, 9 LEd(2d) 799, 83 SCt 792 (1963). There is an indication that the pendulum might be swinging away from the wide use of the habeas corpus writ. By a six to three decision in July, 1976, the Supreme Court of the United States affirmed that a person found guilty of violating a state law was not entitled to federal habeas corpus consideration when he had an opportunity at the state level to fully and fairly litigate his claim that evidence was seized illegally in violation of the Fourth Amendment. Stone v. Powell, 428 US 465, 49 LEd(2d) 1067, 96 SCt 3037 (1976).

lief after he had served some time in the state reformatory, claiming that his constitutional guarantee of the assistance of counsel was not properly granted at the state court trial. In a habeas corpus proceeding, the action is brought against the person or persons who are responsible for the custody of the person requesting relief.

§ 1.17 Summary

The Constitution of the United States is the political foundation of the United States government. It was written and adopted after careful consideration and after experiments had been made with other forms of alliances among the colonies.

The United States Constitution is composed of seven articles, the first three of which separate the powers of government. Amendments have been adopted in accordance with the terms of the Constitution. These amendments when adopted became a part of the Constitution and have the same binding effect as the original Constitution.

The people of the thirteen states relinquished, by way of the Constitution, certain enumerated powers to the federal government established by that Constitution. These powers once delegated cannot be withdrawn. The extent to which powers were granted continues to be the subject of debate and court interpretation reaching from the time the Constitution was ratified by the states to the present.

Although certain powers are delegated to the federal government, many powers, including the police power, remain primarily in the states. However, limitations in exercising these powers have been placed on the states by the specific provisions of the Constitution and by court decisions.

The first ten amendments to the Constitution, known as the Bill of Rights, were adopted and became effective in 1791, two years after the Constitution was ratified. These forbid the abridgment of individual rights by Congress and other agents of the United States Government. When adopted, they did not apply to the states. Today, most of the provisions of the Bill of Rights are now made applicable to the states through the Fourteenth Amendment.

The due process clause of the Fifth Amendment is a part of

the Bill of Rights and applies to agents of the United States
Government. The due process clause under which the federal
courts review the actions of state agents is a part of the Fourteenth Amendment which was adopted in 1868.

Because of the broad interpretation of the Fourteenth
Amendment due process clause by the Supreme Court, state
officials as well as federal officials must look to the United
States Supreme Court for decisions clarifying constitutional
standards. States may, through legislative acts or court decisions, require more strict standards, but the states cannot
establish standards which do not meet the minimum standards
established by the federal courts or federal legislation.

Chapter 2

SPEECH, PRESS AND ASSEMBLY*

> Congress shall make no law ... abridging the freedom of speech, or of the press; or the right of the people peaceably to assemble, and to petition the Government for a redress of grievances.
>
> FIRST AMENDMENT

Section

§ 2.1 Introduction

Many portions of our Bill of Rights have antecedents traceable to the Magna Charta or centuries-old English common law tradition. This is not so with the First Amendment. Freedom of speech, press, religion, and assembly is a legal concept born on American soil.[1] The merger of Church and State in England furnished a fertile ground for religious and political repression. Censorship of the press through licensing originated with the efforts of the Church to suppress heretical writings. By virtue of a decree issued by the Court of the Star Chamber in 1585, no book could be printed or published in England until reviewed and licensed by the Archbishop or a delegate. The function of licensing was to weed out all printed materials

---

* by Jacqueline R. Kanovitz

[1] Bryant, THE BILL OF RIGHTS 81 (1965).

containing unorthodox religious thought or criticism of the Crown.[2] The history of this period is replete with instances of books being burned, printing presses destroyed, and authors being carted off to prison. Licensing laws came to an end in 1694.[3] But the lifting of licensing did not usher in an era of literary freedom. Political dissent was now stifled by means of rigorous enforcement of seditious libel laws. The offense of seditious libel consisted of merely speaking out against public officials. During the heyday of repression, a man could be punished for the crime of seditious libel if he read objectionable material, heard it read and laughed at it, or repeated it to another.[4]

The framing of a Bill of Rights was the first order of business facing the Congress that met after the ratification of the Constitution. The foundations for a strong central government had been laid. Now curbs were required to assure that the frightening English experience would never be repeated on this side of the ocean. In delineating the rights of free citizens in their relations with government, it was no coincidence that freedom of speech, press, religion, and assembly were positioned first. Our colonial forefathers had the vision to realize that without freedom of the mind, no other freedoms would be secure. Through the First Amendment, they sought to carve out a zone of intellectual liberty removed from federal control. With the adoption of the Fourteenth Amendment, which provides, among other things, that no state shall deprive any person of *liberty* without due process, First Amendment limitations were made binding on the states.[5]

The nation has now experienced two centuries of internal stability under one Constitution. When viewed from the perspective of world history, this is a remarkable accomplishment. The First Amendment has been a singularly important factor. When citizens can openly criticize their government and advocate change, changes are made through orderly political processes. In every age, dissident groups have existed. The presence of a vocal minority furnishes evidence that democracy is working. Although protest may have an un-

[2] *Id.* at 98-100.
[3] *Id.* at 94.
[4] *Id.* at 115.

[5] Gitlow v. New York, 268 US 652, 69 LEd 1138, 45 SCt 625 (1925).

settling flavor, experience has taught that when the channels of peaceful debate are closed, discontent will ultimately find expression in socially less acceptable forms. When grievances exist, they must be aired—if not through the press and on speakers' platforms, then by riots upon the streets. The First Amendment provides a safety valve through which the pressures and frustrations of a heterogeneous society can be ventilated. Professor Emerson has identified another vital function that free speech serves in the life of a democracy:

> [F]reedom of expression is an essential process for advancing knowledge and discovering truth. An individual who seeks knowledge and truth must hear all sides of the question, consider all alternatives, test his judgment by exposing it to opposition, and make full use of different minds.... The reasons which make open discussion essential for an intelligent individual judgment likewise make it imperative for rational social judgment.[6]

A general knowledge of the First Amendment is a minimum training ingredient that a nation firmly committed to the value of free expression has a right to expect of those who enforce its laws.

§ 2.2   General observations about the First Amendment

The First Amendment commands that "Congress shall make no law ... abridging the freedom of speech...." Does Congress violate this mandate by enacting a law making it a crime to threaten (by words or symbolic speech) the life of the president?[7] Are a citizen's First Amendment rights *abridged* if he is arrested for trespassing while distributing political tracts on the walkways of a private shopping center?[8] The text of the First Amendment does not directly answer these problems. "Freedom of speech" is not a self-defining concept; nor does the term "abridge" point unequivocally to the types of regulatory interferences that are beyond the power of government.

[6] Emerson, THE SYSTEM OF FREEDOM OF EXPRESSION 6, 7 (1969).

[7] Watts v. United States, 394 US 705, 22 LEd(2d) 664, 89 SCt 1399 (1969).

[8] Hudgens v. NLRB, 424 US 507, 47 LEd(2d) 196, 96 SCt 1029 (1976).

That the Constitution does not confer an unqualified right to speak out at all times and places and on every conceivable subject has never been seriously questioned. Mr. Justice Oliver Wendell Holmes dramatized this point in his now-famous quotation:

> The most stringent protection of free speech would not protect a man in falsely shouting fire in a theatre and causing a panic.[9]

Once one makes the inevitable concession that an unlimited speech privilege is neither workable nor desirable, the crucial issue to be faced is where to draw the line. For several decades the Supreme Court, in search of a general theory of First Amendment interpretation, experimented with a number of formulistic solutions, such as the bad tendency test,[10] the clear and present danger doctrine,[11] and the compelling interest standard.[12] Each of these formulations proved themselves to be, if of any utility at all, capable of application in limited areas only.[13] In recent years, the Supreme Court appears to have abandoned an attempt to find a comprehensive formulistic solution for all First Amendment problems, and to have adopted a pragmatic *"ad hoc* interest balancing" technique under which individual and social interests in freedom of expression are balanced against competing considerations of social policy.[14] These various tests and approaches will be explored in greater detail shortly. But first, a survey of the range of endeavors encompassed within the scope of free speech privilege is appropriate.

§ 2.3   Range of endeavors included within free expression

1. The right to formulate and hold beliefs

The formulation of ideas, thoughts, beliefs and opinions is antecedent to, but an integral part of, expression. It is difficult

[9] Schenck v. United States, 249 US 47, 52, 63 LEd 470, 39 SCt 247 (1919).

[10] Gitlow v. New York, 268 US 652, 69 LEd 1138, 45 SCt 625 (1925).

[11] Schenck v. United States, 249 US 47, 52, 63 LEd 470, 39 SCt 625 (1919).

[12] NAACP v. Alabama, 357 US 449, 2 LEd(2d) 1488, 78 SCt 1163 (1958).

[13] Brennan, *The Supreme Court and the Meiklejohn Interpretation of the First Amendment,* 79 HARVLREV 11 (1965).

[14] See, e.g., Branzburg v. Hayes, 408 US 665, 33 LEd(2d) 626, 92 SCt 2646 (1972).

to conceive of any government practice more horrendous than official thought control. What a citizen chooses to believe is intimate and personal, and beyond the reach of his government. The First Amendment creates an absolute immunity from government coercion to affirm or disavow a belief. In *West Virginia State Board of Education* v. *Barnette*,[15] the celebrated case invalidating a compulsory flag salute statute, the Court stated:

> If there is any fixed star in our constitutional constellation it is that no official, high or petty, can prescribe what shall be orthodox in politics, nationalism, religion, or other matters of opinion or force citizens to confess by word or act their faith therein. If there are any circumstances which permit an exception, they do not now occur to us.

Freedom of expression, then, begins with freedom of belief.

2. *The right to communicate ideas, opinions and information*

An uncommunicated belief, however, has little impact outside the mental life of the person embracing it. It would be a strange order that protected the right to hold a belief but not the right to relay it. The First Amendment affords extensive protection to the right to communicate ideas, opinions and information. But in the nature of things, this right cannot be as complete and absolute as the right to harbor a thought. Communication gives rise to a possibility of conflict between freedom of expression on the one side and competing norms, goals and values of society on the other. It is for this reason that social controls may become necessary. However, we are not concerned at this point with the scope of permissible government intervention in speech matters, but with surveying the range of possible activities which fall within the free speech privilege.

There is an almost infinite variety of mediums for self-expression and communication with others, the boundaries limited only by human inventiveness and imagination. Though the Constitution makes specific reference to the freedom of

---

[15] 319 US 624, 87 LEd 1628, 63 SCt 1178 (1943).

"speech" and "press," no one today would seriously contend that journalistic and public speaking endeavors constitute the only expressive mediums with a claim to free speech protection, to the exclusion of art, music, drama, motion picture films and the like. It is impossible to compile an exhaustive list of enterprises that come within the purview of the First Amendment, but a sampling is in order. The Supreme Court has recognized as legitimate free speech undertakings the right to send mail,[16] to stage live dramatic productions,[17] to exhibit motion pictures,[18] to solicit membership for an organization,[19] to engage in picketing,[20] to hold a parade or march,[21] or a sit-in demonstration,[22] and to participate in countless other activities in which written, verbal or pictorial messages are being communicated to others. But the list does not stop here. Practically any devised method for expressing ideas, verbal or otherwise, presents a protectible claim unless it collides with an important societal interest, in which case the court must strike a balance.

3. "Pure speech" v. "speech plus"

It does not follow necessarily, however, that all conduits for self-expression and communication of ideas must be given the same degree of constitutional immunity. Those modes of expression which involve a higher risk of bringing the communicator into conflict with the rights of other citizens lend themselves more readily to regulation. The Supreme Court has, on occasion, applied the descriptive labels of "pure speech" and "speech plus" to differentiate amongst possible communications techniques, the "plus" component having reference to the amount of physical behavior that accompanies the message's delivery. For example, a newspaper editorial would be "pure speech" while a public parade would be "speech plus."

---

[16] Procunier v. Martinez, 416 US 396, 40 LEd(2d) 224, 94 SCt 1800 (1974).

[17] Schacht v. United States, 398 US 58, 26 LEd(2d) 44, 90 SCt 1555 (1970).

[18] Burstyn v. Wilson, 343 US 495, 96 LEd 1098, 72 SCt 777 (1952).

[19] Thomas v. Collins, 323 US 516, 89 LEd 430, 65 SCt 315 (1945).

[20] Thornhill v. Alabama, 310 US 88, 84 LEd 1093, 60 SCt 736 (1940).

[21] Edwards v. South Carolina, 372 US 229, 9 LEd(2d) 687, 83 SCt 680 (1963).

[22] Brown v. Louisiana, 383 US 131, 15 LEd(2d) 637, 86 SCt 719 (1966).

If these labels serve any useful purpose, their purpose is limited to focusing attention upon the fact that mediums for communication involving higher levels of public involvement are more likely to give rise to law enforcement problems, create community frictions (if only in the use of facilities), and pose problems for which a degree of regulatory intervention may be required that would be wholly unnecessary if a different speech medium, involving a lesser degree of public conduct, were employed for imparting the same message. There is, to be sure, a vast world of difference between a message contained in a newspaper, or on a leaflet, and one on a picket sign being carried by several hundred marchers as they walk down a busy street. Mass pickets, street rallies, marches and sidewalk demonstrations, even if well organized, are likely to cause serious problems of traffic congestion, elevation of noise levels, and inconvenience of other citizens seeking to use these same public facilities, to say nothing of the risk of possible riots and disorders. For this reason, citizens who desire to make extraordinary uses of the public streets as forums for communicating ideas stand in a constitutionally less favorable posture than those who employ mediums involving lesser degrees of public involvement to get their messages across.[23] It is not because the message in the newspaper is any more "pure" than the one on the picket sign; it is simply that the newspaper editorial poses fewer regulatory problems.

Local governments, being charged with the responsibility of regulating the uses of streets and other public facilities for the safety and convenience of the entire community, have a right to insist upon advance notice of open-air gatherings as a means of allocating limited facilities, preparing a time schedule and assuring that there will be adequate policing of such events. Accordingly, a permit requirement, as a means of attaining these goals, has been held reasonable in relation to parades and outdoor meetings,[21] but an unconstitutional burden upon speech when applied to the privilege of publishing or pub-

---

[23] Cox v. Louisiana, 379 US 536, 13 LEd(2d) 471, 85 SCt 453 (1965).

[21] Cox v. New Hampshire, 312 US 569, 85 LEd 1049, 61 SCt 762 (1941).

licly distributing newspapers and informational handbills.[25] The latter activities simply do not pose the type of regulatory considerations justifying this form of limitation.

4. "Symbolic speech conduct"

Mute, symbolic acts can be and frequently are a highly dramatic and effective vehicle for relaying a message to others. The Supreme Court has recognized the communicative potential of expressive acts and has, on no less than four occasions, accorded silent conduct the status of constitutionally protected speech. Protected under the category of "symbolic speech conduct" have been the right to display a red flag as a symbol of opposition to organized government;[26] the right to refuse, on reasons of conscience, to salute and pledge allegiance to the American flag;[27] the right to sit quietly in a segregated public facility in silent disapproval of its discriminatory practices;[28] and the right to wear a black arm band in school as a symbol of opposition to war.[29] In each of these cases the mute acts were intended to impart a message and no one observing the conduct could have misunderstood its thrust.

But the immunity given symbolic speech conduct is somewhat less pervasive than in the case of "pure speech," or speech in verbal form. In affirming the conviction of one who had burned his draft card as a symbolic act of protest to the Vietnam war, the Supreme Court in *O'Brien* v. *United States*[30] laid down a three-pronged test for determining when an individual can be punished for engaging in physical conduct employed as a substitute for words: (1) the government must have a substantial interest in regulating the *noncommunicative* aspects of the conduct; (2) its interest must be unrelated to the suppression of any message associated therewith; and (3) the means adopted to promote that interest must be no more

---

[25] Lovell v. City of Griffin, 303 US 444, 82 LEd 49, 58 SCt 666 (1938); Schneider v. Town of Irvington, 309 US 147, 84 LEd 155, 60 SCt 146 (1939).

[26] Stromberg v. California, 283 US 359, 75 LEd 1117, 51 SCt 523 (1931).

[27] West Virginia State Bd. of Educ. v. Barnette, 319 US 624, 87 LEd 1628, 63 SCt 1178 (1943).

[28] Brown v. Louisiana, 383 US 131, 15 LEd(2d) 637, 86 SCt 719 (1966).

[29] Tinker v. Des Moines School Dist., 393 US 503, 21 LEd(2d) 731, 89 SCt 733 (1969).

[30] 391 US 367, 20 LEd(2d) 672, 88 SCt 1673 (1968).

restrictive than necessary for the accomplishment of the government's legitimate ends.

The line drawn in *O'Brien* makes sense. The killing of a public official is in no sense free speech though committed for the sake of dramatizing opposition to his policies, and this is so although the whole world understands this to be the message. In *O'Brien* there was a strong national interest in the effective administration of the draft requiring that selective service cards be preserved—a government interest having nothing to do with the suppression of any message of verbal opposition to the war likely to accompany such acts. In light of this, O'Brien could be punished for burning his draft card even though the forbidden act was in his case a symbolic substitute for speech.

Most jurisdictions today have statutes punishing certain forms of flag treatment thought to be objectionable—physical defacement, defilement, mutilation and contemptuous treatment being the acts most frequently singled out. Since a man's conduct with reference to a flag invariably reveals his attitudes toward it and those things it symbolizes, flag handling necessarily involves "symbolic speech conduct." The only government interest at issue in fixing norms of conduct with respect to how citizens handle flags owned by them is the interest in national unity and consensus—preserving the flag as an "unalloyed symbol" of national pride and patriotism. But these interests, even if valid, are inseparable from the message communicated by the act of mishandling it. The absence of a government interest in regulating conduct apart from the expressive element associated with it, precludes the government from treating flag abuse as a crime under the *O'Brien* analysis. This would seem to be the thrust of the Supreme Court's most recent decisions on point. The Court overturned convictions for burning a flag,[31] wearing a replica of it on the seat of trousers,[32] and displaying it in an upside down position with a peace symbol pasted on it.[33] Only in the last case, however, did the Court face the *O'Brien* question.

[31] Street v. New York, 394 US 576, 22 LEd(2d) 572, 89 SCt 1354 (1969).

[32] Smith v. Goguen, 415 US 566, 39 LEd(2d) 605, 94 SCt 1242 (1974).

[33] Spence v. Washington, 418 US 405, 41 LEd(2d) 842, 94 SCt 2727 (1974).

5. The right to gather and receive information

Recognition of a right to formulate ideas, beliefs and opinions and to communicate them to others draws with it, as a necessary corollary, the right to receive, listen to, read and observe communications originating with others. The First Amendment right of citizens to *receive* information supplied the justification for invalidating a post office statute requiring persons to affirmatively request delivery of "communist political propaganda" sent to them from abroad.[34] But this right is not absolute, and the government can, for example, ban travel to certain foreign countries, thereby restricting the free flow of information concerning that country, if the action is undertaken in the interest of national security.[35]

The right to acquire information takes on special importance when the person asserting that right is a member of the press, but even here the right is limited. Representatives of the media are not, for example, free to demand access to the scenes of crime or disaster where their presence might disrupt law enforcement efforts.[36] By the same token, newsmen may be compelled to give testimony before a grand jury though the disclosure of confidential sources may handicap their news gathering capacity.[37] They may also be prohibited from attending or publishing information about trials if such restrictions are necessary to protect a defendant's right to receive a fair trial before an impartial jury.[38] But a discriminatory denial of access to the scene of newsworthy events, based upon a disagreement with the points of view represented by the excluded members, would raise serious equal protection problems.[39]

§ 2.4   Regulation of speech content

For centuries leading up to the American Revolution, the English Crown had shielded itself from public criticism, first,

---

[34] Lamont v. Postmaster General, 381 US 301, 14 LEd(2d) 398, 85 SCt 1493 (1965).

[35] Zemel v. Rusk, 380 US 1, 14 LEd(2d) 179, 85 SCt 1271 (1965).

[36] Branzburg v. Hayes, 408 US 665, 33 LEd(2d) 626, 92 SCt 2646 (1972) (dicta); Quad-City Community News Service, Inc. v. Jebens, 334 FSupp 8 (SDIo 1971).

[37] Branzburg v. Hayes, 408 US 665, 33 LEd(2d) 626, 92 SCt 2646 (1972).

[38] Sheppard v. Maxwell, 384 US 333, 16 LEd(2d) 600, 86 SCt 1507 (1966).

[39] Quad-City Community News Service, Inc. v. Jebens, 334 FSupp 8 (SDIo 1971).

by setting up machinery for censorship of the press, and in later years, by rigorous prosecutions under the seditious libel laws. Those who drafted the Constitution were well-versed in history and familiar with the English legacy of political repression. When they wrote, "Congress shall make no law . . . abridging the freedom of speech . . . ," they were concerned primarily with protecting the freedom to criticize government.[40]

The Supreme Court did not seriously commence the task of interpreting the First Amendment until the World War I period. Wars are not the most fortunate occasions for civil liberties and the timing left an imprint on First Amendment development. In 1917, Congress had enacted a comprehensive speech-control measure, known as the Espionage Act, placing pervasive legal controls on expression regarded as a danger to the nation's war effort. One, Schenck, was convicted under the Act for circulating writings among men called up for the draft, urging them to resist conscription. In affirming his conviction, Mr. Justice Oliver Wendell Holmes wrote:

> We admit that in many places and in ordinary times the defendants in saying all that was said in the circular would have been within their constitutional rights. But the character of every act depends upon the circumstances in which it is done. . . . The question in every case is whether the words used are used in such circumstances and are of such a nature as to create a *clear and present danger* that they will bring about the substantive evil that Congress has a right to prevent.[41] (Emphasis added.)

The "clear and present danger" test remained the guiding standard against which government-imposed restrictions upon expression would be tested for several decades. Under the *Schenck* test, speech loses its constitutional protection and becomes amenable to legal controls or punishment only where the utterances give rise to a clear and present danger of some social injury or harm. In recent years the danger test has fallen into disuse; nor has any other test of general applicability emerged to replace it.

[40] Chaffee, Free Speech in the United States 18-20 (1941).

[41] Schenck v. United States, 249 US 47, 63 LEd 470, 39 SCt 247 (1919).

Professor Meiklejohn, a noted First Amendment theorist, has suggested that there should be gradations of free speech protection under his hierarchical ordering, political expression would receive the maximum protection descending to idle chatter at the bottom.[42] While it is perhaps possible to discern three grades of speech protection (fully protected, unprotected and marginally protected speech), the Supreme Court has never developed a ranking system along Meiklejohn value lines. At the risk of over-simplification, the pattern of legal protection today is that all expression is equally secured by the First Amendment unless (1) it comes within one of the "excluded" categories, or (2) it presents only a marginal free speech claim. With the disappearance of the danger test, the Supreme Court adopted the technique of definitionally excluding from the First Amendment some forms of expression, most notably obscenity, "fighting words," incitement to violence, and threats. (The excluded categories will be discussed shortly.)

More recently, there has emerged a commercial speech category that falls somewhere betwixt and between. The central concern of the First Amendment is the flow of ideas and information. Speech unconcerned with this interest apparently enjoys only a second-class form of citizenship within the free speech structure.[43] Commercial speech occupies the major spot in this hybrid category. The government may regulate or ban advertisements on a particular matter if the regulation serves the public interest. This accounts for the tobacco industry's inability to ward off the regulatory ban on media advertising of tobacco products.[44] There is no such pervasive power in the case of noncommercial speech. Majoritarian interests and values have never been deemed sufficient to justify imposing a forced silence on the minority. The First Amendment, in the main, disables the government from making it a crime to speak on a given subject or to advocate a particular belief. The fol-

[42] Meiklejohn, POLITICAL FREEDOM (1960).

[43] Pittsburgh Press v. Pittsburgh Comm'n on Human Relations, 413 US 376, 37 LEd(2d) 669, 93 SCt 2553 (1973); Bigelow v. Virginia, 421 US 806, 44 LEd(2d) 600, 95 SCt 2222 (1975).

[44] See cases cited in note 43 supra.

lowing speech areas, however, have been excluded from the First Amendment.

1. Obscenity—substance and procedure

Since 1957 it has been established that obscenity is not within the ambit of constitutionally protected free speech. In *Roth v. United States*,[45] the case so holding, the Supreme Court advanced the following rationale:

> All ideas having even the slightest redeeming social importance— unorthodox ideas, controversial ideas, even ideas hateful to the pre- vailing climate of opinion—have the full protection of the [First Amendment] guaranties, unless excludable because they encroach upon the limited area of more important interests. But implicit in the history of the First Amendment is the rejection of obscenity as utterly without redeeming social importance.

Having determined that obscene utterances are without constitutional protection, the Supreme Court became em- broiled in a struggle, which would consume more than a decade, to devise a legal test of obscenity that could command the approval of at least a majority of its members. The first time anything like real consensus was reached occurred in 1973 when a majority of the Court settled upon a triple-headed formulation which remains the test today. Under the holding of *Miller v. California*,[46] before a motion picture or literary work can be written out of the First Amendment on the basis of its being obscene, three elements must coalesce.

Applying contemporary community standards, the work viewed as a whole must (1) appeal to the prurient interests of the average person; (2) portray in a patently offensive way specific types of "hard-core" sexual conduct previously defined by applicable state law; and (3) lack any serious literary, artistic, political or scientific value. The *Miller* test furnishes more concrete and manageable standards than any of its predecessors. It requires that the assessment of obscenity be made on the basis of the entire work rather than isolated paragraphs, scenes or pictures. The work taken as a whole

[45] 354 US 476, 1 LEd(2d) 1498, 77 SCt 1304 (1957).

[46] 413 US 15, 37 LEd(2d) 419, 93 SCt 2607 (1973).

must satisfy the three criteria. State legislatures are required to give concrete meaning to their legal definitions of obscenity by enumerating specific types of "hard-core" sexual behavior that must be found in a work before it is stripped of legal protection. The *Miller* Court offered the following examples of the types of materials that a legislature might appropriately proscribe:

(a) Patently offensive representations or descriptions of ultimate sexual acts, normal or perverted, actual or simulated.
(b) Patently offensive representations or descriptions of masturbation, excretory functions, and lewd exhibition of the genitals.

Conspicuously absent from this list is simple nudity unaccompanied by lewd or pornographic gesturings, an area that the Supreme Court apparently intended to remain outside the scope of permissible obscenity regulation. Even in the face of patently offensive depictions of hard-core sexual acts, no work can be condemned as obscene and taken outside the First Amendment if, upon an evaluation of the material in its entirety, it is found to contain any serious literary, artistic, political or scientific value. But the fact that the descriptions of hard-core sexual acts are contained in printed words rather than pictures is not determinative of the obscene or protected character of the work. A book deficient on all three *Miller* criteria has no more claim to free speech protection than a work that illustrates the same conduct by pictures.[47]

The proclamation that obscenity was not constitutionally protected put the handwriting on the wall, but the pornography industry continued to wage legal battles in the hopes the Supreme Court would recant and carve out an exception in the case of consenting adults. Time and again the argument was made that the First Amendment secures to every adult in society the inalienable right to consume any communicative materials that may appeal to him. It necessarily follows from this, so the argument proceeds, that the law's involvement with obscenity must be limited to those situations where children are involved or where necessary to prevent improper imposi-

[47] Kaplan v. California, 415 US 115, 37 LEd(2d) 492, 93 SCt 2680 (1973).

tions upon an unwilling adult audience. Some credence was given to this position by *Stanley v. Georgia*,[48] a case in which the Supreme Court held that the government is without power to make it a crime for one to possess obscene matter *in the privacy of his home.* But all hopes that *Stanley* spelled a new and more liberal attitude toward the obscenity issue were dashed by a series of cases handed down in a span of the next four years that made it abundantly clear that *Stanley* turned upon the home environment and could not be read any more broadly than its facts. In *United States v. Reidel*,[49] the Supreme Court ruled that the scope of permissible legal involvement in the commercialization of obscenity outside the home is not dependent upon the patron's characteristics. Reemphasizing that obscenity is not constitutionally protected speech, the Court extrapolated from this that the regulatory power outside the home embraced even consenting adults. *Reidel* dealt with a post office regulation against the sending of obscene materials through the mails, but its impact reaches to "adult" book stores, movie houses and other businesses catering to the baser instincts of an adult clientele.[50] The Supreme Court rulings have completely withdrawn all legal protection from the smut-purveying industry.

Local governments have broad latitude in experimenting with methods for halting the flood of obscenity. Both criminal and civil enforcement procedures are available. In the case of motion pictures, legislatures may require film exhibitors to submit all films to a civil review board prior to holding a public showing, provided that the legal machinery established incorporates procedural safeguards which place the burden on the government to seek prompt judicial review of all censorship decisions.[51] Enforcement through a system of prior restraint has the advantage of halting obscene movies before they are

[48] 394 US 557, 22 LEd(2d) 542, 89 SCt 1243 (1969).

[49] 402 US 351, 28 LEd(2d) 813, 91 SCt 1410 (1971).

[50] Paris Adult Theatre I v. Slaton, 413 US 49, 37 LEd(2d) 446, 93 SCt 2628 (1973); United States v. 12 200-Ft. Reels of Super 8 mm Film, 413 US 123, 37 LEd(2d) 500, 93 SCt 2665 (1973); United States v. Orito, 413 US 139, 37 LEd(2d) 513, 93 SCt 2674 (1973).

[51] Freedman v. Maryland, 380 US 551, 13 LEd(2d) 649, 85 SCt 734 (1965).

ever publicly shown. Alternatively, local governments can abandon any effort to screen in advance and rely upon criminal obscenity statutes to punish offenders after a violation has occurred.

Because the *Miller* standard for separating punishable obscenity from constitutionally protected free speech is narrow, technical and requires painstaking scrutiny of the work as a whole, the Supreme Court has determined that these evaluations are best left to a judicial setting, and accordingly, has minimized the role of law enforcement officers in making discretionary judgments on obscenity matters. There is no right to seize allegedly obscene books, films or pictures incident to a lawful arrest based upon probable cause, even though the arresting officer has personally viewed the material and regards it as pornographic in every sense of the word. In *Roaden* v. *Kentucky*,[52] a sheriff, after viewing a film at a drive-in theatre and satisfying himself that it was obscene, arrested the manager and seized the film. The Supreme Court reversed the conviction on the grounds that, absent a prior judicial determination of the obscenity question, the seizure was illegal. On the other hand, where a judge accompanied the police officer to the movie theatre and personally viewed the film before signing a warrant for its seizure, the procedure was upheld.[53]

These cases make it clear that searches and seizures of literary material must conform to higher standards of reasonableness than searches for contraband in general. No seizure is justified unless made pursuant to a warrant issued by a magistrate after an *ex parte* determination of probable cause to believe that specific items are obscene under the *Miller* test. A personal viewing by the issuing magistrate is a desirable precautionary measure whenever practicable. Where it is not feasible for the judge to evaluate the materials personally, the proper course to be followed is to present the magistrate with detailed and concrete factual data regarding the types of hard-core sexual acts portrayed, their quantitative and qualitative aspects, and their relationship, if any, to the plot, leaving it to the magistrate to draw the appropriate legal conclusions.

[52] 413 US 496, 37 LEd(2d) 757, 93 SCt 2796 (1973).

[53] Heller v. New York, 413 US 483, 37 LEd(2d) 745, 93 SCt 2789 (1973).

It will not do for the officer to supply the magistrate with no more than his conclusory assertions that the *Miller* standards were met. His role is to supply the judge with factual data and the magistrate's is to evaluate it in light of legal standards.

The Supreme Court has established special procedures surrounding the execution of obscenity search warrants. The Fourth Amendment requirement that search warrants must particularly describe the "things to be seized" is applied most rigorously when the "things" are literary works. A general warrant authorizing the seizure of "all obscene publications" found at a particular location is not an adequate description. The language is constitutionally deficient because it attempts to delegate to the executing officer the power to make on-the-spot obscenity determinations, a power properly exercisable by an issuing magistrate alone.[54]

Where the purpose of a search warrant is to obtain criminal evidence, the police may not seize all copies found on the premises of each periodical, book or film mentioned in it.[55] The seizure of multiple copies of each item is constitutionally objectionable because it interferes unnecessarily with the dissemination of materials that may later be adjudicated innocent and that, at the point of seizure, are still clothed with a constitutional presumption of innocence. A single copy of each item is sufficient for evidentiary purposes. Moreover, where the sole copy of a film is taken, the court must, upon application of the exhibitor, return it to him in order to permit copying so that he may continue to show it until the final outcome of his trial.[56] No movie can be suppressed until it has been adjudicated obscene in an adversary proceeding. Should the exhibitor continue showing it before his trial, the police may not return and raid the picture house for the sake of seizing the film again.[57] Even though subsequent showing may constitute separate indictable offenses, the only constitutionally

---

[54] Marcus v. Search Warrant, 367 US 717, 6 LEd(2d) 1127, 81 SCt 1708 (1961); A Quantity of Copies of Books v. Kansas, 378 US 205, 12 LEd(2d) 809, 84 SCt 1723 (1964).

[55] Heller v. New York, 413 US 483, 37 LEd(2d) 745, 93 SCt 2789 (1973).

[56] *Id.*

[57] Bradford v. Wade, 386 FSupp 1156 (NDTex 1974), Llewelyn v. Oak land County Prosecutor's Office, 402 FSupp 1379 (EDMich 1975); Universal Amusement Co., Inc. v. Vance, 404 FSupp 33 (SDTex 1975).

appropriate reason for seizure at this point is evidentiary; but the first film supplies this need. Law enforcement agencies may not seek to shut down a movie theatre by repeated raids and seizures occurring at a point in the criminal process where the enterprise is presumed to be innocent.

2. "Fighting words"

In *Chaplinsky* v. *New Hampshire*,[58] a man was convicted for addressing the following language to a city marshal in a face-to-face confrontation on a city street: "You are a God damned racketeer" and "a damned Fascist." Previous to this, the Supreme Court had observed that "resort to epithets or personal abuse is not in any proper sense communication of information or opinion safeguarded by the Constitution. . . ." [59] But *Chaplinsky* was the first case to apply this dicta and affirm a conviction for what the Court styled "fighting words." Subsequent cases have reaffirmed the holding in *Chaplinsky* that "fighting words" fall outside the perimeter of free speech protection and they have sought to clarify the scope and content of this exclusion. It is not enough that the words used are offensive to the hearer or that they may in fact provoke a violent retaliation.[60] If the listener's reaction were determinative of the question, no one could safely articulate unpopular or controversial beliefs, since every such idea is likely to antagonize at least some members of the public. The "fighting words" exception does not measure the speaker's right to express his ideas by the boiling point of his audience. Indeed, this exclusion is not concerned with the communication of ideas or information at all. The only messages falling within the speech category carved out by *Chaplinsky* are verbal insults and direct personal abuse.

The *Chaplinsky* definition of "fighting words," as interpreted by subsequent decisions, is composed of two aspects— one dealing with speech content and the other with the circum-

---

[58] 315 US 568, 86 LEd 1031, 62 SCt 766 (1942).

[59] Cantwell v. Connecticut, 310 US 296, 309, 84 LEd 1221, 60 SCt 900 (1940) (dicta).

[60] Edwards v. South Carolina, 372 US 299, 9 LEd(2d) 697, 83 SCt 680 (1963); Cox v. Louisiana, 379 US 536, 13 LEd(2d) 471, 85 SCt 453 (1965); Street v. New York, 394 US 576, 22 LEd(2d) 572, 89 SCt 1354 (1969); Bachellar v. Maryland, 397 US 564, 25 LEd(2d) 570, 90 SCt 1312 (1970).

stances under which it is uttered. Fighting words are (1) personally abusive, insulting or derisive remarks, (2) addressed at another to his face under circumstances inherently likely to provoke an immediate violent response.[61] Verbal abuse tends in all cases to offend the sensibilities of the listener, but this quality alone does not furnish a basis for punishment. It is the inherent likelihood that such language will trigger an immediate violent response that removes it from the First Amendment and places it within the domain of state regulatory power. This likelihood can be known only by examining the actual words used in the total context in which they are uttered. The same language strung together in sequence may constitute "fighting words" in one context and protected speech in another.

In *Lewis* v. *City of New Orleans*,[62] the Supreme Court struck down, as violative of the First Amendment, a local ordinance making it an offense to "curse or revile or use obscene or opprobrious language toward or with reference to any member of the city police while in the actual performance of his duties." The deficiencies of this ordinance are apparent when compared to the *Chaplinsky* definition. It attempts to make verbally abusive language *per se* a punishable offense when addressed to an officer. But it is not the abusive nature of the language alone that brings on legal condemnation; words lose their constitutional protection under *Chaplinsky* only when uttered under circumstances inherently likely to provoke the listener to retaliate with physical violence. The New Orleans ordinance failed to take account of anything besides the words. Though it is unlikely that any well-trained police officer could be provoked to a point of violence by bullying language coming from a child or feeble old lady, the ordinance made their conduct criminal. Denouncing the statute as void on its face, the Supreme Court declined to consider the constitutional status of the words actually spoken by the defendant in this case.

A similar result was reached in *Gooding* v. *Wilson*,[63] where the Supreme Court upset the conviction of an anti-war pick-

---

[61] Lewis v. New Orleans, 415 US 130, 39 LEd(2d) 214, 94 SCt 970 (1974); Gooding v. Wilson, 405 US 518, 31 LEd(2d) 408, 92 SCt 1103 (1972).

[62] 415 US 130, 39 LEd(2d) 214, 94 SCt 970 (1974).

[63] 405 US 518, 31 LEd(2d) 408, 92 SCt 1103 (1972).

eter, who upon being asked to stop blocking an induction center entrance, had turned upon the officer and snarled:

> White Son of a B----, I'll kill you. You Son of a B----, I'll choke you to death. You Son of a B----, if you ever put your hands on me again, I'll cut you all to pieces.

The snag here, as in *Lewis*, was the overbreadth of the statute. The legislature had failed to observe the narrow constitutional definition of "fighting words" and had sought to punish abusive language without regard to the context or likelihood of its precipitating a physical confrontation. The legislature must provide more sensitive tools before speech punishment can be meted out.

Law enforcement officers cannot be faulted when convictions like *Lewis* and *Gooding* are overturned. It is one thing to ask that an officer practice restraint in evaluating whether personal insults measure up to "fighting words"; to suggest that the officer go beyond this and make a proper assessment regarding the statute's constitutionality borders on the extravagant. Neither moral nor civil liability attaches to the good faith enforcement of a law later declared unconstitutional.[64] The best advise this author can give to an officer who has been subjected to verbal abuse of the type punishable under *Chaplinsky* is to make the arrest and let the defendant thrash out the statutory problems in court.

3. Use of profanity in public

Despite dicta in earlier cases suggesting that profanity was not embraced in free speech, at the first opportunity in which this issue was squarely presented, the Supreme Court completely backed off. *Cohen* v. *California*[65] arose out of an incident in which an anti-war protester appeared in a courthouse wearing a jacket with the message "F--k the Draft!" displayed in bold face print across it. He was arrested and convicted under a state statute making it an offense to "wilfully disturb the peace or quiet . . . by offensive conduct." In analyz-

---

[64] § 11.8 *infra*.

[65] 403 US 15, 29 LEd(2d) 284, 91 SCt 1780 (1971).

ing his conduct, the Supreme Court first undertook to ascertain whether his crude and tasteless display fell within any of the excluded speech categories previously recognized. It rejected the notion that his language was unprotected on the basis of obscenity because the word "f--k" in the context used lacked any prurient appeal. Nor was his conviction sustainable as an application of the *Chaplinsky* test since no one reading it could have regarded the words as an insult addressed at him.

Having eliminated the traditional areas where speech control is allowable, the Supreme Court addressed the central issue—whether the First Amendment permits the government to make the use of vulgar, "four-letter" words in public, without more, a punishable offense. After a searching analysis of the problem, the Supreme Court arrived at the conclusion that it is beyond the government's province to "cleanse public debate to the point where it is grammatically palatable" or to establish what is an orthodox or acceptable word. In the Court's opinion, there was no difference between a claimed power to protect the public from exposure to particular words which might be offensive and a power to protect the public from particular ideas having this quality. In neither case does the power exist.

4. *Threats*

Free speech protection is designed to assist the free flow of ideas and information. This function serves to delineate the boundaries of the constitutional privilege. Spoken threats make no contribution to the wealth of knowledge. No possible social benefit could flow from according First Amendment status to utterances calculated to intimidate. Before a man can be punished for uttering menacing language, however, a genuine threat must be made. In *Watts* v. *United States*,[66] a young man, in the course of an anti-war rally, took the floor and said:

> They always holler at us to get an education. And now I have already received my draft classification as 1-A and I have got to report for my physical this Monday coming I am not going. If they

[66] 394 US 705, 22 LEd(2d) 664, 89 SCt 625 (1969).

ever make me carry a rifle the first man to get in my sights is L.B.J.
They are not going to make me kill my black brothers.

He was indicted and convicted under a federal law making it a
crime for any person to "knowingly and willfully . . . [make]
any threat to take the life of or inflict bodily harm upon the
President. . . ." The Supreme Court reversed on the grounds
that the statement, viewed in its proper context and considering
its conditional nature, amounted to no more than a "very crude
offensive method of stating a political opposition to the President." Political criticism does not forfeit its protected status
because it is tasteless, caustic or hyperbolic. Watts' message
was neither intended nor understood as embodying a genuine
threat upon the life of the President.

5. *Incendiary speech—herein, speech endangering national
security or local law and order*

Perhaps the most volatile First Amendment issues of the
twentieth century have centered upon a reconciliation of free
speech with national security interests. At what point is the
government justified in stepping in and putting a halt to speech
perceived as a threat to the internal order or the political
stability of the country? Local communities also face this problem, though on a lesser scale. Speech is a potent force in impel-
ling action. A hotheaded, street-corner orator can trigger a
local community riot. At some point along the line, it is legitimate for government to intervene and curtail utterances calculated to disrupt the internal order of the national or local
community. The problem reduces itself to a delicate task of
constitutional line-drawing, establishing a point of permissible
government intervention that is neither too early nor too late.
But the Supreme Court has not always been consistent in its
approach and the constitutional line has fluctuated.

During the aftermath of World War I, in a period of widespread national hysteria and broad public intolerance of revolutionary creeds and radical political doctrines, the Supreme
Court's regard for civil liberties reached an all-time low-water
mark. In the 1925 case of *Gitlow* v. *New York*,[67] the Supreme

[67] 268 US 652, 69 LEd 1138, 45 SCt
625 (1925).

Court ruled that advocating or teaching the overthrow of organized government by unlawful means was so inimical to the public welfare and the utterances so pernicious and dangerous that state legislatures could crush such doctrinal rumblings in an embryonic stage. It mattered not, in the Court's opinion, that the defendants in this case had never advocated any concrete actions, let alone immediate ones, directed toward accomplishing the government's overthrow. If the propagandizing efforts struck at the foundations of organized government, the government could "extinguish the spark without waiting until it has enkindled the flame or blazed into conflagration." The *Gitlow* case gave virtually no protection to free speech. It authorized government intervention at the earliest possible phase, the instant that the "dangerous" doctrine surfaced, and whether the doctrine was in fact dangerous or not required no more substantiation than the government's own paranoia.

A half-century later, in the case of *Brandenburg v. Ohio*,[68] also involving a prosecution under a state criminal syndicalism law, the Supreme Court drew the line of allowable expression much closer to the point of action. Under *Brandenburg*, advocacy of the use of force and violence exceeds the scope of free speech protection and becomes subject to the regulatory power of government only where such advocacy is both (1) directed toward inciting or producing *imminent* lawless action, and (2) is likely to incite or produce such action.

The story of the long and tortured constitutional path from *Gitlow* to *Brandenburg*, involving as it does the "clear and present danger" test and the Communist trials of the McCarthy era, is one that must be unfolded and understood by any serious student of the First Amendment. But this investigation will be postponed for the time being.[69] Our immediate task is to discover what the First Amendment means today.

On the national level, *Brandenburg v. Ohio* spells a much greater level of tolerance for the propagandizing of revolutionary political creeds and radical doctrines. On the local level, it operates as a boundary indicator establishing the point

[68] 395 US 444, 23 LEd(2d) 430, 89 SCt 1827 (1969).   [69] See § 2.5 *infra*.

at which regulatory intervention is permissible to avert a local disturbance. An arrest for engaging in incendiary speech is authorized under the *Brandenburg* test only where (1) the utterances are addressed to a specific audience; (2) the speaker intends to stir his audience to action; (3) he urges the listeners to perform some *specific, concrete* and *immediate* acts of force, violence or unlawfulness; and (4) an outbreak appears imminent.

In the only case to apply *Brandenburg* in a face-to-face crowd encounter, the Supreme Court concluded that the police had failed to make a proper assessment of the situation. *Hess v. Indiana* [70] grew out of a campus anti-war demonstration. The police were attempting to move a reluctant crowd of about 150 spectators off the streets and onto the sidewalks to restore traffic. At this point, Hess, who was standing on the sidewalk while facing the group that had already moved off the street, was heard to utter in a loud voice, "We'll take the f---ing street later (or again)," the final words of his sentence being muffled by other noise. He was immediately arrested and charged with disorderly conduct. The Supreme Court gave two separate reasons for reversing his conviction. First, Hess's statement did not appear to be addressed to any particular person or group. Consequently, it could not be said that "he was *advocating*, in the normal sense, any action." And second, even if Hess could be regarded as having exhorted the crowd to take some action, his message, as the Court read it, urged future action ("We'll take the - - - street later") and lacked the quality of immediacy required under the *Brandenburg* test. Absent proof that Hess's language was both intended to and likely to produce an imminent disorder, he was not subject to arrest for his words.

The foregoing discussion has identified the four major areas excluded from free speech protection—obscenity, "fighting words," violence incitement, and threats. Virtually all other subjects of human discourse are fully arrayed with

[70] 414 US 105, 38 LEd(2d) 303, 94 SCt 326 (1973). See case in Part II.

First Amendment protection—the unorthodox and offensive along with commonly-shared beliefs. The Supreme Court, over the years, has been extremely uncordial in its treatment of regulatory measures burdening matters of speech content. Though it is now established that governments may impose neutral restrictions upon the time, place or manner of public speaking,[71] there is little room for regulatory interference in the marketplace of ideas. This is true no matter how laudable the government's motives may be and even though the regulation serves a valid public interest. In *Miami Herald Publishing Co. v. Tornillo*,[72] a Florida "right of reply" statute was invoked which provided that any newspaper assailing the good character or public record of a candidate for political office was required, on the candidate's request, to furnish him equal space, free of charge, in which to respond to the newspaper's attack. The statute's purpose was to assure full and unbiased news coverage on vital election matters. The Supreme Court, in what is one of the rare modern cases to command unanimous agreement, voted to strike down this statute on the ground that "no government agency—local, state or federal —can tell a newspaper in advance what it can print and what it cannot." Mr. Chief Justice Burger, author of the opinion, wrote:

> The choice of material to go into a newspaper, and decisions made as to . . . content of the paper, and treatment of public issues and public officials—whether fair or unfair—constitutes the exercise of editorial control and judgment. It has yet to be demonstrated how governmental regulation of this critical process can be exercised consistent with First Amendment guarantees. . . .

Much case law has emerged out of regulations affecting speech in public places. Aside from the electronic communications media and the press, the primary public speaking forums —the streets, sidewalks and parks of the nation—are in the hands of government ownership. The First Amendment's content neutrality principle precludes the government from pro-

[71] See § 2.8 *infra*.
[72] 418 US 241, 41 LEd(2d) 730, 94 SCt 2831 (1974).

moting some ideas to the exclusion of others through the selective granting and withholding of access to the public forum. Restrictions upon access to public free speech forums must remain neutral in their impact upon varying points of view, both as written by legislatures and administratively enforced.[73]

§ 2.5   The rise and decline of the "clear and present danger" doctrine

In 1919, the case of *Schenck* v. *United States* [74] came before the Supreme Court. Schenck had been convicted under the Espionage Act for distributing circulars to men called up for the draft, which criticized the war effort and urged the reader to resist conscription. At the time of his appeal, the nation had not yet recovered a peacetime mentality. Mr. Justice Oliver Wendell Holmes, writing for the Court, affirmed Schenck's conviction and issued an opinion with four words in it that would influence the course of First Amendment interpretation for decades to come—"clear and present danger." Holmes wrote:

> We admit that in many places and in ordinary times the defendants in saying all that was said in the circular would have been within their constitutional rights. But the character of every act depends upon the circumstances in which it is done.... The question in every case is whether the words used are used in such circumstances and are of such a nature as to create a *clear and present danger* that they will bring about the substantive evils that Congress has a right to prevent.[75] (Emphasis added.)

Within a few years it became apparent to Mr. Justice Holmes that he had set loose a potential Frankenstein monster in the hands of a Court swept up in the post-war tides of a nation beset by frenzy and hysteria. The waves of violence and labor unrest of the early 1920's created a nationwide panic that all the social evils of the times were being stirred up by the Communists as part of an underground conspiracy to destroy the Republic. State legislatures, responding to the

[73] Southeastern Promotions, Ltd. v. Conrad, 420 US 546, 43 LEd(2d) 448, 95 SCt 1239 (1975).

[74] 249 US 47, 63 LEd 470, 39 SCt 247 (1919).

[75] *Id.* at 52.

national paranoia, in rapid succession began to enact criminal anarchy and criminal syndicalism statutes, the thrust of which was to make it a crime to advocate or teach the doctrine that organized governments should be overthrown by force and violence. A rash of prosecutions directed against left-wing radicals followed.

In a number of cases handed down in the early years following *Schenck,* the majority of the Court, bowing to considerations of political expediency, affirmed convictions under the guise of applying the clear and present danger doctrine, but without any serious effort to determine as a fact whether an actual danger was really caused by the speech.[76] Mr. Justice Holmes, joined by Mr. Justice Brandeis, eschewed these misapplications of the clear and present danger test and, in a number of dissenting opinions, tried to explain the role they conceived for the danger test. In *Abrams* v. *United States,*[77] Holmes, dissenting, made it clear that in his opinion, suppression of speech could be resorted to by government only as a last-ditch effort—when conditions were so critical that no time remained to avoid the evil which the speech threatened by meeting it with counterarguments. And in *Whitney* v. *California,*[78] Holmes and Brandeis joined issue with the majority. Concerning the clear and present danger test, they wrote:

> Fear of serious injury cannot alone justify suppression of free speech and assembly. Men feared witches and burnt women. It is the function of speech to free men from the bondage of irrational fears. To justify suppression of free speech there must be reasonable ground to fear that serious evil will result if free speech is practiced. There must be reasonable ground to believe that the danger apprehended is imminent. There must be reasonable ground to believe that the evil to be prevented is a serious one. . . . [E]ven advocacy of violation [of the law], however reprehensible morally, is not a justification for denying free speech where the advocacy falls short of incitement and there is nothing to indicate that the advocacy would be immediately acted on. . . .
>
> Those who won our independence by revolution were not cow-

---

[76] *E.g.,* Gitlow v. New York, 268 US 652, 69 LEd 1138, 45 SCt 625 (1925).

[77] 250 US 616, 63 LEd 1173, 40 SCt 17 (1919).

[78] 274 US 357, 71 LEd 1095, 47 SCt 641 (1927).

ards. They did not fear political change. They did not exalt order at the cost of liberty. To courageous, self-reliant men, with confidence in the power of free and fearless reasoning applied through the processes of popular government, no danger flowing from speech can be deemed clear and present, unless the incidence of the evil apprehended is so imminent that it may befall before there is an opportunity for full discussion. If there be time to expose through discussion the falsehood and fallacies, to avert the evil by the processes of education, the remedy to be applied is more speech, not enforced silence. Only an emergency can justify repression.[79]

In *American Communications Ass'n, C.I.O.* v. *Douds*,[80] a majority of the Court gave at least a formal endorsement to the Holmes-Brandeis interpretation of the meaning of the danger test. But the endorsement came too late. McCarthyism had already swept the nation. The time for the greatest test of the danger doctrine had arrived. In *Dennis* v. *United States*,[81] the top echelon American Communist Party leaders appealed their conviction of conspiring to violate the Smith Act by teaching and advocating, along with organizing the Party to teach and advocate, the overthrow of the United States government. In his dissenting opinion, Mr. Justice Douglas argued that the prosecution mustered no evidence to establish the strength and tactical position of the Communist Party in the United States. The trial judge instructed the jury that it should bring back a guilty verdict if it found that the defendants had the intent to "overthrow . . . the Government of the United States by force and violence as speedily as circumstances would permit." The Supreme Court voted six to two to affirm the conviction on a record wholly devoid of proof that the Communist Party, as then constituted, posed any clear, present or immediate danger to the nation, or that the doctrines propagandized constituted a present threat. The majority rejected the requirement that the danger must be both *clear* and *present* in all cases before speech control measures can be applied. They restated the clear and present danger test so as to make the seriousness of the threatened

[79] *Id.* at 376, 377.
[80] 339 US 382, 94 LEd 925, 70 SCt 674 (1950).
[81] 341 US 494, 95 LEd 1137, 71 SCt 857 (1951).

harm a factor that could offset its lack of immediacy. Mr.
Chief Justice Vinson quoted Chief Judge Learned Hand:

> "In each case [courts] must ask whether the *gravity of the evil,
> discounted by its improbability,* justifies such invasion of free speech
> as is necessary to avoid the danger." [82] (Emphasis added.)

Having watered down the danger doctrine, they applied it to
the facts and determined that when "a group aiming at [the
government's] overthrow is attempting to indoctrinate its
members and to commit them to a course whereby they will
strike when the leaders feel the circumstances permit," the
extreme seriousness of the threatened harm compensated for
its lack of immediacy, and the government could take action
to crush such a conspiracy "even though doomed from the
outset because of inadequate numbers."

The recasting of the danger doctrine, making the seriousness of the threatened harm and its immediacy factors offset
each other, so distorted it that not only was the *Dennis*
formulation never again mentioned by the Court, the re-
shaping of the test to accommodate momentary expediencies
left such an aftertaste that within a few short years, "clear
and present danger" language passed into legal oblivion. No
more would this phrase appear in any Supreme Court majority
opinion. In the context of incitive utterances, the area of
the doctrine's most important application, the *Brandenburg* case [83] emerged as the new test for indicating the point
of allowing government intervention. But when the actual
language of the *Brandenburg* case is closely scrutinized—that
the government may put a halt to the advocacy of force and
violence only where it is "directed to inciting or producing
imminent lawless action and is likely to incite or produce such
action" [84]—the "new" test does not differ markedly from the
danger doctrine as originally conceived by its two architects.
Brandenburg re-establishes the necessity that the danger be
an immediate (present) one in all cases and postpones the point
of government intervention until the last possible moment.

---

[82] *Id.* at 510.
[83] Brandenburg v. Ohio, 395 US 444,
23 LEd(2d) 430, 89 SCt 1827 (1969).

Review § 2.4(5) *supra.*
[84] *Id.* 395 US at 447.

The differences between the Holmes-Brandeis conception of the danger test and the *Brandenburg* formulation appear more semantic than functional. But if the Supreme Court intended to return to the views of Holmes and Brandeis, why did it not say so in "clear and present danger" terms? The only plausible explanation for the Supreme Court's deliberate failure to make specific reference to the danger test, while at the same time enunciating a "new" test so similar to it, is a desire to disassociate the test from some of its less remarkable applications, particularly in times of national hysteria. In order to avoid resurrecting the whole body of legal precedents associated with this test, including applications that the Court preferred to leave silently interred, the easier solution was to find new rubric with which to reincarnate the doctrine.

But even if *Brandenburg* has covertly re-established the danger test with regard to incitive utterances, the doctrine has definitely lost its foothold in other areas where it formerly applied. In its heyday, the clear and present danger test was looked upon as a test of general First Amendment application.[85] This function has now been taken over by *"ad hoc interest balancing."* Interest balancing is more an approach, or method, for resolving First Amendment issues that a standard, or formula, indicating which way the case should be decided. It represents the prevailing approach applied by the Supreme Court in recent years for resolving First Amendment controversies in areas where formulistic tests do not exist. Formulistic solutions exist to determine whether literary works are obscene,[86] whether utterances are "fighting words,"[87] or whether advocacy of violence has exceeded the limits of speech protection,[88] but how does the Supreme Court set about resolving a novel issue for which there are no previous standards or controlling precedents? How, for instance, does it decide whether a sanitation ordinance prohibiting the distribution of handbills on city streets violates the

[85] *See, e.g.,* Thomas v. Collins, 323 US 516, 89 LEd 430, 65 SCt 315 (1945); Bridges v. California, 314 US 252, 86 LEd 192, 62 SCt 190 (1941).

[86] Miller v. California, 413 US 15, 37 LEd(2d) 419, 93 SCt 2607 (1973).

[87] Chaplinsky v. New Hampshire, 315 US 568, 86 LEd 1031, 62 SCt 766 (1942).

[88] Brandenburg v. Ohio, 395 US 444, 23 LEd(2d) 430, 89 SCt 1827 (1969).

First Amendment? [59] Or whether Congress can impose a ceiling upon the amount private individuals can contribute toward the support of a political candidate? [90] It could ask whether the regulated activity poses a clear and present danger of injuring a substantial public interest. In the past it was common to see the question posed this way.

But the answer in modern times is arrived at by balancing the conflicting interests. Under *ad hoc* interest balancing, the constitutionality of a regulatory measure which in some manner burdens free speech is determined by comparing the First Amendment losses inflicted upon those affected by the regulation in issue with the social gains or benefits on the other side. If the First Amendment losses appear, on balance, to be the greater, the regulation will be struck down as unconstitutional. If the balance falls in the opposite direction, the free speech claims will be subordinated to the larger public interest that the regulation serves. This is perhaps an oversimplification of the balancing approach, but it affords some insight into the methods applied by the Supreme Court in evaluating whether a regulatory measure that adversely affects free speech interests does violate the First Amendment.

Putting an example may help to clarify the process. Suppose that a newspaper reporter is able to gain the confidence of a militant revolutionary group and prints a story, based upon an anonymous interview, about the organization's weapon arsenal and future revolutionary plans. He is then subpoenaed to appear before a grand jury investigating the organization's activities. He refuses to appear and identify the members on the grounds that legal compulsion to disclose his news sources violates his First Amendment rights. To determine the validity of this claim, the Court must assess the impact of compulsory disclosure on the journalist's First Amendment interests and compare this with the countervailing public interest in fair, effective law enforcement and the investigation of criminal matters. Having made the comparison, the Court will pass a judgment with respect to which of these two interests are

[59] Schneider v. Town of Irvington, 309 US 147, 84 LEd 155, 60 SCt 146 (1939).

[90] Buckley v. Valeo, 424 US 1, 46 LEd(2d) 659, 96 SCt 612 (1976).

paramount. On the First Amendment side, compelling a professional journalist to divulge before a grand jury the identity of a confidential news source may handicap his efforts to gather news in the future by making his sources reluctant to supply such information. On the other side of the controversy, however, is the social interest in effective crime detection and the vital role that the grand jury plays in this process. The grand jury must have access to relevant information. Balancing the conflicting First Amendment and social interests at stake in this controversy, the Supreme Court, in *Branzburg v. Hayes*,[91] determined that the social importance of pursuing and prosecuting crimes reported by the press took precedence over "the consequential, but uncertain, burden on news gathering that is said to result from insisting that reporters . . . respond to relevant questions put to them in the course of a valid grand jury investigation or criminal trial." Hence, the reporter could be made to testify.

§ 2.6   "Void for vagueness" doctrine and the First Amendment

Three long-haired and bearded youths are spotted on foot in a residential area wearing dark glasses and carrying an attache case. They do not appear to have any fixed destination. An officer stops them and asks them to give an account of what they are doing. They are unable to do so. He thereupon arrests them under a statute making it an offense, among other things, to "loiter or stroll around from place to place without any lawful purpose or object." The youths appeal their conviction and it is reversed. Two questions should have percolated by this time. First, what has all this to do with the First Amendment, and second, even if there is a connection, why was the conviction reversed?

The answer lies in the "void for vagueness" doctrine—a doctrine applicable to all criminal statutes, but one which applies with special vigor and force to laws operating in the First Amendment area. A vague criminal law, one which fails to mark out the boundaries of the conduct defined as "crimi-

[91] 408 US 665, 33 LEd(2d) 626, 92 SCt 2646 (1972).

nal," offends fundamental notions of due process. Where a defendant is charged with violating such a statute, he can raise what is known as the "void for vagueness" defense. The policy considerations underlying the void for vagueness doctrine are several.

The first is *fair notice* or warning to would-be actors so that conscientious citizens bent upon obeying the law can ascertain what conduct should be avoided. No man should be made to bear the risk of punishment for doing an act that he could not reasonably have ascertained in advance was forbidden by the law. "A statute which either forbids or requires the doing of an act in terms so vague that men of common intelligence must necessarily guess at its meaning and differ as to its application" [92] necessarily lays a booby trap for the innocent. But fair notice is not the only policy consideration at stake and is perhaps less important than the others, since few citizens scrutinize the statute books before embarking upon a contemplated course of action. Perhaps more significant is the danger of *arbitrary and erratic application*. Even a conscientious officer will find it difficult to act in an impartial and neutral manner if the statute he is charged with enforcing fails to provide clear, precise and objective guidelines for determining when a violation has occurred. If the officer is left to speculate what conduct falls within and without the vaguely marked boundaries of a poorly drafted law, the play of subjective influences is virtually inevitable. Such a situation is intolerable in a nation governed by laws and not men.

The risk that vague laws lend themselves to irregularities in the course of administration was precisely the factor that prompted the Supreme Court in *Papachristou* v. *City of Jacksonville* [93] to nullify a municipal ordinance which made it an offense, among other things, to "wander or stroll about from place to place without any lawful purpose or object." The reasons put forth by the Court for attaching a vagueness label to this ordinance, however, were broad enough to knock out vagrancy and loitering statutes nationwide. Condemned

[92] Connally v. General Construction Co., 269 US 385, 391, 70 LEd 322, 46 SCt 126 (1921).

[93] 405 US 156, 31 LEd(2d) 110, 92 SCt 839 (1972).

as objectionable was the fact that this ordinance (1) failed to give fair notice to potential offenders who would be subject to arrest when taking a leisurely stroll, sitting on a park bench, or seeking shelter from the elements in the doorway of a building; (2) encompassed innocent activity that is part of the amenities of life in a free society; (3) invited arbitrary and erratic applications by failing to provide adequate guidelines whereby law enforcement authorities might distinguish between innocent and unlawful conduct; and (4) watered down Fourth Amendment "probable cause" standards by sanctioning arrests on no more than an officer's suspicion that the party arrested had committed, or was about to commit, some other more serious crime.

Legislatures have purposely kept the elements of vagrancy or loitering obscure so that such laws may be effective tools for crime prevention, delegating to the policeman on the beat discretion to determine when a suspicious-looking character if left at large may pose a threat to society. But this type of discretion the Constitution does not allow. *Papachristou* suggests that the higher the discretionary element in *any* criminal statute, the more vulnerable it is to attack on void for vagueness grounds. Consequently whenever a choice exists between invoking a tight and narrow statute covering the exact conduct and one with a higher discretionary element, the officer should always prefer the former. Though an officer risks neither moral nor civil sanctions when he discretionally acts in good faith in enforcing an unconstitutional law, the public interest is best served when officers enforce the more narrow statutes. Convictions are less likely to be overturned.

Problems of vagueness are compounded when the law operates on the fringes of the First Amendment. The mere existence of a vague law may have an *in terrorem* or deterrent impact on the exercise of free speech rights. As Mr. Justice Marshall has put it, " 'uncertain meanings inevitably lead citizens to steer far wider of the unlawful zone' . . . than if the boundaries of the forbidden area were clearly marked." [94] By

[94] Grayned v. City of Rockford, 408 US 104, 33 LEd(2d) 222, 92 SCt 2294 (1972).

this he meant that citizens, faced with a law of unclear meaning, may be induced to forgo assertion of protected free speech rights rather than hazard possible arrest and conviction and ultimately be vindicated only after a costly and time-consuming appeal. Through the verbal imprecision of the legislature, an abridgment of free speech has resulted. Because vague statutes tend to chill conduct well beyond the zone of their permissible application, the Supreme Court has imposed stricter standards of tolerable statutory vagueness where free speech interests are at risk [95] and has permitted constitutional attacks upon such statutes with no requirement that the defendant show his conduct could not have been regulated by a statute drawn with the requisite narrow specificity.[96]

It is not the purpose of this section to make law enforcement officials experts in detecting when statutes are unconstitutionally vague. This is a judicial function. But a sampling of cases may be useful, first, to explain why in some cases an offender may escape punishment even though his conduct exceeds the boundaries of free speech protection, and second, to suggest the wisdom of invoking narrow and tightly drawn statutes containing objective guidelines describing the conduct made punishable, as opposed to those calling for discretionary judgments or subjective assessments of the facts, where an opportunity presents itself for making a choice between the two.

A comparison of the cases of *Coates v. City of Cincinnati*[97] and *Cameron v. Johnson*[98] underscores the features that increase the risk of a successful vagueness attack. In *Cameron*, the Supreme Court found no unconstitutional vagueness in a statute making it unlawful for "any person, singly or in concert with others, to engage in picketing or mass demonstrations in such a manner as to obstruct or unreasonably interfere with free ingress or egress to and from" any public building. However, in *Coates*, involving an ordinance making it unlaw-

[95] Smith v. California, 361 US 147, 4 LEd(2d) 205, 80 SCt 215 (1959).
[96] Coates v. City of Cincinnati, 402 US 611, 29 LEd(2d) 214, 91 SCt 1686 (1971) (White concurring); Gooding v. Wilson, 405 US 518, 31 LEd(2d) 298, 92 SCt 1103 (1972).
[97] 402 US 611, 29 LEd(2d) 214, 91 SCt 1686 (1971).
[98] 390 US 611, 20 LEd(2d) 182, 88 SCt 1335 (1968).

ful for "three or more persons to assemble . . . on any side-walks, . . . and there conduct themselves in a manner annoy-ing to persons passing by," the vagueness challenge prevailed. Both statutes were designed to cope with a similar type of problem—public inconvenience. But the *Cameron* statute was narrower in two respects than the *Coates* ordinance: (1) it pro-hibited conduct in a fixed location only (entrances to public buildings), and (2) the forbidden behavior (obstructing or un-reasonably interfering with ingress and egress) was unrelated to the points of view being expressed by the offender. Though some discretion was required to determine whether an ob-struction or unreasonable interference had been occasioned, determinations concerning whether the statute had been vio-lated depended upon objectively observable physical events as opposed to assessments of the impact of the picketer's message. The *Coates* ordinance, on the other hand, made the pivotal arrest decision turn upon the officer's assessment of whether or not the participants in the street assembly had "annoyed" persons passing by.

There is a vast world of difference between "obstruct" and "annoy" as the crucial fact to be established before free speech rights are halted. "Obstruct" circumscribes the discretionary element to a minimum and forces enforcement decisions to be made upon the basis of physically observable facts wholly unrelated to the offender's message. Unlike *obstruct*, an as-sessment of whether participants in a street assembly have *annoyed* others, interjects a much more subjective element and invites consideration of the offender's message as well as his physical behavior. "Annoy" is a term without any inherent objective content. It involves an emotional reaction to a stimulus, but not all persons react alike. What may be annoy-ing to some may not be so to others. Annoyance, like beauty, has a content that exists only in the eyes of the beholder. The *Coates* ordinance called upon the enforcing officer to make a subjective assessment of the impact of the offender's *words*, as well as his behavior, upon those who might be in the vicinity, but turned him loose without any criteria upon which to base his determination. The subjectivity implicit in a statute authorizing regulatory intervention into sensitive speech matters, upon the basis of a stimulus-reaction incapable of objective verification and varying from person to person, creates an extreme risk of enforcement irregularities. It lends itself too readily to censorial applications because the officer disagrees with the views being expressed. Legislatures may not vest an officer with enforcement discretion to disrupt speech because he is annoyed by what is being said or thinks others might be so annoyed.

At the risk of over-generalization, some conclusions can be drawn with regard to those statutory features that evoke void for vagueness responses in a First Amendment setting:

(1) An ordinance which invites or permits an enforcement decision to be based in part upon considerations of message or speech content runs a much higher risk of judicial invalidation than one which confines the officer's enforcement discretion to physically observable acts and behavior divorced from the offender's message.[99]

(2) Ordinances forbidding disruptive speech activity in a geographically limited zone, such as in front of a school or courthouse, or other public building, are more likely to withstand a vagueness attack than one of citywide application, because the level of disruption required to support an affirmative enforcement decision is tied to an object referent—the physical needs of the locale for unobstructed access (in a *Cameron*-type of ordinance) or freedom from acoustical interference as in the case of an anti-noise law.[100]

(3) Words like "annoying," "offensive" and similar terms involving a stimulus-response which varies from person to person and is incapable of objective determination on the basis of physical fact data are almost certain to bring on judicial condemnation when used as a statutory criterion for law enforcement intervention into speech-

---

[99] Cox v. Louisiana, 379 US 536, 13 LEd(2d) 471, 85 SCt 453 (1965).
[100] Grayned v. City of Rockford, 408 US 104, 33 LEd(2d) 222, 92 SCt 2294 (1972).

related matters. Such standards lend themselves too readily to censorial applications.

(4) Another consideration, not apparent from *Cameron* and *Coates*, but developed in several other decisions, is the importance to the public of having the particular conduct regulated and the extent to which it is possible for the legislature to minimize the discretionary element without at the same time sacrificing a vital public interest such as preventing violence and disorders.[101] In *Smith* v. *Goguen*,[102] the Court observed:

> There are areas of human conduct where, by the nature of the problems presented, legislatures simply cannot establish standards with great precision. Control of the broad range of disorderly conduct that may inhibit a policeman in the performance of his official duties may be one such area, requiring as it does an on-the-spot assessment of the need to keep order.... But there is no comparable reason for committing broad discretion to law enforcement officials in the area of flag contempt.... [N]othing prevents a legislature from defining with substantial specificity what constitutes forbidden treatment of United States flags....

Courts are more willing to uphold a legislative delegation of discretion to make *ad hoc* enforcement decisions where important public interests like safety are at stake, and where it is not possible to anticipate and detail in advance the range of factual variants that might implicate this interest. In sum, the attachment of a vagueness label to a statute depends, in part, upon a judicial assessment of the societal benefits and risks that accompany a delegation of enforcement discretion when operative in a First Amendment setting.

§ 2.7   Parades, pickets and public assemblies—the right to communicate

The mass street demonstration was a style of protest that became a signpost of the 1960's and early 1970's. For the poor, for those alienated from the mainstream of American

---

[101] Parker v. Levy, 417 US 733, 41 LEd(2d) 439, 94 SCt 2547 (1974).

[102] 415 US 566, 39 LEd(2d) 605, 94 SCt 1242 (1974).

life who lack funds to enlist media support for their cause, it is the only available channel for dramatizing a grievance and bringing it to public attention. It is on the streets and sidewalks that police officers face their most important First Amendment responsibilities. The officer is in the unenviable position of having two conflicting, though equally imperative, roles to play. As a protector of the public peace, his responsibilities are very familiar to him. But he is also a guardian of the rights guaranteed by the First Amendment, a role not as clear. When a community confrontation is threatened, it is easier for an officer to arrest the few whose views have offended others than to placate the increasingly intolerant and potentially unruly crowd of spectators.

But considerations of momentary expediency should not be allowed to obscure other interests at stake. To a speaker delivering a soapbox oration or a protest demonstrator who has invested a good deal of sincere emotional energy, the frustration of his efforts to communicate his grievances to the public, by reason of his arrest, serves as a further manifestation that changes in the existing order cannot come about by peaceful means. Regulatory intervention into free speech activities, therefore, becomes a very ticklish affair. If an officer commits an error affecting the rights of a group already estranged, patterns of alienation and resentment deepen. It is critical that law enforcement officers develop an awareness of their First Amendment "enforcement/guardian" responsibilities.

§ 2.8   —The streets as a public forum

The constitutional guarantee of freedom of expression would be of limited importance if it did not carry with it some assurance of the availability of means to reach a suitable audience. Public streets, sidewalks and parks have traditionally served this need. They afford to those who lack the financial resources to rent private halls or buy television time a free public forum from which to broadcast their grievances. Indeed, the Supreme Court has stated that these open-air facilities are "so historically associated with the exercise of First Amendment rights that access to them for the purpose of exercising such rights cannot constitutionally be denied broadly and absolutely."[103]

The recognition of the First Amendment's right of access to streets, parks and other open places poses regulation problems. Free expression or assembly is not the sole community interest at stake in the use of open-air public facilities, and when free speech conflicts with competing uses, reasonable accommodations must be made. A parade inevitably disrupts normal traffic patterns. Leaflets produce litter. Loud and raucous noises intrude upon the desires of others for mental tranquility. The First Amendment does not deprive local authorities of the power to impose *reasonable* restrictions upon free speech access to open-air public facilities in an effort to reconcile conflicting public and private demands upon their use. A municipality in the exercise of its police power may regulate the time, place and manner of using public streets for the purpose of holding outdoor parades, speeches or mass assemblies.[104] An ordinance banning parades in the downtown business area during peak traffic hours,[105] or banning demonstrations between the hours of 8 p.m. and 8 a.m. when most city dwellers have retired to their homes for relaxation and quiet,[106] is a constitutionally appropriate measure. Local authorities, moreover, need not open the entire city as a public, free speech forum. Under a properly drawn statute, a community could limit or deny access to select areas where the public interest in orderly governmental functioning demands a minimum level of noise and distraction. Concerning the constitutionality of location restrictions, the Supreme Court has said:

> The nature of the place, "the pattern of its normal activities, dictates the kinds of regulations of time, place, and manner that are reasonable." Although a silent vigil may not unduly interfere with a public library, . . . making a speech in the reading room almost certainly would. That same speech should be perfectly appropriate in a park. The crucial question is whether the manner of expression

[103] Food Employees Local 590 v. Logan Valley Plaza, Inc., 391 US 308, 20 LEd(2d) 603, 88 SCt 1601 (1968).

[104] Cox v. New Hampshire, 312 US 569, 85 LEd 1049, 61 SCt 762 (1941).

[105] Houston Peace Coalition v. Houston City Council, 310 FSupp 457 (SDTex 1970).

[106] Abernathy v. Conroy, 429 F(2d) 1170 (4thCir 1970).

is basically incompatible with the normal activity of a particular place at a particular time. . . . [I]n assessing the reasonableness of the regulation, we must weigh heavily the fact that communication is involved; the regulation must be narrowly tailored to further the State's legitimate interest.[107]

Because of the special characteristics of the school environment, local authorities may declare the public streets and sidewalks adjacent to schools off limits for noisy diversionary activity during the hours when classes are in session.[108] Hospital districts, jail yards, firehouses and court facilities represent similarly protectable locations.[109] But a regulation designed to restrict noise activity to a level compatible with a school or hospital would be wholly inappropriate in the context of a municipal transportation terminal where the public is freely invited and noise and bustling is commonplace.[110] The constitutionality of restrictions burdening speech because of the locale depends upon an analysis of the characteristics of the place and its needs for tranquility and quiet. The right of First Amendment access to open-air public facilities can be withdrawn only when the regulated conduct is incompatible with the facility's primary use.

Local governments need not be insensitive to the desires of their inhabitants for tranquility, comfort and privacy when they take shelter in their homes. City dwellers need some place where they can retreat from the noise and activity of their surroundings. A municipality has fairly ample police power to protect the repose of citizens in the sanctuary of their homes. An ordinance prohibiting persons from ringing doorbells of private residences for the purpose of soliciting sales without a previous request has been upheld as constitutional even in its application to national magazine salesmen.[111] Though the Supreme Court has never faced the issue squarely,

[107] Grayned v City of Rockford, 408 US 104, 33 LEd(2d) 222, 92 SCt 2294 (1972).

[108] Id.

[109] Adderley v. Florida, 385 US 39, 17 LEd(2d) 149, 87 SCt 242 (1967); Cameron v. Johnson, 390 US 611, 20 LEd(2d) 182, 88 SCt 1335 (1968); Cox v. Louisiana, 379 US 559, 13 LEd(2d) 487, 85 SCt 476 (1965).

[110] Wolin v. Port Authority, 392 F(2d) 83 (2ndCir 1968); Kuszynski v. City of Oakland, 479 F(2d) 1130 (9thCir 1973); Chicago Area Military Project v. City of Chicago, 508 F(2d) 921 (7thCir 1975).

[111] Beard v. Alexandria, 341 US 622, 95 LEd 1233, 71 SCt 920 (1951).

a number of lower federal courts have upheld restrictions upon residential picketing.[112]

But citizens cannot expect the same measure of legal protection for their mental tranquility when they venture on the open streets. The government can regulate open-air speech behavior in the interest of protecting inhabitants from unwelcome points of view only when they are forced into the role of a "captive audience," lacking protective mechanisms to defend their own sensibilities. A local government may not, for instance, defend an ordinance prohibiting drive-in theatres from showing films displaying nudity, on the grounds that the pictures are visible from public places, and the measure is necessary to protect inhabitants from exposure to sights that may be offensive to them.[113] The simple retort is that no one is forced to look, and if he finds a sight distasteful, he can readily avert his eyes. Since travelers upon the public streets have ample means at their own disposal to avoid being subjected to unpleasant *visual* matter, the police power of local governments is correspondingly diminished. Blaring *noises*, however, raise different policy considerations. There is no way users of the street can avoid listening to overbearing sounds and are, with respect to disturbingly loud noises, indeed a "captive audience." As a result, it is proper for local governments to enact anti-noise measures. The Supreme Court has upheld an ordinance prohibiting the operation upon any public street of sound trucks, loud speakers or other sound amplification equipment emitting raucous noise.[114]

The police power of local governments extends to the enactment of traffic control measures. Ordinances prohibiting demonstrators from blocking ingress or egress to buildings, or obstructing the free flow of traffic, are constitutionally permissible.[115] But restrictions burdening speech in the interest of promoting local sanitation have not been received as cordially.

[112] Garcia v. Gray, 507 F(2d) 539 (10thCir 1974). *See also*, Gregory v. City of Chicago, 394 US 111, 22 LEd(2d) 134, 89 SCt 946 (1969) (Black concurring). *But see*, People Acting Through Community Effort v. Doorley, 468 F(2d) 1143 (1stCir 1972).

[113] Erznoznik v. City of Jacksonville, 422 US 205, 45 LEd(2d) 125, 95 SCt 2268 (1975).

[114] Kovacs v. Cooper, 336 US 77, 93 LEd 513, 69 SCt 448 (1949).

[115] Cameron v. Johnson, 390 US 611, 20 LEd(2d) 182, 88 SCt 1335 (1968).

Prohibiting citizens from distributing informational handbills and leaflets in public is not a constitutionally permissible method of keeping litter off the city streets.[116] Alternatives less burdensome to speech must be adopted for promoting cleanliness.

The foregoing discussion demonstrates that local communities are not devoid of the necessary power to confine First Amendment conduct within boundaries compatible with metropolitan living. But even the presence of a sufficient regulatory interest will not buttress an ordinance that makes invidious distinctions based upon the massage that the speaker seeks to communicate.[117] In *Police Department* v. *Mosley*,[118] the Supreme Court invalidated a Chicago ordinance banning all picketing and demonstrating within 150 feet of school premises during class hours *except* for labor picketing. Mr. Justice Marshall wrote:

> [U]nder the Equal Protection Clause, not to mention the First Amendment itself, government may not grant the use of a forum to those people whose views it finds acceptable but deny use to those wishing to express less favored or more controversial views. And it may not select which issues are worth discussing or debating in public facilities. There is an 'equality of status in the field of ideas,' and government must afford all points of view an equal opportunity to be heard. Once a forum is opened up to assembly or speaking by some groups, government may not prohibit others from assembling or speaking on the basis of what they intend to say. Selective exclusions from a public forum may not be based on content alone, and may not be justified by reference to content alone.

Though the city of Chicago may have had a valid interest in seeking to protect its schools from noisy disruptions, labor picketing is no less disruptive than other picketing, and consequently, the existence of a *preferential classification* defeated the whole regulatory scheme. Whatever power the government may have to restrict access to a public forum, it

---

[116] Schneider v. Town of Irvington, 309 US 147, 84 LEd 155, 60 SCt 146 (1939).

[117] Police Dep't v. Mosley, 408 US 92, 33 LEd(2d) 212, 92 SCt 2286 (1972).

[118] *Id.*

must be employed in an even-handed, consistent and uniform manner. The theme that government must treat all demonstrations alike, regardless of their views, pervades the field of enforcement as well as the legislative function. The Supreme Court has, on several occasions, overturned convictions under "content neutral" laws, upon finding that they have been enforced in an impermissible manner.[119] Though an ordinance banning parades in the downtown business district during peak traffic hours is a constitutionally appropriate exercise of police power, unless it is uniformly applied to all, it may not be invoked against any. If the authorities look aside during a St. Patrick's Day parade, they will find themselves hard-pressed to justify later arrests of less favored groups for engaging in similar conduct.

There are numerous alternatives open to local communities to minimize the noise, disruption and inconvenience accompanying parades, rallies and outdoor demonstrations. The problems experienced by communities during the 1960's and early 70's stemmed, in large part, not from the lack of adequate regulatory power, but from a failure upon the part of local legislative bodies to channel this power in the proper direction. A precise and narrowly drawn ordinance prohibiting residential demonstrations after 8 P.M., or requiring a permit in order to hold an outdoor assembly, would solve a multitude of problems. In the one case, community inconvenience during hours of repose is completely avoided, while in the other, advance notice assures the presence of adequate policing to keep the meeting orderly. Unfortunately, all too frequently legislatures have neglected to address themselves to these needs. As a result, law enforcement officials may arrive on the scene after a demonstration has already gotten under way, and in policing the event, are forced to rely upon vague and loosely-drafted "breach of the peace" and "disorderly conduct" statutes. Such statutes are ill-adapted to the needs of law enforcement in a First Amendment setting.[120] Their

---

[119] Cox v. Louisiana, 379 US 536, 13 LEd(2d) 471, 85 SCt 453 (1965); Flower v. United States, 407 US 197, 32 LEd(2d) 653, 92 SCt 1842 (1972).

[120] Cox v. Louisiana, 379 US 536, 13 LEd(2d) 471, 85 SCt 453 (1965); Gregory v. City of Chicago, 349 US 111, 22 LEd(2d) 134, 89 SCt 946 (1969) (Black concurring).

principal deficiency is that they require the officer to make an educated guess whether the demonstrators have exceeded the boundaries of free speech protection and whether regulatory intervention would be proper. As has already been noted, the presence of a large discretionary element in statutes operating in a First Amendment context gives rise to a substantial void for vagueness risk,[121] and invites the possibility of challenge. There were numerous incidents during the 1960's and 70's where such challenges were successful.[122] As a result, communities were plagued by disruptive street assemblages that they were *statutorily* ill-equipped to control. The solution lies in the direction of precise and narrowly drawn laws prohibiting specific conduct, such as noisy demonstrations in front of schools, obstructing the public passage, picketing in residential areas, and activities of a similar nature. Such laws take the guesswork out of law enforcement and clearly point out the boundaries of the impermissible.

§ 2.9   —Indoor public forum

Because recruiting stations, welfare offices and other governmental buildings frequently house the seats of authority against which protest is directed and afford an opportunity to bring pressures to bear directly upon the source, they are popular targets for groups with grievances. The interiors of buildings have not traditionally been regarded as appropriate forums for protest. A high degree of decorum and order is necessary for the proper conduct of official business. Nevertheless, the influx into public buildings of persons claiming the right to utilize the facilities for organizational recruiting, pamphleteering, hanging placards, soliciting petition signatures, and other speech-connected activities, has made it necessary for the courts to begin considering the extent to which the Constitution guarantees the right to an *indoor public forum.*

Whatever right exists to invade the interior of public buildings for purposes of expression or protest, it is certainly less extensive than the free speech privilege assertable in open-air

---

[121] Review § 2.6. *See also* § 2.12 *infra.*

[122] Cox v. Louisiana, 379 US 536, 13 LEd(2d) 471, 85 SCt 453 (1965).

public facilities where noise, crowds and congestion are far more commonplace.[123] The government, no less than a private landowner, has the power to maintain a working environment conducive to the orderly conduct of its business.[124] The right to free expression cannot be exercised at the expense of the primary purpose a facility is designed to serve.[125] Accordingly, protesters would not be justified in entering public buildings in such numbers as to overburden the capacity of the facility;[126] in behaving in a loud or boisterous fashion during working hours; or in engaging in any other type of conduct that materially disrupts normal business routine.[127]

In analyzing the extent to which free speech activity inside public buildings is constitutionally privileged, three factors are paramount: (1) whether the building is open to the public; (2) the relevance of the claimant's message to the selected building or the audience found inside it; and (3) the extent to which the method of communication being utilized interferes with the normal business routinely conducted upon the premises.[128] Openness to the public is a threshold requirement. There is no First Amendment right to demand access to a jailhouse or other public facility to which the general public is excluded.[129] But an open-door policy alone is not sufficient to convert the interiors of a government building into a general free speech forum. Normally, there is no right to invade the interior of a public building for purposes of protest and communication, unless the message has some special relationship either to the building or the persons found within it. Though the First Amendment may privilege a welfare rights organizer to enter the waiting room of a public welfare office for the

---

[123] Massachusetts Welfare Rights Org. v. Ott, 421 F(2d) 525 (1stCir 1969).

[124] Adderley v. Florida, 385 US 39, 17 LEd(2d) 149, 87 SCt 242 (1967); Cameron v. Johnson, 390 US 611, 20 LEd(2d) 182, 88 SCt 1335 (1968).

[125] Cameron v. Johnson, 390 US 611, 20 LEd(2d) 182, 88 SCt 1335 (1968); Massachusetts Welfare Rights Org. v. Ott, 421 F(2d) 525 (1stCir 1969); LeClair v. O'Neil, 307 FSupp 621 (D Mass 1969).

[126] State v. McNair, 178 Neb 770, 135 NW(2d) 463 (1965).

[127] LeClair v. O'Neil, 307 FSupp 621 (D Mass 1969).

[128] Unemployed Workers Union v. Hackett, 332 FSupp 1372 (D RI 1971); Reilly v. Noel, 384 FSupp 741 (D RI 1974); Albany Welfare Rights Org. v. Wyman, 493 F(2d) 1319 (2ndCir 1974).

[129] Adderley v. Florida, 385 US 39, 17 LEd(2d) 149, 87 SCt 242 (1967).

purpose of distributing informational leaflets to the applicants who frequent it since the message is addressed to them, a similar invasion would not be justified if the message were of general public interest and an equally relevant audience were accessible outside on the streets.[130]

But even though the public is invited to enter, and the message is relevant to the business conducted upon the premises or to persons who frequent the building, consideration must still be given to the extent to which the method of communication selected interferes with the primary government function which the building was designed to serve. On two separate occasions, the Supreme Court has recognized the right to engage in mute, passive and unobtrusive expression inside public buildings. In *Brown v. Louisiana,*[131] the Supreme Court held that a group of Black youths could not be arrested for refusing to leave a segregated reading room of a public library which they had entered for the purpose of staging a quiet and orderly sit-in demonstration. And in *Tinker v. Des Moines Independent School District,*[132] the Court ruled that a student could not be expelled for wearing a black arm band on school property as a symbol of his opposition to the Vietnam War. In both cases, the mode of indoor protest involved no obstruction or interference with the normal transaction of routine business.

These two cases do not suggest that silent protest is the only type of speech permissible inside public buildings. Lower federal courts have approved the use of indoor public forums for more active forms of expression such as distributing leaflets, enlisting signatures on petitions, conversing with persons waiting for business, and, even in some cases, singing and chanting.[133] But in each case, the Court found that because of the nature of the locale, the specific activity did not cause serious interference with normal routine. Conduct which might be entirely permissible in a large and bustling municipally-operated transportation terminal [134] might be inappropriate and off limits in a compact and business-like welfare

---

[130] See cases cited in note 128 *supra.*

[131] 383 US 131, 15 LEd(2d) 637, 86 SCt 719 (1966).

[132] 393 US 503, 21 LEd(2d) 731, 89

SCt 733 (1969).

[133] See cases cited in note 128 *supra.*

[134] Wolin v. Port Authority, 392 F(2d) 83 (2ndCir 1968).

office.[135] Developing case law indicates that the interiors of public buildings are not necessarily foreclosed to speech-related conduct which involves voice, movement and activity. The focal point of the inquiry is on the "publicness" of the locale, the relevance of the message, and the extent to which its delivery disrupts normal business patterns.

§ 2.10   —First Amendment privilege on private property

The constitutional admonition against abridging free speech is addressed to the government at all of its various levels. The government, as a property owner, must operate with deference to the First Amendment. But outside the narrow boundaries carved in *Marsh v. Alabama*,[136] there is no corresponding limitation upon how a private landowner chooses to enjoy his property. In *Marsh*, a Jehovah's Witness was arrested for trespassing when she distributed religious leaflets on the streets of Chickasaw, Alabama. Although Chickasaw appeared to be an ordinary municipality, it was in fact a company-owned town. The corporate proprietors owning the town furnished all normal municipal services, including police and fire protection, street maintenance, sewage disposal, etc. The Supreme Court reversed the trespass conviction. The substance of its ruling was that where a private entrepreneur assumes *all* the physical and functional characteristics of a municipal entity, he becomes saddled with a First Amendment burden no less than that of government.

For a brief period from 1968 to 1976 the doctrine of *Marsh v. Alabama* was expanded to include the parking facilities and pedestrian walks of private shopping center complexes on the theory that these too had government-like characteristics. In the case of *Food Employees Local 590 v. Logan Valley Plaza, Inc.*,[137] the Supreme Court drew an analogy between the walkways of a private shopping center and the streets of a municipal business district and ruled that the former, though privately owned, were available to members of the public for First Amendment uses. *Logan Valley Plaza* was subsequently

[135] LeClair v. O'Neil, 307 FSupp 621 (D Mass 1969).
[136] 326 US 501, 90 LEd 265, 66 SCt 276 (1946).
[137] 391 US 308, 20 LEd(2d) 603, 88 SCt 1601 (1968).

distinguished and limited, and finally overruled. In *Hudgens v. National Labor Relations Board*,[138] handed down in 1976, the Supreme Court abandoned *Logan Valley Plaza* and decided that shopping center owners are not constitutionally compelled to submit to free speech claims by members of the public.

The constitutional guarantee of free speech is a guarantee only against abridgment by government and affords no redress against the corporate proprietors of a shopping center complex. The latter remain at liberty to bar, flatly or on a selective basis, persons desiring to come upon the premises for the purpose of picketing, handbilling, soliciting or any other First Amendment business. Should the owner of a commercial establishment request police assistance in expelling a free speech claimant, the officer should have no hesitation in lending his support. Although the *Hudgens* case did not expressly overrule *Marsh v. Alabama*, whether it remains good law today is of little practical importance because *Marsh* is now limited to its facts, and its facts—a company-owned town—are extremely rare indeed. The rule that emerges is that private property is not constitutionally available for picketing, handbilling, marching or any other orderly form of First Amendment activity, unless the owner is willing to voluntarily submit to this use. An entry upon private property without the consent of the owner remains a trespass even though committed in a misguided belief that a speech-connected purpose makes the entry lawful.

§ 2.11   —Controlling demonstrations through permits

Local authorities frequently look upon open-air assemblies as something like a First Amendment nuisance that communities are obliged to put up with. Such a negativism ignores the vital role that public assemblies have traditionally played and continue to play in the national life. A democratic society must afford a vehicle for public airing of grievances. The question becomes how to avoid community inconvenience

---

[138] 424 US 507, 47 LEd(2d) 196, 96 SCt 1029 (1976).

and disruption while, at the same time, recognizing the First Amendment right to protest in a public forum.

Advance planning and scheduling, sound resource allocation decisions, and adequate policing are the keys to constitutional allocation of accommodations. When the police are at the scene of a demonstration, directing traffic and mingling with the crowd, problems of community inconvenience and disruption are minimized. Unfortunately, communications are sometimes strained and voluntary cooperation cannot be relied upon to produce the notice necessary to activate pre-planning. The most practical solution to this problem is a permit or licensing system. A permit offers several decided advantages. First, it puts legal compulsion behind the requirement that protest groups give the authorities sufficient advance notice to allow provision for adequate policing. Second, the wait may dampen the enthusiasm of groups more interested in disruption than orderly communication of their views. Third, it puts local authorities in a position to exercise a supervisory role in the scheduling of times and places, thus avoiding the problem of demonstrations during peak traffic hours or two groups competing for the same facility. And finally, it affords an opportunity to pass on the costs of special policing from the public to the permit applicants as part of the licensing fee.[139]

But there are limits to what can be accomplished through a permit system. The Constitution does not sanction the use of permits as a regulatory tool for sifting out, in advance, groups that may pose serious peace-keeping problems, nor the denial of a license in order to keep them off the streets.

The requirements for a constitutionally valid permit system are relatively stringent. The ordinance establishing the system must be narrowly drawn and must define in detail the powers and duties of the responsible administrator.[140] The time, place, duration and manner of using open-air public facilities for speech purposes represent valid administrative considerations in the granting or withholding of a permit.[141] They are con-

[139] Cox v. New Hampshire, 312 US 569, 85 LEd 1049, 61 SCt 762 (1941).

[140] Lovell v. City of Griffin, 303 US 444, 82 LEd 949, 58 SCt 666 (1938); Kunz v. New York, 340 US 290, 95 LEd 280, 71 SCt 312 (1951); Niemotko v. Maryland, 340 US 268, 95 LEd 267, 71 SCt 325 (1951).

[141] Lovell v. City of Griffin, 303 US 444, 82 LEd 949, 58 SCt 666 (1938).

siderations in which the officer in charge may be delegated limited administrative discretion. But permit ordinances allowing discretionary denials for reasons other than those relevant to time scheduling, resource allocation, traffic congestion, noise or related considerations stand on a shakier foundation.[142] The Supreme Court has invalidated an ordinance requiring the administrator to evaluate the character of the applicant, the nature of his organization, and the effect of a permit on the general welfare of the community;[143] and another inviting consideration of the proposed demonstration's impact upon "the public welfare, peace, safety, health, decency, good order, morals or convenience" of the community.[144] These standards bear little relationship to problems of resource allocation and scheduling. More important, they give a free hand to the administrator to determine in advance what views may be publicly aired. This feature is constitutionally intolerable.

It is understandable that communities would prefer to avoid situations having a potential for outbreaks and violence. This cannot be accomplished, however, through the denial of a permit. In *Hague v. C.I.O.,*[145] the Supreme Court struck down a New Jersey municipal ordinance which authorized the director of public safety to withhold a permit to use open-air public facilities if, in his opinion, it would prevent riots, disturbances or disorderly assemblages. The Court pointed out that such an ordinance could conceivably result in the suppression of all views since "the prohibition of all speaking would undoubtedly 'prevent' such eventualities." In *Kunz v. New York,*[146] the Supreme Court invalidated a New York licensing regulation authorizing the administrator to withhold approval if the applicant had in the past "ridiculed or denounced other religious beliefs." The applicant in *Kunz* had been denied a permit because his intemperate religious views had, on a past occasion, caused a serious public disorder. The Supreme Court felt that this was not an appropriate consideration in denying

[142] See cases cited in note 140 *supra.*
[143] Staub v. Baxley, 355 US 313, 2 LEd(2d) 302, 78 SCt 277 (1958).
[144] Shuttlesworth v. City of Birmingham, 394 US 147, 22 LEd(2d) 162, 89 SCt 935 (1969).
[145] 307 US 496, 83 LEd 1123, 59 SCt 954 (1939).
[146] 340 US 290, 95 LEd 280, 71 SCt 312 (1951).

him a permit to speak. For those schooled in peacekeeping, the *Kunz* case may appear a rather startling decision. But Mr. Justice Blackmun has explained why license administrators may not be authorized to delve into what an applicant has said or done in the past, or what his ideological position may be, as a basis for deciding whether to grant a permit. He stated:

> [A] free society prefers to punish the few who abuse rights of free speech *after* they break the law than to throttle them and all others beforehand. It is always difficult to know in advance what an individual will say, and the line between legitimate and illegitimate speech is often so finely drawn that the risks of freewheeling censorship are formidable.[147]

If the applicant's prior conduct or past history for creating disturbances cannot be used as a standard for denying his application, quite clearly the apprehension of a hostile community reception of his views is an inappropriate basis.[148] Where local authorities anticipate an incident because of community intolerance or an adverse local sentiment, the solution lies in routing the demonstrators through a less volatile portion of the town and deploying sufficient police manpower to keep the peace.[149] The right to peacefully advocate unpopular ideas may not be sacrificed to the threat of a hostile community reception.[150]

The first requirement of a constitutionally valid permit system is, then, that the ordinance be narrowly drawn and establish clear, concrete and relevant criteria to control the administrator's discretion. The criteria must relate primarily to considerations of facility allocation and problems of scheduling. The second requirement pertains to the actual manner of administration. It is not enough that the legislature establishes "content neutral" standards governing the issuance of

---

[147] Southeastern Promotions, Ltd. v. Conrad, 420 US 546, 559, 43 LEd(2d) 448, 95 SCt 1239 (1975).

[148] See Bachellar v. Maryland, 397 US 564, 25 LEd(2d) 570, 90 SCt 1312 (1970); Collins v. Chicago Park Dist., 460 F(2d) 746 (7thCir 1972). *See also,* Blasi, *Prior Restraints on Demonstrations,* 68 MICHLREV 1482 (1970).

[149] Blasi, *supra* note 148.

[150] Gregory v. City of Chicago, 394 US 111, 22 LEd(2d) 134, 89 SCt 946 (1969).

permits. Responsible administrators must *in fact* apply these criteria in a uniform, consistent and equal manner. A permit may not be denied because the administrator considers the applicant's views offensive;[151] nor may this result be accomplished indirectly by manipulating demonstration routes or times to cut down a group's exposure. If the city allows a St. Patrick's Day or Veteran's Day parade to pass through the main business district streets, it would scarcely be an equal application of the law to confine a less popular group to side streets and dark alleys.[152] Favoritism has no place in the enforcement of a parade permit scheme.

The final requirement relates to procedural safeguards. A constitutionally valid permit sysem must incorporate procedural safeguards designed to assure prompt processing of applications and expeditious judicial review of adverse permit rulings.[153] Timeliness is an important aspect of effective political protest, and overly cumbersome, time-consuming application procedures can stifle dissent as effectively as outright censorship. For this reason, a permit regulation will be deemed constitutionally deficient unless it incorporates sufficient procedural safeguards to assure that (1) applications do not get bogged down in a mass of bureaucratic red tape, and that (2) avenues exist for prompt judicial review and correction of abuses of administrative discretion.

§ 2.12   —Policing of open-air gatherings

Even with a well-functioning permit system, some incidents are inevitable when groups with opposing ideologies meet on the public streets. The question that arises is: when is regulatory intervention into ongoing speech constitutionally appropriate? But before undertaking to discuss this matter, a word of caution is appropriate.

Before halting a speaker or group of demonstrators, the officer should carefully scrutinize his own motives. If he is

---

[151] Shuttlesworth v. City of Birmingham, 394 US 147, 22 LEd(2d) 162, 89 SCt 935 (1969); Houston Peace Coalition v. Houston City Council, 310 FSupp 457 (SD Tex 1970).

[152] Houston Peace Coalition v. Houston City Council, 310 FSupp 457 (SD Tex 1970).

[153] Southeastern Promotions, Ltd. v. Conrad, 420 US 546, 43 LEd(2d) 488, 95 SCt 1239 (1975).

undertaking the arrest because the individual is a Communist or a Black, or is espousing a philosophy that the officer disapproves, the conviction will not stand. A police officer must erase from his own mind who the group is or what its ideological position is, and focus entirely upon what its conduct consists of on this particular occasion. There are few practices that will alienate a minority group more completely or jeopardize a conviction more certainly than discriminatory or selective enforcement of laws in a First Amendment setting. Even though there may be a narrowly drawn statute prohibiting individuals from demonstrating in the exact location, the conviction will not be permitted to stand if the rules have been waived for other, more favored groups.[154] In his official conduct, the officer must be able to put aside his own personal prejudices and enforce one law for all groups alike.

Mention has already been made of the variety of legal controls available to local communities for the regulation of public assemblies.[155] If there exists a precise and narrowly-drawn statute forbidding picketing in close proximity to schools, courthouses, jails or like facilities; an anti-noise law; an ordinance prohibiting demonstrations without a permit; or a similar regulatory measure making specific conduct illegal, the officer has unquestionable authority to invoke the law and halt violating speech behavior without waiting for signs of a community outbreak. Traffic control measures of general application may also be enforced against participants in a demonstration. Concerning this, the Supreme Court has stated:

> One would not be justified in ignoring the familiar red light because this was thought to be a means of social protest. Nor could one, contrary to traffic regulations, insist upon a street meeting in the middle of Times Square at rush hour as a form of freedom of speech or assembly. Governmental authorities have the duty and responsibility to keep their streets open and available for movement. A group of demonstrators could not insist upon the right to cordon off a street, or entrance to a public or private building, and allow no one to pass who did not agree to listen to their exhortations.[156]

[154] Cox v. Louisiana, 379 US 536, 13 LEd(2d) 471, 85 SCt 453 (1965); Flower v. United States, 407 US 197, 32 LEd(2d) 653, 92 SCt 1842 (1972).

[155] Review § 2.8 *supra*.

[156] Cox v. Louisiana, 379 US 536, 554-5, 13 LEd(2d) 471, 85 SCt 453 (1965).

A number of communities have enacted statutes making it a punishable offense to obstruct the public passage. The Louisiana statute is typical of its kind and provides:

> No person shall wilfully obstruct the free, convenient and normal use of any public sidewalk, street, highway, bridge, alley, road or other passageway, or the entrance, corridor, or passage of any public building ... by impeding, hindering, stifling, retarding or restraining traffic or passage thereon or therein.[157]

A carefully drawn statute like the one above is a valid exercise of police power, and if applied equally to all groups alike, would support a conviction of demonstrators who walk several abreast forcing pedestrians off the sidewalks, obstruct ingress or egress to buildings, or interfere with normal traffic patterns.[158] The chief danger to convictions under "obstructing public passage" statutes is past enforcement patterns. These measures are rarely enforced consistently and uniformly against all groups. Once local authorities tolerate some demonstrations that disrupt normal street uses, this lays a basis for equal protection arguments by others, thereby making it difficult for convictions to stick.[159]

The employment of general disorderly conduct, breach of the peace, and "failure to move on" statutes in a First Amendment setting raises several distinct problems calling for fuller treatment. Initially, there is a consideration of the statute's vulnerability under the void for vagueness doctrine.[160] If this hurdle can be surmounted, and many cases fail on this basis without ever reaching the merits, the next inquiry is whether the statute was properly applied.

1. Refusal to move on

Statutes authorizing the police to arrest individuals for refusing to obey their orders to disperse or "move on" should be used with extreme caution as speech control measures.

---

[157] LaRevStatAnn § 14:100.1 (Cum Supp 1962).

[158] Cameron v. Johnson, 390 US 611, 20 LEd(2d) 182, 88 SCt 1335 (1968); Shuttlesworth v. City of Birmingham, 382 US 87, 15 LEd(2d) 176, 86 SCt 211 (1965) (by implication).

[159] See cases cited in note 154 *supra*.

[160] Review § 2.6 *supra*.

Unless the statute sets forth in specifics the circumstances under which an officer may issue such an order, the statute will not pass the void for vagueness standards. Legislatures may not delegate to police officers an unbridled discretion to issue on-the-spot orders halting demonstrations, coupled with the authority to arrest those who disobey. An ordinance that leaves the terms and conditions upon which citizens can use the streets for speech-related purposes to the unfettered discretion of a police officer could easily be bent into a vehicle for arresting persons whose ideologies or physical appearances may offend him.[161] Even though the officer may be acting solely in the interest of keeping peace, a valid conviction cannot result if the statute violates due process vagueness standards.

Shuttlesworth v. *City of Birmingham* [162] is the leading case on point. Shuttlesworth, a civil rights leader, and several companions were standing outside a department store during the period of a protest boycott. An officer approached the group and told them to move on and clear the sidewalk. The others left but Shuttlesworth stayed behind and, when he questioned the officer's authority, he was arrested under an ordinance which made it an offense, among other things, to "stand . . . upon any street or sidewalk of the city after having been requested by any police officer to move on." The Supreme Court experienced no hesitation in reversing his conviction. The thrust of its ruling was that legislatures may not delegate to police officers authority to arrest those who disobey their orders to disperse and, at the same time, furnish them with no objective standards or guidelines as to when such an order may issue. The reason for this was explained by Mr. Justice Black in a different case:

> [U]nder our democratic system of government, lawmaking is not entrusted to the moment-to-moment judgment of the policeman on his beat. Laws, that is valid laws, are to be made by representatives chosen to make laws for the future, not by police officers whose duty is to enforce laws already enacted and to make arrests only

---

[161] Shuttlesworth v. City of Birmingham, 382 US 87, 15 LEd(2d) 176,

86 SCt 211 (1965).
[162] *Id.*

for conduct already made criminal.... To let a policeman's command become equivalent to a criminal statute comes dangerously near making our government one of men rather than of laws.[163]

Statutes making it an offense to disobey an order are not constitutionally objectionable if coupled with standards controlling *when* an order may be made. Had the Birmingham ordinance made it an offense to "obstruct the free passage upon any public street and remain after having been requested by an officer to move on," the vagueness objection would have been removed.[164] There is a critical difference between this statute and the Birmingham ordinance as written. Now the officer is required to observe specific acts declared unlawful by the legislature (obstructing the public passage) preliminary to issuing an order, the violation of which becomes grounds for arrest.

The point of this discussion is that law enforcement officers have no inherent authority to issue arrest-triggering orders at will and no legislature can give it to them. But since law enforcement officers have no way of judging the constitutionality of the laws they enforce, a simple rule of thumb may avoid entanglement:

> *If the demonstrators are in a place where they have a legal right to be and are conducting themselves in a peaceful and lawful manner, an officer cannot make their conduct a criminal offense by ordering them to disperse and arresting them if they refuse.*[165]

2. Disorderly conduct and breach of peace

A group of civil rights demonstrators, headed by a respected civil rights leader, march two abreast in an orderly manner from city hall to the mayor's residence to press for busing reforms. As they walk, they chant prayers and songs. Residents begin coming out of their homes and a large crowd

---

[163] Gregory v. City of Chicago, 394 US 111, 22 LEd(2d) 134, 89 SCt 946 (1969).

[164] Shuttlesworth v. City of Birmingham, 382 US 87, 15 LEd(2d) 176, 86 SCt 211 (1965) (dicta).

[165] Brown v. Louisiana, 383 US 131, 15 LEd(2d) 637, 86 SCt 719 (1966); Wright v. Georgia, 373 US 284, 10 LEd(2d) 349, 83 SCt 1240 (1963).

of bystanders congregates on the sidewalks. The police officers assigned to the march attempt to keep the two groups separate. The mood of the spectators gradually changes. As the crowd swells, its language becomes rougher and tougher. Jeers and insults are followed by the hurling of rocks and eggs. The police dodge these missiles and attempt to catch those persons in the crowd who are throwing them. Though the demonstrators maintain their decorum in the face of all of this, the spectators are dangerously close to a riot. What are the police to do now?

Unfortunately this scenario has played in virtually every community. Though the theme of the protest may vary from time to time and from place to place, when hotly-contested issues are debated in a public forum, a spark may sometimes ignite. At what point may the police halt speech in the interest of averting local violence and disorder?

At the inception, a distinction must be made between those cases where the speaker or group engages in boisterous, intemperate, antagonistic or disorderly behavior, and those cases in which the threat to the public peace arises out of a hostile audience-reaction to the *theme* of an orderly First Amendment protest. The latter situation is frequently referred to as the problem of "mob censorship" or the "heckler's veto." Different regulatory responses are called for in each of these situations.

The propriety of arresting a speaker or group of demonstrators, on charges of disorderly conduct or for causing a breach of the peace, depends upon three primary considerations:

(1) the conduct of the speaker or group engaged in First Amendment behavior,
(2) the reaction of the audience, and
(3) the availability of police manpower at the scene to avert a possible crisis situation.

These factors are interrelated. Their interplay can be seen by a comparison of the two leading cases of *Feiner v. New York*[166] and *Cox v. Louisiana*.[167]

---

[166] 340 US 315, 95 LEd 295, 71 SCt 303 (1951).

[167] 379 US 536, 13 LEd(2d) 471, 85 SCt 453 (1965).

In the *Feiner* case, Feiner, a university student, delivered a soapbox oratory to a racially mixed crowd of about eighty persons on a busy street in downtown Syracuse, New York. The audience filled the sidewalks and spread out into the street. Pedestrians were inconvenienced and were forced to walk into traffic. In the course of his speech, Feiner, in a loud, high-pitched voice, attacked the mayor of Syracuse as a "champagne-sipping bum"; made some derogatory remarks about President Truman and certain local political officials; and then urged the Blacks in the audience to "rise up in arms and fight for their rights." The audience was restless, and there was some pushing, shoving and angry muttering. At least one man indicated that if the police did not get Feiner down, he would do it himself. There were only two police officers present at this time. Feiner was requested several times by the police to stop speaking, and when he continued in the face of an impending riot, he was arrested on a charge of disorderly conduct. In affirming his conviction, the Supreme Court said:

> We are aware that the ordinary murmurings and objections of a hostile audience cannot be allowed to silence a speaker, and are also mindful of the possible danger of giving overzealous police officials complete discretion to break up otherwise lawful public meetings. "A state may not unduly suppress free communication of views, religious or other, under the guise of conserving desirable conditions." But we are not faced here with such a situation. It is one thing to say that the police cannot be used as an instrument for the suppression of unpopular views, and another to say that, *when as here the speaker passes the bounds of argument or persuasion and undertakes incitement to riot*, they are powerless to prevent a breach of the peace.[168]

The crucial factor in *Feiner* was that Feiner himself was intentionally provoking the situation. The audience was not reacting intolerantly or unreasonably to what Feiner was saying; he was intentionally inflaming them by urging them to "rise up in arms and fight." There were only two police officers available at the scene to keep the peace, and the audience was threatening to get out of hand. Under these circumstances, the

---

[168] Feiner v. New York, 340 US 315, 320-21, 95 LEd 295, 71 SCt 303 (1951).

police were justified in arresting Feiner without first attempting to placate an enraged bystander audience that outnumbered them forty to one.

Cox v. *Louisiana*, the second case, presents a somewhat different situation. In *Cox*, 2,000 Black university students assembled at the state capital and marched in an orderly fashion, two abreast and stopping for traffic lights, to the courthouse. The purpose of the demonstration was to protest the jailing of twenty-three fellow students who had been arrested on the previous day for picketing a segregated lunch counter. The students were at all times decorous and well-behaved. When the students reached the courthouse, they sang "God Bless America," pledged allegiance to the flag, prayed briefly, sang two "freedom songs," and then prepared to listen to a speech delivered by Cox, their advisor and a Field Secretary for CORE. The local authorities had been given advance notice of this demonstration the evening before, and seventy-five to eighty combined firemen and police officers had been stationed between the demonstrators and a crowd of 100 to 300 curious white spectators who had gathered on the sidewalk to watch. According to the Court, the mood of the demonstrators was never hostile, aggressive or unfriendly. Rather, they behaved in a polite and orderly manner throughout. As in *Feiner*, there was some grumbling and jeering on the part of the audience, but there was no showing that the police detachment at the scene was inadequate to control any possible outbreaks that might arise. At the end of his speech, Cox urged the students to go uptown and "sit in" at various segregated lunch counters. The sheriff, deeming the last appeal to be inflammatory, took a power megaphone and ordered the demonstrators to go home. When the order was ignored, the police began to explode tear gas shells into the crowd of demonstrators; the group soon broke up. Cox was later arrested and charged with breach of the peace. On appeal, the Supreme Court reversed his conviction, holding that Cox and his supporters had not engaged in any conduct which the state of Louisiana could punish as a breach of the peace. Their singing and chanting, while it may have been loud, was not disorderly or riotous. The tenseness, the angry mutterings, grumblings and jeerings from the onlookers, though probably of the same magnitude as in *Feiner,* were not attributable to anything that Cox and his followers had said. If First Amendment rights are not to be sacrificed because of local hostilities to their assertion, the police, in a case like *Cox,* have a clear-cut duty to arrest the hecklers and not the speaker.

On the basis of *Feiner* and *Cox,* some guidelines for police action can be drawn. If the speaker is deliberately attempting either to incite or to antagonize his audience, the police may break up the assembly and arrest the speaker or group when the situation threatens to get out of hand. In the more modern terminology of the *Brandenburg* case,[169] the police may intervene to avert a disturbance the speaker is attempting to ignite when (1) the speech is directed toward producing *immediate* lawless action, and (2) an uncontrollable outbreak is threatened. On the other hand, if the speaker or group is not responsible for the hostile attitude of the listeners, aside from the fact that they are peacefully expressing unpopular views, the police have a clear obligation to do everything to keep the audience in line so that the meeting will be allowed to continue. A meeting held in a lawful manner does not lose its constitutional protection because an unsympathetic audience threatens to retaliate with violence.[170] If the police have adequate advance notice of the event, certainly there would be no excuse for depriving a group of its constitutional right to peaceably assemble by failure to provide adequate police protection.[171]

Occasionally, however, miscalculations can occur as to the strength of the peace-keeping force needed at the scene of a demonstration. Even in the face of what appears to be a manpower shortage, the police at the site should do everything within their power to contain the hecklers until reinforcements arrive. Only at the point when the situation appears wholly

[169] Brandenburg v. Ohio, 395 US 444, 23 LEd(2d) 430, 89 SCt 1827 (1969). Review § 2.4 *supra.*

[170] Gregory v. City of Chicago, 394 US 111, 22 LEd(2d) 134, 89 SCt 946 (1969).

[171] Williams v. Wallace, 240 FSupp 100 (ND Ala 1965); Cottonreader v. Johnson, 252 FSupp 492 (ND Ala 1966). *See also* Chapple, *Freedom of Assembly,* 55 JCRIMLC&PS 425 (1964).

unmanageable, should thought be given to the possibility of halting protected speech as a means of peace-keeping. Unquestionably, in the face of an impending riot, the police would be justified in enlisting the voluntary cooperation of the demonstrators in averting a crisis, even though not of their own making. In the event that this request is refused, a difficult decision must be reached for which there is no authoritative guidance. The Supreme Court has never made its position clear whether the police may arrest orderly protest demonstrators who refuse to stop speaking when requested to do so in the face of an impending riot. *Gregory v. City of Chicago* [172] posed this question but the Court's holding fell short of answering it. Comedian Dick Gregory led a group of civil rights demonstrators on an orderly protest march through a Chicago residential area. Approximately one hundred Chicago police officers had been assigned to accompany them. As they marched, the Gregory group was met by a crowd of approximately 1,000 hostile spectators. The police made a commendable effort to keep the two groups separate, but the onlookers became increasingly more unruly and began hurling rocks, eggs and bottles at the marchers. The demonstrators, nevertheless, maintained their decorum and made no effort to retaliate in kind. Fearful that the situation was rapidly becoming riotous, the police five times requested Gregory and his group to leave the area, offering an escort and protection. Some of the marchers left. Those who remained were arrested and charged with disorderly conduct. The Supreme Court, in a sparse one-page opinion written by Mr. Chief Justice Warren, reversed the conviction, stating that there was no evidence in the record to indicate that the marchers had at any time behaved in a disorderly manner.

Granting that peaceful demonstrators are not vicariously responsible for the lack of restraint shown by spectators and cannot be arrested on charges of *disorderly conduct* because spectators threaten to riot, the case leaves unanswered whether peaceful demonstrators may be arrested on some *other* grounds when, in the face of a threatened civil disorder, they

[172] 394 US 111, 22 LEd(2d) 134, 89 SCt 946 (1969).

refuse to obey a police request to stop demonstrating. Until this question is resolved, the solution lies in "protective custody." Where all reasonable efforts to pacify a hostile crowd of spectators have failed, and the police are no longer able to maintain order, to avoid bloodshed and property damage, the police should ask the demonstrators to cooperate voluntarily in stopping their protest, and if this is not forthcoming, take them into custody for their own protection but without preferring charges.

Since the Constitution protects the right to engage in peaceful protest, but not the right to disrupt a meeting, consideration should never be given to halting speech conduct until after a conscientious attempt has been made to arrest those who are directly responsible for causing the disturbance and until after the situation is out of hand. Even though arresting the speaker or demonstrators who have occasioned the crowd to gather may appear the simplest and most expeditious solution to the problem of maintaining law and order on the streets, suppressing free speech is a terrific price to pay for averting minor disturbances. Where it is the hostile reception and not the speech itself that menaces the public peace, peace-keeping efforts should be focused upon the crowd and the right to speak preserved until a point is reached where it is impossible for the speech to continue because the necessary order no longer exists.

§ 2.13   Summary and practical suggestions

Freedom of expression is essential to democratic ideals and institutions. The constitutional guarantees contained in the First Amendment are binding upon all levels of government but not on private property owners. Freedom of expression includes the right to formulate ideas, opinions and beliefs; the right to communicate them by virtually every known medium including, in some cases, mute symbolic acts; and the right to gather and receive information from others. In the nature of things, the last two rights are not as complete and absolute as the first. The constitutionality of measures burdening free speech rights is tested in modern times by *ad hoc* interest balancing under which conflicting First Amendment and public interests are compared, and a balance struck with the weightier interest prevailing.

In terms of mediums of communication, governments have far more latitude in regulating speech delivery mediums that make extensive use of open-air facilities, such as parades, pickets and public assemblies (often referred to as "speech plus" mediums), than in the case of expressive mediums that rely to a lesser extent on public conduct to reach the desired audience. The reason for the distinction lies in the greater degree of public inconvenience which the former pursuits occasion. The First Amendment does not deprive local governments of the power to place reasonable regulations upon the use of streets, sidewalks, parks and other public facilities for speech purposes. Permits are appropriate regulatory devices for allocating physical facilities and scheduling times. Local communities may similarly enact measures modulating noise levels or banning disruptive speech activity in school and hospital zones, residential neighborhoods and the like.

One of the primary purposes of the First Amendment was to remove government control over speech content. It remains true today that there is less judicial tolerance for legislative attempts to limit *content* of speech than for laws regulating the *manner of presentation*, such as laws exacting permits for all public assemblies. There are a limited number of speech subject matter categories from which free speech protection has been withdrawn. Obscenity, "fighting words," threats and violence incitement fall outside the ambit of First Amendment concern and may be regulated and punished. But as to the vast range of other subject matters falling within the First Amendment, regulatory controls based upon content are, almost without exception, constitutionally repugnant. This limitation is addressed to police officers also. In the enforcement of laws, officers must carefully guard against even an appearance of prejudice and must concentrate solely upon conduct, disregarding ideologies and points of view being expressed. The void for vagueness doctrine precludes legislative delegation of extensive on-the-spot enforcement discretion. Laws operative in a First Amendment setting must contain clear, precise and objective guidelines whereby law enforcement officers can distinguish between innocent and unlawful conduct. Whenever a choice exists between invoking a narrow statute covering specific conduct (such as obstructing the public passage or picketing in a school zone) or a statute with a higher discretionary element (such as breach of the peace or disorderly conduct), the officer should always prefer the former because such statutes are less likely to be vulnerable to void for vagueness attacks.

In policing public assemblies, the officer should bear in mind that ordinances purporting to authorize arrests for refusing to obey his command may be unconstitutional and that, in any event, if the demonstrators are in a place where they have a legal right to be and are conducting themselves in a peaceful and lawful manner, he cannot make their conduct a crime by ordering them to disperse and arresting them if they disobey. Where a speaker or group of demonstrators attempts to provoke a riot by advocating immediate acts of violence, the police can halt the meeting and arrest the participants if a disruption of order appears imminent. But where the speaker or his group remains decorous, but an outbreak is threatened because a crowd, hostile to his views, is intent on disrupting the meeting, the police must make every possible effort to protect the right to speak and may request that First Amendment activities be suspended only when efforts to quiet the crowd have failed, and an uncontrollable outbreak is imminently threatened.

Chapter 3

AUTHORITY TO DETAIN AND ARREST*

The right of the people to be secure in their persons, houses, papers, and effects, against unreasonable searches and seizures, shall not be violated, and no Warrants shall issue, but upon probable cause, supported by Oath or affirmation, and particularly describing the place to be searched, and the persons or things to be seized.

FOURTH AMENDMENT, 1791

§ 3.1   Historical development of the law of arrest—England

Under English common law, sheriffs and constables appointed by the Crown were the only designated peace officers. These sheriffs and constables had the authority to call upon ordinary citizens to form a *posse comitatus* and to assist in making an arrest. As the duty to protect society was largely the responsibility of the private citizen, the citizen as well as designated peace officers, had the power of arrest. Unlike the statutory authority possessed by the private citizen today,

* by John C. Klotter

102

under common law the private citizen had power that was equal in nearly all respects to that of the appointed sheriff or constable. Sheriffs, constables, and private individuals had a duty and responsibility to carry out without delay the command of a warrant issued by a judicial officer. Where no warrant was obtained, a distinction was drawn in the law of arrest between felonies and misdemeanors.

Great latitude was given the officer or citizen in making an arrest for a felony. In the case of a felony, an officer or a private citizen acting without a warrant could make an arrest if a felony were committed in his presence or view, or if he had reasonable grounds to believe that the person to be arrested had committed the felony. Under this common law interpretation, a peace officer or private person who had reasonable grounds to believe that a felony had been committed could make an arrest even though the crime in fact was not committed in his presence and even though the person suspected might later prove to be innocent.

At common law, an arrest for an offense less than a felony could not be made without a warrant unless it involved a breach of the peace. Although actual personal violence was not an essential element of a breach of the peace, there must have been some violation of public order or public decorum. For example, shooting, hollering, cursing or using vile and obscene language was considered a breach of the peace, while mere drunkenness without any other disturbance was not considered a breach of the peace to justify an arrest without a warrant.

Many of the arrest practices developed in England prior to the adoption of our Constitution were brought to this country by the colonists and form a part of our legal tradition. Due to necessity and changing conditions most states, by statute, have modified and deleted some of the more technical requirements of the common law of arrest. For example, most states have deleted the requirement that a misdemeanor be a breach of the peace in order for the police to make a warrantless arrest. Nonetheless, the fundamental and substantive protections developed under the common law for those suspected of having committed a crime remain unchanged today and are embodied in the philosophy of the Fourth Amendment. Referring to this historical basis in *Henry v. United States,* Mr. Justice Douglas observed:

> The requirement of probable cause has roots that are deep in our history. The general warrant, in which the name of the person to be arrested was left blank, and the writ of assistance, against which James Otis inveighed, both perpetuated the oppressive practice of allowing the police to arrest and search on suspicion. . . . And as the early American decisions both before and immediately after its [the Fourth Amendment] adoption show, common rumor or report, suspicion or even "strong reason to suspect" was not adequate to support a warrant for arrest.

History has played a large role in molding our legal institutions. The decisions of the Supreme Court of the United States today are to a great extent the result of the development and refinement of common-law concepts and practices followed several centuries ago.

§ 3.2   Constitutional provisions

The Constitution of the United States and the constitutions of all of the respective states have provisions concerning arrest, search and seizure. The Fourth Amendment to the Constitution, which was adopted in 1791, provides as follows:

> The right of the people to be secure in their *persons,* houses, papers, and effects, against unreasonable searches and seizures, shall not be violated, and no Warrants shall issue, but upon probable cause, supported by Oath or affirmation, and particularly describing the place to be searched, and the *persons* or things *to be seized.* (Emphasis added.)

Although this section is often referred to as the search and seizure provision of the Constitution, it also protects individuals from illegal seizures of their persons—i.e., arrests. Both the express terminology of the amendment and the historical context of its adoption lead to this conclusion. In the 1959 *Henry* case the Supreme Court dispelled any uncertainty which might previously have existed as to the status

---

[1] 361 US 98, 4 LEd(2d) 134, 80 SCt 168 (1959). See Part II of this book.

of illegal arrest under the Fourth Amendment in the following language:

> [I]t is the command of the Fourth Amendment that no warrants either for searches or *arrests* shall issue except upon "probable cause. . . ." (Emphasis added.)

Prior to 1962, federal arrests, searches and seizures were governed by the standards embodied in the Fourth Amendment, while similar state procedures were judged by a more flexible standard embraced in the due process clause of the Fourteenth Amendment. In 1963, however, the Supreme Court of the United States in *Ker* v. *California*[2] held that arrests by state and local police officers are to be judged by the same constitutional standards as apply to the federal government. Hence, in order for an arrest to be valid today, the police must comply with the provisions of the Fourth Amendment as well as their own state constitutions and statutes.

§ 3.3 "Arrest" defined

Each state has a statute or code authorizing a peace officer to make an arrest. For example, the Kentucky Revised Statute states:

> (1) A peace officer may make an arrest in obedience to a warrant, or without a warrant when a felony or misdemeanor is committed in his presence or when he has reasonable grounds to believe that the person being arrested has committed a felony.[3]

The Illinois Code, which allows officers to make arrests for misdemeanors not committed in their presence, provides that: A peace officer may arrest a person when:

> (a) He has a warrant commanding that such person be arrested; or
> (b) He has reasonable grounds to believe that a warrant for the person's arrest has been issued in this State or in another jurisdiction; or
> (c) He has reasonable grounds to believe that the person is committing or has committed an offense.[4]

---

[2] 374 US 23, 10 LEd(2d) 726, 83 SCt 1623 (1963).

[3] KY REV STAT ANN §431.005(1) (1975).

[4] ILLREVSTAT ch 38, §107-2 (1975).

Although the state and federal statutes and codes include provisions specifying when a peace officer may make an arrest with or without a warrant, few of these statutes attempt to define arrest. One exception is the Illinois Code, which defines arrest as follows:

"Arrest" means the taking of a person into custody.[5]

Because most of the statutes fail to define arrest, it is necessary to look to court decisions, treatises and encyclopedias for definitions. Some of the more common definitions include the following:

(a) "The term 'arrest' has a technical meaning, applicable in legal proceedings. It implies that a person is thereby restrained of his liberty by some officer or agent of the law, armed with lawful process, authorizing and requiring the arrest be made. It is intended to serve, and does serve, the end of bringing the person arrested personally within the custody and control of the law, for the purpose specified in, or contemplated by, the process."[6]

(b) An arrest is the taking of another into custody for the actual or purported purpose of bringing the other before a court, or of otherwise securing the administration of the law.[7]

(c) An arrest is the taking, seizing, or detaining of the person of another, (1) by touching or putting hands on him; (2) or by any act that indicates an intention to take him into custody and that subjects him to the actual control and will of the person making the arrest; or (3) by the consent of the person to be arrested.[8]

Arrest has also been judicially defined as the taking, seizing or detaining of the person of another, by touching or by putting hands upon him, in the execution of process or any act indicating an intention to arrest.

None of these definitions is entirely satisfactory. Arrest is a term which eludes precise definition. Basically, it is a legal conclusion used to describe the complex series of events which

---

[5] IllRevStat ch 38, §102-5 (1975).
[6] Hadley v. Tinnin, 170 NC 84, 86 SE 1017 (1915), quoting Lawrence v. Buxton, 102 NC 131, 8 SE 774 (1889).
[7] Restatement(2d) of Torts §112 (1965).
[8] 5 AmJur(2d) Arrest §1 (1962).

have in fact taken place. The law defines the elements necessary to constitute an arrest. Whether or not all of these elements are present in a given situation depends upon the facts of each case, including the mental attitude of the officer, the circumstances under which he confronts the person, the reasonable reaction of that person to the officer's action and a multitude of other actions which cannot be conveyed by a bland definition.[9]

An illegal arrest, contrary to the belief of some, does not deprive the court of jurisdiction to try the offender.[10] An indictment may be returned even though the arrest was illegal. On the other hand, the determination as to whether the officer's actions amount to a legal arrest becomes very important in some cases. Frequently, the success or failure of the state in its prosecution of a case will depend entirely upon the legality of the officer's arrest.

For example, the determination as to whether the arrest was legal becomes very important where the court is considering a motion to suppress evidence. If an arrest is illegal, the search incident to that arrest is not authorized and any evidence secured thereby will not be admissible in court. In some instances this suppression of evidence will have the same effect as depriving the court of jurisdiction to try the offender. If the only evidence which the state has to convict an armed robbery suspect is a gun, stocking, and large roll of bills taken from his person during a search incident to an illegal arrest, the offender will go free. Therefore, it is imperative that the officer thoroughly understand the meaning of the word "arrest."

§ 3.4   Elements necessary to constitute an arrest

Although it is difficult, if not impossible, to frame a definition of an arrest which will apply in all circumstances, the following common elements must be considered in order to understand the court's reasoning in determining when the acts of the officer are considered an arrest.

---

[9] United States v. Rodgers, 246 FSupp 405 (ED Mo 1965).

[10] Frisbie v. Collins, 342 US 519, 96 LEd 541, 72 SCt 509 (1952).

1. Real or assumed legal authority

To constitute an "arrest" as the term is used in criminal law, the restraint of the liberty of the individual must be either under actual authority of an officer or assumed authority. An officer is exercising assumed authority when he acts under a void warrant or makes an arrest for a misdemeanor not committed in his presence, where such is not authorized by the statutes of his state. In *District of Columbia* v. *Perry*,[11] a Maryland state trooper pursued a speeder across the state line into the District of Columbia where he ultimately halted the car. While the Maryland trooper was checking the motorist's license, a member of the District of Columbia police force arrived at the scene. Upon being informed by the Maryland officer that the motorist was driving in excess of the local speed limit and was believed to be intoxicated, the District of Columbia officer arrested him. The court held that the arrest was illegal since the Maryland officer had no authority to make an arrest in the District. The District of Columbia officer was likewise without authority to make a valid arrest because neither the speeding nor driving while intoxicated, both misdemeanors, were committed in his presence. There was an arrest in fact when the District of Columbia officer took the speeding motorist into custody under assumed legal authority, but the arrest was illegal because it was not in compliance with local statutes.

2. Intention

The intention of the arresting officer to take a person into custody is one of the basic elements which distinguishes an arrest from lessor forms of detention. Although the intent of the officer is an important factor in every arrest, specific or actual intent is not necessary. For example, under certain circumstances a court may infer from the officer's conduct an intent to take a person into custody, when in fact no such intention existed. Hence, in a false arrest case, the officer cannot escape liability by stating that he didn't intend to make the

---

[11] 215 A(2d) 845 (DC 1966).

arrest, if the circumstances indicated that the officer did in fact take the person into custody.

3. Custody and control

To constitute a technical arrest, the arrested party must come within the actual custody and control of the officer. The person to be arrested may come within the custody and control of the law (1) by submission, or (2) by a manual caption as evidenced by some touching of the body.[12] If the person submits voluntarily to the control of the officer, he is under arrest as much as if the officer had subdued and handcuffed him. It is not necessary that there be an application of actual force, manual touching, or physical restraint visible to the eye, so long as the person arrested understands that he is in the power of the one arresting him and submits to his control. In fact, mere words on the part of the officer can constitute an arrest if they are coupled with an intent on behalf of the officer to restrain and if they in fact cause a person to be restrained of his liberty.

One court has explained "custody and control" by stating that no actual force is necessary to constitute an arrest if the arresting officer intends to take the person into custody and supports his intention by an unequivocal act, such as keeping the arrested person in sight and controlling his actions. However, the court continued,

[O]ne person can no more arrest another by simply telling him to "consider himself under arrest" and then turning on his heel and leaving that person free to go his own way, than one can commit a homicide by merely telling another to consider himself dead.[13]

Some writers have stated that an intention to submit on the part of the arrestee is essential to constitute an arrest. If this were true in all situations, a person who was unconscious or intoxicated could not be placed under arrest. A person may be arrested for intoxication where there is actual seizure and

[12] Bankers Ass'n v. Cassady, 264 Ky 378, 94 SW(2d) 622 (1936); State v. Dunivan, 217 MoApp 584, 269 SW 415 (1925).
[13] Berry v. Bass, 157 La 81, 102 So 76 (1924).

restraint even though he does not understand or intend to be arrested.

Even with the definitions and guidelines obtained from various cases it is often difficult to determine whether an arrest has been consummated. Depending as it does on the intention of the officer making the arrest and the person arrested in some instances, the determination is often a question of fact to be resolved by a jury.

§ 3.5　Arrest under the authority of a warrant

The primary and most basic source of authority to arrest, recognized under the common law and under modern statutes, is that of a warrant. This is the only authority expressly sanctioned by the Constitution of the United States. The Fourth Amendment sets forth the standards under which a warrant may be issued:

> [N]o warrant shall issue but upon probable cause, supported by Oath or affirmation, and particularly describing ... the persons or things to be seized.

Most state statutes or codes have provisions to the effect that a peace officer may arrest where he has a warrant commanding him to make such an arrest. For example, the Illinois Code provides:

> A peace officer may arrest a person when: (a) He has a warrant commanding that such person be arrested; ... .[14]

Similarly, the California statute states: "A peace officer may make an arrest in obedience to a warrant. . . ." [15] Even without such statutory authorization, this right would exist by virtue of the common law.

The function of an arrest warrant is to protect private citizens from the harassment of unjustified arrests, incarcerations and criminal prosecutions. At common law it was expected that most arrests would be made under a warrant and only in exceptional situations was authority extended to permit an

---

[14] IllRevStat ch 38, §107-2(a) (1975).　　[15] CalPenalCode §836 (1970).

arrest without it. The common-law preference for arrests made under the authority of a warrant is embodied in the Fourth Amendment. The chief objection to the warrantless arrest is that it bypasses

> ... the safeguards provided by an objective predetermination of probable cause, and substitutes instead the far less reliable procedure of an after-the-event justification for the arrest or search, too likely to be subtly influenced by the familiar shortcomings of hindsight judgment.[16]

Wherever it is at all practicable, the officer should obtain a warrant before acting. The Supreme Court has indicated that in doubtful or marginal cases where probable cause for an arrest is not clearly made out, action under a warrant will be sustained where one without it will fail. The Court stated:

> "[T]he informed and deliberate determinations of magistrates empowered to issue warrants ... are to be preferred over the hurried action of officers...."[17]

Aside from constitutional considerations, there is a very practical reason why police officers should, wherever time permits, obtain a warrant before making an arrest. If the warrant is proper on its face and the officer does not abuse his authority in executing the arrest, he will be protected against civil liability for false arrest or false imprisonment, even though it is later determined that the arrest was unjustified.[18]

§ 3.6   Requirements for a valid arrest warrant

To be valid and executable, the warrant must comply with definite standards or requirements. Some of these requirements are constitutional requirements, while others are either statutory or judicially determined. If any one of the requirements is lacking, the warrant is invalid, and an arrest made under that warrant, as well as the search incidental to that ar-

---

[16] Beck v Ohio, 379 US 89, 13 LEd(2d) 142, 85 SCt 223 (1964).

[17] United States v. Ventresca, 380 US 102, 13 LEd(2d) 684, 85 SCt 741 (1965), quoting United States v.

Lefkowitz, 285 US 452, 76 LEd 877, 52 SCt 120 (1932).

[18] Alexander v. Lindsey, 230 NC 663, 55 SE(2d) 470 (1949).

rest, is unauthorized. The most common requirements for a valid arrest warrant are discussed below.

1. The warrant must be supported by "probable cause."

Probably the most important requirement is the Fourth Amendment direction that "... no warrant shall issue but upon probable cause ..." The Supreme Court of the United States has defined probable cause as follows:

> Probable cause exists where "the facts and circumstances within [the arresting officers'] knowledge and of which they had reasonably trustworthy information [are] sufficient in themselves to warrant a man of reasonable caution in the belief that" an offense has been or is being committed. [Citation omitted.] [19]

This probable cause must be found to exist by a magistrate or other judicial officer. In order for the warrant to serve the protective function which it was designed to achieve, the magistrate, in issuing the warrant, must (1) evaluate the evidence presented against the person suspected of having committed a crime, and (2) determine whether, in his impartial judgment, the charges against the individual are sufficiently supported to justify placing him in custody.

(a) Sufficiency of information

As the magistrate must make this determination on the basis of the evidence presented to him in the complaint, he must be supplied with sufficient information to support an independent judgment that probable cause exists to justify the issuance of an arrest warrant. Although the peace officer is not required to furnish evidence sufficient to establish guilt beyond a reasonable doubt, he must supply more than mere suspicions or conclusions. The complaint must indicate in detail some of the reasons and facts that support the officer's conclusion that a crime has in fact been committed and that the person to be arrested did in fact commit the crime.

For example, in the case of *Whiteley* v. *Warden*,[20] the arrest and the incidental search were held invalid because nothing

[19] Draper v. United States, 358 US 307, 3 LEd(2d) 327, 79 SCt 329 (1959).

[20] 401 US 560, 28 LEd(2d) 306, 91 SCt 1031 (1971).

more than the peace officer's conclusion that a crime had been committed was given to the magistrate. The basis for the arrest warrant issued by the justice of the peace was a complaint which stated:

> "I, C. W. Ogburn, do solemnly swear that on or about the 23 day of November, A.D., 1964, in the County of Carbon and State of Wyoming, the said Harold Whiteley and Jack Daley, defendants, did then and there unlawfully break and enter a locked and sealed building. . . ."

In reversing the conviction, the Supreme Court of the United States pointed out that the complaint consisted of nothing more than the complainant's conclusion that the individuals named perpetrated the offenses described in the complaint. Although the officers in this case had more information at their disposal, they did not furnish it to the magistrate who issued the warrant. The Court reaffirmed the reasoning that the magistrate must base his decision on the information he has available when the warrant is issued.

The amount of pre-arrest information necessary to obtain a warrant is no greater than that required to make an arrest without a warrant. In fact, there has been some indication in recent Supreme Court decisions that the "probable cause" requirement for a warrant may be even less exacting than the "reasonable grounds" for making an arrest without a warrant.[21] The Supreme Court has recognized that affidavits are drafted by nonlawyers in the midst of criminal investigations. If the constitutional requirement of probable cause were given an overly technical construction by magistrates and judges, a principal incentive now existing for the procurement of arrest warrants would be destroyed.[22]

In *Spinelli v. United States*,[23] the Court summarized the standards to be applied in determining probable cause:

---

[21] Aguilar v. Texas, 378 US 108, 12 LEd(2d) 723, 84 SCt 1509 (1964).

[22] United States v. Ventresca, 380 US 102, 13 LEd(2d) 684, 85 SCt 741 (1965). Also see rule 4(b) of the Federal Rules of Criminal Procedure which provides that "The finding of probable cause may be based upon hearsay evidence in whole or in part."

[23] 393 US 410, 21 LEd(2d) 637, 89 SCt 584 (1969).

In holding as we have done, we do not retreat from the established propositions that only the probability, and not a prima facie showing, of criminal activity is the standard of probable cause . . . ; that affidavits of probable cause are tested by much less rigorous standards than those governing the admissibility of evidence at trial . . . ; that in judging probable cause issuing magistrates are not to be confined by niggardly limitations or by restrictions on the use of their common sense . . . ; and that their determination of probable cause should be paid great deference by reviewing courts. . . .

(b) Use of informants

In recent years there have been many court decisions concerning the propriety of using hearsay evidence in determining if probable cause exists. Closely related is the legality of using information to support the probable cause determination without disclosing the informant who supplied the information to the officer.

In the case of *Aguilar* v. *Texas*,[24] the United States Supreme Court reaffirmed previous decisions stating that the affidavit for the arrest warrant may be based on hearsay information and need not reflect the direct personal observation of the affiant. The Court, however, went on to explain that the magistrate must be informed of some of the underlying circumstances from which the informant concluded that a crime had in fact been committed. In 1965, in *United States* v. *Ventresca*,[25] the Court again placed the stamp of approval on the use of undisclosed informants, but cautioned that recital of some of the underlying circumstances in the affidavit is essential if the magistrate is to perform his function.

But in 1969, the Supreme Court in *Spinelli* v. *United States*[26] warned against carrying the use of undisclosed informants too far and reversed a case because the affidavit had not sufficient information for the issuing magistrate to conclude that probable cause existed.

If information obtained from an unnamed informant is to be used in obtaining an arrest warrant, and especially if this information is the only basis for determining probable cause,

---

[24] 378 US 108, 12 LEd(2d) 723, 84 SCt 1509 (1964).
[25] 380 US 102, 13 LEd(2d) 684, 85 SCt 741 (1965).
[26] 393 US 410, 21 LEd(2d) 637, 89 SCt 584 (1969).

the affiant must establish (1) that the informant is reliable and (2) that the information from the informant is credible. When probable cause for an arrest warrant is based solely on an informer's unverified report, reliability of the informer is crucial.[27]

In addition to establishing reliability of the informant, the affiant, usually the officer, must make certain that the information from the informant was not just rumor or suspicion. The criminal activity must be described in such detail that the magistrate can reasonably conclude that the information is credible.[28]

The United States Supreme Court has made it clear that it is not essential that the informant be one who has given reliable information in the past;[29] however, to avoid problems it is preferable to establish clearly the reliability of the informant and obtain definite statements concerning the basis of the informant's information. Where the informant has not given valid information on a previous occasion, the officer should verify the information and make an independent investigation to obtain additional "probable cause."

2. *The affidavit for the warrant must be supported by oath or affirmation.*

This Fourth Amendment requirement is a prerequisite to conferring jurisdiction on the magistrate over the person of the defendant. Some person must swear to the facts and circumstances which are described in the affidavit. Although it is the responsibility of the magistrate or other judicial officer to make certain that the affidavit is given under oath, it is advisable that the police officer who is submitting the affidavit, if necessary, remind the magistrate of this requirement. Although the officer would probably not be held liable if he executed the warrant which was not given under oath, any evidence obtained as a result of this arrest warrant and an

---

[27] United States v. Manning, 448 F(2d) 992 (2ndCir 1971).

[28] United States v. Drew, 436 F(2d) 529 (5thCir 1971).

[29] United States v Harris, 403 US 573, 29 LEd(2d) 723, 91 SCt 2075 (1971).

incidental search would be inadmissible if the defense could show that the oath was not given.

3. The person to be seized must be particularly described.

A third requirement included in the Fourth Amendment is that the person to be seized must be particularly described. As stated by the American Law Institute:

> An arrest under a warrant is not privileged unless the person arrested (a) is a person sufficiently named or otherwise described in the warrant and is, or is reasonably believed by the actor to be, the person intended, or (b) although not such person, has knowingly caused the actor to believe him to be so.[30]

The usual method of designating the person to be arrested is to insert his name in the warrant. Although the name on the warrant does not necessarily have to be spelled exactly as the true name is spelled, so long as it identifies the person to be arrested, it must at least be similar. For example, the Supreme Court has held that a warrant that authorized the arrest of the person designated as "James West" without providing any further designation or description would not justify the arrest of "Vandy M. West" who had never been known by the name appearing on the warrant, and who in no way caused the mistake, irrespective of the fact that "Vandy West" was the intended subject of the warrant.[31] A warrant which leaves a blank for the arresting officer to fill in the name violates the Fourteenth Amendment standards of particularity. If the name is not known, the warrant must include a description which is sufficient to identify with reasonable certainty the person to be arrested. This may be done by describing his occupation, his personal appearance, peculiarities, place of residence, or other means of identification.[32]

There has been much unnecessary confusion concerning the use of the "John Doe" warrants. A warrant that authorizes the arrest of "John Doe," without any further description or identification of the person to be arrested, is a nullity. It is

[30] RESTATEMENT(2d) OF TORTS §125 (1965).
[31] West v. Cabell, 153 US 78, 38 LEd 643, 14 SCt 752 (1894).
[32] People v. Montoya, 255 CalApp-(2d) 137, 63 CalRptr 73 (1967).

obvious that such a warrant does not particularly describe "the person to be seized." A warrant is valid, however, if it is drafted to authorize the arrest of "John Doe," and provides an adequate description which will identify the person to be arrested. For example, the California Court of Appeals in the *Montoya* case agreed that:

> The weight of authority holds that to meet the constitutional requirements, a "John Doe" warrant must describe the person to be seized with reasonable particularity.

The court in that case went on to find that the description of the defendant as a "white male about, 30 to 35 years, 5'10", 175 pounds, dark hair, medium build," did not meet the constitutional requirements of reasonable particularity.

On the other hand, where the warrant directed officers to arrest "John Doe, a white male with black wavy hair and stocky build observed using a telephone in apartment 4C, 1806 Patricia Lane, East McKeesport, Pennsylvania," the Third Circuit Court of Appeals held that there was sufficient physical description coupled with the precise location at which the person could be found to make the John Doe warrant valid.[33] The court in so holding explained that "the technical requirements of elaborate specificity once exacted under common law pleadings have no place in this area."

The best procedure is to make every effort to determine the name and/or alias of the person to be arrested. If this is not possible and a John Doe arrest warrant is issued, the peace officer should try to include all identifying information, especially that information which is peculiar to the individual to be arrested.

4. The warrant must state the nature of the offense.

Judicial and legislative decisions have added requirements not specifically enumerated in the Constitution. One of these is that the warrant must state the nature of the offense. The offense need not be stated in the same detail as would be necessary in the indictment or information, but the warrant must

[33] United States v. Ferrone, 438 F(2d) 381 (3rdCir 1971).

include language specifying the nature of the offense with sufficient clarity to advise the subject of the accusation.

5. The warrant must designate the officer or class of officers who are directed to comply with the order of the court.

Generally the warrant may be directed to a specific officer or to a class of officers. Some statutes require that the warrant be directed to all peace officers in the state. For example, the Illinois Code states:

> The warrant shall be directed to all peace officers in the State. It shall be executed by the peace officer, or by a private person specially named therein, and may be executed in any county in the State.[34]

It is preferable to have such a provision in the warrant so that all officers within the class have authority to execute the warrant.

An arrest warrant may also be addressed to a specific private person unless there is a statute which prohibits this. This person must be expressly named on the warrant because he does not fall within the class of officers authorized by statute to execute a warrant.

6. The warrant must be issued in the name of the state or United States.

Although certain powers are delegated to *local* officials by the state constitution or statute, the police power rests primarily with the state. Thus, the name of the state must appear on the warrant, even if the warrant is issued by a county or city official. A warrant issued by a Federal official must have "United States" on it.

7. The warrant must be issued and signed by a neutral and detached judicial officer.

An arrest warrant must be issued by a neutral and detached judicial official. The United States Supreme Court has determined that an attorney general is not neutral and de-

---

[34] IllRevStat ch 38, §107-9(e) (1975).

tached, and a warrant issued by the attorney general, even though he is authorized by statute to do so, is not valid.[35]

In *Coolidge*, the Court made it quite clear that neither law enforcement officers nor prosecutors may issue warrants, noting:

> Without disrespect to the state law enforcement agent here involved, the whole point of the basic rule so well expressed by Mr. Justice Jackson is that prosecutors and policemen simply cannot be asked to maintain the requisite neutrality with regard to their own investigations—the "competitive enterprise" that must rightly engage their single-minded attention.

Although some law enforcement officers, with special permission, still issue arrest warrants in a few states, this practice is clearly condemned and should be abandoned.

There is still doubt concerning the authority of a court clerk to issue an arrest warrant. The majority of the Justices of the United States Supreme Court in the case of *Shadwick v. City of Tampa* [36] agreed that a court clerk was a neutral and detached person and was authorized to issue an arrest warrant for the arrest of persons charged with breach of a municipal ordinance. This reasoning, however, has not received full support from the states. Justice Powell, writing for the majority in the *Shadwick* case, explained that when the clerk is an employee of the judicial branch of the city and disassociated from the role of law enforcement, he may issue an arrest warrant for a violation of the municipal ordinance even though he is not a judge or an attorney.

This decision should be considered with caution as the Court emphasized that the clerk's neutrality had not been impeached and was in fact not questioned. Also, the capability of the clerk to determine "probable cause" was not questioned. The door was left open to challenge a clerk's ability to determine whether probable cause exists for a requested arrest or search.

The best procedure is for a person who is "neutral and detached" and who is qualified by education and experience

---

[35] Coolidge v. New Hampshire, 403 US 443, 29 LEd(2d) 564, 91 SCt 2022 (1971). See Part II of this book.

[36] 407 US 345, 32 LEd(2d) 783, 92 SCt 2119 (1972).

to issue the arrest warrant. The whole purpose of requiring a judicial officer to issue the warrant is to be certain that a disinterested and qualified person makes this important decision. If the issuance of a warrant is only a ministerial act to be performed by an untrained clerk, the purpose is defeated.

Not only must the warrant be issued by a judicial officer, it must also be signed *after* it has been completed. A warrant signed and later filled in is in fact a "traveling warrant," which was condemned by the framers of the Constitution. In some states, the warrant must include the name of the issuing official and also the title of his office.

8. Additional state requirements.

In addition to the preceding requirements, states may have other requirements. For example, some states require that the warrant itself must state the date when issued and the municipality or county where issued; others require that the amount of bail be inserted on the warrant itself. Because statutes in some states require additional information to be on the warrant, it is essential that the peace officer consult the applicable statutes of his state.

§ 3.7   Execution of the warrant

Even though the warrant has been properly issued on a showing of probable cause, and sufficiently describes the person to be arrested, the arrest will not be legal unless the warrant is properly executed. Some of the requirements to be met in executing the warrant are listed below. In addition, the local statutes must be consulted to determine the authority and duties of the arresting officer. If all the requirements under state and federal law are complied with, the arrest will be legal, the officer will be protected, and the evidence secured incident to the arrest will generally be admissible.

1. The executing officer must be specifically named or come within the class designated on the warrant.

A warrant addressed to a particular officer by name or designation of his office must be served by such officer or his duly authorized deputy. If the warrant is addressed to a particular class of peace officers, it must be served by an officer who falls within that class. If an arrest warrant is addressed to a private person, he must execute the warrant and may not appoint someone to execute the warrant for him.

Today, the common practice is to issue an arrest warrant to "all peace officers in the state." Such a warrant can be executed by anyone within that class. If, however, as was the earlier practice and still the practice in some areas, a warrant is issued to a sheriff, he, being the highest peace officer within the jurisdiction, may deputize others to execute it, or his regular deputies may execute the warrant on the theory that they are acting through the sheriff.[37]

2. *The warrant must be executed within the jurisdictional limits.*

The validity of an arrest under a warrant depends on the territorial jurisdiction of the issuing official. Most modern statutes contain provisions authorizing the execution of a warrant in any county of the state, even though it was issued by a magistrate in another county. In the absence of a statute conferring state-wide authority on issuing magistrates, a warrant may not be executed outside the county of its origin.

Under our federal system, the issuing state is powerless to authorize an arrest outside its territorial jurisdiction. A warrant for arrest issued in one state may not be executed in another state unless the second state has by statute conferred validity on out-of-state warrants. A warrant issued in one state may, however, *indirectly* serve as the basis for an arrest in the second state even in the absence of special legislation. For example, knowledge that a warrant has been issued for John Smith's arrest in state *A* may furnish reasonable grounds for a police officer in state *B* to believe that a felony has been committed and to justify Smith's arrest in state *B*. In such a case, it is not the warrant but the reasonable inference which a police officer in the second state may properly draw from the fact of its issuance that forms the basis of the arrest.

[37] Ex parte Rhodes, 48 LaAnn 1363, 20 So 894 (1896).

In addition, an out-of-state warrant may serve as the basis for issuing a fugitive warrant in another state.

3. The arresting officer should make known his purpose.

As a general rule, the arresting officer should make known his purpose and the cause of the arrest. Some states have statutes requiring the officer to inform the person to be arrested of the cause of the arrest and the fact that a warrant has been issued. If possible, the officer should make it clear that he is making an arrest and that he has authority to do so. This is particularly important if the officer is not in uniform.

There are logical exceptions to this rule. If the person to be arrested flees or forcibly resists before the officer has an opportunity to advise him or if the giving of such information will imperil the arrest, such notice is not required. Also, if the person to be arrested purposely makes it impossible for the officer to make known his purpose—for example, by fleeing to another part of the house to hide—he cannot complain that the officer did not inform him of the intended arrest. Where a police officer had attempted unsuccessfully to advise the suspect by phone from an adjoining apartment, and the suspect hid under a bed when the officers knocked on the door, "it was not unreasonable to dispense with an announcement of presence and purpose."[38]

4. The officer usually must show the arrest warrant or advise the arrestee that the warrant has been issued.

Under the common law rule which has been adopted in a number of states, a warrant must be in the possession of the arresting officer and shown to the person arrested if so demanded. The officer does not have to show the warrant before the arrest, especially if the officer reasonably believes that showing the warrant would be dangerous to him or others or would imperil the making of the arrest. For example, where the arrestee resists arrest at the outset and there is danger of his escape, the officer is not bound to exhibit the warrant until

[38] Kirvelaitis v. Gray, 513 F(2d) 213 (6thCir 1975).

the prisoner is secured.[39] In such a case, after the person has submitted to the arrest or acquiesced, the officer, if requested, should acquaint the arrestee with the cause of the arrest either by stating the substance of the warrant or by reading it to him.

Because of the need for quick action in our highly mobile society, there has been a trend in recent years to relax the common-law requirement regarding the display of the warrant. The federal rules [40] and most modern state codes contain provisions to the effect that the officer need not have the warrant in his possession at the time of the arrest, but after the arrest, if the person arrested so requests, the warrant shall be shown to him as soon as practicable. The Kentucky Code, which is similar to most modern codes, provides:

> A warrant of arrest may be executed by any peace officer. The officer need not have the warrant in his possession at the time of arrest, but in that event he shall inform the defendant of the offense charged and the fact that the warrant has been issued, and upon request show the warrant, or a copy of it, to the defendant as soon as possible.[41]

§ 3.8   Arrest without a warrant

Neither the Fourth Amendment to the Constitution nor the constitutional provisions of the various states contains any express reference to the right to arrest without a warrant. But it was recognized early in the common law that under certain circumstances it was impractical, if not impossible, to obtain a warrant. The common law attempted to strike a balance between the interests of the community in protecting itself and the rights of citizens to be free from unjustified arrests, and in certain situations authority was extended to permit arrest without a warrant.

The exceptions to the rule requiring a warrant were based on the strictest necessity. The common law permitted a peace officer to make an arrest for a felony committed in his presence. In addition, because of the social importance of apprehending a felon while he was then available, an officer was allowed to make an arrest if he had reasonable grounds to be-

[39] Crosswhite v. Barnes, 139 Va 471, 124 SE 242 (1924).

[40] FRCrimP 4(d)(3) (1975).
[41] KyRCrimP 2.10(1) (1971).

lieve that a felony had been committed and that the person to be arrested had committed it. The right to make an arrest without warrant for a misdemeanor was narrowly confined to those circumstances in which prompt action on the part of the peace officer or private citizen was necessary to prevent a breach of the peace or to maintain public order. Before an arrest was authorized, the law required that the person making the arrest actually witness the commission of a misdemeanor amounting to a breach of the peace.

In 1975 the United States Supreme Court reemphasized and restated the reason for authorizing an arrest without a warrant in these terms:

> Maximum protection of individual rights could be assured by requiring a magistrate's review of the factual justification prior to any arrest, but such a requirement would constitute an intolerable handicap for legitimate law enforcement. Thus, while the Court has expressed a preference for the use of arrest warrants when feasible, . . . it has never invalidated an arrest supported by probable cause solely because the officers failed to secure a warrant. [Citations omitted.] [42]

The common-law distinction between felony and misdemeanor arrests is preserved in most states today, and the legality of an arrest without a warrant, in many instances, may turn upon the issue of whether the offense for which the arrest was made constitutes a felony or a misdemeanor.

§ 3.9   Arrest without a warrant in felony situations

1. Definition of a felony

The statute of each state defines the authority to arrest for a felony and, in some states, classifies the various crimes into felonies or misdemeanors. Thus, a police officer, especially one who operates in a state which distinguishes felonies and misdemeanors for arrest purposes, should acquaint himself with the statutes of his state.

The Uniform Arrest Act defines a felony as any crime

---

[42] Gerstein v. Pugh, 420 US 103, 43 LEd(2d) 54, 95 SCt 854 (1975).

which is or may be punished by death or imprisonment in a state prison. As the laws in most states do not provide for imprisonment in a state institution unless the term is at least one year, it is generally agreed that an offense is a felony if the penalty attached is at least one year and the incarceration is in a state institution rather than a local jail. An offense, however, may be designated by statute as a felony even though it does not carry a year's incarceration. Thus an offense is considered a felony when (1) the statute provides that it is a felony, or (2) there is no such designation, but the offense is punishable by imprisonment in a state prison.

Although there is apparent concensus in the technical definition of a felony and misdemeanor, all semblance of uniformity disappears when these terms are used or applied to concrete areas of criminal conduct. What may be regarded as a felony in one state, may constitute a misdemeanor in another. Except for the crimes of murder, robbery and rape, generalizations in the area are unreliable. Therefore, the legislative designations in the particular jurisdiction must be carefully examined. If the state statute does not specifically enumerate the felonies, the officer should go through the statutes and codes and designate the felonies as such.

2. Authority to arrest

The states are uniform in authorizing by statute or judicial decision, a peace officer to arrest without a warrant when he has reasonable grounds to believe that a felony has been committed and that the person to be arrested has committed it. A small number of states add an additional requirement limiting this authority to those situations where it is impractical to obtain a warrant before making the arrest. For example, the Texas Code provides that:

> Where it is shown by satisfactory proof to a peace officer, upon the representation of a credible person, that a felony has been committed, and that the offender is about to escape, so that there is no time to procure a warrant, such peace officer may, without warrant, pursue and arrest the accused.[43]

[43] TexCodeCrimProAnn art 14.04 (1966).

The code provisions authorizing warrantless arrests for felonies do not spell out what is meant by "reasonable grounds to believe." The term "reasonable grounds" does not appear in the Fourth Amendment but is often used interchangeably with the term "probable cause." Technically, "probable cause" refers to the minimum knowledge that a judicial officer must have before issuing an arrest warrant, and "reasonable grounds" refers to the knowledge that an officer must possess prior to making a valid arrest without a warrant. Nevertheless, the courts have often referred to "probable cause" when defining the minimum knowledge that an officer must possess to make a constitutionally valid arrest without a warrant, and the reader should not be confused by this usage.

In requiring that the arresting officer possess reasonable grounds to believe in the guilt of a suspect, the Constitution seeks to safeguard citizens from unfounded charges of crime. At the same time, its standards are intended to be sufficiently flexible to permit efficient law enforcement. Because of the need to compromise between these two opposing interests, the Constitution does not demand infallibility from the arresting officer.

"Reasonable grounds" lies somewhere on the evidentiary scale between good faith suspicion and proof beyond a reasonable doubt. The rule of "probable cause" or "reasonable grounds" makes allowances for some mistakes on the part of an arresting officer. The fact that subsequent events and information may prove that the person arrested has not actually committed a felony makes no difference as long as appearances at the time of the arrest are such as to lead a police officer reasonably to conclude that a felony has been committed, and that the person he is about to arrest is responsible for the felony.

3. Determining "reasonable grounds"

"Reasonable grounds" depends on the facts and circumstances of each case. In determining whether an officer has reasonable grounds for an arrest, the information to be considered is that which is available to him at the time of the arrest. An arrest cannot be justified by what a subsequent search produces, but must stand or fall solely on the basis of the facts possessed by the officer at the precise moment of the arrest. According to the RESTATEMENT OF TORTS, the nature of the crime, the chance of escape, and the harm to others if the suspect escapes are all relevant factors to be considered by an officer in determining whether grounds for a warrantless arrest exist.[44]

A completely satisfactory definition of what constitutes "reasonable" is impossible to formulate. One court has characterized reasonable grounds as "the sum total of layers of information and the synthesis of what the police have heard, what they know and what they observe as trained officers." In determining whether reasonable cause exists in a particular case, the test most frequently employed in the federal courts is that set forth by the Supreme Court in *Draper v. United States:* [45]

> Probable cause exists where "the facts and circumstances within [the arresting officers'] knowledge and of which they had reasonably trustworthy information [are] sufficient in themselves to warrant a man of reasonable caution in the belief that" an offense has been or is being committed.

Judge Warren Burger, while serving as a member of the District of Columbia Circuit Court, went a little further and indicated that the police officers may call on their experience in determining if reasonable grounds exist.

However, the best guidelines for police action are found not in the legal definitions given by the courts, but in the factual situations where probable cause has been found to exist. In making a felony arrest, a police officer may rely on information from a wide variety of sources. The most common sources include the officer's personal observations, informants' tips, reports from other officers or law enforcement agencies, leads furnished by the victim of the crime, physical evidence found at the scene of the crime, and past criminal records of suspects.[46] Reliable information may be obtained from many

[44] RESTATEMENT(2d) OF TORTS §119, comment j. (1965).

[45] 358 US 307, 3 LEd(2d) 327, 79 SCt 329 (1959).

[46] LaFave, ARREST: THE DECISION TO TAKE A SUSPECT INTO CUSTODY, 265-299 (1965).

other sources. The more information obtained from whatever source, the better are the officer's chances of showing that reasonable grounds for the felony arrest exist.

(a) Personal observations of the arresting officer

When a police officer observes the actual commission of a felony there is no question whether he has adequate grounds to arrest without a warrant. But criminals seldom commit crimes in the presence of law enforcement officers. Frequently the police officer only observes acts which are suspicious. For example, he might observe a car with a motor running in an industrial complex, and, as he approaches, the car moves on. Or he might observe a man running down the street late at night carrying a bag. In instances such as these the officer does not have probable cause or reasonable grounds to believe that a felony has been committed or that these individuals have committed or are intending to commit a felony. Therefore, an arrest under these circumstances would be illegal as the Constitution does not permit an arrest on suspicion only.

Nevertheless, an officer would be lax in his duties if he allowed suspicious circumstances such as these to pass without further inquiry or investigation. Where circumstances justify it, further inquiry may produce sufficient additional information to justify an arrest.[17] Where the totality of the circumstances—which could include the time of the day or night, the area, attempted flight by the suspect, the known record of the suspect and other factors known to the officer—collectively lead the officer in light of his experience to reasonably believe a felony has been committed, the arrest is justified.[18]

Consider the following example of reasonable grounds based upon the personal observation of the arresting officer. A District of Columbia officer observed three persons standing in the shadow of a building "passing and changing" packages. As the area was considered by the police to be high in narcotics traffic, the officer decided to investigate. When he told the men that he would like to talk with them for a min-

[17] See §3.14, *infra*, concerning police authority to detain.
[18] Green v. United States, 259 F(2d) 180 (DC Cir 1958), *cert. denied*, 359 US 917, 3 LEd(2d) 578, 79 SCt 594 (1959).

ute, one of the men shouted, "F - - - you," and ran. The officer gave chase. About a block away, the suspect tried to crawl underneath a Volkswagen parked at the curb. After the second command to come out, the suspect emerged from under the Volkswagen and, as he did so, the police officer observed a bag of heroin lying in plain view under the suspect. The defendant claimed that there were no reasonable grounds for his arrest for disorderly conduct and, therefore, the heroin had been obtained by an illegal search and seizure.

The United States Court of Appeals for the District of Columbia Circuit held that there were reasonable grounds for the arrest, adding:

> We reiterate that we are not deciding that defendant was guilty of disorderly conduct, a decision that would require a determination concerning community standards. The standard that governs arrest does not require proof enough to convict. The police officer's probable cause for arrest may stand even though the prosecutor needs additional evidence for the preliminary hearing or the trial.[49]

(b) Informers' tips

Tips received from informers frequently afford an invaluable source of pre-arrest information, especially in the vice areas where a premium is put on secrecy. Without the leads furnished by confidential informants, many crimes would go undetected. The Supreme Court has expressly sanctioned the use of this type of information in making a warrantless arrest.[50] As a safeguard against lying or inaccurate informers, the police should make an independent investigation whenever feasible to substantiate the report before making an arrest.

Where the arrest is based in whole or in part on an informer's word, an important factor is the reliability of the source. Some considerations relevant to the question of reliability are the length of time the officer has known or dealt with the informer, his general character and reputation, the number of tips received from him in the past, the accuracy of the in-

---

[49] Von Sleichter v. United States, 472 F(2d) 1244 (DC Cir 1972).

[50] Draper v. United States, 358 US 307, 3 LEd(2d) 327, 79 SCt 329 (1959).

formation previously given, and whether the informer is a volunteer or is paid for his knowledge.[51] The Supreme Court has held that detailed information from a paid informant who had a past history of supplying reliable tips regarding violations of narcotics laws was sufficient in itself to furnish probable cause for an arrest without a warrant.[52]

Although it is preferable to have an informer who has given correct information in the past and to corroborate this information, there are times when the arresting officer must rely solely on an unknown informer's tip. If the circumstances justify it, the officer may rely upon an informant even if the informant's identity is not known to the officer. For example, where an assailant assaulted an FBI officer and took his gun, money and credentials, an elderly male, who told the police officers that he didn't want to get involved, said that he saw the offender on the second floor of a certain house. The anonymous informant did not state that he had seen the offense being committed nor that he had seen the youth fleeing the scene. Following the informant's lead, the officers made the arrest and retrieved the gun taken from the agent.

At the trial the defendant moved to suppress the gun and other evidence found in the apartment on the grounds that the police did not have probable cause for arrest, primarily because the officers were not justified in relying on information received from an informant who was not known to the officers. In upholding the arrest, the majority of the justices of the Seventh Circuit followed this rationale:

> The fact that one of the neighbors was willing to supply this information, albeit in a guarded manner, to us raises a presumption of reliability on which the police properly could and did rely.
> . . . In view of the exigencies of the situation and considering the practical aspects of obtaining any information at all in the particular neighborhood, the police had probable cause [reasonable grounds] to make the arrest.[53]

On the other hand, the officer cannot always depend on the

---

[51] Comment, *Informer's Word as the Basis for Probable Cause in the Federal Courts*, 53 CALLREV 840 (1965).

[52] Draper v. United States, 358 US 307, 3 LEd(2d) 327, 79 SCt 329 (1959).

[53] United States v. Ganter, 436 F(2d) 364 (7thCir 1970).

informer's tip alone supplying information for probable cause. For example, information obtained from unsworn statements of a jail prisoner; a first-time informer whose reliability has not been established; or an anonymous tip received over the telephone would probably require some independent investigation and corroboration before an arrest could be made. Corroborating data might come from the suspect's prior record of arrest or convictions for the same type of offense, his association with known violators, furtive conduct such as flight when approached by police officers, the receipt by the officer of similar reports from others, or a combination of these elements.

What if probable cause (or reasonable grounds) is based on a tip which is ultimately proved untrue? In a 1974 case a defendant, convicted of interstate transportation of stolen securities, claimed that evidence seized after his arrest was inadmissible because the arresting FBI agent acted solely on the basis of information from his supervisor who, in turn, had received the informer's false statement.[54] The informer had advised the supervisor that he had personally observed stolen securities in the defendant's possession but the informer admitted at trial that he had never seen the defendant before. The FBI officer was not aware that the informant had lied, and the defense counsel conceded that the facts related in the affidavit attached to the post-arrest complaint form supported a finding of probable cause if true.

In upholding the arrest and resulting search, a majority of the court explained that:

> The discrepancy between what the informer may have told the FBI and what was actually proved at trial may not now be used to invalidate an arrest, absent any showing of fraud or deceit on the part of the law enforcement officials involved. [Citation omitted.] "[P]robable cause is not defeated because an informant is later proved to have lied, as long as the affiant accurately represents what was told him."

If the FBI officer had any inkling that the informer was giv-

[54] United States v. Garofalo, 496 F(2d) 510 (8thCir 1974).

ing false information or ever if he should have known from the circumstances that the evidence was questionable, not only would the evidence be inadmissible but also, the officer would be subject to civil or criminal action.

The question often arises whether it is necessary to disclose the informant who has supplied the reasonable grounds necessary to make a felony arrest. Following the rationale of the probable cause cases, the Supreme Court decided in at least one case that the officer need not disclose the identity of the informant "if the trial judge is convinced, by evidence submitted in open court . . . that the officers did rely in good faith upon credible information supplied by a reliable informant." [55] Mr. Justice Stewart, speaking for the majority explained, however, that in such instances the officers must be able to inform the court of the underlying circumstances from which the officers concluded that the informant was credible and reliable.

(c) Information from other officers or law enforcement agencies

The police department of a large metropolis operates as a closely coordinated unit in which fast and accurate dissemination of information is essential to efficient law enforcement. Frequently, an officer receives a message over the police radio, directing him to go to a certain place and arrest a certain person without informing him of any reasons for the arrest. Certainly, no one would seriously contend that this officer had probable cause to believe in the guilt of the person arrested. Nevertheless, the Constitution does not require that the arresting officer personally, independent of his police colleagues, have knowledge of all the facts necessary to constitute probable cause.[56]

Probable cause in such a circumstance must be evaluated on the basis of the collective information of the police rather than that of the officer who performs the act of arrest.[57] Where words heard over a police radio form the basis of the arrest-

[55] McCray v. Illinois, 386 US 300, 18 LEd(2d) 62, 87 SCt 1056 (1967).
[56] Draper v. United States, 358 US 307, 3 LEd(2d) 327, 79 SCt 329 (1959).
[57] Smith v. United States, 358 F(2d) 833 (DC Cir 1966).

ing officer's probable cause, the sending officer must have reasonable grounds on which to base his message. A contrary rule would permit the police to do indirectly what the Constitution forbids them from doing directly, by publishing a report on the police radio.

In the case of *Whiteley v. Warden*,[58] an arrest warrant which was issued without probable cause was the basis for a bulletin sent to an officer in another county. The officer in the other county, relying upon the radio message that a warrant was outstanding, made the arrest and incidental search. The state claimed that even though the warrant was invalid since it was not supported by probable cause, the police officer who relied upon the radio bulletin in making the arrest nevertheless made a legal arrest and resulting search. The Supreme Court held that if the initial warrant is defective, an arrest made by another officer solely on the basis of a radio message stating the warrant has been issued is also defective. The Court agreed, however, that the arresting officers who relied upon the information received over the police radio were certainly protected from civil and criminal liability. The Court explained:

> We do not, of course, question that the Laramie police were entitled to act on the strength of the radio bulletin. Certainly police officers called upon to aid other officers in executing arrest warrants are entitled to assume that the officers requesting aid offered the magistrate the information requisite to support an independent judicial assessment of probable cause. Where, however, the contrary turns out to be true, an otherwise illegal arrest cannot be insulated from challenge by the decision of the instigating officer to rely on fellow officers to make the arrest.

The same reasoning was applied in the case of *United States v. Impson*[59] where the arrest was made by a Wichita Falls, Texas, police agent at the telephonic request of a U.S. Secret Service agent. Here there was no arrest warrant. The court reiterated that there is no question that the arresting officer in another area can act on the basis of information which has been relayed to him by police transmission facilities; however,

[58] 401 US 560, 28 LEd(2d) 306, 91 SCt 1031 (1971).   [59] 482 F(2d) 197 (5thCir 1973).

the prosecution must show that the officer who made the telephonic request himself had reasonable grounds for the arrest.

(d) Past criminal record of a suspect

The past criminal record of a suspect standing alone can
never constitute probable cause for an arrest.[60] Any other rule
would deprive all ex-convicts of the protections of the Fourth
Amendment and subject them to arrest at will. Nevertheless, a
police officer may properly consider a suspect's record in conjunction with other information in deciding whether there
are adequate grounds for arrest.

(e) Physical evidence found at the scene of a crime

Whether physical evidence found at the scene of a crime,
standing alone, can justify an arrest depends upon the type
of evidence involved. For example, a handkerchief bearing
the initials "JS" found a few inches from a murder victim
would not furnish reasonable cause for a felony arrest of a
"John Smith" in the absence of some stronger evidence to implicate him in the crime. On the other hand, fingerprints taken
from the shattered window of a burglarized jewelry store,
which had been washed just prior to closing, if they matched
with a set of prints on file with the police, would furnish
sufficient cause to make an arrest.[61]

In a case where a tavern proprietor reported that a burglar
tried to pry open the side door of the tavern with a screwdriver and that another burglar wore gloves, the use, as evidence, of a screwdriver and gloves found in a field where the
suspect had been running was admitted as justifying the arrest.[62]

Other examples of evidence which have been considered
sufficient to furnish reasonable grounds are a billfold found
at the scene of the crime with the victim's name, and a de-

---

[60] Beck v. Ohio, 379 US 89, 13
LEd(2d) 142, 85 SCt 223 (1964).

[61] State v. Callas, 68 Wash(2d) 542,
413 P(2d) 962 (1966).

[62] People v. Allen, 17 Ill(2d) 55, 160
NE(2d) 818 (1959). See Klotter &
Meier, Criminal Evidence for Police
§13.3(b), Anderson Publishing Co.
(2d ed 1975).

scription of the car observed at the scene of the crime, including the license number, make, and color.

(f) Reports of victims or eye-witnesses

It is seldom that the police catch a criminal in the act of committing a crime. The license number of a car used in a hold-up, the physical description of an assailant, or the victim's identification of a picture taken from the rogue's gallery are frequently the best and only leads which the police may have into an unsolved crime. Victims and eye-witness observers may and do in many instances furnish reliable information. For example, in *United States* v. *Masini*,[63] a bookstore proprietor who had been alerted by the police that passers of counterfeit $20 bills were active in the area became suspicious when a man entered his store and purchased two paperback books using a $20 bill which did not look or feel right. He immediately telephoned the police and accompanied them on a search for the man. The suspect was found in a hotel lobby and, upon being identified by the proprietor, was placed under arrest. The arrest was upheld.

§ 3.10 Arrest without a warrant in misdemeanor situations

At common law, a breach of the peace was the only non-felony for which a warrantless arrest was authorized. The common law developed in an agrarian society where the problems of law enforcement were relatively simple. But modern experience in urban areas with heavy crime rates has demonstrated the need for reconsideration of the rule. Efforts of law enforcement agencies in apprehending, for example, petty thieves and others who had committed misdemeanors not amounting to a breach of the peace, were being unduly hampered by the strictness of the common-law rule.

In response to the changing needs of the community, most states either by statute or judicial decision have enlarged the powers of the police to make warrantless arrests for misdemeanors. In most states it is no longer required that the offense for which the arrest is made constitute a breach of the peace.

---

[63] 358 F(2d) 100 (6thCir 1966).

The statutes generally provide that a peace officer may arrest without a warrant any person who has committed a misdemeanor in his presence.

Unlike a felony arrest, the common law and the law in most states today leave no room for a reasonable mistake on the part of an officer making a warrantless arrest for a misdemeanor. The common-law distinction between felonies and misdemeanors and the requirement that the misdemeanor be actually committed in the presence of the officer have been criticized in recent years as demanding of a police officer a decision which even judges find difficult.

A growing number of states have enlarged the powers of the police officer to make arrests without warrants for misdemeanors.[64] For example, the Illinois Code provides that:

A peace officer may arrest a person when:
(a) He has a warrant commanding that such person be arrested; or
(b) He has reasonable grounds to believe that a warrant for the person's arrest has been issued in this State or in another jurisdiction; or
(c) He has reasonable grounds to believe that the person is committing or has committed an offense.[65]

The term "offense" is defined as the violation of any penal statute of the state or ordinance of a political subdivision of the state. This statute and the statutes of approximately a half-dozen other states make it possible for police officers to make an arrest for a misdemeanor upon reasonable grounds or probable cause even if the misdemeanor is not committed in their presence.

In addition to these, some states authorize peace officers to make warrantless arrests for misdemeanors not committed in their presence under certain special conditions such as: "the offender will flee if not immediately apprehended"; "he

[64] These are among the state statutes authorizing misdemeanor arrests even if the offense is not committed in the officer's presence:
ArizRevStatAnn §13-1403 ¶2 (1956).
HawRevStat §803-5 (Supp 1975).
IoCodeAnn §755.4(2),(3) (1949).
LaCodeCrimProAnn art 213(3) (Supp 1976).
NyCrimProL §140.05 (1971).
WisStat §968.07(1)(d) (1971).
[65] IllRevStat ch 38, §107-2 (1975).

will destroy or conceal evidence of the commission of the offense if not apprehended immediately"; or "he may cause injury to himself or others or damage to property if not apprehended."[66]

Other states authorize warrantless arrests for misdemeanors not committed in the officer's presence only for certain specified or classes of misdemeanors.[67] An example is the Oregon statute which authorizes an arrest on probable cause for a Class A misdemeanor.[68]

Although there is a recognizable trend toward broadening a peace officer's misdemeanor arrest powers, the majority of states still require that the misdemeanor be actually committed in his presence and that the arrest take place immediately or in close pursuit. Any deviation must be by statutory enactment.

1. "Misdemeanor" defined

The Uniform Arrest Act defines a misdemeanor as "any crime or violation of a municipal ordinance which is not classified as a felony." Unless the offense is defined as a felony, or unless it is punishable by at least one year in the penitentiary, the offense must be treated as a misdemeanor. Many states by statute specifically set out which crimes are felonies so that there will be no doubt as to the procedure to be followed; however, in many instances the officer must determine on the spot whether the offense is a felony or a misdemeanor. If in doubt, the offense should be treated as a misdemeanor for the purposes of arrest and search. Since the arrest privileges for misdemeanors are generally more restricted than those for felonies, the officer will be protected if he mistakenly employs the misdemeanor procedure for what later turns out to be a felony.

---

[66] KAN STAT ANN §22-2401(c)(2) (1974).
NEBREVSTAT §29-404.02(2) (1975).
NCGENSTAT §15A-401(b)(2) (1975).
UTCODEANN §77-13-3(3) (1975).
WYSTATANN §7-12.3 (CumSupp 1975).

[67] DC CODEANN §23-581 (1973).
MDANNCODE art 27, §594B(d),(e) (1976).
WASHREVCODEANN §10.31.100 (Supp 1975).
[68] ORE REV STAT §133.310(1)(a) (1973).

2. "In the officer's presence" defined

Determining the precise meaning of the phrase "in the officer's presence" has caused the courts considerable difficulty. In *Miles v. State*,[69] the Oklahoma court said:

> An offense is committed in the presence of an officer, within the meaning of the statute authorizing an arrest without a warrant, only when he sees it with his eyes or sees one or more of a series of acts constituting the offense, and is aided by his other senses. An offense is likewise deemed committed in the presence of the officer where the offense is continuing, or has not been fully consummated at the time the arrest is made.

In order for an offense to be considered to have taken place within the presence of the arresting officer, he must be made aware of its commission through one or more of his senses. He must perceive the acts which make up the offense while they take place and not merely learn of the event at a later date. The offense must still be in progress when the officer reaches the scene in order for him to make a warrantless arrest for a misdemeanor in most states. If the offense has terminated before he arrives, under the usual statute the officer would be required to obtain a warrant before making the arrest. The officer need not witness the entire misdemeanor; if any part of the offense is still in progress when he reaches the scene, the arrest may be made.

For example, in *People v. Foster*,[70] the defendant allegedly assaulted a shopkeeper who retreated into her store, bolted the door and called the police. When the police arrived at the store, the defendant was kicking at the shop door and screaming insults and threats at those inside. The shopkeeper emerged with blood still streaming from her nose and told the police that the defendant had attacked her. The defendant violently resisted arrest, kicking and scratching. It required five officers to finally subdue her and to place her under arrest. In commenting on the legality of the arrest, the court stated,

[69] 30 OklaCrim 302, 236 Pa 57 (1925).   [70] 10 NY(2d) 99, 176 NE(2d) 397 (1961).

It would be a strange law that would hold such an arrest illegal on the ground that the underlying assault had not been perpetrated in the officer's presence. A more reasonable view is that the affray was still in progress when the police came. Blood was flowing, a mob had gathered, the accused was kicking at the door to get another crack at her victim. What has the statutory requirement of sworn information and warrant to do with all this? To prevent irresponsible arrests of presumably innocent citizens, the statute demands that the officer, unless the misdemeanor be committed in his presence, have assurance in the form of a sworn complaint. None of us would strike from the law that reasonable requirement. But the requirement and its purpose are satisfied when as here the visible signs of a continuing assault are right in front of the policeman's eyes. Here there was presented to his consciousness adequate information that what he saw was the last phase of an assault.

If the entire offense has been completed before the police officer arrives on the scene, and order has been restored, under most state statutes the officer would have to procure a warrant before making an arrest.

3. Necessity for quick action

In addition to witnessing the misdemeanor for which the arrest is made, most states require that the officer make the arrest immediately or after close pursuit. If for some reason the officer is delayed or unable to make the arrest until a later time, he must obtain a warrant. For example, frequently a patrolman pursues a speeder who manages to avoid him by crossing the state line. If on the following day, or even a few hours later, the patrolman catches the speeder again within the state, no arrest can be made unless the officer has taken steps in the meantime to obtain a warrant, or unless the speeder is again violating the law.

§ 3.11   Authority to enter premises to make an arrest without a warrant

A man's home is his castle, and an entry should not be made even to make an arrest unless there is a clear need to do so. Some abuses by police officers have necessitated that the courts lay down some general guidelines for officers to follow in making warrantless entries into private rooms and hotels to effectuate an arrest. In the case of *United States* v. *Lindsay*,[71] a United States Appeals Court reversed a robbery conviction because the warrantless entry into a motel room in which the defendant was found violated the standards established in a previous case. In 1970 the same Court of Appeals for the District of Columbia established certain standards which have been recognized in other courts. Although the court agreed that these standards are not binding, they do give some guidelines which are helpful.[72]

In the *Dorman* case, the D.C. Circuit Court of Appeals recognized that often there is an urgent need which will justify entry without a warrant to make an arrest. The court then listed seven factors which are material in determining whether this urgent need exists:

> First, that a grave offense is involved, particularly one that is a crime of violence. . . .
>
> Second, and obviously inter-related, that the suspect is reasonably believed to be armed. . . .
>
> Third, that there exists not merely the minimum of probable cause, that is requisite even when a warrant has been issued, but beyond that a clear showing of probable cause, including "reasonably trustworthy information," to believe that the suspect committed the crime involved.
>
> Fourth, strong reason to believe that the suspect is in the premises being entered.
>
> Fifth, a likelihood that the suspect will escape if not swiftly apprehended.
>
> Sixth, the circumstance that the entry, though not consented, is made peaceably. Forcible entry may in some instances be justified. . . .
>
> Another factor to be taken into account . . . relates to time of entry—whether it is made at night. . . .

It is again emphasized that these criteria do not apply in all cases. However, in the *Lindsay* case the majority of the judges seemed to base their decision on the fact that the entry was not justified because there was no strong reason to believe

---

[71] 506 F(2d) 166 (DC Cir 1974). Also see United States v. Shye, 492 F(2d) 886 (6th Cir 1974).   [72] Dorman v. United States, 435 F(2d) 385 (DC Cir 1970).

that the suspect was in the dwelling and that there was no substantive evidence indicating that the appellant was the robber.

## § 3.12	The citation and summons in law enforcement

The making and completion of an arrest consume many hours of police time. The person charged with an offense must be taken to the police station, a complaint must be filed against him, he must be booked, and finally, provision must be made for his release on bail or on his own recognizance. Frequently, however, the needs of adequate law enforcement may be met by issuing a citation or summons rather than physically arresting every minor lawbreaker. Although the practice of issuing citations and summons was first practiced without statutory sanction, today most states include provisions for the issuance of citations or summons in state statutes or codes.

The terms "citation" and "summons" are sometimes used interchangeably.[73] A citation, or summons, as used by the law enforcement officer, is nothing more than a written notice directing a person to appear in court at a stated time and place to answer for an offense charged in the notice. There is often confusion as to the status of a person who has been issued a citation, summons, or notice to appear. The issuance of a citation is not an arrest; it is an alternative to an arrest. One author has appropriately characterized it as a "courtesy" substitute for an arrest.[74] The person may or may not be arrested at the time the citation is issued, depending upon the wording of the statute which permits the issuance of the citation.

Although the term was used in Roman Law, the issuance of a traffic or other misdemeanor citation is a practice of relatively recent origin. It is a very useful device in modern law enforcement and should be resorted to whenever feasible. Some of the advantages of a citation over a physical arrest of minor lawbreakers are that it—

[73] Traditionally, the summons is a will issued by a court directing the sheriff or other proper officer to notify the person named that an action has been commenced against him in court. When used in the statutes, such as those discussed, the summons is issued, not by a judge, but by a police officer. See BLACK'S LAW DICTIONARY 1604 (4th ed 1968).

[74] Houts, FROM ARREST TO RELEASE 84 (1958).

(1) saves the officer the considerable time and trouble involved in taking an individual in to the police station;

(2) does not impose the unnecessary indignity of bodily arrest upon those who are not criminals in any real or serious sense; and

(3) will help to elevate the public image of the law enforcement officer by lessening the antagonism between the public and the police.

Many states have enacted specific statutes authorizing the use of citations for certain types of offenses. These statutes generally provide either that the citation may be issued *instead* of making a physical arrest, or that the citation may be issued after a person is already arrested.[75] For example, Kentucky Revised Statute provides:

> A peace officer may issue a citation *instead* of making an arrest for a misdemeanor committed in his presence, if there are reasonable grounds to believe that the person being cited will appear to answer the charge. The citation shall provide that the defendant shall appear within a designated time. [Emphasis added.][76]

Under this statute the citation is issued in lieu of making a physical arrest.[77]

In some other states the wording of the statute differs. For example, the Ohio Rules of Criminal Procedure provide that:

> In misdemeanor cases where a person *has been arrested* with or without a warrant, the arresting officer, the officer in charge of the detention facility to which the person is brought or the superior of either officer, without unnecessary delay, may release the *arrested* person by issuing a summons when issuance of a summons appears

---

[75] One possible exception is in the Georgia Code where §27-222 specifically provides that "a law enforcement officer may arrest persons accused of violating any law or ordinance . . . [relating to motor vehicles] by issuance of a citation . . . ." Even here it is questionable that the mere writing could be considered an arrest.

[76] Ky Rev Stat Ann §431.015(1) (1975).

[77] Some of the other states that provide for issuance of a citation, summons or notice in lieu of arrest are DelCodeAnn tit.11, §1907 (1974). IllRevStat ch 38, §107-11 (1975). IoCodeAnn §321.485(2) (Supp 1975). KanStatAnn §22-2408 (Supp 1976). LaCodeCrimProAnn art 211 (1967). NyCrimProL §150.20(2) (Supp 1976).

reasonably calculated to assure the person's appearance. . . . [Emphasis added.] [78]

Under the provisions of this and similar statutes, the issuance of the notice to appear, called a summons in this statute, follows the arrest and is employed as a substitute for an immediate hearing before the magistrate.[79]

As a general rule, the citation does not enlarge the officer's authority to make an arrest without a warrant in the case of a misdemeanor. An officer can issue a citation only if he has the authority to arrest in the first instance. For example, the Illinois Code provides that:

> Whenever a peace officer is authorized to arrest a person without a warrant he may instead issue to such person a notice to appear. [80]

Therefore, under the law prevailing in most states today, a police officer could not issue a citation for a misdemeanor which was not committed in his presence.

Where the use of a citation is authorized, provision is made in one of several ways to enforce compliance on the part of the individual cited. The statutes usually provide that if the defendant fails to appear voluntarily in response to the citation, a complaint may be made before the magistrate and a warrant for his arrest will be issued. The Uniform Arrest Act provides a one hundred dollar fine or a thirty day jail sentence as additional punishment for those who willfully fail to heed a notice to appear.

Although the citation is used primarily in traffic cases there is no good reason why it cannot be employed for other types of offenses. Where the facts indicate a high probability that the offender will honor the citation and appear in court, issuance of a citation is the preferable procedure to follow. However, where the violator indicates that he will not respond to the citation, or where he is intoxicated, disorderly or dangerous to the public, a physical arrest should be made.

[78] UHRCRIMP 4Г (Supp 1976).
[79] CALPENALCODE §853.6 (Supp 1977).
COLOREVSTATANN §42-4-1505 (1973).
CONNGENSTATANN §6-49a (1958).
INDANNSTATCODE §9-4-1-131 (Supp 1976).
[80] ILLREVSTAT ch 38, §107-12(a) (1975).

§ 3.13　Fresh pursuit as extending the power of arrest

As a general rule, the peace officer has no official power to apprehend offenders beyond the boundaries of the county or district for which he has been appointed. However, both the common law and most statutes recognize a limited exception to this rule when an officer is in "fresh" or "hot" pursuit of a suspect who is fleeing to avoid apprehension. The doctrine of fresh pursuit arose out of necessity; and the instances of its application are becoming more frequent today as the means of rapid transportation improve.

Fresh pursuit has been defined as "pursuit without unreasonable interruption" or "the immediate pursuit of a person who is endeavoring to avoid arrest." At common law the doctrine of fresh pursuit applied only to felony cases. Although a few states retain the common-law limitation, the majority of the states recognize the right of a peace officer to pursue one who has committed any offense, including a misdemeanor, across corporate or county lines anywhere *within* the state if the pursuit is immediate and continuous.

Because of the nature of our federal system, no state can confer on its officers any power which is effective in another state. Before a peace officer can act as an officer of another state, there must be a statute existing in the second state which confers authority on an officer entering that state in fresh pursuit.

In recent years there has been a trend among the states toward increased cooperation in the area of law enforcement. Many states have adopted the Uniform Fresh Pursuit Act or similar legislation permitting law enforcement officers from other states who enter their state in fresh pursuit to make an arrest. For example, the Iowa Code provides:

> Any member of a duly organized state, county, or municipal law-enforcing unit of another state of the United States who enters this state in fresh pursuit, and continues within this state in such fresh pursuit, of a person in order to arrest him on the ground that he is believed to have committed a felony in such other state, shall have the same authority to arrest and hold such person in custody, as has any member of any duly organized state, county, or municipal law enforcing unit of this state, to arrest and hold in custody

a person on the ground that he is believed to have committed a felony in this state. [81]

A few states extend the privilege to out-of-state officers to make an arrest in fresh pursuit only on a reciprocity basis. An officer entering one of these states can make an arrest only if his own state has adopted similar legislation which would permit an officer from the second state to make an arrest in fresh pursuit there. To understand the exact territorial limits of his authority, an officer should be familiar not only with his local statutes, but with the fresh pursuit statutes of all neighboring states.

The right of fresh pursuit across state boundary lines is generally confined by statute to felonies. An officer pursuing a fleeing misdemeanant must end his pursuit at the state line. Illinois is one of the few states which permits out-of-state law enforcement officers in fresh pursuit to cross its borders in order to make an arrest for a misdemeanor. There seems to be no logical reason why other states should not authorize fresh pursuit arrests for misdemeanors as well as felonies.

Because of the differences in the laws of the various states, the officer who might have the opportunity to follow a suspect into another state on fresh pursuit must know the laws of the surrounding states. The fact that the officer's own state authorizes officers from other states to come into that state in fresh pursuit and make either felony or misdemeanor arrests does not mean that the other bordering states reciprocate. For example, although a peace officer from the states surrounding the state of Illinois may enter Illinois and make an arrest for a misdemeanor, officers from Illinois do not have that same privilege in the surrounding states. A police officer from Illinois entering Kentucky on fresh pursuit has very little protection because the Commonwealth of Kentucky has not adopted any uniform fresh pursuit act. Therefore, in Kentucky, the Illinois officer has only the authority to arrest as a private citizen, and as a private citizen he may make an arrest only when a felony in fact has been committed. In this situa-

---

[81] IoCodeAnn §756.1 (1949).

tion, the officer entering the neighboring state while in fresh pursuit of a speeder is merely another speeder.

§ 3.14   Police authority to detain

For many years police administrators and judges have been wrestling with the question surrounding the right of the police officer to stop a suspect under circumstances where there were not sufficient grounds for an actual arrest. Although it was common practice for police officers to stop and question a suspect under such circumstances, the courts and legal writers were, until recently, sharply divided as to whether such a right in fact existed and, if it did exist, its precise limitations. There is still much confusion in this area, but police officers today can act with substantial authority. In the case of *Terry v. Ohio,*[82] the Court squarely faced this problem and laid down some general rules.

The facts of the *Terry* case are very similar to those of thousands of other cases where police officers are confronted with situations which require that they take some action. Here, while patrolling the streets in downtown Cleveland, the officer observed three men "casing a job, a stick-up." The activities of the suspects—looking in the store window, walking a short distance, turning back, peering in the same store window and returning to confer—caused the officer to determine that a further inquiry was justified. He therefore approached the three men, identified himself as a police officer and asked their names. When the men mumbled something in response to his inquiry, the officer grabbed the petitioner, spun him around, and patted down the outside of his clothing. Feeling a pistol in the pocket of Terry's overcoat, the officer reached inside the overcoat but was unable to remove the gun. He ordered Terry to remove the overcoat and then retrieved a .38-caliber revolver. He testified that he only patted the men down to see whether they had weapons.

The Court acknowledged that the question before them was a difficult and troublesome one. In approving the detention of the suspects, the majority of the Court held:

---

[82] 392 US 1, 20 LEd(2d) 889, 88 SCt 1868 (1968). See Part II of this book.

A police officer may in appropriate circumstances and in an appropriate manner approach a person for purposes of investigating possibly criminal behavior even though there is no probable cause to make an arrest.

Thus, the Supreme Court has upheld the authority of the police officer to stop or detain a person when he observes unusual conduct which leads him reasonably to conclude in light of his experience that criminal activity may be afoot. The Court went on to explain that if he has this right to detain, he must necessarily have the right to protect himself and others while conducting a carefully limited search of the outer clothing in an attempt to discover weapons which may be used to assault him.

This does not authorize a police officer to detain anyone on mere suspicion. The officer must be able to articulate the reasons for his belief that criminal activity was being planned or was in the process of being executed. The Court did say, however, that the officer could give weight to his experience, and to the reasonable inferences which he is entitled to draw from the facts, in light of that experience.

The authority to detain as explained in the *Terry* case is not based upon any state statute or constitutional provision as such. The Court explained that this was in fact a stop and a seizure within the meaning of the Fourth Amendment, but that such detention in the circumstances that existed here was "reasonable." [83]

The scope of the *Terry* stop and frisk doctrine was examined by the United States Supreme Court in 1972. The Court, in the *Adams* case,[84] approved the stopping and questioning of a suspect after an informant had advised the officer that the suspect was carrying narcotics and had a gun stuck under his belt. Part of the officer's information was received from an informer, while in *Terry* the information to justify the stop was obtained by personal observation. The majority (six to three) of the Court in *Adams* logically determined that

---

[83] The scope of the frisk doctrine is discussed in Chapter 4 which deals with search and seizure (at §4.16).

[84] Adams v. Williams, 407 US 143, 32 LEd(2d) 612, 92 SCt 1921 (1972).

"the subtleties of the hearsay rule should not thwart an appropriate police response."

Since the *Terry* case was decided by the Supreme Court, many lower courts have rendered decisions interpreting this case. In some instances the lower courts have found that officers have abused the privilege to detain as discussed in the *Terry* case, while others have recognized practical necessities and have approved stopping motorists as well as pedestrians under the *Terry* reasoning.

The *Terry* rationale and the general authority to arrest on reasonable grounds can often be combined to give the officer authority to stop and then arrest. In certain circumstances, the suspicion of the officer may be aroused, but he does not have the authority to make an arrest because he doesn't have the required reasonable grounds. Often, however, he does have the authority as defined in the *Terry* case to detain the suspect. If during the period of detention, additional facts are uncovered which supply reasonable grounds or probable cause to arrest, the arrest, of course, can be consummated.

The officer who is well acquainted with the authority to ask questions as explained in the *Terry* case and the authority to arrest can, in the vast majority of the cases, reasonably determine if the proper procedure is to detain, arrest, or take no immediate action.

Although the detention in the *Terry* case involved a pedestrian on the street, there is no reason why the same rationale could not be applied where the detention is to be in a building. The Bronx County Supreme Court in New York has logically reasoned that the "stop and frisk" rationale must also apply within private living quarters.[85] The court in this case explained that the dangers in a closed apartment are even greater than they are on a sidewalk. Again, the court pointed out that the officers must, of course, be able to point to specific facts upon which to base their belief that criminal activity was afoot.

Recent cases have removed some of the doubt concerning the authority of a police officer to detain without making

[85] People v. Henry, Bronx Co. Supreme Ct., N.Y., decided Oct. 20, 1968.

an arrest, nevertheless, the officer is still limited not only as to the initial detention but as to the length of the detention. In any event, he must act reasonably and not overstep his authority.

1. Legislation

In an attempt to add clarity to an area fraught with confusion, a few states had, prior to the *Terry* decision, adopted legislation defining and limiting the right to stop and question. Since the decision in *Terry* v. *Ohio*, additional states have adopted legislation clarifying the right of the officer to detain and to frisk. Two examples of such legislation are here discussed.

(a) The Uniform Arrest Act

The Uniform Arrest Act adopted by the Interstate Commission on Crime contains the following provisions concerning detention:

> I. A peace officer may stop any person abroad whom he has reasonable ground to suspect is committing, has committed or is about to commit a crime, and may demand of him his name, address, business abroad and whither he is going.
> II. Any person so questioned who fails to identify himself or explain his actions to the satisfaction of the officer stopping him may be detained and further questioned and investigated.
> III. The total period of detention provided for by this section shall not exceed two hours. Such detention is not an arrest and shall not be recorded as an arrest in any official record. At the end of the detention period the person so detained shall be released unless arrested and charged with a crime.

This provision has been adopted by Rhode Island, New Hampshire and Delaware. The constitutionality of the detention provisions of the Uniform Arrest Act has been upheld by the Supreme Courts of both Delaware and Rhode Island, but the Supreme Court of the United States has not reviewed a case in which this issue was presented. The Delaware and Rhode Island courts, in construing the statute, attempted to distinguish the procedures authorized by the act from the technical arrest. They explained that the detention is not recorded as an arrest and the person is not formally charged with a crime.

Although this provision has not been specifically upheld by the Supreme Court of the United States, the stopping which is authorized by this act was upheld in the *Terry* case discussed in the previous section. However, the Supreme Court did not approve the two-hour detention period and the constitutionality of this section of the act remains open to speculation.

(b) The "Stop and Frisk" Act

In response to demands of law enforcement agencies for a greater measure of certainty in the area of permissible investigatory conduct, the New York Legislature in 1964 enacted a statute which is commonly referred to as the "Stop and Frisk" Act. This act, as amended, provides:

> 1. In addition to the authority provided by this article for making an arrest without a warrant, a police officer may stop a person in a public place located within the geographical area of such officer's employment when he reasonably suspects that such person is committing, has committed or is about to commit either (a) a felony or (b) a misdemeanor defined in the penal law, and may demand of him his name, address and an explanation of his conduct.
>
> . . . .
>
> 3. When upon stopping a person under circumstances prescribed in subdivisions one and two a police officer or court officer, as the case may be, reasonably suspects that he is in danger of physical injury, he may search such person for a deadly weapon or any instrument, article or substance readily capable of causing serious physical injury and of a sort not ordinarily carried in public places by law-abiding persons. If he finds such a weapon or instrument, or any other property possession of which he reasonably believes may constitute the commission of a crime, he may take it and keep it until the completion of the questioning, at which time he shall either return it, if lawfully possessed, or arrest such person. [86]

Provisions of the Stop and Frisk Act do not permit an officer to stop and question on mere caprice or whim. The test employed under the act is "reasonable suspicion." An officer is

[86] NYCRIMPROL §140.50 (Supp 1973). Analogous to former NYCODE CRIMPRO §180-a (1964).

justified in detaining one whom he "reasonably suspects" is committing, has committed, or is about to commit certain specified crimes.

In the case of *Sibron v. New York*,[87] the Supreme Court of the United States discussed the New York Stop and Frisk Act. The Court acknowledged that the state is free to develop its own law to meet the needs of local law enforcement and may call the standards it employs by any name it may choose. But the Court went on to explain that the state may not authorize police conduct which violates Fourth Amendment rights regardless of the labels which it attaches to such conduct. Applying this reasoning, the Supreme Court refused to make any pronouncement on the facial constitutionality of the New York Stop and Frisk Act but did not find that it was unconstitutional as applied in this particular case. In upholding the stop, the Court stated in *Sibron*:

> We have held today in *Terry v. Ohio* . . . that police conduct of the sort with which section 180-a deals must be judged under the Reasonable Search and Seizure Clause of the Fourteenth Amendment.

In a concurring opinion Mr. Justice Harlan stated that the statute is certainly not unconstitutional on its face.

It is clear from the cases that states may enact legislation setting out the standards to be followed by police officers when stopping persons for investigation purposes. Such statutes, of course, must not violate constitutional standards. And with or without such a statute, the officer must be prepared to give specific and articulable facts which, taken together with rational inferences from those facts, reasonably warrant the intrusion.

To be so prepared the officer should make contemporaneous and detailed records concerning the activities which led him reasonably to conclude the person was committing or had committed the criminal offense.

Since the decisions in the *Terry* and the *Sibron* cases, state legislatures have been confronted with questions relating to the need for a stop and frisk statute. In view of the *Terry*

[87] 392 US 40, 20 LEd(2d) 917, 88 SCt 1889 (1968).

case, where the stop and frisk was authorized without a statute in Ohio, it has been argued that a stop and frisk statute is unnecessary. Others contend, however, that a stop and frisk statute gives legislative approval to the procedure which is authorized, and should be adopted, if only for setting out more exact standards. Several states have been convinced by the latter argument and have adopted stop and frisk statutes.

2. Motorists

Because automobiles are frequently used both as a means for perpetrating a crime and as an instrument of escape, the courts in recent years have had to reckon with the special problems involved in the detention of motorists. Strictly speaking, stopping a moving vehicle comes closer to the definition of arrest than does a casual approach to a pedestrian on the street. When a pedestrian is confronted by a police officer who wants to ask a few questions, he can generally continue on his course during the conversation. On the other hand, when the driver of a motor vehicle is forced off the road or directed to stop by a siren, his freedom of locomotion has been impeded without his consent for the duration of the interview.

The decisions of the Supreme Court on whether the mere stopping of an automobile constituted arrest are somewhat confusing. In the case of *Henry v. United States*,[88] the Supreme Court held that an arrest is complete when the car is stopped and that at or before this time the police officer must have reasonable grounds to believe that the crime has been committed. The authority of the *Henry* decision was weakened by the fact that the Government conceded on appeal that the stopping of the car amounted to arrest and by the fact that the stop was made by FBI agents who do not have the same authority as local police officers. In a case decided the following year,[89] the Court, by implication, held that the mere approach of an officer to make an inquiry of the occupants of the car does not of itself constitute an arrest.

There is no doubt that a police officer may arrest the driver of an automobile under the same authority that he can make

---

[88] 361 US 98, 4 LEd(2d) 134, 80 SCt 168 (1959).

[89] Rios v. United States, 364 US 253, 4 LEd(2d) 1688, 80 SCt 1431 (1960).

an arrest of a pedestrian—that is, if he has a warrant of arrest; if he has reasonable grounds to believe that a felony has been committed; or if a misdemeanor is committed in his presence. But in many instances it is desirable to have the right to stop an automobile for the purpose of asking questions on grounds which might not amount to a basis for arrest.

(a) Reasonable suspicion of criminal activity

Although the facts in the case of *Terry v. Ohio*[90] concerned the detention of a pedestrian on a street, there seems to be no valid reason why this same reasoning cannot be applied in an automobile situation. At least one Federal Circuit Court of Appeals has logically decided that the *Terry* reasoning will apply when detaining the driver of an automobile.[91] In this case, officers, while patrolling the streets at 3:30 A.M., noticed a car containing two men driving slowly through the streets located off the main highway. Noticing that the car had an out-of-county license, the officers kept the vehicle under surveillance for a period and noted that it moved slowly by several business establishments which were closed. They stopped the car, and one of the officers asked an occupant of the car to step out. While the occupant was leaving the car, he bumped into some object on the floor which gave a noise of metal hitting metal. The officer then shined his light inside and saw the ends of two pry bars sticking out of a sack on the floor of the car.

The defendant Carpenter was convicted by the state court of burglary and possession of burglary tools. A motion was made at the trial to exclude the evidence because the original stopping was illegal, the defendants claiming there was no authority to arrest. The court, however, rejected this argument and applied the *Terry* reasoning, stating:

> In applying the *Terry* analysis to the facts of this case, it seems clear that the police officers were "reasonable" in the initial "seizure" of Carpenter. It was an early morning hour in a small town where unidentified cars do not routinely travel at that time. The car had out of county license plates. There had been a series of burglaries

[90] 392 US 1, 20 LEd(2d) 889, 88 SCt 1868 (1968).

[91] Carpenter v. Sigler, 419 F(2d) 169 (8thCir 1969).

in the town. During the period of surveillance by the officers the car moved very slowly past closed business establishments and pursued a rather erratic course through the streets of the town. These facts taken together all point to sufficient justification for stopping the Carpenter auto and requiring the occupants to identify themselves.

In the absence of a reasonable suspicion, does the rationale of the *Terry* case, or any other reasoning, justify the stopping of vehicles near the Mexican-United States border to determine if aliens are in the vehicle? In the case of *United States v. Brignoni-Ponce,*[92] the United States Supreme Court refused to approve the routine stopping of vehicles unless the stopping officer is "aware of specific articulable facts, together with rational inferences from these facts, that reasonably warrant suspicion" that a vehicle contains illegal aliens.

But what about a situation where, instead of roving police stopping the cars, the border patrol establishes checkpoints on roads leading away from the border? In the case of *United States v. Martinez-Fuerte* and a companion case,[93] the Supreme Court distinguished between roving patrols and temporary or permanent roadblocks set up some distance from the border in an effort to apprehend smugglers who transport illegal aliens into the United States. In both of these cases, the border patrol had established checkpoints on a major highway away from the Mexican border for the purpose of briefly questioning the occupants of vehicles to determine if aliens were being illegally transported. In one case, the roadblock was set up with a court order, but in the other case, no court order was acquired before the roadblock was established. The Court found that it made no legal difference and upheld this practice as not violating the Fourth Amendment. In summarizing the holding, the Supreme Court said:

> [W]e hold that stops for brief questioning routinely conducted at permanent checkpoints are consistent with the Fourth Amendment and need not be authorized by warrant. The principal protection of Fourth Amendment rights at checkpoints lies in appropriate limita-

[92] 422 US 873, 45 LEd(2d) 607, 95 SCt 2574 (1975).

[93] 428 US 543, 49 LEd(2d) 1116, 96 SCt 3074 (1976); Sifuentes v. United States, same citation.

tions on the scope of the stop. See *Terry* v. *Ohio*, 392 U.S. at 24–27. . . . We have held that checkpoint searches are constitutional only if justified by consent or probable cause to search. . . . And our holding today is limited to the type of stops described in this opinion. "[A]ny further detention . . . must be based on consent or probable cause." . . . None of the defendants in these cases argues that the stopping officers exceeded these limitations.

In reaching the conclusions, the Supreme Court emphasized the necessity of weighing the public interests against the Fourth Amendment interest of the individual. The majority explained that the intrusion into the rights of the individual are sufficiently minimal that no particularized reason need exist to justify this intrusion.

In distinguishing between the random roving patrol stops which are not authorized and the checkpoint stops which are authorized, the Supreme Court emphasized that in the latter instance motorists using the highways are not taken by surprise because they know or may obtain knowledge of the location of the checkpoints, and because the checkpoint operations both appear to, and actually involve, less discretionary enforcement activity. It must be kept in mind that this detention, as authorized in the *Martinez-Fuerte* case, is limited to the particular facts of that case, that is, border patrol stops.

(b) License and registration checks

One issue that has been repeatedly brought to the attention of the courts involves the right of a police officer to stop a motor vehicle to check the driver's license or the car's registration, mechanical condition or weight. Does the law allow a police officer to stop a motor vehicle on less reasonable grounds than those required to stop a pedestrian? Does the fact that a motorist is using the highway lessen the rights guaranteed to him under the Fourth Amendment?

Frequently, the right to stop a motorist to check his driver's license or to determine if he has a legitimate registration certificate is expressly granted by the state statute. It has been argued that without the power to conduct license checks, the police would have no way of apprehending and eliminating unqualified drivers whose licenses had been revoked or suspended due to prior traffic offenses. On this basis, the courts have given officers the authority to detain motorists, and have held that such detention does not amount to a technical arrest.

In *City of Miami v. Aronovitz*,[94] the Florida court noted that the owner of an operator's license exercised a privilege granted by the state and subject to the reasonable regulations of the use of the highway common to all citizens. The highest court of the Commonwealth of Kentucky reached the same results in recognizing the right of officers to set up roadblocks for the purpose of ascertaining whether operators of motor vehicles were licensed.[95]

Perhaps the best rationale for a limited detention of motorists is included in the majority decision of the Nebraska Supreme Court in the case of *State v. Holmberg*.[96] In this case, officers acting under the authority of a Nebraska statute stopped a camper-pickup and asked the driver to exhibit his operator's license and registration card. While checking the license and registration, the officer smelled and saw evidence of marijuana. The defendant contended that even the momentary stopping of the motorist for an inspection constituted an arrest and required probable cause. He argued that because the officer interfered with his freedom of movement without probable cause, the evidence should not be admitted.

The argument that the United States Supreme Court, in *United States v. Brignoni-Ponce*, foreclosed the right of a state to authorize a detention to check driver's licenses was rejected by the Nebraska Supreme Court with the following explanation in the *Holmberg* case:

> This statute is intended to give the officers mentioned therein the power to enforce laws regulating the operation of vehicles or the use of the highways. The licensing laws are safety measures applicable to the use of all roads or highways within the state. It would be most unusual to have an observable indication of a licensing violation of a moving vehicle. Stopping the vehicles for inspection is the only practical method of enforcement. . . .

[94] 114 S(2d) 784 (Fla 1959).
[95] Commonwealth v. Mitchell, 355 SW(2d) 686 (Ky 1962).
[96] 194 Neb 337, 231 NW(2d) 672 (1975).

In all of the cases recognizing the authority of peace officers to stop motor vehicles to check driver's licenses and registration certificates, the courts warn against using this as a subterfuge or ruse to check for violations of other laws. In the *Holmberg* case, the majority of the Nebraska Supreme Court members indicated that they would have no hesitancy in holding a detention arbitrary and unreasonable if the facts should disclose that the stop was a mere pretext for other reasons. That court, as well as others, also pointed out that when the driver has produced his license and registration card, and they are in proper form, he must promptly be allowed to continue on his way unless the officer becomes aware of a reasonable probability of a violation of the law that may justify further detention. If the automobile is lawfully stopped, the officer may arrest for other violations when these occur in his presence.[97]

§ 3.15 Summary

The outcome of a case may often depend on how the officer handles the arrest. If the officer oversteps his authority, the exclusionary rule which will be discussed in the following chapter may preclude the use of all evidence gained as a result of the arrest in any subsequent trial.

As a general rule, an officer may make an arrest under the authority of an arrest warrant, or without a warrant if an offense is committed in his presence and, in the case of a felony, if he has reasonable grounds to believe that the person whom he is about to arrest has committed the crime. The preferable method of making an arrest is by the authority of an arrest warrant. To be valid, the warrant must meet the constitutional and statutory requirements. The United States Constitution specifically requires that the warrant (1) be issued upon probable cause, (2) be supported by oath or affirmation, and (3) particularly describe the persons to be seized. Other requirements have been added by legislation or case decisions.

Although the Constitution contains no exceptions, the courts have recognized the necessity of making arrests with-

[97] Cox v. State, 181 Tenn 344, 181
SW(2d) 338 (1944).

out warrants. Generally an arrest without a warrant will be found valid in a felony case if the officer can show that he had reasonable grounds to believe that a felony was committed and that the person he arrested committed the felony. In determining such reasonable grounds, he may use facts obtained from his personal observation, certain informers' information, information from other departments or other agencies, the past criminal record of the suspect, and physical evidence.

In the usual misdemeanor case, the officer cannot make the arrest unless the misdemeanor is committed in his presence. In order for the offense to be considered as taking place within the presence of the officer, he must be made aware of its commission through one or more of his senses. Some state legislation has extended the authority to arrest without a warrant in misdemeanor situations to make it possible for the officer to arrest validly if he has reasonable grounds to believe that a misdemeanor has been committed.

To conserve the time of the police as well as of the person who has violated a law, the legislatures and courts have sanctioned the use of the citation and summons. Although the statutes differ in wording, a citation is not considered an arrest, but an alternative to an arrest. The citation is used primarily in traffic cases, but it should be used whenever possible to bring those accused of other minor violations before the courts.

Because a state cannot confer any official power which would be effective in another state, fresh pursuit of an offender is usually authorized within the state, but into another state, only if approved by the host state. The right of fresh pursuit across state boundary lines is generally confined by statutes to felonies. There are, however, a few states that authorize out-of-state law enforcement officers to cross state borders in order to make an arrest for a misdemeanor. Most states still do not have fresh pursuit legislation, and, absent such legislative authority, an officer from another state making an arrest acts only in the capacity of a private citizen.

In some instances the officer does not have the authority to arrest, but does have the authority to detain. In a few states the authority to detain has been granted by statute, but even without a statute, such a detention is justified under recent court decisions when the officer observes unusual conduct which leads him reasonably to conclude, in light of his experience, that criminal activity may be afoot.

Recognizing that special problems arise concerning the stopping of automobiles, the courts have authorized officers to stop automobiles to check driver's licenses or automobile registrations. In most jurisdictions, the right of an officer to stop a car in order to check the driver's license is expressly granted by statute, and the statutes have been upheld. The right to stop a car to check the driver's license does not, however, give the officer the right to conduct a search. In addition, an officer may detain a motorist when he reasonably suspects criminal activity may be afoot.

Chapter 4

SEARCH AND SEIZURE*

The right of the people to be secure in their persons, houses, papers, and effects, against unreasonable searches and seizures, shall not be violated, and no Warrants shall issue, but upon probable cause, supported by Oath or affirmation, and particularly describing the place to be searched, and the persons or things to be seized.

FOURTH AMENDMENT, 1791

§ 4.1   Historical development of search and seizure laws

In order to understand our present constitutional provisions and the interpretations made by the various courts concerning search and seizure, the history of this protection must carefully be studied. As the laws concerning search and seizure were greatly influenced by the laws and customs of England, both the English background and the American background are necessarily included in this study.

* by John C. Klotter

160

Although the use of search warrants appears not to have been known in early English common law, the use of the search warrant gradually crept into the administration of the English government to the point that until 1766, the person, property and premises of the individual were subject to practically unlimited searches and seizures. At first the use of search warrants was confined to stolen goods; but it came to be used indiscriminately for other types of evidence. In 1766 the English House of Commons passed resolutions condemning the use of "general warrants."

The United States Supreme Court, in an early case referring to the general warrant and the condemnation of such warrants by the English Parliament, stated:

> It was welcomed and applauded by the lovers of liberty in the colonies as well as in the mother country. It is regarded as one of the permanent monuments of the British Constitution, and is quoted as such by the English authorities on that subject down to the present time.[1]

As this rule was being developed in England, events were taking place in this country which, to a great extent, determined the future of search and seizure laws. Five years prior to the condemnation of the general warrant by the House of Commons, an incident took place in America which brought the necessity for *specific provisions* for the protection of an individual's security, personal liberty and private property to the attention of those who would later write our Constitution.

In a crowded Boston courtroom in February, 1761, a group of merchants denounced the general warrants which gave the English soldiers authority to search any ship, store or house. The issue before the court was the admissibility of evidence obtained by the Crown through a writ of assistance or general warrant, a device frequently employed by the authorities to search for smuggled goods. At that time writs of assistance, as they were called, were issued with little restraint. They empowered the authorities to search virtually any house or any other building on a mere suspicion that goods subject to sei-

---

[1] Boyd v. United States, 116 US 616,
29 LEd 746, 6 SCt 524 (1886).

zure might be found there. No showing of probable cause was required.

James Otis, an attorney who had previously served as attorney general for the Colony of Massachusetts, represented the merchants. He called the writ of assistance "the worst instrument of arbitrary power, the most destructive of English liberty, and the fundamental principles of law, that was ever found in an English law book." John Adams, who heard the arguments in the case said later, after he had become President of the United States, "Every man of the crowded audience appeared to me to go away as I did, ready to take up arms against the writs of assistance. Then and there was the first scene of the first act of opposition to the arbitrary claims of Great Britain. Then and there the child of independence was born." [2]

Fifteen years after this case the colonies declared their independence. In 1789 the Constitution was ratified, and in 1791 the Fourth Amendment was adopted to ensure that the personal security and private property of the individual would be protected against invasion by the federal government.

§ 4.2   Constitutional provisions

Even prior to the adoption of the Constitution many of those who objected to its ratification criticized the absence of a provision protecting the people against unreasonable searches and seizures. This was understandable as the writs of assistance were fresh in the minds of those who advocated the inclusion of a Bill of Rights. Led by James Madison, the First Congress initiated legislation to protect the people against unreasonable searches and seizures. After ratification in 1791, this became the Fourth Amendment to the Constitution and provided that:

> The right of the people to be secure in their persons, houses, papers, and effects against unreasonable searches and seizures, shall not be violated, and no Warrants shall issue, but upon probable cause, supported by Oath or affirmation, and particularly describing the place to be searched, and the persons or things to be seized.

[2] WORKS OF JOHN ADAMS, vol II, app A, pp 523-525.

Like other provisions of the Bill of Rights, the Fourth Amendment would have little meaning without judicial interpretation. For example, the word "unreasonable" as used in the Amendment could allow many searches or could restrict searches to those with warrants only. Other terms which must be interpreted before the provision will have meaning include "persons," "houses," "papers," "effects," "probable cause," "particularly describing" and even the word "searched." In hundreds and even thousands of cases the courts have attempted to define the meaning of these terms as used in this section of the Constitution, and thereby define the scope of this protection. To make this protection more understandable, a few of the more important cases are included in Part II of this book.

The constitutions of the several states uniformly imposed restraints on state actions similar to the restrictions imposed by the United States Constitution. For example, the constitution of Texas has the following provision:

> The people shall be secure in their persons, houses, papers and possessions, from all unreasonable searches or seizures, and no warrant to search any place, or to seize any person or thing, shall issue without describing them as near as may be, nor without probable cause, supported by oath or affirmation.[3]

The state constitutions would also have very little meaning without judicial interpretation. The state courts have often disagreed among themselves as to the scope and application of the constitutional provisions; and the state courts have likewise disagreed with the federal courts. However, as will be indicated in future paragraphs, where there is such disagreement the interpretation by the Supreme Court of the United States will prevail and this will be binding insofar as minimum standards are applied to the states.

The federal constitutional provisions place limitations on the federal officials and, by way of the Fourteenth Amendment, on state officials. In addition, the state constitutions as interpreted by the state courts place limitations on the powers

---

[3] TexConst art 1, §9.

of the state officials. However, neither the federal provisions nor the state provisions are applicable to searches and seizures by private persons, as these are limitations upon governmental rather than private activities.

§ 4.3 The exclusionary rule

The exclusionary rule simply stated is, "Evidence obtained by an unreasonable search and seizure will not be admissible in court." This rule that evidence be excluded when the Fourth Amendment is violated is not a provision of the Fourth Amendment itself but is a rule that has been framed by the courts. The exclusionary rule, especially as it relates to search and seizure, is a product of the United States courts and is not followed in England or in the other nations whose system of law is based on Anglo-Saxon sources.

There are arguments for and against the exclusionary rule. In England and Canada, evidence is admitted even though obtained in violation of the search and seizure provisions. The reason for the common law or English rule has been succinctly stated by English judges as follows:

> I think it would be a dangerous obstacle to the administration of justice if we were to hold [that] because evidence was obtained by illegal means, it could not be used against a party charged with an offense. . . . It, therefore, seems to me that the interests of the State must excuse the seizure of documents, which seizure would otherwise be unlawful, if it appears in fact that such documents are evidence of a crime committed by anyone. . . .[4]

And in another case:

> In their Lordships' opinion the test to be applied in considering whether evidence is admissible is whether it is relevant to the matters in issue. If it is, it is admissible and the court is not concerned with how the evidence was obtained.[5]

In 1955, the Supreme Court of California summarized, before rejecting them, the reasons for refusing to adopt the exclusionary rule:

[4] Elias v. Pasmore, [1934] 2 KB 164, AllERRep 380.

[5] Kuruma v. Reginam, [1955] 2 WLR 223, 1 AllER 236.

The rules of evidence are designed to enable courts to reach the truth and, in criminal cases, to secure a fair trial to those accused of the crime. Evidence obtained by an illegal search and seizure is ordinarily just as true and reliable as evidence lawfully obtained. The court needs all reliable evidence material to the issue before it, the guilt or innocence of the accused, and how such evidence is obtained is immaterial to that issue. It should not be excluded unless strong considerations of public policy demand it.[6]

. . . .

Despite the persuasive force of the foregoing arguments, we have concluded, . . . that evidence obtained in violation of the constitutional guarantees is inadmissible. . . . We have been compelled to reach that conclusion because other remedies have completely failed to secure compliance with the constitutional provisions on the part of police officers with the attendant result that the courts under the old rule have been constantly required to participate in, and in effect condone, the lawless activities of law enforcement officers.

The argument for not adopting the exclusionary rule was succinctly stated by Justice Cardozo of the New York Court of Appeals, when he commented, "The criminal is to go free because the constable has blundered."[7]

Those who advocate the application of the exclusionary rule argue that this is the only means by which the provision of the Fourth Amendment can be protected. This reasoning will be developed in the paragraphs which follow.

§ 4.4   —Adoption of rule by federal courts in Weeks v. United States

For many years the American courts followed the common law doctrine in all cases and authorized the use of evidence even though it was obtained in violation of the search and seizure provisions. But in 1914, the Supreme Court, in *Weeks v. United States*,[8] unequivocally rejected the common law rule, and specifically held that evidence obtained by unreasonable search and seizure would be excluded in the federal courts.

In the *Weeks* case, a United States marshal, working with local police officers, seized from the defendant's home some

---

[6] People v. Cahan, 44 Cal(2d) 434, 282 P(2d) 905 (1955).
[7] People v. Defore, 242 NY 13, 150 NE 585 (1926).
[8] 232 US 383, 58 LEd 652, 34 SCt 341 (1914).

letters and envelopes which were subsequently used as evidence against the defendant. The defendant was found guilty on a federal charge of using the mails to defraud. On appeal, the Supreme Court held that in a federal prosecution, the Fourth Amendment barred the use of evidence secured through illegal search and seizure.

This exclusionary rule, which initially was applicable only to federal courts, was later adopted by state courts as a means of forcing compliance with the provisions of the Fourth Amendment. Notwithstanding the argument that the rights of private citizens could be protected against illegal searches by criminal prosecution of the offending law enforcement officers, or by action for damages, the courts were convinced that these measures had failed, and that it was necessary to exclude the evidence obtained by illegal search in order to remove the incentive for law enforcement officers to violate the Fourth Amendment.

The *Weeks* decision, however, did not prohibit the use in federal courts of evidence illegally obtained by *state* officers. But, in extending the application of the exclusionary rule, the Court, in 1920, held that if a federal officer seized documents illegally, his knowledge acquired in that action could not be used in obtaining other evidence.[9] And finally in 1960, the door was closed to the use of *all* such illegally obtained evidence in federal courts when the court ruled that evidence obtained by state officers in violation of the Fourth Amendment could not be used in federal courts.[10]

As late as 1949, the Supreme Court refused to apply the exclusionary rule to the states. In *Wolf* v. *Colorado*,[11] the Court stated:

> We have no hesitation in saying that were a State affirmatively to sanction such police incursion into privacy it would run counter to the guarantee of the Fourteenth Amendment. But the ways of enforcing such a basic right raise questions of a different order. How such arbitrary conduct should be checked, what remedies

[9] Silverthorne Lumber Co. v. United States, 251 US 385, 64 LEd 319, 40 SCt 182 (1920).

[10] Elkins v. United States, 364 US 206, 4 LEd(2d) 1669, 80 SCt 1437 (1960).

[11] 338 US 25, 93 LEd 1782, 69 SCt 1359 (1949).

against it should be afforded, [and] the means by which the right should be made effective, are all questions that are not to be so dogmatically answered as to preclude varying solutions which spring from an allowable range of judgment on issues not susceptible of quantitative solution.

In the *Wolf* case the Court reviewed the actions taken by the various state courts and summarized their positions. In the summary, the Court noted that of the forty-seven states which had passed on the exclusionary rule, thirty-one rejected the rule and sixteen states were in agreement with it. The Court also pointed out that of ten jurisdictions within the United Kingdom and the British Commonwealth of Nations, none had held evidence obtained by illegal search and seizure inadmissible. The concluding paragraph of the majority opinion in *Wolf* summarized the holding with:

> We hold, therefore, that in a prosecution in a State court for a State crime the Fourteenth Amendment does not forbid the admission of evidence obtained by unreasonable search and seizure.

However, Justice Murphy, one of the four dissenting justices, reiterated the reasons for adopting the exclusionary rule and making it applicable to the states through the Fourteenth Amendment. He pointed out that if the search and seizure clause were to be enforced there were three available devices: judicial exclusion of illegally obtained evidence; criminal prosecution of the violators; and civil action against violators in the action of trespass. He concluded that only the first remedy is effective, stating:

> The conclusion is inescapable that but one remedy exists to deter violations of the search and seizure clause. That is the rule which excludes illegally obtained evidence. Only by exclusion can we impress upon a zealous prosecutor that violation of the Constitution will do him no good. And only when that point is driven home can the prosecutor be expected to emphasize the importance of observing constitutional demands in his instructions to the police.

Despite the definite statement by the majority that the Fourteenth Amendment did not forbid the admission in state courts of evidence obtained by an unreasonable search and seizure, a series of cases decided between 1949 and 1961 displayed a clear change in judicial attitude toward the opposite position. In 1956 the exclusionary rule was extended when a federal officer was enjoined by a federal court from presenting in a state court evidence previously held inadmissible in a federal court because it had been illegally seized by the federal officer.[12]

§ 4.5   —Extension of rule to all courts in Mapp v. Ohio

In 1961, two centuries after James Otis made his denunciation of the writs of assistance, the exclusionary rule reached maturity when the Supreme Court extended the rule to every court and law enforcement officer in the nation.[13] By the decision in *Mapp v. Ohio*, the Supreme Court made it clear that henceforth evidence obtained by procedures which violated Fourth Amendment standards would no longer be admissible in state or federal courts against the party whose rights were violated.

On May 23, 1957, three Cleveland police officers arrived at Dollree Mapp's residence in the City of Cleveland, pursuant to information that a person who was wanted for questioning in connection with a recent bombing was hiding in Miss Mapp's home, and that there was a large amount of obscene paraphernalia hidden there also. After telephoning her attorney, Dollree Mapp refused to admit the officers without a search warrant. Three hours later, the officers returned with reinforcements and again sought entrance. When she did not come to the door, one of the doors was forcibly opened and the policemen gained entry. Miss Mapp demanded to see the search warrant, and a paper, claimed to be the warrant, was held up by one of the officers. She grabbed the paper and placed it in her bosom. A struggle ensued in which the officers recovered the piece of paper and handcuffed Miss Mapp. A search was conducted of the entire apartment, including the bedroom, living room, kitchen, dinette, and basement of the building. The obscene materials, for the possession of which

[12] Rea v. United States, 350 US 214, 100 LEd 233, 76 SCt 292 (1956).

[13] Mapp v. Ohio, 367 US 643, 6 LEd(2d) 1081, 81 SCt 1684 (1961). See Part II for portions of this case.

the defendant was ultimately convicted, were discovered as a result of that widespread search.

The state contended that even if the search were made without authority or otherwise unreasonably, it was not prevented from using the unconstitutionally seized evidence at the trial because *Wolf* v. *Colorado supra*, had authorized the admission of such evidence in a state court and also that the state of Ohio did not follow the exclusionary rule. After a discussion of other applicable cases, the Court flatly declared the application of the exclusionary rule to all the states, saying:

> Today we once again examine *Wolf's* constitutional documentation of the right to privacy free from unreasonable state intrusion, and, after its dozen years on our books, are led by it to close the only courtroom door remaining open to evidence secured by official lawlessness in flagrant abuse of that basic right, reserved to all persons as a specific guarantee against that very same unlawful conduct. We hold that all evidence obtained by searches and seizures in violation of the Constitution is, by that same authority, inadmissible in a state court.

The exclusionary rule, defined in the *Weeks* case as a matter of judicial implication, was made applicable in the federal courts in 1914. Between the years 1914 and 1961, the Supreme Court said the rule was not applicable to the states by reason of the Fourteenth Amendment, and then reversed itself and said the rule was to be made effective against the states.

The decision in the *Mapp* case in 1961 left no doubt that the exclusionary rule prohibited the use of evidence obtained in violation of the Fourth Amendment in both federal and state courts. This ruling, together with previous decisions of the Supreme Court, made it mandatory that state officials comply with the search and seizure standards as enunciated by the United States Supreme Court and, in some instances, federal district courts. In addition, state and local officers must comply with decisions of state courts where these limitations are greater than those imposed by the federal courts.

This ruling should not be interpreted to mean that all searches are unreasonable. However, because of the inability of state and federal courts to clearly announce rules concerning search and seizure, and the failure of officers, knowingly or unknowingly, to follow even those rules that are clear, thousands of cases have been disposed of without even reaching the stage where guilt or innocence is considered.

§ 4.6 —Application and modification of the rule

Since 1961, efforts have been made to convince members of the Supreme Court that the exclusionary rule should be reversed or at least modified. Many legal scholars have argued that the exclusionary rule has not proved workable and has done more harm than good. Professor John H. Wigmore, for example, has consistently criticized the wisdom of the rule, and has pointed out the illogic of a rule which reprimands the police officer by freeing the lawbreaker.[14] More recently, action has been taken by members of interested organizations to amend these restrictive rules.[15] A brief review of the arguments pro and con will bring this issue more in focus.

Justice Murphy, in his dissenting opinion in the case of *Wolf* v. *Colorado*,[16] argued that there are only three ways by which the Fourth Amendment search and seizure protection may be enforced:

> If we would attempt the enforcement of the search and seizure clause in the ordinary case today, we are limited to three devices: judicial exclusion of illegally obtained evidence; criminal prosecution of violators; and civil action against violators in the action of trespass.

He goes on to say—and other justices agree—that only one of these is effective, and that is judicial exclusion of illegally obtained evidence.

In other cases the judges and attorneys have rested the reasoning for the exclusionary rule on two enunciated judicial cases: 1) the "imperative of judicial integrity" requires the exclusion of tainted evidence, and 2) the exclusion of illegally seized evidence will deter unlawful police conduct.[17]

---

[14] 8 Wigmore, EVIDENCE §2184a (3d ed 1961).

[15] See Amici Curiae brief prepared by the Americans for Effective Law Enforcement, Inc. in the case of Wolff v. Rice, 428 US 465, 49 LEd(2d) 1067, 96 SCt 3037 (1976).

[16] 338 US 25, 93 LEd 1782, 69 SCt 1359 (1949).

[17] United States v. Peltier, 422 US 351, 45 LEd(2d) 374, 95 SCt 2313 (1975).

In regard to the first reason, those who favor the exclusionary rule explain that for the courts to authorize the use of evidence obtained in violation of one of the amendments to the Constitution would place the court in the position of approving violations of the Constitution.

The rationale for the second foundation is that if the police officer and the prosecutor realize that evidence obtained in violation of the Fourth Amendment will be inadmissible, police officers will be instilled with the necessity of taking a greater degree of care toward the rights of an accused. It is further urged that the officers and prosecutors will make greater efforts to learn and apply the laws relating to search and seizure.

Today it is claimed by some criminal justice personnel that the foundation on which the exclusionary rule was built has become quicksand. Numerous cases are cited where pertinent evidence is excluded and criminals released, even where the officer acted in good faith and with a reasonable degree of training and education concerning the search and seizure laws.[18]

Some arguments have been advanced from time to time for modifying the exclusionary rule.

(1) There is no provision in the Constitution or the Fourth Amendment which requires or indicates that evidence should be excluded merely because it has been obtained in violation of the court standards. This is a judicial rule. It is not required by the Constitution and is not followed in other countries whose laws are based on the Anglo-Saxon model.

(2) Society and the law-abiding citizen are denied the protection of the law. The price paid for the exclusionary rule is much too high; the right to be protected from criminal attack should be considered along with the protection of the rights of the person accused of crime.

---

[18] Bivens v. Six Unknown Fed. Narc. Agents, 403 US 388, 29 LEd(2d) 619, 91 SCt 1999 (1971).

(3) The laws relating to search and seizure are so complex
that the officer not trained in law cannot comprehend
them. If the police officer is to be deterred from violating the search and seizure protections, they must
be made clear enough so that the average person can
understand them. This is not the case, however; the
laws are so complex and fraught with such variables,
depending on the factual situation, that even judges
cannot understand them. Often there are conflicts between concurring and dissenting judges in a single
opinion and the federal reviewing courts do not agree
with the state courts.[19]

(4) Police officers are more informed today and the harsh
methods for "policing the officer" are no longer justified. Today more than four hundred schools in the
United States offer education to police officers and other
criminal justice personnel. Although no amount of
formal police training will make the policeman an expert in the law of search and seizure, the training for
police officers, not only in the technicalities regarding
search and seizure, but also regarding the rights of
individuals in general, is at least as comprehensive as
that given to members of other professions. To continue to use the argument that the exclusionary rule
"polices the policeman" no longer has merit.

There is some indication that the rule, if not abandoned,
will not be expanded. In a 1974 case[20] before the Supreme
Court, that Court refused to allow a grand jury witness to
invoke the exclusionary rule, indicating that this would unduly
interfere with the effective and expeditious discharge of the
grand jury's duties. In this case the majority of the Supreme
Court indicated some disillusionment with the exclusionary
rule in their conclusions that:

In sum, the rule is a judicially created remedy designed to safeguard

[19] Nedrud, THE CRIMINAL LAW (1975).

[20] United States v. Calandra, 414 US 338, 38 LEd(2d) 561, 94 SCt 613 (1974).

Fourth Amendment rights generally through its deterrent effect, rather than a personal constitutional right of the party aggrieved.

Despite its broad deterrent purpose, the exclusionary rule has never been interpreted to proscribe the use of illegally seized evidence in all proceedings or against all persons. As with any remedial device, the application of the rule has been restricted to those areas where its remedial objectives are thought most efficaciously served.

Although refusing to abandon the exclusionary rule, the Supreme Court in July, 1976, rendered a decision which greatly reduces the application of the rule.[21] Acknowledging that the exclusionary rule is a judicially created means of effectuating the rights secured by the Fourth Amendment, the Court again reiterated its position that the rule has never been interpreted to proscribe the introduction of illegally seized evidence in all proceedings against all persons. In the case of *Stone* v. *Powell* and its companion case, *Wolff* v. *Rice*, the defendants in two separate trials claimed that evidence obtained as a result of an allegedly illegal search should not have been admitted into court. In both cases, the defendants had an opportunity to, and did in fact appeal to higher state courts where their claims were denied.

Habeas corpus actions were brought in federal courts to have the state court convictions set aside based upon the exclusionary rule. The question as stated by the United States Supreme Court is whether state prisoners—who have been afforded the opportunity for full and fair consideration of the reliance upon the exclusionary rule with respect to seized evidence by the state courts at trial on direct review—may invoke their claim again on federal habeas corpus review.

Rather than facing the exclusionary rule issue directly, the Supreme Court decided the case on the habeas corpus question. However, in so doing, the Court weighed the value of the exclusionary rule and the cost of extending it to collateral reviews.

Finding in *Stone* v. *Powell* that habeas corpus relief is not appropriate in such cases, the Court concluded:

[21] Stone v. Powell, 428 US 465, 49 LEd(2d) 1067, 96 SCt 3037 (1976).

> In sum, we conclude that where the State has provided an oppor-
> tunity for full and fair litigation of a Fourth Amendment claim, a
> state prisoner may not be granted federal habeas corpus relief on
> the ground that evidence obtained in an unconstitutional search or
> seizure was introduced at his trial. In this context the contribution
> of the exclusionary rule, if any, to the effectuation of the Fourth
> Amendment is minimal and the substantial societal costs of appli-
> cation of the rule persist with special force.

This case did not reverse previous cases which established
the exclusionary rule. On the other hand, it certainly limited
application of the rule. Probably as importantly, the Supreme
Court again questioned the value of such a rule in modern
society.

In another case [22] decided the same day as *Stone v. Powell*,
the majority found that the judicially created exclusionary rule
should not be extended to forbid in civil proceedings of one
sovereign (here, the Federal Government) the use of evidence
seized by a criminal law enforcement agent in another sovereign (here, the state government), since the likelihood of deterring law enforcement conduct through such a rule is not
sufficient to outweigh the societal cost imposed by the exclusion.

Although the exclusionary rule is still applicable, there are
at least four exceptions to the application of the rule at the
present time: (1) The application of the rule does not prevent
use of illegally seized evidence in grand jury proceedings.[23]
(2) It does not require that the trial court exclude such evidence from use for impeachment of a defendant.[24] (3) It does
not forbid in certain instances in civil proceedings the use of
evidence illegally seized.[25] (4) The evidence may be used if the
defendant does not object to its use.[26]

One reason the exclusionary rule was adopted was to pre-

---

[22] United States v. Janis, 429 US 874, 49 LEd(2d) 1046, 96 SCt 3021 (1976).

[23] United States v. Calandra, 414 US 338, 38 LEd(2d) 561, 94 SCt 613 (1974).

[24] Walder v. United States, 347 US 62, 98 LEd 503, 74 SCt 354 (1954).

[25] United States v. Janis, 429 US 874, 49 LEd(2d) 1046, 96 SCt 3021 (1976).

[26] Henry v. Mississippi, 379 US 443, 13 LEd(2d) 408, 85 SCt 564 (1965).

vent officials—purposely or negligently—from violating rights protected by the Fourth Amendment. If the exclusionary rule is modified or its application further restricted, law enforcement officers must continue to make every effort to understand thoroughly the rules regarding search and seizure and to apply them in a professional manner. Failure to do so will most certainly result in a return to the strict application of the rule.

The various methods by which evidence may be legally seized are discussed in the sections which follow.

§ 4.7   Search with a valid search warrant

One method of making a search which is universally recognized as legal is to search with a valid warrant. Both the United States Constitution and the constitutions of the various states describe the circumstances under which search warrants may be issued. They generally provide, "No warrants shall issue, but upon probable cause, supported by oath or affirmation, and particularly describing the place to be searched and the persons or things to be seized." No other means of making a search is mentioned in the Constitution.

When it is practicable, the best method of making a search is with a search warrant. Generally speaking, an officer who proceeds under the authority of a warrant regular and valid upon its face is protected against both civil and criminal liability.

1. Definition of a search warrant

A search warrant has been defined as an order in writing in the name of the state, signed by a judicial officer in the proper exercise of his authority, directing a peace officer to search for personal property and to bring it before the court.

2. Requirements for a search warrant

A search warrant cannot be issued unless it meets the requirements as set forth in the Constitution. Also, search warrants must meet other requirements as determined by the courts in order for the search warrant to be legal and the evidence seized thereunder to be admissible in the court.

For a warrant to be valid:

(a) *The proper official must issue the warrant.*

In most instances the statutes specifically authorize the issuance of a warrant and name the officials who may issue the warrant. For example, the Criminal Code of Illinois provides: [A]ny judge may issue a search warrant. . . ." [27]

The issuance of a search warrant is a function of the judicial branch of government. Therefore, a practice whereby a member of the police department or a district attorney has the authority to issue a search warrant is probably improper. [28] Where a judicial officer has *limited* authority under the statute to issue warrants in *restricted* cases, obviously a warrant issued by such official for searches which would be outside his authority would not be legal and the evidence secured thereunder would be inadmissible.

Although the Supreme Court has justified the issuance of an arrest warrant by a clerk when the arrest is for a violation of the municipal ordinance, there is no such authority for the issuance of a search warrant by a clerk. [29] And where the statute provides that a search warrant may be issued by a district court judge or a supreme court judge, a warrant signed by the clerk of the court rather than the judge is invalid. [30]

Apparently in a few jurisdictions, prosecuting attorneys and even police officers have been authorized to issue search warrants. This practice was found improper in a 1971 case. [31] In that case warrants were signed and issued by the attorney general acting as a justice of the peace. The majority of the court agreed with the petitioner's claim that the warrant was invalid as not being issued by a "neutral and detached magistrate." The Court emphasized the reason for the rule that the warrant must be issued by a "neutral and detached magistrate" with this statement:

[27] ILLREVSTAT ch 38, §108-3 (1975).
[28] In White v. Simpson, 28 Wis(2d) 590, 137 NW(2d) 391 (1965), a statute permitting the district attorney to issue arrest warrants was declared unconstitutional, and in State v. Paulick, 277 Minn 140, 151 NW(2d) 591 (1967), a state statute authorizing a clerk to issue a warrant was declared invalid.
[29] See §3.6 and cases cited under ¶7.
[30] State v. Cochrane, 84 SD 538, 173 NW(2d) 495 (1970).
[31] Coolidge v. New Hampshire, 403 US 443, 29 LEd(2d) 564, 91 SCt 2022 (1971). See case in Part II.

Without disrespect to the state law enforcement agent here involved, the whole point of the basic rule. . . is that prosecutors and policemen simply cannot be asked to maintain the requisite neutrality with regard to their own investigations. . . .

In a move to speed up the process of securing search warrants, the state of California enacted legislation giving peace officers authority to sign the judge's name to search warrants after obtaining judicial permission over the telephone. In such case, the same degree of proof must be presented by telephone to the judge as is required in a face-to-face request by police for search warrants.

(b) A warrant may be issued only for authorized objects.

There is nothing in the Constitution which limits the type of evidence that can be seized under a warrant. However, the United States Supreme Court in several early cases adopted what came to be called the "mere evidence" rule. One of these cases, *Gouled* v. *United States*,[32] held that searches for and seizures of items to be used as "mere evidence" of crime would not be authorized unless the government could assert some superior right to the property. From this grew the rule which was later codified in the Federal Rules of Criminal Procedure, that warrants could be issued only for stolen or embezzled property, property used as a means of committing a crime, or contraband goods.

The "mere evidence" rule was challenged and expressly overruled in the case of *Warden* v. *Hayden*.[33] In that case, Justice Brennan, speaking for the majority, rejected the proposition that the Constitution limits searches and seizures to fruits of the crime, weapons by which escape of the person arrested might be effected, and property, the possession of which is a crime. The majority explained:

We come, then, to the question whether, even though the search was lawful, the Court of Appeals was correct in holding that the seizure and introduction of the items of clothing violated the Fourth Amendment because they are "mere evidence." The distinction

[32] 255 US 298, 65 LEd 647, 41 SCt 261 (1921).

[33] 387 US 294, 18 LEd(2d) 782, 87 SCt 1642 (1967).

made by some of our cases between seizure of items of evidential value only and seizure of instrumentalities, fruits, or contraband has been criticized by courts and commentators. The Court of Appeals, however, felt "obligated to adhere to it." . . . We today reject the distinction as based on premises no longer accepted as rules governing the application of the Fourth Amendment.

Following this decision, Congress amended the Federal Code by inserting this language:

> In addition to the grounds for issuing a warrant in section 3103 of this title, a warrant may be issued to search for and seize any property that constitutes evidence of a criminal offense in violation of the laws of the United States.[34]

With this amendment federal warrants may now be issued for "mere evidence" in addition to the other articles previously mentioned.

Some state legislatures, recognizing the arbitrary distinction of types of evidence which could be seized, broadened the authority by statute even before the *Warden* case. For example, in Illinois a statute was enacted which provides that the search warrant may be issued for seizure of . . . "any instruments, articles or things which have been used in the commission of, or which may constitute *evidence* of, the offense in connection with which the warrant is issued." [35] (Emphasis added.)

Due primarily to inertia, some states still have provisions which limit the type of evidence which can be seized under a warrant. If the state still has these limitations, they must be followed.

(c) *The warrant must be issued "on probable cause."*

(i) Definition and explanation

The Fourth Amendment to the Constitution and the state constitutions provide that no warrant shall issue but upon "probable cause." Many efforts have been made to define probable cause as required by this provision of the Constitu-

---

[34] 18 USC §3103a (1970).   [35] ILLREVSTAT ch 38, §108-3(a) (1975).

tion and many cases have been decided determining not only the meaning of probable cause, but the evidence necessary in order for the judicial officer to determine that probable cause exists.

The Supreme Court, in the case of *Dumbra v. United States*,[36] made this statement concerning the probable cause requirements:

> [I]f the apparent facts set out in the affidavit are such that a reasonably discreet and prudent man would be led to believe that there was a commission of the offense charged, there is probable cause justifying the issuance of a warrant.

Probable cause cannot be justified by what the subsequent search discloses. Rather, the determination of existence of probable cause is not concerned with the question of whether the offense charged has been committed in fact or whether the accused is guilty or innocent, but only with whether the issuing official has reasonable grounds for his belief. The judicial officer has the responsibility for determining whether probable cause exists. If the facts set out in an affidavit are such that a reasonable, discreet and prudent man would be led to believe that the accused had committed a crime and that the articles described can be found at the place described, the issuance of a search warrant is justified.

The issuing magistrate, before determining that probable cause exists, must have facts which go beyond mere suspicion but which need not constitute clear evidence. Therefore, the facts available to the affiant must be made known to the magistrate so that he may make an intelligent and independent decision. Unless he is personally aware of the facts, he may take into account only that information which is supplied to him. As to the right of the magistrate to rely on his own experience, the majority of the justices in the District of Columbia Circuit Court commented:

> But we must take into account that a magistrate, experienced in these matters, is entitled to draw inferences from acts which to the un-

---

[36] 268 US 435, 69 LEd 1032, 45 SCt 546 (1925).

initiated and unskilled would be seemingly innocent acts. "Although in a particular case it may not be easy to determine when an affidavit demonstrates the existence of probable cause, the resolution of doubtful or marginal cases in this area should be largely determined by the preference to be accorded to warrants." [37]

In the usual case, the affiant is a police officer or an agent, but information may be furnished to the issuing official by a private citizen. For example, the affidavit of a police officer, even though insufficient in itself, when supported by the sworn testimony of a landlord was adequate in one case to establish probable cause.[38]

As was discussed in an earlier paragraph, probable cause for the issuance of a search warrant must be judged on the basis on what was before the issuing judge. While an invalid search warrant will not be made valid by what the subsequent search discloses, neither will a valid search warrant be attacked if no evidence is found. To state this differently, if the facts given to the judge who issued the search warrant were adequate at the time to establish probable cause for the issuance of the warrant, later evidence which contradicts that given in the affidavit does not in itself invalidate the search warrant.[39]

(ii) Standard of proof

There are many issues relative to the "probable cause" requirement. Two have received particular attention over the years. One of these concerns the standard or degree of proof necessary to support a finding of probable cause. This is discussed here. The other matter concerns the use of informants, both disclosed and undisclosed, and will be discussed in the next subsection.

Probable cause is just what it says. That is, there must be sufficient facts to indicate that the articles described are *probably* located at the place described. Absolute certainty is not required in determining probable cause. Something less than "beyond a reasonable doubt" is necessary, but more than mere

[37] United States v. Berry, 463 F(2d) 1278 (DC Cir 1972).

[38] State v. Valde, 225 NW(2d) 313 (Io 1975).

[39] Hunt v. Swenson, 466 F(2d) 863 (8thCir 1972).

suspicion is required. In the case of *Brinegar v. United States*,[40] the Supreme Court stated that there is a large difference between the two things to be proved (guilt and probable cause), as well as the tribunals which determine them. This Court also made it clear that a lesser quanta of proof is required to establish probable cause than to establish proof beyond a reasonable doubt.

Though proof beyond a reasonable doubt is not the necessary standard of proof for probable cause, a clearly conclusary statement by the affiant is not sufficient. For example, where the sole support for a warrant was the sworn statement of a sheriff that the defendant "did then and there lawfully break and enter a locked and sealed building" the warrant was invalid.[41] The conviction was set aside because the affidavit stated a mere conclusion of the officer. The Supreme Court made this comment concerning probable cause in the *Whiteley* case:

> The decisions of this Court concerning Fourth Amendment probable-cause requirements before a warrant for either arrest or search can issue require that the judicial officer issuing such a warrant be supplied with sufficient information to support an independent judgment that probable cause exists for the warrant.

The strict legal rules regarding the use of hearsay evidence to prove guilt beyond a reasonable doubt do not apply in determining probable cause for a search warrant. Hearsay may be the basis for the issuance of a warrant so long as there is a substantial basis for crediting the hearsay.[42]

Finally, in regard to the degree of proof necessary to substantiate probable cause for a search warrant, the Supreme Court in *Ventresca* has indicated that if there are doubts, they should be decided in favor of finding the warrant valid.

(iii) Use of informants

Much of the information to support probable cause comes

---

[40] 338 US 160, 93 LEd 1879, 69 SCt 1302 (1949).

[41] Whiteley v. Warden, 401 US 560, 28 LEd(2d) 306, 91 SCt 1031 (1971).

[42] United States v. Ventresca, 380 US 102, 13 LEd(2d) 684, 85 SCt 741 (1965).

from informants and is, therefore, hearsay. Although such hearsay may be used, the officer or affiant must establish that the hearsay information is reliable and credible. The issuing official will also evaluate the information in view of his own experience and judgment. He will take into consideration the corroborative information furnished by the police officer and compare the specific allegations with the circumstances surrounding the alleged offense.

There are many varieties and types of informants. Despite the fact that much attention has been devoted to the use of undisclosed informants, in many instances the information to support probable cause is from reputable lay citizens, public officials or other law enforcement officials.

A recent series of cases has upheld the use of information from undisclosed informants in supporting the search warrant. Before such hearsay evidence can be used, however, certain conditions must be met.[43] In one of these cases, *Aguilar* v. *Texas*,[44] the United States Supreme Court explained that the magistrate must be informed of the underlying circumstances from which the informant concluded that the information was reliable and the informant credible and in *Spinelli* v. *United States*,[45] the conviction was set aside because the underlying circumstances were not explained in enough detail. There, the court said that if the informant's tip is not corroborated, the issuing official must be given sufficient information for him to reach an independent conclusion that the informant was credible and his information reliable.

The two-pronged standard for testing the use of evidence from an undisclosed informant was summarized by the judges of the Eighth Circuit Court in these words:

> In *Aguilar* the Supreme Court laid down a two-pronged standard for testing the credibility of an informant's tip upon which a magistrate is asked to rely: (1) The magistrate must be given some of the underlying circumstances from which the affiant concluded that the informant was credible or that his information was reliable; and

[43] Jones v. United States, 362 US 257, 4 LEd(2d) 697, 80 SCt 727 (1960).

[44] 378 US 108, 12 LEd(2d) 723, 84 SCt 1509 (1964).

[45] 393 US 410, 21 LEd(2d) 637, 89 SCt 584 (1969).

(2) he must be given some of the underlying circumstances from which the informant reached the conclusions conveyed in the tip.[46]

In this case the court found that a statement that the informant "has always been found to be reliable and accurate" was not sufficient.

Some of the earlier cases left doubt as to whether the affiant was required to show that the undisclosed informant had given reliable information on past occasions. Any doubt concerning this matter was eliminated when, in 1971, the Supreme Court agreed that under certain circumstances it was not necessary to prove that the undisclosed informant had proved trustworthy in the past. The majority opinion used this explanation:

> To be sure there is no averment in the present affidavit, as there was in *Jones*, that the informant had previously given "correct information," but this Court in *Jones* never suggested than an averment of previous reliability was necessary.[47]

In the *Harris* case the Supreme Court again admonished lower courts for taking a negative attitude toward the issuance of search warrants. The majority suggested that the lower courts pay heed to such statements made in the *Ventresca* case and that they give more credit to the officer's reputation and experience.

Reiterating the rationale of previous cases, the Fifth Federal Circuit Court refused to find an affidavit insufficient because it did not aver that the informant was reliable. There the court placed some weight on the fact that the informant supplied indicia of reliability by giving information which was against his penal interests.[48]

Not only may the issuing official take into consideration the experience of the officer-affiant, but he may also consider the experience of the informant. In one instance, where the informant had previously provided information resulting in

[46] United States v. Cummings, 507 F(2d) 324 (8thCir 1974).

[47] United States v. Harris, 403 US 573, 29 LEd(2d) 723, 91 SCt 2075 (1971).

[48] United States v. Barfield, 507 F(2d) 53 (5thCir 1975).

arrests and seizures of large quantities of marijuana, the Second Circuit Court affirmed the use of information from the informant even though much of the information he received was obtained through the sense of smell.[49]

Do the rules relating to unnamed informants apply as well to disclosed informants? The majority of one circuit court logically distinguished between the use of information from an informant who was in fact named and an undisclosed, unnamed informant. There, the justices noted that they had discovered no case that extends the requirements of credibility and reliability, as required for an undisclosed informant, to identified bystanders or victims who are eyewitnesses to a crime.[50] No such requirements need be met. The rationale behind requiring a showing of credibility and reliability is to prevent searches based upon an unknown informant's tip that may not reflect anything more than idle rumor or irresponsible conjecture. This is not so in relation to named informants or eyewitnesses to the crime.

This series of cases has been frequently misinterpreted regarding the disclosure of informants. There are, of course, instances where the informer must be disclosed if it is necessary to a fair defense. This is quite different from disclosing the informer who has not participated in the crime but only gives information on which probable cause for the search warrant is based. In the case of *Nutter v. State*,[51] the state court defined the circumstances under which the informer must be disclosed. The court explained that the state has a privilege to withhold from disclosure the identity of persons who furnish information to police officers concerning the commission of crimes. The court went on to say, however:

> On the issue of guilt or innocence and upon demand by the defendant, the trial court may, in the exercise of its judicial discretion, compel such disclosure upon determination that it is necessary and relevant to a fair defense. Factors to be considered in ascertaining whether such disclosure is necessary and relevant to a fair defense

[49] United States v. Pond, 523 F(2d) 210 (2dCir 1975).

[50] United States v. Burke, 517 F(2d) 377 (2dCir 1975). Also see United States v. Unger, 469 F(2d) 1283 (7thCir 1973).

[51] 8 MdApp 635, 262 A(2d) 80 (1970).

include the nature of the crime charged; the importance of the informer's identity to a determination of innocence, as for example, whether or not the informer was an integral part of the illegal transaction and the possible significance of his testimony; and the possible defenses. Whether the privilege must yield depends on the facts and circumstances of the particular case. But if the informer testifies for the State the privilege may not be invoked by it.

(d) The warrant must be "supported by oath or affirmation."

The Fourth Amendment to the Constitution includes a requirement that the warrant be supported by oath or affirmation. Although this responsibility is placed upon the issuing official, it is often necessary that the official be reminded of this requirement. If this requirement is not met, the evidence obtained under the warrant will not be admitted into court. Therefore, not only the police officer but the prosecutor should make certain that this provision is carried out. Unless the affidavit on which the search warrant is based is supported by oath or affirmation, the warrant is issued unlawfully and the search conducted thereunder is unlawful.[52]

There is a presumption that the warrant is supported by oath and affirmation. However, this presumption is rebuttable and the defense may introduce evidence showing that no oath was administered.

(e) The place to be searched and the things to be seized must be "particularly" described.

The Fourth Amendment to the Constitution and the various state constitutional provisions include a requirement that not only the place to be searched be particularly described, but that the property to be seized also be particularly described. The Constitution does not define the word "particularly" and again we must go to the cases.

It is not necessary to have a legal description such as would be required on a deed of conveyance. The Constitution requires that the premises be defined with practical accuracy. However, the description must be sufficiently definite so as

---

[52] Rose v. State, 171 Ind 662, 87 NE 103 (1909).

to clearly distinguish the premises from all others. It must be such that the officer executing the warrant can, with reasonable effort, identify the exact place to the distinction of all others. The name of the owner of the house is not necessary, unless this is needed to identify the particular house.

Describing the house as a certain number on a certain street is usually sufficient but is not necessarily required, if the premises are otherwise so described that they can be readily identified. Where there are two streets in the same city bearing identical names and numbers, or more than one building at the designated street number, a description giving only the number and street would not be sufficient, as it would not exclude others. Obviously, a search warrant directing officers to search all places would be clearly illegal, and a search warrant with the description of the premises left blank, to be filled in by the officer making the search, is illegal. It is this type of general warrant that the Fourth Amendment was designed to prohibit.

Some courts are very technical in requiring that the description be specific. For example, the United States District Court for the Eastern District of Michigan found a warrant invalid because it failed to sufficiently identify the place to be searched in that it did not indicate that the building was a two-family dwelling.[53]

The constitutional provisions require that the "places" must be described and that the "things" to be seized must also be described. If the warrant fails to adequately describe the property to be seized, any seizure made under the warrant will be inadmissible.[54] The officer must, therefore, obtain as specific a description of the goods as is reasonably possible under the circumstances. For the protection of both the officer and the citizen, the warrant should describe the property that is to be seized with such particularity as to clearly identify it, and thereby prevent the seizure of other property. Also, the courts apparently require a less descriptive warrant for gambling devices than for stolen goods.[55] And apparently weapons,

[53] United States v. Esters, 336 FSupp 214 (ED Mich 1972).

[54] Giles v. United States, 284 Fed 208 (D NH 1922).

[55] Nuckols v. United States, 99 F(2d) 353 (DC Cir 1938).

narcotics or other contraband would not require the same detailed and precise descriptions as would books and documents.[56]

In the *Stanford* case, the United States Supreme Court found that a description which described property sought as "books, records, pamphlets, cards, receipts, lists, memoranda, pictures, recordings and other written instruments concerning the Communist Party of Texas" was too sweeping to be *particular* within the meaning of the Fourth Amendment.

In order to avoid having the search declared illegal and the evidence obtained thereunder rendered inadmissible, the officer should take care to specifically designate the exact premises to be searched, including the area within the premises. He should also obtain as nearly as possible the description of the things to be seized therefrom.

There is case law justifying a search of persons on the premises when the warrant to search the premises is executed, but it is preferable to include in the warrant a description of the person to be searched. In such case, the description of the person to be searched should be as clear as possible, such as that for an arrest warrant. A warrant authorizing without further description the search of any person on the premises would probably be invalid.

Some state statutes include additional requirements. For example, the state of Illinois requires that the warrant shall state the time and date of issuance. The officer must be familiar with the state codes concerning the requirements for a search warrant. Obviously, another requirement is that the signature of the issuing official be on the warrant. The warrant is not complete until signed and it cannot be amended once the signature has been affixed to the warrant. The magistrate cannot by his subsequent signing of the warrant legalize the search made under the unsigned warrant.

3. Execution of the search warrant

When the warrant has been properly issued by the issuing official, the police officer has no choice but to execute the war-

---

[56] Stanford v. Texas, 379 US 476,
13 LEd(2d) 431, 85 SCt 506 (1965).

rant. In executing the warrant and in proceeding in the manner in which the warrant directs, the officer is carrying out the orders of the court. If the warrant is valid on its face, has been issued by the proper official, and is executed properly, the officer is protected from civil liability as well as criminal prosecution.

Even *with* the warrant, the officer must follow certain procedures in order for the execution to be lawful and the evidence to be admissible in court. These procedures are set out below:

(a) *The warrant must be executed by an officer so commanded.*

As the warrant is an order of the court it can only be executed by the person designated by name or class. If, as is true in the usual case, the warrant is issued to a class of officers, it may be executed by any officer in that class. Many statutes now provide that the warrant shall be directed for execution to all peace officers of the state. If the warrant is directed for execution to a certain peace officer, other officers may assist in the execution.

(b) *The warrant must be executed within time limitations.*

In absence of statute, the constitutional guarantees are violated where the warrant is not executed within a reasonable time. The term "reasonable" has not been specifically defined, however. Obviously the warrant must be executed while there is still probable cause that the items to be sought are on the described premises. If there is evidence that the described property has been removed from the premises, then the search warrant may not be used as a weapon or form of coercion upon the person or premises against whom it is directed.

To avoid unnecessary confusion, many of the states by legislative action have designated the time within which a warrant may be executed. For example, the Illinois criminal code provides that the warrant shall be executed within ninety-six hours from the time of issuance. Rule 41 of the Federal Rules provides that the warrant shall command the officer to search forthwith the place named for the property specified and that the warrant may be executed and returned only within ten days after its date. A warrant not executed within the time limitations as provided by the statute, or not executed within a reasonable time, is void. If the statutes limit the execution of the warrant to the daytime, unless certain conditions are met, a warrant executed in violation of the state statute would be illegally executed and the evidence obtained thereunder inadmissible.

A federal case held that a search initiated in the daytime under a daytime search warrant may continue into the night-time for so long as reasonably necessary for completion.[57]

(c) Only necessary force may be used in executing a warrant.

By common law and under the statutes, the officer is justi-fied in using necessary force to execute the warrant. The United States Code provides that in executing a warrant an officer has the authority to break both outer and inner doors if, after giving notice of his authority and purpose and de-manding entrance, he is refused admittance.[58] If the occupant denies admittance to the premises, the officer may use such force as is reasonably necessary to gain entry. Denial of ad-mission does not have to be specific but may be inferred from the surrounding circumstances, as when a person known to be inside refuses to come to the door. Once inside, the search-ing officer may use such force as is necessary to gain entrance into closets, rooms or other places. In such case the force should be used only if the occupant refuses to provide access to the place to be searched.

The courts have placed more importance on life and safety than on the execution of the search warrant. Therefore, deadly force or force which may cause serious bodily injury is not reasonable nor authorized. If, however, the person in charge of the premises or the person who is described in the search warrant threatens the officer with deadly force, the officer may use such force to seize the person and search him. If the of-fense involved is a misdemeanor, the officer would find it

---

[57] United States v. Joseph, 278 F(2d) 504 (3dCir 1960).

[58] 18 USC §3109 (1970).

extremely difficult to justify the use of deadly force merely to execute the search warrant.

If no one is in charge of the premises, the officer may nevertheless carry out the instructions of the court in searching the premises described. In some instances where there is no need for prompt action, it is advisable to seek entrance from a neighbor or delay until the occupant can admit the police officers. Although this is apparently not a legal requirement, it might be preferable to breaking down doors unnecessarily.

(d) Prior notice and demand should usually precede forcible entry.

Some statutes require that prior notice and demand be given before entry, while other statutes are silent on the subject. Even where there is no statute, most courts by case law require that prior notice be given unless an exception exists. The purpose of the entry announcement, or as some courts call it the "knock and announce" rule, is to protect the privacy of the individual, to avoid needless destruction of property of occupants who are willing to voluntarily admit the police, and to shield the officers from attack by surprised residents.[59] Notwithstanding the fact that notice of entry is generally preferable and often required, case law has recognized the anarchism of the notice rule in an era of indoor plumbing. The experienced officer recognizes that it takes only a few seconds for a person to destroy evidence. And the danger of giving the person accused of a serious crime the time to injure the officer is readily recognized.[60]

Acknowledging the need to make a speedy entrance, especially in drug cases, several states have enacted what is known as "no-knock" provisions in their statutes. The Federal Drug Abuse, Prevention, and Control Act of 1970 included such legislation, but this was repealed in 1974 due, in part, to apparent abuse by enforcement officers. The passing of the 1970 Act and the later amendment to that Act caused some unnecessary confusion in the minds of many officers.

---

[59] United States v. Beale, 436 F(2d) 573 (5thCir 1971) and Sabbath v. United States, 391 US 585, 20 LEd(2d) 828, 88 SCt 1755 (1968).

[60] Jackson v. United States, 354 F(2d) 980 (1stCir 1965).

First, this Act applied only to federal officers, and the repeal, therefore, did not affect the vast majority of officers. Secondly, case law existed prior to the Act and has been reemphasized since the amendment.

In the case of *Miller v. United States*,[61] an exception for exigent circumstances such as immediate physical danger, flight, or destruction of evidence was discussed. And in 1956, the California Supreme Court, in the case of *People v. Maddox*,[62] allowed unannounced entry despite a provision in the state statute which provided that notice be given.

Some states, such as Nebraska, have statutes authorizing the issuance of no-knock warrants where evidence exists showing the necessity. The statute provides:

> The judge or magistrate may so direct only upon proof under oath, to his satisfaction, that the property sought may be easily or quickly destroyed or disposed of, or that danger to the life or limb of the officer or another may result, if such notice be given; . . .[63]

If a no-knock warrant is obtained, information must be included in the affidavit in order to justify the court in issuing this type of warrant.[64]

In a 1974 case, the Circuit Court of Appeals for the Second Circuit listed three exceptions to the requirement that the officer must knock, announce his authority and purpose, and be refused admittance before he can break in.[65] There the Circuit Court stated that the United States Supreme Court has acknowledged the three exceptions, namely: (1) where persons within already know of the officer's authority and purpose; (2) where the officers are justified in the belief that persons within are in imminent peril of bodily harm; or (3) where those within, made aware of the presence of someone outside, are then engaged in activity which justifies the officers in belief that an escape or the destruction of evidence is being attempted.

---

[61] 357 US 301, 2 LEd(2d) 1332, 78 SCt 1190 (1958).

[62] 46 Cal(2d) 301, 294 P(2d) 6 (1956).

[63] NebRevStat §29-411 (1975).

[64] State v. Daniels, 294 Minn 323, 200 NW(2d) 403 (1972).

[65] United States v. Artieri, 491 F(2d) 440 (2dCir 1974).

The court justified the entry without a knock under the exigent circumstance rule on the grounds that the agents had reasonable grounds to believe and did believe that the defendant was likely to be armed, and the fact that the officers knocked loudly, paused for three seconds, and entered. This was sufficient notice, where the suspect was an experienced narcotics violator and obviously would be aware of the authority and purpose.

(e) Only the property described may be seized.

The warrant particularly describes things to be seized. Only those things described can be seized under the authority of a warrant. If other property is seized, the authority for such seizure must be found elsewhere. The right of the police officer to seize property not described in the warrant will be discussed in a later section.

Many statutes and codes require that agents executing a search warrant serve a copy of the warrant on the person in charge of the premises. The question that arises is that if the warrant is not left with the person in charge, does this make the seizure illegal and the evidence inadmissible? At least one federal circuit court has decided this question. In the case of *United States* v. *McKenzie* [66] the Sixth Circuit Court found that the defendant's argument that the search was fatally defective because he was not served with a copy of the warrant until the day after the search was without merit.

In addition to the requirements mentioned for executing the search warrant, other requirements may be included in the statutes or code of the state. Therefore, the officer should be acquainted with all the statutory provisions in his state concerning execution of the warrant.

4. Search of person on premises where person not described in the warrant

From previous paragraphs it can be deduced that if the officer is aware that a person will be on the premises and the

---

[66] 446 F(2d) 949 (6thCir 1971).

personal property sought can be hidden on the person, that person should be described in the warrant. In some instances the officer does not know who will be on the premises and cannot describe him in the warrant. This often poses a problem for the executing officer. To fail to search the person on the premises could place the officer's personal safety in jeopardy or result in the concealment of the sought-after items.

This last situation arose in the case of *United States* v. *Micheli*[67] which was before the First Circuit Court in 1973. Here, the agents armed with a warrant searched the building for counterfeit bills and paraphernalia. During the course of the search, they seized evidence from a briefcase carried onto the premises by the co-owner of the printing press housed in the building. While the court agreed with the general proposition that a warrant to search premises does not permit a personal search of one who merely happens to be present at the time, it nevertheless justified the search of the briefcase. The majority found the seizure to be reasonable because the briefcase belonged to the co-owner of the press who was not a mere visitor or a passerby who suddenly found his belongings vulnerable to a search of the premises.

A concurring judge in this case argued that this limitation was not necessary. He indicated that the rule, as he saw it, is that once probable cause for a search warrant was presented to the magistrate and a search warrant issued, the police officer should have authority to search anywhere on the premises, including those present, when it was reasonable to believe that the persons harbored matter described in the warrant.

Some state statutes, such as that in Wisconsin, specifically provide that the person executing the warrant may reasonably detain and search a person on the premises to protect the officer or to prevent the disposal or concealment of items particularly described in the warrant.[68] In the absence of such statute, the cases of each state must be closely scrutinized to determine the authority to search the persons on the premises. Even if there is no such authority to search under the warrant, there are still alternatives to the police officer. First, if grounds

---

[67] 487 F(2d) 429 (1stCir 1973).   [68] WisStatAnn §968.16 (1970).

for arrest are apparent at the time the search is initiated or if these grounds develop as the search progresses, the arrest can be made, and the search incidental to the arrest may legitimately follow. Secondly, if there is not sufficient information for reasonable grounds to justify an arrest, there may be sufficient reasonable cause to believe that criminal activity is afoot, justifying a "stop and frisk." [69]

5. Return of the warrant

An officer who acts under a search warrant and seizes property must make return of all things which he seizes. The federal code provides that the warrant may be executed and returned within ten days after its date. Although there is some indication that failure to comply strictly with the statute may not make the warrant void, certainly this requirement should be followed. An example of a statute which gives clear instructions as to the procedure to be followed is that of Illinois:

> A return of all instruments, articles or things seized shall be made without unnecessary delay before the judge issuing the warrant or before any judge named in the warrant or before any court of competent jurisdiction. An inventory of any instruments, articles or things seized shall be filed with the return and signed under oath by the officer or person executing the warrant. The judge shall upon request deliver a copy of the inventory to the person from whom or from whose premises the instruments, articles or things were taken and to the applicant for the warrant. [70]

6. Advantages in searching with the search warrant

The first part of the Fourth Amendment prohibits unreasonable searches and seizures, and it goes on to set out the requirements for a search warrant. In the early discussion of this provision it was argued that no search would be justified without a warrant as there was no provision in the Constitution for a search without a warrant. Although in exceptional cases the courts have recognized the necessity of allowing searches *without a warrant*, this is not the preferred method.

Advantages of a search with a warrant include:

[69] United States v. Peep, 490 F(2d) 903 (8thCir 1974).

[70] IllRevStat ch 38, §108-10 (1975).

(a) Evidence obtained under a warrant is more likely to be admitted than evidence obtained by a search incidental to arrest.

There is a definite indication, especially in the more recent cases, that the courts are encouraging the use of search warrants in preference to searches without the warrant. In *United States v. Ventresca*,[71] the Court made this comment concerning the search warrant:

> In *Johnson v. United States* and *Chapman v. United States,* the Court, in condemning searches by officers who invaded premises without a warrant, plainly intimated that had the proper course of obtaining a warrant from a magistrate been followed and had the magistrate on the same evidence available to the police made a finding of probable cause, the search under the warrant would have been sustained.

In indicating the encouragement given the officers to use the warrant the Court stated:

> A grudging or negative attitude by reviewing courts toward warrants will tend to discourage police officers from submitting their evidence to a judicial officer before acting.

The courts are recognizing that one of the reasons that warrants are not requested by enforcement agents is the reluctance of judicial officers to issue warrants in fear of a reversal by a higher court and the frequency of the courts declaring the search warrant invalid at the trial of the case. Officers who have had such experience recognize that, in many instances, search warrants have been found invalid because of some technicality, and the evidence obtained thereunder has been held inadmissible in the trial of the case. Much of this appears to be due to the failure of the issuing official to follow proper procedures in issuing the warrant. These recent Supreme Court cases, however, would tend to encourage a more positive attitude concerning the recognition of the validity of the search warrant by the courts. The encouragement to use the

[71] 380 US 102, 13 LEd(2d) 684, 85 SCt 741 (1965).

search warrant has also been evidenced by some provisions of the state codes. For example one state statute directs: "No warrant shall be quashed nor evidence suppressed because of technical irregularities not affecting the substantial rights of the accused." [72]

(b) *The officer is better protected when the search warrant is used.*

Generally, the officer acting under a search warrant is protected from civil and criminal liability if the warrant is valid on its face. This means that if the warrant has the necessary information included on it and is properly signed, the officer is protected in executing the warrant even though it is determined later that there was no probable cause for that warrant or the warrant was not supported by oath or affirmation. There is one exception to this rule; that is, if the officer is aware that the warrant has been issued by an official who does not have authority to issue the warrant, he may still be civilly or criminally liable.

§ 4.8   Search incidental to a lawful arrest

1. Rationale for exceptions

Although the search under the search warrant is preferred and there are no specific exceptions in the Fourth Amendment or in the constitutions of the various states, the law has long recognized the power of an arresting officer to search the person of the arrestee and the surrounding premises that are under his control. This search incident to a lawful arrest is one of the exceptions to the rule that the search must be made with a search warrant. As a matter of fact, more searches are made under this authority than under any other authority. There is no question but that such a search must be authorized if the law is to be enforced, as it is impractical to obtain warrants in all instances.

This right to make the search incident to the lawful arrest has been repeatedly recognized by all the courts including the

---

[72] ILLREVSTAT ch 38, § 108-14 (1975).

Supreme Court of the United States. In the case of *United States v. Rabinowitz*,[73] the Court specifically recognized the authority to search incidental to a lawful arrest. In this case, the defendant was convicted of selling, possessing and concealing forged and altered obligations of the United States with intent to defraud. Armed with valid warrants for arrest, the government officers, accompanied by two stamp experts, went to the defendant's place of business, a one room office open to the public. The officers thereupon arrested the defendant under the authority of the arrest warrant, and over his objections, searched the desk, safe, and file cabinets located in the office for an hour and a half. They found and seized 573 stamps with overprints forged, along with some other stamps which were subsequently returned to the defendant. In upholding the search for and seizure of the stamps, the Supreme Court stated:

> It is unreasonable searches that are prohibited by the Fourth Amendment. [Citation omitted.] It was recognized by the framers of the Constitution that there were reasonable searches for which no warrant was required. The right of the "people to be secure in their persons" was certainly of as much concern to the framers of the Constitution as the property of the person. Yet no one questions the right, without a search warrant, to search the person after a valid arrest. The right to search a person incident to arrest always has been recognized in this country and in England.

If the officer understands the reason for this exception to the general rule, he will have much less difficulty determining the application of the rule. The reason for the rule was explained by Justice Frankfurter in the dissenting opinion of *Rabinowitz*. Justice Frankfurter stated:

> What, then, is the exception to the prohibition of the Fourth Amendment of search without a warrant in case of a legal arrest, whether the arrest is on a warrant or based on the historic right of arrest without a warrant if a crime is committed in the presence of the arrester? The exception may in part be a surviving incident of the historic role of "hue and cry" in early Anglo-Saxon law. [Citation omitted.] Its basic roots, however, lie in necessity. What is the

[73] 339 US 56, 94 LEd 653, 70 SCt 430 (1950).

necessity? Why is search of the arrested person permitted? For two reasons: first, in order to protect the arresting officer and to deprive the prisoner of potential means of escape, . . . and, secondly, to avoid destruction of evidence by the arrested person.

In recognizing this necessity, the courts have approved searches where the searches are necessary to protect the officer and to avoid destruction of the evidence.

2. Requirements

Although the courts have uniformly adopted the rule which allows a search incidental to a lawful arrest, they have established specific requirements. These requirements are discussed here.

(a) The arrest must be lawful.

The first and most important requirement is that the arrest itself must be a lawful arrest. If the arrest is not lawful, then the resulting search is not lawful and the evidence so obtained is inadmissible.

If the arrest and resulting search incidental to that arrest is to be upheld, all of the legal requirements discussed in the previous chapter regarding arrest must be met. The officer can expect that the defense attorney, if possible, will show that the arrest was illegal and thus destroy all lawful basis for the search.

(b) Only certain articles may be seized.

As is the case of the search with a warrant, there are limitations as to the type of article which can be seized without a warrant as an incident to a lawful arrest. Because of recent decisions, restrictions on the types of articles which can be seized have been relaxed. As explained in the previous section, in the case of *Warden v. Hayden* (n. 33), the United States Supreme Court reversed previous decisions and held that there was no constitutional prohibition concerning the seizure of "mere evidence." Prior to that time, the federal courts and state courts had followed the rule that only fruits of the crime, means of committing the crime, and weapons to effect an escape could be seized. Since that decision "mere evidence" as well as fruits of the crime, the means of committing the crime, and weapons may be seized as an incident to an arrest by federal officers.

Because state statutes and some state court decisions are not consistent, there is still conflict as to the type of evidence which may be seized by state officers for use in state courts. Some states by statute have provided for the seizure of specific items when the search is made incidental to an arrest. For example, the Illinois Code provides that:

> When a lawful arrest is effected a peace officer may reasonably search the person arrested and the area within such person's immediate presence for the purpose of:
> (a) Protecting the officer from attack; or
> (b) Preventing the person from escaping; or
> (c) Discovering the fruits of the crime; or
> (d) Discovering any instruments, articles, or things which may have been used in the commission of, or which may constitute evidence of, an offense.[74]

Under such a statute, "mere evidence" as well as the fruits of the crime and instruments used in the commission of the crime may be seized. And the *Hayden* decision makes it clear that such seizure does not violate constitutional provisions.

Notwithstanding the *Hayden* rule, some states by statute or court decision still restrict the seizure to fruits of the crime, means by which it was committed, and weapons to effect an escape. Unless such statutes or state court decisions are changed, the search for "mere evidence" would be unauthorized. As pointed out by the U.S. Supreme Court, there is no rational reason for such rule, but some states, because of negligence or lack of understanding, have failed to take action which would remove these restrictions. As a result where such state statutes and court decisions exist, the seizure is limited. The state officer must therefore look to the state statutes and state decisions to determine if there are any additional restrictions as to the articles which can be seized incidental to a lawful arrest.

---

[74] IllRevStat ch 38, §108-1 (1975).

(c) *The search must be made contemporaneously with the arrest.*

If the reasons for the search incidental to a lawful arrest are studied, a requirement that the search be made contemporaneously with the arrest is understandable. When the arrest takes place the officer has the authority to search the person arrested and the immediate area in order to protect himself and to deprive the prisoner of the means of escape. After the prisoner is safely in his jail cell, the search cannot be justified as the necessity no longer exists. The second reason for justifying the search is to avoid destruction of the evidence by the persons arrested. If the arrestee is safely behind bars, there is no danger of this. A search warrant can be obtained for searching for that evidence.

In a 1965 incident in Kentucky the defendant was arrested by a state trooper for improper passing in an automobile on a public highway. Having arrested the defendant for improper passing and having no operator's license, the trooper searched his person and placed him in the police cruiser that was parked nearby. The officer then called the police barracks requesting a wrecker and talked with the defendant for a few minutes. He then returned to the car and searched it, locating seven cases of whiskey in the trunk of the car. The appellant was indicted for the offense of transporting alcoholic beverages for the purposes of sale in a dry territory. After discussing the law on the subject, the Kentucky Court of Appeals (now the Kentucky Supreme Court) held that:

> The case at bar did not offer facts of an extreme emergency. Appellant had been arrested, searched and placed in another car. If the arresting officer was interested in a search of the automobile, he might have obtained, upon proper ground, a search warrant.[75]

The search was declared illegal in this case and the judgment was reversed.

In determining what is contemporaneous, most of the opinions have indicated that the search should follow the arrest

[75] Lane   v.   Commonwealth,   386 SW(2d) 743 (Ky 1965).

and not precede it. Where it is the arrest that confers the power to make the incidental search, there is, of course, the question as to when the arrest occurs. It is not necessary that the officer place the person under arrest by so stating; however, this is advisable. Also, there are some cases which justify the search even though it precedes the formal arrest. For example, the Virginia Supreme Court decided that when probable cause exists for arrest, a contemporaneous search may be conducted either before or after the arrest.[76]

There is some indication that the contemporaneous limitations are being less strictly applied, especially where the officer honestly and reasonably believes the delay might be dangerous or lead to destruction of evidence.[77] To avoid any problems, the best practice is to advise the person apprehended that he is being arrested, and to make the contemporaneous search immediately or as soon as practicable.

(d) *The arrest upon which the search is based must be in good faith.*

If the arrest in fact is a sham or subterfuge, even though it is supported by probable cause or an arrest warrant, and is executed merely as an expedient to further the chief aim of searching the premises for evidence, the search will not be upheld. A good example of this is the case of *United States* v. *Pampinella.*[78] Here the federal officers, knowing that the defendant was leaving town, arrested his wife on a warrant charging husband and wife with harboring a criminal. After the arrest of the wife under an arrest warrant, the officers found a machine gun in a locked suitcase in the closet. The court, even though recognizing that the arrest was lawful, held the search was unreasonable because the arrest was a pretext to search for some sort of evidence against the defendant. In reaching the conclusion that this arrest was a hoax or subterfuge in order to make a search, the court noted the fact that several days after the search the defendant was charged

---

[76] Italiano v. Commonwealth, 214 Va 334, 200 SE(2d) 526 (1973).

[77] United States v. Jenkins, 496 F(2d) 57 (2dCir 1974).

[78] 131 FSupp 595 (ND Ill 1955).

with illegal possession of the gun and the harboring charges against both the defendant and the wife had been dropped.

3. Area of search

A difficult problem is presented when the search is made incident to a lawful arrest. Here, neither the place to be searched nor the things to be seized are particularly described. The courts have recognized that the search incident to arrests made, under appropriate circumstances, extend beyond the person of the one arrested to include the premises under his immediate control. The question then arises as to what does the term immediate control mean? Does this mean the entire house? Does it mean the automobile driven by a person who has been arrested? Does this mean the house and all of the outbuildings when the arrest has taken place in the yard? In the following paragraphs, each of these situations will be discussed.

(a) Person arrested

In *United States* v. *Robinson* and a companion case,[79] the United States Supreme Court held that a full search incident to a lawful custodial arrest is authorized and no further justification is needed. In approving the search incidental to a lawful arrest the Supreme Court affirmed that:

> It is well settled that a search incident to a lawful arrest is a traditional exception to the warrant requirements of the Fourth Amendment. This general exception has historically been formulated into two distinct propositions. The first is that a search may be made of the person of the arrestee by virtue of the lawful arrest. The second is that a search may be made of the area within the control of the arrestee.

The majority rejected the argument that the search incident to the lawful arrest depends upon the probability of discovering fruits or further evidence of the particular crime for which the arrest is made. They explained that the justification for the

---

[79] United States v. Robinson, 414 US 218, 38 LEd(2d) 427, 94 SCt 467 (1973). Also Gustafson v. Florida, 414 US 260, 38 LEd(2d) 456, 94 SCt 488 (1973).

authority to search incident to a lawful arrest rests quite as much on the need to disarm the suspect in order to take him into custody as it does on the need to preserve evidence on his person for later use at trial.

Despite the ruling in *United States* v. *Robinson*, some state courts have restricted the search of the person incident to a lawful arrest. By a four to three majority, the California Supreme Court held that a full warrantless search of the person incidental to an arrest for a minor offense cannot be justified.[80] The Hawaii Supreme Court also found unreasonable a search incident to a minor offense arrest that would have been proper under the *Robinson* and *Gustafson* rule.[81] The Oregon court, after first refusing to go along with the *Robinson* ruling, later abandoned its own rule that such searches can be no broader than necessary and agreed to follow the *Robinson* rule in order to "avoid further confusion."[82]

In spite of some decisions to the contrary, the majority rule which now exists is that an officer who has proper authority to make an arrest may make a full search of the arrestee and seize evidence, even though such evidence has no direct connection with the arrest.

(b) Premises where arrest made

Prior to the case of *Chimel* v. *California* in 1969,[83] there was some confusion concerning the scope of the search where the arrest was made on the premises. In the case of *Harris* v. *United States*,[84] the Supreme Court, quoting from a previous case, held that the search of a dwelling place was justified as an incident to arrest. In the *Harris* case the petitioner was arrested in the living room and a search was made of the entire apartment. During the search, which continued for five hours,

---

[80] People v. Brisendine, 13 Cal(3d) 528, 119 CalRptr 315, 531 P(2d) 1099 (1975); People v. Longwill, 123 CalRptr 297, 538 P(2d) 753 (1975).

[81] State v. Kaluna, 55 Haw 361, 520 P(2d) 51 (1974).

[82] State v. Florance, 270 Ore 169, 527 P(2d) 1202 (1974).

[83] 395 US 752, 23 LED(2d) 685, 89 SCt 2034 (1969). See Part II for this case.

[84] 331 US 145, 91 LEd 1399, 67 SCt 1098 (1947) quoting Agnello v. United States, 269 US 20, 70 LEd 145, 46 SCt 4 (1925).

illegally possessed draft classification cards were obtained. Though it was conceded that this evidence was in no way related to the crime for which petitioner was initially arrested, he was convicted and the conviction was upheld. There, the court reasoned that the petitioner was in exclusive possession of a four-room apartment, and his control extended to the bedroom in which the draft cards were found.

Mr. Justice Murphy, in his dissenting opinion in the *Harris* case, condemned the search of the full apartment as an incident to the lawful arrest, arguing that this was not the intent of the courts in authorizing the search without a search warrant. Also, some state courts refused to go along with the *Harris* decision and limited the search incident to a lawful arrest to the immediate area of the arrest.[85]

Probably one of the most far-reaching decisions of the United States Supreme Court during the 1968–69 term was the decision in *Chimel* v. *California, supra*. In the *Chimel* case, police officers arrested the petitioner with an arrest warrant and, incidental to this arrest for burglary, made a physical search of the entire residence. The facts in the case were very similar to the facts of the *Harris* case, where FBI agents made a search of the entire apartment on the basis of a lawful arrest. In this *Chimel* case, the Supreme Court reviewed and discussed the *Harris* and other cases and specifically reversed prior decisions stating, "It is time, for reasons we have stated, to hold that on their own facts, and insofar as the principles they stand for are inconsistent with those that we have endorsed today, they are no longer to be followed."

The Court did not state that a search cannot be made as an incident to a lawful arrest, but merely limited the scope of such a search. The Supreme Court, in setting out the proper extent of a search incident to an arrest, noted,

> When an arrest is made, it is reasonable for the arresting officer to search the *person* arrested in order to remove any weapons that the latter might seek to use in order to resist arrest or effect his escape. [Emphasis added.]

[85] Benge v. Commonwealth, 321 SW(2d) 247 (Ky 1959).

Besides authorizing the search of the person arrested, the Court approved a limited search for evidence.

> In addition, it is entirely reasonable for the arresting officer to search for and seize any evidence on the arrestee's person in order to prevent its concealment or destruction. And the area into which arrestee might reach in order to grab a weapon or evidentiary items must, of course, be governed by a like rule.

In this *Chimel* case the Court also defined the term "immediate control" which had been used loosely in other cases. In defining this term the Court said,

> There is ample justification, therefore, for a search of the arrestee's person and the area "within his immediate control"—construing that phrase to mean the area from which he might gain possession of a weapon or destructible evidence.

To summarize, the Supreme Court has determined that when a legal arrest is made, the arresting officer or officers may search the *person* of the defendant for weapons or evidence and in addition may search the area into which the defendant might reach *to obtain a weapon* or *to destroy evidence*.

In an August, 1969 case,[86] the Maryland Court of Special Appeals was faced with making a determination as to the area which could be searched without violating the "reach" provisions of the *Chimel* case. The court rejected "the arm's length" restrictions which had been advocated by some judges and defense attorneys and held that the area is not limited to an arm's length radius encircling the arrestee at the moment of his arrest. Specifically, the court said,

> But as the search is tested by its reasonableness and its scope is justified by the need to protect the arresting officer and to prevent the destruction of evidence, we cannot construe *Chimel* [v. *California*] to mean that the area is confined to that precise spot which is at arm length from the arrestee at the moment of his arrest. He may well lunge forward or move backward or to the side and thus into an area in which he *might* grab a weapon or evidentiary items then within his reach before the officer could, by the exercise of rea-

[86] Scott v. State, 7 MdApp 505, 256 A(2d) 384 (1969).

sonable diligence, restrain him. We think that *Chimel* requires that the State show that the search was conducted and items were seized in an area "within the reach" of the arrestee in this concept, as for example, by evidence as to the location of the items with respect to the whereabouts of the arrestee, the accessibility of the items and their nature.

The Maryland court made it clear, however, that the search would not reasonably extend to a locked drawer explaining:

> It would seem that a seizure of a weapon or destructible evidence in a locked drawer in the immediate presence of the arrestee in the literal sense would be beyond the permissible scope of a search.

According to at least one court, then, the area of search incident to a lawful arrest extends to the area where the arrestee might lunge in order to reach a weapon or destroy evidence. Obviously, the scope of the search will depend on the facts of each case.[87]

(c) Automobile

This discussion concerns the search of an automobile as an incident to the lawful arrest. Further justification for the search of the automobile will be discussed in other sections.

The search of an automobile *incident to an arrest* is justified on the same grounds as the search of the premises. That is, the search incident to the arrest is justified for two reasons. First, in order to protect the arresting officer and to deprive the prisoner of means of escape, and secondly, to avoid destruction of evidence by the arrested person. As pointed out, the search incident to arrest is limited to the area within the immediate control of the arrestee. But what is the immediate control? When a person is operating a motor vehicle, the whole thing is apparently under his control or within his possession. Interpreting this very liberally, some early decisions held that the entire automobile may be searched as an incident to a lawful arrest.

It is generally recognized that the arresting officer may pro-

---

[87] Also see United States v. Melville, 309 FSupp 829 (SD NY 1970), in which the court found that "special circumstances" would justify a search even beyond the "lunge" area.

tect himself and, when conditions justify, search the person of the driver when a traffic arrest is made. Even under earlier decisions, however, he could not generally search the entire car in the usual *traffic* arrest situation.

It is generally conceded that the *Chimel* case reduced the permissible area of a search incident to an arrest in automobile situations.[88] There is disagreement among the courts, however, as to application of the rule of the *Chimel* case. For example, the Eighth Circuit Court stated that the permissible search area includes the area into which the arrestee might leap.[89] Thus, the court upheld the search of the back seat of an automobile while the arrestee, a grand larceny suspect, stood within "leaping" distance of the car. But the Oklahoma Court of Criminal Appeals in the case of *Fields* v. *State*[90] held that the *Chimel* case applied to a search of the car and that the search of the glove compartment of the car shortly after the arrest was not properly incident to the arrest.

In the case of *State* v. *Keith*[91] the Oregon Court of Appeals acknowledged that the *Chimel* case had greatly restricted searches of automobiles incident to arrest, but justified the search of the automobile by explaining that the vehicle here was seized as an instrumentality of the crime and, therefore, could be searched for further evidence of that crime without the necessity of a warrant.

Generally, the arresting officer may search the person of the driver of the car when an arrest is made. Even under the *Chimel* ruling he may also search the "lunge" area or the area within the reach of the arrestee. In such situations he may search for weapons or destructible evidence. In view of recent cases it is very difficult to justify the search of the entire car as an incident to arrest. Therefore, a search of the part of the automobile that is not within the reach of the arrestee must be based on other grounds.

An automobile parked in the driveway adjacent to a house can not be searched as an incident to an arrest when the arrest

---

[88] Ramon v. Cupp, 423 F(2d) 248 (9thCir 1970).

[89] In re Application of Kiser, 419 F(2d) 1134 (8thCir 1969).

[90] 463 P(2d) 1000 (OklaCrim 1970).

[91] 2 OreApp 133, 465 P(2d) 724 (1970).

is consummated in the house. In the case of *Coolidge v. New Hampshire*,[92] the Supreme Court of the United States made it clear it would not extend the area of search incident to an arrest to include the search of an automobile parked near a house. The Court, referring to the *Chimel* case, pointed out that there is no way in which the arrestee could conceivably have gained access to the automobile after the police had arrived on his property and made the arrest in the home.

(d) Area other than where arrest made

If the arrest takes place outside the residence, the house usually cannot be the subject of an incidental search. In the case of *Vale v. Louisiana*,[93] the defendant was arrested on the front steps of his house. In this case, the Supreme Court held that the warrantless search of the inside of the house could not be justified as an incident to the arrest. The Court said that even if the *Chimel* case is not accorded retroactive effect, no precedent of the Court could sustain the constitutional validity of the search in this case.

Where the arrest is made outside the residence, the search of the person is authorized to protect the officer and to prevent destruction of the evidence. Additionally, the search can extend to the area into which the arrestee may reach. Under the more recent decisions, however, the search of out-buildings generally would not be justified unless they were within the immediate reach of the arrestee.

An interesting case concerning a search incident to an arrest was the case of *United States v. Alberti*.[94] The defendant was located in the garage and then lured by misrepresentation into his apartment so that the arrest could be made and search could be made of the premises. The court here held that under the circumstances the search was unreasonable and the evidence must be excluded.

(e) Arrestee's clothing

For some time, a practical question has been posed by police

---

[92] 403 US 443, 29 LEd(2d) 564, 91 SCt 2022 (1971).

[93] 399 US 30, 26 LEd(2d) 409, 90 SCt 1969 (1970).

[94] 120 FSupp 171 (SD NY 1954).

who make an arrest and then search the clothing of the arrestee after he is lodged in the jail. In a 1974 case the United States Supreme Court again expressed the view that the Fourth Amendment prohibits only unreasonable searches and approved a search of clothing of the person after he has been arrested and put in jail.[95]

In this case, the defendant was arrested shortly after 11 p.m., and immediately taken to jail. The next morning new clothes were purchased for him, and his clothing was taken and held as evidence. An examination of the clothing revealed paint chips matching the samples that had been taken at the scene of the break-in. The defendant objected to the introduction of the evidence claiming that neither the clothing nor the results of the examination were admissible because the warrantless seizure of the clothing was invalid under the Fourth Amendment. The trial judge didn't agree. He admitted the evidence and the defendant was found guilty.

The Court of Appeals reversed and disallowed the admission of this evidence because the warrantless seizure of the defendant's clothing was after the administrative process and mechanics of arrest had come to a halt. The Supreme Court of the United States, reversing the Court of Appeals, held that the search and seizure of the clothing did not violate the Fourth Amendment, and explained that:

> [O]nce the accused is lawfully arrested and is in custody, the effects in his possession at the place of detention that were subject to search at the time and place of his arrest may lawfully be searched and seized without a warrant even though a substantial period of time has elapsed between the arrest and subsequent administrative processing, on the one hand, and the taking of the property for use as evidence, on the other.

The Court cautioned that there is, of course, a time when the Fourth Amendment would prohibit post-arrest seizures of the effects of the arrestee. But in this case the seizure of the clothes had been reasonable under the circumstances.

[95] United States v. Edwards, 415 US 800, 39 LEd(2d) 771, 94 SCt 1234 (1974).

Justices Stewart, Brennan, and Marshall dissented, arguing that the search which occurred ten hours after the arrest, at a time when the administrative processing and mechanics of arrest had come to an end, was unconstitutional under the Fourth Amendment.

§ 4.9   Waiver of constitutional rights

In accord with the general principle which allows a person to waive his constitutional rights, the rights protected by the Fourth Amendment to the Federal Constitution and the state provisions concerning search and seizure may be waived. However, these constitutional rights are considered to be waived only after careful evaluation. The cases are not in complete agreement as to what amounts to a consent, but some definite rules have been developed. Federal courts have taken the approach that every reasonable presumption against waiver of the fundamental constitutional rights will be taken.

Recognizing that a search may be conducted with the consent of the individual concerned, the following principles must be kept in mind.

1. The consent must be voluntary.

To be constitutionally adequate, the consent must be given without force, duress or compulsion of any kind.[96] The government has the burden of proving that the consent was voluntary and the proof must be clear and positive. Mere submission to authority is not voluntary consent. For example, if the officer says, "You don't mind if I conduct a search of your premises, do you?", and the owner of the premises makes no answer, this is not a voluntary consent.

In a 1973 case,[97] the defense very persuasively argued that if warnings, such as the *Miranda* warnings, must be given before a person can waive his Fifth Amendment rights, the same

---

[96] United States v. Fowler, 17 FRD 499 (SD Cal 1955).

[97] Schneckloth v. Bustamonte, 412 US 218, 36 LEd(2d) 854, 93 SCt 2041 (1973). See United States v. Watson, 423 US 411, 46 LEd(2d) 598, 96 SCt 820 (1976), where the majority of the United States Supreme Court again held that defendant did not have to know that he could have withheld his consent to a search.

reasoning should apply in regard to the waiver of Fourth Amendment rights. The specific case before the Supreme Court of the United States concerned the admissibility of three stolen checks obtained from the trunk of an automobile by officers who asked the driver if they could search the trunk. Without any advice from the police that he did not have to waive his Fourth Amendment rights, the driver said, "Sure, go ahead."

The defendant moved to suppress the introduction of the evidence on the ground that the material had been acquired through an unconstitutional search and seizure. The Federal District Court reasoned that the State was under an obligation to demonstrate not only that the consent was uncoerced but that it was given with an understanding it could be freely and effectively withheld. On appeal by the prosecution, the Supreme Court of the United States reversed the Circuit Court of Appeals decision and held in effect that the *Miranda* type of warning is not required in a search and seizure situation.

The majority in *Schneckloth* reaffirmed the rule that the consent must be voluntary, but included the following statement regarding the warning:

> Our decision today is a narrow one. We hold only that when the subject of a search is not in custody and the State attempts to justify a search on the basis of his consent, the Fourth and Fourteenth Amendments require that it demonstrate that the consent was in fact voluntarily given, and not the result of duress or coercion, express or implied. Voluntariness is a question of fact to be determined from all the circumstances, and while the subject's knowledge of a right to refuse is a factor to be taken into account, the prosecution is *not* required to demonstrate such knowledge as a prerequisite to establishing a voluntary consent. [Emphasis added.]

The warning that the police officer must look to *state* as well as federal rules bears repeating. The New Jersey Supreme Court rejected the consent principles set forth in the *Schneckloth* case, claiming this new test a "drastic departure" from previous decisions.[98] In New Jersey the state must show that

---

[98] State v. Johnson, 68 NJ 349,
346 A(2d) 66 (1975).

the person involved *knew* that he had a right to refuse to accede to the request for the consent search. Officers are again cautioned that, if the state has by statute or court decision required stiffer restrictions, those restrictions must be adhered to if based on the state constitutional provision.

There is still some conflict among authorities concerning the validity of a waiver where the officer advises the person in charge of the premises that a warrant will be applied for if permission to search is not granted. One federal court has indicated that it is not coercion if the officer only points out that he will apply for a warrant if the consent to search is denied.[99] The view of the majority was that the advice given by the law enforcement agent was well-founded since he could in fact apply for a warrant. This should be distinguished from the situation where the officer claims he *has* a warrant and will use it if consent to search is not given, when in fact he does *not* have a warrant or has a warrant that is unserviceable.[100] To avoid the risk of later challenge, the officer should not even mention the search warrant unless he in fact has one.

2. *Extensiveness of search is limited to exact words of consent.*

Since the officers are acting under a waiver of constitutional rights, the court requires that they carefully observe any limitations placed upon the consent either directly or by inference. Therefore, a consent to search a portion of one's premises is not a consent to search other portions.

The question also arises as to the withdrawal of the consent. Some authorities state that after the commencement of the search by voluntary consent, the consent may not be withdrawn. But in the case of *Strong v. United States*,[101] the court found that the defendant may revoke his consent during the process of the search.

If the person giving consent agrees to allow officers to search his house for one item, this does not convey the consent to search for other items. For example, consent by a resi-

---

[99] United States v. Faruolo, 506 F(2d) 490 (2dCir 1974).

[100] Middleton v. Commonwealth, 502 SW(2d) 517 (Ky 1973); Bumper v. North Carolina, 391 US 543, 20 LEd(2d) 797, 88 SCt 1788 (1968).

[101] 46 F(2d) 257 (1stCir 1931).

dent for officers to search his house for narcotics does not authorize examination of bookkeeping ledgers in the house. The judges of the Seventh Circuit agreed with the defendant that a "consent search" may be limited by the person giving consent, and the limitations must be observed. Also, this was not a situation where evidence of a different crime was discovered in plain view, as the ledgers had to be opened before there was any indication of a violation.[102]

It has been argued that where the person authorizes the search and later withdraws this consent, the officer is placed in the position of being led into making the search without a warrant, when he possibly would have made efforts to obtain the warrant had he not been authorized to search without it. This argument is persuasive but the apparent trend is to the contrary. In recent cases concerning the waiver of constitutional rights (as, for example, in the self-incrimination situation), the courts have allowed the consentor to withdraw his consent at any time. In view of these decisions, it would seem that the search must be discontinued when the consent is withdrawn, unless the search can be justified on other grounds.

3. *The person giving the consent must have the capacity to consent.*

The most serious problem confronting the officer who is contemplating the consent search is whether the person who gives consent is legally qualified to do so. This situation arises in the case of landlords, joint tenants, partners, spouses or agents.

The general rule as reaffirmed in recent Supreme Court cases is that "the consent of one who possesses common authority over the premises or effects is valid against the absent, non-consenting person with whom the authority is shared."[103] Under this rule, a valid consent to search premises may be given by a person who has immediate and present right to possess those premises. This third-party consent does not rest upon the law of property but upon the reasonableness of rec-

---

[102] United States v. Dichiarinte, 445 F(2d) 126 (7thCir 1971).

[103] United States v. Matlock, 415 US 164, 39 LEd(2d) 242, 94 SCt 988 (1974).

ognizing that the absent party assumes the risk that a co-inhabitant might permit a search.[104]

The immediate and present right to possess premises may or may not coincide with the legal right to pass title to the property, but in any event, the constitutional right to be free from unreasonable searches and seizures protects the possessory right, not the legal title. As a result, the landlord lacks the legal capacity to authorize a consent search that would be valid against a tenant of the leased premises. Even a roomer in a roominghouse is a tenant under this rule, and only he can give consent. This includes the tenant at sufferance who has not paid his room rent, but is still allowed to stay in the room.

The same reasoning appears to be true concerning business partners. In the case of *United States* v. *Sferas,*[105] the court held:

> [T]he rule seems to be well established that where two persons have equal rights to the use or occupancy of premises, either may give consent to a search, and the evidence thus disclosed can be used. . . .

The consent of one probably would not extend to a desk or other facility reserved exclusively for the use and control of another partner.

It is quite common for the officer to arrive at the residence of the suspect and find that the suspect is not home. He often is advised, however, that a member of the family is present. The question then arises as to whether the member of the family, whether it be the wife, a child, or a parent, can waive the constitutional protection and consent to the search of the residence of the suspect. The decisions of the various courts have not been in agreement, especially as to the authority of the wife to consent to the search. From the decisions, however, we can come to some general conclusions.

(a) Consent by the spouse

Although some courts are still holding to the contrary, the "modern authority" as mentioned in one case is that the wife

---

[104] Coolidge v. New Hampshire, 403 US 443, 29 LEd(2d) 564, 91 SCt 2022 (1971).

[105] 210 F(2d) 69 (7thCir 1954).

is in the same position as a tenant in common and can consent to the search of the premises occupied by both. In the case of *United States* v. *Thompson*,[106] the United States Court of Appeals for the Fifth Circuit stated that it was abandoning the forty-year-old rule that a wife cannot consent to the search of the couple's apartment, and authorized such a search. The court went on to say, however,

> Our holding that a wife can consent to a search of the premises she shares with her husband is limited to those premises under mutual control. The issue of whether a wife can consent to the search of premises reserved exclusively for the husband is not before us.

Even those states which have been reluctant to abandon the rule that the wife alone may not give a valid consent to search the house when the search is directed to the absent spouse, have recently accepted the "modern authority." [107] Recognizing the trend toward equalization of the rights and obligations of men and women, the spouses who jointly occupy premises are now generally considered as tenants in common.

Even if the consenting party is not the spouse, but only acting in this capacity, a consent to the search of her paramour's room is valid, according to the Tenth Circuit Court of Appeals.[108] Here, the woman who claimed she was the defendant's wife consented to a search of the hotel room where the officers found a zipper bag containing contraband. The defendant claimed that since the woman was not his wife, although she had lived with him for three years, she had no authority to permit the search of the room. The court said:

> We believe that the rule that a wife may give consent to search premises that she has a right to use and occupy equal to that of her husband, . . . extends to the present circumstances and is equally applicable to the search of the zipper bag.

There remains confusion concerning the authority of the wife (or husband) to consent to a search of the part of the

[106] 421 F(2d) 373 (5thCir 1970).
[107] Commonwealth v. Sebastian, 500 SW(2d) 417 (Ky 1973); Yuma Co. Attorney v. McGuire, 111 Ariz 437, 532 P(2d) 157 (1975).
[108] White v. United States, 444 F(2d) 724 (10thCir 1971).

premises used *exclusively* by the other. One court decided that a wife cannot consent to the search of a rented garage which was leased entirely by the husband and not jointly occupied.[109] On the other hand, where the husband and wife had mutual use of the bedroom and the wife had access to the dresser drawer located in the room, the wife's consent to take evidence from the dresser drawer was upheld.[110] If the facts indicate that one spouse has *exclusive* control over a portion of the premises or a particular container, reliance on consent by the other spouse may jeopardize the seizure. To be certain the evidence will be admissible, consent should be obtained from the party who has control, or the area should be guarded by an officer until a search warrant is obtained.

(b) Consent by the parent

The general rule is that a minor child's possessory right in the family home is only that which he derives from the parent, and that the parent may authorize the consent search valid against the child. Where a room was occupied jointly by the defendant and his two younger brothers, the First Circuit Court of Appeals had no difficulty in finding that the mother could give consent to search the room.[111] In the *Peterson* case, the majority found that even though the minor child considered a room exclusively his, the mother had access and complete control over the entire premises and, therefore, had the authority to consent.

The majority rule is that adult children who live in the house and have exclusive use of a particular room are treated as tenants in common as to the area used by all. Also, the parent, or anyone else who has common access to an area of the home may consent to a search of that area.[112]

(c) Consent by a minor child

An officer cannot rely on a consent given by a minor child. First, it would be very difficult to prove that the child under-

[109] United States ex rel. Cabey v. Mazurkiewicz, 312 FSupp 11 (1969).

[110] People v. Stacey, 58 Ill(2d) 83, 317 NE(2d) 24 (1974).

[111] United States v. Peterson, 524 F(2d) 167 (4thCir 1975).

[112] People v. Bunker, 22 MichApp 396, 177 NW(2d) 644 (1970).

stood the fact that he didn't have to give consent, and secondly, the minor child's interest in the property is not that of a tenant in common. It would seem, however, that an adult child who has the status of a joint tenant or resident does have authority to consent to the search of the area used jointly.

(d) Consent by school authorities

Although there is still some confusion as to whether the principal can consent to the search of a student's locker, in at least one case such a seizure was upheld.[113] There the court upheld its previous ruling and declared that the locker belonged to the school and that the student had no right to exclusive dominion over it. The court pointed out that the principal, as a representative of the municipal owners of the locker, has a duty to inspect it whenever a suspicion of illegal use arises. As there may be circumstances where the facts differ, it is preferable to get a warrant in this situation.

Before leaving the consent searches, it should be mentioned that when someone leaves articles in another's house or in another's care, the person who has custody of such article may consent to a search of that article.[114]

As the burden of proof is on the prosecution to show that the consent was given voluntarily, this consent should be obtained in writing when possible and should be witnessed by more than one person. If forms are used, they should be readily available at all times.

The law enforcement officer should recognize that the courts will give weight to the fact that the consent was given by the very young or the very old person or by one who has difficulty in understanding the English language. In such cases, the courts will be less ready to accept the consent to search.

§ 4.10   Search of movable vehicles and objects

The guarantee of freedom from unreasonable searches and seizures recognizes a necessary difference between the search of a dwelling house, for which a warrant may readily obtain,

---

[113] People v. Overton, 24 NY(2d) 522, 249 NE(2d) 366 1969).

[114] Marshall v. United States, 352 F(2d) 1013 (9thCir 1965).

and the search of a ship, boat, wagon, airplane or other movable object, where it is not practical to secure a warrant, because the object may be quickly moved out of the jurisdiction in which the warrant must be sought. The most often-quoted case which stated what has become known as the "moving vehicle" rule is *Carroll* v. *United States*.[115]

Following this decision and some contemporaneous decisions which distinguished between search of a vehicle and search of a house or other permanent structure, there was some doubt, especially in lower courts, about the moving vehicle doctrine.[116] Much of this doubt was laid to rest when the Supreme Court, in 1970, reaffirmed the right of officers to search a vehicle which is moving or about to be moved out of the jurisdiction, provided that there is probable cause to believe that the vehicle contains articles the officers are entitled to seize.

In the case of *Chambers* v. *Maroney*,[117] the police officers received a report that a filling station had been robbed. After receiving a description of the getaway car and a partial description of suspects who had been seen in the area, they stopped a station wagon answering the description of the car about two miles from the holdup site and arrested the occupants. During the course of the search of the car, the police found concealed, in a compartment under the dashboard, two .38-caliber revolvers and, in the right-hand glove compartment, an amount of small change and cards bearing the name of the attendant of another station which had been reported robbed at an earlier time.

At the trial, the materials taken from the station wagon were introduced over the objection of petitioner's counsel. Because the search was made some time after the arrest, the court quickly disposed of the search incident to the lawful arrest, saying that such a search was in violation of the Constitution. The Supreme Court, however, pointed out that there were other alternative grounds for the search in this case.

Relying heavily upon the *Carroll* case, the Supreme Court

---

[115] 267 US 132, 69 LEd 543, 45 SCt 280 (1925).

[116] Husty v. United States, 282 US 694, 75 LEd 629, 51 SCt 240 (1931).

[117] 399 US 42, 26 LEd(2d) 419, 90 SCt 1975 (1970). See case in Part II.

stated that the Government recognized a necessary difference
between a search of a store, dwelling house or other structure,
in respect of which a proper official warrant may readily be
obtained, and a search of a ship, motorboat, wagon or automobile for contraband goods where it is not practical to secure
a warrant. The following paragraph taken from the case ex-
plains the "probable cause-moving vehicle" doctrine:

> In enforcing the Fourth Amendment's prohibition against unrea-
> sonable searches and seizures, the Court has insisted upon probable
> cause as a minimum requirement for a reasonable search permitted
> by the Constitution. As a general rule, it has also required the judg-
> ment of a magistrate on the probable-cause issue and the issuance
> of a warrant before a search is made. Only in exigent circumstances
> will the judgment of the police as to probable cause serve as suf-
> ficent authorization for a search. *Carroll* holds a search warrant
> unnecessary where there is probable cause to search an automobile
> stopped on the highway; the car is movable, the occupants are
> alerted, and the car's contents may never be found again if a war-
> rant must be obtained. Hence an immediate search is constitutionally
> permissible.

The ruling in the *Chambers* case is a very fortunate one for
the investigator. Because the *Chimel* ruling restricted the
search incident to arrest to the immediate area, it is obvious
that more reliance must be placed on the search under the
moving vehicle doctrine.[118]

The United States Supreme Court in December, 1975, affirmed the action it took in the *Chambers* case on facts which
were very similar to those in that earlier case. In *Texas* v.
White,[119] officers searched the automobile after the suspect had
been arrested and the car driven by an officer to the station
house. The Texas Court of Criminal Appeals, in a three to
two decision, reversed the conviction on the ground that the
evidence of four checks was obtained without a warrant in
violation of the defendant's Fourth Amendment rights. The

---

[118] Chimel v. California, 395 US 752, 23 LEd(2d) 685, 89 SCt 2034 (1969). For a state case approving the moving vehicle search, see People v. Williams, 383 Mich 549, 177 NW(2d) 151 (1970). For a pre-Chambers case, see People v. Kuntze, 371 Mich 419, 124 NW(2d) 269 (1963).

[119] 423 US 67, 46 LEd(2d) 209, 96 SCt 304 (1975).

United States Supreme Court, with two justices dissenting, however, disagreed in these terms:

> In *Chambers* v. *Maroney* we held that police officers with probable cause to search an automobile on the scene where it was stopped could constitutionally do so later at the station house, without first obtaining a warrant. There, as here, "the probable-cause factor" that developed on the scene "still obtained at the station house." . . . The Court of Criminal Appeals erroneously excluded the evidence seized from the search at the station house in the light of the trial judge's finding . . . that there was probable cause to search [the defendant's] car.

The justification for this exception to the requirement that a search warrant must be obtained is that, because the vehicle is moving, or about to be moved, from the jurisdiction, there is no possibility of getting a search warrant even if probable cause for the warrant exists. Therefore, there are three requirements which must be met if the search is to be justified under this exception:

1. The officer must have probable cause which would justify a search warrant if one could be obtained.
2. The vehicle must be moving or about to be moved.
3. The facts must indicate that a warrant may not be readily obtained.

As a minimum, the officer must have facts or information which would authorize the issuance of a search warrant, had application been made for one. Although the officer need not go before the judicial officer and prove probable cause before the search, he must have facts or information which would warrant a person of reasonable caution to believe that an offense had been, or was being, committed, and that articles which are subject to seizure were in the vehicle to be searched.

The doctrine is generally applied when an automobile is searched without a warrant; however, the same rationale may justify the search of a boat, plane, truck-trailer or mobile home. The Eighth Circuit Court found little difference between the search of an automobile and the search of a trailer where exigent circumstances existed. Cautioning that exigent circumstances must exist, and that there must be a pressing need for a prompt search, the justices of the Eighth Circuit nevertheless approved the search of a tractor-trailer.[120] If exigent circumstances are present and probable cause exists, there is no reason why a search of aircraft is not constitutionally permissible.[121] The Tenth Circuit Court also found that a search of a mobile home for marijuana fell within the exigent circumstances doctrine of *Chambers* v. *Maroney* where probable cause existed and the mobile home was about to be moved from the jurisdiction.[122]

Although the *Carroll* doctrine has been frequently referred to as the "automobile exception," some courts are now applying the logic where other types of movable objects are involved. For example, the California Supreme Court found a degree of similarity between a motor vehicle and a package being shipped by air freight. That court concluded that the exemption to the warrant requirements explained in *Chambers* v. *Maroney* applies to such a package.[123] And the Eighth Circuit Court had no difficulty in applying the rationale to the search of a duffel bag when probable cause existed, and the item was movable.[124] That court commented:

> A current line of cases indicates that the special rationales developed by the Supreme Court in the automobile search area are equally applicable to other movable items such as the duffel bag involved here.

A majority of the United States Court of Appeals for the Fifth Circuit, sitting *en banc*, approved the warrantless search in a credit union office of purses belonging to the manager who had admitted juggling accounts. The court there con-

---

[120] United States v. Bozada, 473 F(2d) 389 (8thCir 1973). Also see Lederer v Tehan, 441 F(2d) 295 (6thCir 1971), where the court approved the search of a "U-Haul" truck.

[121] United States v. Sigal, 500 F(2d) 1118 (10thCir 1974).

[122] United States v. Miller, 460 F(2d) 582 (10thCir 1972).

[123] People v. McKinnon, 7 Cal(3d) 399, 103 CalRptr 897, 500 P(2d) 1097 (1972).

[124] United States v. Wilson, 524 F(2d) 595 (8thCir 1975).

cluded that the reasoning of *Chambers* transcends its factual setting sufficiently to justify the search.[125]

In other cases, courts have justified searches of suitcases in transit where exigency justified such search.[126] Like reasoning applied where the baggage is in the possession of the traveler. In the case of *United States* v. *Mehciz*,[127] the Ninth Circuit Court of Appeals upheld the search of an overnight suitcase taken from the defendant as he alighted from a plane. Referring to the Supreme Court expression in *Chambers* that there is a difference between houses and cars, the Court reasoned that there is also a corresponding constitutional difference between a house and a suitcase. In these cases the justification for the search is "probable cause plus exigency." It does not matter whether there is probable cause for a physical arrest of the person.

Because of the "exigent circumstances" reasoning, efforts have been made to extend the *Carroll* warrantless search exceptions to residences and other fixed premises. The *Carroll* doctrine, even when interpreted to include goods in transit such as duffel bags, suitcases, boxes or trunks, requires that the vehicle or article be movable. Evidence must also show that it would be difficult, if not impossible, to obtain a warrant. The Supreme Court has clearly pointed out in these cases that there is a difference between the search of a store, dwelling house or other structure, and the search of a ship, motor boat, wagon or automobile. Nevertheless, there seems to be a movement by some state and lower federal courts to extend the "exigent circumstances" reasoning to a search of the premises.

The Nebraska Supreme Court, indicating that exigent circumstances justified immediate action, approved the search of an apartment where officers overheard conversations which led them to realize that heroin was already in the apartment and would be ready for distribution before a warrant could be

---

[125] United States v. Hand, 516 F(2d) 472 (5thCir 1975).
[126] United States v. Evans, 481 F(2d) 990 (9thCir 1973); People v. McKinnon, 103 CalRptr 897, 500 P(2d) 1097 (1972); State v. Wolfe, 5 WashApp 153, 486 P(2d) 1143 (1971).
[127] 437 F(2d) 145 (9thCir 1971).

obtained.[128] Here, the court found that there was probable cause for a search warrant, but because of the exigent circumstances, the search of the suspect's premises was made without the warrant.

Although the Nebraska Supreme Court refers to cases to justify this decision, the authority to enter fixed premises for the purpose of searching for evidence of crime, even though exigency exists, appears to be beyond the rationale of the *Carroll-Chambers* doctrine. There is case law to support officers' entering premises in fresh pursuit to make an arrest, but this authority is based upon different reasoning and would not include the right to make a search of the premises without making the arrest.[129] Future cases will, no doubt, determine if exigency will justify a warrantless intrusion into premises for the exclusive purpose of searching for evidence of crime. Until the Supreme Court acts in this area, however, police officers should not rely on existing authority.

Since the *Chambers* case, many searches have been made under the moving vehicle doctrine examined there, and most of these have been upheld.[130] However, in the case of *Coolidge v. New Hampshire* decided on June 21, 1971,[131] the Supreme Court made it clear that this doctrine could not be applied unless the specific requirements were met. The Court approved the *Chambers* reasoning with this paragraph:

> As we said in *Chambers,* "exigent circumstances" justify the warrantless search of "an automobile *stopped on the highway,*" where there is probable cause, because the car is "movable, the occupants are alerted, and the car's contents may never be found again if a warrant must be obtained."

But the Court explained that this justification for a warrant-

---

[128] State v. Patterson, 192 Neb 308, 220 NW(2d) 235 (1974). Also see State v. McGuire, 13 ArizApp 539, 479 P(2d) 187 (1971), authorizing a warrantless entry on similar facts, and United States v. Jetters, 342 US 40, 96 LEd 59, 72 SCt 93 (1951), where no exceptional circumstances resulted in suppression of seized contraband as evidence.

[129] State v. Pope, 192 Neb 755, 224 NW(2d) 521 (1974).

[130] United States v. Sutton, 341 FSupp 320 (WD Tenn 1972); Merrill v. United States, 463 F(2d) 521 (7thCir 1972).

[131] Coolidge v. New Hampshire, 403 US 443, 29 LEd(2d) 564, 91 SCt 2022 (1971). See Part II.

less search would not apply where the defendant has been arrested and lodged in jail, where there was no evidence the car was about to be moved from the driveway of the defendant's home, and where there was no evidence that the car was being used for illegal purposes. The Court logically reasoned that the opportunity for a search was thus hardly "fleeting."

There is quite a difference of opinion as to what constitutes "exigent circumstances" or "fleeting." In the case of *Cardwell v. Lewis*,[132] a murder suspect's automobile was taken from the public parking lot a short distance from the police station where he was placed under arrest. The next morning, paint scrapings were taken from his car, and a cast of a tire impression made at the crime scene compared with the tires on the car. The defendant was found guilty in state court but the United States District Court, in a habeas corpus proceeding, concluded that the seizure and examination of the respondent's car violated the Fourth and Fourteenth Amendments. The Federal Circuit Court of Appeals affirmed, agreeing that the evidence should not have been admitted as the search was not justified.

On appeal by the prosecution, four members of the Supreme Court, referring to the *Carroll-Chambers* line of decisions, agreed that "exigent circumstances" existed, and that:

> Under circumstances such as these, where probable cause exists, a warrantless examination of the exterior of a car is not unreasonable under the Fourth and Fourteenth Amendments.

After finding that probable cause existed at the time the car was taken from the public lot, these four justices in *Cardwell v. Lewis* determined that the impoundment of the automobile did not render the examination of the exterior unreasonable, as:

> We do not think that, because the police impounded the car prior to the examination, which they could have made on the spot, there is a constitutional barrier to the use of evidence obtained thereby. Under the circumstances of this case, the seizure itself was not unreasonable.

[132] 417 US 583, 41 LEd(2d) 325, 94 SCt 2464 (1974).

The Court distinguished this case from the *Coolidge* case on the grounds that the Coolidge car was parked on the defendant's driveway and the seizure would have required an entry upon private property, while in this case the automobile was seized from a public place where access was not meaningfully restricted. In reference to the exigent circumstances, the Court held that the exigency may arise at any time, and the fact that the police might have obtained a warrant does not negate the possibility of the current situation's necessitating prompt police action.

Mr. Justice Powell concurred in the result on somewhat different reasoning. Consequently, the lower federal court's judgments were reversed and the state conviction was left standing. Four Justices of the Supreme Court dissented, reasoning that the moving vehicle doctrine applies only where the officers do not have reasonable opportunity to obtain a warrant. According to the dissenters, there was absolutely no likelihood that the respondent could have either moved the car or meddled with it during the time necessary to obtain a search warrant.

Although four members of the Supreme Court (with one member agreeing on other grounds) upheld the obtaining of evidence from a moving vehicle even though the officers might have had an opportunity to obtain the warrant, the better practice and the one which should be followed is to obtain a warrant where time permits. This will make it unnecessary to rely as heavily upon the *Chambers* moving vehicle doctrine and the risk of having the evidence rejected will not be as great.

§ 4.11　Seizure without a search (plain view)

Provisions of the Fourth Amendment to the Federal Constitution and the provisions of the state constitutions protect persons against unreasonable searches and seizures. Therefore, where there is no search required, the constitutional guarantee is not applicable. The guarantee applies only in those instances where the seizure is assisted by a necessary search. A series of federal and state cases has affirmed the rule that a seizure of contraband or instrumentalities of the crime in plain view is not a violation of the Fourth Amendment where the officers are on the premises lawfully. This exception to the rule that the officer must have a warrant was well stated in the case of *United States* v. *McDaniel.*[133] In this case the court made the following comment:

> [I]f, without a search and without an unlawful entry into the premises, a contraband article or an article which is needed by the police, is seen in the premises, the police are not required to close their eyes and need not walk out and leave the article where they saw it. Any other principle might lead to an absurd result and at times perhaps even defeat the ends of justice.

Although the rule is clear that it is not a search for an officer to seize what is open and visible to the eye when seen from a place where the officer is entitled to be, there is some question as to the lawfulness of the officer's presence on the premises. An officer lawfully present may use the evidence which is seized where he sees the objects by looking through an open door, an open window, or an open transom. In the *Harris* case,[134] the Court approved the seizure of draft cards when a search was made incidental to a lawful arrest and the object of the search was canceled checks, commenting:

> Nor is it a significant consideration that the draft cards which were seized were not related to the crimes for which petitioner was arrested. Here during the course of a valid search the agents came upon property of the United States in the illegal custody of the petitioner. It was property to which the Government was entitled to possession. . . . Nothing in the decisions of this Court gives support to the suggestion that under such circumstances the law-enforcement

---

[133] 154 FSupp 1 (DC Cir 1957). Also see Coolidge v. New Hampshire, 403 US 443, 29 LEd(2d) 564, 91 SCt 2022 (1971).

[134] Harris v. United States, 331 US 145, 91 LEd 1399, 67 SCt 1098 (1947). See also, State v. Bagley, 286 Minn 180, 175 NW(2d) 448 (1970), quoting Abel v. United States, 362 US 217, 4 LEd(2d) 668, 80 SCt 683 (1960), where seizure of goods not described in the warrant was approved, the Court em-phasizing, "When an article subject to lawful seizure properly comes into the officer's possession in the course of a lawful search it would be entirely without reason to say he must return it because it was not one of those things it was his business to look for." For another case authorizing seizure of marijuana "in plain sight," see United States v. Lozaw, 427 F(2d) 911 (2dCir 1970).

officials must impotently stand aside and refrain from seizing such contraband material.

Such seizures are authorized where the officer is on the premises lawfully or if he can observe the contraband or illegally possessed goods from a position where he is not a trespasser, but if the officer does become a trespasser on property which is under the protection of the Fourth Amendment, his action then amounts to an illegal search and seizure. He cannot use information so obtained to procure a warrant, nor can he seize the evidence without a warrant.

In a 1952 opinion, the United States Supreme Court held that the use of field glasses or a telescope did not amount to a trespass.[135] Also, the fact that the property is hidden by the darkness of night and is revealed only by the use of a flashlight does not necessarily mean the property was found by a search. Stating this more dramatically, the Fifth Circuit Court, in 1971, commented: "The plain view rule does not go into hibernation at sunset." There the justices agreed that the aid of a flashlight did not transform a nighttime observation into a search.[136]

Many state courts have upheld the seizure of contraband or instrumentalities seized from a private automobile without a search. One such case is the case of *Clark* v. *Commonwealth*.[137] In this case the officer stopped the car when he noticed that the car was sitting very low in the back, and the driver was having some difficulty in steering. As he approached the car, he saw a case and some cans of beer on the floor of the car where the back seat had been removed. The court, in affirming the seizure of this contraband, stated:

> There was no unlawful search under the evidence presented. When the troopers approached appellant's car in order to make their investigation, it is undenied the beer in the back part was in plain

---

[135] On Lee v. United States, 343 US 747, 96 LEd 1270, 72 SCt 967 (1952)

[136] Walker v. Beto, 437 F(2d) 1018 (5thCir 1971), quoting Marshall v. United States, 422 F(2d) 185 (5thCir 1970), where the use of a flashlight was approved, the court commenting,

"Regardless of the time of day or night, the plain view rule must be upheld when the viewer is rightfully positioned, seeing through eyes that are neither accusatory nor criminally investigatory."

[137] 388 SW(2d) 622 (Ky 1965).

view. The constitutional guaranty which affords protection from an illegal search does not prohibit a seizure without a warrant where there is no need of a search; that is, where the outlawed object discovered is visible, open and obvious to any one who even casually looks about his surroundings.

Evidence can be seized where there is no search, and information obtained under these conditions may be used to obtain a warrant. But it must be remembered that, in order to seize evidence under this exception so that the evidence will be admissible, the officer must be lawfully present on the premises and observe the illegally possessed or contraband goods. If he is a trespasser, or if he is illegally on the premises when he observes the contraband or illegally possessed goods, there is a search and a seizure in violation of the constitutional provisions.

This "seizure without a search" reasoning or the "plain view" doctrine has been applied in many cases and in many situations. For example, the Ninth Federal Circuit Court of Appeals approved the seizure of an envelope containing what appeared to be a Treasury check from the outside pocket of a pedestrian where the officer recognized the check was made out to another person, and he had probable cause to believe the check to be stolen.[138] The court again noted:

> It has long been settled, however, that objects falling within "the plain view of an officer who has a right to be in the position to have that view are subject to seizure and may be introduced into evidence."

The Eighth Circuit, in affirming the plain view doctrine, held that where officers are on the premises to execute a search warrant for stolen diamonds, they could legitimately seize $9,000 packaged in (St. Louis Bank) wrappers.[139] And the Seventh Circuit justified the seizure of marked bills during execution of a search warrant which described heroin and narcotics paraphernalia.[140] The dissenting judge in that case,

[138] United States v. Sedillo, 496 F(2d) 151 (9thCir 1974).
[139] United States v. Golay, 502 F(2d) 182 (8thCir 1974).
[140] United States v. Jones, 518 F(2d) 384 (7thCir 1975).

with some justification, argued that the seizure was not legal because the prosecution failed to prove that the officers immediately recognized the marked money or a piece of paper with a name and phone number on it as being stolen or contraband.[141]

Although the apparent trend is to apply the plain view exception rather broadly, the two requirements that are always present are that: (1) the officer have a prior justification for intrusion, and that (2) it be immediately apparent that the stolen or contraband evidence is recognized as such at the time the officer makes the seizure.[142]

§ 4.12   Search by a private individual

The constitutional prohibitions against unreasonable searches operate against official action. Therefore, where evidence has been unlawfully seized by a private person with no official knowledge or without collusion, the evidence may generally be used by the prosecution. A private person who unlawfully enters the premises may be subject to civil suit or even criminal action, but the evidence may nevertheless be used. According to the decisions, such a search and seizure is outside the scope of constitutional protection. Obviously, should the court find that a law enforcement officer participated in the search in any way or had knowledge that the search was to be made, the evidence would not be admissible.[143] Even if the police "stand idly by" while a private person acts and the police have knowledge of the action, there is a good possibility that the exclusionary rule will apply.[144]

However, in one case, the Seventh Circuit Court of Appeals

[141] However, see United States v. Canestri, 518 F(2d) 269 (2dCir 1975), where the court approved seizure of unregistered weapons even though the officers did not know at the time that the weapons were not registered.

[142] United States v. Gray, 484 F(2d) 352 (6thCir 1973). Also see United States v. Sellers, 520 F(2d) 1281 (4thCir 1975), holding that officers could make "protective sweep" of apartment, seize evidence in plain view, or use information for a search warrant.

[143] Lustig v. United States, 338 US 74, 93 LEd 1819, 69 SCt 1372 (1949); see Coolidge v. New Hampshire, 403 US 443, 29 LEd(2d) 564, 91 SCt 2022 (1971).

[144] Stapleton v. Superior Ct., 73 CalRptr 575, 447 P(2d) 967 (1968).

pointed out that the inspection by a carrier (airlines) official, without the participation of state or federal authority is not a government search.[145] But where the agent had already called the Drug Enforcement Administration and was told that agents would be there shortly, there was too much government participation, and the exclusionary rule was enforced.[146]

In another case, the court conceded that the question was a close one but approved the seizure of a sawed-off shotgun from a motel room by the motel manager after the 2 P.M. check-out time had passed, and the defendant had been arrested by police officers on another charge.[147] Before action of a private individual can be attributed to the Government, some degree of government instigation or knowledge must be shown.[148]

There seems to be no question that the exclusionary rule does not apply where a private person without any official authority makes the search. An issue which has been becoming more difficult, however, is whether the exclusionary rule should be applied where railroad police, private contract police, investigators or school authorities make the search.

Airline agents are not—according to the Nebraska Supreme Court—law enforcement officers. Therefore, a senior passenger agent who seized marijuana from baggage in the baggage room did not violate the Constitution and the evidence was admissible. The court said the constitutional provisions against unreasonable searches and seizures applies only to governmental agents and not to private persons.[149] But action by school officials was held to be "state action" rendering the Fourth Amendment applicable through the Fourteenth when marijuana was seized from a high school student.[150] The Court of Appeals of New Mexico held,[151] however, that even though

---

[145] United States v. Issod, 508 F(2d) 990 (7thCir 1974).

[146] United States v. Newton, 510 F(2d) 1149 (7thCir 1975).

[147] United States v. Parizo, 514 F(2d) 52 (2dCir 1975).

[148] United States v. Luciow, 518 F(2d) 298 (8thCir 1975).

[149] State v. Skonberg, 194 Neb 554, 233 NW(2d) 919 (1975).

[150] State v. Mora, 307 S(2d) 317 (La 1975). *But see*, State v. Buccino, 282 A(2d) 869 (Del 1971).

[151] Doe v. State, 88 NM 347, 540 P(2d) 827 (1975).

this was state action the same rules should not apply in school discipline cases as apply in other situations. Thus, the court adopted this rule:

> [W]e adopt the standard that school officials may conduct a search of the student's person if they have a reasonable suspicion that a crime is being or has been committed, or they have reasonable cause to believe that the search is necessary in the aid of maintaining school discipline.

With the trend toward licensing private security personnel by state agencies, there is a good chance that such licensed personnel will be considered "official" so that the exclusionary rule will apply.

§ 4.13   Premises protected by the Fourth Amendment

The Fourth Amendment and the provisions of the various state constitutions protect the right of the people to be secure in their persons, houses, papers and effects. Courts have been called upon in many instances to define what premises and areas are protected by this provision. The term "houses" has been interpreted very broadly to include any dwelling, whether it be a mansion, a small house, apartment, or hotel room. The house is protected even though it is temporarily unoccupied as in the case of a summer or weekend home. However, once a dwelling has been vacated, as when a tenant checks out of a hotel, it is not protected. The protection also extends to a place of business.[152]

Not only does the protection extend to the house itself, but also to the curtilage. The curtilage has been defined as the open space situated within a common enclosure and belonging to the dwelling house. It has also been defined as the space which is necessary and convenient and is habitually used for family purposes, including a yard, a garden, or even a field which is near to and used in connection with the dwelling. It is often difficult to define the area included within the curtilage, but certainly the yard around the house is included and protected under the Fourth Amendment and the state

[152] United States v. Rabinowitz, 339 US 56, 94 LEd 653, 70 SCt 430 (1950).

provisions. In one case a farmyard over 200 feet from the residence was protected. The enclosed backyard of the residence has been considered as a part of the curtilage as well as a Finnish bath house adjacent to the dwelling house, and a smoke house associated with the dwelling house and located inside the yard fence.

Although the provisions have been applied broadly, in a leading federal case an area fifty to one hundred yards from the defendant's residence was held to be "open fields" and *not* protected by the Constitution.[153] Other examples of areas not protected are a cave and a shack not within the curtilage of the house.

The comment in the case of *Katz v. United States*[154] that the Fourth Amendment protects people, not places, left some questions as to whether the "open fields" doctrine would still be applicable. However, Mr. Justice Harlan in his concurring opinion in that very case indicates that it probably will be applicable, stating:

> On the other hand, conversations in the open would not be protected against being overheard, for the expectation of privacy under the circumstances would be unreasonable.

In the opinion of the majority of one federal court, the "open field" doctrine is still applicable. In the case of *United States v. Watt*,[155] decided in 1970, the United States District Court for Northern California was of the opinion that the "open fields" doctrine as announced in *Hester* could be applied to allow the seizure of narcotics from a vacant lot.

Some state courts have not followed the interpretation of the federal courts, especially where the wording of the state constitution differs from that of the Fourth Amendment. For example, in Mississippi the constitutional protection of "persons, house and possessions," was held to prohibit the search of open fields and woods without a warrant.[156]

---

[153] Hester v. United States, 265 US 57, 68 LEd 898, 44 SCt 445 (1924).

[154] 389 US 347, 19 LEd(2d) 576, 88 SCt 507 (1967).

[155] 309 FSupp 329 (ND Cal 1970).

[156] Falkner v. State, 134 Miss 253, 98 So 691 (1924).

As late as 1975, the Nebraska Supreme Court *recognized* the "open fields" doctrine with the statement:

> The Fourth Amendment applies to searches of a person or his house, papers, or effects. This does not encompass a field which is approximately 75 feet behind a house which the defendant had not yet finished constructing and had not yet moved into.[157]

Agreeing that the "open fields" doctrine still prevails, the Fifth Circuit Court approved the seizure of a suitcase buried in a chicken coop in an open field and the opening of the suitcase without first obtaining a warrant.[158]

Notwithstanding these recent comments from the various courts, confusion still exists as the result of the unnecessarily vague wording of the *Katz* case. As a consequence, the Wisconsin State Supreme Court reasoned that the *Katz* decision did not affect the open fields doctrine,[159] but the U.S. District Court for Western Wisconsin believed that the *Katz* decision abolished reliance on the common law property concepts and placed "open fields" and "curtilage" in the *same* search and seizure category.[160]

The District of Columbia Court of Appeals, applying the *Katz* rationale, upheld the use of evidence obtained after a police officer on routine patrol peered through a crack in a closed hotel room door and saw a man inside apparently preparing to inject himself with heroin.[161] The court, agreeing that *Katz* departed from adherence to the concept of a constitutionally protected area and analyzed the police surveillance techniques therein involved from the broader perspective of a defendant's reasonable expectation of privacy, applied the rule to cut both ways. Although recognizing that the hotel room is a constitutionally protected area, the court explained that the crack in the door was readily apparent and accessible to anyone walking along the hall and that "what a person knowingly exposes to the public even in his own

---

[157] State v. Poulson, 194 Neb 601, 234 NW(2d) 214 (1975).

[158] United States v. Brown, 473 F(2d) 952 (5thCir 1973).

[159] Conrad v. State, 63 Wis(2d) 616, 218 NW(2d) 252 (1974).

[160] United States ex rel. Gedko v. Heer, 406 FSupp 609 (WD Wis(1975).

[161] Borum v. United States, 318 A(2d) 590 (DC 1974).

home or office is not a subject of Fourth Amendment protection."

Even though the open field doctrine as now applied has some limitations, it is still operative, and in fact, it could be argued that the *Katz* doctrine, if anything, has expanded the areas of search.

§ 4.14   Standing to challenge the search

Although the *Mapp* case said that the only courtroom door remaining open to evidence secured by illegal search has been closed, it seems there is still a crack which has not, as yet, been closed. If the premises are searched and the evidence is incriminating against a party who does not have standing to challenge the search, the evidence may be used against him. The reasoning is that the defendant's rights have not been violated and he may therefore not complain of the unreasonable searches and seizure or prevent the fruits thereof from being used against him. There is no doubt that the person whose rights were violated may complain, but the party who had no substantial possessory interest in the premises searched may not complain.

In the case of *Jones v. United States*,[162] the Court expressed the rule in this paragraph:

> In order to qualify as a "person aggrieved by an unlawful search and seizure" one must have been a victim of a search or seizure, one against whom the search was directed, as distinguished from one who claims prejudice only through the use of evidence gathered as a consequence of a search or seizure directed at someone else.

The courts have been liberal in determining who is a person "aggrieved." In the *Jones* case the Court held that the defendant had standing to suppress, even though he testified that his home was elsewhere, that he paid nothing for the use of the apartment where the narcotics were found, and that he had been allowed to use the apartment as a friend of the tenant of the apartment.

This view was confirmed in 1963 when the United States

[162] 362 US 257, 4 LEd(2d) 697, 80 SCt 725 (1960).

Supreme Court approved the admission into evidence of narcotics obtained as a result of an illegal arrest and search. The
Court approved the use of the evidence because the right to
privacy of the person complaining was not invaded.[163] The
California Supreme Court has apparently differed with the
United States Supreme Court and now accords standing to
suppress to anyone whenever there has been an unreasonable
police search and seizure of any kind.

This "no standing" doctrine was followed where the search
was of another person. In the case of *State* v. *McConoughey*,[164]
the Minnesota Supreme Court refused to reverse a decision
where such a search was challenged. The court pointed out
that when the search is made of another person, the defendant
has no standing to object to the search.

This same reasoning was applied where a car in which the
defendant was not riding was searched. Although a money
order machine found in the car was used in evidence against
the defendant, he could not be heard to complain, the court
explaining:

> The record is devoid of evidence indicating any interest, owner-
> ship, or otherwise, of [defendant in the car] such as to afford him
> standing to complain of its search. Only one whose Fourth Amend-
> ment right of privacy has been violated may object to the intro-
> duction of the fruits of an illegal search.[165]

Other examples of instances where courts have admitted
evidence when the defendant was unable to show that he
had a property right or possessory interest in the place being
searched assist in understanding this exception. In a Kentucky
case, the Court of Appeals upheld the seizure of a revolver
from the hallway of another person's home where the defendant did not show any property rights or possessory interests in the house from which the revolver was seized.[166]

---

[163] Wong Sun v. United States, 371 US 471, 9 LEd(2d) 441, 83 SCt 407 (1963).

[164] 282 Minn 161, 163 NW(2d) 568 (1968).

[165] Cassady v. United States, 410 F(2d) 379 (5thCir 1969). Also see State v. McFarland, 195 Neb 395, 238 NW(2d) 237 (1976), which held that a thief in possession of a stolen car had no standing to object to a search of the car.

[166] Geary v. Commonwealth, 503 SW(2d) 505 (Ky 1972).

Nor did the U.S. Court of Appeals for the Tenth Circuit find any legal obstacle to the admission of narcotics against the defendant when the narcotics were seized from the defendant's sister's automobile.[167]

It must be noted that even though the evidence is admitted as to the party who has no standing to suppress, the search is nevertheless illegal under the Constitution.

§ 4.15   Search after lawful impoundment

Often the police officer has the duty and responsibility to impound a car that has been abandoned, is blocking traffic, is illegally parked, or for some other reason.[168] In such instances the officer is often required, either by law or by regulation, to search the vehicle and make a list of the contents of the vehicle before impounding it. The question then arises as to the use of the contents as evidence where the possession of such contents constitutes a crime.

The rationale for the seizure of contraband or other articles from an impounded car is sound. Such a seizure is justified on the ground that the officer who has the duty of impounding the car for his own protection and for the protection of the owner should inventory the contents to safeguard the owner and protect against false claims of loss. As pointed out by the Nebraska Supreme Court in *State* v. *Wallen*,[169] if during a proper inventory of the contents of an impounded vehicle, evidence of crime is discovered, such evidence may be used to support a charge for the crime indicated.

The courts have cautioned that the seizure of evidence on the impounded car theory is only legitimate if the car is in fact legally impounded. It is preferable to impound the car under the authority of a state or federal law. If there is no such law, then a departmental order defining the circumstances under which the car should be impounded often can be relied upon. The court, in the case of *Heffley* v. *State*,[170] warned that: "If, however, the policing conduct indicates that the intention is

---

[167] United States v. Galvez, 465 F(2d) 681 (10thCir 1972).

[168] *E.g.*, DistColumTraf & VehReg §91.

[169] 185 Neb 44, 173 NW(2d) 372 (1970).

[170] Heffley v. State, 83 Nev 100, 423 P(2d) 666 (1967).

exploratory rather than [for an] inventory, the fruits of that search are forbidden."

The Nebraska court in the *Wallen* case compared the seizure of articles from an impounded car with a seizure without a search. The court explained that the taking of the inventory, a reasonable precaution, did not constitute an unreasonable seizure any more than in any other case where the police stumble on the evidence of crime in the pursuance of duty.

One of the most often quoted cases concerning the authority to seize articles from an impounded car is the case of *Cooper v. California*.[171] In that case the defendant was arrested for violation of the narcotics laws and his automobile seized by police officers pursuant to the California statute authorizing state officers to seize vehicles used unlawfully to transport narcotics. The Supreme Court approved the search of the car a week after the arrest even though there was no search warrant. Where the car is seized and impounded pending forfeiture proceedings, it would be unreasonable, according to the majority, to hold that the police, having to retain the car in their garage for such a length of time, had no right, even for their own protection, to search it.

In the *Cooper* case the state law specifically provided for forfeiture of the car to the state if the car was used for unlawful transportation of narcotics. The Ninth Circuit Court of Appeals refused to apply this doctrine when the officers were not under a mandatory duty to hold the car.[172] Most courts, however, do not require that the impoundment be under state law.[173]

Probably because of the wide differences in the opinions of lower courts concerning the seizure of articles from an impounded car, the Supreme Court in 1976 finally acted and placed a limited stamp of approval on this procedure.[174] In the *Opperman* case an automobile was towed to the city impound lot after it had been parked illegally overnight. From

---

[171] 386 US 58, 17 LEd(2d) 730, 87 SCt 788 (1967).

[172] Ramon v. Cupp, 423 F(2d) 248 (9thCir 1970).

[173] State v. Montague, 73 Wash(2d) 381, 438 P(2d) 571 (1968).

[174] South Dakota v. Opperman, 428 US 364, 49 LEd(2d) 1000, 96 SCt 3092 (1976).

outside the car, the police officer observed a watch on the dashboard and some items of personal property located in the back seat. At his direction, the car was unlocked and a standard inventory form was used to inventory the contents. From the glove compartment, which was unlocked, marijuana was seized and used in evidence. After conviction in the lower court, the Supreme Court of South Dakota reversed the conviction, concluding that the evidence had been obtained in violation of the Fourth Amendment as made applicable to the states by the Fourteenth.

The United States Supreme Court reversed the decision of the South Dakota Supreme Court and held that the evidence was properly admitted. In approving this procedure in limited circumstances, the Court first distinguished between automobiles and homes or offices in relation to the Fourth Amendment protections, and then approved the seizure of evidence from an impounded car under the facts of the case. The majority pointed out that the police were indisputably engaged in a caretaker search of the lawfully impounded automobile, and there was no suggestion of investigatory motive on the part of the police. In the concluding paragraph these words were used:

> On this record we conclude that in following standard police procedures, prevailing throughout the country and approved by the overwhelming majority of courts, the conduct of the police was not "unreasonable" under the Fourth Amendment.

Two *caveats* are in order: 1) The *Opperman* decision does not give *carte blanche* authority to search all impounded cars. The decision was limited to the facts of that case. 2) The respective states, under their own constitutional authority, may proscribe additional limitations. The investigator in each state must be familiar with the limitations of that state when those limitations are based on state constitutional provisions rather than on the Fourth Amendment of the Federal Constitution.

Because state courts are not consistent in recognizing or applying the impounded car doctrine, and may add additional restrictions by way of the state constitutions, a review of state decisions is necessary. A few are discussed here as examples.

Some states authorize an inventory search of the entire automobile including the trunk when there has been in fact a legitimate impounding of the car. For example, the New Mexico Court of Appeals approved the inventory search of an automobile in lawful custody, including the items in the trunk as well as items in plain view.[175] On the other hand, the Kentucky Court of Appeals agreed that the officers may close and lock a car and seize whatever is in plain view during the process, but that they may not open compartments or containers within the vehicle.[176]

The Wisconsin Supreme Court, in suppressing evidence obtained after an inventory was made of the impounded car, acknowledged that cases from other jurisdictions are divided on the question of whether making an inventory of the contents of an impounded car is actually a search. But in the view of the majority, the protection of the police from claims of theft and protection of the defendant's property usually does not require an inspection of closed suitcases and containers.[177]

Both the judges and the police must recognize the reason for authorizing the seizure of contraband and illegally possessed property identified during a legitimate inventory. Seizure of such property should be, and is, authorized by the majority of the courts. This is not an extension of any rule but merely an application of the accepted rule that the officers may seize evidence coming to their attention when they are in a position legally to observe it. The police must realize that the impoundment doctrine does not justify a search into all parts of the car, including the hubcaps, or a seizure of what may be inside the upholstered part of the car.

§ 4.16   Stop and frisk seizures

A new chapter was written into the complicated search and seizure law in 1968 when the Supreme Court decided the

[175] State v. Vigil, 86 NM 388, 524 P(2d) 1004 (1974).
[176] City of Danville v. Dawson, 528 SW(2d) 687 (Ky 1975).
[177] State v. McDougal, 68 Wis(2d) 399, 228 NW(2d) 671 (1975).

case of *Terry* v. *Ohio*.[178] For many years there had been doubt as to whether a police officer could stop a suspicious person on the street and ask questions without making a formal arrest. Even more uncertain was the authority to frisk the suspect for weapons. In the *Terry* case, which has been discussed more thoroughly in a previous section, a police officer stopped a suspect on a downtown Cleveland, Ohio street when he observed the suspect and two other men casing a job. Without putting the suspect under arrest, the police officer patted down the outside clothing of the suspect for weapons and later removed a pistol from the suspect's overcoat pocket. After holding that the detention was justified under the circumstances, the Court concluded that the revolver seized from *Terry* was properly admitted into evidence against him. The Court was careful to distinguish this from a search incident to a lawful arrest, explaining:

> Suffice it to note that such a search, unlike a search without a warrant incident to a lawful arrest, is not justified by any need to prevent the disappearance or destruction of evidence of crime. . . . The sole justification of the search in the present situation is the protection of the police officer and others nearby, and it must therefore be confined in scope to an intrusion reasonably designed to discover guns, knives, clubs, or other hidden instruments for the assault of the police officer.

It is emphasized that the frisk authorized in the detention situation is only for the protection of the officer and is limited to a patting down rather than a full-scale search. In a companion case to the *Terry* case,[179] the United States Supreme Court refused to extend the frisk doctrine to a small package of narcotics found by an officer when he patted down the suspect. The Court reasoned that where there is a self-protective search for weapons, the officer must be able to point to particular facts from which he reasonably inferred the individual was armed and dangerous. Also, the patting down

---

[178] 392 US 1, 20 LEd(2d) 889, 88 SCt 1868 (1968). This case is discussed in §3.14 as it relates to the authority to detain without making an arrest.

[179] Sibron v. New York, 392 US 40, 20 LEd(2d) 917, 88 SCt 1889 (1968).

for weapons was distinguished from a patting down for small items such as packages containing narcotics.

As was inevitable, the lower courts have been called upon to further interpret the *Terry* ruling. One of the questions left unanswered by *Terry* was whether an article which did not feel like a knife or a club but could be a dangerous weapon could be seized. A second question was whether the officer, while in the process of seizing a weapon, could seize other articles which were not dangerous. In the case of *People v. Collins*,[180] the California Supreme Court was able to lay down a rule as to one of these questions. In holding that in some instances the officer can pat down the suspect for a "sap" (such as a bag of sand) which could be used as a weapon, the court explained the test thusly:

> Accordingly, we hold that an officer who exceeds a pat-down without first discovering an object which feels reasonably like a knife, gun, or club must be able to point to specific and articulable facts which reasonably support a suspicion that the particular suspect is armed with an atypical weapon which would feel like the object felt during the pat-down.

In that case the court referred the matter back to the lower court, so that the prosecution could meet the burden of pointing to specific and articulable facts to justify the intrusion.

There is some evidence to indicate that if the officer, in good faith, pats down a suspect and discovers some object which feels like a weapon, and in order to protect himself reaches into the suspect's pocket to obtain the weapon, but in addition or instead of a weapon finds other contraband, the use of such contraband would be legitimate.[181] For example, the California Supreme Court[182] held that a watch found by police officers in the pocket of the suspect was admissible where the officers honestly believed that the watch might have been a knife. The majority of the court agreed that the seizure of the watch did not violate the principles of *Terry v. Ohio*.

---

[180] People v. Collins, 1 Cal(3d) 658, 83 CalRptr 179, 463 P(2d) 403 (1970).

[181] People v. Woods, 6 CalApp(3d) 832, 86 CalRptr 264 (1970)

[182] People v. Mosher, 1 Cal(3d) 379, 82 CalRptr 379, 461 P(2d) 659 (1969).

In the landmark *Terry* case the officers observed conduct on the street which justified the stop and the pat down for weapons. There, a pistol was seized. In the later *Adams* case,[183] a gun was seized from the waistband of a suspect while the suspect was sitting in his car. Lower courts have been requested to determine if the stop and frisk rule applies in other specific situations such as stopping automobiles.

The majority members of the Ninth Circuit Court of Appeals agreed that under certain circumstances officers are justified in stopping vehicles even though they do not have probable cause to make an arrest.[184] In the *Untermyer* case, the police officer was patrolling in a residential area in which burglaries had been recently committed. He observed a suspect walk from a darkened home to a foreign car that was parked nearby, enter the passenger side, and drive a short distance before the headlights were turned on. The court concluded that "the unusual circumstances and [defendant's] unusual conduct were such as to lead the local police officer 'reasonably to conclude in light of his experience that criminal activity may be afoot,' " and affirmed the marijuana possession conviction.

Following like reasoning, the Fifth Circuit Court, specifically referring to the *Terry* and *Adams* cases, approved the stopping of a car where an armed robbery victim told police that one of the attackers was wearing a "bush" or jungle hat and further described the attackers, and where the officers saw passengers meeting the descriptions in a car which exceeded the speed limit and failed to stop at an intersection. The court found that even if the officer could not search the occupants of the car following the issuance of a traffic citation, he could frisk these occupants under the "stop and frisk" authority.[185]

But mere curiosity does not equate with reasonable suspicion that criminal activity may be afoot. Not every car may be stopped and the occupants frisked—even at three o'clock in the morning. Thus, where the record disclosed nothing to indicate the officer had any reason to believe there was danger

---

[183] Adams v. Williams, 407 US 143, 32 LEd(2d) 612, 92 SCt 1921 (1972).

[184] Untermyer v. Hellbush, 472 F(2d) 156 (9thCir 1973).

[185] United States v. Edwards, 469 F(2d) 1362 (5thCir 1972).

to anyone's safety when he ordered the occupant of the back seat of a car to get out, and the officer then frisked him, the frisk and seizure of counterfeit bills were illegal.[186]

From the foregoing it can be concluded that in the proper circumstances the officer may frisk a person who has been detained for weapons, such as a gun or knife. If such weapons are found, they may be used in evidence. Although there is little law on the point, it would seem that the officer can seize weapons other than knives if he can articulate his reasons for believing that the particular suspect has small weapons, such as razor blades, in his possession which might be harmful to the officer. Some courts have upheld the use of other evidence found while the officer was searching for weapons.

Although the *Terry* type of seizure of evidence has been approved in many cases, some justices are becoming critical of overzealous police activity.[187] As pointed out in previous paragraphs, the United States Supreme Court's approval of the *Terry* stop and frisk has been very helpful to police officers. Before this case there was much confusion regarding the right of the police to stop without probable cause. If this type of police practice is to continue to receive court approval, the officer must constantly be cautious that he does not overstep the line and use this procedure as a subterfuge for making an illegal search. Obviously, if the detention and frisk are a subterfuge, evidence obtained will be properly excluded.

§ 4.17 Search of pervasively regulated business

With the decision of the Supreme Court in the case of *United States* v. *Biswell*,[188] new doors are open to inspectional searches or, perhaps one could say, old doors are reopened.

In the *Biswell* case a treasury agent, acting under authority of the Gun Control Act of 1968, requested entry into a locked gun storeroom and was admitted after showing the owner the provisions of the section. The Act authorizes entry during business hours into the premises for the purpose of inspecting or examining records and documents required to be kept on

[186] United States v. Johnson, 463 F(2d) 70 (10thCir 1972).
[187] United States v. Thomas, 314 A(2d) 464 (DC 1974).
[188] 406 US 311, 32 LEd(2d) 87, 92 SCt 1593 (1972).

firearms or ammunition stored by the dealer at such premises.

The Circuit Court of Appeals reversed the lower court which allowed the admission in evidence of two sawed-off rifles which the owner was not licensed to possess. The Circuit Court reasoned that the Act was unconstitutional because it authorized warrantless searches of business premises. The Supreme Court, however, reversed the holding of the intermediate court explaining that close scrutiny of the traffic in firearms is justified and that this limited threat to the dealer's expectations of privacy is reasonable. The majority stated:

> When a dealer chooses to engage in this type of pervasively regulated business and to accept a federal license, he does so with the knowledge that his business records, firearms and ammunition will be subject to effective inspection.

This same reasoning apparently applies to licensed dealers in alcoholic beverages.[189]

§ 4.18   Summary and practical suggestions

The events of history make it clear that searches must be restricted if we are to enjoy individual freedom and the right of privacy. On the other hand, the courts have recognized the necessity of seeking out and prosecuting the violators of the laws of the states and the nation. Although the courts have revised and reversed their decisions over a period of time, they do agree in certain instances. In interpreting the Constitution, the courts have established certain rules of procedure that must be followed by police officers. An officer who knows and understands the rules and the reasons for these rules will be more successful in his profession.

In summary, then, the courts have established certain procedural rules, some of which are as follows:

    a. Evidence is generally excluded if the search is illegal.

    b. The preferred method of search is with a valid search

---

[189] Colonnade Catering Corp. v. United States, 397 US 72, 25 LEd(2d) 60, 90 SCt 774 (1970).

warrant. The courts have indicated that preference will be given to searches under a valid search warrant.

c. Some searches are "reasonable" without a warrant. Among these are: (1) A search incidental to a lawful arrest; (2) A search where a legal waiver has been voluntarily given; (3) A search of a moving vehicle or other movable object where exigent circumstances exist; (4) A search made in an area or under circumstances which the courts have found not to be within the scope of the constitutional protection.

d. In some cases evidence may be seized when no search is required. If the officer is legally in a position where contraband or illegally possessed articles are in plain view, these articles may be seized. This sometimes includes seizure of articles from impounded automobiles.

e. In order to challenge the search the party must have standing to suppress, i.e., he must have a substantial possessory interest in the property searched to justify his challenge.

f. As the constitutional prohibitions limit official action, articles seized by private individuals with no official knowledge may be admitted into evidence even if the search is illegal or would violate the Fourth Amendment if carried out by an officer.

g. Under the proper circumstances an officer may stop and frisk a suspect for weapons. Evidence legitimately obtained in this manner is usually admitted into evidence.

Over the years the courts and legislatures have placed many restrictions on the seizure of evidence, whether it be under a search warrant or by way of one of the exceptions. The officer who seizes articles which are to be used in evidence should be so familiar with the specific rules and requirements that he can select and articulate the grounds for making the search at the time he makes it. It is very dangerous to conduct the search and seize articles and then look for a peg to hang the seizure on. Recognizing that the seizure will be challenged, he must be prepared to justify the search and/or seizure when it is challenged in court.

Chapter 5

WIRETAPPING AND EAVESDROPPING*

To safeguard the privacy of innocent persons, the interception of wire or oral communications where none of the parties to the communication has consented to the interception should be allowed only when authorized by a court of competent jurisdiction and should remain under the control and supervision of the authorizing court. Interception of wire and oral communications should further be limited to certain major types of offenses and specific categories of crime with assurances that the interception is justified and that the information obtained thereby will not be misused.

CONGRESSIONAL FINDINGS, OMNIBUS CRIME CONTROL
AND SAFE STREETS ACT OF 1968.

* by John C. Klotter

IV. REPORT OF THE NATIONAL COMMISSION FOR THE REVIEW
OF FEDERAL AND STATE LAWS RELATING TO WIRETAPPING
AND ELECTRONIC SURVEILLANCE

§ 5.1   Introductory remarks

The problems relating to the admissibility of evidence
obtained by way of wiretapping and eavesdropping are of
relatively recent origin when compared to constitutional protections such as that against self-incrimination or the right
to counsel. Decisions and legislation of the last two decades
have so changed the law concerning wiretapping and eavesdropping that the law prior to that time has little more than
historical significance. However, without a study of that history it would be difficult to understand the provisions of the
federal and state statutes and the rationale for the Supreme
Court decisions interpreting the statutes.

In order to interpret the laws relating to wiretapping and
eavesdropping, it is essential that the search and seizure laws
be researched first. Before Congress enacted the 1968 legislation relating to wiretapping and electronic surveillance,[1] the
Supreme Court handed down decisions which mandated specific safeguards. These decisions were based on the Fourth

---

[1] Title III of the Omnibus Crime
Control and Safe Streets Act of 1968,
part of which was codified at 18 USC
ch 119, §§ 2510–2520 and amended in
1970. Hereafter cited as the Crime
Control Act or as 18 USC §———.
See Part II of this book for a complete
reprint of Title III.

Amendment search and seizure provisions and, in effect, require that any legislation be compatible with constitutional safeguards enunciated in all previous search and seizure decisions.

Because the separate laws relating to wiretapping and eavesdropping have developed along different lines, it is necessary to discuss each of them separately. This is so even though the 1968 federal legislation includes provisions concerning both wiretapping and eavesdropping. In order to make this somewhat complicated material more understandable, the chapter is divided into four general categories. After a general discussion concerning the development of electronic listening devices and the ethics concerning law enforcement listening, the division will be as follows: in part I the constitutional history of law enforcement wiretapping is developed; in part II the law and history relating to eavesdropping is discussed; in part III current federal and state statutory laws are explained, and in part IV, a summary of the findings and recommendations of the National Commission for the Review of Federal and State Laws Relating to Wiretapping and Electronic Surveillance are stated and explained.[2]

§ 5.2   Electronic listening devices

To our colonial forefathers, a search and seizure meant an actual physical intrusion into their homes and a ransacking of their private papers and effects by law enforcement officers. Modern invention and technology have produced far more refined and sophisticated techniques for gaining access to information relating to criminal activity. The twentieth century has witnessed the development of electronic listening and surveillance devices which have revolutionized law enforcement. No longer is it necessary for the police to stand under windows or physically enter homes to learn about the activities which transpire inside.

[2] In 1976, the National Commission for the Review of Federal and State Laws Relating to Wiretapping and Electronic Surveillance (hereinafter cited as the Commission) submitted a report of its findings and recommenda- tions, entitled ELECTRONIC SURVEIL- LANCE REPORT, published by the U.S. Government Printing Office. This publication will be referred to as the NWC REPORT.

There have appeared accounts in the newspapers about wireless transmitters, the size of sugar cubes or smaller, which can be disguised as martini olives to pick up and transmit sound by means of their toothpick aerials.[3] Experts in the fields of electronics and acoustics predict that in the near future, systems will be available which utilize ultrasonic and electromagnetic waves capable of penetrating any structural material and monitoring conversations held within.[4]

Despite accounts of sophisticated eavesdropping devices, there is some indication that in practical situations their use is often very limited.[5] Even if the devices are successfully installed, they are often ineffective. The transmission may be inaudible, or too much sound, including background noise, may be transmitted making the conversations difficult to understand. Studies indicate that body recorders are only 75% functional, and transmission by body microphones is often inaudible.[6] The report of the Commission also indicates that range is very often short; the devices cannot be used in heavily built-up areas; and movements of the person wearing the device interfere with transmission.

The extent to which wiretap and other electronic surveillance equipment has been employed by law enforcement agencies in crime detection activity was largely undetermined until 1976. Section 2519, title 18 of the United States Code requires that annual reports be submitted to the Director of the Administrative Office of the United States Courts each year. These reports indicate that 4334 court orders authorizing electronic surveillance were issued for the period 1968 to 1974.[7] Most of these orders were issued in cases involving espionage, kidnapping, extortion, and vice crimes such as gambling and narcotics.

These figures do not, of course, include instances where wiretap or eavesdrop equipment was used to overhear and/or record communications where one party to the communication gave consent. As will be explained later in this chapter, the 1968 legislation, as amended, does not prohibit the use of

[3] Comment, *Eavesdropping and the Constitution,* 50 MINNLREV 378 (1965).
[4] *Id.*

[5] NWC REPORT, p. 43.
[6] *Id.* at 44.
[7] *Id.* at 266 (Table F-1)

electronic surveillance equipment to intercept a wire or oral communication where one party to the communication has given prior consent. Nor does the law require that this type of surveillance be reported to the administrative office of the United States courts.

Because of Title III of the Crime Control Act's prohibition against the manufacture, sale and advertising of devices for other than official use, there has been a noticeable drop in the manufacture and marketing of such devices.[8] The act does not prohibit the sale of surveillance devices to authorized agencies, and sophisticated equipment is available for law enforcement official use.

§ 5.3   Ethics of law enforcement listening

Electronic eavesdropping and surveillance, even when employed for legitimate law enforcement ends, involve a considerable danger to individual privacy and security of the innocent as well as the guilty. There has yet to be invented a listening device that will distinguish between criminals and innocent citizens, or which will tune off during private conversations and pick up only those pertaining to illegal schemes.

The ethics of law enforcement listening in crime detection has received vigorous debate and comment from legislators, judges, professors and those engaged in the daily business of police work. On the side of those who champion individual liberty, these modern investigatory techniques have been likened to the Nazi Gestapo and the Red Police. Mr. Justice Holmes, one of the early leading critics of law enforcement wiretapping on the Supreme Court bench, characterized the practice as a "dirty business" and expressed the opinion that "it is a less evil that some criminals should escape than that the government should play an ignoble part."[9] In the view of Mr. Justice Douglas, the techniques of electronic investigation are more serious and objectionable than the writs of assistance, which came under attack in colonial days, since the victim is never aware that the police are delving into the inti-

[8] *Id.* at 23.
[9] Olmstead v. United States, 277 US   438, 470, 72 LEd 944, 48 SCt 564 (1928) (Holmes, J., dissent).

macies of his private life.[10] Even Mr. Justice Frankfurter, who was one of the staunch "conservatives" on the Court, on occasion found cause for alarm. In one of his dissenting opinions he cautioned that crime detection was becoming a dirty game in which the "dirty business" of criminals is outwitted by the "dirty business" of law officers, and he predicted that the use of electronic short-cuts in crime investigation would breed disrespect for the law, encourage lazy, immoral conduct on the part of the police, and in the long run undermine effective law enforcement in this country.[11]

Proponents of liberal investigatory policies, on the other hand, have stressed the fact that crime in the United States is on the increase, that the security of society is at stake, and that electronic tools of investigation are necessary, perhaps indispensable, weapons in the arsenal of the police. Crime generally takes place in secrecy and behind closed doors. The jet-age criminal is an extremely shrewd, crafty and evasive fellow. Particularly in the areas of organized crime and threats against the national security, detection would be virtually impossible without the gifts of modern science. It would be unrealistic to deprive the police of electronic investigatory apparatus and tie them to eighteenth century methods of crime detection.

In the "findings" of a congressional committee report included in Title III of the 1968 act, this statement is included:

(c) Organized criminals make extensive use of wire and oral communications in their criminal activities. The interception of such communications to obtain evidence of the commission of crimes or to prevent their commission is an indispensable aid to law enforcement and the administration of justice.[12]

In the opinion of many professional police administrators there is no available substitute for wiretapping and electronic listening in combatting crime in metropolitan areas.

Although some judges have indicated that there is a need

[10] Douglas, THE RIGHT OF THE PEOPLE 151 (1958).

[11] On Lee v. United States, 343 US 747, 760–61, 96 LEd 1270, 72 SCt 967 (1952).

[12] PubL 90–351 § 801. This statement was reaffirmed by a majority of the Commission. NWC REPORT, p. 3.

for extra vigilance in the supervision of electronic eavesdropping, the rights protected are those enumerated in the Fourth and Fifth Amendments, and if the safeguards surrounding those rights are carefully honored, there is no constitutional reason why law enforcement personnel should not be authorized to use electronic devices in carrying out their responsibilities.

I. WIRETAPPING HISTORY

§ 5.4   Constitutionality of law enforcement wiretapping

The constitutional legality of wiretapping first reached the Supreme Court in the landmark case of *Olmstead* v. *United States*.[13] The setting of the case was against the background of organized crime in the Prohibition Era. Olmstead was the ringleader of a gigantic, multi-million-dollar conspiracy to violate the National Prohibition Act. The scheme involved more than seventy persons and was spread over several states. For over five months federal agents worked religiously in gathering evidence. The information that led to the discovery of the conspiracy was obtained almost entirely by tapping the telephone wires leading to the homes and offices of some of the key figures involved in the liquor scheme. Olmstead was convicted and appealed to the Supreme Court, contending that the use of wiretap evidence violated his Fifth Amendment right not to be compelled to be a witness against himself, and his Fourth Amendment immunity against unreasonable searches and seizures. By a narrow five to four vote, the Court decided to affirm his conviction. Chief Justice Taft, who delivered the majority opinion, quickly disposed of the Fifth Amendment argument by pointing out that the defendant had not been *compelled* to talk over the telephone. He had done so voluntarily even though unaware that his conversations were being monitored.

Olmstead's Fourth Amendment argument caused considerably more difficulty. Chief Justice Taft reviewed the his-

[13] 277 US 438, 72 LEd 944, 48 SCt 564 (1928).

torical context in which the Fourth Amendment was adopted and its particular phraseology, and concluded that the proscription was limited to searches and seizures of *material* things—the person, his house, his papers, and his effects. Nothing of a tangible or physical nature had been taken here. The evidence procured was obtained purely by the sense of hearing. The officers had not committed a trespass upon any property belonging to the defendant in installing the wiretap apparatus. Olmstead had no proprietary interest in the telephone lines outside his house. In talking over the telephone, he had intended to project his voice outside the confines of the room, and neither the wires themselves nor the messages passing over them were within the protective bounds of the Fourth Amendment. Chief Justice Taft concluded by saying that if Congress disagreed with the wisdom of the decision, it was up to Congress to change the law.

The *Olmstead* decision, though criticized in many circles, was not effectively overruled until a series of cases was handed down in 1967. In *Berger* v. *New York*,[14] the Supreme Court made the following observation with respect to *Olmstead:*

> The basis of the decision was that the Constitution did not forbid the obtaining of evidence by wiretapping unless it involved actual unlawful entry into the house. Statements in the opinion that a conversation passing over a telephone wire cannot be said to come within the Fourth Amendment's enumeration of "persons, houses, papers, and effects" have been negated by our subsequent cases as hereinafter noted. They found "conversation" was within the Fourth Amendment's protection, and that the use of electronic devices to capture it was a "search" within the meaning of the Amendment, and we so hold.

The final blow to *Olmstead* was dealt several months later in *Katz* v. *United States*[15] where the Court stated that the underpinnings of the 1928 ruling had been so eroded by subsequent decisions that the trespass doctrine enunciated in *Olmstead* could no longer be regarded as controlling. *Katz* and *Berger*, taken together, made it clear that telephone conversations were

---

[14] 388 US 41, 18 LEd(2d) 1040, 87 SCt 1873 (1967). See Part II for a reprint of this case.

[15] 389 US 347, 19 LEd(2d) 576, 88 SCt 507 (1967).

entitled to Fourth Amendment protection. It is significant, however, that in neither of these cases did the Supreme Court state without qualification that wiretapping was *absolutely* forbidden under the Constitution. The thrust of both decisions, rather, indicated that wiretapping was akin to the conventional search and might be tolerable if circumscribed by adequate procedural safeguards.

§ 5.5 Early federal legislation concerning wiretapping

The *Olmstead* decision of 1928, holding that wiretapping did not violate the Fourth Amendment, was not accepted gracefully by many congressmen. As a result, legislation was introduced in 1929 and again in 1931 which would have made such wiretapping illegal. This proposed legislation did not receive congressional approval, but six years after the *Olmstead* decision, Congress, under its broad powers to regulate state and foreign commerce, passed the Federal Communications Act of 1934.[16] The primary purpose of the law was to transfer jurisdiction over wire and radio communications to the newly formed Federal Communications Commission, and there is considerable evidence that Congress was not thinking in terms of law enforcement wiretapping at all. However, the bill did pass, and included within it was the following provision:

> [N]o person not being authorized by the sender shall intercept any communication and divulge or publish the existence, contents, substance, purport, effect, or meaning of such intercepted communication to any person. . . .[17]

Section 501 of the same act imposed a fine not exceeding $10,000, or a prison term not exceeding one year, or both, for wilful or knowing violation of section 605.

Although section 605 of the Federal Communications Act of 1934 has now been amended and superseded by Title III of the Omnibus Crime Control and Safe Streets Act of 1968, a discussion of the application of the 1934 act is necessary. Because of the confusion which resulted from this legislation and the

---

[16] Codified at title 47 of the United States Code.   [17] 47 USC § 605 (1964).

interpretation placed upon it, the law relating to wiretapping was, to say the least, perplexing until 1968.

§ 5.6   Exclusion of wiretap evidence in federal courts

Although section 605 of the 1934 Communications Act discussed in the previous section, included no provisions about the exclusion of evidence obtained in violation of this statute, it was given this interpretation in early decisions by the Supreme Court. In the first *Nardone* case,[18] the defendant was convicted in a federal court of smuggling intoxicating liquor, largely on the basis of wiretap evidence overheard by federal agents who had intercepted his telephone messages. On appeal, the defendant contended that in view of section 605, transcripts of the intercepted telephone communications should not have been admitted into evidence. The government, on the other hand, argued that section 605 did not apply to investigatory tapping by federal law enforcement officers, and that, in any event, exclusion of evidence was not the appropriate remedy to enforce the statute.

Giving the 1934 enactment its first judicial construction, the Supreme Court held that the plain meaning of the statutory language, "no person," included federal agents and prohibited them from engaging in precisely the type of conduct which had led to the conviction in this case. Testimony in court as to the content of the intercepted communication was a "divulgence" within the meaning of section 605. The Court continued by saying that to allow testimony in the face of the statutory prohibition would be to sanction the commission of a federal crime in a federal court of law.

Although the Supreme Court applied the exclusionary rule to wiretap evidence and, by way of the *Nardone* decision, excluded wiretap evidence in federal criminal prosecutions, it did not overrule the *Olmstead* decision. In *Nardone*, the Supreme Court held the evidence inadmissible, not because the conduct of the officers violated the Fourth Amendment, but because the conduct violated a *federal statute*.

---

[18] Nardone v. United States, 302 US 379, 82 LEd 314, 58 SCt 275 (1937).

A series of Court decisions following the first *Nardone* decision further expanded the wiretap exclusionary rule. The lesson that the federal government agents learned in the first *Nardone* decision was that they could not make direct use of evidence obtained by illegal wiretapping. At the second trial of Nardone,[19] the direct wiretap evidence was not used, but evidence procured *indirectly* through knowledge gained by means of the forbidden interceptions played a vital role in the government's case. On the second appeal the Supreme Court again reversed, holding that the exclusionary rule goes beyond merely prohibiting the reception in court of testimony concerning the exact words resulting from the tap. To remove all incentive to violate the statute, leads and other "derivative" evidence which became accessible as a result of illegal interceptions could not be used to obtain a federal conviction.

Another decision in 1939 further restricted the use of wiretap evidence by providing that even if the telephone wires are all in one state the federal law is applicable and evidence is not admissible in federal court.[20] And in 1950, in the well-known *Coplon* case,[21] the rule was extended even further. In this case Judith Coplon, a government employee, was tried for turning over documents to a foreign agent. Reversing the conviction, the Court wrote a new rule into the law. This provided that the burden of proof is on the defendant to show that wiretapping is used, but then the burden shifts to the prosecution to show that wiretapping did not *lead* to evidence used in court. Stated differently, the case held that if the defense can show that wiretapping has been used, the prosecution must show that the evidence to be introduced by the government was not obtained by wiretapping, but by other means.

It can be concluded that although the federal statutes prior to 1968 did not specifically prohibit the use of wiretap evidence, the federal courts made it clear that such evidence, obtained in violation of section 605 of the Federal Communications Act, was not admissible in federal cases. This applied not only to the tapes themselves but to "derivative" evidence, or evidence

[19] Nardone v. United States, 308 US 338, 84 LEd 307, 60 SCt 266 (1939).
[20] Weiss v. United States, 308 US 321, 84 LEd 298, 60 SCt 269 (1939).
[21] United States v. Coplon, 185 F(2d) 629 (2dCir 1950).

obtained as a result of the wiretap. In addition, a federal officer who violated section 605 could be prosecuted for such violation.

§ 5.7   Exclusion of wiretap evidence in state courts

As was indicated in the previous section, the law was quite clear that evidence obtained in violation of section 605 of the Federal Communications Act was not admissible in federal court. However, the law as to the admissibility of evidence in state court was far from clear. Had the Supreme Court of the United States made the wiretap exclusionary rule applicable to the states, such confusion would not have existed. In the case of *Schwartz v. Texas*,[22] the Supreme Court was called upon to determine whether wiretapping by state and local officers came within the proscription of the federal statute, and if so, whether section 605 required the same remedies for its vindication in state courts. In answer to the first question, the Court flatly stated that section 605 made it a federal crime for *anyone* to intercept telephone messages and divulge what he learned. The Court went on to say that a state officer who testified in state court concerning the existence, contents, substance, purport, effect or meaning of an intercepted conversation violated the federal law and committed a criminal act. In regard to the second question, however, the Supreme Court felt constrained by due regard for federal-state relations, and answered in the negative. Mr. Justice Minton, who delivered the majority opinion, stated that the Court would not presume Congress intended to supersede state rules of evidence in the absence of a very clear manifestation of congressional intent.

Because the Supreme Court refused to apply the exclusionary rule to wiretap evidence that was being used in state courts, the states respectively had to make this decision for themselves. As could have been anticipated, there was little uniformity in the resulting rules. Not only did the state statutes differ, but the court decisions in the states differed in interpretation of the statutes. According to hearings held before a congressional committee in 1961, six states authorized wiretapping by stat-

[22] 344 US 199, 97 LEd 231, 73 SCt 232 (1952).

ute, 33 states imposed total bans on wiretapping, and 11 states had no definite statute on the subject. To devote the space necessary to discuss each statute would not be justified. For examples of extremes, however, a statute in Pennsylvania will be compared with a statute in New York.

The Pennsylvania statute provided that no communications by telephone or telegraph could be intercepted without permission of both parties.[23] It also specifically prohibited such interception by public officials and provided that evidence obtained could not be used in court.

The lawmakers in New York, recognizing the need for legal wiretapping, authorized wiretapping and eavesdropping by statute. Even prior to the 1968 federal law authorizing certain wiretapping, a New York law authorized the issuance of an *ex parte* order upon oath or affirmation for limited wiretapping.[24] The statute required that the order must specify the duration of the wiretap and must identify the particular telephone number before the message could be intercepted. The aim of the New York law was to allow court-ordered wiretapping and eavesdropping but to have safeguards similar to those required in search and seizure situations. The New York law was found to be constitutional by the New York State Supreme Court in 1962.[25] Other states, including Oregon, Maryland, Nevada and Massachusetts enacted similar laws which authorized court-ordered wiretapping.

To add to this legal disarray, the vast majority of the states permitted wiretapping evidence to be received in court even though obtained in violation of the state laws and of section 605 of the Federal Communications Act.[26] However, some states, such as Rhode Island, enacted statutory exclusionary rules which provided that illegally procured wiretap evidence was incompetent in civil as well as criminal actions.[27] It is under-

---

[23] Former PaStatAnn tit.18, § 3742 (1957); see now tit. 18 §§ 5701–5705 (Supp 1976).

[24] Former NYCCrimP § 813-a (1942); see now NYCrimPL §§ 700.05–700.70 (1971).

[25] People v. Dinan, 11 NY(2d) 350, 183 NE(2d) 689 (1962).

[26] *E.g.*, see Griffith v. State, 111 S(2d) 282 (Fla 1959); Application for Order Permitting Interception, 207 NY Misc 69, 136 NYS(2d) 612 (1955).

[27] RIGenLawsAnn § 11-35-13 (1949); see now §§ 11-35-21 – 11-35-24 (Supp 1976).

standable that the law enforcement officer could be confused.

As late as 1961, the United States Supreme Court refused to make the wiretapping exclusionary rule applicable to states. In the case of *Pugach* v. *Dollinger*,[28] the defendant was indicted in New York for burglary, assault and conspiracy. About two weeks before the trial was to be held in state court, Pugach brought suit in a federal district court to enjoin state officers from using evidence obtained by wiretapping. The lower federal court refused to enjoin the use of the evidence, and the case finally got to the Supreme Court. The United States Supreme Court compared the case with the *Wolf* v. *Colorado*[29] case and expressed the view that the federal court should not interfere in the prosecution of the state criminal proceeding where the only purpose was to provide an additional means of vindicating any privacy rights created by section 605.

It is difficult to summarize the law concerning the use of wiretap evidence in state courts prior to the case of *Berger* v. *New York*[30] in 1967. Briefly, the situation was this: in some states wiretapping was prohibited, and the use of such evidence in court was prohibited by statute; in some states wiretapping was prohibited, but evidence obtained thereby was admissible in state courts; and in a third group of states, wiretapping was authorized by statute when procedural safeguards were complied with. If the state court authorized the use of wiretap evidence, the United States Supreme Court would not reverse the decision.

To the enforcement officer the situation was frustrating. The police officer who used a wiretap and testified in court concerning its use, even though it was authorized by state law, was subject to prosecution for violation of the 1934 Federal Communications Act.[31] If he denied in court the use of the wiretap, he was subject to prosecution for perjury. If he refused to answer on self-incrimination grounds, his testimony would lose its value.

By way of the decisions in *Berger* and *Katz* v. *United*

---

[28] 365 US 458, 5 LEd(2d) 678, 81 SCt 650 (1961).

[29] 338 US 25, 93 LEd 1782, 69 SCt 1359 (1949).

[30] 388 US 41, 18 LEd(2d) 1040, 87 SCt 1873 (1967).

[31] Benanti v. United States, 355 US 96, 2 LEd(2d) 126, 78 SCt 155 (1957).

States,[32] the Supreme Court made it clear that its past decisions holding that wiretapping was not within the purview of the Fourth Amendment were no longer applicable. In the *Berger* case the Court pointed out in detail the shortcomings of the New York statute authorizing wiretapping and eavesdropping. The Court made it abundantly clear that the Fourth Amendment protected houses, papers and effects against unreasonable searches and seizures, and that this included telephonic communications. In the *Katz* case the same Court emphasized that the Fourth Amendment governs not only the seizure of tangible items but extends as well to the recording of oral statements. Therefore, any state statute which authorizes the use of wiretap evidence must be so drafted as to comply with all of the requirements of the Fourth Amendment as interpreted by the Supreme Court of the United States.

II. EAVESDROPPING HISTORY

§ 5.8 Eavesdropping in general

The law relating to eavesdropping developed along much different lines than that relating to wiretapping. While the wiretapping law is an outgrowth of the twentieth century development of electronic listening and surveillance devices, eavesdropping is as old as man himself. In fact, eavesdropping was a common-law crime, the essence of which consisted of listening under walls, windows, or eaves in order to vex or annoy another by spreading slanderous rumors against him.[33] The eavesdropper was that unsavory character who snooped around under eaves to satisfy his prurient interest in gossip. Modern science has provided him with more dignified and sensitive tools for plying his trade. By means of parabolic microphones, wireless radio transmitters and other electronic listening equipment, private conversations can be picked up and monitored miles away from where they are spoken.

Whereas wiretapping limitations were based primarily on statutory provisions following the enactment of section 605 of

---

[32] 389 US 347, 19 LEd(2d) 576, 88 SCt 507 (1967).

[33] 4 Blackstone, COMMENTARIES ch 13, § 5.

the Federal Communications Act of 1934, in eavesdropping the protection has grown up primarily around an expanding interpretation of the Fourth Amendment. There was no federal law prohibiting eavesdropping, such as the 1934 act which prohibited wiretapping.

The state and federal court decisions relating to eavesdropping handed down during the past forty years have not only established rules concerning law enforcement "bugging" but have provided guidelines for recent legislation. Therefore, a brief discussion of those cases is essential if the legislation is to be understood.

§ 5.9 Eavesdropping and the Fourth Amendment

As was explained in Chapter Four, evidence obtained by an illegal search and seizure in violation of the Fourth Amendment has been excluded in federal courts since 1914. The question relating to eavesdropping is whether the overhearing of conversations by way of a listening device, or "bug," planted in a house or office is within the purview of the Fourth Amendment protection.

The constitutional foundation of the modern law of eavesdropping was laid down by the Supreme Court in the classic *Olmstead* decision of 1928.[34] Although this case related to a wiretap, the reasoning of the case was applied in the later case of *Goldman* v. *United States*,[35] in which the Supreme Court extended the reasoning beyond the traditional wiretap situation. In the *Goldman* case, investigators were able to pick up the entire conversation which took place in an adjoining office by means of a sensitive detectaphone held against a partition wall. Transcripts of the conversation were admitted in evidence over the defendant's objection that the receipt violated the Fourth Amendment. The Court reasoned that since there was no physical trespassory entry by the police into the defendant's home or office, there was no Fourth Amendment invasion. If the listening had been accomplished as a direct result of a Fourth Amendment intrusion, the bounds of permissible law

---

[34] Olmstead v. United States, 277 US 438, 72 LEd 944, 48 SCt 564 (1928).

[35] 316 US 129, 86 LEd 1322, 62 SCt 993 (1942).

enforcement eavesdropping would have been transgressed, and the exclusionary rule would have come into operation.

Goldman stood for the proposition that there is no inherent constitutional defect in surreptitious law enforcement eavesdropping as such. According to that holding, the listening becomes objectionable only when the police commit a physical trespass onto a constitutionally protected area while installing or using an eavesdropping device.

The line of demarcation between permissible investigation and invasion of a constitutional right was a thin one under the interpretation in *Goldman*. This thin line was defined in the case of *Silverman v. United States*,[36] where the Court held that the constitutionally protected area had been invaded. In that case, law enforcement agents, suspecting that the defendant had been operating a gambling establishment, inserted a microphone with a foot-long spike into a common wall until the spike made contact with a heating duct in the premises occupied by the defendant. Here the spike mike actually penetrated the wall of the defendant's office. The Court held that this was a physical trespass into the constitutionally protected area and, therefore, distinguishable from the *Goldman* situation.

With the abandonment of the trespass concept in the later *Katz* case,[37] the spike mike cases have only historical significance. In *Katz*, FBI agents established through observation that there were grounds to believe that the defendant was using a certain public telephone to transmit gambling information interstate. They attached an electronic listening and recording device to the outside of the booth from which he habitually placed his calls. Since the surveillance technique employed involved no physical penetration of the telephone booth, and since the device recorded only one side of the telephone conversation, it was argued by the government that there was no violation of the Fourth Amendment nor of section 605 of the Communications Act. The government's position was buttressed by a previous lower court decision that such use of electronic bugging was not prohibited by the Fourth Amendment.[38]

[36] 365 US 505, 5 LEd(2d) 734, 81 SCt 679 (1961).

[37] Katz v. United States, 389 US 347, 19 LEd(2d) 576, 88 SCt 507 (1967).

[38] United States v. Borgese, 235 FSupp 286 (1964).

Although the government urged that its agents relied upon the decisions in *Olmstead* and *Goldman* and argued that there was no technical trespass such as was condemned in the *Silverman* case, the Supreme Court refused to heed the arguments. In rejecting the old physical trespass distinction, the Court held in *Katz:*

> We conclude that the underpinnings of *Olmstead* and *Goldman* have been so eroded by our subsequent decisions that the "trespass" doctrine there enunciated can no longer be regarded as controlling.

Since the decision in the *Katz* case, there is no question but that the Supreme Court considers eavesdropping by electronic devices, or bugging, to fall within the ambit of the Fourth Amendment. Therefore, all of the safeguards which apply when the seizure is of tangible goods will apply when the seizure is of verbal evidence.

§ 5.10 Eavesdropping and state law

Some of the states recognized the need for law enforcement surveillance prior to the time it was recognized by Congress. These states also acknowledged that something had to be done to make clear the circumstances where electronic surveillance could be utilized. Several jurisdictions, notably Massachusetts, Nevada and New York experimented with the feasibility of bringing eavesdropping under judicial supervision through a system of court orders.[39]

One such law was included in the former New York Code of Criminal Procedure.[40] It authorized certain judges to issue an *ex parte* order for eavesdropping upon oath or affirmation of a district attorney, the attorney general or an officer above the rank of sergeant, stating that there is reasonable ground to believe that evidence of crime may thus be obtained. One requirement was that the order particularly describe the person or persons whose communications, conversations or discussions were to be overheard or recorded along with the purpose thereof. Although the New York effort was hailed by many as

[39] MassGenLawsAnn ch 272, § 99 (1959).

    NevRevStat § 200.650 (1957).

    NYPenalL §§ 738–745 (1957).

[40] Former NYCCrimP § 813-a (1942).

the solution to the current eavesdropping dilemma, the majority of the Supreme Court did not agree.

In the case of *Berger v. New York*,[41] the New York law was challenged as being in conflict with the protections of the Fourth Amendment. In that case, Berger, the petitioner, was convicted on two counts of conspiracy to bribe the chairman of the New York State Liquor Authority. Much of the evidence was obtained by way of recording devices installed in offices of the conspirators. This eavesdropping, or bugging, was performed pursuant to an order obtained from the Justice of the New York Supreme Court as provided by state law. After making it clear that the conversations overheard came within the protection of the Fourth Amendment, the United States Supreme Court found several fatal defects in the law as applied.

Specifically, the Court's objections were: (1) The statutory provisions respecting the showing of probable cause for the issuance of the order lacked the necessary Fourth Amendment safeguards in not requiring an allegation of the particular crime for which the investigation was conducted and a description of the particular conversation sought; (2) the duration of the order, two months, did not comply with the requirements of prompt execution; (3) no mandatory termination date was placed on the eavesdropping order; and (4) the statute did not contain the requirement that notice be given to the suspect before execution, nor was the omission cured by a showing of special facts or exigent circumstances. The Court did not say in the *Berger* case that state statutes could not be enacted authorizing eavesdropping, but it did imply that such statutes must provide safeguards that are required by the Fourth Amendment.

To confuse matters further, some states had no legislation concerning eavesdropping, while other states imposed a total ban on the practice. One such state was Illinois. In that state, as in some others, an eavesdropper is defined as:

> [A]ny person, including law enforcement officers, who operates or participates in the operation of any eavesdropping device. . . .[42]

---

[41] 388 US 41, 18 LEd(2d) 1040, 87 SCt 1873 (1967).

[42] ILLREVSTAT ch 38, § 141-1(b) (1975).

Under these statutes, eavesdropping is not authorized even though it meets the constitutional requirements as stated in the *Berger* and *Katz* decisions.

From the foregoing discussion, it is evident that the states may by statute enact legislation which provides more stringent safeguards than that required by federal laws or federal court decisions. On the other hand, state legislation concerning eavesdropping which does *not* provide for the constitutional safeguards as interpreted by the Supreme Court will be declared unconstitutional, and evidence obtained thereunder will be inadmissible in court.

§ 5.11   Informers with concealed transmitters

Prior to and following the *Katz* and *Berger* cases, enforcement officers used recorders and small microphones to overhear and record conversations between officers and suspects or between informers and suspects. This procedure has been challenged repeatedly, but it has been uniformly upheld. Several cases are discussed in order for the reader to have a better understanding of the law as it applies in different situations.

In an early case in 1952, the United States Supreme Court set out the rationale which served as a guide for the important cases that followed. In *On Lee v. United States*,[43] a Narcotics Bureau undercover agent wearing a small microphone and an antenna concealed in his overcoat entered the laundry of an old acquaintance. Unknown to the suspect, a second narcotics agent was stationed outside with a radio receiver set tuned in to that conversation. At the trial, the second agent was permitted to testify as to matters overheard. This procedure was challenged on the ground that it was an illegal search and seizure in violation of the Fourth Amendment. The United States Supreme Court rejected this argument. The rationale for admitting the evidence was that since the agent with the transmitter had entered the place of business with the consent, if not the implied invitation, of the petitioner, the petitioner could not complain when the agent arranged for transmission of the conversation

[43] 343 US 747, 96 LEd 1270, 72 SCt 967 (1952).

he could have related personally. The fact that the transmitter was concealed did not bring the situation within the ban of the Fourth Amendment.

In the 1963 case of *Lopez* v. *United States*,[44] the Supreme Court reconsidered its holding in *On Lee*. The facts of the *Lopez* case were similar to those in *On Lee* except that only one officer was involved, and the conversation was taped rather than transmitted by way of a microphone. An Internal Revenue agent who had been offered a bribe was instructed by his superior officers to "play along." Outfitted with a miniature tape recorder, the agent went to the defendant's office and obtained incriminating evidence which was subsequently used to convict the defendant. On appeal, the United States Supreme Court affirmed the conviction, explaining that the petitioner took the risk that the officer would accurately reproduce the comments in court, whether by a faultless memory or mechanical recording.

Many similar decisions were handed down by the United States Supreme Court and lower courts prior to the 1968 wiretapping and electronic surveillance statutes. In 1966, the United States Supreme Court upheld the use of recordings of conversations between a police officer and a Mr. Osborn, one of James Hoffa's attorneys.[45] In this case, two federal district court judges had authorized the Federal Bureau of Investigation to conceal a recorder on the local police officer's person in order to get evidence concerning an attempt to bribe a member of the jury panel in the James Hoffa trial.

And in 1968, the United States Court of Appeals for the Tenth Circuit approved the recording of an airport conversation between the suspect and an informer who had a transmitter hidden in his clothing.[46] Relying heavily on Mr. Justice White's concurring opinion in the *Katz* case, the majority of the judges reasoned that to allow a person to record a conversation between himself and another does not violate any

---

[44] 373 US 427, 10 LEd(2d) 462 83 SCt 1381 (1963).

[45] Osborn v. United States, 385 US 323, 17 LEd(2d) 394, 87 SCt 429 (1966).

[46] Holt v. United States, 404 F(2d) 914 (10thCir 1968).

Fourth Amendment protection.[47] Decisions similar to these were handed down by the United States Court of Appeals for the Fifth Circuit in *Dancy* v. *United States* [48] and by the Washington Supreme Court in *State* v. *Wright*.[49]

Following the passage of the 1968 Crime Control Act, the constitutionality of using information obtained from an informant who had a concealed transmitter on his person when talking with the suspect was again challenged.[50] In the *White* case the suspect was convicted of narcotic law violations. At the trial, evidence of incriminating statements made by the defendant and recorded by government agents was admitted. A government informant had consented to have a transmitter fixed to his person prior to talking with the defendant. One agent had the informant's consent to be in the kitchen closet where he heard the conversation. A second agent recorded the conversation from outside the house by means of a radio receiver. Although the prosecution was unable to locate and produce the informant at the trial, the trial court accepted testimony of the two agents. The defendant was found guilty in the lower court, but the Circuit Court of Appeals held that the testimony of the agents was impermissible under the Fourth Amendment and reversed the conviction.

Mr. Justice White wrote the majority opinion for the United

[47] See Katz v. United States, 389 US 347, 19 LEd(2d) 576, 88 SCt 507, in which Mr. Justice White added a footnote to his concurring opinion stating: "In previous cases, which are undisturbed by today's decision, the court has upheld as reasonable under the Fourth Amendment, admission at trial of evidence obtained (1) by an undercover police agent to whom a defendant speaks without knowledge that he is in the employ of the police, Hoffa v. United States, 385 US 293; (2) by a recording device hidden on the person of such informant, Lopez v. United States, 373 US 427; and (3) by a policeman listening to the secret micro-wave transmissions of an agent conversing with the defendant in another location, On Lee v. United

States, 343 US 747. When one man speaks to another he takes all of the risks ordinarily inherent in so doing, including the risk that the man to whom he speaks will make public what he has heard. . . . It is but a logical and reasonable extension of this principle that a man takes the risk that his hearer, free to memorize what he hears for later verbatim repetitions, is instead recording it or transmitting it to another."

[48] 390 F(2d) 370 (5th Cir 1968).

[49] 74 Wash(2d) 355, 444 P(2d) 676 (1968).

[50] United States v. White, 401 US 745, 28 LEd(2d) 453, 91 SCt 1122 (1971). See Part II for portions of this case.

States Supreme Court which concluded that this procedure did not violate the Fourth Amendment, reversing the Court of Appeals. The Court again explained the reasoning for such a holding, stating:

> For constitutional purposes, no different result is required if the agent, instead of immediately reporting and transcribing his conversation with the defendant, either (1) simultaneously records them with electronic equipment which he is carrying on his person, . . . (2) or carries radio equipment which simultaneously transmits the conversations either to recording equipment located elsewhere or to other agents monitoring the transmitting frequency.

The Court also held that for constitutional purposes it makes no difference if the informer is unavailable for trial. This may raise evidentiary problems or pose issues of prosecutorial misconduct but does not present Fourth Amendment issues.

From the foregoing cases it is safe to state that there is no federal constitutional objection to the use of electronically recorded or transmitted conversations with others, whether accomplished by a police agent or a paid informant, if one party to the conversation is aware of and agrees to the recording. Nor does this practice violate the terms of Title III of the 1968 Crime Control Act. This practice is nothing more than recording what the hearer could memorize for later verbatim repetition.

But, even if the use of electronic surveillance equipment is permitted under the federal law, a state statute or constitutional provision may prohibit this use. For example, a majority of the Michigan Supreme Court held that the warrantless police monitoring of conversations between the defendant and an informer, by way of a radio transmitter concealed on the informer's person, violated the *state's* constitutional prohibition against unreasonable searches and seizures.[51] That state court acknowledged that while the United States Supreme Court found no Fourth Amendment prohibition against similar conduct in the *White* case, it placed a more restrictive interpretation on this practice under the Michigan Constitution.

[51] People v. Beavers, 393 Mich 554, 227 NW(2d) 511 (1975).

III. LEGISLATION AND COURT DECISIONS RELATING TO INTERCEPTION OF WIRE OR ORAL COMMUNICATIONS

§ 5.12 Events leading up to the 1968 wiretapping and electronic surveillance statutes

Soon after *Olmstead* v. *United States* [52] where the Supreme Court decided that wiretapping did not violate the provisions of the Fourth Amendment, efforts were made to enact legislation on a national level to regulate wiretapping. Such legislation was introduced in 1929 and 1931 and finally became a part of the Federal Communications Act in 1934.[53] From the beginning the 1934 act resulted in legal chaos. Much of the confusion was caused by the fact that the act did not have a provision which specifically excluded evidence obtained in violation of the statute and the fact that the act did not specifically apply to enforcement officers. Further confusion was brought about when the Supreme Court decided that evidence obtained in violation of the act would be inadmissible in federal courts but not state courts.

Because of a series of state cases, the rules regarding wiretapping and the use of wiretap evidence varied from state to state. And evidence which could be admitted in some states could not be admitted in federal courts. In order to clarify the rules concerning the use of wiretap and eavesdrop evidence, several states enacted legislation which authorized wiretapping and eavesdropping under court order. However, the Supreme Court in the *Berger* case decided that the New York statute was too broad, resulting in a trespassory intrusion into constitutionally protected areas and, therefore, in violation of the Fourth and Fourteenth Amendments. The Court, however, after pointing out in what respects the Fourth Amendment was infringed, implied that a statute could be drawn to meet the Fourth Amendment requirements.

It was evident that the only solution was for Congress to enact a comprehensive law designed to regulate wiretapping and eavesdropping on a uniform nationwide basis. In drafting

[52] 277 US 438, 72 LEd 944, 48 SCt 564 (1928).   [53] Review § 5.5, *supra*.

this legislation it was necessary to incorporate all of the safeguards referred to in the Supreme Court decisions. For that reason the law is replete with requirements which are designed to make it constitutionally sound.

The various sections of Title III of the 1968 Crime Control Act are discussed in detail in following sections. Briefly, it was anticipated that the following purposes would be accomplished by the Act: [54]

a. Prohibit nonconsensual private wiretapping and bugging (with some exceptions).

b. Permit private intercepts with the consent of one party to the conversation if not done to commit a tort or crime and not prohibited by state law.

c. Permit interceptions by communications common carriers (including firms which conduct major portions of their business by telephone) if necessarily incident to the rendition of services or the protection of rights or property of the communications common carrier.

d. Set up a federal court order system for wiretapping or bugging to obtain evidence of specified offenses.

e. Set similar standards for an optional state court order system for wiretapping or bugging.

f. Prohibit federal nonconsensual law enforcement wiretapping and bugging except under court order.

g. Prohibit state nonconsensual law enforcement wiretapping and bugging unless authorized under a state statute providing a court order system at least as restrictive as the federal system.

h. Permit federal law enforcement intercepts with the consent of one party to the conversation.

i. Permit state law enforcement intercepts with the consent of one party to the conversation unless prohibited by state law.

j. Expressly disclaim any intent to regulate federal wiretap or bugging in security cases.

k. Authorize recovery of civil damages for unauthorized wiretapping or bugging.

l. Require annual reports for federal and state court ordered wiretapping and bugging.

[54] NWC REPORT, p. 40.

It is significant that the 1968 law does not confer an absolute right to privacy from wiretapping and eavesdropping. Implicit in the command of the Fourth Amendment, according to the courts, is a recognition that the individual citizen's rights are subject to limited curtailment in carefully scrutinized situations. Basically, what the law does is to extend the conventional warrant system to electronic investigations. Because of the unique method of seizing evidence, however, it was necessary that Congress spell out the procedure to be followed in obtaining a wiretapping or eavesdropping order.

§ 5.13   Interception of wire or oral communications

The Omnibus Crime Control and Safe Streets Act of 1968, 18 U.S.C. §§ 2510–2520, generally prohibits interception of wire or oral communications, but makes reference to exceptions which are covered in other provisions of the law. Section 2511 provides for a fine of $10,000 or five years imprisonment, or both, for anyone who

> willfully intercepts, endeavors to intercept, or procures another person to intercept or endeavor to intercept a wire or oral communication; (b) willfully uses, endeavors to use, or procures any other person to use or endeavor to use any electronic, mechanical, or other device to intercept certain oral communications; (c) willfully discloses, or endeavors to disclose, to any other person the contents of any wire or oral communication, knowing or having reason to know that the information was obtained through the interception of a wire or oral communication in violation of this subsection, or (d) willfully uses, or endeavors to use, the contents of any wire or oral communication, knowing or having reason to know that the information was obtained through the interception of a wire or oral communication in violation of this subsection.

In effect, this section prohibits interception of wire or oral communications other than in compliance with detailed statutory procedure as well as disclosure of the contents of such communications when known to be illegally obtained. Interception is defined as "the aural acquisition of the contents of any wire or oral communication through the use of any electronic, mechanical, or other device." [55] Section 2511 covers not

---

[55] 18 USC § 2510(4) (1970).

only wiretapping but also eavesdropping, and reaches both federal and state investigations.

After stating that the interception of wire and oral communications is generally prohibited, the law makes certain specific exceptions. Recognizing the practical need to intercept wire and oral communications, Congress provided for exceptions for (a) employees of communications common carriers, (b) employees of the Federal Communications Commission, (c) law enforcement officers with prior consent of one party, and (d) private persons with prior consent of one party. In each of these exceptions, however, there are limitations on the authority granted.

The provision which is of extreme importance to police officers is subsection (2) (c), providing:

> (c) It shall *not* be unlawful under this chapter for a person acting under color of law to intercept a wire or oral communication, where such person is a party to the communication or one of the parties to the communication has given prior consent to such interception. [Emphasis added.] [56]

This clear statement of the authority for law enforcement officers to intercept wiretap or oral communications where one party to the communication consents makes it possible for the officer to act with more confidence. In intercepting communications with the consent of one party, it is not necessary that a judge approve the interception.

The third subsection of section 2511 provides that the prohibition stated in the first section does not apply in certain national defense situations. This gives the President the authority to intercept wire or oral communications in order to obtain foreign intelligence which would protect the nation against actual or potential attack. Such interception is authorized without the prior authority of a judicial officer .

The exception authorizing law enforcement officers to intercept wire or oral communications when one party consents has been upheld by the Supreme Court. [57] In the *White* case the

---

[56] 18 USC § 2511(2)(c) (1970).   745, 28 LEd(2d) 453, 91 SCt 1122
[57] United States v. White, 401 US   (1971).

point was made that Title III of the Crime Control Act appears to reflect little more than the Court's prior decisions.

However, the scope of the third subsection [58] which authorizes the President to intercept communications to obtain foreign intelligence has been limited by court decisions. Mr. Justice Powell, speaking for the majority of the United States Supreme Court in the case of the *United States* v. *United States District Court*,[59] concluded that the law does not give the government any more authority than it had before its enactment, and that the President's *domestic* security role must be exercised in a manner compatible with the Fourth Amendment. Therefore, the law does not authorize electronic surveillance in domestic security cases without compliance with the other provisions of the wiretapping legislation.

§ 5.14   Manufacture, distribution, possession and advertising of wire or oral communication interception devices

As a means of preventing violations of the law, 18 U.S.C. § 2512 provides for a maximum fine of $10,000 or imprisonment of not more than five years, or both, to any person who manufactures, assembles, possesses, sells or advertises for sale any device, knowing or having reason to know that the design of such device renders it primarily useful for the purpose of surreptitious interception of wire or oral communications. This provision is only effective, however, if the manufacturer, assembler, possessor or seller knows or has reason to know that such device will be sent through the mail or transported in interstate or foreign commerce.[60]

A necessary exception is included in this section which authorizes manufacture, assembly, or sale of such devices where they are for lawful use to agents or employees of the United States, a state, or a political subdivision thereof.

---

[58] 18 USC § 2511(3) (1970).

[59] 407 US 297, 32 LEd(2d) 752, 92 SCt 2125 (1972).

[60] The Commission concluded that "Title III's prohibition against the manufacture, sale, and advertising, etc., of devices primarily useful for surreptitious electronic surveillance has resulted in a notable drop in the manufacture and marketing of such devices." NWC REPORT, p. 23.

§ 5.15   Confiscation of wire or oral communication interception devices

To make it more unprofitable to violate the law, section 2513 provides for the confiscation by the government of electronic, mechanical, or other devices used, sent, carried, manufactured, assembled, possessed, sold or advertised in violation of the law. This section provides that such confiscation shall be by such officers, agents or other persons as authorized or designated by the Attorney General.

§ 5.16   Immunity of witnesses

Section 2514 provided that a court at the request of a United States Attorney and with the approval of the Attorney General could give immunity to persons testifying concerning violations enumerated in section 2516. When such immunity was given, under the provisions of law the judge could then require the person to testify and hold him in contempt of court for failure to comply with this order. This section was held to be constitutional.[61]

In 1970, however, Congress saw fit to repeal this section of the statute, the effective date of the repeal to be four years following the 60th. day after the date of enactment (Oct. 15, 1970). The repeal did not affect any immunity to which any individual was entitled under the section by reason of any statement or other information given before such date. The subject matter concerning the immunity of witnesses is now covered under 18 U.S.C. §§ 6002 and 6003.

§ 5.17   Prohibition of use of evidence of intercepted wire or oral communications

The failure of Congress to specify in previous legislation that evidence obtained in violation of the law would be inadmissible in court led to untold confusion. As the drafters of Title III of the Crime Control Act were familiar with this confusion, they included a provision which prohibits the use

---

[61] In re Dec., 1968 Grand Jury v. United States, 420 F(2d) 1201 (7thCir 1970).

of direct evidence or derivative evidence if the provisions of the act are violated. Specifically, the law states:

Whenever any wire or oral communication has been intercepted, no part of the contents of such communication and no evidence derived therefrom may be received in evidence in any trial, hearing, or other proceeding in or before any court, grand jury, department, officer, agency, regulatory body, legislative committee, or other authority of the United States, a State, or a political subdivision thereof if the disclosure of that information would be in violation of this chapter.[62]

This makes it clear that no evidence obtained directly or indirectly as a result of an intercepted wire or oral communication in violation of the provisions of the chapter may be used in any proceeding in any court or hearing. This applies to evidence obtained by federal, state or local officers and in federal, state and local courts.

This exclusionary remedy enacted by Title III exceeds Fourth Amendment requirements in several relevant particulars. First, it encompasses proceedings for which exclusion is not required under the Fourth Amendment. In *United States v. Calandra,*[63] the Supreme Court held that the Fourth Amendment does not require suppression of unlawfully seized evidence from grand jury proceedings, and that, therefore, a witness ordered to testify could not refuse on the grounds that the inquiry was derived from evidence obtained in the course of an unlawful search and seizure. But because grand jury proceedings are specifically mentioned in the enumeration of prohibited uses under section 2515, a contrary resolution was reached when the same question arose in connection with illegally intercepted conversations.[64]

A second difference hinges upon the types of transgressions that lead to the imposition of evidentiary sanctions. Title III of the Crime Control Act contains a detailed array of procedural requirements governing the procurement and execution of listening orders, some of which were drafted to satisfy

[62] 18 USC § 2515 (1970).
[63] 414 US 338, 38 LEd(2d) 561, 94 SCt 613 (1974).
[64] Gelbard v. United States, 408 US 41, 33 LEd(2d) 179, 92 SCt 2357 (1972).

the constitutional mandate of *Katz* and others of which go beyond. In *United States* v. *Giordano* [65] the Supreme Court categorically rejected the argument that the Title III exclusionary remedy was limited to cases in which the government fails to observe a procedural requirement founded on the Constitution.

In ruling that evidentiary sanctions may be invoked in some cases where the omitted requirement is purely statutory in origin, the Court stated the test to be whether the requirement constituted a "central safeguard" in the prevention of abuses. For example, the statutory requirement that all applications for intercept orders initiate with the personal approval of the Attorney General, or of an assistant attorney general specially designated by him, was held to be such a safeguard, whereas the directive that all wiretap applications correctly identify the authorizing official was held not to be "central." [66] Though evidentiary sanctions will not be invoked by every inconsequential failure to conform strictly to the mandates of the law, every effort should be made to do so, since it is impossible to tell in advance of adjudication which ones a court will consider important.

§ 5.18 Authorization for interception of wire or oral communications

Subsection (1) of section 2516 sets out the procedures by which a federal investigating agency may apply for an order authorizing wire or oral communications interceptions. This section provides that the Attorney General, or any assistant attorney general specially designated by the Attorney General, may authorize an application. Although the Department of Justice developed extensive procedures for complying with the law, this procedure broke down in one case where the Attorney General's name had been affixed by an executive assistant in his office. The Supreme Court set aside a conviction on the ground that the only delegation of approving authority per-

---

[65] 416 US 505, 40 LEd(2d) 341, 94 SCt 1820 (1974).

[66] United States v. Chavez, 416 US 562, 40 LED(2d) 380, 94 SCt 1849 (1974).

mitted under section 2516 was from the Attorney General to one of his nine assistant attorneys general.[67]

This decision set the tone for future litigation involving governmental failures to comply with the detailed statutory procedures with this comment:

> Congress intended to require suppression where there is a failure to satisfy any of those statutory requirements that directly and substantially implement the congressional intention to limit the use of intercept procedures to those situations clearly calling for the employment of this extraordinary investigative device.

But where the appropriate prosecuting official in fact approved the application, it is not necessary that he make a personal appearance in court to present the application to the issuing magistrate.[68]

Under section 2516, applications can be made only if interception could provide evidence of a violation of specific laws. Generally a federal officer may apply for a court order to authorize interception if there is probable cause to believe that there is a violation of (a) the national security laws; (b) the serious felony statutes such as those relating to murder, kidnapping, robbery or extortion; (c) laws relating to organized crime and gambling; (d) narcotics laws, or other laws specified in the Chapter. In addition, application can be made for such an order where the interception may provide evidence of conspiracy to commit any of these offenses.[69]

Section 2516 confers power only on the Attorney General, or his specifically designated assistant attorney general, to authorize an application for a court order. As indicated in the *Giordano* case, this does not give authority to an executive assistant. On the other hand, if the Attorney General personally approves the application, but it is erroneously cited

---

[67] United States v. Giordano, 416 US 505, 40 LEd(2d) 341, 94 SCt 1820 (1974). As a result of this case, eavesdropping evidence was lost in hundreds of federal cases. For a complete discussion, see NWC REPORT, p. 56.

[68] United States v. Pacheco, 489 F(2d) 554 (5thCir 1974).

[69] The Commission believes that Title III of the Crime Control Act should be amended to permit the Attorney General to designate experienced U.S. Attorneys or Federal Strike Force Chiefs to sign the application for a Title III authorization. NWC REPORT, p. 10.

in the order that an assistant attorney general was the authorizing official, this identification does not require suppression of the wiretap evidence when the Attorney General himself has actually given the approval.[70]

Although Chapter 119 is complete in itself as to the authority to obtain court orders in federal cases, it is effective in the states only if supplemented by state laws. Section 2516(2) provides that the principal prosecuting attorney of any state or the principal prosecuting attorney of any political subdivision of the state may make application to a state court judge for an order authorizing interception, but only if this is authorized by a state statute. If the state statute does authorize interception, application for an order authorizing or approving the interception of wire or oral communication by state investigative or law enforcement officers may be made. The application is limited to interceptions which may provide or have provided evidence of the commission of the offense of murder, kidnapping, gambling, robbery, bribery, extortion, or dealing in narcotic drugs, marijuana, or other dangerous drugs, or other crimes dangerous to life, limb or property, and punishable by imprisonment for more than one year, or any conspiracy to commit any of the foregoing offenses. At least 22 states have enacted legislation to make it possible to take advantage of this federal act.[71] In the states where there is no enabling legislation, a state officer who intercepts communications is subject to penalty the same as any other "person" as defined in section 2510. And, of course, evidence obtained in violation of the Act is not admissible in state court.

§ 5.19 Authorization for disclosure and use of intercepted wire or oral communications

Section 2517 was included to make it clear that law enforcement officers who obtain evidence in accordance with the provisions of the act may legally disclose the information and

---

[70] United States v. Chavez, 416 US 562, 40 LEd(2d) 380, 94 SCt 1849 (1974).

[71] By the end of 1974 a total of 22 states and the District of Columbia had statutory provisions for court-approved electronic surveillance. Some states, however, prohibit such surveillance even though the federal statute authorizes it. NWC Report, p. 266 Table F-2).

use the evidence to the extent appropriate to the proper performance of their official duties. This section also makes abundantly clear that derivative evidence obtained as a result of the legal interception can be used during the investigation and in any criminal proceeding.

The section goes even further and provides that the officer is not limited to the use of evidence described in the order authorizing the interception but may use other evidence incidentally obtained during the authorized interception. As an example, if the officer obtains an order authorizing the interception of a wiretap communication for the purpose of obtaining evidence of narcotics violations, but during that authorized interception obtains evidence of a kidnapping, this may be used when authorized or approved by a judge of competent jurisdiction. Such use can be compared with the seizure of tangible evidence not described in the search warrant but observed by the police officer who is executing a legitimate search warrant.

§ 5.20   Procedure for interception of wire or oral communications

Section 2518 [72] designates the procedures which must be followed in obtaining an order authorizing the interception of wire or oral communications. Because it is necessary to protect the constitutional rights of individuals, the procedure for obtaining an order is detailed and comprehensive. The procedures closely resemble those which have been traditionally employed for obtaining the conventional search warrant.

1. Application for interception order

All applications for orders permitting the interception of wire or oral communications must be authorized by the Attorney General or an assistant attorney general specially designated by him in the case of federal investigations, or by the principal prosecuting officer of the state or of its political subdivisions in the case of state and local investigations. It must be made in writing upon an oath or affirmation before

[72] 18 USC § 2518 (1970).

the appropriate federal or state judge, as the case may be, and must include the following information:

(a) the identity of the law enforcement officer making the application, and the officer authorizing it;

(b) a statement of the facts relied upon by the applicant warranting the issuance of an order, including details as to the particular offense which has been, is being, or is about to be committed; a particular description of the nature and location of the facilities from which or the place where the communication is to be intercepted, the identity of the persons whose communications are to be overheard or recorded; and a description of the types of communications sought;

(c) facts concerning whether or not other investigative procedures have been tried and failed or why they appear unlikely to succeed if tried or would be too dangerous; and

(d) the anticipated period of time for which the interception is required to be maintained;

(e) facts concerning all previous applications involving any of the same persons, facilities or places and the action taken by the judge on the same.

This section has generated as much litigation as any section in the Chapter. The law requires that the identity of the person, if known, committing the offense and whose communications are to be intercepted be included in the application. Searching for means to challenge wiretap orders, attorneys have claimed that (a) if a person is not named in the application, evidence obtained as a result of the order will not be admissible against him, and (b) failure to include the name of a known offender whose communication is expected to be overheard renders the intercepted conversations inadmissible at the trial.

In *United States* v. *Kahn* [73] the Supreme Court construed the statutory requirement that the application and order identify the persons, if known, who are committing the offense and whose communications are to be intercepted. Federal authorities, having probable cause to believe that one Irving Kahn was using specified telephones to conduct an illegal gambling business, secured a court order authorizing the interception

[73] 415 US 143, 39 LEd(2d) 225, 94 SCt 977 (1974).

of "wire communications of Irving Kahn and others as yet unknown." In the course of executing the order, the agents overheard several conversations between Kahn's wife and known gambling figures, implicating her in the illegal operation. Indictments were obtained against both Kahns. On behalf of Mrs. Kahn it was urged that the conversations in which she participated should be suppressed because the government could have discovered her complicity and named her in the application had it made a thorough investigation prior to applying for the listening order. The Supreme Court ruled that a full investigation, in advance of seeking an order, into the possibility that all likely users of a particular telephone were engaging in criminal activities was unnecessary.

The statute requires the naming of particular individuals in the application and order only when law enforcement authorities have probable cause to believe that that person is committing the offense for which wiretap authority is sought. Since the government had no reason to suspect Mrs. Kahn of complicity until after the interception had been conducted, the failure to name her in the application was not an error. The Court further held that, when a wiretap order is properly issued, intercept authority is not limited to conversations in which the person specifically named in the order is a party. Conversations between Mrs. Kahn and others whose identities were unknown in advance of interception were properly admissible into evidence under the language of the order and under section 2518.

The Fifth Circuit Court of Appeals agreed that failure to name specific persons not known to be involved at the time of the surveillance application should not lead to the suppression of the evidence against them.[74] On the other hand, the Fourth Circuit Court of Appeals, referring to the strict interpretation of the statute mentioned in *Giordano*, decided that FBI agents' failure to include in a wiretap application the name of a *known* offender whose communications they *expected* to overhear rendered the offender's intercepted conversations inadmissible at the trial.[75] Here the court explained that compliance with the identification requirements contained in 18

[74] United States v. Doolittle, 507 F(2d) 1368 (5thCir 1975).

[75] United States v. Bernstein, 509 F(2d) 996 (4thCir 1975).

U.S.C. § 2518(1)(b)(iv) assist both the Executive and Judicial branches to carry out their oversight and review functions.

Section 2518 also requires that the application contain a full and complete statement as to whether or not other investigative procedures have been tried and failed, or why they reasonably appear to be too dangerous or unlikely to succeed if tried. Again, giving the statute a strict interpretation, the Ninth Circuit Court of Appeals reversed a conviction because the FBI agents' only statement was that "knowledge and experience in investigating other gambling cases convinced them that normal investigative procedures were unlikely to succeed." [76] The court said this failed to justify the need for wiretap on a suspected gambling operation.

This court in *Kalustian* pointed out that in order to satisfy 18 U.S.C. § 2518(1)(c), the application must inform the issuing official of every technique which is customarily used in police work in investigating the type of crime involved and must explain why each of them has either been unsuccessful or is too dangerous or unlikely to succeed because of the particular circumstances of that case. The Fifth Circuit several months later approved a less stringent standard. The majority held that a "full and complete statement of underlying circumstances" satisfied 18 U.S.C. § 2518(1)(c). [77]

2. Determination of judge

According to section 2518(3) the judge to whom the application is submitted may issue an *ex parte* order authorizing or approving the interception if he determines on the basis of the facts submitted [78] that there is probable cause to believe that:

[76] United States v. Kalustian, 529 F(2d) 585 (9thCir 1975).

[77] United States v. Cacace, 529 F(2d) 1167 (5thCir 1975). (Parts of the affidavit found to be adequate are included in the case and can be compared with the inadequate affidavit in *Kalustian*.)

[78] In discussing the issuance of an *ex parte* order, the Commission commented that, "There has been no evidence heard to contradict the finding of the drafters of Title III that vital differences between ordinary searches and searches by electronic surveillance devices require that wiretap applications be reviewed by higher level judges rather than judges of limited jurisdiction who normally issue ordinary search warrants." NWC Report, p. 12.

(a) an individual has committed, is committing, or is about to commit one of the enumerated offenses;

(b) communications concerning that offense will be obtained through such interception;

(c) normal investigative procedures have been tried and have failed or reasonably appear unlikely to succeed if tried or would be too dangerous; and

(d) the facilities from which, or the place where, the interception will occur are being used in connection with the commission of such offense, or are leased to, listed in the name of, or commonly used by such person.

Congress, according to the Third Circuit Court of Appeals, did not intend to require a higher degree of probable cause for a wiretap than that ordinarily required for a search warrant.[79] The court held that the facts contained in the wiretap application met the standards for what constitutes probable cause.

3. Specifications in order

The order must specify:

(a) the identity of the individual, if known, whose communications are to be intercepted;

(b) the nature and location of the communications facilities or place where authority to intercept is granted;

(c) a description of the type of communication sought to be intercepted and the particular offense to which it relates;

(d) the identity of the agency authorized to intercept and the person authorizing the application; and

(e) the period of time during which such interception is authorized.[80]

4. Duration and minimization

The listening order may not remain in effect any longer than is necessary to achieve the objectives of the authorization and in any event no longer than *thirty days*. It should be

---

[79] United States v. Falcone, 505 F(2d) 478 (3dCir 1974). The Eighth Circuit reached a similar conclusion in United States v. Brick, 502 F(2d) 219 (8thCir 1974).

[80] 18 USC § 2518(4) (1970).

promptly executed and the interception should be conducted in such a manner as to minimize the interception of communications not otherwise subject to interception. There is no limit on the number of extensions which can be granted, but each extension requires the same information and showing of probable cause as the original application. The order and any extensions thereof automatically terminate upon the attainment of the authorized objective.[81]

In several cases the courts have attempted to interpret what is meant by "minimization" of the interception of communications not otherwise subject to interception. Apparently there is no hard and fast formula for minimization, and the requirement is satisfied if the court, in reviewing the government procedures, concludes that on the whole the agents have shown a high regard for the right of privacy and have done all they reasonably could to avoid unnecessary intrusions.[82]

5. Emergency interceptions

Congress contemplated that situations may occasionally arise where the time factor is such as to make it impossible or impracticable for the investigating officer to make application for an order prior to engaging in listening. He cannot always anticipate in advance where or when a conversation will occur and once the sound waves dissipate, the evidence is lost forever. The concession made for emergency situations, is nevertheless, a limited one.

To prevent abuse of the privilege where no necessity exists, the responsible officer must make a reasonable determination that (a) an emergency exists with respect to conspiratorial activities characteristic of organized crime or threatening the national security, requiring that an interception be made before an authorization can be obtained, and that (b) there are grounds upon which such an order could be entered in ac-

---

[81] 18 USC § 2518(5) (1970).

[82] United States v. Bynum, 485 F(2d) 490 (2dCir 1973); United States v. James, 494 F(2d) 1007 (DC Cir 1974); and United States v. Armocida, 515 F(2d) 29 (3dCir 1975). The Commis-

sion, after reviewing many cases, recommended that "no hard and fast minimization guidelines can be drafted, nor is there a need to do so." NWC REPORT, p. 12.

cordance with the standards set out in the federal statute. If these two conditions are satisfied, the listening may be conducted in the absence of an order, provided that the officer makes application for an order approving what has transpired within *forty-eight* hours thereafter. In the event that no application is sought or the application for an approval order is denied, all overheard or recorded communications will be treated as having been obtained in violation of the law for purposes of admissibility.[83]

6. Recording of communications to assure authenticity

Although not mandatory under the law, section 2518(8) does provide as a rule of policy that recordings should be made of every intercepted communication, if possible. The purpose of this requirement is to assure completeness and accuracy and to safeguard against error. The recording, moreover, must be made in such a way as to protect it from editing or other alterations. Immediately upon the expiration of the period of the order or any extensions thereof, the recording must be transmitted to the judge issuing the order and sealed under his direction. Custody of the recordings shall be wherever the judge orders. The presence of the seal on the recording, or a satisfactory explanation for its absence, is a prerequisite for its introduction into evidence at a trial. But since the police are not required to make a recording in every case, the absence of a seal on a recording would probably not foreclose an officer from testifying in court on the basis of his own recollection of what he directly heard. The only consequence is the forfeiture of the ability to utilize the recording itself as evidence. The advantage of having this testimony in recorded form and of being able to utilize it in court lies in the fact that it is a more cogent and convincing mode of presenting the evidence.

---

[83] 18 USC § 2518(7) (1970). The majority members of the Commission determined that this emergency provision had not been used in very many cases. Nevertheless they recommended that it be left in the law and, in fact, enlarged so as to allow electronic surveillance in other cases, such as hijacking or kidnapping, as a means of preventing death or serious bodily harm. NWC REPORT, p. 15.

7. Pre-use notice

Before the contents of any intercepted wire or oral communication, or any evidence derived therefrom, may be received into evidence at any trial, hearing or other proceeding in a federal or state court, each party must be furnished, at least *ten days* in advance, with copies of the records of the communications, the court order and accompanying application.[84] Once this disclosure has been made, the party will be in a better position to raise such objections to its receipt as are authorized by law. Essentially, this requirement amounts to a mandatory form of discovery.

8. Motion to suppress

On the basis of the information disclosed to him by virtue of the pre-use notice requirement, a party aggrieved by the interception may move to suppress the communications themselves and all evidentiary fruits flowing therefrom on the grounds that:

> (i) the communication was unlawfully intercepted;
> (ii) the order of authorization or approval under which it was intercepted is insufficient on its face; or
> (iii) the interception was not made in conformity with the order of authorization or approval.[85]

The motion should be made before the trial, hearing or proceeding unless there is no opportunity to make it or the person was unaware of the grounds of the motion. If the motion is granted, the evidence will be excluded from the proceeding.

A final provision of section 2518 authorizes the United States to appeal from an order granting a motion to suppress the use of evidence. This appeal must be made within thirty days after the date the order was entered and must be diligently prosecuted. This provision is a unique provision but should prove worthwhile as far as the prosecutor is concerned. Because the prosecutor has the specific authority to appeal, a

---

[84] 18 USC § 2518(9) (1970).   [85] 18 USC § 2518(10) (1970).

judge might be more inclined to evaluate the facts more carefully before denying the use of the evidence.

§ 5.21   Reports concerning intercepted wire or oral com-
munications

Another unique feature of the wiretap legislation is that it
requires reports concerning the activities governed by it. Because of the controversy concerning intercepted communications, an effort is apparently being made to determine if such
interceptions are in fact necessary and effective.

Section 2519 requires that the judge who issued or denied
the order shall make a report for the Administrative Office of
the United States Courts concerning orders issued under the
act. This report must be submitted within thirty days after the
expiration of the order and must include in addition to the fact
that the order was issued, the offense, the identity of the investigative agency, the nature of the facilities, and other pertinent information concerning the order.

In addition, the Attorney General and the prosecuting attorneys of the states and political subdivisions must submit a
report once each year to the Administrative Office of United
States Courts. This report must include in addition to a summary of previously reported information, the number of arrests resulting from interceptions, the number of trials, the
number of convictions, and a general assessment of the importance of the interceptions. The Director of the Administrative Office of United States Courts must in turn report to
Congress each year concerning the number of applications and
orders authorized and other information designated in the
section.

§ 5.22   Recovery of civil damages

In addition to the criminal sanctions and the exclusion of
evidence obtained in violation of the law, a third mode of enforcement is incorporated. Section 2520 affords any person
whose wire or oral communication has been intercepted, disclosed, or used in violation of the law, a civil cause of action
for damages against those responsible for the infraction. This
section affords the person whose rights have been invaded a

minimum guaranteed recovery of $100 a day for each day of violation, or $1,000, whichever is higher. If provable damages are in excess of that amount, the person is entitled to recover the actual damages sustained. In addition, the law authorizes recovery of punitive damages and reasonable attorney and litigation expenses.

This section has a provision to protect the officer who in good faith relies on a court order or on the other provisions of the statute when intercepting communications. An officer who obtains proper authorization for eavesdropping or wiretapping or who acts in accordance with the other provisions of the law is immune from a civil suit or criminal prosecution, even though the order turns out to be deficient.

§ 5.23   Constitutionality of Title III of the 1968 Crime Control Act as amended

It was inevitable that the Title III provisions of the Crime Control Act authorizing interception of communications would be challenged in court. Although the United States Supreme Court has not expressly ruled on the matter of constitutionality, it seems to be settled that federal legislation and the state laws modeled on it comply with the requirements of the Fourth Amendment. Title III has successfully run the gauntlet of constitutional attack in nine of the eleven United States Courts of Appeals, after having been raised in as many federal district courts.[86] With one exception, all decisions handed down to date have found the 1968 Act to be in compliance with the guidance established in *Berger* and *Katz*. In the one case which held otherwise at the trial level, the decision was reversed on appeal.[87] This impressive record dispels virtually all doubt as to the constitutional status of the 1968 enactment as amended.

[86] United States v. Tortorello, 480 F(2d) 764 (2dCir 1973); United States v. Cafero, 473 F(2d) 489 (3dCir 1973); United States v. Bobo, 477 F(2d) 974 (4thCir 1973); United States v. Harris, 460 F(2d) 1041 (5th Cir 1972); United States v. Martinez, 498 F(2d) 464 (6thCir 1974); United States v. Cox, 462 F(2d) 1293 (8thCir 1972); United States v. Cox, 449 F(2d) 679 (10thCir 1971); United States v. James, 494 F(2d) 1007 (DC Cir 1974). Also see NWC Report, p. 6.

[87] United States v. Whitaker, 343 FSupp 358 (ED Pa 1972), *rev'd*, 474 F(2d) 1246 (3dCir 1973).

Certainly the framers of this legislation made every effort to incorporate all of the safeguards required by the Fourth Amendment and due process clause. It is evident that *Berger*, *Katz* and other cases were studied to determine what the courts considered to be requirements for an act which would withstand constitutional challenge.

The fact that the courts have generally upheld the statute as constitutional does not settle the issue forever. In the lower federal courts the major issues concerning court-authorized electronic surveillance have centered around minimization and suppression. These issues will no doubt be brought up again. Also, there has been criticism concerning consensual electronic surveillance. It is anticipated that this, too, will be challenged in future cases. However, as of the date of this printing, the legislation has not been declared unconstitutional.

§ 5.24　Permissible warrantless listening

Federal wiretapping and electronic surveillance legislation has provided law enforcement agencies with sources of crime information which had been previously unavailable. Although the law condemns some electronic surveillance, it does not condemn all warrantless listening. Some of the statutorily approved exceptions have been mentioned previously. The purpose of this section is to bring together and examine those instances where listening, recording or using electronic devices without first obtaining a warrant still remains permissible.

1. Listening not involving the interception of any wire or oral communication

Application for a court order authorizing listening is required under 18 U.S.C. § 2516(1) only where *"an interception of a wire or oral communication"* is contemplated. Excluded from statutory coverage are those instances where listening is accomplished without the aid of any sound amplifying or bugging apparatus.

In *United States* v. *McLeod*,[88] a government agent on four separate occasions stood a few feet from the defendant while

---

[88] 493 F(2d) 1186 (7thCir 1974).

she was placing a call at a public telephone and, without the aid of any listening device, overheard her give out sports wagering information. The defendant objected to the use of this information on the ground that the government had failed to obtain an order authorizing interception of her communications. The Seventh Circuit, observing that no "interception" had taken place, ruled that a listening order was unnecessary. A similar result was reached in *United States* v. *Sin Nagh Fong*[89] where agents staked out in an adjoining motel room and heard the defendant's conversation next door without the aid of any artificial voice magnifying equipment.

It would appear from these cases that where an agent is standing in a place where he has a lawful right to be at the time, he need not procure a warrant to eavesdrop on conversations audible to him without electronic or mechanical assistance.

2. Pen registers

A pen register is a device attached to a telephone line, usually at the phone company's central office, which records on paper all outgoing numbers dialed from a particular phone and then cuts off without determining whether the call has been completed and without monitoring the actual conversation. As there is no interception of a communication, the general conclusion is that this type of registration of numbers is not covered by existing legislation. A number of cases have held that no special separate authority is needed when a pen register is used in conjunction with a wiretap that has been approved according to the statutory requirements.[90]

Quoting from cases from the Ninth and Tenth Circuits, the Illinois Appellate Court agreed that telephone company employees violated neither federal nor Illinois law by placing an electronic monitoring device on the phone line of a "blue box." This device did not record any conversations but merely ascertained the long distance number dialed from the defendant's

---

[89] 490 F(2d) 527 (9thCir 1974).
[90] United States v. Brick, 502 F(2d) 219 (8thCir 1974); United States v. John, 508 F(2d) 1134 (8thCir 1974); United States v. Barnard, 490 F(2d) 907 (9thCir 1973). See also, Application of the United States for an Order, 407 FSupp 398 (WD Mo 1976).

phone, a function which the blue box prevented ordinary phone equipment from accomplishing.[91]

3. Radio messages over public frequencies

In *United States* v. *Hall*,[92] the Ninth Circuit ruled that the criminal messages transmitted between a radio sending and receiving set are not protected against warrantless interception by law enforcement officers. The existence of a few wires within the sets was not sufficient, in the court's opinion, to cause the messages to be regarded as a wire communication. And since persons broadcasting over an ordinary frequency have reason to know that their conversations are audible to any whose receiver is tuned to that station, the protection accorded oral communications was not applicable. This court concluded, however, that a message transmitted between a mobile radio unit and a land-line telephone is a wire communication and would be subject to statutory control.

4. Bumper beepers

A device which is colloquially called a "bumper beeper" is a small radio transmitter which can be attached to or placed in an object, whose location can then be fixed by triangulations of receivers or otherwise. It is used by law enforcement agents to keep track of moving vehicles or other moving objects. Since the bumper beeper transmits a radio signal rather than spoken words, most courts have logically held that it does not involve an "interception" of either a wire or oral communication.[93] The Fifth Circuit, however, with little explanation concluded that "the installations of an electronic device on a motor vehicle is a search within the meaning of the Fourth Amendment."[94] That court expanded on this premise and added that all evidence obtained by an exploitation of the "primary illegality" must be suppressed. Fortunately, this expansion of the exclusionary rule is only the opinion of one

---

[91] People v. Smith, 31 IllApp(3d) 423, 333 NE(2d) 241 (1975), quoting Bubis v. United States, 384 F(2d) 643 (9thCir 1967) and Brandon v. United States, 382 F(2d) 607 (10thCir 1967).

[92] 488 F(2d) 193 (9thCir 1973).

[93] NWC REPORT, p. 120.

[94] United States v. Holmes, 521 F(2d) 859 (5thCir 1975).

court. It seems illogical and unnecessary to deprive law enforcement of this necessary investigative tool.

5. *Consent and participant listening*

The necessity for obtaining a court order authorizing the interception of a wire or oral communication is dispensed with under 18 U.S.C. § 2511(2)(c) where one of the parties to the communication either participates in the interception or has given his prior consent to the government's listening. Section 2511(2)(c) is a codification of the pre-*Katz* case law. It was enacted by Congress during a period of legal uncertainty. Many read the *Katz* decision as a tacit overruling of the one-party consent cases. Congress thought otherwise. Acting upon the premise that government listening does no violence to the Fourth Amendment when one of the parties has authorized it or cooperated in its accomplishment, Congress exempted consent and participant listening from the prior warrant requirements.

In retrospect, it appears that the congressional analysis of the Fourth Amendment is correct. Doubts that may previously have existed as to the legal foundations of the consent exception have now been dispelled by *United States* v. *White*,[95] mentioned earlier. Though White's arrest occurred prior to the enactment of the Crime Control Act, as a post-*Katz* decision reaffirming the continued constitutional vitality of the one-party consent cases, the ruling establishes by implication, the constitutional validity of the legislation. Law enforcement officers may, therefore, safely proceed under section 2511(2)(c) in monitoring or recording wire or oral communications without obtaining a court order if one of the parties to the conversation has consented to this being done, and this is so even though the surveillance target is unaware that the interception is taking place.

6. *National security surveillances*

For several decades prior to the enactment of controlling legislation, the Justice Department acting with presidential

---

[95] 401 US 745, 28 LEd(2d) 453, 91 SCt 1122 (1971).

approval had engaged in electronic surveillance as part of its national security intelligence gathering. The constitutional justification for warrantless national security surveillances was based upon a claim of executive privilege. At a time when the government's thesis regarding national security investigations had never been approved or disapproved by the Supreme Court, Congress enacted the Crime Control Act.

Interpreting the language of the act as an affirmative grant of authority by Congress excusing the government from its normal obligation to secure a warrant in the conduct of national security surveillances, the Attorney General approved the use of wiretapping against a *domestic* organization conspiring to bomb government property. The legality of the government's actions was challenged in *United States v. United States District Court*.[96]

The government argued that 18 U.S.C. § 2511(3) contained an affirmative grant of surveillance power to the President, exercisable without prior judicial authorization. The Supreme Court did not agree. Mr. Justice Powell speaking for the majority first concluded that the Act did not give the government any more authority than it had before passage, and that Congress only attempted to make clear that the Act did not legislate with respect to national security surveillances. After this conclusion was reached, the Court reasoned that a President's domestic security role must be exercised in a manner compatible with the Fourth Amendment. In determining that the government could not conduct electronic surveillances in domestic security cases without court approval, the Court concluded that:

> [T]he Government's concerns do not justify departure in this case from the customary Fourth Amendment requirement of judicial approval prior to initiation of a search or surveillance.

The Court emphasized that its holding in this case applied only to *domestic* aspects of national security and in no way limited the other provisions of the statute. The Court further

---

[96] 407 US 297, 32 LEd(2d) 752, 93 SCt 2125 (1972).

noted that there are sufficient differences between national security surveillances and ordinary criminal investigations that Congress might want to consider enacting different standards for the issuance of warrants in domestic security cases than are presently found in Title III of the Crime Control Act.

IV. REPORT OF THE NATIONAL COMMISSION FOR THE REVIEW OF FEDERAL AND STATE LAWS RELATING TO WIRETAPPING AND ELECTRONIC SURVEILLANCE

§ 5.25   Findings and recommendations of the Commission

Since the findings and recommendations of the National Commission for the Review of Federal and State Laws Relating to Wiretapping and Electronic Surveillance will have some bearing on future legislation and decisions, a summary of these findings and recommendations is included. A report of that Commission, which was established under the 1968 Act, was filed on April 30, 1976.

First, the Commission found that the considerations which led Congress to provide procedures for court authorization of electronic surveillance for law enforcement are still applicable. Further, the Commission found that the court-authorized electronic surveillance under Title III of the Crime Control Act has effectively assisted law enforcement in investigations of organized crime offenses, including narcotics distribution, major fraud schemes, and other similar activities of an on-going conspiratorial nature.

Not only did the Commission recommend that the provisions remain for court-ordered wiretaps and eavesdrops, it also recommended that law enforcement should use these tools more extensively in criminal investigations of substantial significance to the public interest, particularly when investigating narcotics importation and distribution, theft, and fencing.

To improve effective use of legal electronic surveillance, the Commission recommended that: (1) law enforcement personnel be given additional training in techniques for the use of electronic surveillance; (2) Congress consider limited expansion of the list of federal crimes for which electronic surveillance orders may be obtained; (3) states which have a significant rate of the types of crimes normally committed by organized criminals should enact legislation consistent with Title III of the Crime Control Act; (4) states should provide for state-wide oversight and centralization of resources for the use of electronic surveillance in law enforcement; (5) there should be greater cooperation between federal and state law enforcement agencies; (6) Title III should be amended to authorize the Attorney General to designate specific United States attorneys and Federal Strike Force Chiefs as authorized to apply for court-ordered wiretapping; (7) state wiretapping legislation should include a provision directing telephone companies to cooperate with law enforcement.

While agreeing that the legislation had achieved its purpose, the Commission nevertheless recommended the following changes in the statutory procedures of Title III: (1) in lieu of an arbitrary limitation on the number of time extensions authorizing electronic surveillance, section 2518 should be amended to require, as a prerequisite to an extension, a showing of some special reason to continue such surveillance; (2) section 2518 should be amended to require that the explanation of exhaustion of alternative investigative techniques include consideration of the particular facts of the case under investigation, insofar as practicable; (3) Title III should require that a court order for electronic surveillance expressly authorize entry upon a private place or premises to install an electronic device, if such entry is necessary to execute the warrant; (4) section 2518 should be amended to require the oral notification of a judge prior to installation of an emergency electronic surveillance; (5) a provision requiring notification of persons intercepted and identified in the course of the electronic surveillance should be added; (6) the exclusionary rule provided by Title III should be retained regardless of the fate of such a rule with respect to case law or law enforcement searches generally, but that it not be expanded beyond the specific Title III provisions; (7) the law with respect to the legal requirements for the use of bumper beepers and pen registers be clarified; (8) Title III should be amended to permit the defendant to appeal the denial of a motion to suppress at the trial level even though he has entered a plea of guilty.

Finally, the Commission recommended that operations

governed by the provisions of Title III be reviewed periodically to determine their effectiveness in law enforcement and to determine if they are effective in stemming private illegal surveillance.[97]

§ 5.26 Summary

A majority of the Supreme Court justices who decided the early cases refused to bring wiretapping within the ambit of the Fourth Amendment. However, federal legislation in 1934 made wiretapping illegal. The law itself did not provide for exclusion of evidence obtained in violation of its provisions, but the Supreme Court, after the enactment of the 1934 statute, decided that evidence obtained in violation of the wiretap law would be inadmissible in federal courts. Confusion was created when the Court refused to apply this court-adopted exclusionary rule to state courts, and as a result, state laws relating to wiretapping and the admission of wiretap evidence were not uniform.

Because there was no federal eavesdropping statute comparable to the wiretap provisions of the Federal Communications Act of 1934, the protection concerning eavesdropping grew up primarily around an expanding interpretation of the Fourth Amendment. After first deciding that eavesdropping without a physical trespass did not violate the Fourth Amendment, the United States Supreme Court reversed its past decisions and in 1967 abandoned the trespass distinction. In that year the same Court held that a New York statute which authorized the interception of communications when approved by judicial authority was invalid since it did not meet the requirements of the Fourth Amendment.

To bring some uniformity out of the confusion, Congress enacted Title III of the Omnibus Crime Control Act of 1968, 18 U.S.C. §§ 2510–2520. This carefully drawn legislation generally prohibits interception of wire or oral communications but makes some specific exceptions. It authorizes inter-

---

[97] Other recommendations were made but these are the primary recommendations that are of interest to law enforcement and criminal justice agencies. Copies of the Commission's ELECTRONIC SURVEILLANCE REPORT are available from the U.S. Government Printing Office.

ception of wire or oral communications by enforcement officers if (a) one party consents; (b) a judicial officer by an *ex parte* order authorizes the interception; or (c) an officer determines that an emergency situation relating to national security or organized crime exists, provided he obtains judicial approval later.

The state officer has the authority to proceed under a court order only if a state statute so authorizes. The federal code does not make such interception legal in those jurisdictions which have clear statutory mandates forbidding the same. To make it possible for the officer to make full use of the law, the states must enact measures designed to safeguard individual rights under a system of court orders which comply with the guidelines established by the federal law. In the absence of such legislation, all wiretapping and eavesdropping by state investigative individuals except by consent of one party is illegal, and the fruits thereof tainted beyond use in any state proceedings.

The law specifically provides that evidence obtained in accordance with its mandates will be admissible in court, while evidence obtained in violation of the provisions will not be admissible. It further authorizes the recovery of civil damages by a person whose communications have been unlawfully intercepted.

Many court cases concerning the constitutionality of the law have been decided, but it has not been declared unconstitutional. Cases have made it clear, however, that if wiretap and eavesdrop evidence is to be admitted, the statute must be strictly complied with.

Some warrantless surveillance is not covered by statute and, therefore, is not prohibited by it. For example, listening which does not involve the *interception* of any wire or oral communications, using the pen register, and listening with the consent of one party is not prohibited by federal law.

Although the enforcement officer is restricted in obtaining evidence by intercepting wire or oral communications, certain evidence obtained in this manner may be used if the laws are observed. To make the most effective use of this law enforcement tool, all officers, and especially administrators and investigators, should be thoroughly familiar with state and federal statutes. Also, definite procedures for obtaining wiretap orders should be established with the prosecuting attorney and the judicial officers. If state legislation has not been enacted, steps should be taken to encourage this enabling legislation.

Chapter 6

INTERROGATIONS AND CONFESSIONS*

> A confession is voluntary in law if, and only if, it was, in fact, voluntarily made. . . . But a confession obtained by compulsion must be excluded whatever may have been the character of the compulsion, and whether the compulsion was applied in the judicial proceeding or otherwise.
>
> Mr. Justice Brandeis
> Ziang Sung Wan v. United States,
> 266 US 1, 14 (1924)

Section

§ 6.1   Introductory remarks

The law concerning interrogations and confessions is not set out in any precise point in the Constitution but derives from a mixture and fusing of several different provisions, with primary emphasis today on the Fifth Amendment privilege against self-incrimination and the Sixth Amendment guarantee of the right to counsel. As a means of enforcing the rights and privileges protected by the Fourth, Fifth, and Sixth

* by John C. Klotter

299

Amendments, confessions are excluded from criminal prosecutions if obtained in violation of the rules which the courts have established.

The traditional approach to confessions and interrogations stressed the aspect of voluntariness and trustworthiness. When confessions were thrown out, it was traditionally because the court found that the confession was not freely and voluntarily made. Coercion and duress made the statements inherently suspect, and for this reason due process of law required exclusion.

A confession must pass at least five hurdles before it may be received as evidence in a court of law. First, it must pass the traditional test of voluntariness and trustworthiness. Secondly, it must meet those requirements established by the Supreme Court in the *McNabb* and *Mallory* cases,[1] the so-called "delay in arraignment" test. More recently the Supreme Court has established additional requirements known as the *Miranda* requirements.[2] The courts have decided that a confession may be tainted by an illegal arrest or an illegal search. And failure to provide counsel may make the confession inadmissible. Each of these will be discussed in the sections that follow.[3]

These strict requirements limit the use of confessions, but questioning is a valuable technique in investigating offenses when used properly. Contrary to what some attorneys claim, statements from suspects are admissible. In fact, the Supreme Court in the *Miranda* case specifically pointed out that under certain conditions, statements may be obtained and used as evidence.[4] Everyone involved in the criminal justice process should be thoroughly familiar with not only the restrictions placed upon questioning by officials, but also the reason for

---

[1] McNabb v. United States, 318 US 332, 87 LEd 819, 63 SCt 608 (1943); Mallory v. United States, 354 US 449, 1 LEd(2d) 1479, 77 SCt 1356 (1957), which is reprinted in Part II of this book.

[2] See generally Miranda v. Arizona, 384 US 436, 16 LEd(2d) 694, 86 SCt 1602 (1966).

[3] In *Miranda* the Court required that the accused be advised as to both his Fifth Amendment right against self-incrimination and his Sixth Amendment right to counsel. 384 US at 467-73. The Sixth Amendment right to counsel is discussed in more detail in Chapter 8, *infra*.

[4] *Id.* at 478. The portions of the text of this case included in Part II of this book should be carefully read.

these restrictions. To protect society as well as the rights of the accused, criminal justice personnel also must be able to determine when questioning is proper and when it is preferable not to use it as an investigatory tool.

§ 6.2   The free and voluntary rule

At early common law an admission or confession was nonetheless admissible as evidence of guilt despite the fact that it was the product of force or duress. As a result, enforcement officers, rather than conducting a thorough investigation to establish guilt, resorted to torture in order to extract a confession from the accused. As society became more humane, these methods fell into disrepute. Given sufficient torture, even an innocent man might confess to a crime he had not committed. It was this risk that led to the ultimate abandonment of the common-law rule and the substitution both in England and the United States of what came to be known as the "free and voluntary" rule.

1. Statement of the rule

The free and voluntary rule is generally stated to be as follows:

> A confession of a person accused of crime is admissible in evidence against the accused only if it was freely and voluntarily made, without duress, fear, or compulsion in its inducement and with full knowledge of the nature and consequences of the confession.[5]

An Illinois case in 1926 gave this formulation of the rule:

> Confessions are competent evidence only when they are voluntarily made. . . . Generally speaking, a confession is regarded as voluntary when it is made of the free will and accord of the accused, without fear or any threat of harm, or without promise or inducement by hope or reward.[6]

2. Reasons for the rule

The historic justification for the rule was that only voluntary confessions could be relied on as trustworthy. After the

---

[5] AMJUR, Evidence § 482 (1939).   [6] People v. Fox, 319 Ill 606, 150 NE 347 (1926).

adoption of the Fifth Amendment with its provisions regarding self-incrimination, the courts began to express disagreement with the traditional rationale. In the 1897 case of *Bram v. United States*,[7] the Supreme Court stated that the competency of a confession as evidence was controlled by the self-incrimination clause of the Fifth Amendment. The following quotation is found in the opinion:

> In criminal trials, in the courts of the United States, whenever a question arises whether a confession is incompetent because [it is] not voluntary, the issue is controlled by that portion of the Fifth Amendment . . . commanding that no person "shall be compelled in any criminal case to be a witness against himself."[8]

This approach was approved by the majority in the *Miranda* case as the proper test to be employed in reviewing confessions from state courts as well, but there were four dissenters. Mr. Justice White, joined in his dissent by Justices Harlan and Stewart, stated that the rule announced by the majority was without support either in history or in the language of the Fifth Amendment. According to their views, the privilege against self-incrimination, as developed at common law, prohibited only compelled *judicial* interrogations. They found no authority for extending the privilege to out-of-court confessions and felt that the test of voluntariness should be maintained.

The free and voluntary rule advocated by the dissenters in *Miranda* is a more flexible approach than the position taken by the majority. Nevertheless, regardless of whether the courts adopt the traditional rationale or the view that ties the confession in with the protection against self-incrimination, voluntariness is still a crucial factor bearing on its competency as evidence.

3. Factors to consider in determining whether a confession is voluntary

Standards of voluntariness have been developed on a case by case basis without any attempt to formulate an all-inclusive

[7] 168 US 532, 42 LEd 568, 18 SCt 183 (1897).   [8] *Id.* at 542.

definition. Such factors as the characteristics of the suspect, including his ability to resist various inducements, the length of the interrogation, and the techniques employed have been considered relevant by the courts in their inquiry. The *Miranda* case holding that a confession is inadmissible if the police have neglected to inform the suspect of his right to counsel and to remain silent, has partially superseded the pre-existing case law on voluntariness. To the extent that the requisite warnings are not given, *Miranda* impels an automatic exclusion of any statement made. While this will undoubtedly take care of a number of cases where duress or coercion was formerly at issue, a vast area remains where voluntariness is still important.

The *Miranda* case does not rule out the possibility that the accused might intelligently waive his right to counsel and to remain silent and elect to make a statement. Certainly on the question of waiver, the criteria of voluntariness developed in prior decisions will continue to play a vital role. Furthermore, once there has been an effective waiver, the future conduct of the interrogation must still be carried out in conformity with the established rules governing voluntariness. Thus, while *Miranda* has alleviated the necessity for judicial inquiry into voluntariness when no warnings have been given, once the appropriate caution has been given and the accused nevertheless confesses, the older decisions relating to voluntariness retain their vitality in assisting the courts in determining admissibility.

Some of the factors which have been considered relevant by the courts in determining if the confessions are voluntary include the following:

(a) Use of force

Instances of physical brutality and the use of third degree methods to obtain a confession are rare, but unfortunately they still occur. These are the cases that reach the courts and tarnish the name of law enforcement. The majority in the *Miranda* case cited a recent incident in New York where a witness under interrogation was kicked and burned with a lighted cigarette butt. Such conduct will render a confession inadmissible even though independent evidence exists which substantiates the truth of the confession.[9] It is regrettable that conduct like this, though undoubtedly an exception today, is responsible for tightening the rules on interrogation in general.

(b) Threats or promises

Not only will actual physical force make a confession inadmissible, but threats of bodily harm or other threats that would cause a suspect to make statements against his will may also make a confession incompetent. In the case of *Payne v. Arkansas*[10] the United States Supreme Court reversed the conviction of a nineteen-year-old boy accused of murder because he had been held incommunicado for three days and was told that a mob was outside the jail to "get him."

In another case a threat by police officers to bring the accused's invalid wife to headquarters for questioning which prompted the accused to confess to murder was grounds for reversal.[11] And even a threat to a public employee that he could be removed from office if he did not cooperate made a confession inadmissible.[12]

The investigator must also be careful about making promises of leniency. A promise by the officer or the prosecutor to reduce or to drop the charge may result in a confession being inadmissible as involuntary.

(c) Psychological coercion

Although all courts have recognized that physical force will taint a confession and make it involuntary, there has been less harmony in the past concerning the use of trickery or psychological coercion in obtaining a confession. In the *Miranda* case[13] Mr. Chief Justice Warren observed that coercion can be mental as well as physical, and that the interrogation can become unconstitutional through the use of sufficient psychological pressure as well as physical duress. Warren

[9] Brown v. Mississippi, 297 US 278, 80 LEd 682, 56 SCt 461 (1936).
[10] 356 US 560, 2 LEd(2d) 975, 78 SCt 844 (1958).
[11] Rogers v. Richmond, 365 US 534, 5 LEd(2d) 760, 81 SCt 735 (1961).

[12] Garrity v. New Jersey, 385 US 493, 17 LEd(2d) 562, 87 SCt 616 (1967).
[13] Miranda v. Arizona, 384 US at 448.

cited, with disapproval, certain practices recommended in various police manuals and texts as contributing to the success of interrogations. Specifically he referred to techniques which are designed to put the subject in a psychological state where his story is but an elaboration of what the interrogator purports to know already—namely, that the suspect is guilty. In condemning these procedures, the Chief Justice warned:

> It is obvious that such an interrogation environment is created for no purpose other than to subjugate the individual to the will of his examiner. This atmosphere carries its own badge of intimidation. To be sure, this is not physical intimidation, but it is equally destructive of human dignity. . . . Unless adequate protective devices are employed to dispel the compulsion inherent in custodial surroundings, no statement obtained from the defendant can truly be the product of his free choice.[14]

Where the psychological coercion is combined with force and prolonged questioning, the confession may be inadmissible under the "totality of circumstances" test. In this regard the United States Court of Appeals for the Eighth Circuit determined that the confession of a murder defendant who had been questioned without nourishment about 25 times while handcuffed in a small hot room in the presence of six officers was involuntary under this test.[15] The majority, while admitting that the defendant was not a model prisoner and that there was substantial testimony indicating that he participated in a brutal killing in the penitentiary, still refused to justify the admission of the confession stating:

> We remain a government of laws, and those charged with law enforcement have a special responsibility to see that the guilty as well as the innocent are given the protection of the Constitution. If we depart from this principle, we deal the administration of justice a heavy blow.[16]

(d) *Application of the free and voluntary rule to the states through the Fourteenth Amendment*

If the highest court of a state upholds a confession as having been freely and voluntarily given, can the Supreme Court of

---

[14] *Id.* at 457-58.
[15] Stidham v. Swenson, 506 F(2d) 478 (8thCir 1974).
[16] *Id.* at 482.

the United States review this decision? This question was answered affirmatively in *Brown* v. *Mississippi* in 1936.[17]

In the *Brown* case the defendant and two other Negroes were charged with murder and offered pleas of "not guilty." During the investigation, the deputy sheriff and several other men accused the defendant of the crime. When he denied his guilt they seized him and twice hanged him by a rope to a limb of a tree. When he was let down the second time, he still protested his innocence and was tied to a tree and whipped. Finally he was released. A day or two later, the deputy and another person severely whipped the defendant again declaring that they would continue to whip him until the defendant confessed. The defendant then agreed to confess to such a statement as the deputy would dictate and he did so, after which he was delivered to the jail. Notwithstanding the fact that the whippings were admitted, the confessions were held to be admissible and the defendant was found guilty.

In reversing the decision of the state court, the United States Supreme Court stated the question as follows:

> The question in this case is whether convictions, which rest solely upon confessions shown to have been extorted by officers of the state by brutality and violence, are consistent with the due process of law required by the Fourteenth Amendment of the Constitution of the United States.[18]

The Court answered the question in the negative saying that confessions obtained in this manner were not freely and voluntarily given and a conviction based upon such a confession could not stand. The Court added:

> The state is free to regulate the procedure of its courts in accordance with its own conceptions of policy, unless in so doing it offends some principle of justice so rooted in the traditions and conscience of our people to be ranked as fundamental. . . . The rack and torture chamber may not be substituted for the witness stand. The state may not permit an accused to be hurried to conviction under mob domination—where the whole proceeding is but a mask—without supplying corrective process.[19]

[17] 297 US 278, 80 LEd 682, 56 SCt 461 (1936).

[18] *Id.* at 279.
[19] *Id.* at 285-86.

Under the authority of the Fourteenth Amendment, the Supreme Court will review the facts surrounding a confession taken by state officers, and will reverse a decision based upon a confession if the standards do not comply with those established by that Court.

(e) *Standards of proof*

The Supreme Court has on many occasions reiterated the rule that only voluntary confessions may be admitted at the trial to determine guilt or innocence. A question which until recently had been left in doubt, however, concerned the standard of proof required in determining if a confession is voluntary. Quite a bit of light was shed on this question in the recent case, *Lego* v. *Twomey*.[20]

In this case a pre-trial suppression hearing was conducted to determine if instructions given in the lower court met the voluntariness standards. The judge in the lower court had not found the confession voluntary "beyond a reasonable doubt" and the defendant argued that this made the admissibility of the confession erroneous. The Supreme Court, however, disagreed. The majority spokesman explained that the defendant is presumed innocent, and the burden falls on the prosecution to prove guilt beyond a reasonable doubt; but, the Court continued, "This is not the same burden that applies in determining the admissibility of a confession." In clearly stating the rule the Supreme Court commented:

> When a confession challenged as involuntary is sought to be used against a criminal defendant at the trial, he is entitled to a reliable and clearcut determination that the confession was in fact voluntarily rendered. Thus the prosecution must prove at least by a *preponderance of the evidence* that the confession was voluntary. (Emphasis added.)[21]

The Court resolved that the states are free, pursuant to their own law, to adopt higher standards such as the "beyond a reasonable doubt" standard, but that such a strict standard is not required by the Constitution.

---

[20] 404 US 477, 30 LEd(2d) 618, 92 SCt 619 (1972).   [21] *Id.* at 489.

Although state courts may require a higher standard than the preponderance of evidence test put forth by the Supreme Court in *Lego*, a Federal Court of Appeals cannot apply a tougher confession voluntariness standard.[22]

After discussing the ruling in the *Lego* case, the majority of the justices of the Fourth Circuit interpreted the mandate as follows:

> Upon this reading of *Lego*, the directions of *Inman* must be revised to admit those confessions into evidence where voluntariness is demonstrated by a preponderance of the evidence rather than the higher degree of proof.[23]

§ 6.3   The delay in arraignment rule

1. *Statement and discussion of rule*

In addition to the free and voluntary rule, the federal courts and some of the state courts have rejected confessions even though obtained freely and voluntarily where there was a delay in taking the person apprehended before a judicial officer as required by statute. Every state, as well as the United States, has a statute or code provision which provides that the person arrested must be taken "without unnecessary delay" or "forthwith" before the nearest available commissioner or other committing officer.

Prior to 1943, the fact that there had been delay in taking the accused before a committing magistrate did not in and of itself render the confession invalid. This delay was merely one of many factors which the courts would take into account in determining whether the confession was in fact freely and voluntarily given.

In the 1943 case of *McNabb* v. *United States*,[24] the Supreme Court for the first time began to insist on a strict and literal compliance with the federal rule requiring that prisoners be taken before a magistrate without undue delay. The case involved the murder of federal officers who were investigating

---

[22] United States v. Johnson, 495 F(2d) 378 (4thCir 1974). See also United States v. Cox, 485 F(2d) 669 (5thCir 1973).

[23] 495 F(2d) at 383.

[24] 318 US 332, 87 LEd 819, 63 SCt 608 (1943).

a ring of bootleggers in Tennessee. Following the shooting, several members of the McNabb family were arrested by federal officers and later jailed. They were questioned intermittently over a period of several days and finally made incriminating statements. During the period of the questioning, they were not, so far as the record showed, taken before a United States commissioner or judge as required by the federal code. The Supreme Court in reversing their conviction rested its holding purely on the ground that evidence secured through a disregard of procedures established by Congress could not be allowed to stand.

Apparently the *McNabb* rule was somewhat forgotten, for in 1957 there was, to put it mildly, an expression of surprise when a rape conviction was set aside because the accused had not been brought before the judicial officer as required by the federal code. In the case of *Mallory* v. *United States*,[25] the Supreme Court vigorously reaffirmed the *McNabb* rule and dispelled all doubt regarding its future application in the federal courts. The complaining witness in the *Mallory* case had gone to the basement of her apartment house to wash some laundry. Having difficulty in detaching a hose, she sought help from the janitor, who lived in a basement apartment with his wife, two grown sons, a younger son, and the petitioner, his nineteen-year-old half-brother. The janitor was not at home but the petitioner, who was alone in the apartment at the time, detached the hose and returned to his quarters. Shortly thereafter, a masked man, whose general features were identified to resemble those of the petitioner, and his two grown nephews attacked the woman.

The petitioner and one of his grown nephews disappeared from the apartment house shortly after this rape was committed. The petitioner was apprehended between 2:00 and 2:30 P.M. the following afternoon along with his older nephews who were also suspects. After questioning by the police, the three suspects were asked to submit to lie detector tests about 4:00 P.M. The operator of the polygraph was not located for about two hours during which time the suspects received

[25] 354 US 449, 1 LEd(2d) 1479, 77 SCt 1356 (1957).

food and drink. The petitioner was questioned starting about 8:00 P.M., and about one hour and a half later he stated that he might have done it. An attempt was made to reach the United States commissioner after 10:00 P.M., but when the commissioner was not located Mallory was requested to repeat the confession, which he did. Between 11:30 P.M. and 12:30 A.M. he dictated the confession to a typist. He was not brought before the United States commissioner until the next morning.

Notwithstanding this delay the confession was admitted into court, Mallory was found guilty of rape, and the jury imposed the death sentence. In reversing the conviction, the Court said:

> We cannot sanction this extended delay, resulting in confession, without subordinating the general rule of prompt arraignment to the discretion of arresting officers in finding exceptional circumstances for its disregard. In every case where the police resort to interrogation of an arrested person and secure a confession, they may well claim, and quite sincerely, that they were merely trying to check the information given by him. . . . It is not the function of the police to arrest, as it were, at large and to use an interrogation process at police headquarters in order to determine whom they should charge before a committing magistrate on "probable cause."[26]

Here the Court did not even consider the free and voluntary rule but reversed the confession merely because there had been a delay in bringing the accused before the United States Commissioner.[27]

2. Application in federal courts

The *McNabb* rule of 1943 was the result of a federal case involving the murder of a federal officer. Mallory was charged with rape, but because the alleged crime occurred in the District of Columbia, it was tried in federal court and the

[26] *Id.* at 455-56.

[27] It is interesting to note that Mallory was not reprosecuted on this charge since there was little evidence without the confession. However, in May, 1960, he was prosecuted in Philadelphia on a charge of rape and burglary, found guilty of burglary and aggravated assault. He was sentenced to serve twenty years on the burglary charge and eighteen months on the assault count, with sentences to run consecutively.

Federal Rules were followed. The statute which required that persons arrested be taken without unnecessary delay before the United States Commissioner applied only to federal courts. Therefore, the *McNabb-Mallory* rule, that in federal courts and in federal procedures a confession will not be admissible if obtained during that period when the arrested person should, according to federal law, have been brought before a federal judicial officer, as originally published, was limited to federal courts and did not apply in state courts.

3. *Application to the states*

Prior to *Miranda* the Supreme Court of the United States had not reversed a state court decision solely on the ground that the confession was obtained during a delay in arraignment. However, in the case of *Culombe* v. *Connecticut*,[28] one of the factors considered by the Supreme Court in reversing a state decision was the delay in arraignment.

The wording of the *Miranda* case mandates that the "delay in arraignment" rule be applied to state court proceedings. Justice Warren, writing for the majority, asserted that the *McNabb-Mallory* rule had received little consideration in the past quarter of a century, but that

> These supervisory rules, requiring production of an arrested person before a commissioner without unnecessary delay and excluding evidence obtained in default of that statutory obligation, were nonetheless responsive to the same considerations of the Fifth Amendment policy that face us now as to the States.[29]

Tying this rule with the decision in a previously decided case, Justice Warren continued:

> Our decision in *Malloy* v. *Hogan* . . . necessitates an examination of the scope of the privilege in state cases as well. In *Malloy*, we squarely held the privilege applicable to the States, and held that the substantive standards underlying the privilege applied with full force to the state court proceedings.[30]

---

[28] 367 US 568, 6 LEd(2d) 1073, 81 SCt 1860 (1961). See Part II for portions of this case.

[29] Miranda v. Arizona, 384 US at 463.

[30] *Id.* at 463-64.

This answered the question which many police officials, prosecutors and judges had been considering: that is, when would the *McNabb-Mallory* rule be made applicable to the states. Although there has been no decision specifically concerning this issue since *Miranda*, and there may not be one because of the other requirements of the *Miranda* case, it is anticipated that if a state case reaches the Supreme Court on the delay in arraignment rule exclusively, this rule will be made applicable to the states through the Fourteenth Amendment.

4. Determining "without unnecessary delay"

Because the *Mallory*[31] case did not state or define what was an "unnecessary delay," hundreds of cases have been decided in an attempt to reach a definition. In *Mallory* the petitioner was apprehended at about 2:30 in the afternoon but no attempt was made to reach the United States Commissioner until after 10 P.M. This delay was too long, but there were some factors which aggravated the situation. One was the fact that the Commissioner was in the same building as the federal agents who apprehended and interviewed the suspect and was readily available.

The Supreme Court has determined that it is not an unnecessary delay if the suspect voluntarily confesses while the police are awaiting the time when the Commissioner's office will be open. This is a *necessary* delay and would not affect the admissibility of the confession. Also, if the delay occurs after the confession, the delay will not make the confession inadmissible if the confession were made voluntarily and the other safeguards met.[32]

Congress, recognizing that the *Mallory* rule was not only ambiguous but placed an unnecessary burden on law enforcement officers, enacted legislation in 1968 which modified the *McNabb-Mallory* requirements. The part of that act which deals with the problem is as follows:

> In any criminal prosecution by the United States or by the District of Columbia, a confession made or given by a person who is a

[31] Mallory v. United States, 354 US at 450-51.

[32] United States v. Mitchell, 322 US 65, 88 LEd 1140, 64 SCt 896 (1944).

defendant therein, while such person was under arrest or other detention in the custody of any law-enforcement officer or law-enforcement agency, shall not be inadmissible solely because of delay in bringing such person before a commissioner or other officer empowered to commit persons charged with offenses against the laws of the United States or of the District of Columbia if such confession is found by the trial judge to have been made voluntarily and if the weight to be given the confession is left to the jury and if such confession was made or given by such person within *six hours* immediately following his arrest or other detention: *Provided, That* the time limitation contained in this subsection shall not apply in any case in which the delay in bringing such person before such commissioner or other officer beyond such six-hour period is found by the trial judge to be reasonable considering the means of transportation and the distance to be traveled to the nearest available such commissioner or other officer.[33]

This in effect states that a confession shall not be inadmissible in a federal court solely because the confession was obtained during the delay in arraignment. The act establishes the time as six hours between arrest and the making of the confession but gives the judge discretion to admit the confession even if more than six hours have elapsed if the judge finds the delay reasonable.

Because of the six hours mentioned in the Omnibus Crime Control Act, some attorneys representing defendants who gave voluntary statements claimed that if a person is detained more than six hours, a confession after that time is inadmissible for that reason. Two United States Courts of Appeals have disagreed.[34] A majority of the members of each court indicated that the six-hour period as established by Congress was a period in which a confession can be obtained and not be challenged solely because of delay in bringing the person before a magistrate. But if a longer delay occurs, it merely constitutes another factor to be considered by the trial judge in determining voluntariness.

A state court, the Indiana Court of Appeals for the First District, agrees that a delay of more than six hours (26 hours

[33] Omnibus Crime Control and Safe Streets Act of 1968 § 701(c), 82 Stat 210. This section of the act is found in 18 USC § 3501(c) (1970).

[34] United States v. Hathorn, 451 F(2d) 1337 (5thCir 1971); United States v. Halbert, 436 F(2d) 1226 (9thCir 1970).

in this case) should not by itself render a confession obtained during that period inadmissible.[35] In interpreting the state law, which is identical to the federal law, the Indiana court confirmed that the delay is but one factor to be considered in determining the admissibility of a confession taken more than six hours after the defendant's arrest.

"Unnecessary delay" depends upon the facts and circumstances of each case. If, as in the *Mallory* case, the judicial officer is readily available, the arrest is made during the office hours of the judicial officer, and there is no justification for not taking the person arrested before him for a hearing, the delay will probably be considered an unnecessary delay. On the other hand, if the arrest is made in the evening when no judicial officer is available, or if the arrest is made some distance from the judicial officer so that it is not practical to take the person arrested before the officer within the six-hour period, the delay will probably be considered necessary, and a confession, even if obtained during the period of delay, will be admitted if other requirements are met.

§ 6.4 Warning and waiver requirements (Miranda rule)

Up to this point two rules relating to the admissibility of confessions have been discussed: (1) The traditional "free and voluntary" rule, and (2) the later "delay in arraignment" rule. In 1966 the Supreme Court of the United States, by way of judicial decision, established further requirements which must be met before a confession is admissible into evidence.[36]

1. Statement and discussion of warning and waiver requirements

In the *Miranda* case the Supreme Court not only reversed the decision of a lower court which had upheld the use of a confession, but affirmatively enumerated warnings that must be given by enforcement officials. In summarizing the many points discussed in the case, the majority concluded that when

---

[35] Apple v. State, —— Ind App ——, 304 NE(2d) 321 (1974).

[36] Miranda v. Arizona, 384 US 436, 16 LEd(2d) 694, 86 SCt 1602 (1966).

an individual is taken into custody or otherwise deprived of his freedom by the authorities and is subject to questioning, he must be given the following warnings:

(1) "You have the right to remain silent and say nothing."
(2) "If you do make a statement, anything you say can and will be used against you in court."
(3) "You have the right to have an attorney present or to consult with an attorney."
(4) "If you cannot afford an attorney, one will be appointed for you prior to any questioning if you so desire."[37]

Not only must these warnings be given initially, but opportunity to exercise these rights must be afforded throughout the questioning. If the accused indicates at any stage of the questioning that he does not wish to be interrogated or that he wishes to consult an attorney, the questioning must stop.

The rights may be waived, but the waiver must be made voluntarily, knowingly and intelligently. However, a valid waiver will not be presumed simply from the silence of the accused after the warnings are given. Also, a waiver will not be considered as voluntary if there is valid evidence that the accused was threatened, tricked or cajoled.

Although the case in which these requirements were established is known as the *Miranda* case, there were in fact four cases incorporated into the decision. The confessions in the case of *Miranda* v. *Arizona* and each of the three companion cases, *Vignera* v. *New York*, *Westover* v. *United States* and *California* v. *Stewart*, were declared inadmissible by the United States Supreme Court. In *Miranda* and *Vignera*, the decisions of the state courts were reversed because the accused had not been effectively warned of his right to remain silent and of his right to have counsel. In *Westover* the confessions were inadmissible even though the defendant had been warned of his rights by the FBI agents prior to the taking of the statements, because the federal authorities were the

---

[37] *Id.* at 444. The Supreme Court left the door open for an exception when it stated: "However, unless we are shown other procedures which are at least as effective in apprising ac- cused persons of their right of silence and in assuring a continuous opportu- nity to exercise it, the . . . safeguards must be observed." *Id.* at 467.

beneficiaries of the pressures applied during the local in-custody interrogation, where no warnings were given. And in the *Stewart* case, the United States Supreme Court affirmed the action of the California Supreme Court which had rejected the confession because the warnings were not given.

To obtain a complete understanding of the case it should be read in its entirety, and all of the facts of the four cases studied. Here, only the facts relating to *Miranda* are stated and discussed. Ernesto Miranda was arrested on March 13 by Phoenix police officers and taken to the interrogation room where he was questioned by two police officers. He was not advised that he had a right to have an attorney present, but signed a statement that the confession was made voluntarily and was advised that the statement "may be used against him." After two hours he confessed to kidnapping and rape. The confession so obtained was admitted at the trial and he was sentenced to 20 to 30 years' imprisonment.

The Arizona Supreme Court affirmed the conviction, and appeal was taken to the United States Supreme Court. The United States Supreme Court reversed the Arizona Supreme Court decision and declared the confession inadmissible. That majority decided that Miranda was not apprised of his right to counsel nor effectively of his right not to be compelled to incriminate himself. Also, that the typed statement indicating the confession was voluntary, did not approach the knowing and intelligent waiver required to relinquish constitutional rights.

The format of the *Miranda* case is unusual. Ordinarily the facts of the case are stated at the beginning, with the reasoning coming after the facts, and the court decision coming last. The *Miranda* decision starts with a discussion of the rules, with page after page of an account of other cases, tactics used by police officers, police literature and rules to be followed in future cases, and ends with the facts of the four cases.

Although two constitutional questions—the right to counsel and self-incrimination—were both discussed throughout the case, the Supreme Court of the United States made it clear that the decision was predicated on the Fifth Amendment privilege against self-incrimination. Referring to the Fifth

Amendment in at least a half-dozen places, the Court included this remark:

> In order to combat these pressures and to permit a full opportunity to exercise the *privilege against self-incrimination*, the accused must be adequately and effectively apprised of his rights and the exercise of those rights must be fully honored. [Emphasis added.] [38]

2. Judicial interpretation of "custodial interrogation"

In several instances the majority in the *Miranda* case limited the warning and waiver requirements by prefixing these with such words as,

> the prosecution may not use statements, whether exculpatory or inculpatory, stemming from *custodial interrogation* of the defendant unless it demonstrates the use of procedural safeguards effective to secure the privilege against self-incrimination. [Emphasis added.][39]

And in another place the summary statement includes this conclusion:

> We hold that when an individual is taken into *custody* or otherwise deprived of his freedom by the authorities *and subjected to questioning*, the privilege against self-incrimination is jeopardized. [Emphasis added.][10]

In the case "custodial interrogation" is defined as:

> We mean *questioning* initiated by law enforcement officers after a person has been taken into *custody* or otherwise deprived of his freedom of action in any significant way. [Emphasis added.][11]

These words do not, of course, answer questions which have arisen in specific cases since *Miranda*. A series of cases has made it abundantly clear, however, that unless the accused is in custody or otherwise deprived of his freedom in a significant way, the warnings are not required. For example, a statement made to a police officer who arrived at the scene and said, "What happened?" was held admissible, the court say-

[38] *Id.* at 467.   [10] *Id.* at 478.
[39] *Id.* at 444.   [11] *Id.* at 444.

ing that this was not a custodial interrogation since the officer made no effort to take the defendant into custody.[42] And a statement made to an officer at a bar was held to be admissible when the suspect was free to leave.[43] Even a police station interrogation was held not to be an "in custody" interrogation under the circumstances in the case of *Freije* v. *United States*[44] decided by a Federal Circuit Court of Appeals. The court in that case explained, "We do not think the situation in this case could be held within *Miranda's* definition of custody." The court went on to reason that:

> Questioning of a witness can not be characterized as "custodial interrogation" simply because it occurs at a police establishment, ... since she never attempted to leave the presence of the police, it can not be said that her presence at Headquarters was against her will.[45]

On the other hand, the Supreme Court of the United States in a case decided in 1969 held that a statement taken at the home of the suspect without the *Miranda* warnings was not admissible.[46] Here, however, the Court pointed out that the officer admitted that the accused was not free to leave when he was questioned in his bedroom in the early hours of the morning.

A fine line exists as to whether a suspect is in "custody" or not in custody so as to make the *Miranda* advice necessary. Some additional cases will help to clarify this issue. In one case the Illinois Appellate Court for the First District held that it was not error to admit the exculpatory statements made by the defendant to the police who went to the home of the defendant after he called the police and told them that his wife had just shot herself or had been shot by someone else.[47] A majority of the members of the court refused to exclude the statement given to the officers when they arrived and said,

[42] Truex v. State, 282 Ala 191, 210 S(2d) 424 (1968); People v. Routt, 100 IllApp(2d) 388, 241 NE(2d) 206 (1968).

[43] State v. Zachmeier, 151 Mont 256, 441 P(2d) 737 (1968).

[44] 408 F(2d) 100 (1stCir 1969).

[45] *Id.* at 103, quoting Hicks v. United States, 382 F(2d) 158, 162 (DC Cir 1967).

[46] Orozco v. Texas, 394 US 324, 22 LEd(2d) 311, 89 SCt 1095 (1969).

[47] People v. Williams, 14 IllApp(3d) 789, 303 NE(2d) 585 (1973).

"What happened?" Such statements are admissible as responses to general on-the-scene questioning by the police as to facts surrounding the crime.

The Texas Court of Criminal Appeals confirmed what other courts have decided on many occasions: that stopping a traffic offender is not necessarily taking "custody" of the person.[48] Since the traffic offender was not in custody, under the facts of this case, his response to the officer's question about possession of a weapon, as a traffic ticket was being written, was not the product of a custodial interrogation.

On the other hand a gambling suspect—although not formally arrested—who was surrounded at his place of business with twenty armed agents was in custody, and evidence obtained after he had been asked if he had any concealed weapons nearby was not admissible according to the Fifth Circuit Court of Appeals.[49]

3. Adequacy of warning

In the *Miranda* case the majority of the Supreme Court stated, "He must be warned prior to any questioning," and then continued with some specific warnings that are required and which are stated in the previous paragraphs. In that same paragraph, however, the Court included the statement, "Unless other effective means are adopted to notify the person of his right to silence and to assure that the exercise of the rights will be scrupulously honored,"[50] the measures must be followed. The question then arises: what if the suspect is warned of his rights, but the warnings are not in the specific terminology used in the *Miranda* case?

Although some courts soon after the *Miranda* case demanded that the warnings be given in the exact words of *Miranda*, the trend is away from this strict rule. In the *Williams*[51] case, the Seventh Circuit decided that a statement by the police that "We have no way of furnishing you with an

[48] Wussow v. State, 507 SW(2d) 792 (Tex 1974).

[49] United States v. Castellana, 488 F(2d) 65 (5thCir 1974).

[50] Miranda v. Arizona, 384 US at 479.

[51] United States ex rel. Williams v. Twomey, 467 F(2d) 1248 (7thCir 1972).

attorney, but one will be appointed for you, if you wish, if and when you go to court," made the confession inadmissible.

On the other hand the Fourth Circuit Court of Appeals took a conflicting stand, holding that the requirements of *Miranda* are satisfied by advice to the in-custody suspect that if he cannot afford an attorney, a court will appoint one for him.[52]

The Hawaii Supreme Court felt that the Fourth Circuit's reasoning was more persuasive than the Seventh Circuit's, and held that the warning, "If you cannot afford an attorney, the court will appoint one for you," was sufficient.[53] In so doing the Hawaii court overruled previous state cases to the contrary. At least one other federal circuit has indicated that the warnings need not be in the exact words of *Miranda*.[54] In 1974 the United States Supreme Court refused to review this much litigated issue. Justice Douglas, noting the division of lower courts over the issue, pointed out that the issue was certainly "certworthy."

In the summary in the *Miranda* case, where the requirements were specifically stated, the majority of the Supreme Court used the phrase, "He must be warned . . . that anything he says *can* be used against him."[55] Because of this, many of the cards with the warnings printed thereon included such wording. In another part of the decision, however, the same judges required that "the right of the accused to remain silent must be accompanied by the explanation that anything said *can* and *will* be used against the individual in court."[56]

Because of the inconsistency in wording, cases have gone to appeal because the defendants claimed that the warning should have included "can and will" rather than "may, could be, or can." The Ninth Circuit Court of Appeals held that the language "anything you say *can* be used against you in court" met the requirements and that the defendant's contention that "can and will" be substituted was without merit.[57] The

[52] Wright v. North Carolina, 483 F(2d) 405 (4thCir 1973).

[53] State v. Maluia, 56 Haw 428, 539 P(2d) 1200 (1975). See also United States v. Olivares-Vega, 495 F(2d) 827 (2dCir 1974).

[54] United States v. Lamia, 429 F(2d) 373 (2dCir 1970).

[55] Miranda v. Arizona, 384 US at 444.

[56] *Id.* at 469.

[57] Davis v. United States, 425 F(2d) 673 (9thCir 1970).

Fifth Circuit Court of Appeals found that the difference between using "can" and "can and will" was inconsequential and upheld a confession where "can" was used.[58]

The rationale followed by the justices in some of the cases discussed—that if the words convey the substance of the warning and make the suspect aware of his constitutional right, a confession should not be held inadmissible merely because it was not in the exact form stated in *Miranda*—appears to be sound. On the other hand, to avoid any possibility of the confession being held inadmissible, it is preferable to read the statement verbatim, and use the terms "can and will" rather than "could be" or "can" or "may." Make sure that the accused understands the warnings and be able to articulate in court the facts indicating that the suspect did in fact receive the warnings and understood them.

There is some evidence that the courts will place a less strict interpretation on the *Miranda* requirements. However, until the Supreme Court of the United States decides in this matter, it is preferable to use the exact words as used in the case and as stated in previous paragraphs.

4. Waiver after warning

In *Miranda* the majority members of the Supreme Court included some definite statements about the waiver. Among these are the following:

> [A] valid waiver will not be presumed simply from the silence of the accused after warnings are given or simply from the fact that a confession was in fact eventually obtained. . . .
>
> . . . .
>
> [A]ny evidence that the accused was threatened, tricked, or cajoled into a waiver will, of course, show that the defendant did not voluntarily waive his privilege. . . .
>
> . . . .
>
> Opportunity to exercise these rights [self incrimination and counsel rights] must be afforded to him throughout the interrogation. After such warnings have been given, and such opportunity afforded him, the individual may knowingly and intelligently waive these rights and agree to answer questions or make a statement. . . .[59]

---

[58] United States v. Grady, 423 F(2d) 1091 (5thCir 1970).

[59] Miranda v. Arizona, 384 US at 475, 476, 479.

The Court goes on to explain that the prosecution must demonstrate that warnings and waiver have been given and that the statements made by the defendant were made voluntarily, knowingly and intelligently. A valid waiver will not be presumed simply from the silence of the accused after warnings are given, nor will a waiver be considered as voluntary if there is valid evidence that the accused was threatened, tricked or cajoled. Not only must the warnings be given initially, but opportunity to exercise these rights must be afforded throughout the questioning. If the accused indicates at any stage of the questioning that he does not wish to be interrogated, or that he wishes to consult with an attorney, the questioning must stop.

Few believed that the matter of waiver would end with the *Miranda* decision. One question which has reoccurred frequently is whether or not the interrogation must cease forever once the person in custody indicates he wishes to remain silent. After quite a few lower court decisions, the Supreme Court in December, 1975 ruled that the police may resume questioning a suspect who has exercised his right to remain silent as long as they respect the suspect's right to stop answering questions at any time.[60]

In Mr. Justice Stewart's opinion, there is nothing in the *Miranda* decision that requires a police officer to cease questioning forever once a defendant expresses his wish to remain silent. Nevertheless, *Miranda* must be read in light of the Court's intention to afford a person in custody the opportunity to cut off questioning at any time.

In the *Mosley* case the defendant was taken into custody on robbery charges and given the full *Miranda* warnings. After the suspect indicated that he did not want to answer any questions, his request was honored and the questions ceased. Some two hours later he was questioned by officers from the homicide bureau about a killing in an unrelated robbery with which he had not been charged. At the second questioning he was given fresh *Miranda* warnings and confessed to the second crime. On appeal, however, he claimed

[60] Michigan v. Mosley, 423 US 96,
46 LEd(2d) 313, 96 SCt 321 (1975).

that he should not have even been questioned the second time after he had exercised his right to remain silent. The majority found that the defendant's rights were fully protected and upheld the conviction.[61]

To the two dissenting justices, Justice Brennan and Justice Marshall, this was a distortion of *Miranda's* constitutional principles, and the process used here eroded the *Miranda* rights.[62]

This should not be interpreted as opening the door to a procedure which would allow the officer to discontinue questioning when the suspect has asserted his rights and then, at some later time, continue the questioning. Unless the suspect of his own volition indicates later that he desires to waive his rights and make a statement, or unless some unusual circumstances justify additional questions, the questioning should discontinue once the accused has exercised his right to remain silent.

5. Effect of legislative acts on Miranda requirements

In an obvious attempt to negate some of the strict requirements placed on investigators by the Supreme Court, the United States Congress in 1968 added several sections to the Omnibus Crime Control Act. Paragraphs (a) and (b) from section 3501 of Title 18 of the United States Code, derived from the Omnibus Crime Act, relate directly to the warnings as required in the *Miranda* case. These provisions of the act are as follows:

(a) In any criminal prosecution brought by the United States or by the District of Columbia, a confession, as defined in subsection (e) hereof, shall be admissible in evidence if it is voluntarily given. Before such confession is received in evidence, the trial judge shall, out of the presence of the jury, determine any issue as to voluntariness. If the trial judge determines that the confession was voluntarily made, it shall be admitted in evidence and the trial judge shall permit the jury to hear relevant evidence on the issue of voluntariness and shall instruct the jury to give such weight to the confession as the jury feels it deserves under all the circumstances.

(b) The trial judge in determining the issue of voluntariness shall

[61] *Id.* at 107.   [62] *Id.* at 111.

take into consideration all the circumstances surrounding the giving of the confession, including (1) the time elapsing between arrest and arraignment of the defendant making the confession, if it was made after arrest and before arraignment, (2) whether such defendant knew the nature of the offense with which he was charged or of which he was suspected at the time of making the confession, (3) whether or not such defendant was advised or knew that he was not required to make any statement and that any such statement could be used against him, (4) whether or not such defendant was advised prior to questioning of his right to the assistance of counsel, and (5) whether or not such defendant was without the assistance of counsel when questioned and when giving such confession.

The presence or absence of any of the above-mentioned factors to be taken into consideration by the judge need not be conclusive on the issue of voluntariness of the confession.[63]

Paragraph (a) makes the traditional voluntary test the sole criterion of the admissibility of a confession in federal court. Paragraph (b) delineates the factors which shall be considered in determining the issue of voluntariness. The mandatory requirements of *Miranda* are to be considered by the trial judge but they *"need not be conclusive* on the issue of voluntariness of the confession." These paragraphs direct that the trial judge take all of these factors, as well as others, into consideration, but that they only be considered as they reflect on the voluntariness of the confession. A confession may therefore be admissible under this act even if the technical requirements of *Miranda* are not met.

The first question that comes to mind is whether or not the legislative body has the authority to change the requirements as established by the Supreme Court when those requirements are based upon a constitutional provision. When this provision was added to the statutory laws of the United States, some legal authorities, including the criminal law committee of the Federal Bar Association, argued that this was squarely in conflict with the Supreme Court decision in *Miranda* and therefore unconstitutional. Other students of constitutional law disagree, arguing that the Supreme Court

[63] Crime Control Act, *supra* note 33, § 701(a) & (b), *codified* at 18 USC § 3501(a) & (b) (1970).

has criticized legislative bodies for not taking action to establish procedural guidelines.[64]

Those who argue that this provision is constitutional point out that in the *Miranda* case the majority encouraged legislative bodies to take action using this terminology:

> Congress and the States are free to develop their own safeguards for the privilege, so long as they are fully as effective as those described above in informing accused persons of the right of silence and in affording a continuous opportunity to exercise it.[65]

Surprisingly, the United States Supreme Court, as of the date of this printing, has not decided on the constitutionality of this section of the federal code. However, the Tenth Circuit Court of Appeals has considered this section and concluded that the trial judge properly relied on section 3501 in admitting the confession of a counterfeiting defendant who claimed that she was not advised of her right to counsel and that the police continued to interrogate her when she asked for a lawyer.[66] The ruling, which in effect re-establishes the voluntary test but enumerates some factors which the judge must consider in determining voluntariness, is not in violation of the Constitution. This is a decision of but one circuit court of appeals. Therefore, it is not safe to rely upon this reasoning until the Supreme Court acts in this matter.

§ 6.5 Exclusion of confession as a means of enforcing the Fourth Amendment

Up to this point three avenues of challenging the admissibility of confessions have been discussed. To review:

(1) Confessions are inadmissible unless the prosecution can show that they are free, voluntary and trustworthy; (2) if the defense can prove to the satisfaction of the court that the confession was obtained during an unnecessary delay in arraignment, the confession will not be admitted; and (3) with some exceptions, the prosecution must demonstrate that the

---

[64] United States v. Wade, 388 US 218, 18 LEd(2d) 1149, 87 SCt 1926 (1967).

[65] Miranda v. Arizona, 384 US at 490.

[66] United States v. Crocker, 510 F(2d) 1129 (10thCir 1975).

Miranda warnings (or equivalent) were administered, and that the defendant waived his rights before the evidence will be admissible in court.

This fourth avenue of challenge relies on the "fruit of the poisonous tree" doctrine or what is sometimes called the *Wong Sun* doctrine.[67] Simply stated, this rule provides that if the confession is derived immediately from an unlawful arrest or unlawful search, the confession is "tainted" and neither it nor its fruits may be used against the defendant whose Fourth Amendment rights were violated.

In the case of *Wong Sun* v. *United States*,[68] an oral statement implicating one of the accused was held inadmissible because of an unlawful entry and an unauthorized arrest. The facts of this case are complicated, and the case should be read to fully understand the significance. Because of the complicated facts and the complexity of the decision, it has earned the name of "The Chinese Puzzle Case." Over the objection of the accused, statements made orally by one of the petitioners in his bedroom at the time of the arrest and search were admitted into evidence at the trial.

The court found that the arrest was illegal, as not based upon probable cause, that the incidental search was therefore illegal, and that the oral confession made at the time was not admissible. The judge reasoned that such statements were fruits of the agents' unlawful action, and that the exclusionary prohibition relating to evidence obtained by illegal search extends to the indirect as well as the direct products of such invasions.

Although denying the use of a confession obtained immediately after an illegal arrest, the Supreme Court in the *Wong Sun* case allowed into evidence a second confession taken after the suspect had been released on his own recognizance. Here the United States Supreme Court said the taint had dissipated sufficiently so that the confession would be considered voluntary and admissible. The Sixth Circuit Court

---

[67] The name being derived from Wong Sun v. United States, 371 US 471, 9 LEd(2d) 441, 83 SCt 407 (1963).

[68] 371 US 471, 9 LEd(2d) 441, 83 SCt 407 (1963).

of Appeals has decided, however, that where the unlawful arrest was followed by a detention of some 42 hours after which time the defendant finally confessed, the confession was inadmissible.[69]

Many other lower court decisions were rendered between 1963 when the *Wong Sun* case was handed down and 1975. However, the United States Supreme Court did not again fully consider the doctrine until the case of *Brown* v. *Illinois*[70] in 1975. The question presented in the *Brown* case was whether an illegal arrest and search tainted the confession obtained after the warnings and procedures required by *Miranda* had been met. Here the defendant was arrested without probable cause in what the court defined as a clearly investigatory arrest. Prior to questioning, however, the officers properly advised him of his rights, and the accused voluntarily agreed to make statements to the police. The prosecution claimed that since the defendant had waived his rights voluntarily, the fact that there was an illegal arrest preceding the advice should not taint the confession.

Mr. Justice Blackmun, speaking for the majority, noted that there was a causal connection between the illegality of the arrest and the confession, and that giving the *Miranda* warnings by themselves does not attenuate the taint of an illegal arrest. The majority of the Court in effect agreed that the Fifth Amendment rights are protected by giving the *Miranda* warnings, but that this in itself does not protect the Fourth Amendment rights; that despite *Miranda* warnings the Fourth and Fourteenth Amendments require the exclusion from evidence of statements obtained as the fruits of an arrest which the arresting officer knows, or should have known, was without probable cause and unconstitutional.

§ 6.6 Corroboration

Under early English law, confessions were admissible even if there was no other evidence to prove guilt of the accused. According to the writers of the period, this led to some persons' being found guilty when in fact there was no crime. In

[69] Hale v. Henderson, 485 F(2d) 266 (6thCir 1973).

[70] 422 US 590, 45 LEd(2d) 416, 95 SCt 2254 (1975).

this country the rule is generally adopted that if the state relies upon the confession, it must also have evidence independent of the confession to show the *corpus delicti;* that is, the fact that the crime charged has in fact been committed. This does not mean, as some seem to argue, that it is necessary to produce the body in a homicide case. It is sufficient if the outside proof together with the confession satisfies the jury beyond a reasonable doubt that a crime in fact has been committed. Some states have by statute codified this requirement and require that the *corpus delicti* be proved by independent proof.

In the case of *Burton v. United States*[71] decided in 1968, the Supreme Court determined that an admission of an extra-judicial confession of a co-defendant who did not take the stand deprived the defendant of his rights under the Sixth Amendment confrontation clause. That Court cautioned that such co-defendant's confession could not be used even if only for the purpose of corroborating statements made in the defendant's own confession.

In a more recent case the Supreme Court has again been called upon to determine if a statement made by the defendant's co-defendant could be offered into evidence by a police officer who took this statement from the co-defendant who did not testify himself.[72] Speaking for the majority, Mr. Justice Rehnquist refused to reverse the conviction where it was clear beyond a reasonable doubt that guilt was manifested by the defendant's confession and the comparatively insignificant effect of the co-defendant's admission. The mere finding of a violation of the *Burton* rule in the course of the trial does not, according to this decision, automatically require reversal of the ensuing criminal conviction. The Court's conclusion was that the "minds of the average jury" would not have found the state's case significantly less persuasive had the testimony containing the co-defendant's admissions been excluded. The admission into evidence of these statements, therefore, was at most harmless error.

[71] 391 US 123, 20 LEd(2d) 476, 88 SCt 1620 (1968).

[72] Schneble v. Florida, 405 US 427, 31 LEd(2d) 340, 92 SCt 1056 (1972).

§ 6.7   Derivative evidence

Many of the older state court decisions and a few state statutes authorized the use of evidence obtained as the result of an otherwise invalid confession. For example, if a confession were obtained from a murder suspect by the use of force and duress, and in the confession the suspect told where the murder weapon was hidden, the earlier cases allowed such evidence to be used at the trial. However, in 1962 the California Supreme Court equated evidence discovered as the result of an involuntary confession with evidence discovered as the result of an unreasonable search and seizure and held that such evidence was not admissible. The court in the case of *People* v. *Ditson*[73] stated:

> It follows that the reason for the common law rule permitting the introduction of real evidence discovered by means of an involuntary confession—that such evidence tends to prove the trustworthiness of the confession—must now be deemed Constitutionally indefensible, and hence that the rule must be abandoned.

Since *Miranda*, the "fruit of the poisonous tree" doctrine unquestionably applies to real evidence obtained by means of an invalid confession. After discussing the warnings which must be given prior to questioning, the Court declared:

> But unless and until such warnings and waiver are demonstrated by the prosecution at trial, *no* evidence obtained as a result of interrogation can be used against him. [Emphasis added.][74]

Just how far does the fruit of the poisonous tree doctrine extend? For example, will the testimony of the witness be excluded when the identity of that witness has been disclosed by the illegally obtained confession? In an often misunderstood and misquoted decision, the United States Supreme Court in 1974 determined that the exclusionary rule which prohibits the admission of certain statements when the *Mi-*

---

[73] 57 Cal(2d) 415, 20 Cal Rptr 165, 369 P(2d) 714 (1962). See also Lee v. State, 428 SW(2d) 328 (Tex 1968), which held that a license plate obtained indirectly by the illegal confession was not admissible into evidence.

[74] Miranda v. Arizona, 384 US at 479.

randa warning is not given, did not apply to the in-court testimony of a witness who was discovered as a result of no-warning questioning.[75] In this case the defendant was arrested for raping and severely beating a forty-three-year old woman. Before the commencement of the interrogation, the police asked the defendant if he knew what crime he had been arrested for, if he wanted an attorney, and if he understood his constitutional rights. The defendant replied that he did understand the charge, that he did not want an attorney, and that he understood his rights. The police advised him further that any statements he might make could be used against him at a later date but did not advise him that he would be furnished counsel free of charge if he could not pay for such services himself.

During the questioning, the defendant, in relating an alibi, stated that he was with a friend, one Robert Henderson, at the time of the crime. The police, however, elicited from Henderson information tending to incriminate the defendant.

Prior to the trial the defendant made a motion to exclude Henderson's testimony because the defendant had revealed Henderson's identity without receiving the full warnings mandated by the *Miranda* decision. This motion was denied and Henderson testified. Following the affirmance of the conviction, the defendant sought *habeas corpus* relief which the federal district court granted, finding that Henderson's testimony was inadmissible because of the *Miranda* violation. The United States Court of Appeals affirmed.

A majority of the members of the United States Supreme Court, in reversing the lower federal courts and approving the admission of the testimony, made these comments in relation to the testimony of the witness:

> This Court said in *Miranda* that statements taken in violation of the *Miranda* principles must not be used to prove the prosecution's case at trial. That requirement was fully complied with by the state court here: respondent's statements, claiming that he was with Henderson and then asleep during the time period of the crime were not admitted against him at trial. . . .

[75] Michigan v. Tucker, 417 US 433, 41 LEd(2d) 182, 94 SCt 2357 (1974).

Just as the law does not require that a defendant receive a perfect trial, only a fair one, it can not realistically require that policemen investigating serious crimes make no errors whatsoever. The pressures of law enforcement and the vagaries of human nature would make such an expectation unrealistic. Before we penalize police error, therefore, we must consider whether the sanction serves a valid and useful purpose.[76]

Although the Court concluded that it would serve no useful purpose to apply the exclusionary rule to the testimony given by Henderson and held that Tucker had been properly convicted of rape, the Court did not go so far as to hold that it is not necessary to administer the *Miranda* warnings. The Supreme Court cautioned that if the *Miranda* warnings are *not* administered, or at least if compliance with the *Miranda* principles are not proved by the prosecutor, statements will not be admitted into evidence. On the other hand, if the failure to advise the suspect of his right to have appointed counsel, as in this case, has no bearing on the reliability of a witness, the testimony of the discovered witness should not be excluded.

In the *Tucker* case the Supreme Court made reference to the strong interest of our justice system in making available to the courts all relevant and trustworthy evidence and to the fact that society has an interest in effective prosecution of criminals. That Court also reminded that the case of *Harris v. New York*[77] held the failure to give the suspect the full *Miranda* warnings did not prevent use of his statements to impeach his testimony at trial, and that such failure does not make evidence inadmissible for all purposes. Nonetheless, unless the Supreme Court goes further, it is preferable to follow the rule which holds that tangible evidence obtained as a direct result of an illegal confession will not be admitted in court.

On the other hand, if the record clearly shows that the statements taken from the accused during the police interrogation were not involuntary, the use of a witness discovered

---

[76] *Id.* at 445-46.

[77] 401 US 222, 28 LEd(2d) 1, 91 SCt 643 (1971).

by the police as a result of the accused's statements will be allowed.

§ 6.8   Admissible statements

Too often the investigator, after reading the Supreme Court decisions, feels that all statements will be inadmissible. However, the Supreme Court in the *Miranda* case emphasized that it did not purport to find all confessions inadmissible. In making this point the Court remarked:

> Confessions remain a proper element in law enforcement. Any statement given freely and voluntarily without any compelling influence is, of course, admissible in evidence. . . . There is no requirement that the police stop a person who enters a police station and states that he wishes to confess to a crime, or a person who calls the police to offer a confession or any other statement he desires to make. Volunteered statements of any kind are not barred by the Fifth Amendment and their admissibility is not affected by our holding today.[78]

The Court, in calling attention to specific instances where interrogation would be valid, held that when investigating crimes the officer may inquire of persons not under restraint. Also, on-the-scene questioning as to facts surrounding a crime or other general questioning of citizens in the fact-finding process is not affected by the holding. This type of questioning was distinguished from the questioning of a suspect, since in this situation the compelling atmosphere inherent in the process of in-custody interrogation is not necessarily present.

The *Miranda* case requires that warnings be given to a person in custody and who is to be *subjected* to *interrogation*. It does not require that a person be warned if he voluntarily makes a statement without interrogation or other compelling influences. Therefore, if a person who is not being questioned and who is not being otherwise influenced to make a statement voluntarily does so, there is no requirement that he be stopped and the warning be given.

This rule was reaffirmed in a 1976 case when the Supreme

[78] Miranda v. Arizona, 384 US at 478.

Court decided that it is not necessary to give the warnings called for in *Miranda* to a taxpayer who is under criminal tax investigation where the taxpayer is not in custody.[79] The petitioner in the *Beckwith* case argued that he was placed in a position which would be legally equivalent to that in the *Miranda* situation and, therefore, statements made should not have been admitted unless the *Miranda* warnings had been given. The Court was not persuaded by this argument since the questioning, even though of a criminal nature, was in the home of the defendant and the defendant was not in custody. The Court said:

> Although the "focus" of an investigation may indeed have been on Beckwith at the time of the interview in the sense that it was his tax liability which was under scrutiny, he hardly found himself in the custodial situation described by the *Miranda* Court as the basis for its holding.[79a]

In an even more recent case [80] the Supreme Court found that a person is not necessarily in custody even in a police environment. In admitting the confession the majority held:

> In the present case, however, there is *no* indication that the questioning took place in a context where respondent's freedom to depart was restricted in any way. He came voluntarily to the police station, where he was immediately informed that he was not under arrest. At the close of a one-half hour interview respondent did in fact leave the police station without hindrance. It is clear from these facts that Mathiason was not in custody "or otherwise deprived of his freedom of action in any significant way."

The Court warned that in some special circumstances a suspect's will may be overborne by law enforcement agents even when he is not in custody. When such a claim is advanced, the Court explained, the record should be examined to determine if the confession met the voluntariness requirements.

Empirical investigation has established that suspects do

[79] Beckwith v. United States, 425 US 341, 48 LEd(2d) 1, 96 SCt 1612 (1976).

[79a] *Id.* at 347.

[80] Oregon v. Mathiason, —— US ——, 50 LEd(2d) 714, 97 SCt 711 (1977).

make statements even after the warnings have been administered. Questioning of suspects and witnesses remains a valuable tool in the effective prosecution of violators. Evidence also indicates that violators are successfully prosecuted without using the questioning techniques condemned in the *Miranda* case. Police officers and prosecutors have learned when to use the confession as an effective tool and when to rely upon other investigative measures.

In the sections that follow, other examples of situations where statements have been upheld as admissible are stated and discussed.

§ 6.9   Use of confession for impeachment purposes

If a confession is found to be inadmissible to help establish the prosecutor's "case in chief" because the *Miranda* warnings were not administered, is that confession nevertheless admissible to impeach the credibility of the defendant if he takes the stand in his own behalf? This was the question presented to the United States Supreme Court in *Harris* v. *New York*[81] in 1971. In the *Harris* case the defendant was charged with selling heroin. Recognizing that the *Miranda* requirements were not met, the prosecutor did not offer statements allegedly made by the defendant to show defendant's guilt. However, when the defendant took the stand in his own defense and made statements contrary to the pretrial statements made to the police, the pre-trial statements were offered in evidence to impeach the testimony of the defendant. The extrajudicial confession was admitted at the trial for the limited purpose of impeaching the in-court testimony of the defendant. The jury was instructed to use the statement only to assess the defendant's credibility and not as evidence of guilt.

Chief Justice Burger, speaking for the majority of the Supreme Court used these words in approving the use of the confession for the limited impeachment purpose:

> Every criminal defendant is privileged to testify in his own defense or to refuse to do so. But that privilege cannot be construed

[81] 401 US 222, 28 LEd(2d) 1, 91 SCt 643 (1971).

to include the right to commit perjury. . . . Having voluntarily taken the stand, petitioner was under an obligation to speak truthfully and accurately, and the prosecution here did no more than utilize the traditional truth-testing devices of the adversary process.[82]

The majority of the Supreme Court in 1975 reiterated its approval of the limited use of custodial statements for impeachment purposes.[83] Again the Supreme Court approved the use of the confession by the prosecution when used for rebuttal purposes to impeach the credibility of the defendant who took the stand in his own behalf.

While custodial statements inadmissible under *Miranda* may nonetheless be admissible for limited impeachment purposes, silence of the accused after warnings may not be used for impeachment purposes. In the case of *United States v. Hale,*[84] the accused was arrested for robbery and transported to the police station where he was advised of his right to remain silent. During the questioning, an officer inquired as to the source of the money found on the person of the suspect. The suspect made no explanation and in fact said nothing during this questioning period, but while testifying in his own behalf at the trial, he explained how he came into possession of the money found on his person.

In an effort to impeach the defendant's explanation of his possession of the money, the prosecutor caused the defendant to admit on cross-examination that he had not offered the exculpatory information to the police at the time of his arrest. The government argued that since the defendant chose to testify in his own behalf at the trial, it was permissible to impeach his credibility by proving that he had chosen to remain silent at the time of arrest. However, after reviewing the law on the subject the majority decided that no reference could be made to the respondent's silence.

In view of this and other cases decided since *Miranda*, the police are not justified in relying on the "tacit confession" in proving guilt of the suspect, or even for impeachment purposes.

---

[82] *Id.* at 225-26 (footnote omitted).
[83] Oregon v. Hass, 420 US 714, 43 LEd(2d) 570, 91 SCt 1215 (1975).
[84] 422 US 171, 45 LEd(2d) 99, 95 SCt 2133 (1975).

§ 6.10 Use of statements made at grand jury hearings

Finding that judicial inquiries and custodial interrogations are not equivalents, the United States Supreme Court in 1976 refused to exclude incriminating statements made to a grand jury hearing even though the *Miranda* requirements were not met where the statements were used in a subsequent prosecution of the witness for perjury.[85]

During the course of a grand jury investigation into narcotics traffic, the witness, Mandujano, denied any knowledge of such traffic. He specifically denied discussing the purchase of heroin with money advanced to him by an undercover agent. The falsity of the statement was conceded but the defendant claimed that the testimony before the grand jury should be suppressed because the government failed to provide the warnings called for by *Miranda*. The district court granted his motion to suppress and the court of appeals affirmed. The government appealed to the United States Supreme Court, where the decision was reversed and remanded.

It is apparent that there is a reluctance on the part of the majority of the Supreme Court to extend the *Miranda* rationale. According to the Supreme Court, the lower courts "erroneously applied the standards fashioned by this Court in *Miranda*." The warnings enumerated in *Miranda*, in the Court's words, "were aimed at the evils seen by the Court as endemic to police interrogation of a person in custody." They need not be followed in other situations.

§ 6.11 Non-official questioning

The requirements of warning and waiver as established by the *Miranda* case are based on the Fifth Amendment self-incrimination protection. The constitutional prohibitions against self-incrimination only operate against official action. Therefore, in the absence of state involvement, volunteered statements made to private citizens are admissible even if no *Miranda* warnings are given.[86]

[85] United States v. Mandujano, 425 US 564, 48 LEd(2d) 212, 96 SCt 1768 (1976).

[86] United States v. Casteel, 476 F(2d) 152 (10thCir 1973); Commonwealth v. Mahnke, —— Mass ——, 335 NE(2d) 660 (1975), *cert. denied*, 425 US 959 (1976).

In Chapter Four a series of cases holding that the Fourth Amendment prohibitions operate only against official action was discussed. The conclusion was that seizure of evidence by a private person is admissible even though the seizure would have been unreasonable if carried out by a law enforcement officer. The same reasoning applies where statements are made to a private individual.

Nevertheless, as the free and voluntary rule is based in part on a rule of evidence (the evidence must be trustworthy), the defendant would have grounds for challenge if force were used by a private citizen. On the other hand, if the challenge is predicated only on the *Miranda* rule or the delay in arraignment rule, the statements made to the private person would no doubt be admissible.

It is interesting to note that at the second trial of Ernesto A. Miranda, a confession made to his mistress was admitted. The Arizona Supreme Court found that the mistress was not obligated to administer the warnings as set out by the Supreme Court in the earlier *Miranda* case.[87]

Quite clearly if there is any official involvement, the private citizen exception would not be applicable. It is apparent that the question of official involvement will be a recurring one, especially as private security people are licensed by state agencies.

§ 6.12   Standing to challenge admissibility

In the discussion relating to search and seizure, it was pointed out that a person whose Fourth Amendment rights are not violated cannot complain when illegally seized evidence is used against him. This general reasoning applies in regard to Fifth Amendment self-incrimination rights.

In an Illinois case police officers arrested A for robbery and questioned him about other persons involved in robberies in that area. After A implicated B, B was arrested, and without the *Miranda* warnings he told the police during the investigation that the defendant had committed crimes in that area. The defendant claims that the evidence against him

[87] State v. Miranda, 104 Ariz 174, 450 P(2d) 364 (1969).

should have been suppressed because it was obtained by un-lawful interrogation of the two other suspects. The Supreme Court of Illinois disagreed and upheld the conviction. The basis of the court's reasoning was that the rights protected by *Miranda* are violated only when evidence obtained without the required warnings and waiver is introduced against a person whose own questioning produced the evidence.[88]

§ 6.13　Admissibility of a second confession after an inadmissible first confession

Will a tainted first confession make a second confession inadmissible which has been obtained after all the safeguards have been complied with? This question was thoroughly discussed in the case of *Payne* v. *State*[89] in 1960. In this case the defendant was charged with first degree murder. He was denied a hearing before a magistrate, was not advised of his right to remain silent, was held for three days without counsel, advisor or friends, was denied food for long periods of time, and was finally told by the chief of police that thirty or forty people wanted to get him. During the period he made a statement in which he admitted the crime. Later he was requested to re-enact the crime, and in doing so he repeated in effect what he had said in the confession several hours before.

The question concerned the admissibility of the statements he made while re-enacting the crime and testimony concerning this re-enactment. The court, after considering the law in such a situation, held that if a confession is obtained by methods which would make it involuntary, subsequent confessions while the accused is under the operation of the same influence are also involuntary. The court went on to say that once a confession made under improper influence is obtained, the presumption arises that a subsequent confession of the same crime flows from the same influences, even though made to a different person than the one to whom the first was made. Of course, this presumption can be overcome, but the prosecution must have sufficient evidence to do so. If it can

---

[88] People v. Denham, 41 Ill(2d) 1, 241 NE(2d) 415 (1968).

[89] 231 Ark 727, 332 SW(2d) 233 (1960).

be shown by the prosecution that the influences operating when the first confession was made did not exist when the later confession was made, the second confession may be admissible. However, the evidence to rebut this presumption must be clear and convincing.

Would like reasoning apply if the second confession were made to another law enforcement agency? This is similar to the situation which occurred in the case of *Westover* v. *United States*, which was decided in the same opinion as *Miranda*. Here the FBI agents interrogated the accused after they had warned him of his right to remain silent and his right to have an attorney. However, prior to this interrogation, Westover had been in the custody of local police for over fourteen hours and had been interrogated at length during that period. The Court declared that despite the fact that the FBI agents had given warning prior to their interview, from Westover's point of view the warning came at the end of the interrogation process, not at the beginning, and that under these circumstances an intelligent waiver of constitutional rights cannot be assumed.

But if at the first interview the defendant makes no incriminating statements or as one court put it, does not "let the cat out of the bag," the fact that improper procedures were followed at the first interview does not necessarily contaminate the second interview.[90] The New Jersey Supreme Court, citing other cases including the case of *Commonwealth* v. *Marabel*,[91] ruled that as the defendant said nothing damaging during the first interview where warnings were not given, the fact that there were no warnings did not taint a later confession where the proper warnings were given before the confession was made.[92]

As a matter of correct practice the warning should be given prior to any interrogation. If police officers receive the suspect after he has been in the custody of another department, the interrogation should not proceed unless the accused knowingly and intelligently waives his rights.

[90] See United States v. Begay, 441 F(2d) 1136 (10thCir 1971); United States v. Trabucco, 424 F(2d) 1311 (5thCir 1970).

[91] 445 Penn 435, 283 A(2d) 285 (1971).

[92] State v. Melvin, 65 NJ 1, 319 A(2d) 450 (1974).

§ 6.14　Summary and practical suggestions

In this chapter the historical development of the rule concerning free and voluntary confessions was discussed. This rule developed over a period of many years and is recognized in all state and federal courts, as well as in England. Of more recent origin is the so-called "delay in arraignment" rule, which was established by the *McNabb* and *Mallory* cases. This rule was rejected by most of the state courts. However, since the decision in *Miranda* v. *Arizona* the delay in arraignment rule is also applied to the state courts via the Fourteenth Amendment.

In 1966 the United States Supreme Court added additional requirements to those established by previous court decisions and statutory enactments.[93] In the *Miranda* case the Supreme Court held that unless other safeguards are adopted, the person in custody must be warned prior to questioning that he has a right to remain silent, that anything he says can and will be used against him in a court of law, that he has the right to the presence of an attorney, and that if he cannot afford an attorney, one will be appointed for him prior to any questioning if he so desires. Additionally, opportunity must be afforded the person questioned to exercise these rights. The Fifth Amendment self-incrimination rights may be waived but they must be knowingly and intelligently waived.

A confession is also considered incompetent and inadmissible if it immediately follows an illegal arrest or search, even if it meets the other requirements. In this regard, offering the *Miranda* warnings after an illegal arrest or search does not cure the Fourth Amendment violation. In addition, the courts have excluded confessions as a means of enforcing the Sixth Amendment "right to counsel" protection. This is discussed in the following chapters.

A confession standing alone will not form the judicial basis for a conviction. Additional outside proof must be introduced to satisfy the jury beyond a reasonable doubt that a crime has in fact been committed.

[93] See Miranda v. Arizona, 384 US 436, 16 LEd(2d) 694, 86 SCt 1602 (1966).

If a confession is found not to meet the required standards, not only will the confession often be inadmissible for the prosecution's case in chief, but real evidence derived from that confession will probably not be admitted either. However, a witness located as a result of an involuntary confession will probably be allowed to testify if his testimony otherwise meets the legal requirements.

The *Miranda* decision and post-*Miranda* decisions have made it clear that warnings are not required in all cases. If the person is not in "custody" or is not "questioned," statements voluntarily given may be admitted even if no warning was given. And even though in-custody statements may be inadmissible under *Miranda*, for the prosecutor's case in chief, they may be used to impeach a testifying defendant's credibility when not claimed to be coerced. However, evidence that the defendant remained silent during police interrogation, and after warnings were given, may not be used to impeach the testifying defendant's credibility.

A confession may be found by the court to be inadmissible against the person whose rights were violated, but some courts have approved the introduction of evidence against persons other than those whose questioning produced the confession. And the *Miranda* requirements only apply where there is official action. If a confession is obtained by one acting solely in a non-official capacity, that statement may be admitted without the necessity of administering the *Miranda* warnings.

There is a presumption that a second confession, obtained after an involuntary first confession, was induced by the same forces which made the first confession inadmissible. However, this presumption in some instances can be overcome by the prosecution.

The courts have established strict rules concerning the admissibility of confessions, but these rules do not prohibit all interrogation, and the investigator should continue to use interrogation as an investigative device. Experience has demonstrated that a large percentage of the persons accused of crime will confess voluntarily, even after being warned as required by *Miranda*. The investigator and administrator must make certain that the warning is given in detail however.

In many instances other methods can be used in conducting the investigation so that it will not be necessary to depend upon the interrogation and a confession. Where a case can be prosecuted without the confession, it is preferable to use the other means available. Despite these restrictions, interrogation is still a useful and legitimate tool in crime investigation.

Although the terms "interrogation" and "confession" have been used throughout this chapter, it is suggested that other terminology be substituted. The terms were used here since they are generally recognized by police personnel and prosecutors. However, apparently some members of the public, and especially some writers, associate these terms with force and duress. To avoid any misunderstanding it is preferable to "talk with" the suspect rather than to "interrogate" him. And it is better to refer to the disclosures as "statements," "remarks," or "comments."

Chapter 7

SELF-INCRIMINATION AND RELATED ISSUES*

No person ... shall be compelled in any criminal
case to be a witness against himself, ...

FIFTH AMENDMENT, 1791

§ 7.1   Pre-constitutional development of the self-incrimination privilege

The rule that a man shall not be compelled to furnish evidence against himself has a long history. Before the year 1236 the accused in a criminal case was required to be sworn, but there was no questioning by the judge. The act of taking the oath was a ritual, and the decision of guilt or innocence was determined not on what was said but on the correct pronunciation of the oath.

* by John C. Klotter

343

In the year 1236, the ecclesiastical courts adopted a new procedure which required that the accused who was under an oath to speak the truth must answer specific questions asked him by the judge. The Star Chamber Statute of 1487 sanctioned the examination of the accused under oath at his trial, and the practice of putting the suspect under oath without any formal charge against him was a favorite method in heresy and sedition trials.[1] However, after the abolition of the Star Chamber and the High Commission in Seventeenth Century England, all ecclesiastical courts were forbidden to administer any oath whereby a party might be obliged to accuse himself of any crime.

By the end of the reign of King Charles II, the claim that no man was bound to incriminate himself on any charge in any court was generally conceded by the English judges. But it was not until after 1700 that the privilege was fully recognized in England.

§ 7.2   Provisions of state constitutions and the Fifth Amendment of the United States Constitution

At the time of the formation of the Union, the principle that no person could be compelled to be a witness against himself had become entrenched in the common law. It was, therefore, understandable that as the original states developed their constitutions, this concept was preserved. In fact, five of the original thirteen states guarded this principle from legislative or judicial change by incorporating it into their constitutions. North Carolina, Pennsylvania and Virginia included the provisions concerning self-incrimination in their constitutions in 1776. Massachusetts included the provision in its constitution in 1780, and New Hampshire in 1784. The remainder of the states extended this protection even though it was not specifically mentioned in their constitutions.[2]

Although this privilege had been included in the constitutions of some of the original thirteen states, the privilege was not included in the Federal Constitution as originally adopted. It was made a part of the Constitution by inclusion in the Fifth

---

[1] 8 Wigmore, Evidence § 2250 (1961).

[2] See Twining v. New Jersey, 211 US 78, 53 LEd 97, 29 SCt 14 (1908).

Amendment in 1791. The part of the Amendment which specifically protects the privilege against self-incrimination reads as follows:

> [N]or shall [any person] be compelled in any criminal case to be a witness against himself, . . .

All of the states except New Jersey and Iowa have state constitutional provisions relating to self-incrimination. In most states the wording is like that in the Federal Constitution, but in others the wording is somewhat different. For example, in Kentucky the constitution provides that:

> In all criminal prosecutions the accused . . . cannot be compelled to give evidence against himself. . . .[3]

Although the term "give evidence" could be interpreted to be broader in application than "be a witness," these terms have generally been interpreted to give the same protection.

§ 7.3 Application of the Fifth Amendment privilege against self-incrimination to the states

The question arose early as to whether the privilege against self-incrimination was a right protected against state action by the Fourteenth Amendment. In other words, if the state courts determined that the self-incrimination privilege was not violated, did the federal courts have the authority to reverse the decision under the provisions of the Fifth Amendment as applied to the states through the Fourteenth? Early cases answered this with a definite no.[4]

The United States Supreme Court, in rejecting the claim that this privilege is protected by the Fourteenth Amendment against abridgment by the states remarked:

> [T]he exemption of compulsory self-incrimination is not a privilege or immunity of National citizenship guaranteed by this clause of the Fourteenth Amendment against abridgment by the States.

Even as late as 1947 the majority on the Court refused to

---

[3] KY. CONST. § 11.

[4] Twining v. New Jersey, 211 US 78, 53 LEd 97, 29 SCt 14 (1908).

apply the Fifth Amendment privilege against self-incrimination in state cases. The Court said in the *Adamson* case:[5]

> It is settled law that the clause of the Fifth Amendment, protecting a person against being compelled to be a witness against himself, is not made effective by the Fourteenth Amendment as a protection against state action on the ground that freedom from testimonial compulsion is a right of national citizenship, or because it is a personal privilege or immunity secured by the Federal Constitution as one of the rights of man that are listed in the Bill of Rights.

Four judges, Justices Black, Douglas, Murphy, and Rutledge dissented. Justice Black, argued:

> [H]istory conclusively demonstrates that the language of the first section of the Fourteenth Amendment, taken as a whole, was thought by those responsible for its submission to the people, and by those who opposed its submission, sufficiently explicit to guarantee that thereafter no state could deprive its citizens of the privileges and protections of the Bill of Rights.

More than half a century after the *Twining* case, the Supreme Court completely reversed the *Twining* decision, and in *Malloy v. Hogan*,[6] held that the Fifth Amendment protection against self-incrimination is made applicable to the states through the Fourteenth. In 1959 the petitioner Malloy was arrested during a gambling raid in Hartford, Connecticut. He pleaded guilty to the crime of pool-selling, a misdemeanor, and was sentenced to one year in jail and fined $500. About sixteen months after his guilty plea, the petitioner was ordered to testify before a referee appointed by the Superior Court of Hartford County to conduct an inquiry into alleged gambling and other criminal activities in the county. He refused to answer any questions on the grounds that it would tend to incriminate him.

The Superior Court adjudged him in contempt and committed him to prison until he was willing to answer the questions. The Connecticut Supreme Court of Errors held that the Fifth Amendment privilege against self-incrimination was not

---

[5] Adamson v. California, 332 US 46, 91 LEd 1903, 67 SCt 1672 (1947).

[6] 378 US 1, 12 LEd(2d) 653, 84 SCt 1489 (1964).

available to a witness in a state proceeding. The Supreme Court of the United States reversed the decision, asserting:

> We hold today that the Fifth Amendment's exception from compulsory self-incrimination is also protected by the Fourteenth Amendment against abridgment by the States.

To reinforce the holding in the *Malloy* case, the Supreme Court in 1965 reversed another conviction because the trial court commented upon the failure of the accused to testify on his own behalf.[7]

By making the self-incrimination guarantee of the Fifth Amendment applicable to the states by way of the Fourteenth, the Supreme Court also mandated that the standards to be applied are those as determined by the Supreme Court and other federal courts. State courts, in interpreting their own state constitutions, may establish additional, more restrictive requirements, but the state may not establish requirements that are less restrictive than those established by the Supreme Court of the United States via the Fifth Amendment.

§ 7.4   Expansion of the privilege to include pretrial situations

The Fifth Amendment provision concerning self-incrimination provides that no person shall be compelled in any *criminal case* to be a witness against himself. When interpreted literally this would mean only that a person shall not be required in a court proceeding in which he is a defendant to give evidence against himself. If this reasoning were followed, coerced confessions obtained prior to the trial of the case would not be considered as violating the self-incrimination privilege.

There has been much discussion concerning the relationship between the self-incrimination privilege and the confession rule. The late Dean Wigmore in his treatise on evidence made this statement regarding confessions and self-incrimination:

> The history of the two principles is wide apart, differing by one hundred years in origin, and derived through separate lines of precedents. . . . If the privilege, fully established by 1680, had

[7] Griffin v. California, 380 US 609, 14 LEd(2d) 106, 85 SCt 1229 (1965).

sufficed for both classes of cases there would have been no need in 1780 for creating a distinct rule about confessions. . . . So far as concerns practice, the two doctrines have not the same boundaries. The privilege covers only disclosures made under legal compulsion; the confession rule covers statements made anywhere, including statements made in court.[8]

Notwithstanding this reasoning, today the self-incrimination privilege does extend to out-of-court as well as in-court situations. All doubt concerning the application of the Fifth Amendment privilege against self-incrimination was laid to rest in the case of *Miranda* v. *Arizona*.[9] After discussing the development of the self-incrimination rule, Chief Justice Warren, speaking for the majority, stated:

> Today, then, there can be no doubt that the Fifth Amendment privilege is available outside of criminal court proceedings and serves to protect persons in all settings in which their freedom of action is curtailed . . . from being compelled to incriminate themselves.[10]

§ 7.5   Scope of the self-incrimination protection [11]

What can an accused person be compelled to do without violating the self-incrimination provisions? Does this protection extend to such practices as the taking of fingerprints and photographs? As the rule developed in England, the prohibition was against compelling an accused to disclose his guilt or to testify to facts subjecting him to punishment. The privilege was expressed in our constitutions by such words as "to be a witness against himself" or "to give evidence against oneself." Some authorities have argued that the protection extends only to testimonial compulsion and that no other compelled conduct, however unlawful or inadmissible on other grounds, is within the protection of the privilege. Most authorities, however, agree that the protection extends to documents and other evidence of a testimonial or communicative nature.

Traditionally, the self-incrimination protection extends to

---

[8] 8 Wigmore, EVIDENCE, § 2266 (1961).

[9] 384 US 436, 16 LEd(2d) 694, 86 SCt 1602 (1966).

[10] *Id.* at 467.

[11] See §§ 7.13 to 7.17 of this chapter for a discussion of additional restrictions predicated on the Due Process Clauses of the Constitution.

private papers, and the accused generally cannot be forced to bring private papers before the court. However, this does not apply to papers or books owned by the government or required to be maintained by government agencies. For example, passports are the property of the United States Government, and a defendant cannot refuse on self-incrimination grounds to make them available for use in court. The United States Court of Appeals for the Second Circuit defined the limits of the self-incrimination protection as it relates to books and papers in these terms:

> The Fifth Amendment can only be invoked to protect books or documents under certain circumstances. Simply stated, the privilege can be invoked to protect one's own books which are in one's own possession and which are self-incriminatory: The guaranty does not apply without this tripartite unity of ownership, possession and self-incrimination.[12]

If papers and documents are truly private, they are protected by the Fifth Amendment as well as the Fourth. On the other hand, if the papers, records or books are involved in a business, and others have knowledge of these records, they are not private within the meaning of the Constitution.[13] While personal diaries, letters, private writings made solely for personal use, or communications to a person occupying family or privileged relationships are protected by the Constitution, business records which the law requires to be maintained may be seized without violating the Fifth Amendment protection.[14]

Professor McCormick, in discussing the scope of the privilege and commenting on the rule as expounded by Wigmore (widely accepted in recent opinions) concluded that:

> The accused without breach of the privilege may be fingerprinted and photographed, deprived of his papers and other objects in his possession, may be physically examined, may have his blood and

---

[12] United States v. Falley, 489 F(2d) 33 (2dCir 1973).

[13] Fisher v. United States, 425 US 391, 48 LEd(2d) 39, 96 SCt 1569 (1976) held that a taxpayer's Fifth Amendment privilege against self-incrimination is not violated by the enforcement of a summons initiated by the Internal Revenue Service for the production of an accountant's work papers. This is true even though the papers prepared by the accountant were turned over to the taxpayer's attorney. See also United States v. Bennett, 409 F(2d) 888 (2dCir 1969).

[14] Id.

other bodily fluids taken for test without his consent, may be required to give a specimen of his handwriting, may be compelled to assume positions taken by the perpetrator of the crime, and may be forced to participate in the police lineup, to stand up for identification, put on articles of clothing, or display a scar or a limp. The list is illustrative, not exhaustive.[15]

Some of the specific situations which concern the police and prosecutor are discussed in the following paragraphs.

1. Fingerprinting and photographing

It has long been recognized that the taking of fingerprints and photographs for identification purposes does not violate the self-incrimination protections. The United States Court of Appeals for the District of Columbia said this was elementary when the person is in lawful custody. The exact words of the court were:

> We find no error in the admission of the palm print of Smith taken the day before trial for purposes of comparison with the palm print on the victim's credit cards. Unlike the situation in *Bynum* v. *United States*, appellant here was in lawful custody at the time the prints were recorded. And it is elementary that a person in lawful custody may be required to submit to photographing and fingerprinting as part of routine identification processes. [Citations omitted.] [16]

There are indications that the taking of fingerprints by force would not be permissible unless there is a valid arrest. And only necessary force may be used. If there is unusual resistance, it is preferable to obtain a court order before taking the prints.

2. The police lineup and other confrontations for identification

The police lineup and "confrontation for identification" prior to trial have been challenged on at least three constitutional grounds. Although the courts have generally agreed that this procedure does *not* violate the self-incrimination provisions of the Fifth Amendment, the majority of the Supreme

[15] C. McCormick, EVIDENCE § 126 (1954).

[16] Smith v. United States, 324 F(2d) 879 (DC Cir 1963).

Court decided that a post-indictment criminal lineup is a *critical stage* in a criminal proceeding and that, therefore, counsel may be required.[17] But the lineup or other confrontation does not violate self-incrimination protections. In the *Wade* case Justice Brennan speaking for the majority stated:

> We have no doubt that compelling the accused merely to exhibit his person for observations by a prosecution witness prior to trial involves no compulsion of the accused to give evidence having testimonial significance.

In *Caldwell* v. *United States* [18] the court explained *why* the lineup and confrontation for identification do not violate self-incrimination provisions of the Fifth Amendment, commenting:

> The mere viewing of a suspect under arrest by eye witnesses does not violate this constitutional privilege because the prisoner is not required to be an unwilling witness against himself. There is a distinction between bodily view and requiring an accused to testify against himself.

Similar reasoning was followed by the United States District Court for Eastern Pennsylvania in concluding that the self-incrimination protection was not violated when a suspect was required to have a dental examination.[19] In this case, at the prosecutor's request, the court allowed an examination to determine whether or not the defendant was missing a tooth in the area of his mouth pinpointed by one of the witnesses. According to the majority, the examination was not testimonial or communicative in nature and did not violate either the Fourth or Fifth Amendments.

It has long been held that the compelled display of identifiable, physical characteristics infringes no interest protected by the privilege against compulsory self-incrimination.

---

[17] Stovall v. Denno, 388 US 293, 18 LEd(2d) 1199, 87 SCt 1969 (1967); Gilbert v. California, 388 US 263, 18 LEd(2d) 1178, 87 SCt 1951 (1967); United States v. Wade, 388 US 218, 18 LEd(2d) 1149, 87 SCt 1926 (1967). See Chapter 8, *infra*.

[18] 338 F(2d) 385 (8thCir 1964).

[19] United States v. Holland, 378 FSupp 144 (ED Pa 1974).

3. Use of blood, urine and breath samples for determining alcohol content of the blood

For many years there has been much discussion concerning the use of breath, urine or blood tests to determine the alcohol content of the blood. One of the first cases to consider the constitutionality of forcibly taking blood from a person who has been arrested was *Breithaupt* v. *Abram*.[20] Here a conviction was upheld, the Court holding that under the circumstances, the withdrawal of blood following an arrest for operation of a motor vehicle while under the influence of alcohol, did not offend a sense of justice, and that the withdrawal of the blood and the admission of the blood for analysis did not violate the Fifth Amendment privilege against self-incrimination. The Court reasoned that the protection of the Fourteenth Amendment did not embrace the Fifth Amendment privilege; therefore, this protection did not apply in state proceedings.

The question again arose in the case of *Schmerber* v. *California*.[21] This case very definitely clarified the issue. Schmerber was arrested at the hospital for driving an automobile while under the influence of intoxicating liquor. With the advice of counsel, Schmerber objected to the taking of the blood sample, but it was taken by a physician at the request of a police officer over Schmerber's objection. This evidence was used in the criminal court, and the defendant was convicted of the criminal offense of driving an automobile while under the influence of intoxicating liquor. In appealing his conviction, the defendant asserted, among other things, that his rights were violated, contending that the admission of the analysis as evidence denied him due process of law under the Fourteenth Amendment as well as his privilege against self-incrimination under the Fifth Amendment as made applicable to the states through the Fourteenth.

The Supreme Court of the United States upheld the conviction and again emphasized that the taking of the blood sample was not a violation of the privilege against self-incrimination

---

[20] 352 US 432, 1 LEd(2d) 448, 77 SCt 408 (1957).

[21] 384 US 757, 16 LEd(2d) 908, 86 SCt 1826 (1966). See Part II for a reprint of this case.

and explained that the privilege protects an accused only from being compelled to testify against himself or otherwise to provide the state with evidence of a testimonial or communicative nature. Although reaffirming the rule established in the *Malloy* case, that the Fourteenth Amendment secures against state invasion the same privileges that the Fifth Amendment guarantees against federal infringement, the Court continued with the statement:

> We hold that the privilege protects an accused only from being compelled to testify against himself, or otherwise provide the State with evidence of a *testimonial* or *communicative* nature, and that the withdrawal of blood and use of analysis in question in this case did not involve compulsion to these ends. [Emphasis added].

The Court cautioned that the decision was limited to the facts of the case where the blood sample was taken by medical personnel in a medical environment.

It is interesting to note the Court also upheld the test as not being a violation of the Fourth Amendment because the blood sample was taken after arrest and there was no time to secure a warrant. The majority reasoned that the evidence of the blood alcohol content in this case might have dissipated had the officer been required to take the time to obtain a warrant.

The majority of the state courts find no problem in also holding that evidence of the *refusal* to take a chemical test does not violate the self-incrimination privilege.[22] The reasoning is that since the use of the evidence does not violate the Fifth Amendment privilege of a person, why should the comment upon the failure to take the test violate the privilege? At least one court, the Minnesota Supreme Court, however, differed with the majority in finding that a driving-while-intoxicated defendant's refusal to submit to a chemical test may not be admitted at his trial.[23] This decision was justified partly on the wording of state law and partly on a footnote in the *Schmerber* case in which the Supreme Court noted that it was not deciding whether the admission of the evidence of an accused's refusal to submit to chemical testing would violate any of the accused's constitutional rights.

[22] People v. Ellis, 65 Cal(2d) 529, 55 Cal Rptr 385, 421 P(2d) 393 (1966).

[23] State v. Andrews, 297 Minn 260, 212 NW(2d) 863 (1973).

4. Handwriting specimens

Although there is still some disagreement, most authorities logically reason that the Fifth Amendment does not cover compulsory handwriting, especially where the writing is for identification purposes. In an Oregon case, the highest court of that state affirmed a conviction where handwriting specimens were taken at the police station.[24] The court refused to include this in the protection of the Fifth Amendment. It equated handwriting specimens with fingerprints and photographs, commenting:

> It seems now to be a well accepted fact that handwriting is almost as individualistic and identifying as are fingerprints.
>
> . . . .
>
> [W]e are unable to find a valid reason for holding that a person whose handwriting has been secured for comparison has had his constitutional right to counsel and privilege against self-incrimination invaded.

In 1973, the United States Supreme Court reiterated its previous announcement that the Fifth Amendment self-incrimination provision does not prohibit compelled display of identifiable, physical characteristics; nor did it prevent the grand jury from subpoenaing handwriting exemplars for identification purposes.[25]

Although the courts are agreed that the use of handwriting specimens for comparison purposes does not violate the Fifth Amendment self-incrimination privilege, a practical question arises as to how one can be forced to give handwriting specimens. One method approved in the case of *United States* v. *Doe*[26] is the use of a court order. In this case, when the defendant persisted in his refusal to give a handwriting exemplar, the court held him in civil contempt and ordered that he be held for 30 days or until such time as he purged himself of this contempt by furnishing the required handwriting exemplar. The court further stated that the suspect could be requested to furnish an exemplar consisting of the reproduc-

---

[24] State v. Fisher, 242 Ore 419, 410 P(2d) 216 (1966).

[25] United States v. Mara, 410 US 19, 35 LEd(2d) 67, 93 SCt 777 (1973). See also Trimble v. Hedman, 291 Minn 442, 192 NW(2d) 432 (1971).

[26] 405 F(2d) 436 (2dCir 1968).

tion of the very instrument (a postal money order in this case) that he was accused of stealing.

Since one can be required by the court order to furnish a sample of the handwriting for comparison purposes, *a fortiori*, it is not a violation of the privilege to use handwriting specimens obtained from suspects by subterfuge. Therefore, the courts have upheld the use of handwriting specimens obtained from fingerprint cards, police booking forms, and questionnaires.[27]

5. Voice exemplars for identification purposes

Many courts now accept spectrograph evidence to prove identity in criminal cases.[28] The constitutional question is whether compulsion to produce voice exemplars for such comparison violates the Fifth Amendment privilege against self-incrimination. This was the issue before the Supreme Court in 1973 in the case of *United States v. Dionisio*.[29] In this case the grand jury had subpoenaed about twenty persons, including the respondent, to give voice exemplars for identification purposes. The respondent refused to comply on the basis that this violated his Fifth and Fourteenth Amendment rights. The United States Supreme Court, however, approved the compelled production of voice exemplars, agreeing that since they were to be used for identification purposes and not for the testimonial or communicative content, this procedure did not violate the Fifth Amendment against self-incrimination. It is obvious that a person could not be required to say anything that would be incriminating. On the other hand, if he is required only to say words which are not testimonial or communicative, the Fifth Amendment is not violated.

6. Footprint comparisons and body examinations

At one time, some courts interpreted the self-incrimination provision as prohibiting the police from requiring a suspect

[27] Duncan v. United States, 357 F(2d) 195 (5thCir 1966), Sutton v. Maryland, 4 MdApp 70, 241 A(2d) 145 (1968).

[28] See Klotter & Meier, CRIMINAL EVIDENCE FOR POLICE, § 13.19 (2d ed 1975).

[29] 410 US 1, 35 LEd(2d) 67, 93 SCt 764 (1973).

to place his foot in a footprint cast. Since the *Schmerber* case, this is no longer considered a violation of the Fifth Amendment as there is no testimony or communication involved.

Also applying the *Schmerber* rationale, the courts find no self-incrimination problem with examining a suspect's body for traces of blood,[30] or taking penis scrapings and saliva samples from a suspect.[31]

§ 7.6   Claiming the privilege

In a criminal case the ordinary witness claims the privilege at the trial as each question is asked. This is a personal privilege and must be claimed by the witness who may be incriminated if he answers the question. The privilege is claimed by the witness stating: "I refuse to answer on the grounds that it might incriminate me."

The defense attorney cannot claim the privilege on behalf of his client when the witness is asked a question which, if answered, would incriminate the witness or the client. The witness must claim the privilege himself although he may have an attorney present to advise him when the privilege may be claimed.

The defendant, on the other hand, in effect claims the privilege by refusing to take the stand in a criminal case. If the defendant takes the stand, he waives the privilege as to questions relating to the offense charged.

The defendant may not invoke the privilege for a third party. But a witness other than the defendant may invoke the privilege on his own behalf and refuse to answer questions which might tend to incriminate him. On the other hand, if that witness does not himself invoke the privilege, neither the defendant nor the defendant's attorney may complain.[32]

The privilege may be claimed outside of court when the person questioned refuses to answer questions asked of him by an official. It may be claimed by expressing an intention not to reply or by remaining mute when a question is asked.

---

[30] McFarland v. United States, 150 F(2d) 593 (DC Cir 1945).

[31] Brent v. White, 276 FSupp 386 (ED La 1967).

[32] United States v. Nobles, 422 US 225, 45 LEd(2d) 141, 95 SCt 2160 (1975).

In court the judge, not the person claiming the privilege, must decide whether the witness may invoke the privilege and decline to answer the question on the grounds of possible self-incrimination. In the case of *State* v. *Robbins*,[33] the Maine Supreme Judicial Court, after citing federal cases including United States Supreme Court cases, reiterated the standards to be applied:

> "To sustain the privilege, it need only be evident from the implications of the question, in the setting in which it is asked, that a responsive answer to the question or an explanation of why it cannot be answered might be dangerous because the injurious disclosure could result."

The judge must decide after he has obtained all the facts and, in some instances, after he has interrogated the witness outside the hearing of the jury, whether the answer would in fact incriminate the witness. The judge in his discretion may direct the witness to answer some questions which would not be incriminating, and not to answer other questions which could be of an incriminating nature.

Often the judge has the difficult task of reconciling the conflict between the defendant's right to testimony in his defense and the witness's claim of privilege of silence. In the *Robbins* case, for example, the State Supreme Court found that the judge had abused his discretion by failing to require the recalcitrant witness to answer questions which presented no real threat of incriminating her, where the answers would have contradicted and incriminated the key prosecuting witness. If, on the other hand, the witness's answer would in fact incriminate him, he will not be required to answer even if the evidence is important to a defendant.

§ 7.7   Waiver of the privilege

Although the guarantee of immunity from compulsory incrimination is a personal privilege, it may be waived. Where the accused acts voluntarily he may waive his privilege protected by the self-incrimination provisions, either in court or

[33] 318 A(2d) 51 (Me 1974), quoting
Hoffman v. United States, 341 US 479,
95 LEd 1118, 71 SCt 814 (1951).

outside of court. The burden is on the prosecution to show that the defendant knowingly and intelligently waived the privilege.

At the trial itself, both the accused and the ordinary witness may waive the rights protected by the self-incrimination provisions. However, the procedure in waiving the right differs between the ordinary witness and the defendant.

1. Waiver by the defendant at trial

The accused has the option under the criminal procedure provisions in this country to remain off the stand altogether or to testify. However, by volunteering to become a witness he waives his right as it concerns relevant inquiries about the charge against him.[34] With few exceptions the defendant cannot take the stand and testify in his own behalf and then refuse to answer relevant inquiries on cross-examination. Even at the trial the accused must be made aware that he is waiving his rights and this waiver must be made intelligently and knowingly.

Many states, including Tennessee, had statutes which required that a defendant desiring to testify in a criminal case do so before any other testimony for the defense was heard by the court trying the case. When this procedure is followed, if the defendant refuses to take the stand prior to the time other testimony for the defense is heard, he waives his right to testify in his own behalf.

This requirement that the defendant take the stand first has been challenged.[35] In the *Brooks* case the trial court refused to allow defendant to testify after the defense had called two other witnesses. Appeal was made to the Tennessee Supreme Court which refused to reverse the conviction. In the appeal to the Supreme Court of the United States, the defendant claimed that requiring a defendant to testify first or lose his right to testify violates the Federal Constitution.

The Supreme Court reversed the lower court, deciding that this requirement violates both the self-incrimination protection of the Fifth Amendment and the due process protection

[34] Johnson v. United States, 318 US 189, 87 LEd 704, 63 SCt 549 (1943).

[35] Brooks v. Tennessee, 406 US 605, 32 LEd(2d) 358, 92 SCt 1891 (1972).

of the Fourteenth Amendment. As to the Fifth Amendment protection the Court said, "This rule cuts down on the privilege to remain silent by making its assertion costly." After explaining that the penalty for not testifying first is to keep the defendant off the stand entirely, even though as a matter of professional judgment his lawyer might want to call him later in the trial, the Court concluded by saying: "Petitioner, then, was deprived of his constitutional rights when the trial court excluded him from the stand for failing to testify first."

By this *Brooks* decision the Supreme Court has declared that a procedure requiring the defendant to take the stand before any other testimony for the defense is heard, whether it be state statute or by the rules of the court, is unenforceable as in violation of the Fifth and Fourteenth Amendments.

2. Waiver by the ordinary witness at trial

Unlike the accused, the ordinary witness has no privilege to decline altogether to testify. On the other hand by taking the stand he waives nothing. He makes the choice as each question is asked. However, when the witness has testified to an incriminating fact, he is considered to have waived his privilege as to all further questions relevant to the same transaction.

The decision of the witness not to answer questions on the grounds it may incriminate him is not conclusive, of course. Although the judge should give the claim careful consideration, he makes the final decision as to whether the witness will be required to answer the question.

3. Waiver outside of court

In an out-of-court situation, if the witness or accused refuses to answer questions, neither the police nor the prosecutor can force him to do so. But if the statement is made after waiver and is made knowingly and intelligently, it may be used in court.[36]

---

[36] See Chapter 6, *supra*, concerning interrogations and confessions for the waiver requirement.

§ 7.8   Comment on the failure to testify

Most state legislatures recognized that authorizing the prosecutor to make comments concerning the accused's failure to testify would discourage the exercise of the privilege against self-incrimination and traditionally forbade the counsel for the state to comment on the failure of the accused to testify. However, a few states, including the state of California, at one time by statute authorized such comment when the accused did not take the stand in his own behalf. In 1947 the Supreme Court refused to set aside a conviction in a case where the prosecutor, under the California law, had commented on the failure of the accused to testify.[37]

In spite of this decision, all questions concerning the authority of the prosecutor to comment on the failure of the accused to testify were resolved in the case of *Griffin v. California*.[38] Here the Court held that the trial court and prosecutor were precluded from commenting before the jury upon the defendant's failure to testify in his own behalf. The decision was not surprising as it reiterated the decision of *Malloy* which held that the Fourteenth Amendment secured against state invasion the protections of the Fifth Amendment concerning self-incrimination.

In light of these decisions it is clear that the prosecutor now does not have the right to comment on the defendant's failure to testify, even though such right might be specifically authorized in a state statute.

§ 7.9   Immunity from criminal prosecution

No discussion concerning self-incrimination would be complete without a mention of the immunity statutes which have received so much attention in the last few years. The most publicized example of the value of the immunity statute was the use of this statute in making it possible to sentence the late Salvatore Giancana for contempt. Giancana, reputed to be one of the top men of Chicago's branch of the Cosa Nostra, was granted immunity from prosecution by a federal grand

---

[37] Adamson v. California, 332 US 46, 91 LEd 1903, 67 SCt 1672 (1947).   [38] 380 US 609, 14 LEd(2d) 106, 85 SCt 1229 (1965).

jury investigating the crime syndicate operations. Because he was granted immunity, he had no legal basis for pleading silence for fear of incriminating himself. Therefore, when he continued to refuse to testify, Judge Campbell committed Giancana, for contempt, to the custody of the Attorney General.[39]

The immunity concept is not new. In 1892 the United States Supreme Court was called upon to decide the constitutional sufficiency of the federal immunity statute which provided only that the compelled testimony should not be given in evidence or used in any manner against the defendant in any criminal proceedings. The Court held that this was unconstitutional as it did not give the witness complete immunity; it did not prevent the use of testimony to search out other testimony which might be used against the accused.[40]

If the statute gives complete immunity it is not considered to be unconstitutional. This seems to be a just and fair decision as the purpose of the privilege initially was to protect the individual so that he could not be compelled to be a witness against himself so as to subject him to criminal prosecution. If there can be no prosecution then the reason for the self-incrimination protection no longer exists.

Because of our dual system of government, there has been some confusion concerning the authority of the federal courts to grant immunity from prosecution in the state court, and the corresponding authority of the state court to make a person immune from prosecution in the federal courts. This issue was presented in the case of *Murphy* v. *Waterfront Commission.*[41] Here the petitioner was subpoenaed by the commission and granted immunity from prosecution in either New York or New Jersey. He, however, persisted in his refusal to testify because there was a possibility that the evidence could be used in federal court. The Supreme Court of the United States held that neither a state nor the federal government may use testi-

---

[39] In re Grand Jury Investigation of Giancana, 352 F(2d) 921 (7thCir 1965).
[40] Counselman v. Hitchcock, 142 US 547, 35 LEd 1110, 12 SCt 195 (1892).
[41] 378 US 52, 12 LEd(2d) 678, 84 SCt 1594 (1964). See also In re Zicarelli, 55 NJ 249, 261 A(2d) 129 (1970), holding that a state immunity statute does not violate self-incrimination provisions.

mony given after immunity was granted by either. The effect of the Supreme Court's holding is to leave unimpaired the immunity laws of the states and strengthen the hands of the prosecutors in obtaining valuable evidence, especially in organized crime situations.

The basic question which has been discussed frequently in the lower courts is whether a person can be required to testify after being given immunity by statute. A related question is whether such person must be given *absolute* immunity against *any* future prosecution. Although the first question has been answered affirmatively in past cases, the answer to the second has been in doubt. This question was considered by the Supreme Court in 1972. The majority agreed that absolute immunity is not required before a person can be ordered to testify under the provisions of immunity statutes.[42]

Here the petitioner was ordered to appear before a grand jury to answer questions after he had been granted immunity. Even after immunity had been granted, however, the petitioner refused to answer the questions claiming that the scope of the immunity provided by the statute was not coextensive with the scope of the self-incrimination privilege. He contended that the statute must, at a minimum, grant full "transactional immunity" in order to be coexistent with the privilege, and that a statute which does not afford absolute "immunity from prosecution" is not transactional and not constitutional.

Mr. Justice Powell speaking for the majority of the Court refused to go along with this strict interpretation. In making clear that a statute prohibiting the use in any criminal case of compelled testimony, or any information directly or indirectly derived from such testimony, is consonant with the Fifth Amendment standards, this terminology was used:

> We hold that such immunity from use and derivative use is coexistent with the scope of the privilege against self incrimination, and therefore is sufficient to compel testimony over a claim of the privilege.

[42] Kastigar v. United States, 406 US 441, 32 LEd(2d) 212, 92 SCt 1653 (1972). This case contains an excellent discussion of the history of immunity statutes and of "transactional" and "use" immunity.

The Court held that this prohibition of use of testimony provides a comprehensive safeguard which bars the use not only of the compelled testimony itself, but also the use of any testimony to develop "leads." The case also provides that the prosecution has the affirmative duty to prove that evidence it proposes to use in a future case is derived from a legitimate source wholly independent of the compelled testimony.

In summary, the *Kastigar* case makes it clear that absolute immunity from *all* prosecution is not required, but for an immunity statute to be constitutional it must confer immunity from "use" of the compelled testimony and evidence derived therefrom. Furthermore, in a subsequent criminal prosecution the prosecutor has the burden of proving affirmatively that evidence proposed to be used is derived from a legitimate source wholly independent of the compelled testimony.

§ 7.10   Claiming the privilege in disciplinary situations

The Fifth Amendment of the United States Constitution and the state self-incrimination provisions provide that no person shall be compelled in any *criminal case* to be a witness against himself. Does this protection extend to a situation where public employees are asked to make statements or answer questions regarding job performance? Secondly, may an employee who refuses to waive self-incrimination rights be dismissed for that refusal?

On at least two occasions the United States Supreme Court has considered the question of whether a police officer can be required to choose between exerting his self-incrimination protection or being removed from office for failure to answer questions at a disciplinary hearing. In the case of *Garrity* v. *New Jersey*,[43] police officers were required to answer questions relative to irregularities in handling cases in the municipal courts or be subject to removal from office. The appellant in that case answered the questions, and some of the answers were used in subsequent prosecution for conspiracy to obstruct the administration of the traffic laws. He appealed to the higher courts and finally to the United States Supreme Court

---

[43] 385 US 493, 17 LEd(2d) 562, 87 SCt 616 (1967).

on the grounds that statements coerced in this fashion should not be used against him in a criminal trial. The Court concluded:

> [T]he protection of the individual under the Fourteenth Amendment against coerced statements prohibits use in subsequent criminal proceedings of statements obtained under threat of removal from office, and that it extends to all, whether they are policemen or other members of the body politic.

In a similar case, a New York City police officer was fired because he refused to sign a waiver and refused to testify before a New York County grand jury which was investigating alleged bribery and corruption of police officers in connection with unlawful gambling operations.[44] The question, as stated by the Supreme Court in that case, was "whether a policeman who refuses to waive the protection which the privilege gives him may be dismissed from office because of that refusal."

Under the circumstances stated, the Supreme Court agreed with the previous *Garrity* ruling but explained that in that case the petitioner's testimony was demanded not solely for the purpose of securing an accounting of his performance of his public trust. The Court indicated that if the testimony is to be used exclusively for administrative purposes, and there is a clear indication that the testimony cannot be used for criminal prosecution, the officer *can* be required to answer questions. The Court expressed this in the following manner:

> If appellant, a policeman, had refused to answer questions specifically, directly, and narrowly relating to the performance of his official duties, without being required to waive his immunity with respect to the use of his answers or the fruits thereof in a criminal prosecution of himself, . . . the privilege against self-incrimination would not have been a bar to his dismissal.

Relying on the wording of the *Gardner* case, the Massachusetts Supreme Court has found that Boston police officers who were allegedly involved in unseemly antics during off-duty hours must respond to a police department questionnaire

---

[44] Gardner v. Broderick, 392 US 273, 20 LEd(2d) 1082, 88 SCt 1913 (1968).

concerning their conduct.[45] In that case affidavits alleged that fifteen or twenty Boston police officers, while in Newport, Rhode Island to participate in a Law Day celebration, swam and played in the nude in a swimming pool at the Ramada Inn, punched a customer with a cue stick, broke into the hotel liquor cabinet, used foul and opprobrious language, and left without paying for breakfast.

A deputy superintendent of the Boston Police Department was placed in charge of the investigation. He prepared a questionnaire which required the officers to file a narrative report of the events based upon fifteen questions set forth in the questionnaire. The questionnaire also provided that the officers' answers could not be used in evidence in a criminal prosecution against them. The officers urged that the questionnaires violated their rights guaranteed by the state and federal constitutions and sought injunctive relief. The highest court of the state of Massachusetts quoted the words of the *Gardner* case and refused to grant injunctive relief to the officers. According to that court, requiring the officers to answer the inquiries directed to the activities in Rhode Island does not infringe their Fifth Amendment rights when the evidence is being used in relation to the performance of official duties and not for criminal prosecution.

Succinctly stated, the rule is that where the employee's testimony is demanded solely and exclusively for administrative purposes and the testimony cannot be used for criminal prosecution, the employee can be required to answer the questions and this does not violate the self-incrimination provisions. But an employee cannot be required to choose between exerting his self-incrimination protection or being removed from office for failure to answer questions if the answers or fruits thereof can be used in a criminal trial.

§ 7.11   Implied consent statutes

Recognizing that a good percentage of fatal automobile accidents involve drivers who have been drinking, state legis-

[45] Broderick v. Police Comm'r, _____ Mass _____, 330 NE(2d) 199 (1975), *cert. denied,* 423 US 1048 (1976).

lators, prosecutors and police have attempted to find some valid means of determining if drivers have been operating vehicles under the influence of intoxicants. In 1953 New York enacted the first implied consent statute. Since that time at least twenty-five other states have enacted legislation similar to the New York statute.[46] This law provides that anyone, whether licensed locally, unlicensed, or licensed in another state, is deemed to have given his consent, in return for the driving privilege, to submit to an alcohol test, if there are reasonable grounds to believe that he has been driving while intoxicated. Under the provisions of this statute, if the individual refuses to take the test, his license may be suspended for a period of six months.

Implied consent statutes have been challenged in various states as violating the self-incrimination provisions of the state and federal constitutions, the search and seizure provisions, the equal protection provisions, and due process of law. To date, these laws have been held to be constitutional. In upholding its statute, the Kansas Supreme Court noted that the only question concerns the power of the state first to suspend and later revoke a driver's license of the licensee upon being arrested on a charge of driving a motor vehicle while under the influence of intoxicating liquor, when the driver refuses to submit to one of the statutory tests.[47] The court repeated that this was not a violation of due process, that it was not an act that would shock the conscience, and was not inherently brutal and offensive. The court also held that it did not violate the self-incrimination provisions of either the federal or state constitutions.

The implied consent law was challenged before the highest court in Nebraska in 1966.[48] That court also upheld the validity of the law, stating:

> We conclude that the validity of a sample of blood or urine under the implied consent law is not impaired by a request for legal counsel, or the failure of defendant's counsel to appear before the sample is taken. We do not, by this opinion, intend to impair the right of a defendant to counsel for the purpose of protecting his rights.

[46] See, e.g., NY Veh & Traf Law § 1194 (Supp 1976).
[47] Lee v. State, 187 Kan 566, 358 P(2d) 765 (1961).
[48] State v. Oleson, 180 Neb 546, 143 NW(2d) 917 (1966).

> Our holding, simply stated, is that a defendant loses no rights subject to protection by legal counsel when he is requested to and furnishes a sample of blood or urine for chemical analysis to be used as evidence against him under the implied consent law.

The implied consent and related statutes have also been challenged on the ground that a *comment* on the failure to take the blood alcohol test violates the self-incrimination privilege. For example, in the case of *Newhouse* v. *Misterly*,[49] the defendant, after being arrested for drunken driving, refused to take the breath test or perform other acts as requested by the enforcement officers. At the trial the prosecution introduced evidence of the defendant's refusal to take the test and argued that the refusal showed the defendant was conscious of the fact that the test would indicate use of alcohol. In refusing to invalidate the defendant's conviction, the reviewing court held that the prosecutor and judge could properly comment at the trial on defendant's refusal to submit to the test. The same reasoning was followed in the Louisiana court which held that since bodily evidence itself violates no privilege against self-incrimination, neither does testimony concerning the refusal to give the bodily evidence.[50]

Although the implied consent statute has not been tested in the United States Supreme Court, it would probably be upheld in view of the holding in *Schmerber* v. *California*.[51]

§ 7.12 Compulsory registration as violation of the self-incrimination privilege

Starting with the *Marchetti* case,[52] a series of convictions have been challenged under the self-incrimination provision because the defendants were required by law to register. In the *Marchetti* case the defendant was charged with failure to purchase a wagering stamp as required by federal statute. The defendant argued that when purchasing the stamp which requires that he indicate whether he is engaged in gambling, and in posting the stamp, he is being required to incriminate himself. The United States Supreme Court in reversing the

[49] 415 F(2d) 514 (9thCir 1969).
[50] State v. Pugas, 252 La 345, 211 S(2d) 285 (1968).
[51] 384 US 757, 16 LEd(2d) 908, 86 SCt 1826 (1966).
[52] Marchetti v. United States, 390 US 39, 19 LEd(2d) 889, 88 SCt 697 (1968).

lower court conviction held that if the defendant claims the privilege, it is a complete defense in a criminal prosecution for violations of the federal tax statutes requiring him to register as a gambler. The Court made it clear that persons may be criminally punished for gambling, but that provisions which require persons engaged in wagering to register as such are not enforceable and that persons may not be criminally punished for failure to comply with the requirements if they properly assert the constitutional challenge.

The *Marchetti* reasoning was applied in another case in 1969. This case involved the infamous Dr. Timothy Leary, a former professor at Harvard University, who actively encouraged the use of LSD.[53] In this case the defendant was convicted in federal court of violating the federal statutes governing traffic in marijuana. One section of the law required that a tax be paid on all transfers of marijuana and that the required order form must show the name and address of the transferor and transferee. One of the questions to be decided in the case was whether petitioner's conviction for failure to comply with the transfer tax provisions of the Marijuana Tax Act violated his Fifth Amendment privilege against self-incrimination. The Supreme Court, following the reasoning of the *Marchetti* case, reversed the conviction after finding that the Marijuana Tax Act compelled the petitioner to expose himself to a real and appreciable risk of self-incrimination.

The Court went on to find that he did not in fact waive his privilege of self-incrimination but violated the statutes requiring registration because of fear of criminal prosecution under the state and federal laws. As in previous cases of this type, the Court pointed out that it did not intend to prohibit enforcement of laws prohibiting the importation of narcotics but only that a person could not be forced to register when such registration would subject him to state or federal prosecution.

§ 7.13   Due process considerations

In the previous sections of this chapter the discussion has centered primarily around the Fifth Amendment self-incrimi-

---

[53] Leary v. United States, 395 US 6,
23 LEd(2d) 57, 89 SCt 1532 (1969).

nation provision as it is made applicable to the states by the Fourteenth Amendment due process clause. The remainder of the chapter will be devoted to a discussion of "Due Process" issues.

In some instances police conduct and procedure is challenged as violating more than one provision of the Constitution. For example, the lineup and other pre-trial confrontations for identification are challenged as violating the self-incrimination provision of the Fifth Amendment, the right-to-counsel provision of the Sixth Amendment, and in some instances the due process clauses of the Fifth or Fourteenth Amendments. The same applies to the use of photographs for identification purposes. The taking of blood or other body fluids for the purpose of making a chemical analysis is often challenged as violating the self-incrimination provision, the search and seizure provision, and the due process clauses as well as the right to counsel.

In *Rochin* v. *California* [54] (which is discussed in subsequent paragraphs), police conduct was challenged as violating the Fourth Amendment, the Fifth Amendment self-incrimination provision, and finally, the due process clause of the Fourteenth Amendment. Even if the court finds that the conduct of the police officer is not in violation of self-incrimination provisions, that conduct may be challenged because of a general "due process" violation. Some of these issues will be discussed in the following sections.

§ 7.14   Pretrial confrontation for identification

If the lineup, showup, or other confrontation is so unnecessarily suggestive as to be conducive to irreparable mistaken identification, the procedure violates due process. For example, if the suspect in the lineup is of one race, and five other persons in the lineup are of a different race, this would of course make the procedure unfair and unconstitutional.

In the case of *Foster* v. *California* [55] decided in 1969, a witness to an armed robbery was called to the police station to view a lineup. In the lineup there were three men, including

---

[54] 342 US 165, 96 LEd(2d) 183, 72 SCt 205 (1952).

[55] 394 US 440, 22 LEd(2d) 402, 89 SCt 1127 (1969).

the petitioner. The petitioner was six feet in height while the other two men in the lineup were about five feet, six inches tall. Also, only the petitioner wore a leather jacket which was similar to the one the witness had said he saw on the robber. At the first lineup the witness could not positively identify the robber and he was called to view a second lineup. At the second lineup there were five men in the lineup but petitioner was the only person in the second lineup who had appeared in the first lineup. This time the witness was convinced that petitioner was the man he saw at the scene of the robbery.

The Supreme Court reversed the conviction and condemned this procedure as a violation of the due process clause of the Fourteenth Amendment, saying:

> In the present case the pretrial confrontations clearly were so arranged as to make the resulting identifications virtually inevitable.

Lineup and confrontation situations were considered again by the Supreme Court in a more recent case.[56] In this case the defendant was convicted of rape and sentenced to twenty years' imprisonment. The state's evidence consisted in part of testimony concerning a stationhouse identification of the defendant by the victim. The victim on several occasions viewed suspects in her home or at the police station, some in lineups and others in showups, and was shown between thirty and forty photographs before she identified the defendant. The officers testified that they did not have a full lineup because they were unable to find other persons fitting the petitioner's unusual description, and that they therefore conducted a showup. This showup consisted of two detectives walking the defendant past the victim at police headquarters. At the victim's request the police also directed the petitioner to say, "Shut up or I'll kill you," these words being used at the time of the rape.

Following the stationhouse showup as described, the victim positively identified the defendant and identified him again at the trial. The in-court identification of the defendant was chal-

---

[56] Neil v. Biggers, 409 US 188, 34 LEd(2d) 401, 93 SCt 375 (1972). This case reviews the lineup and confronta- tion cases and their relation to due process; it is reprinted in Part II.

lenged on the ground that the stationhouse identification was suggestive and therefore contaminated the in-court identification.

The Supreme Court by a four-to-four decision affirmed the conviction after reasserting some general guidelines relating to suggestiveness and misidentification. The four members of the Court agreed that the admission of evidence of an identification showup without more does not in itself violate due process. The Court again warned the lower courts not to lose sight of the reason for examining the lineup or showup, explaining that, "the primary evil to be avoided is a very substantial likelihood of irreparable misidentification." The danger, the Court pointed out, is that suggestive confrontations may increase the likelihood of misidentification at trial; but the central question is whether under "the totality of circumstances" the in-court identification was reliable even though the confrontation procedure may have been suggestive. Applying this test to the facts of this case, the affirming Justices agreed that even though the stationhouse identification may have been suggestive, there was "no substantial likelihood of misidentification."

Five factors were listed in *Biggers* to be considered in evaluating the likelihood of misidentification: (1) the witness's opportunity to view the criminal during the crime; (2) the witness's degree of attention; (3) the accuracy of the witness's prior description of the criminal; (4) the level of certainty demonstrated by the witness at the confrontation; and (5) the length of time between the crime and the confrontation.

Apparently the Second Circuit Court of Appeals was inclined to agree that a woman witness may change her mind without making the showup unreliable.[57] That court refused to reverse the conviction of the defendant even though the witness had first identified another man but quickly changed her mind when she was shown the defendant. The court said the prior misidentification is only one factor to be considered and does not of itself render the identification unreliable. The dissenting judges were of the opinion that this was such a

---

[57] Lucas v. Regan, 503 F(2d) 1 (2dCir 1974).

compelling case of likely misidentification that the appellant should have been granted a retrial at which the in-court identification by this witness would have been excluded.

It is obvious that much of this controversy can be avoided if care is taken to conduct the showup, lineup or other confrontation in such a way that there will be no possibility of unfairness or unreliability. If, in conducting the lineup or showup, the procedure could cause the witness to identify the wrong person, the court may find that this procedure violates the due process provisions of the Constitution and refuse to allow the witness to identify the defendant in court.

§ 7.15   Pretrial photographic identification

Closely related to the lineup is the identification by means of photographs. In the case of *Simmons v. United States*,[58] this type of pre-trial identification by means of photographs was challenged as being suggestive and conducive to misidentification and therefore in violation of the due process clause. Snapshots of the suspect had been shown to the five bank employees who had witnessed a bank robbery, and each witness identified Simmons as one of the robbers. The Court refused to prohibit the employment of this technique but cautioned that each case must be decided on its own facts. The reasons stated were:

> [C]onvictions based on eyewitness identification at trial following a pretrial identification by photograph will be set aside on that ground only if the photographic identification procedure was so impermissibly suggestive as to give rise to a very substantial likelihood of irreparable misidentification.

As in the case of the lineup, if the photographs are used in such a way as to suggest to the witness the identification of the suspect, there is a good possibility that the in-court identification at the trial will be contaminated.

Although the statement of the rule is clear, the line as to what is a suggestive photographic identification and what is not suggestive is a fine one. Perhaps some insight can be gleaned by comparing three similar cases. In one case a New

[58] 390 US 377, 19 LEd(2d) 1247, 88 SCt 967 (1968).

York robbery victim observed his attackers before they sprayed a chemical in his eyes and robbed him of a gun.[59] A week later the victim picked out the suspect from a spread of eight photographs, but one of the photographs was different in that it had a date inscribed which was close to the date the victim's gun was recovered. After the victim stated at the trial that he paid no attention to the numbers or dates, the identification of the suspect at the trial was authorized. The use of the photograph was not "unduly suggestive" nor conducive to irreparable mistaken identification, and the identification was approved by the reviewing court.

In a second case, however, the United States Court of Appeals for the Sixth Circuit found that the use of a single photograph was suggestive and denied due process.[60] Here the victim looked at more than twenty mug shots at police headquarters without identifying anyone as the robber. However, after the suspect had been arrested, police showed the victim a single photo of the suspect and he identified that person as the robber. The court found that the use of the single photograph, even after the victim had not identified the suspect from the first twenty, denied due process as there was no compelling circumstances which justified using a single photo.

In a third case witnesses were shown five photographs on one occasion and identified a suspect.[61] Two months later the same witnesses were shown six photographs. The defendant challenged the selection of his photograph by the witnesses at the second display because he was the only person pictured there who was also pictured in the first display. Recognizing the risk of misidentification, the court, however, thought the risk was reduced in this case due to the time factor and the fact that one photograph was in color and one in black and white. Because the court believed there was nothing improperly suggestive in the initial showings to the three witnesses in the case, the defendant's attack on the later photographic display was not persuasive, and the in-court identification was authorized. They found that the in-court

[59] United States v. Counts, 471 F(2d) 422 (2dCir 1973).
[60] Workman v. Cardwell, 471 F(2d) 909 (6thCir 1972).
[61] United States v. Bowie, 515 F(2d) 3 (7thCir 1975).

identification was not the product of a pre-trial procedure so impermissibly suggestive as to give rise to a very substantial likelihood of irreparable misidentification.

From these and other cases it is apparent that care should be taken in establishing identification procedures to avoid the successful challenge of the process.

§ 7.16   Conduct which "shocks the conscience"

As was pointed out in the first chapter, the scope of the due process clause is so broad that a clear-cut definition is impossible. If, for example, the procedure used by enforcement agents offends a "sense of justice," the conviction based upon evidence obtained after such procedures may be reversed by the Supreme Court using the due process clause of the Fourteenth Amendment as a vehicle. One of the best examples of reversal of a conviction on these grounds is stated in the case of *Rochin* v. *California*.[62] In that case, deputy sheriffs having information that the accused was selling narcotics, entered the open door of a dwelling house and forced open the door to the accused's bedroom. Observing two capsules on the night stand next to the bed, the officers asked, "Whose stuff is this?" The accused seized the capsules and put them in his mouth. The officers then attempted to extract the capsules but being unable to obtain the capsules before the accused swallowed them, took the accused to the hospital. At the hospital and at the direction of the officers, a doctor forced an emetic solution through a tube into Rochin's stomach against his will, and this "stomach pumping" produced vomiting. Two capsules obtained in this manner were used against the defendant at the trial and he was found guilty of possessing a preparation of morphine.

After explaining the application of the due process clause, the Court said it was compelled to conclude that the procedure by which this conviction was obtained violates that clause. The Court went on to say:

> This is conduct that shocks the conscience. Illegally breaking into the privacy of the petitioner, the struggle to open his mouth and remove what was there, the forcible extraction of the stomach

[62] 342 US 165, 96 LEd 183, 72 SCt 205 (1952).

contents—this course of proceeding by agents of government to obtain evidence is bound to offend even hardened sensibilities. They are methods too close to the rack and the screw to permit of constitutional differentiation.

This case was reversed, not on the self-incrimination grounds but solely under the authority of the due process clause of the Fourteenth Amendment.

§ 7.17   Use of blood, breath, and urine samples

As was noted earlier, the taking of blood from the body of the suspect for chemical analysis has been challenged as a violation of the Fifth Amendment as made applicable to the states by the Fourteenth. This procedure has also been challenged as a violation of the due process clause of the Fourteenth directly. In the *Schmerber* case, the Supreme Court considered the due process claim but the majority rejected it.[63] The Court distinguished this from the "stomach pumping" of the *Rochin* case. The Court said: "Under such circumstances the withdrawal of blood does not offend that sense of justice of which we spoke in *Rochin v. California*."

A District of Columbia court has reaffirmed the right of enforcement agents to take urine and blood.[64] In so doing the court explained:

> Such physical evidence obtained from the defendant's body has been excluded on constitutional grounds only where the conduct used to obtain evidence was outrageous, unreasonable and offensive to a sense of justice.

Also there is no deprivation of constitutional rights when a person charged with the offense of operating a motor vehicle while under the influence of intoxicating liquor submits to a drunkometer test unless unnecessary force is used.[65]

This is not to say that the taking of blood or urine from the human body will never be challenged as a violation of the due process clause. As was pointed out in the *Schmerber* case,

[63] Schmerber v. California, 384 US 757, 16 LEd(2d) 908, 86 SCt 1826 (1966).

[64] Davis v. District of Columbia, 247 A(2d) 417 (DC App 1968).

[65] Toledo v. Deitz, 3 Ohio St(2d) 30, 209 NE(2d) 127 (1965). See Klotter & Meier, CRIMINAL EVIDENCE FOR POLICE § 13.12 (2d ed 1975).

if the test is administered by such methods as to invite an unjustified element of personal risk of infection and pain, this might be in violation of the due process clause of the Fourteenth Amendment.

§ 7.18   Summary and practical suggestions

The privilege from self-incrimination had become embodied in the common law prior to the adoption of the United States Constitution and the Bill of Rights. To make certain that this privilege would be protected in the future, members of the First Congress included it as part of the Bill of Rights. In addition, provisions concerning self-incrimination are included in the constitutions of all but two of the states.

In the early decisions, courts determined that the privilege as stated in the Fifth Amendment was applicable to the federal agencies only and not to the states. However, after considerable discussion, it was determined in 1964 by the United States Supreme Court in the *Malloy* case that this self-incrimination protection was made applicable to the states through the Fourteenth Amendment, and that the minimum standards would be those stated by the federal courts.

The early decisions left some doubt as to the application of the self-incrimination provisions outside of court. However, in 1966, the *Miranda* decision of the United States Supreme Court made it abundantly clear that the self-incrimination protection would extend to out-of-court as well as in-court situations.

Although the rule prohibiting the admissibility of involuntary confessions developed differently from the rule concerning self-incrimination, the Supreme Court in the case of *Miranda* reiterated the rule that an out-of-court confession which was solicited without proper warning was inadmissible as violative of the Fifth Amendment, and that this protection would be made applicable to the states through the Fourteenth. This case held that self-incrimination protection may be waived in such out-of-court situations, but that it must be knowingly and intelligently waived.

It is generally agreed that the privilege protects an accused only from being compelled to provide the state with evidence of a testimonial or communicative nature. Therefore, the taking of photographs, fingerprints, blood tests, handwriting specimens and other such evidence from persons legally arrested does not ordinarily violate the self-incrimination protections.

The self-incrimination claim is no longer available if the witness is given immunity under a properly drawn and applied immunity statute. If he is given "use" and "derivative" immunity, he can be required to testify, but the evidence cannot be used against him directly or indirectly in any future court proceeding.

The implied consent statutes provide that a person who obtains a driver's license is deemed to give his consent to submit to an alcohol test if there are reasonable grounds to believe that he was driving while intoxicated. Such statutes do not violate the self-incrimination provisions of the federal or state constitutions.

Statutes which require persons to register where such registration subjects them to state or federal criminal prosecution have been held to be unconstitutional. However, these decisions make it clear that there is no intention to prohibit enforcement of criminal laws where the accused is not required to incriminate himself by such registration.

Some enforcement procedures, such as a confrontation for identification prior to trial, have been challenged as violating the self-incrimination provisions, the right-to-counsel provisions, and the due process provisions of the Constitution. If the lineup or other confrontation for identification is conducted in such a way as to be unduly suggestive, the in-court identification will be disallowed because of the due process considerations. Also, conduct such as pumping the stomach has been found to offend a sense of justice and has made evidence so obtained inadmissible.

When establishing and implementing departmental procedures, the administrator must take into consideration the Fifth Amendment self-incrimination protection as well as the due process protections as interpreted by the Supreme Court. Carefully established procedures for the use of the showup and photographs for identification purposes will avoid unnecessary challenges to the in-court identification of the defendant by witnesses.

Chapter 8

ASSISTANCE OF COUNSEL*

In all criminal prosecutions, the accused shall enjoy the right . . . to have the Assistance of Counsel for his defence.

Sᴉxᴛʜ Aᴍᴇɴᴅᴍᴇɴᴛ, 1791

§ 8.1   Historical development of the right to counsel protection

The law relating to counsel for the criminal defendant has developed over a period of several centuries. This development has been influenced by events which transpired in England prior to the settlement of this country and by American colonial history before the Revolutionary War. Because inequities which existed in the mother country and the colonies were familiar to the framers of the United States Constitution, provisions to reduce abuses were included in the Constitution

* by John C. Klotter

of the United States and the constitutions of the various states. One section provides for the assistance of counsel for those accused of crimes.

In England, prior to 1688, a person charged with treason or felony had no right to demand the assistance of counsel to aid him in preparing his defense. Strangely, during this period persons charged with misdemeanors and parties in civil cases were entitled to seek and obtain legal assistance in their behalf. The rule which allowed counsel in misdemeanors but denied it in more serious offenses, was vigorously assailed by seventeenth century English statesmen and lawyers. Its apologists defended the practice on the ground that the court functioned in the place of counsel and provided ample safeguards for the accused. After the English Revolution of 1688, the rule denying counsel in treason cases was abolished, but existing restriction on the right to counsel in other felony cases continued until as late as 1836, when Parliament granted a corresponding right with respect to felony offenses in general.[1]

The historical development of the right to counsel in America does not parallel the English experience. The necessity of legal assistance in criminal cases was recognized at a much earlier date. Following the Declaration of Independence in 1776, the constitutions of several of the thirteen original states incorporated provisions guaranteeing the right to counsel. There is some diversity with respect to the wording of the early constitutional provisions. For example, in Maryland and New York, where provisions were adopted in 1776 and 1777 respectively, the provisions were to the effect that a defendant accused of crime should be "allowed" counsel. In Pennsylvania, New Hampshire, Delaware and Connecticut the accused was accorded the "right to be heard by himself and by his counsel." And in Massachusetts the constitution provided that the defendant should have the "right to be heard by himself or his counsel at his election."[2]

Inasmuch as many of the men who were responsible for drafting the various state constitutional provisions were also involved in the writing of the United States Constitution, it

---

[1] Powell v. Alabama, 287 US 45, 60, 77 LEd(2d) 158, 53 SCt 55 (1932).

[2] Betts v. Brady, 316 US 455, 465, 86 LEd 1595, 62 SCt 1252 (1942).

is not surprising that the Bill of Rights, which was adopted by the first Congress, contained provisions concerning the right to counsel.

§ 8.2　Constitutional provisions concerning the right to counsel

Prior to the adoption of the United States Constitution, many who argued its merits recognized that the document did not include any specific provisions guaranteeing the right to counsel. This omission was considered serious because an inarticulate person might be unjustly convicted through a lack of legal skills in presenting his defense. Therefore, when the Bill of Rights was considered by the first Congress, the right to counsel was included in the draft as part of the Sixth Amendment. The Amendment reads in pertinent part:

> In all criminal prosecutions, the accused shall enjoy the right . . . to have the Assistance of Counsel for his defence.

Like the other provisions of the Bill of Rights, the portions of the Sixth Amendment on counsel were originally intended to apply only to the operations of the federal government. The Amendment was written in broad, general terms without any attempt to define the scope of its application. Consequently, it becomes necessary to examine case law interpretations to determine what the right to counsel means in modern perspective.

In addition to the guarantee contained in the Bill of Rights, forty-nine states have incorporated similar provisions in their own local constitutions. Although these provisions are worded differently, both in substance and application very little distinction exists. For example, article 2, section 9 of the Illinois Constitution states:

> In all criminal prosecutions the accused shall have the right to appear and defend in person and by counsel.

The state and federal constitutional provisions pertaining to counsel for the accused have not changed during the past half-century. However, due to statutory enactments, and more importantly to court decisions, the rights protected have been vastly expanded. The law is much clearer today than in the past. But many questions still remain unanswered.

§ 8.3   Effects of denial of right to counsel

In a previous chapter the statement is made that if counsel is not afforded as required by the Constitution, a confession obtained after counsel is denied will not be admissible. It is explained that the Sixth Amendment right-to-counsel provision is enforced by excluding the confession. In addition, if counsel is denied at the post-indictment lineup or in certain other confrontation-for-identification situations, such denial could contaminate the in-court identification of the accused by the witness.

If, at the preliminary hearing, the accused is not afforded the right to counsel when this is a "critical stage" of the proceeding, a plea of guilty will not be accepted at a future trial of the case. The same reasoning applies where the right-to-counsel requirements are not complied with at the arraignment. The right to assistance of counsel at the criminal trial itself is deemed so fundamental that failure properly to observe that right automatically vitiates any conviction resulting from that trial.[3] This is true even though there is no showing of prejudicial unfairness.

Legally, a conviction obtained without the proper representation by counsel is totally void. Evidence concerning the conviction cannot be admitted in a later "habitual criminal" proceeding (whereby penalties can be increased for subsequent offenses), nor can it be used to impeach the defendant's testimony in any later proceedings.[4]

As failure to follow statutory provisions and court decisions relating to the right to counsel might prohibit the use of a confession or otherwise vitiate a conviction, it is essential that the criminal justice representative be fully aware of the laws relating to the right to counsel, especially as they apply in pretrial situations.

---

[3] Ferguson v. Georgia, 365 US 570, 5 LEd(2d) 783, 81 SCt 756 (1961).

[4] Loper v. Beto, 405 US 473, 31 LEd(2d) 374, 92 SCt 1014 (1972).

§ 8.4 Right to counsel at trial in federal courts in felony cases

The provisions of the Sixth Amendment are clear in stating that the accused shall enjoy the right to have the assistance of counsel for his defense. But does this command impose an affirmative obligation on the part of the court to appoint counsel where the accused does not request assistance or is unable to pay the legal expenses involved? For several decades lawyers debated whether counsel was "required" or only "permitted" and whether, assuming the right did exist, it extended to all felony cases or was limited to "capital" offenses.

The law remained in a state of confusion until 1938 when the Supreme Court partially clarified the rule with respect to federal prosecutions. In the case of *Johnson v. Zerbst*,[5] the Court ruled that in all federal trials of persons charged with crimes of a serious nature, counsel must be appointed for an indigent defendant unless he intelligently waives his right to counsel. The case involved the prosecution of two Marines who were arrested while on leave in Charleston, South Carolina and charged with passing counterfeit bills, a felony under the laws of the United States though not a capital offense. Both men were taken to jail to await action by the grand jury and were indicted some two months later. Although they were represented by counsel at the time of arrest they were unable to secure counsel for the trial. One of them attempted to conduct his own defense, but no counsel was appointed during the trial. They were both found guilty and sentenced to four and one-half years in the penitentiary.

After serving part of the sentence and after the time for appeal had elapsed, one of the defendants, Johnson, brought habeas corpus proceedings in a federal district court. Upon denial of relief the case was appealed to the Supreme Court of the United States. His conviction was reversed and the case remanded to the district court for retrial in conformity with the views expressed by the Supreme Court in its opinion. In reaching the conclusion that the defendant had been deprived of his constitutional rights, the majority stated:

[5] 304 US 458, 82 LEd 1461, 58 SCt 1019 (1938).

Since the Sixth Amendment constitutionally entitles one charged with crime to the assistance of counsel, compliance with this constitutional mandate is an essential jurisdictional prerequisite to a federal court's authority to deprive an accused of his life or liberty. When this right is properly waived, the assistance of counsel is no longer a necessary element of the court's jurisdiction to proceed to conviction and sentence. If the accused, however, is not represented by counsel and has not competently and intelligently waived his constitutional right, the Sixth Amendment stands as a jurisdictional bar to a valid conviction and sentence depriving him of his life or his property.

This case established two important rules concerning the right to counsel during a criminal trial in the federal courts. (1) Counsel must be appointed for an indigent defendant unless there has been a competent waiver. (2) In order to waive counsel the defendant must make an intelligent and informed choice. The mere failure to request counsel does not amount to a waiver. Moreover, since an intelligent waiver presupposes that the accused has knowledge of his rights, there is a duty on the part of the federal courts to fully advise the defendant of his rights.

§ 8.5   Right to counsel at trial in state courts in felony cases

State agents must abide by the dual requirements of their own separate constitutions and the Sixth Amendment of the Federal Bill of Rights. For many years, diversity existed among the states regarding trial counsel for the indigent defendant.[6] The differences today have largely disappeared as a result of federal judicial intervention in the field, but a discussion of state provisions is nonetheless warranted.

The first step toward the establishment of federal standards in the states came in *Powell* v. *Alabama*[7] where the Supreme Court ruled that a defendant in a state criminal trial for a capital offense was denied due process of law as guaranteed by the Fourteenth Amendment by the failure of the trial court to assign him a court-appointed attorney. In holding that counsel must be appointed in all capital trials where the ac-

---

[6] Betts v. Brady, 316 US 455, 86 LEd 1595, 62 SCt 1252 (1942).

[7] 287 US 45, 77 LEd(2d) 158, 53 SCt 55 (1932).

cused is unable to employ counsel and incapable of conducting his own defense, Mr. Justice Sutherland observed:

> The right to be heard would be, in many cases, of little avail if it did not comprehend the right to be heard by counsel. Even the intelligent and educated layman has small and sometimes no skill in the science of law. If charged with crime, he is incapable, generally, of determining for himself whether the indictment is good or bad. He is unfamiliar with the rules of evidence. Left without the aid of counsel he may be put on trial without a proper charge, and convicted upon incompetent evidence, or evidence irrelevant to the issue or otherwise inadmissible. He lacks both the skill and knowledge adequately to prepare his defense, even though he have a perfect one. He requires the guiding hand of counsel . . . .

The *Powell* holding was limited to the assistance of counsel in capital trials and was based on an interpretation of the due process clause of the Fourteenth Amendment.[8]

The next significant right-to-counsel case in state prosecutions was *Betts v. Brady*,[9] decided by the Supreme Court in 1942. The question presented was whether the *Powell* rationale should be expanded to include state felony trials in which life or death was not at issue. The defendant had been indicted in Maryland on robbery, a non-capital felony. He requested that an attorney be appointed at his trial but was advised by the court that counsel for the indigent was available only in prosecutions for murder and rape. The trial resulted in a conviction and the defendant appealed. The Supreme Court, with three justices dissenting, refused to reverse the Maryland court ruling, explaining:

> [W]e are unable to say that the concept of due process incorporated in the Fourteenth Amendment obligates the states, whatever may be their own views, to furnish counsel in every such case.

The *Betts* holding distinguished between state and federal prosecutions. While counsel was required under the Sixth Amendment in all federal trials where a felony was charged, the states under the Fourteenth Amendment were accorded

[8] The due process clause of the Fourteenth Amendment provides" . . . nor shall any *State* deprive any person of life, liberty, or property, without due process of law; . . ."

[9] 316 US 455, 86 LEd 1595, 62 SCt 1252 (1942).

greater leeway, counsel for the indigent being required only in capital crimes. *Betts* remained the settled law until 1963 when the state courts in Florida learned that they could not rely on past precedent in establishing procedural rules regarding the appointment of counsel in non-capital felony cases.

In 1963, often referred to as "the year of Gideon," the Supreme Court handed down the landmark case of *Gideon* v. *Wainwright* [10] overruling *Betts* v. *Brady*. The facts of the case were very similar. Gideon was charged with breaking and entering a poolroom with intent to commit a misdemeanor, a felony under Florida law though not a capital offense. Because it was not a capital crime, the trial court refused his request for counsel and informed him that he would have to conduct his own defense. Gideon was found guilty and sentenced to eight years' imprisonment. He later filed a petition of habeas corpus and the case ultimately reached the Supreme Court of the United States. Gideon challenged that he had been denied his rights under the Sixth and Fourteenth Amendments. The Supreme Court in a five to four decision voted to reverse his conviction. Mr. Justice Black, who wrote the majority opinion, expressly overruled *Betts* v. *Brady*, declaring:

> The right of one charged with crime to counsel may not be deemed fundamental and essential to fair trials in some countries but it is in ours.

Therefore, it was settled once and for all that the states are henceforth required to furnish counsel to an indigent defendant in all felony trials regardless of whether or not capital punishment is at stake. Counsel during the trial is regarded as a fundamental right essential to procedural fairness. A conviction brought about where legal assistance has been denied is a violation of the Fourteenth Amendment and can be attacked by direct appeal or in habeas corpus proceedings.

It is interesting to note that at Gideon's second trial with an attorney representing him, he was adjudged not guilty.

Because the *Gideon* case was given retroactive application, many prisoners in Florida and other states were released. The

[10] 372 US 335, 9 LEd(2d) 799, 83 SCt 792 (1963).

decision has also influenced the administration of justice in a more indirect way.

The question in one case was whether previous convictions obtained in violation of *Gideon* could be considered in determining the length of a convicted defendant's prison sentence. Here, the statute permitted a longer sentence after a second conviction. In the *Tucker* case,[11] the Supreme Court held that a conviction obtained without the proper appointment of counsel cannot be used to enhance punishment after a subsequent conviction.

In another case,[12] the defendant was charged with raping his eight-year-old stepdaughter. The defendant testified for himself and during the process of impeaching his credibility the prosecutor was permitted on cross-examination to interrogate him about his previous criminal record. The defendant challenged the use of such evidence to impeach his credibility because at least some of the previous convictions were constitutionally invalid. Specifically, he argued that since he was denied counsel at two previous trials, these convictions could not be used to impeach his credibility at this trial even though he had already served his time on these previous sentences.

The Supreme Court agreed that previous convictions which are void because of failure to afford the defendant his right to counsel deprive a criminal defendant of due process of law where the prior convictions are used to impeach the credibility of the defendant's testimony at a future trial.

The effect of this decision is to require the prosecutor to review the record of previous convictions of defendants, and for that matter other witnesses, if he intends to use the previous conviction for impeachment purposes. If he finds that the defendant was improperly denied counsel or the conviction is constitutionally void for other reasons, such convictions cannot be used for impeachment purposes.

§ 8.6   Counsel at the arraignment

Once it was conceded that counsel was required during the criminal trial, the next question concerned whether an accused

[11] United States v. Tucker, 404 US 443, 30 LEd(2d) 592, 92 SCt 589 (1972).

[12] Loper v. Beto, 405 US 473, 31 LEd(2d) 374, 92 SCt 1014 (1972).

could insist upon the presence of counsel at state expense during the preliminary stages. Very little in the way of guidance was afforded by the language of the Sixth Amendment which specifies no more than that the accused should enjoy the right to counsel in all "criminal prosecutions." Does the term "prosecution" signify only the actual trial or can it be interpreted in its broader sense to include the prosecution from beginning to end?

The problem of counsel during the arraignment stage was met by the Supreme Court in the case of *Hamilton v. Alabama.*[13] An arraignment is the last official step before the trial. The accused is brought before the court, informed of the charges against him, and given an opportunity to enter a plea of guilty, not guilty or *nolo contendere.* Under the Federal Rules of Criminal Procedure and under the practice in most states, the accused must be advised at the arraignment stage, if not before, that he has the right to counsel.

The *Hamilton* case raised the question whether the defendant is constitutionally entitled to representation by a court-appointed attorney during his arraignment. The defendant in that case had been charged with breaking and entering a dwelling house at night with the intent to ravish. Under Alabama law, an accused was required to enter a plea of insanity at the arraignment or be barred from raising the defense. The Supreme Court held that under these circumstances the arraignment was so critical a stage in Alabama criminal procedure that the denial of counsel at this stage was in itself a denial of due process of law.

The *Hamilton* decision has been cited for the proposition that counsel must be appointed in any arraignment which is a critical stage in the state proceedings. There remains, of course, the possibility that an accused may intelligently and knowingly waive his right, but absent such a waiver, the assistance of counsel is mandatory if crucial decisions must be made at the arraignment. Otherwise, valuable rights can be lost by failure to make a timely assertion.

Many courts have now adopted the reasoning that any ar-

[13] 368 US 52, 7 LEd(2d) 114, 82 SCt 157 (1961).

raignment is a critical stage in a felony case. For example, in
the case of *Hessenauer* v. *People* [14] the court stated:

> It is by now well established that arraignment is a "critical stage"
> in a felony case and that the right to counsel attaches automatically
> before any plea is made or accepted. [Citations omitted.]

Unless it appears from the record that the trial judge specifically offered and the accused knowingly and understandably
rejected the counsel, the finding of a waiver will not generally
be made.

§ 8.7   Counsel at the preliminary hearing

Pushing the criminal process back another step, the preliminary hearing or examination is an earlier procedure followed in most states within a short period after the arrest. At
the preliminary hearing, it is frequently required that the accused be advised of his right to counsel. The primary function
of the preliminary hearing is to afford an opportunity for a
judicial officer to pass upon the sufficiency of the evidence to
hold the accused. If probable cause is lacking, the magistrate
will order the suspect's release. On the other hand, if sufficient
evidence to warrant further proceedings exists, the magistrate
will set bail or otherwise dispose of the case.

In *White* v. *Maryland* [15] the Supreme Court addressed the
question of the right to assigned counsel at the preliminary
hearing. The defendant in that case had been arrested on
charges of murder on May 27, 1960 and was brought before
a magistrate for the first time on May 31. At the preliminary
hearing and without the presence or advice of counsel, the
accused entered a plea of guilty. When brought in for arraignment on September 8, 1960, counsel had still not been appointed, and the proceedings were postponed until an appointment could be made. He was finally arraigned with counsel on
November 25, 1960, and entered a plea of not guilty by reason of insanity. At the trial, the defendant again entered a
plea of not guilty. The guilty plea made during the preliminary

[14] 45 Ill(2d) 63, 256 NE(2d) 791
(1970).

[15] 373 US 59, 10 LEd(2d) 193, 83
SCt 1050 (1963).

hearing was introduced into evidence, and the defendant was convicted and sentenced to death. In reversing the decision, the Supreme Court compared White's predicament to the situation which occurred in the *Hamilton* case, noting the similarities. The Court observed:

> Whatever may be the normal function of the "preliminary hearing" under Maryland law, it was in this case as "critical" a stage as arraignment under Alabama law. For petitioner entered a plea before the magistrate and that plea was taken at a time when he had no counsel.
>
> We repeat what we said in *Hamilton v. Alabama*, that we do not stop to determine whether prejudice resulted: "Only the presence of counsel could have enabled this accused to know all the defenses available to him and to plead intelligently." We therefore hold that *Hamilton v. Alabama* governs and the judgment below must be and is reversed.

Although both the *Hamilton* and *White* cases involved capital offenses, it seems logical to conclude that the reasoning of *Gideon* would make the same rules applicable in other felony prosecutions where the arraignment or the preliminary hearing is a critical stage in the proceedings.

The Pennsylvania Supreme Court has refused to extend the "critical stage" to the prosecution "bring-up" questioning.[16] In a case before that court the majority of the justices decided that a statement made while the defendant was temporarily away from the prison and in the district attorney's office for questioning, was admissible even though no attorney was present. This "bring-up" order was granted after the preliminary hearing was held and the defendant ordered committed to the county prison to await grand jury action. The defendant argued that the "bring-up" order proceeding was a critical stage in the prosecution process at which point he was entitled to be represented by counsel, and that the statement taken at this time could not be used against him. These words were used in explaining why this was not a critical stage of the proceeding:

[16] Commonwealth v. Broaddus, 458 Pa 261, 317 A(2d) 635 (1974).

We view *White* and *Hamilton* as holding a judicial proceeding is a critical stage only in cases where lack of an attorney at the proceeding directly prejudices the accused. Hence, to come within the holding of these two cases the prejudice must have arisen *at* a judicial proceeding.

Concluding that this was not a judicial proceeding, the Pennsylvania Court refused to extend the *Hamilton-White* guarantee to the "bring-up" situation.

§ 8.8   Right to counsel during the investigation—after indictment

Many prosecutors and police administrators expressed shock when the Supreme Court in 1964 reversed a state murder conviction because the accused was not permitted to consult with his attorney after his arrest and while he was being held in custody at the police station. This decision was only the culmination of a trend begun in *Powell* v. *Alabama* [17] and could have been predicted with a fair degree of accuracy on the basis of *Gideon* v. *Wainwright* [18] and later cases. In a period of less than twenty years, the right to counsel had been extended to the trial of all felony cases, then to the arraignment stage, and finally to the preliminary hearing. The "critical stage" approach logically carried this constitutional right back another step to the investigative stage, and it was only a matter of time until the rule would be formally announced by the Supreme Court.

Then came *Massiah* v. *United States*,[19] handed down by the Supreme Court late in the 1963–1964 term. The facts were that a defendant, who had been arrested, indicted and released on bail for violating the federal narcotics laws, placed his confidence in a co-defendant who had agreed to assist the federal authorities in further investigation. With the cooperation of this man, the investigators listened to a conversation between him and the defendant which took place in a car which had been equipped with a radio transmitter. Incriminating statements overheard in this manner were admitted into

[17] 287 US 45, 77 LEd(2d) 158, 53 SCt 55 (1932).

[18] 372 US 335, 9 LEd(2d) 799, 83 SCt 792 (1963).

[19] 377 US 201, 12 LEd(2d) 246, 84 SCt 1199 (1964).

evidence over the defendant's objection that its receipt violated his Sixth Amendment rights. On appeal the Supreme Court reversed the conviction stating:

> We hold that the petitioner was denied the basic protections of that guarantee when there was used against him at his trial evidence of his own incriminating words, which federal agents had deliberately elicited from him after he had been indicted and in the absence of his counsel.

In a case[19a] similar to *Massiah*, the defendant, Williams, made incriminating statements and agreed to take detectives to find the body of the victim, after a warrant had been issued for his arrest in a Davenport courtroom. The statements were made after an attorney had been appointed in Davenport and the detectives agreed not to question Williams until he talked with an attorney in Des Moines where he was being taken by the detectives.

Although the officers did not question the suspect, one commented that "this little girl should be entitled to a Christian burial," and according to the Court, "deliberately and designedly set out to elicit information."

The United States Supreme Court found that there was no need to consider *Miranda* v. *Arizona* (based on the Fifth Amendment), but that Williams was entitled to the assistance of counsel guaranteed by the Sixth and Fourteenth Amendments. After determining that the defendant had not waived his right to counsel, the Supreme Court held the statements and evidence were not admissible and ordered a new trial.

Do the *Massiah* and *Brewer* rulings in effect mean that there may never be a valid waiver of counsel after indictment if counsel has been contacted? In the case of *Moore* v. *Wolff*[20] the majority of the Eighth Circuit judges held that *Massiah* should not be read so broadly as to hold that there may never be a valid waiver of counsel after indictment or arraignment. In this case the defendant was convicted in state court of assault with intent to rape and sodomy, and was sentenced to

---

[19a] Brewer v. Williams, ___ US ___, 51 LEd(2d) 424, 97 SCt 1232 (1977).

[20] 495 F(2d) 35 (8thCir 1974).

concurrent five-year terms of imprisonment. His argument before the United States Court of Appeals on habeas corpus was that his oral incriminating statements made after appointment of counsel but without counsel present were used against him at trial in violation of the Sixth Amendment right to counsel.

The defendant did not challenge the evidence that he received *Miranda* warnings or that he voluntarily made the oral incriminating statements. He argued, however, that after the appointment of counsel, no interrogation can take place without counsel being in fact notified and given an opportunity to be present. Some of the doubts that have existed since the *Massiah* case were answered by the court's ruling that:

> If an accused can voluntarily, knowingly, and intelligently waive his right to counsel before one has been appointed, there seems no compelling reason to hold that he may not voluntarily, knowingly, and intelligently waive his right to have counsel present at an interrogation after counsel has been appointed. Of course, the Government will have a heavy burden to show that the waiver was knowingly and intelligently made, but we perceive no compelling reason to adopt the *per se* rule advocated by the petitioner.

§ 8.9　Right to counsel during the investigation—before indictment

Mr. Justice White's predictions in *Massiah* that the same reasoning would apply in pre-indictment situations became a reality a few weeks later in the celebrated case of *Escobedo v. Illinois.*[21] In the *Escobedo* case the interrogation took place prior to the indictment. Very briefly, the facts were these. The defendant was arrested for the first time and released the same day on a writ of habeas corpus. He told the police nothing at this time. He was rearrested about eleven days later and before making any statement, requested an opportunity to consult with his attorney. His attorney likewise made repeated efforts to gain access to his client. Both men were told that they could not see the other until the police had finished with their interrogation. In the course of the questioning, the

---

[21] 378 US 478, 12 LEd(2d) 977, 84 SCt 1758 (1964). See Part II for a reprint of portions of this case.

defendant stated that another person had committed the shooting, thereby admitting knowledge of the crime and implicating himself in it. At the trial, he moved to suppress the incriminating statements but his motion was denied.

The Supreme Court of Illinois upheld the trial court's ruling on the competency of the statements and the defendant appealed to the United States Supreme Court. The Supreme Court voted five to four to reverse the decision below. Mr. Justice Goldberg, who wrote the majority opinion, adopted the "critical stage" reasoning developed in the *White* and *Hamilton* cases. Stating that the post-arrest interrogation was the stage "when legal aid and advice were most critical" to a criminal accused, Justice Goldberg observed in *Escobedo:*

> In *Gideon v. Wainwright*, we held that every person accused of a crime, whether state or federal, is entitled to a lawyer at trial. The rule sought by the State here, however, would make the trial no more than an appeal from the interrogation; and the "right to use counsel at the formal trial [would be] a very hollow thing [if], for all practical purposes, the conviction is already assured by pretrial examination." [Citation omitted.]

The precise point in the criminal process when the right to counsel attaches and the suspect must be *permitted* to consult with his attorney was stated as follows:

> We hold, therefore, that where, as here, the investigation is no longer a general inquiry into an unsolved crime but has begun to focus on a particular suspect, the suspect has been taken into police custody, the police carry out a process of interrogation that lends itself to eliciting incriminating statements, the suspect has requested and been denied an opportunity to consult with his lawyer, and the police have not effectively warned him of his absolute constitutional right to remain silent, the accused has been denied "the Assistance of Counsel" in violation of the Sixth Amendment to the Constitution as "made obligatory upon the States by the Fourteenth Amendment," and no statement elicited by the police during interrogation may be used against him at a criminal trial.

Clarifying this lengthy sentence, Justice Goldberg concluded with the admonition that:

> [W]hen the process shifts from investigatory to accusatory—when its focus is on the accused and its purpose is to elicit a confession— our adversary system begins to operate, and, under the circum-

stances here, the accused must be permitted to consult with his lawyer.

With *Escobedo*, the right to counsel has been extended to the earliest possible point in the criminal process. Many questions, nevertheless, were left unanswered. Escobedo had *requested* counsel during the interrogation and his request was denied. What if he had been ignorant of his rights and had not made demands on the police? Moreover, Escobedo had already retained his own attorney and was not asking for the assistance of assigned counsel. Would it have made any difference if he had requested the police to furnish him legal assistance at state expense? Finally, Escobedo was being interrogated about a felony. Would his rights have been identical if instead it had been a misdemeanor? These were just a few of the questions that were being asked after the *Escobedo* case.

Directly following the *Escobedo* decision, the state courts in a series of cases attempted to apply the rules developed, but with differing interpretations. In California, the highest court of the state refused to admit any confession where counsel was not granted and there was no warning given to the suspect that he had a right to remain silent or to have counsel present, despite the fact that defendant never indicated during the interrogation that he desired legal assistance.[22] In Illinois, on the other hand, the highest state court on precisely the same facts reached the opposite conclusion, declining to hold a confession inadmissible in the absence of evidence that the accused had requested and been denied an attorney, even though the police had not effectively warned him concerning his constitutional rights.[23] *Escobedo* had created an intolerable situation, and the need for an authoritative clarification was obvious.

On June 13, 1966, the Supreme Court of the United States spoke. Almost everyone versed in the law could have predicted the result. Only the reasoning of the Court was surprising. In *Miranda* v. *Arizona*[24] and its three companion cases, four convictions were reversed because in each instance incriminating statements had been obtained from the defendants under cir-

[22] People v. Dorado, 40 Cal Rptr 264, 394 P(2d) 952 (1964).
[23] People v. Hartgraves, 31 Ill(2d)

375, 202 NE(2d) 33 (1964).
[24] 384 US 436, 16 LEd(2d) 694, 86 SCt 1602 (1966).

cumstances which did not comport with the constitutional standards enunciated by the Court. The reversal was not made to hinge upon the Sixth Amendment right to counsel, but on the Fifth Amendment provisions concerning self-incrimination. The presence of counsel was held necessary as a means of enforcing the immunity against compulsory self-incrimination.

Because of the *Miranda* ruling, it is no longer necessary for the suspect to request counsel during the *custodial interrogation*. The burden is placed on the police to inform the suspect of his constitutional rights and to refrain from asking any further questions unless the accused knowingly waives his right to counsel and to remain silent. Chief Justice Warren, who wrote the majority opinion, summarized the Court's sweeping new mandate as follows:

> If, however, he indicates in any manner and at any stage of the process that he wishes to consult with an attorney before speaking there can be no questioning. Likewise, if the individual is alone and indicates in any manner that he does not wish to be interrogated, the police may not question him. The mere fact that he may have answered some questions or volunteered some statements on his own does not deprive him of the right to refrain from answering any further inquiries until he has consulted with an attorney and thereafter consents to be questioned.[25]

In determining when the warnings must be given and the suspect afforded an opportunity to consult with counsel, the *Escobedo* and *Miranda* cases must be read together. In *Escobedo* the Court stated that when the process shifts from the investigatory to the accusatory, when its *focus is on the accused* and its purpose to elicit a confession, the accused must be permitted to consult with counsel. In the *Miranda* case the Court explained what was meant by custodial interrogation:

> By custodial interrogation, we mean questioning initiated by law enforcement officers after a person has been taken into custody or otherwise deprived of his freedom of action in any significant way.[26]

---

[25] *Id.* at 445.   [26] *Id.* at 444.

Applying these two cases together, the following succinct rule relating to the assistance of counsel results: when a person is taken into custody *and* questioned, he must be *advised* of his right to counsel; when he is questioned with a view to obtaining incriminating statements although he is not in custody, he must be *permitted* to consult with counsel.

But even though a suspect is in custody, he has no right to the presence of counsel at a court-ordered psychiatric examination. The Texas Court of Criminal Appeals and the United States Court of Appeals for the Fifth Circuit agree that a psychiatric examination is not an adversary proceeding.[27] As its sole purpose is to enable an expert to form an opinion as to an accused's mental capacity to form a criminal intent, and not to establish facts showing that the accused committed certain acts which constitute the crime, no counsel is required.

§ 8.10 Counsel at the lineup

Although the lineup is generally considered a part of the investigative stage, because of its importance it is discussed here as a separate section. In 1967 the Supreme Court of the United States extended the right to counsel to the police lineup and other exhibitions of the accused for identification purposes where this stage of the procedure is "critical."[28]

In previous chapters the cases relating to the lineup are reviewed to determine if the procedure violates the self-incrimination provisions of the Fifth Amendment or the due process provisions of the Fifth and Fourteenth Amendments. From that discussion it is apparent that the lineup and other identification confrontations are challenged on three constitutional grounds: self-incrimination, due process, and right to counsel. In this section the cases relating to right to counsel at the lineup or other identification confrontation are considered.

In a decision in which the members of the United States

---

[27] United States v. Williams, 456 F(2d) 217 (1972); Stultz v. State, 500 SW(2d) 853 (Tex 1973).

[28] United States v. Wade, 388 US 218, 18 LEd(2d) 1149, 87 SCt 1926 (1967); Gilbert v. California, 388 US 263, 18 LEd(2d) 1178, 87 SCt 1951 (1967); Stovall v. Denno, 388 US 293, 18 LE(2d) 1199, 87 SCt 1967 (1967). This rule was not made retroactive beyond June 12, 1967.

Supreme Court had little concensus, the lineup was determined to be a critical stage of the proceeding if the in-court identification of the accused could be jeopardized.[29] The Court in this case quickly decided that the lineup does not violate the self-incrimination protections since the defendant is not being compelled to give evidence of a testimonial or communicative nature. As to the right-to-counsel challenge, the majority agreed that an attorney should generally be present at the lineup in order to get evidence to challenge the credibility of the witnesses' future courtroom identification. The reasoning is that if the procedure followed by the police is such as to suggest that a suspect is the one who committed the crime, the in-court identification may be influenced by this procedure so that there will be danger of misidentification at the trial.

Since the counsel's presence at the lineup is merely to equip him to attack the courtroom identification, he has no right to object to the fact that the lineup is being conducted. In fact, the Court specifically left the door open to the establishment of procedures whereby the counsel would not be required to attend the lineup, saying:

> Legislative or other regulations, such as those of local police departments, which eliminate the risks of abuse and unintentional suggestion at lineup proceedings and the impediments to meaningful confrontation at trial may also remove the basis for regarding the stage as "critical."

Contrary to common opinion, the Supreme Court did not hold that the in-court identification in this case would be excluded *per se*, but referred the case back to the lower court in order to give the government the opportunity to establish by clear and convincing evidence that the in-court identifications were based on observations of the suspect other than the lineup identification.

The holding in the *Wade* case also brought with it some unanswered questions. In *Wade*, the lineup was conducted

---

[29] United States v. Wade, 388 US 218, 18 LEd(2d) 1149, 87 SCt 1926 (1967). Seven of the nine judges dissented as to at least part of the primary opinion.

after the indictment. Soon after that case was decided, the
question arose as to whether the same rule would apply to a
police station showup which took place before the defendant
had been indicted or otherwise formally charged with any
criminal offense. This question was considered by the Supreme
Court in the case of *Kirby v. Illinois*.[30]

In the *Kirby* case the petitioner and a companion were
stopped for investigation. When each produced items bearing
the name "Shard," they were arrested and taken to the police
station. There, the arresting officers learned of the robbery of
a person named "Shard" two days earlier. Shard was called
to the station and immediately identified petitioner and his
companion as the robbers. At the time of this confrontation,
the petitioner and his companion were not advised of their
right to counsel, nor did either ask for or receive legal assistance. At the trial, after a pre-trial motion to suppress his
testimony had been overruled, Shard testified as to his previous identification of the petitioner and his companion and
again identified them as the robbers. The defendants were
found guilty, and the conviction was upheld on appeal. They
appealed to the Supreme Court claiming that the pre-indictment confrontation contaminated the in-court identification
and that the *Wade* rule precluded the use of the identification.

Before discussing the constitutional right-to-counsel issue,
the Court again reiterated its past decisions that this in no
way violates the constitutional privilege against compulsory
self-incrimination. As to the due process challenge to the
lineup and confrontation, the Court said the due process
clauses of the Fifth and Fourteenth Amendments forbid a
lineup that is unnecessarily suggestive and conducive to irreparable mistaken identification, but that such was not the
issue here. Also disallowing the right-to-counsel claim, the
Court refused to extend the right-to-counsel protection of the
Sixth Amendment to a pre-indictment identification such as
the one at issue in this case. In the decision which could have

[30] 406 US 682, 32 LEd(2d) 411, 92
SCt 1877 (1972). See Part II for portions of this case.

far-reaching effects in other situations, Mr. Justice Stewart, speaking for the majority, announced:

> The initiation of judicial criminal proceedings is far from a mere formalism. It is the starting point of our whole system of adversary criminal justice. For it is only then that the government has committed itself to prosecute, and only then that the adverse positions of government and defendant have solidified. . . . It is this point, therefore, that marks the commencement of the "criminal prosecutions" to which alone the explicit guarantees of the Sixth Amendment are applicable.

Applying these principles to lineup and confrontation situations, it is apparent that the attorney does not have to be advised when a lineup or confrontation is to be conducted prior to the indictment. However, such confrontation may still be challenged as being in violation of the due process protection, and in some instances it is advisable to have the attorney at the lineup to avoid any in-court challenge.

Following the important *Kirby* decision of 1972, many state and lower federal courts attempted to interpret the *Kirby* rule which states in general terms that there is no constitutional right to an attorney for a pre-indictment or pre-information lineup. In applying this rule, the United States Court of Appeals for the Fifth Circuit found that returning the arrested suspect, who was involved in an accident while driving a stolen car, to the scene for identification was not a violation of his constitutional rights.[31] The show-up identification without counsel present before formal charges are made against the defendant is not in violation of the Sixth Amendment right-to-counsel provisions according to recent decisions.

Following like reasoning the United States Court of Appeals for the Ninth Circuit agreed that returning a suspected bank robber to the bank a short time after the robbery so that employees could observe and identify him was not in violation of the Sixth Amendment even though counsel was not present.[32] At the time of the show-up, no adversary proceeding had been started against the defendant and there were no unduly suggestive circumstances at the show-up.

[31] United States v. Abshire, 471 F(2d) 116 (5thCir 1972).

[32] United States v. Miramon, 470 F(2d) 1362 (9thCir 1972).

The Pennsylvania Supreme Court adopted a standard of procedure that affords the accused a greater protection than the minimal safeguards provided in the *Kirby* case. In that state, the right to counsel attaches at the time of arrest in confrontation for identification situations.[33]

Because the state may, by a court decision or a statutory enactment, provide greater restrictions than established by the Federal Supreme Court, those involved in the criminal justice process must be familiar with both.

By sifting out the pertinent parts of the *Wade, Gilbert, Stovall* and *Kirby* cases, some conclusions can be reached concerning the lineup and other identification confrontations:

(1) The lineup does not violate the self-incrimination provisions.

(2) The accused may waive the right to have counsel at the lineup if he does so voluntarily, knowingly and intelligently.

(3) Unless there is a state provision to the contrary, counsel does not have to be advised concerning a lineup or confrontation if this is conducted prior to the initiation of judicial criminal proceedings.

(4) Absent a knowing and intelligent waiver, the witness's in-court identification following a post-indictment lineup identification of the suspect may be excluded unless the prosecution can show an independent source for the in-court identification.

(5) The defense attorney has no right to participate in or control the conduct of the lineup.

(6) The lineup or the confrontation is still a valuable tool in law enforcement where the witness making the identification will not be called upon to identify the accused at trial, even if counsel is not present.

Another reminder is justified here. Even though counsel may not be required, as in the case of a pre-indictment confrontation or street confrontation, the in-court identification

[33] Commonwealth v. Richman, 458 Pa 167, 320 A(2d) 351 (1974).

may still be contaminated if the procedure is so suggestive as to violate the due process provisions of the Constitution.

Advising counsel that a lineup is to be conducted will probably not impede legitimate law enforcement, and in fact, law enforcement may be assisted by preventing the infiltration of taint into the prosecution's identification evidence. Therefore, the best procedure is to make every effort to advise counsel when a lineup is to be conducted and to allow him to be present at the lineup. If a waiver is contemplated, the accused should be fully advised of his right to have counsel present.

The discussion of the lineup would not be complete if the provisions of the Omnibus Crime Control and Safe Streets Act of 1968 were not included. After hearing arguments that the *Wade* ruling would make it more difficult to identify the accused in court, Congress enacted the following legislation which is part of the Omnibus Crime Control Act of 1968:

§ 3502.   Admissibility in evidence of eye witness testimony
The testimony of a witness that he saw the accused commit or participate in the commission of the crime for which the accused is being tried shall be admissible in evidence in a criminal prosecution in any trial court ordained and established under article III of the Constitution of the United States.[34]

It was apparently intended that this provision would allow eyewitness testimony as to the identity of the accused at the trial even though counsel was not present at the lineup or other confrontation.

Since the right-to-counsel protection is a constitutional guarantee, there is a good chance that the sweeping language of the legislation will be held to be in violation of the Constitution. There will almost certainly be some restrictions, as this language would even allow "in-court" identifications when the due process requirements are violated.[35]

Even though this legislation specifically applies to the admissibility of evidence in federal courts, it seems obvious that it has significance as far as state courts are concerned. If the

[34] 18 USC § 3502 (1970).   [35] See Chapter 7, *supra*, for a discussion of the lineup and due process.

state admits eyewitness testimony even though counsel was not present during the lineup, and if the United States Supreme Court upholds this procedure for federal courts, that Court will find it difficult to reverse state decisions on these grounds. As mentioned previously, the United States Supreme Court is not likely to require stricter standards in state actions than are required in federal actions.

Until this matter is acted upon by the courts, it is recommended that the requirements established by the Supreme Court be followed.

§ 8.11　Counsel for persons charged with misdemeanors

The Sixth Amendment provides that the accused shall enjoy the right to counsel in all criminal prosecutions. For many years this was interpreted to require the appointment of counsel for indigents only in *capital* cases. In 1963 the United States Supreme Court determined that the states must furnish counsel to indigent defendants in all *felony* cases regardless of whether or not capital punishment is at stake. Although some federal appeals courts and some state courts had ruled that the right to counsel existed during the trial of a misdemeanor case,[36] the United States Supreme Court did not take action until 1972. In the case of *Argersinger* v. *Hamlin*,[37] the United States Supreme Court acted on this question and established some specific guidelines as to the right to counsel in misdemeanor cases.

In the *Argersinger* case the petitioner, an indigent, was charged in Florida with carrying a concealed weapon, an offense punishable by a maximum of six months' imprisonment and a $1,000 fine. He was not represented by counsel at the trial where the judge ordered that he serve 90 days in jail. The Florida Supreme Court, following decisions in previous cases, upheld the conviction agreeing that the right to court-appointed counsel extends only to persons charged with offenses punishable by more than six months' imprisonment. The defendant appealed to the Supreme Court of the United

---

[36] *E.g.,* Harvey v. Mississippi, 340 F(2d) 263 (5thCir 1965); People v. Mallory, 378 Mich 538, 147 NW(2d) 66 (1967).

[37] 407 US 25, 32 LEd(2d) 530, 92 SCt 2006 (1972). See Part II for this case.

States claiming that his Sixth Amendment right to counsel as applied to the states by the Fourteenth was violated.

The majority of the members of the United States Supreme Court stated that the problems associated with misdemeanors are often as complicated as felonies and require the presence of counsel to insure the accused a fair trial. Establishing the line where counsel is required if not waived, the Court concluded:

> We need not consider the requirements of the Sixth Amendment as regards the right to counsel where the loss of liberty is not involved, . . .

and:

> We hold, therefore, that absent a knowing and intelligent waiver, no person may be *imprisoned* for any offense, whether classified as petty, misdemeanor, or felony unless he was represented by counsel at his trial. [Emphasis added.]

As a result of this decision, the right to counsel at trial is guaranteed in misdemeanor cases where imprisonment is a possibility to the same extent that right to counsel is guaranteed in felony cases.[38] In a misdemeanor case, therefore, the judge must determine before trial that no imprisonment will be imposed if the case is to be tried without counsel unless counsel is intelligently and competently waived.

The problems created by the *Argersinger* holding are apparent. First, because of the limited number of public defenders, there are insufficient attorneys to represent persons charged with misdemeanors. As a result, in many instances the judges have determined in advance that no imprisonment will be imposed. This in itself has resulted in a weakening of the criminal justice system. Secondly, there is evidence that the waiver of counsel is often openly encouraged by judges. According to a study supported by the Law Enforcement Assistance Administration, compliance with the requirements of the *Argersinger* decision has generally been token in nature.[39]

---

[38] See Gideon v. Wainwright, 372 US 335, 9 LEd(2d) 799, 83 SCt 792 (1963), for the guidelines in felony cases.

[39] A five volume report on "Counsel for misdemeanants" is available at the National Institute of Law Enforcement and Criminal Justice. Washington, D.C.

The establishment of the "possibility of imprisonment" criteria as the test for applying the right to counsel protection is definite, even though somewhat arbitrary. Problems remain concerning the standards to test indigency and criteria to uniformly ascertain where the "no imprisonment" determination will or will not be imposed.

§ 8.12　Juveniles' constitutional right to counsel

On May 15, 1967, the Supreme Court of the United States extended the right-to-counsel privilege to juveniles.[40] The facts of the case are briefly as follows: Gerald Francis Gault, a 15-year-old boy, was arrested and charged with being a delinquent minor after a verbal complaint concerning a telephone call made to a neighbor woman in which the neighbor claimed that Gault had made lewd and indecent remarks. He was not advised at the hearing of his right to counsel, right to confrontation, or privilege against self-incrimination. Also, no one was sworn at the hearing, no transcript was made, and no record of the substance of the proceedings was prepared.

The youth was declared a delinquent and committed to the State Industrial School until he reached the age of 21 unless sooner discharged by due process of law. The Supreme Court of Arizona affirmed dismissal of a petition for a writ of habeas corpus and an appeal was made to the United States Supreme Court.

On the right-to-counsel issue the majority commented:

> We conclude that the Due Process Clause of the Fourteenth Amendment requires that in respect of proceedings to determine delinquency which may result in commitment to an institution in which the juvenile's freedom is curtailed, the child and his parent must be notified of the child's right to be represented by counsel retained by them, or if they are unable to afford counsel, that counsel will be appointed to represent the child.

This wording would seem to indicate that juveniles are guaranteed the right to counsel to the same degree as are adults.

In holding that the self-incrimination provisions also apply

[40] In re Gault, 387 US 1, 18 LEd(2d) 527, 87 SCt 1428 (1967).

to juveniles, the Court injected the right-to-counsel protection, stating:

> We conclude that the constitutional privilege against self-incrimination is applicable in the case of juveniles as it is with respect to adults.

Other comments in the case indicate that with few exceptions the constitutional guarantees afforded adults will also be given to juveniles.

Since the *Gault* decision, questions have arisen as to the waiver of the right to counsel in the case of a juvenile. In the *Gault* case the Court stated that the child and his parents must be notified of the child's right to be represented by counsel. In carrying out this demand the New York Supreme Court ruled that the parents as well as the child must be advised concerning the right to counsel. That court held that unless the juvenile is advised of all his rights in the presence of the parent or a lawyer, so the court can be sure the rights are understood, a juvenile's confession will not stand up in court.[41]

The rule requiring that both the parent and the juvenile be advised concerning the right to counsel has exceptions which have been applied in several courts. For example, a New Jersey juvenile domestic relations court decided that the capacity to waive one's right to counsel cannot be determined by age alone.[42] The court said that although it has been frequently argued that a juvenile is not competent to waive his right to counsel because of his young age, this proposition has been generally rejected by the weight of authority.

To avoid any possibility of taint, it is suggested that the requirements of the *Gault* decision be followed and that the accused juvenile be advised of his rights in the presence of his parents or an attorney.

§ 8.13   Right to counsel on appeal

Not only does the right to counsel protect persons accused of crime prior to trial, it has been expanded to protect the per-

---

[41] In re Aaron D., 30 AppDiv(2d) 183, 290 NYS(2d) 935 (1968).

[42] In re R.M., 105 NJSuper 372, 252 A(2d) 237 (1969).

son who has been convicted in the trial court. Where an appeal is granted as a matter of right, it is unconstitutional for the state to refuse to appoint counsel for indigents.[43]

Having decided that counsel must be appointed for indigent state defendants on their first appeal where the appeal is a matter of right, the Supreme Court was requested in 1974 to expand that right and require counsel for discretionary state appeals and for appeals to the United States Supreme Court. In the case of *Ross* v. *Moffitt* [44] the respondent, an indigent, was represented by a court-appointed counsel at the trial and was convicted of forgery in two separate cases. He appealed as a matter of right to the North Carolina Court of Appeals and was again represented by court-appointed counsel. However, the court refused to appoint counsel for a discretionary review by the North Carolina Supreme Court, and he was denied the appointment of counsel to prepare a petition for certiorari to the United States Supreme Court.

Recognizing that the right to counsel had already been expanded greatly and that the Supreme Court had given extensive consideration to the rights of indigent persons on appeal, Mr. Justice Rehnquist, speaking for the majority, refused to extend that right to the described situation. This decision provides that the due process clause does not require a state to provide the respondent with counsel on his discretionary appeal to the state supreme court nor to the United States Supreme Court. The rationale is that on appeal, not the state, but the defendant initiates the appellate process, seeking not to fend off the efforts of the state's prosecutor but rather to overturn a finding of guilt made by a judge or a jury below.

§ 8.14   Right to counsel at probation or parole revocation hearing

Of special interest to probation, parole and corrections personnel is the case of *Mempa* v. *Rhay* [45] in which the Supreme Court decided that a probationer is entitled to appointment of counsel at a combined probation revocation and delayed

---

[43] *Douglas* v. *California*, 372 US 353, 9 LEd(2d) 811, 83 SCt 814 (1963).
[44] 417 US 600, 41 LEd(2d) 341, 94 SCt 2437 (1974).
[45] 389 US 128, 19 LEd(2d) 336, 88 SCt 254 (1967).

sentencing hearing. Mr. Justice Marshall, speaking for the Court, determined that where a defendant has been convicted and placed on probation, counsel must be appointed to represent him at the probation revocation hearing where the imposition of sentence is a possibility. This is a critical stage of the prosecution proceedings, and a lawyer must be afforded at such a *combined* hearing, whether it be labeled "revocation of probation" or "deferred sentencing." Applying the *Mempa* ruling, the Michigan Court of Appeals held that the accused is entitled to counsel at the probation revocation hearing where sentencing is to be adjudged in the event that the probation is revoked.[46]

In 1972 the United States Supreme Court was called on to determine if this right extended to parole revocation procedures in *Morrissey v. Brewer*.[47] The parole officer in the case had recommended that parole be revoked because of the parolee's continued violation of parole rules. The petitioner claimed that his due process rights as guaranteed by the Fourteenth Amendment were violated because he had received no hearing prior to revocation of the parole. The state responded by arguing that no hearing was required.

In a lengthy decision the Supreme Court of the United States specifically stated that it did not decide the question whether the parolee is entitled to the assistance of retained counsel or to appointed counsel if he is indigent, but did set out other requirements which must be met prior to a parole revocation. Among these are: a) written notice of the claimed violation; b) disclosure to the parolee of evidence against him; c) opportunity to be heard in person and to present witnesses and documentary evidence; d) the right to confront and cross-examine adverse witnesses; e) a neutral and detached hearing body such as a traditional parole board, members of which need not be judicial officers or lawyers; and f) a written state-

---

[46] People v. Brown, 17 Mich App 396, 169 NW(2d) 522 (1969).

[47] 408 US 471, 33 LEd(2d) 484, 92 SCt 2593 (1972). Every probation and parole officer should read this case fully for an understanding of the function of probation and parole as viewed by the United States Supreme Court justices. See Baxter v. Palmigiani, 425 US 308, 47 LEd(2d) 810, 96 SCt 1551 (1976) for a decision denying right to counsel for prisoners charged with misconduct.

ment by the fact finders as to the evidence relied on and reasons for revoking parole.

After setting out these requirements, the Court added that it had no intention of creating an inflexible structure for parole revocation procedures. The Court explained that these were only basic requirements and that the states could formalize their own procedures so long as they complied with these requirements.

The Supreme Court did not specifically require that counsel be authorized at the parole revocation since it did not consider such proceedings to be prosecutorial in nature. However, if the requirements as stated above are to be guaranteed, the parolee may well argue that only with counsel can he be certain that these requirements are met.

After the decision in the *Morrissey* case, the justices were again called upon to determine the necessity of appointing counsel at a probation revocation hearing—this time, where the probationer had been sentenced *at trial*.[48] The Court declared that since the loss of probation, like the loss of parole, is a serious deprivation of liberty, due process must be afforded the probationer already sentenced at trial by entitling him to two hearings as set down in *Morrissey:* (1) a preliminary hearing at the time of detention to determine whether probable cause exists to believe he has violated parole or probation, and (2) a comprehensive hearing prior to any final revocation decision.

Addressing the question of whether indigents in parole or probation revocation hearings have a constitutional right to appointed counsel, the Court considered the informal nature of such hearings, the advocacy of the parole or probation officer, and the "more limited due process rights" of those already convicted of crime, deciding that appointment of counsel in such situations should be decided on a case-by-case basis.

The Kentucky Court of Appeals, looking to the guidelines suggested in the two Supreme Court cases mentioned above, held that a reckless driver is not entitled to be discharged from custody merely because he was not represented by counsel

[48] Gagnon v. Scarpelli, 411 US 778,
36 LEd(2d) 656, 93 SCt 1756 (1973).

at a revocation hearing.[49] In this Kentucky case an habitually reckless driver was given a 180-day contempt sentence for violating a no-driving injunction which was initially suspended. He had no right to counsel at the hearing on the prosecutor's motion to set aside the suspension order, the Kentucky Court explained, as the court was not reviewing an action independent of the original contempt proceeding. The reasoning of the judges was that in this habeas corpus proceeding where the action by the lower Kentucky Court was being challenged, there was not even a suggestion that the driver had not violated the terms of the probation or that there were any mitigating circumstances. He insisted that the mere fact that he was not represented by counsel at the revocation hearing entitled him to be discharged from custody. The court disagreed and refused to grant relief.

To summarize, the United States Supreme Court has interpreted the Constitution to require retained counsel, or appointed counsel for indigent persons, at hearings where deferred sentencing and probation revocation are combined. The Court neither required nor denied counsel at parole or probation revocation hearings where the probationer had been sentenced at trial, but held the presence of counsel at such hearings should be decided on a case-by-case basis. Due process requirements which the Court *did* specify could arguably be fulfilled only with the assistance of counsel in certain situations.

§ 8.15   Effective assistance of counsel

Although the right to counsel has been guaranteed by the Federal Constitution since 1791, this right has been greatly extended in the last decade. Gradually, the right has been expanded to apply at trial in all felony and some misdemeanor cases, and at proceedings prior to and subsequent to the trial proceedings. Recently the quality of representation has been more effectively challenged. Although the Supreme Court has never enunciated any clear standards for courts to follow on

---

[49] Reeder v. Commonwealth, 507 SW(2d) 491 (Ky 1973)

claims of ineffectiveness of counsel, state supreme courts and federal circuit courts have groped for a prescription to apply in this situation. Over a period of time the courts have generally accepted a formula which came to be known as the "mockery of justice" standard. This standard has been defined in these words:

> [A] charge of inadequate representation can prevail "only if it can be said that what was or was not done by the defendant's attorney for his client made the proceedings a farce and a mockery of justice, shocking to the conscience of the Court." [50]

As the scope of the right-to-counsel provisions of both the state constitutions and the U.S. Constitution expanded, the demands to change this test to a more stringent one for the attorney have been forcefully urged. As a result some courts, including the Third, Fifth, Sixth and District of Columbia Circuits,[51] have adopted a more objective standard known as the "reasonably competent" standard. Under this standard if counsel does not exhibit the "normal and customary" degree of skill and knowledge possessed by attorneys who are reasonably knowledgeable of criminal law, the assistance is ineffective, and this fact will furnish grounds for reversal.

It can be readily observed that by applying the recent, more stringent test of the attorney, more cases will be reversed because of the ineffective assistance of counsel. The danger is also clearly evident since the accused could get the benefit of the trial strategy of two different attorneys. The accused could, of course, argue that any counsel who does not persuade the court or jury to find him not guilty is ineffective. It is certain that attorneys do not agree on the best trial strategy in a criminal case. Therefore, if more courts apply the "normal customary skill and knowledge" test, more carefully designed boundaries will have to be developed.[52] Until the Supreme Court of the United States establishes a standard which will

---

[50] Cardarella v. United States, 375 F(2d) 222 (8thCir 1967), quoting O'Malley v. United States, 285 F(2d) 733, 734 (6thCir 1961).

[51] E.g., Beasley v. United States, 491 F(2d) 687 (6thCir 1974); United States v. De Coster, 487 F(2d) 1197 (DC Cir 1973).

[52] See J. J. Finer, *Ineffective Assistance of Counsel*, 58 Cornell LRev 1077 (1973).

be applied uniformly, justice will not be equally dispensed in all jurisdictions. Courts will be even more burdened due to new trials as appeals courts find the representation ineffective with each court applying its own particular set of standards.

§ 8.16   Right to freely communicate with counsel

The right to counsel encompasses the right to communicate with counsel in private. Several cases have established the duty of officers having custody of a suspect to afford him a reasonable opportunity to consult privately with his attorney. No officer has the right to be present and to hear what is said during the interview,[53] nor does the officer have the right to listen or record the conversations by means of "bugging" devices. Conversations between an attorney and his client are said to be "privileged."

In a 1963 decision the Supreme Court of the state of Washington was outspoken in its disapproval of practices which tend to interfere with the right of the accused to consult with counsel in private.[54] The defendant in this case was charged with lewdness and later with second degree burglary and larceny. Being unable to post bond, the defendant remained in the county jail from the time of his arrest until the end of the trial. A room had been provided in the county jail for consultations between prisoners and their attorneys. After several interviews between the defendant and his attorney, it was discovered that their conversations had been recorded by the use of a microphone which had been installed in the conference room. The trial judge refused to dismiss the case but advised that he would exclude any derivative evidence which had come to light as a result of the eavesdropping procedure. In reversing the defendant's conviction, the state Supreme Court stated that effective legal representation could not be obtained without privacy. After citing several cases on point, the court concluded:

> A defendant and his lawyer have a right to talk together by telephone or personal interview without their conversations being

[53] State ex rel. Tucker v. Davis, 9 OklaCrim 94, 130 Pac 962 (1913); see also, 21 AmJur(2d) *Criminal Law* § 312 (1965).

[54] State v. Cory, 62 Wash(2d) 371, 382 P(2d) 1019 (1963).

monitored by the prosecution through a secret mechanical device which they did not know was being used. We do not think that the granting of a new trial is an adequate remedy for the deprivation of the right to counsel where eavesdropping has occurred. . . . It is our conclusion that the defendant is correct when he says that the shocking and unpardonable conduct of the sheriff's officers in eavesdropping upon the private consultations between the defendant and his attorney, thus depriving him of his right to effective counsel, violates the whole proceedings. The judgment and sentence must be set aside and the charges dismissed.

The cases are consistent in holding that the right to counsel includes the right to consult with counsel in private.

§ 8.17 Self-representation rights

With so many decisions relating to the right-to-counsel provisions of the Constitutions, one would think that this matter had been fully litigated. However, it seems that questions are still arising concerning the interpretation of this Sixth Amendment provision. One of the important decisions of the 1974–75 term of the United States Supreme Court related to the defendant's right to serve as his own counsel. After reviewing the history of the right to counsel and the right of self-representation, and after examining the various statutory and state constitutional provisions, six members of the United States Supreme Court concluded that a defendant who truly wishes to defend himself should not be forced to accept the services of an attorney.[55] Some of the facts of this landmark decision will assist in understanding its implications.

Anthony Faretta was charged with grand theft in Los Angeles County, California. A Superior Court judge appointed the public defender to represent Faretta, but before the date of the trial Faretta requested that he be permitted to represent himself. After first ruling that Faretta would be authorized to conduct his own defense, the judge reversed his earlier ruling and again appointed the public defender to represent the accused. Throughout the trial, the judge required that Faretta's defense be conducted only through the appointed attorney.

[55] Faretta v. California, 422 US 806, 45 LEd(2d) 562, 95 SCt 2525 (1975).

At the conclusion the jury found the defendant guilty as charged, and the judge sentenced him to prison. He appealed on the grounds that he had not been granted permission to represent himself. The Supreme Court agreed, pointing out that at the time the Sixth Amendment was adopted, the right of self-representation was recognized in the colonies as well as in England.

Mr. Justice Stewart, who wrote the opinion, included this phrase:

> In sum, there is no evidence that the colonists and the Framers ever doubted the right of self-representation, or imagined that this right might be considered inferior to the right of assistance of counsel. To the contrary [they] always conceived of the right to counsel as an "assistance" for the accused, to be used at his option, in defending himself.

Apparently it does not make any difference if the defendant is equipped to represent himself or not. According to the Supreme Court:

> We need make no assessment of how well or how poorly Faretta had mastered the intricacies of the hearsay rule and the California code provisions that govern challenges of potential jurors on *voir dire*. For his technical legal knowledge, as such, was not relevant to an assessment of his knowing exercise of the right to defend himself.

Three justices, in dissenting to this conclusion, warned that the holding would raise a host of procedural problems. The warning of the minority has proved valid. The United States District Court for Southern New York was asked to determine if the defendant who has counsel also has a right to participate in his own trial as co-counsel. That court found that a defendant does not have a right to the best of two Sixth Amendment worlds—he may have counsel appointed, or waive counsel and conduct his own defense; but he does not have the right to demand both.[56]

In another case,[57] the Court of Appeals for the Second Cir-

---

[56] United States v. Swinton, 400 FSupp 805 (SD NY 1975).

[57] United States v. Armedo-Sarmiento, 524 F(2d) 591 (2dCir 1975).

cuit reversed a conviction because the trial court had disqualified, without the consent of the defendant, an attorney who had indicated a potentially serious conflict of interest. That reviewing court found that the defendant may waive his right to have his retained counsel free from conflicts of interest. The court reasoned that if the defendant can insist on representing himself, as in the case of *Faretta*, he may insist on being represented by a particular attorney even though that attorney has a conflict of interest insofar as his effective representation of the defendant is concerned.

One can conclude from these cases that: 1) the accused has an absolute right to represent himself at the trial even though he may not be qualified to do so; 2) although he may represent himself, he *probably* cannot demand counsel and then choose to be his own co-counsel; 3) the right to manage one's own defense includes the right to choose attorneys who face a serious conflict of interest.

There is no doubt that additional questions will arise. For example, will the Supreme Court allow a person to be put to death who so poorly represents himself as to be deprived of procedural and substantive "due process of law"? Such a question can only be answered in the future.

§ 8.18   Summary and practical suggestions

Under the English common law prior to 1688, there was no right to counsel in felony cases. From the year 1695 when counsel was allowed for the first time in trials for treason until the present there has been a progressive expansion of the right to counsel. This right was deemed to be of such importance that many of the states prior to the writing of the United States Constitution included guarantees in their state constitutions. With the adoption of the Sixth Amendment in 1791, the right to counsel became embodied in the Federal Constitution.

The provision of the Sixth Amendment that in all criminal prosecutions the accused shall have the assistance of counsel for his defense was originally interpreted to mean that an accused was entitled to counsel only during trials in the federal courts. However, after the Fourteenth Amendment was adopted in 1868, the courts began to consider the right to counsel as a fundamental right and, therefore, binding upon the states through the Fourteenth Amendment.

The Sixth Amendment is written in broad generalities. Over the years the courts have been called upon to interpret whether its requirements are satisfied by allowing the accused to employ counsel of his choice and whether the government must furnish counsel to indigents who are unable to retain their own. More pressing has been the question concerning the stage in the criminal process at which the right to counsel attaches. In 1938 the Supreme Court in the *Johnson* case made it clear that the accused must be represented by counsel during trials in the federal courts unless he intelligently and competently waives this right. For many years the Court refused to apply the identical rule to state prosecutions, but in the 1963 case of *Gideon* v. *Wainwright* the *Johnson* rule was made effective against the states also. The precise holding in *Gideon* was that counsel must be provided for indigent defendants in state felony trials unless the right is intelligently waived.

After some years of confusing lower court decisions, the United States Supreme Court in 1972 extended the right-to-counsel protection to trials in misdemeanor cases. This right to have counsel appointed for indigents in misdemeanor situations is limited to misdemeanors where imprisonment is a possibility. As in the case of felony offenses, the right to have counsel in a misdemeanor case may be knowingly and intelligently waived.

The right to have counsel appointed has been extended to the arraignment and to the preliminary hearing when these are critical stages in the criminal process. In 1964, a major stride was taken by the Supreme Court in *Escobedo* v. *Illinois* where the Court held that the right to counsel begins when the police carry out a process of interrogation that lends itself to eliciting incriminating statements. After this point the police can no longer refuse a suspect his request to see his attorney. The scope of the *Escobedo* holding was clarified two years later by the Supreme Court in the 1966 case of *Miranda* v. *Arizona*. Though the case hinged primarily on the privilege against self-incrimination, the Court made some very pertinent observations concerning the right to counsel and established the rule that an accused must be warned of his right to counsel after he is taken into custody and before interrogation, and that he must be informed of his right to appointed counsel if unable to employ his own. Waiver of the right cannot be predicated on the failure of the accused to request counsel.

In 1967 the Supreme Court extended the right to counsel to a lineup or other confrontation-for-identification situation. Here the Court said that because the pre-trial identification may unduly influence the in-court identification at the trial, as a general rule the accused should have an attorney available at the lineup proceeding. It was explained, however, that this right may be knowingly and intelligently waived. Also the Court left the door open for the prosecution to show that the in-court identification was not contaminated by the pre-trial identification procedure.

In an effort to modify the *Wade* holding, Congress in 1968 by legislation provided that eyewitness testimony shall be admissible in the criminal prosecution. This apparently applies even if the attorney is not present at the lineup and even if the right has not been waived. There is some question as to the constitutionality of this legislation.

In 1972 the Supreme Court explained that the *Wade* requirements applied only in a post-indictment confrontation, but these rules do not apply to a police station showup which takes place before the defendant has been indicted or otherwise formally charged with a criminal offense.

One of the rights made applicable to juveniles by the *Gault* decision in 1967 was the right to have the assistance of counsel. The ruling of the majority of the Supreme Court in that case was that the child and his parent must be notified of the child's right to be represented by counsel. Some courts have reasoned, however, that a juvenile, especially an older juvenile, may in certain circumstances waive the right to counsel if he is informed and has average intelligence. The better practice is to advise both the juvenile and his representative concerning the right to counsel.

The right-to-counsel protection of the Sixth Amendment was first limited to counsel at the trial in felony cases in federal court. It has gradually extended to pre-trial proceedings. The right has also been extended to post-trial proceedings involving deferred sentencing, and is to be decided on a case-by-case basis where the parolee or probationer was sentenced previously.

Not only is the accused entitled to have counsel, he is entitled to have at least "reasonably competent" counsel. The courts do not agree as to the standard that should be applied in determining the competency of counsel. Two standards which have been mentioned by various courts are the "mockery of justice" standard and the "reasonably competent" standard.

The fact that the accused is entitled to counsel does not mean that he must be assigned counsel against his will. In 1975 the Supreme Court determined that a state may not constitutionally refuse to allow a defendant to conduct his own defense.

Everyone studying the criminal justice system should be familiar with the cases and statutes describing the right to counsel. Investigators and police administrators should be especially familiar with the law relating to the right to counsel during the investigation.

In the *Escobedo* and *Miranda* cases specific requirements were delineated. However, this should not discourage the use of information legitimately obtained from suspects prior to the formal indictment. Experience has demonstrated that valuable evidence can be obtained by proper questioning without violating the Sixth Amendment constitutional rights. Although the rules established by the courts limit the circumstances under which a confrontation for identification may take place, this investigative technique is proper and valuable when conducted by personnel who are familiar with the limitations.

The administrator should insure that procedures established by the department conform to the legal requirements of the *Escobedo* and *Miranda* cases, as well as to those of the *Wade* and *Kirby* cases.

Chapter 9

DOUBLE JEOPARDY*

[N]or shall any person be subject for the same offence
to be twice put in jeopardy of life or limb . . . .

FIFTH AMENDMENT, 1791

§ 9.1 Introduction

A woman is found in her home, raped, severely beaten and unconscious. She is unable to describe her assailant. A month later the defendant is arrested for this crime and taken to the police station for questioning. Before interrogating him concerning his whereabouts on the night in question, the police advise the defendant of his right to remain silent and his right to counsel, but through oversight, no mention is made of his right to the appointment of counsel if he is indigent. The defendant proceeds to give an alibi, stating that he spent the entire evening with a friend, one Smith. When Smith is contacted by the authorities, he disavows being with the defendant on the night of the rape and reports instead that he saw the defendant for the first time on the following morning, that the defendant's face was severely scratched at that time, and that in response to his inquiries about the scratches, the

* by Jacqueline R. Kanovitz

defendant stated that he had had a "wild time" the evening before with a woman who lived at the victim's address.

At the defendant's trial, the prosecution calls Smith as a witness. The trial judge excludes Smith's expected testimony on the grounds that, since Smith's identity had been revealed to the authorities by the defendant during the course of an interrogation conducted without a full *Miranda* warning, the proffered testimony was the tainted fruits of a *Miranda* violation. (In light of *Michigan* v. *Tucker,*[1] this ruling is erroneous.) The exclusion of Smith's testimony results in an absence of sufficient evidence to identify the defendant as the assailant, and as a consequence, he is acquitted.

May the prosecutor appeal the trial court's erroneous exclusion of Smith's testimony, secure a reversal, and retry the defendant, using Smith as a witness? Alternatively, may it reindict the defendant for the crime of rape and retry him without seeking an appeal? The answer to both questions is no.[2] The reason inheres in the double jeopardy clause of the Fifth Amendment which provides:

> [N]or shall any person be subject for the same offence to be twice put in jeopardy of life or limb . . . .

The historical genesis of the doctrine forbidding multiple prosecutions for the same offense is somewhat obscure. Though the Magna Charta makes no reference to double jeopardy, there is considerable evidence that the doctrine opposed to placing a man twice in jeopardy for the same offense had gained recognition under the English common law by the thirteenth century.[3] It was fully entrenched in English jurisprudence long before the colonial period and was brought to this continent as a part of the common-law legal tradition. The earliest written formulation of the double jeopardy doc-

---

[1] 417 US 433, 41 LEd(2d) 182, 94 SCt 2357 (1974). For a discussion of this case see § 6.7, *supra.*

[2] United States v. Jenkins, 420 US 358, 43 LEd(2d) 250, 95 SCt 1006 (1975); Fong Foo v. United States, 369 US 141, 7 LEd(2d) 629, 82 SCt 671 (1962); Kepner v. United States, 195 US 100, 49 LEd 114, 24 SCt 797 (1904); Ball v. United States, 163 US 662, 41 LEd 300, 16 SCt 1192 (1896).

[3] Bartkus v. Illinois, 359 US 121, 3 LEd(2d) 684, 79 SCt 676 (1959) (Black, J., dissenting).

trine in this country appeared in the *Massachusetts Body of Liberties* of 1641.[4] The Fifth Amendment prohibition against double jeopardy reflects the awareness of those responsible for drafting the Bill of Rights that a legal system which fails to place limits upon the number of opportunities available to government for establishing a defendant's guilt runs a serious risk of abuse.

Despite the central importance of the double jeopardy restraint, it was one of the last significant portions of the Bill of Rights to be made applicable to the states. This occurred in 1969 in the case of *Benton v. Maryland.*[5] In *Benton*, the Supreme Court announced that immunity from double jeopardy constituted a fundamental right and that, henceforth, state double jeopardy practices would be governed by established Fifth Amendment standards.

§ 9.2   Constitutional policies underlying double jeopardy restriction

The deceptively simple statement contained in the Fifth Amendment mandating that governments shall not subject any person to being twice placed in jeopardy for the same offense masks what has been termed a "wilderness of legal complexity."[6] Supreme Court efforts to give coherent meaning and application to this limitation have been remarkably disappointing. Few portions of the Bill of Rights remain murkier or more poorly explored from an analytic standpoint. Any attempt to formulate a concrete body of double jeopardy principles must reflect the fundamental policy considerations underlying the constitutional restriction. We must, therefore, investigate these policy considerations before embarking upon our journey down the convoluted paths of double jeopardy law.

Limiting the number of times a government may subject an accused to jeopardy for a single offense safeguards several distinct interests. The first relates to the emotional well-being

---

[4] J. A. Sigler, Double Jeopardy, 22 (1969).

[5] 395 US 784, 23 LEd(2d) 707, 89 SCt 2056 (1969).

[6] Fisher, *Double Jeopardy: Six Common Boners Summarized*, 15 UCLALRev 81, 81 (1967).

of an accused. Criminal trials represent a heavy personal, as well as financial, strain. An acquittal would not end the emotional ordeal if reprosecution were permissible. The prohibition against double jeopardy reflects society's concern that a man, who has been tried once and either acquitted or convicted, should be able to leave that phase of his life behind him forever and plan his future without overhanging fears and doubts.[7] But more important, an unlimited governmental power to prosecute repeatedly for the same offense increases the probability that innocent persons may be convicted because they are too worn down, either psychologically or financially, to put forth an adequate defense.[8] Although a rule limiting the prosecutor to one attempt at establishing guilt may on occasion result in an erroneous acquittal (for which no appeal is available), a contrary policy would be productive of unnecessary harassment and waste and would jeopardize the security of the innocent. Mr. Justice Black summarized the policy considerations as follows:

> [T]he State with all its resources and power should not be allowed to make repeated attempts to convict an individual for an alleged offense, thereby subjecting him to embarrassment, expense and ordeal and compelling him to live in a continuing state of anxiety and insecurity, as well as enhancing the possibility that even though innocent he may be found guilty.[9]

§ 9.3 Double jeopardy overview

The double jeopardy prohibition embodies a number of related protections which share a common concern with eliminating the danger of excessive or abusive applications of the power to prosecute. Because of the complexity of the subject matter, an overview of the various protections should be set forth before plunging into a more detailed consideration. The Fifth Amendment is primarily concerned with successive or repeated criminal prosecutions and only incidentally with multiple punishments for the same offense.

---

[7] United States v. Candalaria, 131 FSupp 797 (SD Cal 1955).

[8] See generally, Note, *Twice in Jeopardy*, 75 YALELJ 262 (1965) [hereinafter cited as *Twice in Jeopardy*]

[9] Green v. United States, 355 US 184, 187–88, 2 LEd(2d) 199, 78 SCt 221 (1957).

The power of government to bring an individual to trial a second time for the *same offense* is severely limited and depends upon how the first trial terminated. There are three possible modes of termination—an acquittal, a conviction, or a mistrial (*i.e.*, termination before a verdict or final decision is reached).

(1) An accused is placed in jeopardy when his first trial begins. Even though his first trial *ends before a verdict is reached,* having been once placed in jeopardy, he is, in most cases, immune from reprosecution for the *same offense.* An exception is made, however, where there is a "manifest necessity" for halting the first proceedings prior to a verdict.[10]

(2) An accused whose first trial *ends in an acquittal.* gains an unqualified immunity from reprosecution for the *same offense.* This is true even though the acquittal resulted from a trial court error or is based upon an indictment so defective that it would not have supported a conviction had the verdict gone the other way.[11]

(3) An accused whose first trial *ends in a conviction* is secure against new efforts by the government to convict him for the *same offense* in hopes of increasing the punishment. This protection, however, can be relinquished by the accused. Where a convicted defendant successfully attacks his conviction and has it set aside, he becomes subject to reprosecution.[12]

All three of the above protections are predicated upon the second prosecution being brought for the *same offense.*[13]

Within the past decade, the Supreme Court has ruled that the double jeopardy safeguard incorporates the doctrine of "collateral estoppel" and, by virtue of this doctrine, accords an *acquitted* defendant limited protection against later government efforts to convict him of *separate and distinct offenses.*[14]

---

[10] Discussed in § 9.5, *infra.*
[11] Discussed in § 9.6, *infra.*
[12] Discussed in §§ 9.6, 9.7, *infra.*
[13] Discussed in §§ 9.9—9.10, *infra.*

[14] Ashe v. Swenson, 397 US 436, 25 LEd(2d) 469, 90 SCt 1189 (1970). See Part II of this book for a reprint of this important case.

(4) Under the collateral estoppel doctrine, the government is barred from prosecuting a defendant for a *separate and distinct offense* if he was acquitted in an earlier prosecution on the basis of a determination in his favor of a disputed issue of ultimate fact; the same fact is involved in the second prosecution; and the government would be required to secure a contrary determination of this fact in order to obtain a guilty verdict.[15]

Each of these various headings of double jeopardy protection will be discussed in fuller detail in the sections that follow.

§ 9.4 Stage in the prosecution when jeopardy attaches

"Jeopardy" is the danger of conviction and punishment that an accused incurs when he is placed on trial in a criminal action.[16] Although the constitutional language, "jeopardy of life or limb," suggests that the protection is confined to proceedings in which these most serious penalties are authorized, this provision has been construed more broadly than its language and applies to *all* criminal proceedings, including prosecutions for misdemeanors in which no more than a fine is authorized[17] and proceedings before juvenile courts which are, at least in theory, inspired by goals of rehabilitation rather than punishment.[18]

The double jeopardy safeguard does not apply in civil proceedings. Accordingly, there is no constitutional barrier to the legislature's imposing or the government's pressing successive claims against an individual to exact both a civil and a criminal sanction for the same act or violation. The government may, for example, prosecute an individual for smuggling articles into the country in violation of tariff laws, and regardless of the outcome of this trial, institute civil proceedings against him aimed at the forfeiture and confiscation of the smuggled goods.[19] Though two proceedings are involved and two sanc-

---

[15] Discussed in § 9.11, *infra*.

[16] Breed v. Jones, 421 US 519, 44 LEd(2d) 346, 95 SCt 1779 (1975).

[17] Robinson v. Neil, 409 US 505, 35 LEd(2d) 29, 93 SCt 876 (1973).

[18] Breed v. Jones, 421 US 519, 44 LEd(2d) 346, 95 SCt 1779 (1975).

[19] One Lot Emerald Cut Stones v. United States, 409 US 232, 34 LEd(2d) 438, 93 SCt 489 (1972).

tions imposed, the Double Jeopardy Clause is not offended since the second proceeding is civil in nature.

What the Constitution forbids is the second jeopardy. It follows from this that before an accused gains constitutional immunity from prosecution for an offense, he must undergo a first jeopardy. When a Fifth Amendment bar is raised, it becomes necessary to ascertain whether the defendant's original prosecution reached a stage of maturity when "jeopardy" can be said to attach. For unless this stage was once reached, there is no constitutional barrier standing between the accused and the government in its efforts to prosecute him.

Under the English common law and in England today, jeopardy does not attach so as to bar reprosecution until a verdict has been reached.[20] In the United States, jeopardy attaches much earlier in the criminal process. When an accused is tried before a jury, he is placed in jeopardy as soon as the jury has been impaneled and sworn.[21] In non-jury trials, jeopardy attaches after the first witness has been sworn and the court has begun to hear evidence.[22] The vast majority of criminal prosecutions run a normal course ending with an acquittal or a conviction. The critical difference between the English and American attachment rules emerges only in those cases in which the first proceeding terminates in a mistrial without a verdict being reached. In England, a defendant whose first criminal trial ends without a verdict has no legal protection. The government is guaranteed one fair opportunity to present its evidence in full and to receive a judgment on the merits. If, for some reason, it is deprived of this opportunity in the first proceedings, it can reprosecute because no jeopardy has attached under the English rule until there is a verdict.

The rule in the United States is otherwise. It is the act of placing the accused on trial, and not the conclusion of his trial, that provides the foundation for reprosecution immunity. Consequently, where a mistrial is declared after the jury has

---

[20] Note, *Double Jeopardy: The Reprosecution Problem*, 77 HARVLREV 1272, 1273 (1964).

[21] Illinois v. Somerville, 410 US 458, 35 LEd(2d) 425, 93 SCt 1066 (1973);

Downum v. United States, 372 US 734, 10 LEd(2d) 100, 83 SCt 1033 (1963).

[22] Serfass v. United States, 420 US 377, 43 LEd(2d) 265, 95 SCt 1055 (1975).

been impaneled and sworn or, in bench trials, after the presentation of evidence has begun, the American defendant's ordeal is normally at an end.

An exception to the American rule has, however, been carved out in those cases where there is a "manifest necessity" for interrupting the first trial prior to a verdict. This exception, which is the subject of § 9.5, reflects an effort to accommodate the public interest with that of the accused. Even with this exception, a significant difference between English and American attachment principles remains. In the United States, we still regard the power to retry an accused after an initial mistrial as the aberrant case, whereas in England, it is the norm.

None of the steps preliminary to placing the accused on trial constitute jeopardy. The Fifth Amendment limitation is not invoked by an arrest, and even though the accused is released, he may later be taken into custody and made to stand trial. The same is true of a preliminary hearing before a magistrate. Since the accused is not placed in jeopardy when taken before a magistrate for a probable cause hearing, a dismissal of the charges at this juncture lacks Fifth Amendment finality.[23] Similarly, the finding of an indictment, followed by an arraignment and pleading, are pre-jeopardy events. A pretrial dismissal of an indictment, therefore, poses no legal barrier to its later reinstitution.[24] Although repeated arrests, indictments and arraignments on charges never brought to trial could become almost as vexatious as repeated criminal prosecutions, since these procedures arise at a stage in the criminal process before jeopardy has attached, abuses of this type are beyond the scope of the double jeopardy safeguard.

§ 9.5 Double jeopardy consequences of a mistrial

The central concern of double jeopardy is to spare an accused the ordeal of being forced repeatedly to muster his energies in his own defense, a concern reflected in our earlier attachment rule. Regardless of the outcome of his first trial,

---

[23] Collins v. Loisel, 262 US 426, 67 LEd 1062, 43 SCt 618 (1922).

[24] Serfass v. United States, 420 US 377, 43 LEd(2d) 265, 95 SCt 1055 (1975); Bassing v. Cady, 208 US 386, 52 LEd 540, 28 SCt 392 (1908); United States v. Green, 414 F(2d) 1174 (DC Cir 1969).

if it has progressed to a sufficient stage to trigger the attachment rule, the accused ordinarily gains constitutional immunity from retrial for the same offense. This is categorically
true where his first trial ends in an acquittal or an unreversed
conviction. From the standpoint of an accused, retrial on the
same charges is no less distressing when his first trial progresses beyond the point of jeopardy attachment but ends
prior to the rendition of a verdict. The hardship upon the
accused, however, is not the only interest at stake when the
original proceeding ends without a verdict. Respect for law
diminishes whenever the guilty escape punishment; the public interest at stake pressures for recognition of a new opportunity to present in full the incriminating evidence against
the accused and to receive a verdict on the merits. Faced with
these two conflicting interests, the Supreme Court has opted
for a middle course.

Circumstances may arise during the course of a criminal
trial making its completion impossible or impracticable. The
most common reason for discharging a jury without a verdict
is irreconcilable deadlock.[25] Besides this, a juror may die, the
accused may become seriously ill, or any number of untold
events may transpire that call for the granting of a mistrial.

In *United States* v. *Perez*,[26] the Supreme Court determined
that an inflexible approach which would bar reprosecution in
all cases that progress beyond the point of jeopardy but fail
to terminate in a verdict, was neither desirable nor compelled
by the Constitution. Mr. Justice Story, who wrote the *Perez*
opinion, adopted the following test for evaluating the double
jeopardy consequences of a mistrial. Where his first trial ends
prior to a verdict, the government is precluded from retrying
the accused unless

taking all circumstances into consideration, there is a manifest
necessity for the act, or the ends of public justice would otherwise
be defeated.[27]

In confining the government's power to reinstitute pro-

---

[25] Logan v. United States, 144 US
263, 36 LEd 429, 12 SCt 617 (1892);
United States v. Perez, 22 US(9 Wheat)
579, 6 LEd 165 (1824).

[26] 22 US(9 Wheat) 579, 6 LEd 165
(1824).
[27] *Id.* at 580.

ceedings following a mistrial to those cases where there is a "manifest necessity" for concluding the first trial prematurely or where this action is necessitated by the "ends of public justice," Mr. Justice Story attempted to strike a fair balance between the interest of the accused in ending his ordeal after one trial and the interest of the public in pressing forward until a verdict is reached. The test enunciated by Mr. Justice Story in *Perez* has remained the guiding standard against which the double jeopardy consequences of a mistrial are assessed. Cases in which a mistrial may properly be granted without erecting a bar to reprosecution fall within three general groupings.

1. Mistrials attributable to actions of defendant or his counsel

Where the defendant himself moves for a mistrial or consents to one being granted, this ordinarily is sufficient to remove any legal barrier to reprosecution.[28] A request will definitely eradicate all obstacles where the defendant or his counsel bears responsibility for the situation underlying the motion. The same has been held true, however, where the accused seeks a mistrial because of some error attributable to the judge or the prosecutor.[29] A different situation, nevertheless, would be presented should the judge or prosecutor deliberately engage in misconduct to taint the original proceedings and provoke the defendant into moving for a mistrial.[30] In such a case, the defendant's request could scarcely be regarded as a voluntary act waiving the protection of his first jeopardy. Conversely, where the defendant or his counsel deliberately engages in a course of conduct designed to precipitate a mistrial, and one is granted on motion of the prosecution or by the court, the accused will be barred from relying on his former jeopardy as a defense to retrial though the motion was made by another.[31]

[28] United States v. Dinitz, 424 US 600, 47 LEd(2d) 267, 96 SCt 1075 (1976); United States v. Jorn, 400 US 470, 27 LEd(2d) 543, 91 SCt 547 (1971).

[29] United States v. Dinitz, 424 US 600, 47 LEd(2d) 267, 96 SCt 1075 (1976).

[30] See cases cited in note 28, *supra*.

[31] United States v. Jorn, 400 US 470, 487, 27 LEd(2d) 543, 91 SCt 547 (1971) (Burger, C. J., concurring). See also, United States v. White, 524 F(2d) 1249 (5thCir), cert. denied, 426 US 922 (1975).

2. Mistrials granted because conclusion of proceedings has become impossible or severely impracticable

Where there is a "breakdown in judicial machinery"[32] making it impossible or severely impracticable for the original proceedings to be carried on to their normal conclusion, a case of "manifest necessity" is presented, and regardless of which party requests it, a mistrial may be granted without prejudice to the government's power to retry the accused. In this category fall cases where the trial judge,[33] a juror[34] or the accused[35] becomes so ill during the first proceeding as to be unable to continue; where wartime exigencies make it impossible to complete the trial at the time and place set;[36] or where the first jury reaches a deadlock and is unable to bring back a verdict.[37] Cases of true "necessity," where external circumstances beyond the control of the court or the prosecutor have made it virtually impossible to complete the trial, are non-controversial. In such instances, retrial is permissible.

3. Mistrials granted upon discovery of incurable legal defect in proceedings or commission of reversible error

There is no way to categorize the range of contingencies that might arise during the course of a criminal trial requiring a judge to give serious consideration to granting a mistrial. Though the defendant may not actively seek this course, and though there may be no "breakdown in judicial machinery" making completion impossible, circumstances may arise when, giving due consideration to matters of fairness either to the accused or the government, the granting of a mistrial is the only practicable alternative. In *Illinois* v. *Somerville,*[38] the Supreme Court addressed itself to the scope of the "ends of public justice" aspect of the *Perez* test and gave the following summation:

[I]t is possible to distill . . . a general approach, premised on the

---

[32] Wade v. Hunter, 336 US 684, 93 LEd 974, 69 SCt 834 (1949).

[33] Freeman v. United States, 237 Fed 815 (2dCir 1916).

[34] United States v. Potash, 118 F(2d) 54 (2dCir), cert. denied, 313 US 584 (1941).

[35] United States v. Stein, 140 FSupp 761 (SD NY 1956).

[36] Wade v. Hunter, 336 US 684, 93 LEd 974, 69 SCt 834 (1949).

[37] See cases cited in note 25, *supra.*

[38] 410 US 458, 35 LEd(2d) 425, 93 SCt 1066 (1973).

'public justice' policy enunciated in *United States* v. *Perez* .... A trial judge properly exercises his discretion to declare a mistrial if an impartial verdict cannot be reached, or if a verdict of conviction could be reached but would have to be reversed on appeal due to an obvious error in the trial. If an error would make reversal on appeal a certainty, it would not serve 'the ends of public justice' to require that the Government proceed with its proof when, if it succeeded before the jury, it would automatically be stripped of that success by an appellate court. . . .[39]

In the *Somerville* case, a mistrial was granted to the government on its request when, after the jury had been impaneled and sworn, the prosecuting attorney realized that the indictment was fatally deficient. The Supreme Court ruled that granting a mistrial on these facts was justified by the "ends of public justice" since any conviction subsequently obtained would have been reversible on appeal. The same rationale supports the granting of a mistrial when, after a trial is in progress, the judge discovers that a juror is biased [40] or otherwise disqualified to sit,[41] the defendant has failed to plead to an indictment,[42] or for irregularities of a similar nature. But the "ends of public justice" do not sanction the granting of a mistrial where the prosecution has failed to use proper diligence to assure the presence of an important witness,[43] or where, in the course of the government's presentation, unexpected evidentiary weaknesses develop.[44] The government is not entitled to a second opportunity to bolster its case.

Although each of the defendant's prior trials may have been aborted for reasons deemed sufficiently compelling when viewed in isolation, there may be an outer Fifth Amendment limit on the aggregate number of verdictless attempts the government may undertake in an effort to establish guilt. The defendant's interest in ending his ordeal after a series of repeated mistrials must be weighed against the public interest in pressing forward until a verdict on the merits is reached.

[39] *Id.* at 464.
[40] Simmons v. United States, 142 US 148, 35 LEd 968, 12 SCt 171 (1891).
[41] Thompson v. United States, 155 US 271, 39 LEd 146, 15 SCt 73 (1894).
[42] Lovato v. New Mexico, 242 US 199, 61 LEd 244, 37 SCt 107 (1916).

[43] Downum v. United States, 372 US 734, 10 LEd(2d) 100, 83 SCt 1033 (1963).
[44] McNeal v. Hollowell, 481 F(2d) 1145 (5thCir 1973), *cert. denied,* 415 US 951 (1974).

At some point, repeated mistrials become oppressive and finality is constitutionally mandated.[45]

§ 9.6　Double jeopardy consequences of a completed trial

Where an original trial runs its full course and terminates in a verdict, the defendant has measurably more protection than when a mistrial is declared for reasons of "manifest necessity" or in the "interest of public justice."

1. Acquittal

An accused who has been acquitted gains absolute constitutional immunity from reprosecution for the *same offense.*[46] The government, having once failed to persuade the trier of the fact that the defendant is guilty, is not entitled to a second chance. It matters not that the acquittal came about as a result of judicial errors in the interpretation of a criminal statute; mistaken rulings on the admissibility of crucial government evidence; or other erroneous bench determinations that seriously handicap the prosecution or prejudice the presentation of its case.[47] Nor is it significant that the trial leading to an acquittal is brought under a fatally defective indictment. Though an accused may be retried if the defects are discovered in time to move for a mistrial,[48] if they are not detected until after he has been acquitted of the charges, the rule is otherwise.[49] After an acquittal, retrial is constitutionally foreclosed.

A most extreme example of the rule barring retrial after an erroneous acquittal occurred in *Fong Foo v. United States,*[50] where the trial judge prevented the government from completing its evidence by directing a verdict for the accused. The Supreme Court, while indicating strong disapproval of this

[45] Carsey v. United States, 392 F(2d) 810 (DC Cir 1967); Preston v. Blackledge, 332 FSupp 681 (ED NC 1971).

[46] United States v. Jenkins, 420 US 358, 43 LEd(2d) 250, 95 SCt 1006 (1975); Fong Foo v. United States, 369 US 141, 7 LEd(2d) 629, 82 SCt 671 (1962); Green v. United States, 355 US 184, 2 LEd(2d) 199, 78 SCt 221 (1957); Kepner v. United States, 195 US 100, 49 LEd 114, 24 SCt 797 (1904);

Ball v. United States, 163 US 662, 41 LEd 300, 16 SCt 1192 (1896). For a discussion of the meaning of "same offense" see §§ 9.8—9.10, *infra.*

[47] See cases cited in note 46, *supra.*

[48] Illinois v. Somerville, 410 US 458, 35 LEd(2d) 425, 93 SCt 1066 (1973).

[49] Ball v. United States, 163 US 662, 41 LEd 300, 16 SCt 1192 (1896).

[50] 369 US 411, 7 LEd(2d) 629, 82 SCt 671 (1962).

action, ruled nevertheless that the government was not entitled to a second opportunity to present its case against the accused.

The constitutional consideration at stake under the Double Jeopardy Clause is, however, protection against *reprosecution*. The government is not foreclosed from taking an appeal to correct a trial error if the error can be corrected without exposing the accused to retrial. In *United States v. Wilson*,[51] after the jury had brought in a guilty verdict, the trial judge, on a post-trial motion, dismissed the indictment on the basis of unreasonable and prejudicial preindictment delay. The government's efforts to appeal from this ruling were resisted by the defendant who claimed that an acquittal was constitutionally beyond review. The Supreme Court ruled that the Double Jeopardy Clause limits appellate review of an erroneous acquittal only where a reversal would expose the accused to a second trial for the same offense. In an opinion written by Mr. Justice Marshall, the Court said:

> [A] defendant has no legitimate claim to benefit from an error of law when that error could be corrected without subjecting him to a second trial before a second trier of fact.

The trial court's error in this case, in setting aside the jury's verdict of guilt and substituting in its place what in effect amounted to an acquittal, did not require exposing the accused to a second trial as a means of correction. The error could be rectified by remanding the case to the trial court with directions to enter judgment on the original verdict. In *United States v. Jenkins*,[52] handed down on the same day, a trial judge, sitting without a jury, had acted upon an erroneous assumption of law and had reached a determination which in effect amounted to an acquittal. Here the government's appeal was rejected for the reason that, since the defendant had never been adjudicated guilty, the error could not be corrected by such a simple expedient as reversing and remanding with directions to reinstate a finding of guilt. Since there was never an adjudication of guilt, a retrial would be required. The Fifth

[51] 420 US 332, 43 LEd(2d) 232, 95 SCt 1013 (1975).

[52] 420 US 358, 43 LEd(2d) 250, 95 SCt 1006 (1975).

Amendment precludes the government from appealing from an erroneous acquittal in those cases where a retrial is necessary to correct the trial court error.

2. Conviction

Where the defendant is originally convicted, the only interest the government could have in reinstituting proceedings against him is the hope that a later judge or jury might impose a more serious penalty. The Double Jeopardy Clause protects a convicted defendant against reprosecution for the same offense, unless he elects to relinquish this protection by attacking his conviction and having it set aside on appeal.

§ 9.7   Double jeopardy consequences of a successful appeal

Under the English common law prior to the American Revolution, neither the accused nor the Crown could appeal from a judgment in a criminal case. The only remedy available to a prisoner after receiving an erroneous conviction was resort to the King's pardoning power.[53] Gradually, appeals on behalf of the defendant came to be recognized, first as a matter of grace, and later as a matter of right.

With the advent of appellate review, the issue soon arose whether an accused who appealed from a conviction and secured a reversal because of errors committed at his first trial gained constitutional immunity from reprosecution. The Supreme Court answered in the negative.[54] Over the years, various legal theories have been put forward to explain why an accused can be retried for a convicted offense after he has had it overturned on appeal. Mr. Justice Holmes stood alone in his advocacy of the *continuing jeopardy* rationale.[55] Under the Holmes analysis, there is one continuing jeopardy until the proceeding against the accused has been finally resolved. Retrial is permissible under the Holmes view because it is part and parcel of the original jeopardy which continues until a final disposition is made. The difficulty with this analysis is that it goes too far and would equally support retrial after an erroneous acquittal or unnecessary initial mistrial. Being

[53] See Note, 47 YALELJ 489 (1938).
[54] Ball v. United States, 163 US 662, 41 LEd 300, 16 SCt 1192 (1896).

[55] Kepner v. United States, 195 US 100, 49 LEd 114, 24 SCt 797 (1904).

antithetical to double jeopardy policy, it has never commanded support.

In *Green v. United States*,[56] the Supreme Court endorsed a *waiver* theory—that by appealing from his conviction, the accused waived the protection of his first jeopardy in the event it was set aside. This theory, too, has its shortcomings. Since "waiver" connotes a voluntary relinquishment of a right, it is fictional to suggest that an accused is waiving double jeopardy protection and consenting to a retrial when, after an erroneous conviction, he has no real meaningful choice except to appeal. In *United States v. Tateo*,[57] the Supreme Court moved away from the waiver explanation and set forth a more practical justification for permitting retrial after an appellate reversal. The Court stated:

> While different theories have been advanced to support the permissibility of retrial, of greater importance than the conceptional abstractions ... are the implications ... for the sound administration of justice. Corresponding to the right of an accused to be given a fair trial is the societal interest in punishing one whose guilt is clear after he has obtained such a trial. It would be a high price indeed for society to pay were every accused granted immunity from punishment because of any defect sufficient to constitute reversible error in the proceedings leading to conviction. From the standpoint of a defendant, it is at least doubtful that appellate courts would be as zealous as they are now in protecting against the effects of improprieties at the trial or pretrial stage if they knew that reversal of a conviction would put the accused irrevocably beyond the reach of further prosecution. In reality, therefore, the practice of retrial serves defendants' rights as well as society's interest. . . .[58]

That a successful appeal from a conviction opens the door to further criminal proceedings is now established beyond dispute. But how far is the door ajar? Suppose that an accused is originally tried for the crime of first-degree murder, but the jury brings back a verdict of guilty to a lesser included offense, such as second degree murder or voluntary manslaughter. Does a successful appeal from this conviction pave the way to retrial for first degree murder? Or, alternatively, suppose that he is convicted of first-degree murder at his

---

[56] 355 US 184, 2 LEd(2d) 199, 78 SCt 221 (1957).

[57] 377 US 463, 12 LEd(2d) 448, 84 SCt 1587 (1964).

[58] *Id.* at 466.

original trial and given a life sentence. If reconvicted for this offense upon remand after a reversal, may he now be sentenced to death? What new risks, if any, does an accused incur by successfully attacking a conviction?

1. Scope of retrial after appellate reversal of conviction for lesser included offense

The first question, whether an accused who secures the reversal of a conviction for a lesser included offense may be retried for a greater one, was resolved against the government in *Green v. United States.*[59] There the accused, after having been indicted for first-degree murder and found guilty of the lesser included offense of second-degree murder, won a reversal on appeal. The case was remanded and he was again tried for first-degree murder; this time he was convicted of the greater crime. The Supreme Court reversed the first-degree murder conviction on the grounds that retrying him for this offense, after a successful appeal from a second-degree murder conviction, was a violation of double jeopardy. The Court rested this conclusion upon the theory of an "implied acquittal." When the original jurors brought back a verdict of guilty to second-degree murder pursuant to instructions giving them a full opportunity to convict for first-degree murder, they impliedly acquitted him of the more serious crime. The accused could not be forced to relinquish his constitutional protection against a second jeopardy on an implicitly acquitted offense as the price of contesting an erroneous conviction. When the first jury refused to convict him of first-degree murder, his jeopardy for that offense came to an end; the government was constitutionally foreclosed from resurrecting this charge. The *Green* rule, limiting the scope of retrial following an appellate reversal to the convicted offense appealed from when it is less than the indicted offense, has been consistently adhered to.[60]

2. Increased punishment upon retrial for same offense following appeal

The *Green* case did not remove all risks facing an accused who must decide whether to seek appellate review of a con-

[59] 355 US 184, 2 LEd(2d) 199, 78 SCt 221 (1957).

[60] Price v. Georgia, 398 US 323, 26 LEd(2d) 300, 90 SCt 1757 (1970).

viction. Though the Court placed a constitutional ceiling upon the types of offenses for which an accused can be retried following a successful appeal, the question of punishment was never reached. If Green had been convicted of first-degree murder at his original trial and sentenced to life in prison, the reversal of his conviction would open the door to retrial on first-degree murder charges. Suppose he is reconvicted of this offense and this time sentenced to death. Does he have a double jeopardy right to insist upon life imprisonment as the maximum punishment constitutionally inflictable upon retrial sought by him? A pre-*Green* case had decided this issue against the accused.[61]

Twelve years after *Green*, the United States Supreme Court in *North Carolina v. Pearce*[62] again considered the question of whether double jeopardy precludes a trial judge from imposing a more severe punishment upon an accused who is reconvicted of the same offense following a successful appeal and, once more, answered in the negative. But if the harsher sentence is imposed for vindictive purposes or to punish the accused for challenging his conviction by appeal, due process considerations are raised. There is little danger that a harsher sentence will reflect impermissible motives when imposed at the second trial by a jury, since a sentencing jury, unlike a sentencing judge who has been reversed on appeal, has no personal involvement in the prior history of the case and no incentive to increase the punishment for the sake of retaliation. For this reason, the imposition of an enhanced sentence by a jury upon retrial for the same offense following an appellate reversal of the conviction raises no constitutional objections.[63]

But a sentencing judge stands in a different position, particularly if he is the same judge who presided in the original proceedings and whose decision was reversed. A sentencing judge is not constitutionally precluded from increasing the punishment of a defendant in the event that he is reconvicted following a successful appeal, but the judge must guard

---

[61] Stroud v. United States, 251 US 15, 64 LEd 103, 40 SCt 50 (1919).

[62] 395 US 711, 23 LEd(2d) 656, 89 SCt 2072 (1969).

[63] Chaffin v. Stynchcombe, 412 US 17, 36 LEd(2d) 714, 93 SCt 1977 (1973).

against both the fact and the appearance of retaliatory motivations. To assure this, the *Pearce* court laid down two requirements which must be satisfied to sustain a punishment increase: (1) any enhancement of punishment must be based upon objective information concerning conduct of the accused occurring subsequent to the first trial; and (2) the factual data upon which a decision to increase the sentence is based must be made a part of the record. Assuming that both requirements are complied with, neither double jeopardy nor due process are offended when an accused is subjected to an increase in sentence upon a reconviction for the same offense following a successful appeal.

All discussion up to this point concerning limitations upon the power of government to reprosecute an accused following an acquittal, conviction or mistrial, has proceeded on the assumption that the second trial was brought for the *same offense*. Determining when offenses charged at successive trials are the same presents what is the most complex and mind-boggling, yet crucial, issue in the entire field of double jeopardy law. Aside from the narrow boundaries in which the collateral estoppel doctrine operates, immunity from reprosecution depends upon offense identity. The Supreme Court has unfortunately left this important area largely unexplored. Nor is concrete guidance in this matter to be obtained from the legion of conflicting state cases. With this grim introductory note, let us now turn to a consideration of the *same offense* question.

§ 9.8   Same offense—critical concept in search of meaning

An ex-convict is arrested when it is discovered that he has a revolver concealed on his person. The jurisdiction has two relevant statutes—one making it an offense for any person to carry a concealed weapon, and another making it an offense for an ex-convict to have a deadly weapon in his possession. After being tried and convicted of the first crime, he is then placed on trial for the second. At this juncture he interposes a plea of former jeopardy. How should the judge rule?

The answer to this question unfortunately varies both within the federal court system and from state jurisdiction to jurisdiction. It may even diverge within a given jurisdiction depending upon whether the prosecutor attempts to try the several statutory violations at consecutive trials or to join them in a single proceeding thereby seeking multiple convictions and punishments. The reason for this clash stems from a lack of consensus on the most basic and fundamental aspect of the inquiry. Where should the focal point be placed in defining the boundaries of an "offense" for double jeopardy purposes?

Depending upon whether a statutory or behavioral approach is taken to the problem of establishing a double jeopardy definition of an "offense," the concept can have two different levels of meaning. First, a double jeopardy "offense" can be treated as equivalent to a substantive-law offense described in terms of its elements. This accords with its ordinary meaning in the English language and makes the constitutional safeguard substantially mean that an accused shall not be twice tried for the same statutory charge. If this be the correct interpretation of the constitutional language, then the ex-convict in our hypothetical case loses on his plea of former jeopardy, because though his underlying conduct was unitary, it violated two separate sections of the criminal code.

Alternatively, the behavior of the accused can be employed as the index for measuring the number of double jeopardy "offenses." If the underlying behavior establishes the boundaries of double jeopardy "offense," our ex-convict is immune from the second prosecution, for, though two statutes were violated by his gun possession, the offending conduct was unitary.

These two divergent points of reference, behavioral and statutory, form the nucleus of the two principle offense-defining tests currently utilized by the courts—the so-called "same evidence" and "same transaction" tests.

1. "Same evidence" test

The "same evidence" test for determining whether a second prosecution is brought for the "same offense" adopts what amounts to a statutorily-oriented solution to the problem of offense identity. A court applying this test must compare the several indictments for the purpose of determining the evidence required to convict under each of them. The evidence required is, of course, a function of the elements included within the statutory violation charged. Only if the identical elements of proof necessary to obtain a conviction under one statute would equally suffice to obtain a conviction under another will the offenses proscribed by both statutes be regarded as the "same" under this test.[64] Thus, if each statute violated in the course of criminal activity requires proof of one or more elements not shared by the others, the "offenses" are different, even though some elements may overlap and all charges grow out of the same underlying conduct. The prosecutor may, therefore, separately try each such statutory charge.

The "same evidence" test of offense identity affords a bare minimum of protection against reprosecution. Existing penal codes are replete with instances of duplicating and overlapping statutes dealing with slightly different aspects of the same general type of conduct. Sex crimes are a notorious example. An alleged act of forcible intercourse can, depending upon the statutory law of a given jurisdiction, generate ten or more "same evidence" test offenses. Though bizarre, it is conceivable in an evidentiary test jurisdiction that a sex offender might be tried consecutively for assault and battery, rape, fornication, carnal knowledge, seduction, adultery, indecent exposure, lewd and lascivious behavior, and depending upon the victim's age or relationship to the accused, child molesting, impairing the morals of a minor, contributing to delinquency, or incest.[65] Since most of these statutory violations require proof of at least one distinct element not shared by any of the rest, multiple "same evidence" test offenses have allegedly been committed, and the accused can be separately tried for each.

But overlapping statutes dealing with slightly different aspects of the same underlying behavior are not the only area where opportunities for unfairness exist under the evidentiary

[64] Gavieres v. United States, 220 US 338, 55 LEd 489, 31 SCt 421 (1911). See also, for a discussion of the "same evidence" test, *Twice in Jeopardy*, *supra* note 8.

[65] United States ex rel. Brown v. Hendrick, 431 F(2d) 436 (3dCir), *cert. denied*, 402 US 976 (1970). See also, Note, 7 BROOKLYN LREV 79, 82 (1937).

test of an offense. A single criminal act may produce multiple consequences as, for example, where the accused recklessly careens an automobile into a crowd of pedestrians killing several,[66] or robs several individuals at one time and place.[67] Where multiple wrongs of the same general type are committed simultaneously, the requirement that the prosecutor prove the death or injury of a distinct victim at each trial furnishes a sufficient variance in proof to satisfy the "same evidence" test and to allow the prosecutor to proceed for each injury separately.[68] Pushed to its limits, the "same evidence" test has been applied to sanction multiple prosecutions growing out of a single discharge of a gun where the bullet fragmented and struck two persons,[69] and where it entered the body of a pregnant woman, wounding her and killing her unborn child.[70]

The harshness of the "same evidence" test is mitigated to a limited extent by the "included offense" doctrine. When two crimes defined in separate statutes are so related that it is both legally and physically impossible to commit one without necessarily and in all cases committing the other, the relationship between them is one of included offenses.[71] The concept of an included offense is best illuminated by way of example. Suppose that the legislature has defined two crimes, A and B. To procure a conviction for crime A, the prosecutor must establish the existence of three elements, X, Y, and Z, whereas crime B requires proof of elements Y and Z alone. Since all of the elements of crime B are incorporated into crime A, and it is legally impossible to commit A without necessarily com-

---

[66] Holder v. Fraser, 215 Ark 67, 219 SW(2d) 625 (1949).

[67] Gandy v. State, 42 AlaApp 215, 159 S(2d) 71 (1963); People v. Kelley, 168 CalApp(2d) 387, 335 P(2d) 955 (1959); Commonwealth v. Meyers, 193 PaSuper 531, 165 A(2d) 400 (1960); Morgan v. State, 220 Tenn 247, 415 SW(2d) 625 (1949).

[68] State v. Singleton, 66 Ariz 49, 182 P(2d) 920 (1947); Holder v. Fraser, 215 Ark 67, 219 SW(2d) 625 (1949); Murray v. Commonwealth, 289 SW(2d) 203 (Ky 1956); State v. Whitley, 382

SW(2d) 665 (Mo 1964); State v. Varner, 329 SW(2d) 623 (Mo 1959).

[69] Commonwealth v. Browning, 146 Ky 770, 143 SW 407 (1912); Berry v. State, 195 Miss 899, 16 S(2d) 629 (1944).

[70] State v. Shaw, 219 S(2d) 49 (Fla App 1969).

[71] People v. Pater, 267 CalApp(2d) 921, 73 CalRptr 823 (1969); People v. Krupa, 64 CalApp(2d) 592, 149 P(2d) 416 (1944); Johnson v. State, 217 Tenn 234, 397 SW(2d) 170 (1965).

mitting B at the same time, B is an included offense. The simplest example of an included offense relationship is two crimes of different degrees such as first and second-degree murder.[72] Robbery and larceny stand in this relationship, though not different degrees of the same crime. Robbery is defined as the felonious taking of personal property from the possession of the owner by force and fear. It is essentially a combination of two other crimes—assault (putting the victim in fear) and larceny (taking and carrying off his property). Since it is both physically and legally impossible to perpetrate robbery without simultaneously committing an assault plus larceny, the latter are offenses included within the crime of robbery.

The "same evidence" test, read literally, would appear to sanction prosecution on robbery charges following a larceny trial because proof of an additional element is required to obtain a conviction for the former. But the "same evidence" test is modified by the "included offense" doctrine which holds that where one offense is included within another, prosecution for the lesser offense precludes retrial on the greater, and vice versa.[73] The "included offense" exception, however, has a fairly narrow reach.

The case of the ex-convict mentioned at the beginning of this section does not come within the included offense rule. Although possessing a *concealed* weapon and being an *ex-convict* in possession of a weapon share one element (X) in common (weapon possession), a conviction under the first statute requires proof of X plus Y (that the weapon was concealed on the person of the possessor), whereas a conviction under the second statute requires proof of X plus Z (that the possessor was an ex-convict). Possessing a concealed weapon (XY) is not included in the offense of being an ex-convict in possession of a weapon (XZ). Though it will frequently happen that both are committed simultaneously, it is neither legally nor factually impossible to commit one without the

---

[72] Singleton v. United States, 294 Fed 890 (5thCir 1923).

[73] People v. Blue, 161 CalApp(2d) 1, 326 P(2d) 183 (1958); State v. La-bato, 7 NJ 137, 80 A(2d) 617 (1951); State v. Johnson, 112 OhioApp 124, 165 NE(2d) 814 (1960).

other. Witness the case of an ex-convict who possesses a weapon openly. Because these two statutes do not stand in an included offense relationship, successive prosecutions would be permissible in an evidentiary test jurisdiction.[74]

The "same evidence" test was first enunciated in England five years after the American Bill of Rights was adopted.[75] Though some variation of the English test has gained a foothold in the vast majority of American jurisdictions,[76] several courts have abandoned it.[77] The "same evidence" test has recently come under attack as being of limited utility in promoting fundamental double jeopardy policy goals.[78] The test may have been workable several centuries ago when the number of statutory offenses was relatively sparce and each statute covered a broad area of sharply delineated conduct. Under such conditions, there was little likelihood of harassing, multiple prosecutions for the same underlying conduct. But each session of the legislature in modern times brings with it a host of new criminal statutes, frequently enacted without adequate attention to existing laws containing duplicating or overlapping provisions. The multiplication of statutory offenses regulating slightly different aspects of the same general conduct and requiring subtle variations in evidence to convict results in an erosion of double jeopardy protection when the "same evidence" test is applied to determine whether the offense charged at a second prosecution is the same. The Oregon Court of Appeals has recognized this in a recent decision:

> [T]he traditional 'same evidence' test provides virtually no protection against repeated prosecutions based on a single act or course of conduct. A prosecutor is limited only by the number of ways in which the legislature has made the defendant's conduct punishable,

[74] Bell v. Kansas, 452 F(2d) 783 (10thCir), cert. denied, 406 US 974 (1972); State v. Brown, 262 Ore 442, 497 P(2d) 1191 (1972).

[75] Rex v. Vandercomb & Abbott, [1796] 2 Leach 708, 168 EngRep 455.

[76] Twice in Jeopardy, supra note 8, at 269–75.

[77] Ashe v. Swenson, 397 US 436, 25 LEd(2d) 469, 90 SCt 1189 (1970)

(Brennan, J., concurring); People v. White, 390 Mich 245, 212 NW(2d) 222 (1973); State v. Brown, 262 Ore 442, 497 P(2d) 1191 (1972); Commonwealth v. Campana, 452 Penn 233, 304 A(2d) 432 (1973).

[78] See cases cited in note 77, supra. See also, Twice in Jeopardy, supra note 8.

and may indulge in harassment against which the double jeopardy guarantee should protect. He may split his case, so that if the first trial results in an acquittal he can try the defendant again, for essentially the same conduct, before a different jury or, in case of a conviction, he could prosecute further to obtain what he considers a suitable punishment. He can use the first prosecution as a 'trial run,' planning on refining his case if the first prosecution is unsuccessful. As a consequence, a defendant is deprived of the assurance that an acquittal is the end of the matter or that a conviction and sentence is the final measure of his guilt and punishment. Moreover, repeated prosecutions strain the resources of defendants and dissipate those of the courts and prosecutors, and deprive judgments of their finality. Modern commentators are, for these reasons, justly critical of the 'same evidence' test.[79]

2. "Same transaction" test

Disenchantment with the mechanical results of the "same evidence" test has prompted a minority of courts to seek a fresh solution to the problem of establishing a double jeopardy definition of "offense." In quest of a standard more sensitive to the constitutional policy of avoiding harassing reprosecutions, the "same transaction" test has been turned to.[80] The "same transaction" test measures the boundaries of an "offense" by the underlying behavior of the accused and treats each *criminal transaction* as a single unit for prosecution purposes. Where multiple statutory violations are committed in the course of a unitary transaction, this test does not require that any violation go unprosecuted. What it does require is that the various charges be consolidated for trial in one proceeding.[81] This result is endorsed by the American Law Institute Model Penal Code,[82] widely acclaimed by legal scholars,[83] and presently mandated in England.[84] The behavioral approach protects the accused from multiple prosecutions growing out of the same criminal act, transaction or

---

[79] State v. Brown, 262 Ore 442, 497 P(2d) 1191, 1194–95 (1972) (footnotes omitted).

[80] See cases cited in note 77, *supra.*

[81] See cases cited in note 77, *supra.*

[82] ALIModelPenalCode § 1.07(2).

[83] Carroway, *Pervasive Multiple Offense Problems—A Policy Analysis,* 1971 UtahLRev 105 (1971); Kirchheimer, *The Act, the Offense and Double Jeopardy,* 58 YaleLJ 513 (1949); *Twice in Jeopardy, supra* note 8.

[84] Connelly v. Director of Public Prosecutions, [1964] 2AllER 401, AC 1254.

episode. Such a result is to be applauded both because it conserves judicial resources and because it better promotes the policies underlying the double jeopardy safeguard.

The "same transaction" test, however, is not without its difficulties. Although the prosecutor is required to join for trial all charges growing out of the same underlying criminal *act* or *transaction*, the latter concepts do not mark off their own boundaries. Few criminal endeavors consist of a single act. Even the simple undertaking of discharging a gun consists of a series of separate motions—transporting the weapon to the appropriate location, loading it, aiming and firing. It would be nonsense to suggest that each muscular exertion constitutes a separate "act" or unit for prosecution purposes. But what characteristic forges these motions together and makes them a unitary undertaking? The problem becomes more acute if additional facts are added. Suppose that the discharge occurred while the accused was attempting to flee the scene of a robbery just perpetrated by him. To further complicate matters, the bullet ricochets, injuring one by-stander and killing another. How many "criminal transactions" or, in other words, prosecution units, exist under the behaviorally-oriented, offense-defining test?

In a jurisdiction utilizing the "same evidence" test of an offense, the solution is simple, though unsatisfactory from a policy standpoint. No less than three major, substantive legal offenses were committed—armed robbery, assault and battery, and homicide—and since each violation requires different elements of proof to secure a conviction, the accused can be prosecuted three separate times without violating his double jeopardy rights.[85] Unlike a comparison of the elements of proof required to convict, concepts like "act" and "transaction" are not so easily tied down. There are no pre-established boundary lines circumscribing three-dimensional events. Faced with this dilemma, courts favoring a behavioral solution to the question of whether a second prosecution involves the same offense, have tended to place emphasis upon time con-

[85] State v. Moton, 476 SW(2d) 785 (Mo 1972). See also cases cited in note 68, *supra*.

tinuity and singularity of motivating intent.[86] In *People* v. *White*,[87] the Supreme Court of Michigan, after placing the "same transaction" test on a constitutional footing in that jurisdiction, made an effort to set the limits of a transaction-ally-defined offense. White had been accused of forcing a woman into a car, driving her some distance, and ultimately raping her. After having been tried and found guilty of kidnapping, he was charged with felonious assault and rape, and placed on trial a second time over his objection. (Consecutive trials would have been authorized on these facts under the "same evidence" test because different proof elements are required to establish each of the various charges.) The Supreme Court of Michigan ruled that the "same transaction" test was constitutionally compelled in Michigan, and because all three charges arose out of a unitary criminal transaction, the second trial was improper as having been brought for the "same offense."

What made the defendant's separate acts and crimes a "unitary transaction"? The attribute that forged them together as a single prosecution unit, in the Michigan court's opinion, was the fact that they were committed in a continuous time sequence and were motivated by a purpose to accomplish a single criminal objective—rape. Based upon these two criteria, our hypothetical fleeing bank robber can be tried but once for his three robbery-related crimes in jurisdictions which utilize the "same transaction" approach.[88] Would a court applying this test feel compelled to regard his killing of a police officer to avoid arrest, miles removed and hours later, a part of the "same transaction," or would it regard this crime to be too remote?

Though continuity and purpose are somewhat less than ideal as analytic tools for segregating conduct into segments for prosecution, and further refinement is desirable, the behavioral test of an offense is inspired by recognition of the

[86] Neal v. State, 55 Cal(2d) 11, 357 P(2d) 839 (1960); State v. Corning, 289 Minn 354, 184 NW(2d) 603 (1971); State v. Brown, 262 Ore 442, 497 P(2d) 1191 (1972).

[87] 390 Mich 245, 212 NW(2d) 222 (1973).

[88] Smith v. State, 486 P(2d) 770 (Okla 1971).

need for a double jeopardy definition of "offense" more in harmony with underlying double jeopardy policies and represents a step in the proper direction.

§ 9.9 —The Supreme Court's failure to clarify

"Same offense" is the most critical phrase found in the constitutional provision dealing with double jeopardy. If this phrase is read as embodying the "same evidence" test, and "offense," for double jeopardy purposes, is equated with "same statutory charge," protection against multiple prosecutions is relatively narrow, since a resourceful district attorney can normally find two or more statutory provisions applicable to different aspects of virtually any criminal undertaking. But if "same offense" is interpreted more generously as precluding reprosecution on charges growing out of the same underlying behavior or factual episode, the double jeopardy safeguard has a far more expansive application. In this situation, one would expect that the Supreme Court, at some time during the one hundred and eighty-six years since the adoption of the Bill of Rights, would have made its position clear. But such has not been the case. While there has been a smattering of decisions touching upon this problem tangentially or inconclusively, none is authority for a mandatory reading of the Fifth Amendment as incorporating one or the other of the two prevailing offense-defining tests.

In *Gavieres* v. *United States*,[89] the United States Supreme Court declined to overturn a second-trial conviction for insulting a public officer following a previous conviction on charges of public drunkenness, though both arose out of the same factual incident. The Court there quoted the Supreme Court of Massachusetts:

"A conviction or acquittal upon one indictment is no bar to a subsequent conviction and sentence upon another, unless the evidence required to support a conviction upon one of them would have been sufficient to warrant a conviction upon the other. The test is not

[89] 220 US 338, 55 LEd 489, 31 SCt 421 (1911), quoting Morey v. Commonwealth, 108 Mass 433, 434 (1871).

whether the defendant has already been tried for the same act, but whether he has been put in jeopardy for the same offense. A single act may be an offense against two statutes; and if each statute requires proof of an additional fact which the other does not, an acquittal or conviction under either statute does not exempt the defendant from prosecution and punishment under the other."

This sounds like a statement of the "same evidence" test and it is. But *Gavieres* is not authority for reading this test into the Fifth Amendment, because the case arose in the Philippine Islands while they were under American governance. The case is purported to be an interpretation of a statute rather than of the Constitution itself.[90] In *Blockburger* v. *United States*,[91] the Supreme Court reiterated the above-quoted language; but *Blockburger's* indorsement of the "same evidence" test is also inconclusive for the purposes at hand. Blockburger engaged in one commercial transaction which lead to two narcotics charges, one for selling the narcotics without the original stamped package, and the other for selling the same substance without a written order form. But he was not tried consecutively on these charges. Instead, the government joined both in one proceeding.

What Blockburger contested was the Fifth Amendment power of the government to impose consecutive sentences on two charges growing out of a unitary underlying event. The Supreme Court ruled that the "same evidence" test was applicable to determine whether both charges were for the same offense, implying that if they were, consecutive sentencing was impermissible. The Court went on to find, however, that each charge alleged a distinct offense because different proof was required to convict. Since *Blockburger* involved the propriety of imposing consecutive sentences on charges growing out of a unitary transaction when *joined for trial in one proceeding*, the case is not controlling on the constitutionally appropriate definition of an "offense" in the context of *successive trials*. The policy considerations underlying cumulative punishment cases are different from those involved in multiple

[90] Abbate v. United States, 359 US 187, 3 LEd(2d) 729, 79 SCt 666 (1959); Green v. United States, 355 US 184, 2 LEd(2d) 199, 78 SCt 221 (1957). [91] 284 US 299, 76 LEd 306, 52 SCt 180 (1932).

prosecutions, and a test which is appropriate in one class of cases is not necessarily appropriate in the other class.[92]

The central concern of the double jeopardy safeguard is protection against repetitive trials and harassment. As a device for implementing this policy, the "same evidence" test is totally ineffective since it permits the prosecutor to circumvent restrictions upon reprosecution by varying the statutory charges. There is no constitutional necessity that a single, uniform offense-defining standard be established for use in multiple prosecution and cumulative punishment cases alike. The standard should be molded by functional considerations rather than a desire for legal symmetry. As a test for use in multiple prosecution cases, the behavioral approach is superior. It avoids the problem of repetitious prosecutions for the same underlying conduct without, at the same time, sacrificing any legitimate social interest. The public interest in vindicating *all* infractions of the law is amply protected by virtue of the government's ability to join the various charges and try them at one time.

In *Ashe v. Swenson,*[93] decided in 1970, the Supreme Court sidestepped an opportunity to resolve this question once and for all. Six poker players in the basement of a private home were held up by a group of armed, masked bandits. Defendant Ashe was placed on trial under an indictment charging the robbery of Knight, one of the six poker players. He did not dispute the state's proof that an armed robbery had occurred or that property had been taken from Knight. The only controverted issue at trial was whether Ashe had in fact been one of the masked men. The jury returned a verdict of "not guilty due to insufficient evidence." Ashe was then placed on trial, over his objection, for the robbery of Roberts, another of the six players. The second trial ended in a conviction.

After exhausting his state court remedies, Ashe brought federal habeas corpus proceedings, claiming that the second prosecution had violated his double jeopardy rights. Several alternatives were presented to the Supreme Court for dispos-

[92] Neal v. State, 55 Cal(2d) 11, 357 P(2d) 839 (1960); State v. Brown, 262 Ore 442, 497 P(2d) 1191 (1972); *Twice in Jeopardy, supra* note 8.

[93] 397 US 436, 25 LEd(2d) 469, 90 SCt 1189 (1970). See Part II for portions of this case.

ing of this case. It could have seized the opportunity to establish a double jeopardy definition of offense. Had it taken this course and determined that the behavioral test was constitutionally mandated, this would have led to an overturning of the second proceeding as having been brought for the same offense.[94] An alternative reading of the Fifth Amendment as incorporating the evidentiary test would have produced the opposite result.[95] Finally, there was a third solution, the one which the Court in fact took. It could avoid the identity question completely and reverse Ashe's conviction on the basis of the more narrow collateral estoppel doctrine. For Ashe, the individual, it was of little consequence what rationale the Court employed in arriving at its conclusion that his conviction could not stand. But for *Ashe*, the case, its significance as a constitutional precedent would have been far more consequential had the Supreme Court tackled the identity question and made its position clear.

The meaning of "same offense" stands today, as it did in 1970, in controversy and confusion. Though the double jeopardy safeguard has been made applicable to the states through the Fourteenth Amendment, the scope of immunity against reprosecution is by no means uniform throughout the nation and will not be so until the Supreme Court comes to grips with the problem of establishing a constitutional definition of an "offense."

§ 9.10   —Same offense in a dual sovereignty context

The United States consists of fifty-one separate sovereign entities, including the federal government, each separately endowed with the power to try and punish infractions of their own laws. Criminal undertakings may intersect state lines or simultaneously contravene the laws of a state and the federal government. Does a criminal act become more than one offense, for purposes of double jeopardy, when it violates the laws of two sovereignties, albeit identical laws?

This problem is different from that met in the preceding two sections where multiple prosecutions occurred within the

---

[94] *Id.*, (Brennan, J., concurring).   [95] See State v. Moton, 476 SW(2d) 785 (Mo 1972).

confines of one jurisdiction, and the question of offense identity was resolved on the basis of the "same evidence" or "same transaction" test. In a dual sovereignty context, these tests have not been utilized.

1. Successive state and federal prosecutions

The problem of successive prosecutions by a state and the federal government first reached the Supreme Court in *United States* v. *Lanza*.[96] Lanza was convicted by the state of Washington for manufacturing, transporting and having possession of liquor, in violation of a state statute. Following the Washington state conviction, Lanza was tried in a federal court under the Volstead Act for performing the same acts with regard to the same liquor and was again convicted. On appeal to the Supreme Court, the issue centered upon whether the double jeopardy clause of the Fifth Amendment prohibits a second trial before a federal court of an accused who has previously stood trial on identical charges before a state tribunal. A negative answer was given. The Supreme Court responded to the double jeopardy argument by pointing out that, under the federal union, the United States government and the states are separate entities, each separately endowed with the sovereign power to define what conduct amounts to an offense against its peace and dignity. An act denounced as a crime both by a state and by the United States is, therefore, an offense against each; to treat a prior state court prosecution, brought to vindicate an offense against its laws, as a bar to federal enforcement proceedings would operate as a serious encroachment upon the sovereign powers of the federal government. Such a result was not contemplated by the Bill of Rights. If an act simultaneously violates the laws of a state and the United States, the state court cannot immunize the accused from federal accountability by catching and trying him first.

Though *Lanza* established the power of the federal government to try an accused following a state prosecution based

---

[96] 260 US 377, 67 LEd 314, 43 SCt 141 (1922).

on the same conduct and brought for identical charges, a power since reaffirmed,[97] the United States has voluntarily refrained from retrying an accused after state court proceedings except in extraordinary cases. In 1959, Attorney General William P. Rogers made a policy statement that no federal prosecution should be commenced after an acquittal or conviction for the same conduct in a state trial "unless the reasons are compelling," and further indicated that the federal government would in the future make every effort to cooperate with state and local authorities to the end that a single prosecution would occur in the jurisdiction with paramount interest.[98] This represents a sound rule of policy.

Lanza dealt with the power of the federal government to try an accused following a state prosecution on similar charges. In *Bartkus* v. *Illinois*,[99] the same rationale was applied though the sequence of prosecutions reversed. Illinois sought to prosecute an accused for robbing a local bank after he had been previously tried in a federal court and acquitted of this conduct under charges of violating the National Bank Robbery law. The accused raised a plea of former jeopardy, the Illinois Court rejected it, and this trial ended in a conviction. The Supreme Court affirmed on the basis of the dual sovereignty doctrine that an act denounced as a crime under the laws of two separate, sovereign political entities is an offense against each, and each may separately try and punish for the infraction of its laws.

2. Successive state court prosecutions

Criminal transactions may intersect state lines and, in so doing, offend the laws of several states. The dual sovereignty argument for permitting successive prosecutions rests on even firmer ground here than in the case of federal-state concurrence, because now the factor of territorial independence is added to that of political sovereignty. Under our federal system, each state has undisputed power both to define and exact punishment for crimes committed within its borders.

---

[97] Abbate v. United States, 359 US 187, 3 LEd(2d), 729, 79 SCt 666 (1959).

[98] Dept. of Justice Press Release, N.Y.Times, April 6, 1959, quoted in

Hall and Kamisar, MODERN CRIMINAL PROCEDURE 479 (1966).

[99] 359 US 121, 3 LEd(2d) 684, 79 SCt 676 (1959).

Therefore, a criminal proceeding undertaken in one state has no double jeopardy impact upon prosecutions allowable in the courts of a sister state. If the criminal conduct of an accused extends across state lines, he is amenable to separate trials and punishments to the fullest extent authorized under the separate laws of each state involved.[100]

3. Successive prosecutions brought before state and local courts

The dual sovereignty justification for allowing separate prosecutions when the same conduct offends the identical laws of two states, or of a state and the federal government, has no application where the prosecuting authorities stand in the relationship of a state to one of its local political subdivisions. All local units of government are part of the state, created by the state to assist it in discharging its governmental functions, and are not separate sovereign entities. For this reason, a conviction or acquittal in a municipal court would constitute a bar to a subsequent prosecution for the *same offense* in a state court, despite the fact that the conduct is outlawed by both levels of government.[101] For double jeopardy purposes, there is only one prosecuting entity in this situation.

In the next section we encounter the collateral estoppel doctrine. A summary review of the material on offense identity will serve to put the collateral estoppel doctrine in its proper perspective as a related device for implementing the constitutional policy of finality in criminal cases. The double jeopardy safeguard affords as a minimum assurance in all jurisdictions that an accused cannot be retried on the identical statutory charges. This degree of protection obtains whether his first trials ends in a conviction or an acquittal, or, in many cases, even though it eventuates in a mistrial. But a criminal act can, and frequently does, violate more than one section of the penal code. Where multiple overlapping or related statutory violations are committed in the course of one criminal trans-

---

[100] People ex rel. Heflin v. Silberglitt, 2 NYApp(2d) 767, 153 NYS(2d) 279 (1956).

[101] Waller v. Florida, 397 US 387, 25 LEd(2d) 435, 90 SCt 1184 (1970).

action, and consecutive trials are brought for each, application of the double jeopardy safeguard becomes more complicated. There are two alternative theories upon which the second prosecution may be foreclosed: (1) the offenses charged may be regarded as the *same offense*, or (2) the collateral estoppel doctrine may be applicable.

Suppose a man is accused of having raped and then murdered a female victim. The state first places him on trial under an indictment charging rape. The accused does not seek to controvert the state's evidence that the dead woman was raped; instead, he relies upon a defense of alibi. The jury brings in a verdict of not guilty. The accused is thereafter placed on trial under a second indictment charging him with the victim's death. Does the second trial violate his double jeopardy rights? Regardless of the offense-defining test employed by the jurisdiction, on these facts, the answer should be "yes."

In jurisdictions utilizing the "same transaction" test, an affirmative response is required because both charges originated from the same underlying factual episode, causing them to be treated as the "same offense." In jurisdictions subscribing to the "same evidence" test, the second trial is barred, but for an entirely different reason, that being the doctrine of collateral estoppel. The collateral estoppel doctrine, now a constitutionally required aspect of double jeopardy protection, is concerned with identity of *issues* involved in consecutive trials rather than identity of offenses. Though murder and rape would not be considered the "same offense" in jurisdictions subscribing to the "same evidence" test, both trials present a common issue of fact—namely, the defense of alibi.

§ 9.11   Collateral estoppel

The collateral estoppel doctrine holds that where an ultimate issue of fact has been raised and determined in one proceeding, the matter is conclusively established and binding upon the parties in any subsequent litigation between them in which the identical issue may again be called into dispute.[102]

---

[102] Ashe v. Swenson, 397 US 436, 25 LEd(2d) 469, 90 SCt 1189 (1970).

The losing party is denied a second opportunity to make the same factual contention in the hopes of prevailing upon a different judge or jury to accept his rendition of the disputed matter. In the context of criminal prosecutions, this means that if an identical factual issue is determinative of the defendant's guilt of two separate and distinct offenses, and this issue is resolved in the defendant's favor at trial for one offense, the government is foreclosed from prosecuting for the second offense since it can no longer establish his guilt.

The above hypothetical case presents this situation. Even though under the "same evidence" test murder and rape are not the "same offense," a common issue is involved in both proceedings, the asserted alibi. When the first jury brought back a verdict of acquittal in the face of undisputed evidence that a rape had been committed, the only plausible explanation is that it credited the defendant's testimony that he was not present at the scene of the crime. The government is collaterally estopped from seeking to controvert this fact in any subsequent judicial proceeding involving the accused, albeit for a different crime. Since the government would be required to convince a second jury that the accused was in fact present at the scene of the crime to establish the murder charge, the murder prosecution is barred.

The collateral estoppel doctrine is of ancient origin, and is grounded upon considerations of finality. In *Ashe v. Swenson*,[103] it was incorporated into the double jeopardy guarantee. The Supreme Court ruled that double jeopardy rights of an accused are not *confined* to immunity from reprosecution for the same offense; his rights are equally violated when he is forced to stand trial for a *different* offense involving a collaterally-estopped factual contention.

Although both aspects of double jeopardy protection are founded upon similar policy considerations, the contours of these related doctrines are by no means coextensive. The branch of double jeopardy insulating an accused from reprosecution for the same offense is far broader than collateral estoppel. With respect to immunity from reprosecution for the same offense, it is irrelevant whether the first trial ends

---

[103] *Id.*

in a conviction, an acquittal, or in many instances, whether it goes to a verdict at all. Collateral estoppel, or the doctrine opposed to relitigating the *same factual assertions* in consecutive trials brought for different offenses, is, on the other hand, dependent upon all of the following:

(1) The identical parties must be involved in both proceedings.[104]

(2) The first trial must have terminated in an acquittal.[105] (An accused cannot claim any collateral estoppel benefit from a conviction, because a guilty verdict necessarily signifies that the trier of the facts accepted the government's rendition of all disputed factual issues and resolved them adversely to the defendant.)

(3) The acquittal must have turned upon an adjudication in the defendant's favor of a material fact issue that is common to both proceedings.[106]

(4) The basis for the acquittal, or in other words, the specific issue determined in favor of the accused at his first trial, must be reasonably apparent from the pleadings, evidence, instructions or other trial records.[107]

(5) This issue must negate his culpability for the offense charged at the second trial.[108]

Collateral estoppel protection is, thus, fairly confined. Unless the accused can demonstrate that his acquittal on unrelated charges necessarily resolved in his favor a factual contention that precludes criminal responsibility for the offense charged at the second trial, collateral estoppel is no barrier to the second prosecution. Let us return, for the moment, to our hypothetical case about the man accused of raping

---

[104] United States v. Hutul, 416 F(2d) 607 (7thCir 1969), *cert. denied,* 396 US 1012 (1970); People v. LoCicero, 14 NY(2d) 374, 200 NE(2d) 622 (1964).

[105] Bell v. Kansas, 452 F(2d) 783 (10thCir), *cert. denied,* 406 US 974 (1972); United States v. Lopez, 420 F(2d) 313 (2dCir 1969); United States v. Harriman, 130 FSupp 198 (SD NY 1955).

[106] Johnson v. Estelle, 506 F(2d) 347 (5thCir), *cert. denied,* 422 US 1024 (1975). See also Note, 74 HARVLREV 752, 758–59 (1960).

[107] Ashe v. Swenson, 397 US 436, 25 LEd(2d) 469, 90 SCt 1189 (1970); see also Comment, 24 MoLREV 513, 523 (1959).

[108] United States ex rel. Triano v. Superior Court, 393 FSupp 1061 (D NJ 1975), *cert. denied,* 423 US 1056 (1976).

and then murdering a female victim. Suppose that at the original trial where he was indicted for rape, the accused had contested only one issue, that being the sufficiency of the government's evidence to establish that the dead woman had been raped rather than simply molested. An acquittal on this basis, unlike where he prevailed on a defense of alibi, would determine no issue in his favor that would absolve him of homicide. In consequence, the accused, though acquitted of rape, may still be tried for murder.[109]

Where at the first trial, the accused actively litigates several issues, only one of which is pertinent to the offense charged in the second proceeding, application of collateral estoppel is complicated by the fact that criminal juries return general verdicts without elaborating upon the reasons. Had our hypothetical accused both disputed that the dead woman's body showed evidence of rape *and* presented alibi testimony, a general verdict of acquittal could mean, in the alternative, that (1) the jurors remained unconvinced that a rape occurred, or (2) they credited the defendant's testimony that he was not present at the scene of the crime. Only if the jury declined to convict for the second of these two reasons, does the defendant's absolution of rape bar the government from prosecuting him for murder. How does the court determine which of several disputed issues were resolved by the jury in favor of the accused in reaching their not-guilty verdict? This inquiry cannot be avoided if a serious effort is made to apply the collateral estoppel doctrine.

Instruction in this process is found in *Ashe v. Swenson.*[110] When called upon to apply the collateral estoppel doctrine, a trial judge must act upon the assumption that the acquitting jury behaved rationally and must scrutinize the pleadings, evidence, instructions and other relevant matter with an eye to determining "whether a rational jury could have grounded its verdict upon an issue other than that which the defendant seeks to foreclose from consideration." [111] Where only one issue is seriously contested at the original trial, it is reasonable

---

[109] State v. Barton, 5 Wash(2d) 234, 105 P(2d) 63 (1940).

[110] 397 US 436, 25 LE(2d) 469, 90 SCt 1189 (1970).

[111] *Id.* at 444, quoting Mayers & Yarborough, 74 HarvLRev 1, 38–39 (1960).

to assume that the jury, in acquitting the accused, credited his rendition of the disputed fact and found for him on this basis rather than on some uncontroverted matter. This, then, becomes the collaterally estopped factual contention. When there is a vigorous contest on several factual issues, only one of which has consequences in the second prosecution, it is reasonable to assume that the jury found against the government and in favor of the accused on the government's weakest link. When, however, the strength of the government's case on each of the disputed points is, relatively speaking, equal, determining with any degree of precision the basis for acquittal becomes practically impossible. The accused, being unable to demonstrate that his acquittal turned upon the issue he is seeking to foreclose from consideration, must lose on his collateral estoppel defense.

Thus seen, the collateral estoppel doctrine operates in a fairly narrow sphere. It is a rare case where the accused can pinpoint which of several strongly contested issues was resolved in his favor by the jury that acquitted him; and if convicted, he has no recourse to the doctrine at all. The broadening of the concept of double jeopardy to include protection against reprosecution for a separate offense involving a collaterally estopped factual contention does not, therefore, provide an adequate substitute for the Supreme Court's failure to supply a serviceable, uniform, offense-defining test for double jeopardy.

§ 9.12 Summary

The constitutional protection against double jeopardy embodies two related safeguards: (1) it precludes the government from twice trying an accused for the same offense; and (2) it protects the accused from being twice forced to establish the identical factual assertion, albeit in the context of a different offense.

1. Immunity from reprosecution for the same offense

Double jeopardy is primarily concerned with sparing an accused the ordeal and harassment of repeated criminal trials for the same offense. The act of placing an accused in "jeopardy" (i.e., impaneling the jury or, in bench trials, swearing the first witness) is ordinarily sufficient to immunize him against a second trial for the "same offense." This is invariably so where the original trial terminates in an acquittal. An acquittal is final, ending the accused's jeopardy, though it results from an error, unless the error is one capable of correction without further trial proceedings. Where his first trial ends in a conviction, the accused gains a similar immunity. If, however, the accused succeeds in having his conviction set aside, the way is paved for further proceedings; on retrial his new jeopardy is limited to the originally convicted offense. Should he again be found guilty of this offense, the judge at the second trial is not limited by the sentence imposed in the original proceeding, but retaliation against the accused for taking an appeal may not be a factor in increasing his punishment. Where a mistrial is declared in the original proceeding, reprosecution is foreclosed unless the case falls within the "manifest necessity" rule enunciated by the Supreme Court in the *Perez* case.

The foregoing discussion assumes, however, that the second prosecution is brought for the "same offense." For want of an authoritative Supreme Court pronouncement establishing a required double jeopardy definition of "offense," two approaches have emerged. The "same evidence" test, currently employed by a decided majority of the courts, compares the statutory violations charged at successive trials and the proof required to convict under each. Under this test, if each statute violated requires proof of at least one element not embraced in the rest, a distinct "offense" is created for which the accused may be separately tried though the offending conduct is the same. The "same evidence" test gives an extremely narrow interpretation to double jeopardy protection and has been criticized as ineffectual to implement the constitutional policies underlying the double jeopardy safeguard.

The alternative approach, embodied in the "same transaction" test, defines an "offense" for double jeopardy purposes in terms of the underlying conduct, thereby forcing the prosecutor to try all statutory violations committed in the course of a unitary criminal transaction in one proceeding. Where the same conduct violates the laws of two states, or of a state and the federal government, neither of these tests is utilized; each sovereign entity may separately try and punish for the infraction of its laws.

2. Collateral estoppel

A determination that the offense charged at the second trial is not the "same," does not end the inquiry. Double jeopardy can occur though the offense charged at the second trial is different if conviction at the second trial would entail relitigation of a factual assertion resolved adversely to the government's interests in an earlier proceeding. Thus, under the collateral estoppel doctrine, where the accused is acquitted at his first trial on the basis of the resolution in his favor of a disputed factual contention that negates his culpability for the crime charged at his second trial, he is constitutionally immunized from the second prosecution, a protection that exists wholly apart from whether the offenses are the same.

Chapter 10

FAIR AND JUST TRIAL AND HUMANE PUNISHMENT*

> In all criminal prosecutions, the accused shall enjoy
> the right to a speedy and public trial, by an impartial
> jury of the State and district wherein the crime shall
> have been committed, which district shall have been
> previously ascertained by law, and to be informed of
> the nature and cause of the accusation; to be confronted
> with the witnesses against him; to have compulsory
> process for obtaining witnesses in his favor, and to have
> the Assistance of Counsel for his defence.

SIXTH AMENDMENT

§ 10.1   Introduction

An inscription on the walls of the Department of Justice
reads: "The United States wins its points when justice is done

* by Jacqueline R. Kanovitz

459

its citizens in the courts." The criminal justice system, as we know it, did not, like Minerva, the source of wisdom, spring forth full-blown at a single point in history. There was a time in the Western world when a man could be condemned without a trial,[1] and when the most barbaric and inhuman atrocities imaginable were performed in the name of criminal punishment.[2] The first major triumph in the evolution of the Anglo-American criminal justice system occurred at Runnymede in 1215, where King John was forced to capitulate to the demands of his insurgent barons and to sign the historic document known as the Magna Charta. The Magna Charta secured for Englishmen the guarantee that no free man would thenceforth be condemned to death or sent to prison "except by the legal judgment of his peers or by the law of the land."[3] This language echoes a familiar ring. It is the precursor of the due process principle that is enshrined in the Fifth and Fourteenth Amendments to the United States Constitution. Those who drafted our Constitution were not content, however, to rely upon this short-hand phrase alone as a means of constitutionalizing and perpetuating a number of specific procedural safeguards that had, over the centuries, come to be associated with the due process notion. In the Bill of Rights, they elaborated on what process was due. Several of the familiar constitutional safeguards surrounding the prosecution and trial of criminal cases will be canvassed in this chapter: the right to indictment by a grand jury, the assurance of a speedy and public trial, the requirement that the tribunal assembled to pass judgment be an impartial one, the right to be tried before a petit jury, the right to confront and cross-examine adverse witnesses, and the assurance that the punishment inflicted will be neither cruel nor unusual. These limitations are designed to enhance the integrity and reliability of the guilt-determining process and to insure respect for human dignity in the realm of criminal justice.

[1] Douglas, WE THE JUDGES 354 (1956).
[2] 4 W. Blackstone, COMMENTARIES *92.
[3] MAGNA CHARTA, ch 39, reprinted in R. Perry & J. Cooper, SOURCES OF OUR LIBERTIES 17 (1959).

§ 10.2 Speedy trial

The Sixth Amendment guarantee that "the accused shall enjoy the right to a speedy . . . trial" embodies a fundamental safeguard applicable in both federal and state prosecutions.[4] Delays in the administration of justice jeopardize three distinct interests of the accused. The first interest, *physical freedom*, is implicated in all cases where the accused cannot obtain bail release. Prolonged confinement under unwholesome and over-crowded jail conditions offers little of positive value. The disruption of job relationships and family life has an adverse impact on chances of rehabilitation, and is particularly unfortunate for those who are ultimately found to be innocent.[5] Quite apart from whether the accused is incarcerated pending trial, the existence of outstanding untried charges may injure a second interest, his *psychological and emotional well-being*. Criminal accusations damage a man's reputation and standing in the community, curtail employment opportunities, and give rise to future uncertainties. The emotional trauma resulting from disruption of normal life patterns and relationships may produce symptoms of severe anxiety and depression, making the period between accusation and trial a mental nightmare.[6] But the most serious injury is that done to the accused's *capacity to prepare a meaningful defense*. When the wheels of justice grind too slowly, the integrity of the proceedings may be compromised by the intervening death or disappearance of defense witnesses and general dulling of memories.[7] The erosive effects of delay are compounded when the accused is incarcerated pending trial. The special disadvantage of the pretrial detainee was noted in *Smith* v. *Hooey*,[8] where the United States Supreme Court said:

> [I]t is self-evident that "the possibilities that long delay will impair the ability of an accused to defend himself" are markedly increased

---

[4] Klopfer v. North Carolina, 386 US 213, 18 LEd(2d) 1, 87 SCt 988 (1967).

[5] Barker v. Wingo, 407 US 514, 532-33, 33 LEd(2d) 101, 118, 92 SCt 2182, 2193 (1972).

[6] *Id.*; Smith v. Hooey, 393 US 374, 21 LEd(2d) 607, 89 SCt 575 (1969); Klopfer v. North Carolina, 386 US 213, 18 LEd(2d) 1, 87 SCt 988 (1967).

[7] See cases cited in note 6, *supra*.

[8] 393 US 374, 21 LEd(2d) 607, 89 SCt 575 (1969).

when the accused is incarcerated. . . . Confined in a prison, . . . his ability to confer with potential defense witnesses, or even to keep track of their whereabouts, is obviously impaired. And, while "evidence and witnesses disappear, memories fade, and events lose their perspective," a man isolated in prison is powerless to exert his own investigative efforts to mitigate these erosive effects of the passage of time.[9]

Though the speedy trial guarantee was fashioned as a mechanism for protecting the accused against (1) prolonged pretrial incarceration, (2) heightened anxiety and concern, and (3) damage to his defense capacity,[10] society, too, loses when justice is delayed. Delay is a two-edged sword. The general availability and memory of prosecution witnesses are subject to the same time hazards as defense witnesses; the prosecution itself may be shorn of evidence to establish the defendant's guilt.[11] In *Barker v. Wingo*,[12] the Supreme Court elaborated upon the social consequences of tardy justice:

[T]here is a societal interest in providing a speedy trial which exists separate from, and at times in opposition to, the interests of the accused. The inability of courts to provide a prompt trial has contributed to a large backload of cases in urban courts which, among other things, enables defendants to negotiate more effectively for pleas of guilty to lesser offenses and otherwise manipulate the system. In addition, persons released on bond for lengthy periods awaiting trial have an opportunity to commit other crimes. . . . Moreover, the longer an accused is free awaiting trial, the more tempting becomes his opportunity to jump bail and escape. Finally, delay between arrest and punishment may have a detrimental effect on rehabilitation.[13]

When the social costs measured in terms of lost wages, public expense of maintaining pretrial detainees, and providing support for their dependent families are added in, the social consequences of delay are experienced directly by every member of the public.

---

[9] *Id.* at 379-80, 21 LEd(2d) at 612, 89 SCt at 578 (footnote omitted).

[10] See cases cited in note 6, *supra*.

[11] Dickey v. Florida, 398 US 30, 42, 26 LEd(2d) 26, 34-35, 90 SCt 1564, 1571 (1970) (Brennan, J., concurring). See also, Ponzi v. Fessenden, 258 US 254, 264, 66 LEd(2d) 607, 613, 42 SCt 309, 312 (1922).

[12] 407 US 514, 33 LEd(2d) 101, 92 SCt 2182 (1972).

[13] *Id.* at 519-20, 33 LEd(2d) at 110-11, 92 SCt at 2186-87 (footnotes omitted).

§ 10.3 —Stage in criminal process when speedy trial guarantee attaches

A criminal trial is the culmination of a number of procedural phases commencing with the discovery of a crime and proceeding through a detailed investigation, arrest, indictment, arraignment and various other pretrial events, both formal and informal. Snags can develop at each of these stages, and the ultimate result will be to retard the criminal trial.

In *United States* v. *Marion*,[14] the Supreme Court ruled that the Sixth Amendment speedy trial guarantee does not commence to run until after the government has constituted a putative suspect an "accused" either through an arrest, indictment, information or comparable method of proferring formal charges. In excluding delays occurring in the pre-accusatory period from the Sixth Amendment purview, the Supreme Court supported its position by reference to the Amendment's text, "in all criminal cases, the *accused* shall enjoy the right to a speedy . . . trial. . . ." "Accused" is a technical term designating one who already has been charged with crime. Its use symbolized to the *Marion* Court a deliberate decision to postpone attachment of the speedy trial guarantee until after the point of accusation is reached.

Aside from semantic considerations, a policy argument can be raised for excluding from Sixth Amendment computations the interval between commission of an offense and arrest or indictment. The public interest is best served by a detailed and thorough investigation. Premature accusations are scarcely to be encouraged. If law enforcement agencies always operated on a level of maximum efficiency in conducting investigations and making arrests, there would be little need for imposing legal controls regulating the duration of the pre-accusatory period. Experience shows, however, that administrative derelictions occur. The authorities may be slow in commencing an investigation. It is not unknown for a case to lie dormant for no apparent reason long after an investigation is concluded. Or the government may decide for strategic reasons to put off an arrest. Delays in charging a

[14] 404 US 307, 30 LEd(2d) 468, 92 SCt 455 (1971).

suspect may be more damaging than those occurring at a later stage in the criminal process. Without notice of the charges, the accused-to-be has no reason to focus upon his whereabouts during a seemingly uneventful day or to search out witnesses to assist him in reconstructing the past. Few of us are capable of accounting for our conduct at a given hour if called upon to explain months or years later. The suspect's ability to defend can be crippled by delays in charging him.

Marion declined to extend Sixth Amendment speedy trial protection to the period before formal charges have been made. The Supreme Court did, however, acknowledge the existence of two other legal controls operative during this phase of the criminal process. First, there are statutes of limitation which bar prosecution if the charges are not made within a specified fixed time after the crime has been committed. Their purpose is to protect citizens against being forced to defend against stale criminal charges after passage of time may have obscured the basic facts.[15] Statutes of limitation are not flexible; when the period fixed by the legislature has expired, the prosecutor is barred from pressing criminal charges even though the evidence against a particular individual remains unimpaired by passage of time. These statutes do not, however, seriously interfere with law enforcement efforts because they provide ample time for discovery and investigation.

The Due Process Clause, with its assurance of a fair trial, constitutes the second mechanism protecting an accused-to-be against injurious delays in charging him. The boundaries of this protection remain, as yet, unexplored by the Supreme Court. The government in the *Marion* case conceded that a *deliberate* and *prejudicial* delay in charging an accused-to-be, engaged in by the government to obtain some tactical advantage over him, would violate his due process rights. The Supreme Court tacitly agreed, but declined to elaborate.

The lower federal courts have, therefore, been left largely without guidance in fashioning due process protection for

---

[15] Public Schools v. Walker, 76 US(9 Wall) 282, 288, 19 LEd 576, 578 (1870).

suspects complaining of delays in charging them. Two dominant approaches have emerged.[16]

The most prevalent approach, traceable to a series of narcotics cases in the District of Columbia, was stimulated by judicial concern over narcotics investigatory practices. Typically, an undercover agent is given a lengthy assignment, and arrest warrants are not issued until it is completed. Postponing notification of criminal charges until the agent "surfaces" may impair the accused's chances of a fair trial in several different ways. Judge Wright of the District of Columbia Circuit, in a dissenting opinion, has pointed out these risks:

> I suggest that it defies human experience for any man . . . to remember and to identify with absolute conviction the particular 102 faces, as distinguished from hundreds of others, that passed through his mind, many on just one occasion, during the kaleidoscope of his months-long undercover investigation. Indulging the unlikely assumption that he can remember the 102 particular faces, to suggest that he can allocate each face to the appropriate time and place shown in his diary offends credulity.
>
> Viewed from the standpoint of the people the policeman identifies, the situation is even more disconcerting. There is just no way in which an accused can protect himself against the stale charge in the policeman's diary plus the policeman's mental image of him as the offender. The accused has no way of knowing, to say nothing of proving, where he was at the time and on the day the policeman says his diary shows he made a sale of narcotics to the policeman. . . . The people in this subculture simply do not have desk pads and social calendars to assist them in determining where they were at a particular time many months before. . . .[17]

In *Ross v. United States*,[18] the foundation of the narcotics pre-arrest delay cases, the District of Columbia Circuit ruled that a seven months' delay between the alleged narcotics offense and the swearing out of a warrant violated the defendant's due process right. Under the criteria enunciated in

---

[16] *Compare* Robinson v. United States, 459 F(2d) 847 (DC Cir 1972) *with* United States v. Jackson, 504 F(2d) 337 (8thCir 1974), *cert. denied,* 420 US 964 (1975). See also, Hamil-ton v. Lumpkin, 389 FSupp 1069 (ED Va 1975).

[17] Powell v. United States, 352 F(2d) 705, 710-11 (DC Cir 1965) (dissenting opinion).

[18] 349 F(2d) 210 (DC Cir 1965).

Ross and refined by subsequent cases,[19] the Due Process Clause requires dismissal if (1) the government unreasonably puts off making an arrest after its case against a suspect has been completed, and if in consequence, (2) he is prejudiced in his ability to present an adequate defense or, in the alternative, the evidence against him has been so weakened by delay as to be unreliable. Although *Ross* was a response to problems associated with narcotics undercover practices, the same approach has been applied in other factual settings [20] and by circuits other than the District of Columbia.[21]

The second approach to the problem of pre-accusatory delay is a variation of *Ross*. This approach focuses upon the same factors (reasons for delay and prejudice), but employs them in a balancing test under which the need for showing injury is adjusted in proportion to the delay's unreasonableness.[22] Under it, the court considers why the government delayed in presenting charges after its investigation has been concluded.[23] If the government has blatantly abused its powers, the court will dismiss the charges without inquiring into whether the subject has been injured. The need for demonstrating prejudice, however, takes on graduated importance where the reasons for the delay are less culpable.[24]

Neither approach calls upon the government to make hasty and incomplete investigations to speed up the moment of arrest. Nor has the government been penalized for tardy arrests where delay results from inability to locate its suspect.[25] If, however, the whereabouts of the accused-to-be are known,

[19] United States v. Jones, 524 F(2d) 834 (DC Cir 1975), see Part II for a reprint of this case; Robinson v. United States, 459 F(2d) 847 (DC Cir 1972).

[20] United States v. Barket, 530 F(2d) 189 (8thCir 1976); United States v. Parish, 468 F(2d) 1129 (DC Cir 1972); Tynan v. United States, 376 F(2d) 761 (DC Cir 1967).

[21] Acree v. United States, 418 F(2d) 427 (10thCir 1969); United States v. Childs, 415 F(2d) 535 (3dCir 1969); United States v. Lee, 413 F(2d) 910 (7thCir 1969); Whitted v. United States, 411 F(2d) 107 (9thCir 1969); United States v. Capaldo, 402 F(2d) 821 (2dCir 1968); Schlinsky v. United States, 379 F(2d) 735 (1stCir 1967); Terlikowski v. United States, 379 F(2d) 501 (8thCir 1967); United States v. Harbin, 377 F(2d) 78 (4thCir 1967).

[22] United States v. Barket, 530 F(2d) 189 (8thCir 1976); United States v. Jackson, 504 F(2d) 337 (8thCir 1974).

[23] Hamilton v. Lumpkin, 389 FSupp 1069, 1075 (ED Va 1975).

[24] See cases cited in note 22, *supra*.

[25] United States v. Jones, 524 F(2d) 834 (DC Cir 1975).

lower federal court cases suggest that the authorities run some risk if, after reaching an affirmative arrest decision, they postpone charging him.

In exploring developing legal trends which protect suspects against tardy arrests, we have strayed afield from the speedy trial guarantee. The time has now come to return.

§ 10.4 —Criteria for judging when speedy trial is denied

Barker v. Wingo [26] was the first case in which the Supreme Court devoted a serious effort toward establishing criteria for judging when the right to a speedy trial is denied. One option was to establish a specific time within which criminal defendants must be tried. This has in fact been done by a substantial number of legislatures,[27] as well as by courts, pursuant to their supervisory rule-making powers. The Supreme Court declined this invitation. Had the drafters of our Constitution regarded passage of time the only relevant consideration, the Court reasoned, they would have fixed the period themselves. Alternatively, the Court could have adopted the "demand-waiver" doctrine, prevalent in several circuits. Under this doctrine, the accused was treated as having waived his right to complain of any delay which occurred before he demanded that his case be tried. The Supreme Court in *Barker* agreed that the accused's timely efforts to secure a speedy trial were an important factor in determining whether his right to a speedy trial was denied, but it declined to make this the sole factor.

The Supreme Court ultimately adopted a four-pronged balancing test. The factors to be weighed in the balance are: (1) the length of the delay, (2) the reasons for it, (3) the defendant's timely assertion of his rights, and (4) whether he suffered prejudice.

1. Length of delay

The length of the delay is important, not for its own sake, but only as it tends to indicate the likelihood of injury to

[26] 407 US 514, 33 LEd(2d) 101, 92 SCt 2182 (1972).

[27] Kamisar, LaFave & Israel, Modern Criminal Procedure 1059-60 (4th ed 1974).

one of the speedy-trial protected interests—security against (1) oppressively long pretrial confinements, (2) extended periods of anxiety, concern and public censure, and (3) erosion of defensive capacity.[28] The first factor, length of delay, operates primarily as a "triggering mechanism."[29] Unless the lapse of time between accusation and trial is "presumptively prejudicial,"[30] there is no need for extending the inquiry into the other three factors. What constitutes a sufficient delay to warrant further investigation is a relative matter, the primary considerations being the complexity of the case and the types of prosecutorial and defensive evidence likely to be encountered. A presumptively prejudicial delay in the case of an ordinary street crime, for example, would be considerably less than for a complex conspiracy,[31] because less time is required for trial preparation and eye-witness testimony grows stale quicker than documentary evidence. The Supreme Court declined to designate a fixed period requiring a closer look, but indicated that lower federal courts might do so, pursuant to supervisory rule-making powers. Several have. In the District of Columbia, a six months' delay between accusation and trial will trigger an investigation.[32]

The first factor, delay, operates as a red flag signaling the need for a more detailed scrutiny of the record. If the delay has been sufficiently long that some prejudice can be presumed, the inquiry shifts to the problem of fixing responsibility.

2. Reasons for delay

In the second phase of the *Barker* analysis, the court must make a serious effort to locate responsibility. The Sixth Amendment does not protect an accused against self-inflicted delays.[33] Consequently, delays attributable to the accused, or to which he has consented, are disregarded in determining

---

[28] Review §10.2, *supra*.

[29] Barker v. Wingo, 407 US 514, 530, 33 LEd(2d) 101, 117, 92 SCt 2182, 2192 (1972).

[30] *Id.*

[31] *Id.* at 531, 33 LEd(2d) at 117, 92 SCt at 2192.

[32] United States v. West, 504 F(2d) 253 (DC Cir 1974).

[33] United States v. Lustman, 258 F(2d) 475 (2dCir 1958).

whether his right to a speedy trial has been violated.[34] The accused may not complain of lost time resulting from the government's inability to locate him while he was a fugitive;[35] of trial postponements resulting from his own illness;[36] from defense motions seasonably acted upon;[37] or of intervals during which he was mentally incompetent to stand trial.[38] For Sixth Amendment purposes, the only relevant delays are those attributable to the government. The government includes both the prosecutor and the court. The weight assignable to government-caused delays varies with the underlying reason. The Supreme Court admonished:

> A deliberate attempt to delay the trial in order to hamper the defense should be weighed more heavily against the government. A more neutral reason such as negligence or overcrowded courts should be weighed less heavily but nevertheless should be considered since the ultimate responsibility for such circumstances must rest with the government rather than with the defendant. Finally, a valid reason, such as a missing witness, should serve to justify appropriate delay.[39]

Formerly, some courts took the position that an accused serving out sentence in another jurisdiction could not complain of the lack of a speedy trial. In voluntarily committing an act resulting in his imprisonment elsewhere, so the reasoning went, the delay was attributable to him. In *Smith* v. *Hooey*,[40] the Supreme Court took issue with this reasoning. Because extradition procedures exist for securing temporary custody of an out-of-state-prisoner, when he requests a speedy trial and fails to receive one, the fault lies with the government.

The determination that there has been some unexcused

---

[34] Dickey v. Florida, 398 US 30, 26 LEd(2d) 26, 90 SCt 1564 (1970) (Brennan J., concurring); United States v. Ferguson, 498 F(2d) 1001 (DC Cir 1974).

[35] United States v. Simmons, 338 F(2d) 804 (2dCir 1964).

[36] Joy v. United States, 416 F(2d) 962 (9thCir 1969).

[37] United States v. Jones, 524 F(2d) 834, 850 (DC Cir 1975).

[38] United States v. Cartano, 420 F(2d) 362 (1stCir 1970); Nickens v. United States, 323 F(2d) 808 (DC Cir 1963); United States v. Lustman, 258 F(2d) 475 (2dCir 1958).

[39] Barker v. Wingo, 407 US 514, 531, 33 LEd(2d) 101, 117, 92 SCt 2182, 2192 (1972) (footnote omitted).

[40] 393 US 374, 21 LEd(2d) 607, 89 SCt 575 (1969).

delay attributable to the government does not end the inquiry. To evaluate whether this delay violated the speedy trial guarantee, the court must focus upon the last two factors.

3. Assertion of rights

Prior to *Barker*, a majority of the lower federal courts adhered to the so-called "demand-waiver" doctrine, which required the court to disregard all delay which occurred before the accused demanded trial.[41] His silence while the delay continued was treated as a waiver. *Barker* acknowledged that the defendant's "assertion of or failure to assert his right to a speedy trial" was "one of the factors to be considered in an inquiry into the deprivation of the right," [42] but declined to make this the sole factor. The Court added, however, that:

> [T]he failure to assert the right will make it difficult for a defendant to prove that he was denied a speedy trial.[43]

Where the accused is uncounseled and ignorant of his rights or where he is incarcerated pending trial, his failure to make a timely demand will be treated with greater leniency than where he welcomes the delay, hoping that the government will abandon its case against him.[44]

4. Prejudice to defendant

Whether the accused has been prejudiced by reason of the delay in trying him constitutes the final consideration. *Barker* instructs that, in evaluating this factor, consideration should be given to those interests which the speedy trial guarantee was designed to protect.[45]

Extended periods of pretrial incarceration are a serious matter, doubly so when the pretrial detainee is innocent. Consequently, where the accused is incarcerated pending trial, a comparatively shorter period may violate the constitutional

---

[41] Barker v. Wingo, 407 US 514, 524-25, 33 LEd(2d) 101, 114-115, 92 SCt 2182, 2188-89 (1972).

[42] *Id.* at 528, 33 LEd(2d) at 116, 92 SCt at 2191.

[43] *Id.* at 531-32, 33 LEd(2d) at 117-18, 92 SCt at 2192-93.

[44] United States v. Calloway, 505 F(2d) 311 (DC Cir 1974).

[45] Review §10.2, *supra*.

guarantee.[46] The District of Columbia Circuit has adopted an automatic rule requiring dismissal where the accused is confined for more than one year awaiting trial for a nonviolent offense.[47]

Even when the accused remains at large, however, the period between arrest and trial may be a strained and abnormal time for him. Job opportunities may be closed; he may be shunned by his fellow citizens; apprehensiveness over the future may become psychologically immobilizing. Whether these consequences accompany delay in a given case is a relevant subject for inquiry.

The most serious time hazard is the risk that the accused will be handicapped in his ability to put forth an adequate defense. The likelihood that some defense witnesses will die, disappear, or that their testimony will be weakened by normal memory deterioration increases with the passage of time. If the accused is capable of documenting specific instances of evidentiary impairment, his claimed deprivation of a speedy trial is accorded heavy weight. The Supreme Court has noted, however, that:

> Loss of memory . . . is not always reflected in the record because what has been forgotten can rarely be shown.[48]

On this basis, several lower federal courts have been willing to take judicial notice that after an excessive period of time, evidentiary deterioration will set in, and they are willing to presume prejudice, although the accused is unable to point to any specific instances. This presumption has the effect of shifting to the government the burden of establishing the absence of injury.[49]

---

[46] Petition of Provoo, 17 FRD 183 (D Md), aff'd sub nom., United States v. Provoo, 350 US 857, 100 LEd 761, 76 SCt 101 (1955), United States ex rel. Von Cseh v. Fay, 313 F(2d) 620 (2dCir 1963).

[47] United States v. West, 504 F(2d) 253 (DC Cir 1974).

[48] Barker v. Wingo, 407 US 514, 532, 33 LEd(2d) 101, 118, 92 SCt 2182, 2193 (1972).

[49] Smith v. United States, 418 F(2d) 1120 (DC Cir 1969); Chism v. Koehler, 392 FSupp 659 (WD Mich 1975); United States v. Chin, 306 FSupp 397 (SD NY 1969).

5. Application of criteria

Having identified the four factors relevant in evaluating a speedy trial denial claim, the Supreme Court proceeded to develop guidelines for their application. It cautioned:

> We regard none of the four factors identified above as either a necessary or sufficient condition to the finding of a deprivation of the right of speedy trial. Rather, they are related factors and must be considered together with such other circumstances as may be relevant. In sum, these factors have no talismanic quality; courts must still engage in a difficult and sensitive balancing process.[50]

To illustrate the proper application of these criteria, the *Barker* Court labored over them in reference to the case before it. Barker was indicted for murder in 1958 but was not tried until five years later. During the intervening period, the prosecution obtained sixteen separate continuances. (Most of these continuances had been sought to gain time to try an accomplice so that the government would be in a position to compel his testimony against Barker.) Barker raised no objection to the first eleven continuances, which consumed approximately seventy percent of the total five year delay. It was not until after his accomplice was convicted that Barker began actively pressuring for a speedy trial. The Supreme Court characterized this as a "close" case,[51] and proceeded to evaluate the factors. Five years between arrest and trial was an extraordinary period, certainly long enough to trigger a detailed scrutiny. The government's excuse, the desire to convict an accomplice and make him a government witness against Barker, might have justified an appropriate delay, but five years was inexcusably long. Counterbalancing the excessive and inexcused delay, however, was the fact that prejudice was minimal and Barker admitted, through counsel, that he was content to await the outcome of his accomplice's trial, gambling on the hope that if his accomplice were acquitted, the government would abandon its case against him. Barker's claim was denied. The most damaging aspect of his

---

[50] Barker v. Wingo, 407 US 514, 533, 33 LEd(2d) 101, 118, 92 SCt 2182, 2193 (1972).

[51] *Id.* at 533, 33 LEd(2d) at 119, 92 SCt at 2193.

case was his complacency in the face of delay. The Supreme Court said:

> We do not hold that there may never be a situation in which an indictment may be dismissed on speedy-trial grounds where the defendant has failed to object to continuances. There may be a situation in which the defendant was represented by incompetent counsel, was severely prejudiced, or even cases in which the continuances were granted *ex parte*. But barring extraordinary circumstances, we would be reluctant indeed to rule that a defendant was denied this constitutional right on a record that strongly indicates, as does this one, that the defendant did not want a speedy trial. . . .[52]

Where the accused has been subjected to an unconstitutional delay, the only corrective remedy available is to dismiss the indictment and grant trial immunity. The government may not reimburse him for the time by subtracting the delay from any sentence ultimately imposed.[53] Discharging potentially guilty persons without a trial is serious business. This may account for characteristic judicial hesitation to find that the delay has reached constitutional proportions, even though appreciable. In spite of the risks that accompany this remedy, it is perhaps the preferable alternative. The denial of a speedy trial casts doubts upon the accuracy of the guilt-determining process.

§ 10.5   Public trial

The constitutional guarantee of a "public trial" is found in the Sixth Amendment, juxtaposed to the speedy trial requirement. Its precise origin is uncertain. Some have considered this guarantee to be a reaction to the infamous practices of the English Court of Star Chamber, while others have traced it beyond to the tyrannous closed-door sessions in Spain during the Inquisition.[54] Regardless of the historical evil it was set against, the right of a criminal defendant to be tried in open court has come to be regarded as a fundamental ingredient of procedural due process.

[52] *Id.* at 536, 33 LEd(2d) at 120, 92 SCt at 2194.

[53] Strunk v. United States, 412 US 434, 37 LEd(2d) 56, 93 SCt 2260 (1973).

[54] In re Oliver, 333 US 257, 266-69, 92 LEd 682, 690-92, 68 SCt 499, 504-06 (1948).

The advantages ascribed to public trials are several: [55]

(1) The openness of the proceedings to public scrutiny operates as a check upon government excesses or abuses.

(2) Witnesses are more reluctant to give perjured testimony in the presence of an audience.

(3) Unknown persons possessing knowledge of the crime may be drawn to the trial as spectators and may come forward with their knowledge.

(4) Public trials afford citizens an opportunity to learn about the workings of their courts and to evaluate whether the judicial system is functioning adequately.

While general agreement exists concerning the basic value of a public trial, divergent views have been expressed with respect to the court's power to exclude certain classes of spectators. This problem has arisen most frequently in the context of rape and morals trials. According to settled interpretation, the right to a public trial is not absolute, but is subject to limited judicial discretion to restrict attendance in cases of special necessity.[56] The propriety of an order barring some or all of the spectators from the courtroom depends to a large extent on the duration and scope of the order, as well as the reasons for its issuance.[57]

The most obvious restriction upon the public nature of the trial stems from the physical capacity of the courtroom. The constitutional right to a public trial does not require that spectators having no immediate concern with the case be admitted in such numbers as to overcrowd the courtroom and to take up space required for jurors, witnesses, court officers, and friends and relatives of the defendant.[58] Once the limits of the courtroom's seating capacity have been reached, other members of the public seeking admission may be turned away. A trial judge in the exercise of his inherent power to

---

[55] United States v. Kobli, 172 F(2d) 919 (3rdCir 1949); State v. Schmit, 273 Minn 78, 139 NW(2d) 800 (1966); People v. Jelke, 308 NY 56, 123 NE(2d) 769 (1954).

[56] People v. Byrnes, 84 CalApp(2d) 72, 190 P(2d) 290 (1948).

[57] Note, *The Accused's Right to a Public Trial*, 49 COLUMLREV 110, 114-15 (1949).

[58] United States v. Kobli, 172 F(2d) 919 (3dCir 1949).

preserve order and decorum in the courtroom may, by the same token, expel rambunctious spectators.[59]

Human nature being what it is, trials involving sex crimes will arouse morbid curiosities and draw larger crowds of spectators than run-of-the-mill criminal cases. A witness may be embarrassed to testify about intimate details before a gaping group of strangers. The propriety of relaxing the requirement of a public trial where necessary to create an atmosphere in which the witness feels comfortable to testify presents a complex constitutional issue. In the case of juvenile witnesses, exclusion orders have been upheld more readily. There is fairly general agreement that a trial judge temporarily may bar members of the public from the courtroom where reasonably necessary to induce a youthful witness to testify without embarrassment or fright on matters of a delicate nature.[60] The same rule should hold for adult witnesses who are intimidated by large crowds. The criminal trial's primary function is conducting a search for truth. The witness's testimony may be crucial, and the jury should hear it as freely and naturally as possible. When the presence of the public interferes with the trial's truth-finding function, the paramount interest should prevail.

Occasionally, a judge will bar members of the public from the courtroom to protect *them* from exposure to indecent, immoral or sordid testimony. Orders clearing the courtroom to protect the public morals are far more questionable than those made to protect a timid witness. The constitutional mandate of a public trial contains no wholesale exclusion for debased or degenerate crimes. A distinction must be made, however, between juvenile spectators and mature adults. The presence of children in the courtroom is of marginal value in advancing the interests protected by a public trial. Consequently, a judge would be justified in excluding immature persons from the courtroom while testimony unsuitable for their ears is being presented.[61] But an indiscriminate order barring adult members of the public from remaining in the

---

[59] State v. Schmit, 273 Minn 78, 139 NW(2d) 800 (1966).
[60] People v. Jelke, 308 NY 56, 123 NE(2d) 769 (1954).
[61] State v. Schmit, 273 Minn 78, 139 NW(2d) 800 (1966).

courtroom, based solely on the nature of the testimony rather than the needs of the witness, is an infringement upon the accused's right to a public trial.[62]

Trials are public under the Constitution for reasons other than popular entertainment. There is a point at which a trial can become too "public," where it loses its serene and dignified atmosphere. When this occurs, the defendant's constitutional right to a fair trial is compromised. The introduction of television and news cameras into the courtroom, enabling greater numbers to observe, invites serious problems of unnatural distractions and diversions. As a consequence, the great majority of state courts have banned live coverage of criminal trials. In the notorious Billie Sol Estes case, the Supreme Court stated that a criminal defendant is "entitled to have his day in court, not in a stadium, or a city or nationwide arena."[63] The televising of portions of his state criminal trial was held to violate Estes's due process rights. The problem of excessive trial publicity will be met again in § 10.13, infra.

§ 10.6 Right to trial by jury

The petit jury is an ancient and venerable institution. The Magna Charta of 1215 declared that no free man could be condemned to death or sent to prison "except by the legal judgment of his peers."[64] Historians have debated whether the Great Charter's reference to a judgment by peers established for Englishmen the right to trial by jury.[65] Though the foundations of the peer judgment concept may have been laid by the Magna Charta, there is little evidence of any institution even remotely resembling the modern petit jury until

[62] *Id.;* People v. Jelke, 308 NY 56, 123 NE(2d) 769 (1954). *But see* Robertson v. State, 64 Fla 437, 60 So 118 (1912); People v. Nyhus, 19 ND 326, 124 NW 71 (1909).

[63] Estes v. Texas, 381 US 532, 549, 14 LEd(2d) 543, 555, 85 SCt 1628, 1636 (1965).

[64] MAGNA CHARTA, ch 39, reprinted in R. Perry & J. Cooper, SOURCES OF OUR LIBERTIES 17 (1959).

[65] *Id.* at 7-8; 1 F. Pollock & Maitland, THE HISTORY OF ENGLISH LAW BEFORE THE TIME OF EDWARD I, 173 n.3 (2d ed 1909); 2 J. Story, COMMENTARIES ON THE CONSTITUTION OF THE UNITED STATES, 540-41 (4th ed 1873); Frankfurter & Corcoran, *Petty Federal Offenses and the Constitutional Guaranty of Trial by Jury,* 39 HARVLREV 917, 923 (1926).

the fourteenth century.[66] For a time, the jury method of determining criminal guilt existed in competition with several older forms such as "trial by ordeal" and "trial by battle." [67] Gradually, these barbaric practices fell into disuse and the jury system gained pre-eminence. By the time it was transplanted to American soil, the common-law petit jury—an impartial tribunal consisting of twelve laymen assembled to listen to evidence adduced in open court and to render a verdict by unanimous decision—had a tradition dating back several centuries.

William Blackstone, writing in 1768, hailed the jury principle as the "glory of English law" and "the most transcendent privilege which any subject can enjoy or wish for." [68] While Blackstone's accolades may appear extravagant to the twentieth century reader, his sentiments typify eighteenth-century thinking. Those who drafted our Constitution were men of the times; they held the jury principle in such esteem that double precautionary measures were taken. Article III, section 2 of the 1787 Constitution ensured that "[t]he Trial of all Crimes, except in Cases of Impeachment, shall be by Jury. . . ." Two years later, the Sixth Amendment added the further guarantee that "[i]n all criminal prosecutions, the accused shall enjoy the right to . . . trial, by an impartial jury. . . ."

The jury system offers several unique advantages over other methods of adjudicating criminal guilt. First, the jury is a democratic institution. It affords citizens an opportunity to participate in the administration of criminal justice, and through participation, to gain an insight into the workings of their judiciary. Shared responsibility enhances public trust in the integrity of criminal verdicts. Second, the jury, being drawn from a representative cross-section of the community, reflects the conscience of the community and its sense of justice and mercy. The jury thus interjects humanizing qualities into a depersonalized penal system. Finally, and most importantly, the jury constitutes a fundamental safeguard

[66] Id.

[67] Wells, *The Origin of the Petty Jury*, 27 LQRev 347, 357 (1911); see also, Cornish, THE JURY 10-12 (1968).

[68] 3 W. Blackstone, COMMENTARIES *379.

against miscarriages of justice. Mr. Justice White, writing in *Duncan* v. *Louisiana*,[69] summarized the protective function of the jury:

> A right to jury trial is granted to criminal defendants in order to prevent oppression by the Government. Those who wrote our constitutions knew from history and experience that it was necessary to protect against unfounded criminal charges brought to eliminate enemies and against judges too responsive to the voice of higher authority. The framers of the constitutions strove to create an independent judiciary but insisted upon further protection against arbitrary action. Providing an accused with the right to be tried by a jury of his peers gave him an inestimable safeguard against the corrupt or overzealous prosecutor and against the compliant, biased, or eccentric judge. If the defendant preferred the common-sense judgment of a jury to the more tutored but perhaps less sympathetic reaction of the single judge, he was to have it. . . .[70]

Despite the central role which the jury has occupied in the Anglo-American scheme of criminal justice for the past several centuries, it was not until 1968 that state criminal defendants acquired jury trial rights under the United States Constitution coextensive with those enjoyed in a federal court. In *Duncan* v. *Louisiana*,[71] the Supreme Court announced that the Sixth Amendment right to jury trial qualified for protection under the Fourteenth Amendment due process clause and that the states were obliged to furnish jury trials in all cases which, if tried in a federal court, would come within the Sixth Amendment guarantee.

The constitutional right to a jury trial may not be defeated through indirection. In *United States* v. *Jackson*,[72] the Supreme Court struck down the capital punishment provisions of the Federal Kidnapping Act. The Act authorized the jury, upon finding the defendant guilty, to impose the death penalty, but limited the maximum punishment inflictable at a non-jury trial to life imprisonment. The inevitable impact of such enhanced punishment was to discourage defendants from as-

---

[69] 391 US 145, 20 LEd(2d) 491, 88 SCt 1444 (1968).

[70] *Id.* at 155-56, 20 LEd(2d) at 499-500, 88 SCt at 1451 (footnote omitted).

[71] 391 US 145, 20 LEd(2d) 491, 88 SCt 1444 (1968).

[72] 390 US 570, 20 LEd(2d) 138, 88 SCt 1209 (1968).

serting their constitutional right to a jury trial. Legislatures are precluded from establishing one form of punishment applicable to those who assert their right to contest their guilt before a jury, and another less serious form available in other instances. Institutionalized deterrents to requesting trial by jury are offensive to the Sixth Amendment.

§ 10.7   —Offenses for which jury trials are not constitutionally required

At the time the Constitution was adopted, there existed under the English common law a limited number of instances where jury trials were unavailable.[73] The defendant had no right to a jury in cases of "petty offenses."[74] Similar exclusions were common throughout the colonies. But when the Constitution defined the jury trial rights of the accused, it did so in comprehensive language. Article III, section 2 jury-trial protection extended to the "Trial of all Crimes," while the Sixth Amendment mandate embraced "all criminal prosecutions."

Despite this broad and unequivocal language, the Supreme Court has consistently interpreted the Constitution as perpetuating the historical distinction between petty and serious offenses. The major controversies have centered, not on whether petty offenses are subject to a jury trial requirement, but on developing criteria for locating the Sixth Amendment boundary line. The felony-misdemeanor distinction was not a workable tool.[75] Some misdemeanors might be extremely serious, carrying significant penalties and doing measurable reputational damage. In a series of cases, the Supreme Court wavered between an objective one-factor approach based upon punishment severity and more individualized analysis.[76] In *Baldwin* v. *New York*,[77] the matter was finally settled. The Supreme Court held that the best index of how seriously society

---

[73] Frankfurter & Corcoran, *Petty Federal Offenses and the Constitutional Guaranty of Trial by Jury*, 39 HarvLRev 917, 934 (1926).

[74] *Id.*

[75] Callan v. Wilson, 127 US 540, 32 LEd 223, 8 SCt 1301 (1888).

[76] Note, *The Petty Offender's Constitutional Right to a Jury Trial: The Denial in* Duncan v. Louisiana, 36 TennLRev 763 (1969).

[77] 399 US 66, 26 LEd(2d) 437, 90 SCt 1886 (1970).

regards a crime is the punishment it authorizes for the offender. The boundary line between petty and serious offenses for jury trial purposes was fixed at six months' imprisonment. Where the accused faces possible incarceration for a longer period, he has a right to have a jury determine his guilt. The definition of a petty offense as one carrying no more than a six-month penalty was adopted as a rule of administrative convenience. Where the maximum sentence inflictable falls below the six-month limit, the advantages flowing from speedy and inexpensive non-jury adjudications were deemed to offset any possible hardship visited upon a petty offender of being tried without a jury.

Under the common law, there was no right to a jury trial on criminal contempt charges. Contempts were not regarded as crimes and could be tried summarily by the judge without regard to the penalty imposed. The common-law method of trying criminal contempts was deemed to be constitutionally permissible as late as 1968, and individuals were sometimes given long prison terms without the benefit of a jury decision.[78] This practice was doubly oppressive since it placed in the hands of the judge whose orders had been flaunted the power to sit as judge, jury and prosecutor in vindicating his own authority. It was partly for this reason that the Supreme Court in *Bloom v. Illinois*,[79] expanded the jury trial guarantee to serious criminal contempts. Six months is now the maximum sentence that a judge may impose upon a conviction for criminal contempt without impaneling a jury.[80]

There is no right to a jury trial in proceedings before a military tribunal even when brought for serious charges.[81] Nor are jury trials available as a matter of constitutional right in juvenile court proceedings.[82]

---

[78] Green v. United States, 356 US 165, 2 LEd(2d) 672, 78 SCt 632 (1958).

[79] 391 US 194, 20 LEd(2d) 522, 88 SCt 1477 (1968).

[80] Frank v. United States, 395 US 147, 23 LEd(2d) 162, 89 SCt 1503 (1969).

[81] Ex parte Milligan, 71 US(4 Wall) 2, 122, 18 LEd 281, 296 (1886). See also Dennis, *Jury Trial and the Federal Constitution*, 6 ColumLRev 423 (1906).

[82] McKeiver v. Pennsylvania, 403 US 528, 29 LEd(2d) 647, 91 SCt 1976 (1971).

§ 10.8   —Size of jury

The petit or trial jury, as it evolved at common law, consisted of twelve men who were selected at random from the community and whose function was to hear all the evidence in open court and reach a unanimous decision regarding the defendant's guilt or innocence of the charges leveled against him. When the jury concept was brought to America, its common-law characteristics were maintained. This pattern still prevails in the federal courts and in most state systems.

Several decades ago, there was a reform movement to streamline judicial administration, and one suggestion was to reduce the size of petit juries. Several jurisdictions implemented the proposal. In Florida, Louisiana, South Carolina, Texas and Utah, less than twelve-member juries were established for felonies, and in at least eight jurisdictions, misdemeanor juries were reduced to below the traditional common-law number.[83] Until *Duncan* v. *Louisiana*,[84] which incorporated the Sixth Amendment jury trial guarantee into the Fourteenth Amendment guarantee and made it binding upon the states, these local experiments were not a matter of federal constitutional concern. But once the states became subject to Sixth Amendment jury trial mandates, the question was presented whether reductions in jury size were offensive to the United States Constitution.

This issue was brought to a head in *Williams* v. *Florida*,[85] which challenged the constitutionality of the six-man felony jury provided for under Florida law. The Supreme Court was not writing on a clean slate. Earlier cases had suggested that the common-law jury blueprint was embedded within the Sixth Amendment.[86] In *Williams*, however, the Supreme Court reassessed the matter and determined that, history aside, the number twelve was not an immutable corollary of the Sixth Amendment right to a jury trial. Mr. Justice White, who wrote

---

[83] Williams v. Florida, 399 US 78, 99 n. 45, 26 LEd(2d) 446, 459, 90 SCt 1893, 1905 (1970).

[84] 391 US 145, 20 LEd(2d) 491, 88 SCt 1444 (1968).

[85] 399 US 78, 26 LEd(2d) 446, 90 SCt 1983 (1970).

[86] Rasmussen v. United States, 197 US 516, 49 LEd 862, 25 SCt 514 (1905); Maxwell v. Dow, 176 US 581, 44 LEd 597, 20 SCt 448 (1900); Thompson v. Utah, 170 US 343, 42 LEd 1061, 18 SCt 620 (1898).

the majority opinion, determined that the relevant inquiry was not whether a particular feature was buttressed by centuries of tradition, but whether it is critical to the jury's constitutional role. Having cast the inquiry in this form, Mr. Justice White concluded:

> [T]he essential feature of a jury obviously lies in the interposition between the accused and his accuser of the commonsense judgment of a group of laymen, and in the community participation and shared responsibility that results [sic] from that group's determination of guilt or innocence. The performance of this role is not a function of the particular number of the body that makes up the jury. To be sure, the number should probably be large enough to promote group deliberation, free from outside attempts at intimidation, and to provide a fair possibility for obtaining a representative cross-section of the community. But we find little reason to think that these goals are in any meaningful sense less likely to be achieved when the jury numbers six, than when it numbers 12. . . . And, certainly the reliability of the jury as a factfinder hardly seems likely to be a function of its size.[87]

§ 10.9　—Unanimous verdicts

Under the common law, the jury's decision had to represent the unanimous consensus of all its members. If the entire body was unable to agree on one of the two alternatives, a mistrial resulted. A hung jury operates neither as an acquittal nor a conviction; it leaves the door open for further criminal proceedings.[88]

The practice of requiring unanimous verdicts in criminal cases was firmly entrenched in Anglo-American jurisprudence when the Constitution was drafted, and remains the prevailing practice throughout the nation today. Only two jurisdictions have dispensed with the common-law unanimity requirement where there is at stake a possible punishment in excess of a year's imprisonment. In Louisiana, a three-fourths majority vote is sufficient to render a non-capital felony verdict,[89] while in Oregon the concurrence of five-sixths of the jurors is necessary.[90] Though several other jurisdictions have dis-

---

[87] 399 US at 100-01, 26 LEd(2d) at 460, 90 SCt at 1906 (1970).

[88] Review §9.6 supra.

[89] LaStatAnn, CodeCrimPro, art 782 (1966).

[90] OreConst, art 1, §11; OreRevStat §§136.330, 136.610 (1967).

pensed with the need for unanimity in misdemeanor trials, Louisiana and Oregon stand alone in authorizing majority verdicts in felony prosecutions. These local experiments were undertaken in an effort to reduce the frequency of hung juries, thereby eliminating some measure of the costs and delays attendant upon recurring mistrials.[91]

Adaptation of the jury to accommodate diverse local situations was unobjectionable prior to *Duncan v. Louisiana*,[92] since the states were under no federal constitutional compulsion to accord jury trials at all. But the 1968 ruling, applying Sixth Amendment jury trial standards to the states, triggered the need for a fresh look at state majority criminal verdict practices.

The opportunity was presented in *Apocado v. Oregon*,[93] challenging whether jury unanimity was indispensable to a constitutionally valid verdict. (Oregon, it should be recalled, is one of the two jurisdictions authorizing majority verdicts in felony prosecutions.) The Supreme Court split five to four in favor of upholding *state* criminal convictions based upon less-than-unanimous verdicts. When all the concurring and dissenting opinions are tallied, however, five justices (Stewart, Brennan, Marshall, Douglas and Powell) took the position that jury unanimity is a mandatory feature of the Sixth Amendment guarantee of trial by jury, while only four (White, Burger, Blackmun and Rehnquist) subscribed to the contrary view. Mr. Justice Powell provided the pivotal swing vote necessary to create a majority in favor of upholding the Oregon jury practice. He agreed that unanimous verdicts were an indispensable feature of the Sixth Amendment jury trial guarantee as it applied in *federal* proceedings, but rejected as unsound the premise that when a given procedural safeguard is incorporated into the Fourteenth Amendment and made binding upon state jurisdictions, coextensive application is required. He saw no inconsistency in exacting different jury verdict standards in state and federal trials despite the

---

[91] Comment, *Should Jury Verdicts Be Unanimous in Criminal Cases?*, 47 OreLRev 417 (1968).

[92] 391 US 145, 20 LEd(2d) 491, 88 SCt 1444 (1968).

[93] 406 US 404, 32 LEd(2d) 184, 92 SCt 1628 (1972).

Supreme Court's mandate four years before in *Duncan* v. *Louisiana*.[94] Mr. Justice Powell's vote carried the day. *Apocado* v. *Oregon* may embark the Supreme Court upon a trend of defederalizing some other aspects of the Bill of Rights as they apply to the states. In the context of jury trials, the Sixth Amendment requires a unanimous verdict to convict in a federal criminal proceeding, but is satisfied by less when the trial takes place in a state.

§ 10.10   —Composition of the jury

In order to be constituted in conformity with Sixth Amendment requirements, the petit jury must be drawn from a source fairly representative of the community.[95] The systematic exclusion of any cognizable group or class of qualified citizens from the pool of potential jurors is constitutionally offensive.[96] The reasons for the Sixth Amendment's fair cross-section requirement were explained by Mr. Justice Marshall in *Peters* v. *Kiff*,[97] a case challenging the racial composition of the jury pool:

> [A] State cannot, consistent with due process, subject a defendant to indictment or trial by a jury that has been selected in an arbitrary and discriminatory manner, in violation of the Constitution and laws of the United States. Illegal and unconstitutional jury selection procedures cast doubt on the integrity of the whole judicial process. They create the appearance of bias in the decision of individual cases, and they increase the risk of actual bias as well.
>
> . . . .
>
> [T]he exclusion from jury service of a substantial and identifiable class of citizens has a potential impact that is too subtle and too pervasive to admit of confinement to particular issues or particular cases. . . .
>
> [W]e are unwilling to make the assumption that the exclusion of Negroes has relevance only for issues involving race. When any large and identifiable segment of the community is excluded from jury service, the effect is to remove from the jury room qualities of human nature and varieties of human experience, the range of which is unknown and perhaps unknowable. It is not necessary to

[94] 391 US 145, 20 LEd(2d) 491, 88 SCt 1444 (1968). *Duncan* is discussed in §10.6 *supra.*

[95] Taylor v. Louisiana, 419 US 522, 42 LEd(2d) 690, 95 SCt 692 (1975).

[96] *Id.*

[97] 407 US 493, 33 LEd(2d) 83, 92 SCt 2163 (1972).

assume that the excluded group will consistently vote as a class in order to conclude . . . that their exclusion deprives the jury of a perspective on human events that may have unsuspected importance in any case that may be presented.[98]

To place the constitutional cross-section requirement in its operative context, some insight into the jury selection process is required. The mechanics of jury selection can be divided roughly into four phases. The first phase of the selection process is controlled by the legislature. Statutes exist in all states fixing the qualifications for jury service and establishing statutory exemptions. The typical qualifications for jury service include United States citizenship, local residency, a minimum age requirement and, frequently, the attributes of good character and normal intelligence.[99] From the broad population possessing these qualifications, statutory exemptions are carved out. The exemptions reflect considerations of personal hardship or overriding professional commitments. Persons employed in critical occupations such as government officials, medical personnel, ministers, educators and the like commonly receive exempt status under the law.[100] Jury commissioners are appointed to administer the second and third stages of the jury selection process. During the second phase, the commissioners compile a list of potentially qualified jurors. In some instances, the legislature will prescribe the sources from which the names of prospective jurors must be taken (i.e., from voter registration lists or tax rolls). More commonly, however, the system for selecting prospective jurors is left to the jury commissioners' discretion.[101] Where discretion is allowed, jury commissioners often draw their pools from such diverse sources as telephone directories, public utility lists, club and church membership rolls, recommendations of "key men" in the community, and casual conversations with business acquaintances or friends.[102] The names of

[98] *Id.* at 502-04, 33 LEd(2d) at 93-94, 92 SCt at 2168-69 (footnote omitted).

[99] Note, *The Congress, The Court, and Jury Selection: A Critique of Title I and II of the Civil Rights Bill of 1966*, 52 VaLRev 1069, 1072-1074

(1966), [hereinafter cited as *Jury Selection*].

[100] *Id.*

[101] *Id.* at 1075-1080.

[102] *See, e.g.,* Swain v. Alabama, 380 US 202, 13 LEd(2d) 759, 85 SCt 824 (1965).

the persons thus compiled and found qualified are then placed in a jury wheel or similar device.

The third phase of the selection process is based upon chance or lot. When a jury panel is needed, the jury commissioners will hold a public drawing. The *voir dire* examination constitutes the final phase of the culling process and is conducted by the judge. On *voir dire* examination, the prospective jurors are examined for bias and other disqualifying causes. In order to implement the constitutional guarantee of an impartial tribunal, most states give the prosecutor and defense counsel a limited number of peremptory challenges in addition to the right to reject prospective jurors for cause. Out of this process twelve jurors are ultimately selected.

The Sixth Amendment requires that the jury panel be taken from a *source* reasonably designed to produce a fair cross section of the community.[103] This does not mean that the jury actually chosen must constitute a mirror reflection of the community's economic, racial, sexual and ethnic composition.[104] The actual selection of the jury panel, which occurs in the third stage, results from lot or chance. Random chance, however, is unlikely to produce a democratically constituted jury if the selection procedures up to this point have resulted in an unrepresentative pool. Unconstitutional imbalances in the jury wheel may be built into the system by the legislature during the first phase or by the jury commissioners during the second.

1. Juror qualifications and exemptions

Those who sit on the jury have a responsible task to perform. The traits of character, maturity and judgment which make for a qualified juror are not distributed evenly throughout the general population. Consequently, a jury composed by random sampling techniques from the entire body politic, though the most democratic in its makeup, may contain members ill-suited to performing the jury's task. The Sixth Amendment does not preclude the states from establishing qualifi-

---

[103] Taylor v. Louisiana, 419 US 522,   [104] *Id.*
42 LEd(2d) 690, 95 SCt 692 (1975).

cations for jury service so long as (1) the standards set are reasonably related to the goal of obtaining competent jurors, and (2) the members of the community eligible for jury service under the criteria are fairly representative of the whole.[105] The Supreme Court has been hesitant to interfere with local autonomy in setting juror qualifications.[106]

Virtually all states require jurors to be United States citizens, over twenty-one, and capable of understanding English.[107] These qualifications are relevant and have received judicial approval.[108] Requiring jurors to possess "intelligence,"[109] or "sound judgment,"[110] interjects greater subjectivity into the selection process, but this feature alone is not fatal. In *Carter v. Jury Commission*,[111] a jury qualification statute requiring prospective jurors to be "generally reputed to be honest and intelligent and . . . esteemed in the community for their integrity, good character, and sound judgment . . ."[112] was assailed on the grounds that the subjectivity required in applying these standards afforded an opportunity for discrimination against minorities. The Supreme Court, noting that such statutes are of "ancient vintage,"[113] determined that the mere *potential* for abusive applications did not afford a basis for striking the statute down. The courts will, however, correct actual abuses in administering such criteria if abuses in fact occur.

The common-law jury was composed of twelve *men.* Women did not acquire the right to serve on English juries until 1919.[114] The appearance of women on American juries paralleled the English experience. In some states, however, vestiges of the period when women were disqualified from jury service remained in the form of statutes sparing females

---

[105] *Id.*

[106] *See, e.g.,* Carter v. Jury Comm'n, 396 US 320, 24 LEd(2d) 549, 90 SCt 518 (1970).

[107] *Jury Selection, supra* note 99.

[108] Carter v. Jury Comm'n, 396 US 320, 24 LEd(2d) 549, 90 SCt 518 (1970); United States v. Gordon-Nikkar, 518 F(2d) 972 (5thCir 1975); United States v. Guzman, 337 FSupp 140 (SD NY 1972).

[109] *See, e.g.,* ArizRevStatAnn §20-201 (1956).

[110] *See, e.g.,* SCCodeAnn §38-52 (Supp 1968).

[111] 396 US 320, 24 LEd(2d) 549, 90 SCt 518 (1970).

[112] AlaCode, tit. 30, §21 (Supp 1967).

[113] 396 US at 336, 24 LEd(2d) at 561, 90 SCt at 527.

[114] Act of 1919, 9 & 10 Geo. V, c. 71.

the "burdens" of jury duty unless they actively volunteered, or in the form of statutes granting them automatic exemptions.[115] In *Taylor* v. *Louisiana*,[116] handed down in 1975, the Supreme Court announced that legislatively established qualifications and exemptions which operate to exclude females from jury service are not constitutionally acceptable. Mr. Justice White wrote:

> The States are free to grant exemptions from jury service to individuals in case of special hardship or incapacity and to those engaged in particular occupations the uninterrupted performance of which is critical to the community's welfare. It would not appear that such exemptions would pose substantial threats and that the remaining pool of jurors would not be representative of the community. A system excluding all women, however, is a wholly different matter. . . .
>
> . . . .
>
> Accepting as we do . . . the view that the Sixth Amendment affords the defendant in a criminal trial the opportunity to have the jury drawn from venires representative of the community, we think it is no longer tenable to hold that women as a class may be excluded or given automatic exemptions based solely on sex if the consequence is that criminal jury venires are almost totally male. . . .[117]

2. Prospective juror lists

Most state legislatures have not seen fit to designate the source from which prospective juror lists must be compiled but, rather, have left this matter to the jury commissioners' discretion.[118] Note has already been taken of the varied sources from which names of prospective jurors are taken.[119] If the goal is a representative jury, random sampling techniques from an inclusive list of all persons in the community eligible for jury service is the process best calculated to produce such results. The Supreme Court has in the past, however, been satisfied with a good deal less than this.[120] Prior to *Taylor* v.

---

[115] *Jury Selection, supra* note 99, at 1074 n. 31-32, 1076-77 n. 43.

[116] 419 US 522, 42 LEd(2d) 690, 95 SCt 692 (1975).

[117] *Id.* at 534-37, 42 LEd(2d) at 700-02, 95 SCt at 700-01 (citation omitted).

[118] *Jury Selection, supra* note 99, at 1072-80.

[119] See text *supra.*

[120] Carter v. Jury Comm'n, 396 US 320, 332-33, 24 LEd(2d) 549, 559, 90 SCt 518, 525 (1970).

Louisiana,[121] which made emphatic the states' obligation to comply with the fair cross-section requirement, review standards were lax. A constitutional challenge to the methods by which the names of prospective jurors were compiled required proof of *purposeful discrimination* against an identifiable group on account of race, color, religion, national origin or ethnic background.[122] Purposeful discrimination is a formidable fact to establish. In *Swain v. Alabama*,[123] a Negro defendant found guilty of rape and sentenced to death by an all-white jury, attempted to support his claim of intentional exclusion of Negroes by evidence that:

> [W]hile Negro males over 21 constitute 26% of all males in the county in this age group, only 10 to 15% of the grand and petit jury panels drawn from the jury box since 1953 have been Negroes, there having been only one case in which the percentage was as high as 23%. . . . Although there has been an average of six to seven Negroes on petit jury venires in criminal cases, no Negro has actually served on a petit jury since about 1950.[124]

The jury commissioners testified that they compiled their juror pools from "city directories, registration lists, club and church lists, conversations with other persons in the community, both white and colored, and personal and business acquaintances."[125] They denied that racial considerations entered into their selection procedures. The Supreme Court said:

> Venires drawn from the jury box made up in this manner unquestionably contained a smaller proportion of the Negro community than of the white community. But a defendant in a criminal case is not constitutionally entitled to demand a proportionate number of his race on the jury which tries him nor on the venire or jury roll from which petit jurors are drawn. . . . We cannot say that purposeful discrimination based on race alone is satisfactorily proved by showing that an identifiable group in a community is underrepresented by as much as 10%. . . . *Undoubtedly the selec-*

---

[121] 419 US 522, 42 LEd(2d) 690, 95 SCt 692 (1975).

[122] Swain v. Alabama, 380 US 202, 13 LEd(2d) 759, 85 SCt 824 (1965); Hernandez v. Texas, 347 US 475, 98 LEd 866, 74 SCt 667 (1954); Strauder v. West Virginia, 100 US 303, 25 LEd 664 (1880).

[123] 380 US 202, 13 LEd(2d) 759, 85 SCt 824 (1965).

[124] Id. at 205, 13 LEd(2d) at 764, 85 SCt at 827-28.

[125] Id. at 207, 13 LEd(2d) at 765, 85 SCt at 828-29.

tion of prospective jurors was somewhat haphazard and little effort was made to ensure that all groups in the community were fully represented. But an imperfect system is not equivalent to purposeful discrimination based on race. We do not think that the burden of proof was carried by petitioner in this case.[126]

Since *Swain* v. *Alabama*, however, there have been two significant constitutional developments. In *Peters* v. *Kiff*,[127] decided in 1972, the Supreme Court held that a defendant's standing to challenge unconstitutional selection procedures is not dependent upon a showing that he was a member of the allegedly excluded group or that he has been prejudiced in some manner as a result of the exclusion. *Peters* v. *Kiff* paved the way for *Taylor* v. *Louisiana*,[128] handed down three years later, which decreed that "the presence of a fair cross section of the community on venires, panels or lists from which petit juries are drawn is essential to the fulfillment of the Sixth Amendment's guarantee of an impartial jury trial in criminal prosecutions.[129] Though the *Taylor* Court took precautions to point out that

> in holding that petit juries must be drawn from a source fairly representative of the community we impose no requirement that petit juries actually chosen must mirror the community and reflect the various distinctive groups in the population,[130]

the case indicates that the Supreme Court is now willing to assume a greater supervisory role over the composition of state juries. Under the review standards established in *Swain*, purposeful discrimination was required before a defendant could challenge the unrepresentative character of his jury. Though purposeful discrimination could be inferred from consistent underrepresentation of identifiable groups on source lists, such underrepresentation had to be dramatic before a court would draw this inference.[131] *Taylor* v. *Louisiana*,[132] while

---

[126] *Id.* at 208-09, 13 LEd(2d) at 766, 85 SCt at 829-30 (emphasis added) (footnote omitted).

[127] 407 US 493, 33 LEd(2d) 83, 92 SCt 2163 (1972).

[128] 419 US 522, 42 LEd(2d) 690, 95 SCt 692 (1975).

[129] *Id.* at 526, 42 LEd(2d) at 696, 95 SCt at 696.

[130] *Id.* at 538, 42 LEd(2d) at 703, 95 SCt at 702.

[131] *See, e.g.,* Avery v. Georgia, 345 US 559, 97 LEd 1244, 73 SCt 891 (1953).

[132] 419 US 522, 42 LEd(2d) 690, 95 SCt 692 (1975).

not addressing the specific issue, can be read as placing an active duty upon state governments to utilize selection procedures and source lists designed to produce fairly representative juries. It seems improbable that the *Taylor* Court would be willing to affirm a criminal conviction after finding that "the selection of prospective jurors was somewhat haphazard and little effort made to ensure that all groups in the community were . . . represented."[133]

§ 10.11   —Waiver of right to jury trial

The Sixth Amendment provides that "[i]n all criminal prosecutions, the accused shall enjoy the right to a . . . trial by an impartial jury. . . ." No mention is made of the right to waive a jury and plead one's case before a judge. Under the common law of England when our Constitution was adopted, this right was not recognized.[134] Although technically the "consent" of the accused was required before he could be subjected to a jury trial, if he initially was recalcitrant, he would be tortured until he submitted.[135] In 1772, England ceased torturing defendants who refused to consent to trial before a jury, but it was not until decades later that the concept of bench trials gained acceptance.[136] Though bench trials are provided for in the United States, many jurisdictions do not give the accused unrestricted control over whether his case is tried by a jury or a judge. His right to waive trial by jury may be conditioned upon the approval of the court, the prosecutor, or both.[137] In the federal system, waivers are governed by Rule 23(a) of the Federal Rules of Criminal Procedure:

> Cases required to be tried by jury shall be so tried unless the defendant waives a jury trial in writing with the approval of the court and the consent of the government.

In *Singer v. United States*,[138] a defendant, who was forced to undergo a jury trial because the prosecution refused its

---

[133] Swain v. Alabama, 380 US 202, 13 LEd(2d) 759, 85 SCt 824 (1965).

[134] Singer v. United States, 380 US 24, 27-28, 13 LEd(2d) 630, 633-34, 85 SCt 783, 786 (1965).

[135] *Id.*

[136] *Id.*

[137] Note, 51 CORNELLLQ 339, 342-43 (1966).

[138] 380 US 24, 13 LEd(2d) 630, 85 SCt 783 (1965).

consent to his attempted waiver, challenged the constitutionality of Rule 23(a) insofar as it conditioned his right to forego trial by jury upon the government's approval. His theory essentially was that the Sixth Amendment guarantee of a jury trial implied the correlative right to forego the jury and have the case decided by the judge if the accused considered the latter mode of trial more advantageous. Reviewing historical evidence, the Supreme Court concluded that neither the common law nor the Constitution recognized the right to demand trial before a judge sitting without a jury. The Court then proceeded to demolish the defendant's remaining arguments:

> In light of the Constitution's emphasis on jury trial, we find it difficult to understand how the petitioner can submit the bald proposition that to compel a defendant in a criminal case to undergo a jury trial against his will is contrary to his right to a fair trial or to due process. A defendant's only constitutional right concerning the method of trial is to an impartial trial by jury. We find no constitutional impediment to conditioning a waiver of this right on the consent of the prosecuting attorney and the trial judge when, if either refuses to consent, the result is simply that the defendant is subject to an impartial trial by jury—the very thing that the Constitution guarantees him. . . .[139]

§ 10.12　Fair and impartial trial

Regardless of the mode of trial, whether it is before a judge or jury, the accused is entitled to have his guilt determined by an impartial tribunal. The assurance of a fair and impartial trial is a basic ingredient of the due process of law guaranteed by the Fifth and Fourteenth Amendments. With regard to the presiding judge, due process requires that he be detached and disinterested in the outcome. In *Tumey* v. *Ohio*,[110] the Supreme Court set aside a criminal conviction because the judge who tried the case had a direct pecuniary interest in the outcome. (His salary was paid from fees and costs levied against those who were convicted.) This method of compensating the judge offered a potent inducement to resolve doubtful cases in favor of fee-generating guilty verdicts.

---

[139] *Id.* at 36, 13 LEd(2d) at 638, 85 SCt at 790.

[110] 273 US 510, 71 LEd 749, 47 SCt 437 (1927). See also, Ward v. Village of Monroeville, 409 US 57, 34 LEd(2d) 267, 93 SCt 80 (1972).

The accused is entitled to be tried before a neutral and un-biased judge even though he bears responsibility for pre-disposing the judge against him. In *Mayberry v. Pennsyl-vania*,[141] the accused insisted upon representing himself and during the course of a lengthy trial, addressed numerous in-sulting and slanderous remarks to the judge. His excesses included calling the judge a "hatchet man for the state,"[142] a "dirty sonofabitch,"[143] a "tyrannical old dog,"[144] a "bum,"[145] a "nut,"[146] and a "fool."[147] Mayberry repeatedly ignored rul-ings from the bench and voiced his displeasure when his motions were overruled by telling the judge to "shut up" and, "Go to hell."[148] Toward the end of the trial, he became so insolent and abusive that the judge found it necessary to gag him and to remove him temporarily from the courtroom. After the jury had returned a verdict, the judge found the defendant guilty of multiple counts of contempt for his conduct during the trial and sentenced him to between eleven and twenty-two years in prison. Though characterizing this conduct as "a shock to those raised in the Western tradition,"[149] and "not 'befitting an American courtroom,'"[150] the Supreme Court unanimously reversed the contempt convictions on the ground that a trial judge who has been the target of personal abuse should step down at the end of the trial and turn the contempt proceedings over to another judge, one who is "not bearing the sting of . . . slanderous remarks."[151] The accused does not forfeit his right to a fair trial before an impartial tribunal because he deliberately engages in conduct that provokes any bias or prejudice against him.

Where a case is tried before a jury, subtle influences, such as appearing before the jury in prison clothing, may tip the

[141] 400 US 455, 27 LEd(2d) 532, 91 SCt 499 (1971).

[142] *Id.* at 456, 27 LEd(2d) at 535, 91 SCt at 501.

[143] *Id.*

[144] *Id.* at 457, 27 LEd(2d) at 536, 91 SCt at 501.

[145] *Id.* at 458, 27 LEd(2d) at 536, 91 SCt at 501.

[146] *Id.* at 460, 27 LEd(2d) at 537, 91 SCt at 503.

[147] *Id.* at 461, 27 LEd(2d) at 538, 91 SCt at 503.

[148] *Id.* at 458, 27 LEd(2d) at 536, 91 SCt at 502.

[149] *Id.* at 456, 27 LEd(2d) at 535, 91 SCt at 500.

[150] *Id.* at 462, 27 LEd(2d) at 538, 91 SCt at 504.

[151] *Id.* at 466, 27 LEd(2d) at 540, 91 SCt at 505.

delicate balance against the accused. In *Estelle* v. *Williams*,[152] the Supreme Court held that the government may not compel a criminal defendant to stand trial before a jury while dressed in prison garments, because in the layperson's mind prison garments may be associated with guilt.

Fundamental to the notion of a fair trial is the requirement that the defendant's guilt be established on the basis of evidence developed inside the courtroom and on the witness stand where the defendant is protected by counsel and has an opportunity for cross-examination.[153] Jury contacts with out-of-court information concerning the issues involved in a case may reach due process proportions if the exposure occurs under circumstances which create a substantial risk that the jurors' judgments may have been influenced. In *Turner* v. *Louisiana*,[154] the Supreme Court overturned a conviction in which two deputy sheriffs, who had been key prosecution witnesses, functioned as jury custodians during the three-day trial. Although there was no evidence that the deputies actually discussed the case outside the courtroom, the verdict depended, in large measure, upon whether or not the jury credited the testimony of these two witnesses on various disputed facts. The three-day period of close association between the jurors and these two witnesses necessarily had some impact upon the jury's assessment of their testimonial credibility. In light of the fact that the weight to be assigned their testimony was a significant factor in the case, and that the jury may have credited their rendition of disputed facts because of extraneous influences, the integrity of the verdict was called into question and a new trial was required.

The Supreme Court has become increasingly sensitive to potentially harmful irregularities in the jury process. In *Parker* v. *Gladden*,[155] the Supreme Court ruled that the extra-judicial remarks, made by the bailiff to several jury members, to the effect that the accused was a "wicked fellow" and "guilty," violated the defendant's right to a fair trial before an impartial jury.

[152] 425 US 501, 48 LEd(2d) 126, 96 SCt 1691 (1976).

[153] Parker v. Gladden, 385 US 363, 17 LEd(2d) 420, 87 SCt 468 (1966).

[154] 379 US 466, 13 LEd(2d) 424, 85 SCt 546 (1965).

[155] 385 US 363, 17 LEd(2d) 420, 87 SCt 468 (1966).

§ 10.13   —Prejudicial media coverage

The media has traditionally played an influential role in the shaping of public opinion. When the opinion thus molded relates to the guilt or innocence of an untried criminal defendant, there is a head-on collision between freedom of the press and the right to a fair trial. Mr. Justice Frankfurter identified the problem when he inquired:

> How can fallible men and women reach a disinterested verdict based exclusively on what they heard in court when, before they entered the jury box, their minds were saturated by press and radio for months preceding by matter designed to establish the guilt of the accused.[156]

Few cases have captivated public interest as much as the Dr. Samuel Sheppard murder trial of the fifties. Even before formal charges had been placed against Sheppard, the news media had proclaimed his guilt and were pressuring for "justice." For months, the headlines of local newspapers were saturated with stories of his lack of cooperation with the authorities, his refusal to take a lie detector test, his illicit love affairs, interviews with "bombshell witnesses," and other inflammatory revelations. At Sheppard's trial, the courtroom was jammed with news media representatives. To facilitate more detailed coverage, the judge permitted broadcasting equipment to be installed in vacant courthouse rooms. Although media representatives were not permitted to take pictures inside the courtroom while the trial was in session, the jurors and witnesses were rushed by photographers and reporters waiting in the corridors whenever they entered or left. Verbatim records of the trial proceedings along with editorialized comments and reactions were published daily by the newspapers. Newspaper clippings alone filled five volumes.[157] Sheppard's trial was, in the words of the state appeals court, a " 'Roman holiday' for the news media," [158] and in the words of the United States Supreme Court, permeated by a

---

[156] Irvin v. Dowd, 366 US 717, 729-30, 6 LEd(2d) 751, 760, 81 SCt 1639, 1646 (1961) (Frankfurter, J., concurring).

[157] Sheppard v. Maxwell, 384 US 333, 342, 16 LEd(2d) 600, 608, 86 SCt 1507, 1512 (1966).

[158] Id. at 356, 16 LEd(2d) 616, 86 SCt at 1519.

"carnival atmosphere."[159] Sam Sheppard ultimately won a reversal of his conviction.[160] Though his case was extreme, the underlying problem is a recurrent one.

The defendant's right to a fair trial before an impartial tribunal can be eroded by an irresponsible media. Where the community has been bombarded in advance of trial with prejudicial publicity, selecting a constitutionally acceptable jury may become well-nigh impossible.[161]

1. Constitutional standards

In a nation where most citizens either read the newspaper or own radios or televisions, the facts associated with names like Jack Ruby, Watergate, Charles Manson, and Patricia Hearst are likely to come to the attention of virtually all persons qualified for jury service. On a local level, every community periodically has a crime sensation. If by its very nature media exposure to the facts involved in a pending criminal case were enough to disqualify a prospective juror, jury trials would be available in routine cases only. The due process test of impartiality is not whether the prospective juror is totally unfamiliar with the facts and issues involved, or even whether he holds a "preconceived notion as to the guilt or innocence of an accused."[162] The standard is whether "the juror can lay aside his impression or opinion and render a verdict based on evidence presented in court."[163] His affirmations on *voir dire* that he is equal to this task do not, of course, preclude the defendant from controverting the matter.

It is possible to distill from Supreme Court cases several factors relevant to a determination of whether pretrial publicity has exceeded the constitutional danger zone and calls for corrective measures.

---

[159] *Id.* at 358, 16 LEd(2d) at 618, 86 SCt at 1520.

[160] 384 US 333, 16 LEd(2d) 600, 86 SCt 1507.

[161] Rideau v. Louisiana, 373 US 723, 10 LEd(2d) 663, 83 SCt 1417 (1963); Irvin v. Dowd, 366 US 717, 6 LEd(2d) 751, 81 SCt 1639 (1961); United States v. Abbott Laboratories, 369 FSupp 1396 (ED NC 1973).

[162] Irvin v. Dowd, 366 US 717, 723, 6 LEd(2d) 751, 756, 81 SCt 1639, 1642 (1961). See also, Murphy v. Florida, 421 US 794, 44 LEd(2d) 589, 95 SCt 2031 (1975).

[163] See cases cited in note 162, *supra.*

(a) *Substance of publicity*

There is a tremendous difference between the prejudicing influence of a straightforward, factual account of the details of the crime and an editorialized indictment. Sensationalism in crime reporting is journalism at its worst. Even factual reporting can be damaging if it leads to the disclosure of items later ruled inadmissible, such as the existence of a confession.[164] In *Rideau v. Louisiana*,[165] the Supreme Court reversed a conviction where the accused was tried in a community repeatedly exposed to a televised broadcast from the jail, in which he confessed to the details of a brutal rape-murder in response to the sheriff's leading questions. The Court found it conjectural whether Rideau could receive a fair trial after the entire community had seen and heard him admit his guilt in front of television cameras.

(b) *Pervasiveness of publicity*

Quantitative, as well as qualitative considerations are relevant.[166] Where the publicity is pervasive, few can escape exposure; and, though exposure itself is not fatal, it may lead to a prejudiced jury.

(c) *Recentness of publicity*

The length of time between the publicity and the trial has significance.[167] The probability of finding twelve impartial jurors increases when the trial is held months or years after the information flood has subsided.[168] A juror's exposure *during the trial* to extrajudicial reports can be highly damaging; but this is readily preventable.[169] Where the case is controversial or likely to provoke widespread publicity, the judge can sequester, or isolate, the jurors from public contacts while the trial is not in session.[170]

[164] See cases cited in note 162, *supra.*

[165] 373 US 723, 10 LEd(2d) 663, 83 SCt 1417 (1963).

[166] Sheppard v. Maxwell, 384 US 333, 16 LEd(2d) 600, 86 SCt 1507 (1966).

[167] Wansley v. Slayton, 487 F(2d) 90, 93-94 (4thCir 1973).

[168] United States v. Concepcion Cueto, 515 F(2d) 160, 164 (1stCir 1975); United States v. Bowe, 360 F(2d) 1, 12 (2dCir 1966).

[169] See cases cited in note 168, *supra.*

[170] Sheppard v. Maxwell, 384 US 333, 16 LEd(2d) 600, 86 SCt 1507 (1966).

(d) Attitudes revealed on voir dire

The jury lists, if properly compiled, should contain a representative cross section of the community.[171] The attitudes revealed by prospective jurors during their *voir dire* examination, therefore, constitute a good index of community prejudice. In *Murphy v. Florida*,[172] the Supreme Court instructed:

> The length to which the trial judge must go in order to select jurors who appear to be impartial is ... [a] factor relevant in evaluating those jurors' assurances of impartiality. In a community where most veniremen will admit to a disqualifying prejudice, the reliability of the others' protestations may be drawn into question; for it is more probable that they are part of a community deeply hostile to the accused, and more likely that they may unwittingly have been influenced by it.[173]

For six months preceding the trial in *Irvin v. Dowd*,[174] the media bombarded the community with headline stories relating the defendant's confession to six murders and twenty-four burglaries, his previous criminal record, his attorney's plea bargain attempts, the prosecutor's determination to secure the death penalty, *ad nauseam*. The result of the *voir dire* revealed a community sentiment intensely hostile toward the defendant. Ninety per cent of all veniremen examined, by their own admission, were uncertain of their ability to render an impartial verdict based upon the evidence adduced at the trial. Eight of the twelve jurors selected for the case indicated preconceived notions that the defendant was guilty but, despite this, affirmed their ability to act impartially. The Supreme Court reversed the conviction. The *voir dire* examination furnished the triggering factor. The Court said:

> Where so many, so many times, admitted prejudice, such a statement of impartiality [by the jurors actually selected] can be given little weight.[175]

---

[171] Review §10.10, *supra.*

[172] 421 US 794, 44 LEd(2d) 589, 95 SCt 2031 (1975).

[173] *Id.* at 803-04, 44 LEd(2d) at 597, 95 SCt at 2037.

[174] 366 US 717, 6 LEd(2d) 751, 81 SCt 1639 (1961).

[175] *Id.* at 728, 6 LEd(2d) at 759, 81 SCt at 1645.

2. Remedial measures

Even though the community has been saturated with prejudicial pre-trial publicity, several curative measures of varying degrees of efficacy may be available. The first possible corrective is, of course, to conduct a probing *voir dire* examination of each prospective juror in order to eliminate those who entertain a bias or prejudice that might color their verdict. But, as *Irvin* v. *Dowd* shows, where a community has been thoroughly immersed, *voir dire* examinations are unlikely to discover, let alone to eliminate, subliminal prejudices. In such a case, thought must be given to other remedies for disinfecting a hostile community sentiment. One possible solution is to grant a trial continuance until the impact of the adverse publicity has abated. Though delay has antiseptic value as a method for assuring a fair trial, it suffers from one serious drawback. Repairing the damage done to one constitutional right is effected at the cost of injury to another. By the time the case has passed into semi-oblivion, it may no longer be possible to accord the accused a speedy criminal trial.[176] In the tradeoff, the accused has been forced to forgo his right to a speedy trial at the cost of obtaining an impartial tribunal which is no more than his constitutional due.

Where the publicity has been localized, changing the venue of the trial to some other community affords an alternative to delay.[177] In some instances, this method of counteracting prejudicial publicity may be required as a matter of constitutional law.[178] A change of venue is of dubious value, however, where the case has become a nationwide *cause célèbre*. No community is so remote that names like Lee Harvey Oswald are foreign. When contaminating disclosures have been spread across the nation's headlines and television screens until the point of exhaustion, the defendant may be forced into the "Hobson's choice" of accepting a delayed trial or foregoing the jury entirely.

---

[176] Speedy trial guarantee is discussed in §§10.2-10.4, *supra*.

[177] Groppi v. Wisconsin, 400 US 505, 510, 27 LEd(2d) 571, 575-76, 91 SCt 490, 493 (1971). See also, Shep- pard v. Maxwell, 384 US 333, 16 LEd(2d) 600, 86 SCt 1507 (1966).

[178] Groppi v. Wisconsin, 400 US 505, 27 LEd(2d) 571, 91 SCt 490 (1971).

Contaminated disclosures which arise *during the trial* can be counteracted more readily. Once the jury has been impaneled, the judge can issue cautionary instructions to the jurors to refrain from reading or listening to any extrajudicial discussions about the case, or where circumstances indicate that this might not be effective, the judge can isolate the jury from all public contact for the duration of the trial, a remedy known as "sequestration." Even this remedy, however, is not without its flaws. If the jurors are kept from their friends and families for weeks, latent hostilities directed against the defendant may develop.

Probing *voir dire* examinations, trial continuances, changes of venue and sequestration are, at best, palliatives. Their utility in a given case can never be measured precisely, and their use is frequently accompanied by additional public costs, vexatious delays, or sacrifice of some other constitutional rights. Attempting to purify the local climate of opinion, does not offer a realistic solution to the problem.

In England, the problem of sensational crime reporting is kept within bounds by liberal use of contempt powers against irresponsible media representatives. The press and broadcast media in the United States, however, enjoy greater free speech immunity because of the First Amendment. The Supreme Court has given unceremonious reception to the application of contempt powers to control the press.[179] First Amendment rights, however, are not absolute. The resolution of First Amendment controversies calls for a balancing of competing interests.[180] Would the Supreme Court tolerate some restrictions upon the press to protect the accused's right to a fair trial before an impartial jury? In a 1972 case dealing with an unrelated issue, the Supreme Court held out a candle of hope.[181] Four years later, when a Nebraska judge entered a "gag order" restraining media representatives from certain disclosures about a sensational mass murder case then pending, the Supreme Court bit its tongue and, in a unanimous

[179] *See, e.g.,* Pennekamp v. Florida, 328 US 331, 90 LEd 1295, 66 SCt 1029 (1946); Bridges v. California, 314 US 252, 86 LEd 192, 62 SCt 190 (1941).

[180] Interest balancing is discussed in §2.5, *supra.*

[181] Branzburg v. Hayes, 408 US 665, 685, 33 LEd(2d) 626, 641, 92 SCt 2646, 2658 (1972).

opinion, ruled that the Nebraska judge had no business telling the press what crime news it could report.[152] Even though a free press may not always be a responsible one, the Supreme Court's 1976 ruling in the Nebraska press case strongly suggests that the solution must be looked for elsewhere than in commanding the media to abstain from various disclosures.

If the question is asked how the Nebraska media representatives acquired the information the judge was attempting to quiet, the solution becomes apparent immediately. Police, prosecutors, defense attorneys and prospective witnesses are the persons most familiar with the case; they are, therefore, the group most likely to be contacted for "scoops."

In the Dr. Sam Sheppard case,[153] the Supreme Court outlined a number of precautionary measures available to trial judges to protect the integrity of the guilt-determining process:

(1) Prosecutors and defense attorneys are officers of the court and subject to the court's powers of discipline and control. A presiding judge can order opposing counsel to refrain from divulging implicative facts or making prejudicial statements about pending criminal cases.

(2) A witness, once subpoenaed, is amenable to the authority of the court. The presiding judge can admonish prospective witnesses to avoid extrajudicial comments to media representatives until after the trial is completed.

(3) The trial judge, pursuant to his inherent power to preserve order and decorum in his courtroom, can prohibit cameras and broadcasting equipment while the trial is in session. Indeed, this action may be required as a matter of constitutional law.[154]

(4) Finally, the court can use its prestige to recommend to local law enforcement agencies that they promulgate regulations relating to press releases.

Concerning this last suggestion, the American Bar Association has promulgated a model standard for police department

---

[152] Nebraska Press Ass'n v. Stuart, 427 US 539, 49 LEd(2d) 683, 96 SCt 2791 (1976).

[153] Sheppard v. Maxwell, 384 US 333, 16 LEd(2d) 600, 86 SCt 1507 (1966).

[154] Estes v. Texas, 381 US 532, 14 LEd(2d) 543, 85 SCt 1628 (1965).

adoption. The model standard establishes what matters are appropriate subjects for public comment and what information should remain undisclosed. During the investigatory phase and prior to the placing of formal charges, the ABA standards would permit public disclosure of "pertinent facts relating to the crime itself and to investigative procedures."[185] "The identity of a suspect prior to arrest and the results of investigative procedures," on the other hand, should not be disclosed unless "necessary to aid in the investigation, to assist in the apprehension of the suspect, or to warn the public of any dangers."[186]

Between the lodging of formal charges and the final disposition of the case, law enforcement officers would be precluded from making public comments on six subjects: (1) the defendant's prior criminal record; (2) the existence or contents of inculpatory statements or confessions; (3) the defendant's agreement to or refusal to submit to various laboratory tests and their outcome; (4) the identity and/or probable testimony of any prospective witness; (5) the possibility of a plea bargain; and (6) the officer's opinion on the merits of the case or the strength of the government's evidence against the defendant.[187] While the defendant is in custody, law enforcement officers would be required to refrain from posing him for photographs or from making him available to the media for a press conference unless, adequately counseled, he requests such exposure. At the other side of the spectrum, law enforcement officers would be allowed to comment upon: (1) the facts and circumstances surrounding the arrest, including any resistance encountered or weapons used; (2) the nature of any evidence seized at the time of the arrest (other than a confession, admission or statement); (3) the substance of the charges placed against the person arrested; (4) court records in the case; (5) the scheduling or results of any stage in the criminal process; (6) the fact that the accused denies the charges; and (7) the need for public assistance in obtaining evidence.[188] Violation of the American Bar Association standards would be grounds for disciplinary action.[189]

---

[185] ABA Standards, *Fair Trial and Free Press* §2.1(a) (1968).
[186] *Id.*

[187] *Id.* §2.1(c).
[188] *Id.*
[189] *Id.* §2.1(d).

In 1966 the Justice Department adopted a body of guidelines for federal law enforcement officers very similar to the American Bar Association's proposals except with regard to the disclosure of criminal records.[190] The Justice Department rules condemn public disclosures of the existence and content of any inculpatory statements or confessions, expressions of opinion as to the suspect's guilt, the use of inflammatory labels like "mad dog sex killer" or "hoodlum," and disclosure of the existence or results of polygraph tests, ballistics reports, fingerprint analyses or other laboratory-developed evidence. On the matter of prior criminal records, however, the Justice Department has adopted the position that it will neither voluntarily release this information without solicitation nor decline to make it available in the face of a specific request.

Law enforcement agencies would do well to study the American Bar Association and Justice Department models. Since the printing of crime information cannot be suppressed once it gets into the hands of the media, courts and law enforcement agencies must begin riding herd on inflammatory news-leak sources. There is no First Amendment obligation to disclose to the media sources of crime information not available to members of the public in general.[191] If law enforcement agencies restrict press releases along the lines suggested above, significant strides will be made in promoting the fair trial rights of an accused.

§ 10.14   Confrontation of adverse witnesses

The right of an accused to face his accusers in the presence of the tribunal assembled to pass judgment upon him finds its source in the Sixth Amendment:

> In all criminal prosecutions, the accused shall enjoy the right . . . to be confronted with the witnesses against him. . . .

A literal reading of the constitutional language suggests, as a minimum assurance, that those whose testimony is used to

---

[190] Address by Attorney General Nicholas Katzenbach to the American Society of Newspaper Editors, April 16, 1965, reprinted in Hall & Kamisar, MODERN CRIMINAL PROCEDURE 413 (1966).

[191] See, e.g., Quad-City Community News Serv. Inc., v. Jebens, 334 FSupp 8 (SD Iowa 1971).

establish the defendant's guilt must face him in open court. For such a confrontation to occur, the accused must be present too. Hence, there arises in the accused a Sixth Amendment right to attend his trial and to be present during every stage of the proceedings.[192] In the nature of things, however, this right cannot be absolute. The right of attendance is lost if, after the trial is begun, the accused voluntarily absents himself,[193] or conducts himself in such a disruptive manner that it is impossible for the trial to continue with him in the courtroom.[194]

The Sixth Amendment requires the defendant to be confronted by adverse witnesses not solely for the sake of allowing him to peer upon their countenances. The courtroom furnishes the best known laboratory for conducting investigations into the truth. When a witness testifies on the stand, he is subject to three reliability-enhancing conditions that are not present where he makes the same statements at some other time and place.[195] First, the witness is required to testify under oath and under pain of perjury if he deliberately falsifies. Second, the fact-finding tribunal has an opportunity to observe him as he testifies and to evaluate, on the basis of his demeanor, whether he is telling the truth. Finally and most important of all, when the witness gives incriminating testimony in a courtroom atmosphere, the defendant has an opportunity to cross-examine him. Cross-examination is a potent device for exposing testimonial weaknesses. The witness may have had an inadequate opportunity to observe the events to which he testified; his memory may be faulty; narrative imprecisions may have crept into his speech; or his testimony may suffer from an underlying lack of candor or sincerity. Through cross-examination the defendant may be able to bring to the jury's attention infirmities in the witness' cognitive, perceptual, recollective or narrative abilities, or to discredit his truthfulness.

[192] Illinois v. Allen, 397 US 337, 25 LEd(2d) 353, 90 SCt 1057 (1970).

[193] Taylor v. United States, 414 US 17, 38 LEd(2d) 174, 94 SCt 194 (1973).

[194] Illinois v. Allen, 397 US 337, 25 LEd(2d) 353, 90 SCt 1057 (1970).

[195] Chambers v. Mississippi, 410 US 284, 35 LEd(2d) 297, 93 SCt 1038 (1973); California v. Green, 399 US 149, 26 LEd(2d) 489, 90 SCt 1930 (1970).

Cross-examination is the essence of the constitutional right of confrontation. The two guarantees are so interrelated that the Supreme Court, in references to the confrontation clause, has repeatedly alluded to it as assuring the "right to confront and *cross-examine*" as if the latter term appeared directly in the constitutional text.[196] Certainly, it is implicit in it. There would be little reason for guaranteeing the right to confront adverse witnesses if nothing more than a visual encounter were contemplated.

Because confrontation and cross-examination are fundamental mechanisms for testing the reliability of an adverse witness's testimony, the Sixth Amendment assurance is an element of due process and is obligatory on the states.[197]

§ 10.15   Prosecutor's constitutional disclosure obligations

Several decades ago the Supreme Court remarked upon the unique position of the prosecuting attorney in our adversary system of criminal justice:

> The United States Attorney is the representative not of an ordinary party to a controversy, but of a sovereignty whose obligation to govern impartially is as compelling as its obligation to govern at all; and whose interest, therefore, in a criminal prosecution is not that it shall win a case, but that justice shall be done. As such, he is in a peculiar and very definite sense the servant of the law, the twofold aim of which is that guilt shall not escape or innocence suffer. He may prosecute with earnestness and vigor—indeed, he should do so. But, while he may strike hard blows, he is not at liberty to strike foul ones. It is as much his duty to refrain from improper methods calculated to produce a wrongful conviction as it is to use every legitimate means to bring about a just one.[198]

There is an emerging line of authority which imposes an affirmative obligation upon the prosecutor, in some instances, to disclose to defense counsel exculpatory evidence. The trend was begun in a noncontroversial context—the knowing use

---

[196] *See, e.g.,* Chambers v. Mississippi, 410 US 284, 297-98, 35 LEd(2d) 297, 310, 93 SCt 1038, 1047 (1973).

[197] Pointer v. Texas, 380 US 400, 13 LEd(2d) 923, 85 SCt 1065 (1965).

[198] Berger v. United States, 295 US 78, 88, 79 LEd 1314, 1321, 55 SCt 629, 633 (1935).

of manufactured evidence to secure a guilty verdict.[199] The wisdom and justice of setting aside a criminal conviction where the prosecutor has suborned perjury is self-evident. There are at stake two separate considerations, either of which standing alone is sufficient to call for a reversal: (1) deterring insufferable government conduct, and (2) rectifying a dubious verdict. In *Mooney v. Holohan*,[200] the Supreme Court said:

> [Due process] is a requirement that cannot be deemed satisfied . . . if a state has contrived a conviction through the pretense of a trial which in truth is but used as a means of depriving a defendant of liberty through a deliberate deception of court and jury by the presentation of testimony known to be perjured. Such a contrivance by a state to procure the conviction and imprisonment of a defendant is as inconsistent with rudimentary demands of justice as is the obtaining of a like result by intimidation.[201]

In *Alcorta v. Texas*,[202] the *Mooney* principle was extended to a situation where the prosecutor, while not instigating the false testimony, stood by in silence, knowing that a prosecution witness was committing perjury, and made no effort to correct the misimpression. Alcorta, who was accused of murdering his wife, claimed in defense that he did so in a sudden fit of passion aroused when he discovered his wife kissing one Castilleja late at night in a parked car. (Had the jury believed this defense, Alcorta's criminal responsibility would have been reduced from murder to a lesser grade of homicide.) The prosecuting attorney, who previously had been informed by Castilleja that he and the deceased were having an affair, allowed Castilleja to testify on the stand that he had not kissed the accused's wife on the night of her death and that their relationship was simply one of casual friendship. The Supreme Court reversed Alcorta's conviction on the ground that the prosecutor, by failing to correct testimony he knew to be false, became a participant in creating a "false impression" with respect to a material fact.

---

[199] Pyle v. Kansas, 317 US 213, 87 LEd 214, 63 SCt 177 (1942); Mooney v. Holohan, 294 US 103, 79 LEd 791, 55 SCt 340 (1935).

[200] *Id.*

[201] *Id.* at 112, 79 LEd at 794, 55 SCt at 342.

[202] 355 US 28, 2 LEd(2d) 9, 78 SCt 103 (1957).

Alcorta is significant because it marked the beginning of a shift in emphasis. In reversing the conviction, the Supreme Court addressed itself to the question of the verdict's integrity ("false impression") rather than the need for deterring misbehavior. *Alcorta* laid the foundations for the development of a broader disclosure rule. There is a remarkable similarity between a "false impression" resulting from perjured testimony and a "false impression" resulting from the suppression of material evidence. The risk of an erroneous conviction is not appreciably less where the government keeps hidden in its files evidence that might create a reasonable doubt in the mind of the jury than where it knowingly utilizes false testimony.

The transition from a specialized disclosure obligation operating in the realm of perjured testimony to a more generalized responsibility was accomplished in *Brady* v. *Maryland*.[203] Brady and a confederate were accused of perpetrating a murder during the course of a robbery. Brady was tried separately. At his trial, Brady admitted participating in the crime, but appealed to the jury to recommend a life sentence rather than death, contending that it was his confederate Boblit who did the actual killing. Prior to the trial, Brady's attorney had requested the prosecutor to allow him to examine Boblit's extrajudicial statements. The prosecutor turned some of them over to Brady's counsel but withheld from him Boblit's statement in which he confessed to firing the fatal shot. Brady was sentenced to death. The Supreme Court reversed his conviction and issued the following proclamation:

> We now hold that suppression by the prosecution of evidence favorable to an accused upon request violates due process where the evidence is material either to guilt or to punishment, irrespective of the good faith or bad faith of the prosecution.
>
> The principle . . . is not punishment of society for misdeeds of a prosecutor but avoidance of an unfair trial to the accused. . . . A prosecution that withholds evidence on demand of an accused which, if made available, would tend to exculpate him or reduce the penalty helps shape . . . a proceeding that does not comport with

[203] 373 US 83, 10 LEd(2d) 215, 83 SCt 1194 (1963).

standards of justice, even though, as in the present case, his
action is not "the result of guile," . . .[204]

Brady divorced the government's disclosure obligations
from a misconduct analysis and predicated its responsibilities
on a broad recognition that where the government withholds
significant evidence favorable to the accused, the integrity of
the proceeding is compromised. Although the prosecutor's
good faith or bad faith has ceased to be relevant, *Brady* does
not eliminate the need for establishing government complicity
in depriving the accused of a fair trial. The defendant's discovery, after his trial, that favorable evidence existed but
was simply not presented, or even that a prosecution witness committed perjury, is an occasion for sympathy, but not
a constitutional violation unless these evidentiary shortcomings can be linked to the government.[205] The minimum link is
notice.

1. Imputed notice

As a threshold requirement for establishing a constitutionally cognizable claim under *Brady*, the accused must prove
that the prosecutor had notice of favorable evidence and failed
to disclose it. The fatal knowledge, however, need not be
present in the mind of the attorney assigned to prosecute the
case. *Giglio* v. *United States*[206] establishes that knowledge in
the possession of any member of the prosecutor's staff is attributed to all of the others. In *Giglio*, a crucial government
witness testified on cross-examination that he received no
promises of leniency from the government in return for
testifying against his co-conspirator. The truth of the matter
was that an associate in the United States Attorney's office
had promised him leniency, but the promise was unknown
to the government attorney who tried the case. The Supreme
Court held that the breakdown of communications in the
prosecutor's office did not exonerate the government from

---

[204] *Id.* at 87-88, 10 LEd(2d) at 218-
19, 83 SCt 1196-97.
[205] Burks v. Egeler, 512 F(2d) 221
(6thCir 1975).

[206] 405 US 150, 31 LEd(2d) 104, 92
SCt 763 (1972).

its obligation to expose testimony known to be false by any member of the prosecutor's staff. Mr. Chief Justice Burger offered the following analysis:

[W]hether the nondisclosure was a result of negligence or design, it is the responsibility of the prosecutor. The prosecutor's office is an entity and as such it is the spokesman for the Government. A promise made by one attorney must be attributed, for these purposes, to the Government. To the extent this places a burden on large prosecution offices, procedures and regulations can be established to carry that burden and to insure communication of all relevant information on each case to every lawyer who deals with it.[207]

The *Brady* disclosure obligation placed upon the prosecutor is not exhausted when a search of the prosecutor's files and an inquiry of the staff fails to reveal an awareness of the information in question. Lower federal courts have held that evidence in the possession of law enforcement officers in the prosecuting jurisdiction, whether or not revealed to the prosecutor or his staff, falls within the informational domain for which the prosecutor is responsible under the *Giglio* case.[208] In *Barbee v. Warden*,[209] the prosecutor introduced the defendant's revolver into evidence but failed to disclose that ballistics and fingerprint tests performed on it had been negative. Indeed, he was ignorant of this favorable defense evidence because the police, deeming the negative results to be useless to the prosecutor, had failed to pass the laboratory reports along. The Fourth Circuit ruled:

The police are also part of the prosecution, and the taint on the trial is no less . . . [i]f the police allow the State's Attorney to produce evidence pointing to guilt without informing him of other [contradictory] evidence.[210]

The lesson to be learned from *Barbee* is that the police must keep detailed and accurate records of all investigatory results,

[207] *Id.* at 154, 31 LEd(2d) at 108, 92 SCt at 766 (citations omitted).

[208] United States v. Morell, 524 F(2d) 550 (2dCir 1975); Barbee v. Warden, 331 F(2d) 842 (4thCir 1964).

See also, Moore v. Illinois, 408 US 786, 33 LEd(2d) 706, 92 SCt 2562 (1972) (Marshall, J., dissenting).

[209] 331 F(2d) 842 (4thCir 1964).

[210] *Id.* at 846.

whether positive or negative, and when the investigation is concluded they must turn the complete file over to the prosecutor, unpruned of investigatory items which from a law enforcement vantage point represent wasted efforts. There is no advantage to be obtained in withholding from the prosecutor negative lab results, disappointing statements given by possible prosecution witnesses, and items of a similar nature. Keeping the prosecutor ignorant of weaknesses in the government's case will not make it one bit stronger than it is. To the contrary, ignorance may handicap the prosecutor in preparing to meet defense trial strategies, and even in the event of a prosecution victory, the conviction may be vulnerable as a result of the prosecutor's inadvertent failure to discharge his *Brady* or *Alcorta* disclosure obligations.

2. Brady disclosure duty

In *Moore v. Illinois*,[211] the Supreme Court undertook to shed further light on the scope of the prosecutor's obligations under *Brady*. *Brady*, as interpreted through the eyes of *Moore*, is dependent upon three conditions: (1) the prosecutor's failure, whether through inadvertence or design, to comply with a defense request for production of the evidence in the prosecution's possession; (2) the favorable character of the evidence to the defense; and (3) the materiality of the evidence to the issue of guilt or punishment.

3. Request for production

The Supreme Court has always discussed the prosecutor's *Brady* disclosure obligation in the context of a defense request for production of the evidence. Despite language in *Moore* which suggests that a request is necessary to trigger the prosecutor's duty to turn over favorable evidence, the Supreme Court has never been called upon to face the issue squarely. The concensus of lower federal courts appears to be that a request does not mark the outer limits of government responsibility, and that occasions can arise where the

[211] 408 US 786, 33 LEd(2d) 706, 92 SCt 2562 (1972).

prosecutor is under a constitutional obligation to volunteer exculpatory evidence to the accused without defense counsel's prodding.[212] The correctness of these decisions depends upon an evaluation of the function of a request in the *Brady* disclosure scheme.

In a busy prosecution office, the prosecutor cannot be expected to recognize the relevance of every evidentiary item in his files to some possible defense theory. A request "serves the valuable office of flagging the importance of the evidence for the defense."[213] But there are some items of evidence, like an eyewitness's negative identification,[214] that are so obviously relevant and valuable to the defense that a failure to disclose them borders on active concealing. Allowing the prosecutor to stand upon the ceremony of a production request where the evidence's unmistakable value to the defense could not have escaped his attention is nonsense, and it is inconceivable that the Supreme Court would reach such a conclusion, should the issue be squarely presented. The lower federal courts are correct in regarding the absence of a production request as inconsequential where the prosecutor could not fail to appreciate the evidentiary item's material importance to the defense.

4. Favorable character of the evidence and its materiality

Brady's avowed purpose is "not punishment of society for misdeeds of a prosecutor but avoidance of an unfair trial to the accused."[215] In keeping with this, a conviction will not be set aside for a failure to disclose unless the undisclosed evidence is both *favorable* to the accused and *material*. In its broadest sense, any evidence that might be useful to the defendant in creating a reasonable doubt in the minds of the jurors is *favorable* to him. The Supreme Court has never suggested a more stringent test of "favorableness" than this.

---

[212] *See, e.g.*, United States v. Agurs, 510 F(2d) 1249 (DC Cir 1975) (collecting leading cases).

[213] United States v. Keogh, 391 F(2d) 138, 147 (2dCir 1968).

[214] Evans v. Janing, 489 F(2d) 470 (8thCir 1973). See also, Jackson v. Wainwright, 390 F(2d) 288 (5thCir 1968), *Annot*, 34 ALR(3d) 16, 140-50 (1970).

[215] 373 US at 87, 10 LEd(2d) at 218, 83 SCt 1197.

Though it might be useful to the accused to know in advance what evidence the prosecutor intends to use *against him*, *Brady* does not call for complete pretrial discovery. The undisclosed favorable evidence will be regarded as *material* if it could "in any reasonable likelihood have affected the judgment of the jury." [216] Assessments of materiality depend upon a hindsight evaluation of the strength of the evidence presented against the accused at his trial. The prosecutor's failure to disclose that the victim-eyewitness was unable to identify the accused from his mug shot, for example, might be highly material and require reversal if he were the only eyewitness and the circumstantial evidence were weak, but fall short of a *Brady* violation in the face of other positive eyewitness identifications and/or strong circumstantial evidence.[217]

Herein lies the prosecutor's dilemma. While judicial evaluations of the undisclosed evidence's materiality are made on the basis of a hindsight review of the trial record, the prosecutor, in making *Brady* decisions, is not blessed with the gift of hindsight. In the face of genuine doubt as to materiality, an over-generous reading of *Brady* constitutes the more prudent course to take. If the defendant is convicted in spite of the disclosure, the prosecutor's open-file policy has left the government no worse off. If, on the other hand, he is acquitted and the disclosed evidence tipped the scale, this fact by itself confirms that the evidence was material and that, in disclosing it, the prosecutor did no more than his *Brady* duty. On such facts, the conviction obtained through suppression would have been reversible in any event. The disclosure of favorable evidence in borderline cases thus appears to harm the government not at all.

§ 10.16 Cruel and unusual punishment

There was a time in English history when a convicted criminal, as punishment for his offense, might be burned at the stake, boiled in oil, or have his hands or ears cropped off.

---

[216] Giglio v. United States, 405 US 150, 154, 31 LEd(2d) 104, 108, 92 SCt 763, 766 (1972).

[217] *See* Moore v. Illinois, 408 US 786, 33 LEd(2d) 706, 92 SCt 2562 (1972); Evans v. Janing, 489 F(2d) 470 (8thCir 1973).

Blackstone, in his *Commentaries on the Law of England* published in 1769, reported that for the crime of treason, an Englishman might be dragged to the gallows, hung, cut down, disemboweled while still living, and finally put to death by decapitation and quartering.[218] The Eighth Amendment erected a constitutional barrier against the infliction of "cruel and unusual punishments" by the federal government. This limitation is now equally binding on the states.[219]

Notions regarding what constitutes cruel treatment in the realm of penal justice have varied over time. Public hangings, floggings and the cropping off of ears were punishments still in common practice when this nation was founded.[220] In 1779, Thomas Jefferson advocated the castration of any man found guilty of rape, polygamy or sodomy, and the facial mutilation of any woman found guilty of a comparable offense.[221] Judged by twentieth-century standards, Jefferson's proposal sounds fiendish and unspeakable. But to decent thinking men of the eighteenth century, bodily mutilation was regarded as an acceptable punishment for certain types of crimes.[222] What would happen if some state legislature belatedly enacted Thomas Jefferson's proposal today? Should a court, in evaluating the statute's Eighth Amendment constitutionality, look backwards in history to the time of the Constitution's adoption to see how enlightened public opinion in 1791 would have reacted to this measure, or should the court make its assessments on the basis of contemporary penological thoughts and values? To ask this question is to answer it.

The Supreme Court has repeatedly emphasized the Eighth Amendment's "expansive and vital character"[223] and capacity for evolutionary growth.[224] What constitutes "cruel and un-

---

[218] 4 W. Blackstone, COMMENTARIES *92.

[219] Robinson v. California, 370 US 660, 8 LEd(2d) 758, 82 SCt 1417 (1962).

[220] Mr. Justice Brennan traces the history of the Eighth Amendment in his concurring opinion in *Furman v. Georgia*, 408 US 238, 257, 33 LEd(2d) 346, 360, 92 SCt 2726, 2736 (1972).

[221] van den Haag, PUNISHING CRIMINALS 193-4 (1975).

[222] See note 220, *supra*.

[223] Weems v. United States, 217 US 349, 377, 54 LEd 793, 802, 30 SCt 544, 553 (1910).

[224] Trop v. Dulles, 356 US 86, 2 LEd(2d) 630, 78 SCt 590 (1958).

usual punishment" is not linked to eighteenth-century standards. The constitutional meaning of "cruelty" changes as
"public opinion becomes enlightened by humane justice." [225]
If there should ever come a time when civilized standards advance to a point where the death penalty is no longer palatable to the vast majority, these changed attitudes would be
reflected in the Eighth Amendment, and death would become "cruel and unusual punishment." As of 1977, however, this point has not been reached. [226]

The Eighth Amendment prescription against "cruel and
unusual punishment" operates primarily as a check upon the
legislature. It qualifies the legislative power to prescribe punishments in several different respects:

(1) It prohibits the legislature from authorizing unnec-
    essarily cruel methods of punishment.
(2) It precludes the enactment of punishments which,
    though not cruel in themselves, are severely dispro-
    portionate to the offense for which imposed.
(3) It imposes substantive limits upon what can be de-
    fined as a crime.
(4) It forbids the enactment of capital punishment sen-
    tencing systems which allow arbitrary or erratic con-
    siderations to determine which offenders, convicted of
    the same crime, shall go to prison and which shall be
    condemned to die.

In addition to circumscribing legislative judgments, the
Eighth Amendment ban against cruel and unusual punishment operates as a check upon the conduct of corrections
officials. [227]

There is a common thread that binds together these diverse applications of the Eighth Amendment. Mr. Justice
Brennan recognized and summed it up in his concurring opinion in *Furman* v. *Georgia*. [228] He said:

> Ours would indeed be a simple task were we required merely
> to measure a challenged punishment against those that history

---

[225] Weems v. United States, 217
US at 378, 54 LEd at 803, 30 SCt at
553.
[226] *See* Gregg v. Georgia, 428 US
153, 49 LEd(2d) 859, 96 SCt 2909
(1976).

[227] *See, e.g.,* Gates v. Collier, 501
F(2d) 1291 (5thCir 1974).
[228] 408 US at 269-70, 33 LEd(2d)
at 366-67, 92 SCt at 2742.

has long condemned. That narrow and unwarranted view of the Clause, however, was left behind with the 19th century. . . . We know "that the words of the [Clause] are not precise and that their scope is not static." We know, therefore, that the Clause "must draw its meaning from the evolving standards of decency that mark the progress of a maturing society." That knowledge, of course, is but the beginning of the inquiry.

In *Trop* v. *Dulles*, . . . [i]t was said, finally, that:

"The basic concept underlying the [Clause] is nothing less than the *dignity of man*. While the State has the power to punish, the [Clause] stands to assure that this power be exercised within the limits of civilized standards."

. . . At bottom, then, the Cruel and Unusual Punishment Clause prohibits the infliction of uncivilized and inhuman punishments. The State, even as it punishes, must treat its members with *respect for their intrinsic worth as human beings.* A punishment is "cruel and unusual," therefore, if it does not comport with *human dignity*.[229]

§ 10.17   —Unnecessarily cruel methods of punishment

Reflecting over history, one can only be astounded at the humanity with which contemporary society punishes those convicted of crime. Blackstone's account, above, of how English society dealt with those convicted of treason sets one's teeth on edge. Mercifully, such barbaric atrocities as crucifixion, burning at the stake, public vivisection and the like have long since passed from the legal scene. Any efforts to revive them in the United States would be resisted by means of the Eighth Amendment. The constitutional prescription against the infliction of "cruel and unusual punishment" stands as a legal barrier to any method of punishment which inflicts unnecessary pain or suffering upon the offender.[230] Torturing an offender to see how much he can endure is an affront to his dignity as a member of the human race. Equally important, society itself is debased when one of its members is treated as less than a human being.

The death penalty has provided the most controversial Eighth Amendment issue in modern times. During the nineteenth and first half of the twentieth century, the Supreme Court and other courts entertained a number of constitutional attacks upon particular methods of carrying the death

---

[229] *Id.* at 270, 33 LEd(2d) at 366-67, 92 SCt at 2742 (emphasis added). (citations omitted).

[230] Wilkerson v. Utah, 99 US 130, 25 LEd 345 (1879).

sentence into effect, specifically—shooting,[231] electrocution[232] and lethal gas.[233] These cases were brought upon the tacit assumption that death itself was a constitutionally accepted form of punishment. The issue was whether the state had selected an allowable method for carrying out this sentence. In each of these cases, the courts, finding that the method employed involved no unnecessary pain or prolongation of suffering, upheld the method.

In 1972, a death row prisoner petitioned the Supreme Court for certiorari on the basis of his contention that capital punishment *per se* was cruel and unusual punishment. The Supreme Court granted certiorari in *Furman v. Georgia*[234] and reversed Furman's conviction; but the case was anything but decisive on the capital punishment issue. Justices Brennan and Marshall stood alone in their total and unrestricted condemnation of capital punishment. For them, contemporary standards of decency had progressed to a point where death had become a constitutionally unacceptable punishment in any size, shape, manner or form. Mr. Chief Justice Burger, joined by Justices Blackmun, Powell and Rehnquist, disagreed with this analysis. While they expressed deep-seated personal reservations about the morality, and perhaps the efficacy, of capital punishment, they could find no authorization in the Eighth Amendment's language as previously interpreted for declaring death *per se* cruel and unusual punishment. The remaining three Justices—Douglas, Stewart and White—were not yet ready to address the central question of whether capital punishment was outlawed by the Eighth Amendment under any and all circumstances and for every possible crime. For them, it was sufficient to find the Georgia death penalty statute unconstitutional on more narrow grounds. They joined Justices Brennan and Marshall, creating a five-man majority necessary to overturn the Georgia statute; but they did so on the grounds that the legislature's delegation to a sentencing judge or jury of standardless discretion to decide whether a

231 *Id.*

232 In re Kemmler, 136 US 436, 34 LEd 519, 10 SCt 930 (1890).

233 Hernandez v. State, 43 Ariz 424, 32 P(2d) 18 (1934).

234 408 US 238, 33 LEd(2d) 346, 92 SCt 2726 (1972).

convicted offender would receive a life sentence or the death penalty, when combined with the rarity with which the death penalty was in fact imposed, made its infliction upon the few unfortunates who received it an arbitrarily cruel and unusual punishment. Their objections went to the sentencing system and not to the penalty itself. This made the *Furman v. Georgia* capital punishment scoreboard 2–4–3: two found capital punishment constitutionally unpalatable in any form, four were of the opposite view, and three found it unconstitutional *as administered* in Georgia, but expressed no opinion as to its generic constitutionality.

Since the Georgia approach to capital punishment sentencing was a common approach authorized under the laws of some thirty-nine states, the District of Columbia, and various portions of the United States Criminal Code,[235] *Furman's* impact was felt nationwide. The status of capital punishment was left up in the air. Although *Furman* contained nine separate opinions spanning more than two hundred pages, nowhere in the opinions was there a clue as to whether or how capital punishment laws could be made acceptable to a majority of the Court. A moratorium was called on the execution of death row prisoners, and chaos ensued as legislature after legislature scrambled in an effort to devise some capital punishment sentencing scheme that would meet with constitutional approval. Post-*Furman* legislation assumed one of three patterns:[236]

   (1) Mandatory death penalty as an automatic consequence of the conviction of a capital offense;
   (2) Discretionary death penalty coupled with statutory standards controlling the sentencing body's exercise of its discretion; and
   (3) Hybrid statutes combining both approaches.

The long-overdue second round, whereby the new sentencing approaches would be tested, came in 1976, when the

---

[235] *Id.* at 417-18, 33 LEd(2d) 452-53, 92 SCt 2817-18 (Powell, J., dissenting).

[236] Note, *The Response to Furman: Can Legislators Breathe Life Back into Death?*, 23 CLEVESTLREV 172 (1974).

Supreme Court granted certiorari to review death penalties imposed under the diverse post-*Furman* laws of five states.[237] *Gregg* v. *Georgia* [238] settled the matter, once and for all, that the death penalty is not *per se* cruel and unusual punishment in violation of the Eighth Amendment. Implicit in *Gregg* v. *Georgia* and its companion cases, however, is the recognition that death is different from all other forms of punishment, both in its severity and its finality, and that, as a result of these differences, the Eighth Amendment demands more of the government, both procedurally and substantively, before this ultimate penalty may be exacted. These matters are discussed in the sections that follow.

Fines, prison sentences and capital punishment are, for all practical purposes, the only criminal sanctions in contemporary use. They may, indeed, be the only ones that are constitutionally allowable. In *Trop* v. *Dulles* [239] the Supreme Court ruled that Congress may not strip a man of his citizenship to punish him for deserting in times of war. Denationalization was looked upon as a cruelly degrading form of punishment and one which causes acute mental torment and suffering.

§ 10.18   —Excessive punishments

Penalties of a familiar and widely accepted type, such as a fine, prison term or death sentence, may amount to cruel and unusual punishment if the penalty is excessively severe in relationship to the underlying offense for which it is imposed. The Eighth Amendment incorporates notions of punishment-offense proportionality. This dimension of the cruelty clause was first recognized by the Supreme Court in *Weems* v. *United States*.[240] Weems, a government employee, was convicted of falsifying a "public and official document." He

---

[237] Gregg v. Georgia, 428 US 153, 49 LEd(2d) 859, 96 SCt 2909 (1976); Proffitt v. Florida, 428 US 242, 49 LEd(2d) 913, 96 SCt 2960 (1976); Jurek v. Texas, 428 US 262, 49 LEd(2d) 929, 96 SCt 2950 (1976); Woodson v. North Carolina, 428 US 280, 49 LEd(2d) 944, 96 SCt 2978 (1976); Roberts v. Louisiana, 428 US 325, 49 LEd(2d) 974, 96 SCt 3001 (1976).

[238] 428 US 153, 49 LEd(2d) 859, 96 SCt 2909 (1976).

[239] 356 US 86, 2 LEd(2d) 630, 78 SCt 590 (1958).

[240] 217 US 349, 54 LEd 793, 30 SCt 544 (1910).

was sentenced to 15 years' incarceration at hard labor with chains on his ankles, to an unusual loss of his civil rights, and to perpetual surveillance. The Supreme Court ruled that this amounted to cruel and unusual punishment. Though the Court might have disposed of the case on the basis of unnecessary physical pain and suffering attendant upon the sentence, it did not do so. Instead, the Court focused on the lack of proportion between the crime and the punishment, remarking:

> [I]t is a precept of justice that punishment for crime should be graduated and proportioned to [the] offense [charged].[241]

Despite the Supreme Court's clear mandate for treating disproportionately severe punishments as cruel under the Eighth Amendment, courts until recently have been reluctant to set aside sentences on the grounds that they are unconstitutionally excessive.[242] This attitude is, in part, a healthy one. The courts should defer to the superior expertise of the legislature in determining the seriousness of the offense and the appropriate punishment.[243] There comes a point, however, where prudent self-restraint shades off into judicial role abdication. Legislative bodies are not infallible; it is as much the courts' function to interpret and apply the Eighth Amendment as other constitutional provisions.

The capital punishment controversy reawakened scholarly interest in the Eighth Amendment. This reawakening was accompanied by a parallel development: the courts have become less reticent in their review of criminal sanctions for Eighth Amendment excessiveness.[244] One federal appeals court, for instance, has determined that the imposition on a first offender of an indeterminate sentence of from 30 to 60 years' imprisonment for the possession and sale of marijuana, though authorized under Ohio law, was disproportionate to the gravity of the crime and, therefore, unconstitution-

---

[241] *Id.* at 367, 54 LEd at 798, 30 SCt at 549.

[242] *See, e.g.,* Donaldson v Wyrick, 393 FSupp 1041 (WD Mo 1974) (refusing to set aside 99-year sentence for rape).

[243] Note, *The Effectiveness of the Eighth Amendment: An Appraisal of Cruel and Unusual Punishment,* 36 NYULRev 846, 847-48 (1961).

[244] *See, e.g.,* Downey v. Perini, 518 F(2d) 1288 (6thCir 1975); Hart v Coiner, 483 F(2d) 136 (4thCir 1973); Roberts v. Collins, 404 FSupp 119 (D Md 1975).

ally cruel punishment.[245] The process by which the court reached this decision is noteworthy. The court did not apply subjective criteria or rely upon intuition. Instead, it compared Ohio's statutory penalty with penalties imposed for the same offense by other jurisdictions, and with penalties imposed by Ohio for other crimes. This investigation revealed that Ohio's sanctions for marijuana offenses were the most severe in the nation, and even more severe than Ohio penalties for such dangerous felonies as kidnapping, armed robbery, voluntary manslaughter and rape. The court's analytical approach was sound. Not until it was satisfied, by objective indicators, that the Ohio penalty for marijuana possession and sale was unnecessarily severe in light of contemporary practices elsewhere, and irrational within the state's own internal punishment scheme, did the court overturn the Ohio legislature's judgment with regard to how severely marijuana possession should be punished.

Death is, beyond a doubt, the most severe punishment that society can inflict. The determination that death is not in itself cruel and unusual punishment in no way resolves whether this penalty is unconstitutionally excessive with respect to a *particular* offense. In *Gregg v. Georgia*,[246] the Supreme Court, upholding a death sentence imposed upon a defendant convicted of the brutal robbery-murder of two men, made it clear that it was not blanketly approving the death penalty. Mr. Justice Stewart, author of the opinion, wrote:

> [W]e are concerned here only with the imposition of capital punishment for the crime of murder, and when a life has been taken by the offender, we cannot say that the punishment is invariably disproportionate to the crime. It is an extreme sanction, suitable to the most extreme of crimes.[247]

Not satisfied that he had adequately driven home the limitations of his holding, he added in a footnote:

> We do not address here the question whether the taking of a criminal's life is a proportionate sanction where no victim has been

---

[245] Downey v. Perini, 518 F(2d) 1288 (6thCir 1975).

[246] 428 US 153, 49 LEd(2d) 859, 96 SCt 2909 (1976).

[247] *Id.* at 187, 49 LEd(2d) at 882, 96 SCt at 2931-32 (footnote omitted).

deprived of life—for example, when capital punishment is imposed for rape, kidnapping, or armed robbery that does not result in the death of any human being.[248]

Stewart's cautionary language directed at clarifying the scope of the *Gregg* holding makes it a foregone conclusion that any death penalty imposed for a crime other than murder will be challenged for its Eighth Amendment excessiveness, and that the Supreme Court is still a long way from completing its chapter on capital punishment.

AUTHOR'S NOTE: On October 4, 1976, the Supreme Court agreed to hear the case of a convicted rapist who had been sentenced to death under Georgia law. *Croker v. Georgia,* cert. granted, 97 SCt 56 (1975). The defendant argued that death was an excessive and disproportionate penalty for the rape of an adult victim who was otherwise unharmed. On July 29, 1977, as this book went to press, the Supreme Court handed down a decision overturning the sentence. The opinion remains as yet unpublished. Consequently, the author is in no position to assess whether the case stands for the proposition that capital punishment is unconstitutionally excessive for all crimes other than those in which a human life is taken, or whether it stands for a narrower proposition.

§ 10.19   —Punishment of status

The Eighth Amendment contains a substantive limitation on what behavior can be made a punishable offense. In *Robinson* v. *California,*[249] the Supreme Court held that an individual could not be branded a criminal or subjected to penal sanctions, no matter how slight, simply because he occupied a status or condition that was offensive to the community. Robinson had been sentenced to jail under a California statute that made it a crime to *be* a drug addict and authorized conviction without proof that the offender had purchased, sold, used or even possessed narcotic drugs within the State of California, or had been guilty of any antisocial conduct associated with drug addiction. The addict, under this statute, was punishable solely because he *was* an addict

---

[248] *Id.,* n. 35.

[249] 370 US 660, 8 LEd(2d) 758, 82 SCt 1417 (1962).

and not because he committed an overt act. Mr. Justice Stewart, who wrote the majority opinion, observed that narcotics addiction is a disease and stated that it was as barbaric and cruel to punish an individual for this affliction as to make it a crime "to be mentally ill, or a leper, or to be afflicted with a venereal disease."[250]

Most jurisdictions have vagrancy laws. Under the typical statute, a vagrant is defined as one who is able-bodied and lives in idleness without any visible means of support.[251] Subsequent to *Robinson*, numerous vagrancy laws nationwide were successfully challenged on the basis that they punish the "offender" for his status—for *being* a person who is capable of self-support but who lives in idleness and poverty, rather than for *doing* any particular type of act.[252] In *Papachristou* v. *City of Jacksonville*,[253] the Supreme Court invalidated a municipal vagrancy law on the grounds of the "void for vagueness" doctrine.[254] In light of the unceremonious legal treatment that vagrancy laws have been receiving in the courts, it is recommended that police officers forego making vagrancy arrests completely.

In *Powell* v. *Texas*,[255] an effort was made to extend the *Robinson* doctrine beyond pure consideration of status to embrace symptomatic behavior that is a direct manifestation of the nonpunishable status. One, Powell, a self-confessed alcoholic, was convicted of being drunk in a public place. On appeal, he contended that, because he was compelled to drink and once drunk would lose control over his behavior, it was cruel and unusual punishment to impose criminal sanctions on him for appearing drunk in a public place. The Supreme Court was unwilling to take the second step and immunize symptomatic behavior. Mr. Justice Marshall, writing the opinion for a closely divided Court, said:

> The entire thrust of *Robinson's* interpretation of the Cruel and Unusual Punishment Clause is that criminal penalties may be in-

[250] *Id.* at 666, 8 LEd(2d) at 763, 82 SCt at 1420.

[251] *See, e.g.,* NCGenStat §14-336 (1969).

[252] Wheeler v. Goodman, 306 FSupp 58 (WD NC 1969); Goldman v. Knecht, 295 FSupp 897 (D Colo 1969).

[253] 405 US 156, 31 LEd(2d) 110, 92 SCt 839 (1972).

[254] The "void for vagueness" doctrine is covered in §2.6, *supra*.

[255] 392 US 514, 20 LEd(2d) 1254, 88 SCt 2145 (1968).

flicted only if the accused has committed some act, has engaged in some behavior, which society has an interest in preventing, or perhaps in historical common law terms, has committed some *actus reus*. It thus does not deal with the question of whether certain conduct cannot constitutionally be punished because it is, in some sense, "involuntary" or "occasioned by a compulsion." [256]

In *Powell, Robinson* lost its bid to become a significant legal doctrine. It is a rare law that attempts to punish an "offender" purely for *being* the type of person that he is. Almost invariably, the statute will specify some conduct component of the crime. In *Powell,* the conduct was appearing in public while intoxicated. Though Powell may have been powerless to control this conduct because he *was* an alcoholic, a status for which the state of Texas could not punish him, the Supreme Court made it abundantly clear that its *Robinson* decision did not establish a constitutional doctrine of diminished criminal responsibility for addicts and others similarly afflicted.

§ 10.20   —Sentencing discretion in capital punishment cases

The Supreme Court's blow to capital punishment under its 1972 *Furman* v. *Georgia* [257] decision reflected disenchantment not with the penalty itself, but with the process whereby capital punishment was being administered. Under the laws of thirty-eight states, in addition to Georgia, sentencing judges and jurors were entrusted with standardless discretion to determine whether defendants committing the same crime should die or be sent to prison. [258] The result was random and uneven justice. Of the five Supreme Court Justices voting for a reversal in *Furman,* only two, Justices Brennan and Marshall, expressed the view that capital punishment was constitutionally unacceptable under any and all circumstances. The objections of the remaining three, Mr Justices Douglas, Stewart, and White, were directed at the system under which the death

[256] *Id.* at 533, 20 LEd(2d) at 1268, 88 SCt at 2154-55.
[257] 408 US 238, 33 LEd(2d) 346, 92 SCt 2726 (1972).

[258] *Id.* at 417-18, 33 LEd(2d) at 452-53, 92 SCt at 2817-18.

penalty was being administered. Mr. Justice Stewart summed up these objections:

> These death sentences are cruel and unusual in the same way that being struck by lightning is cruel and unusual. For, of all the people convicted of rapes and murders in 1967 and 1968, many just as reprehensible as these, the petitioners are among a capriciously selected random handful upon whom the sentence of death has in fact been imposed. . . . [T]he Eighth and Fourteenth Amendments cannot tolerate the infliction of a sentence of death under legal systems that permit this unique penalty to be so wantonly and so freakishly imposed.[259]

Furman toppled death penalty laws nationwide. Virtually the only jurisdiction to emerge unscathed were the nine states which had theretofore abolished capital punishment. Could the death penalty be salvaged? The alignment of Justices in *Furman* suggested the affirmative, but none of the nine opinions offered insight into how this might be accomplished. Since broad and unguided sentencing discretion had been the death penalty's nemesis, it required no genius to adduce that this feature had to be excised from capital punishment sentencing systems if they were to meet with judicial approval. There were two paths down which a legislature might travel in reaching this result: (1) retain discretionary sentencing but provide standards to guide the sentencing body in exercising its discretion whether to impose a prison sentence or the death penalty; or (2) remove all sentencing discretion and make the death penalty an automatic consequence of the conviction of a capital offense.

Between 1972 and 1976, the year of the second bout, 35 state legislatures met and enacted new death penalty laws.[260] In 1976, the Supreme Court granted certiorari to review the post-*Furman* capital punishment laws of five jurisdictions whose efforts to comply with *Furman* were representative of those adopted nationwide.[261] The results were illuminating. Without attempting to discuss each case individually, it is

---

[259] *Id.* at 309-310, 33 LEd(2d) at 390, 92 SCt at 2762-63 (footnotes omitted).

[260] Gregg v. Georgia, 428 US 153, 49 LEd(2d) 859, 96 SCt 2909 (1976).

[261] See cases cited in note 237, *supra*.

possible to distill from them several required features of a constitutionally valid capital punishment sentencing system.

First, where a person's life is at stake, the Eighth Amendment demands individualized sentencing discretion.[262] The Supreme Court overturned mandatory death penalty laws in two states, citing three separate reasons for its action: (1) mandatory death penalties are, in its opinion, incompatible with contemporary penological values and practices; (2) making death an automatic result of conviction of a particular offense is unlikely to correct the arbitrary selection process condemned by the *Furman* decision (a jury, finding the death penalty unduly harsh on the facts of the case, might avoid it by bringing back a verdict of guilty to a lesser offense or might vote to acquit, thereby reintroducing into the sentencing system the type of capricious sentencing discretion that *Furman* was set against); and (3) mandatory death penalties, by treating "all persons convicted of a designated offense, not as uniquely individual human beings, but as members of a faceless, undifferentiated mass to be subjected to the blind infliction of the [death] penalty,"[263] offended the fundamental constitutional policy underlying the Eighth Amendment—respect for human dignity.

Legislatures in those jurisdictions which had responded to *Furman* by enacting mandatory death penalty laws were, therefore, rapped on the knuckles and sent back to the drawing board with instructions that, where a person's life is at stake, the Eighth Amendment demands that the sentencing body be afforded an opportunity to consider "relevant facets of the character and record of the individual offender [and] the circumstances of the particular offense."[264] The first requirement for a constitutionally valid capital punishment sentencing system is: (1) it must afford the sentencing body discretionary power to show mercy by withholding the death penalty and imposing instead a prison sentence where it feels that mercy is justified.

---

[262] Woodson v. North Carolina, 428 US 280, 49 LEd(2d) 944, 96 SCt 2978 (1976); Roberts v. Louisiana, 428 US 325, 49 LEd(2d) 974, 96 SCt 3001 (1976).

[263] Woodson v. North Carolina, 428 US at 304, 49 LEd at 961, 96 SCt at 2991 (1976).

[264] *Id.*

Unguided sentencing discretion, however, is equally to be avoided. The Eighth Amendment requires *informed* and *controlled* discretion in capital punishment cases. The second and third requirements for a constitutionally valid capital punishment sentencing system are: (2) the sentencing body must be provided with clear and objective guidelines and must focus its attention upon those factors relevant to an imposition of the death penalty; [265] and finally, (3) the sentencing body must be afforded the opportunity to hear information relevant to the exercise of its sentencing discretion. [266]

In *Gregg v. Georgia*, [267] the Supreme Court approved the Georgia legislature's statutory response to *Furman*. The present Georgia law is, therefore, available as a model for jurisdictions which remain uncertain whether their laws are in compliance with Eighth Amendment capital sentencing requirements. Under the present Georgia law, [268] bifurcated, or two-staged, proceedings are employed. During the first stage of a capital trial, the only issue before the judge or jury is whether the defendant committed the capital offense with which he has been charged. His guilt is established in the normal fashion. In the event of a conviction, the trial proceeds to a second phase where the issue before the judge or jury is the appropriate sentence. The Georgia statute lists various aggravating and mitigating circumstances which the sentencing body must consider in arriving at its punishment decision. The aggravating and mitigating factors set forth in the statute are designed to channel the sentencing body's attention to the special characteristics of the offender or circumstances surrounding the commission of the offense which make the case peculiarly appropriate for mercy in sentencing or for the imposition of the death penalty. Among the aggravating circumstances that the sentencing body is directed to consider are whether the defendant was previously convicted of a capital felony, whether he was serving out a life sentence when he committed murder, whether the murder victim was a peace officer, whether the defendant committed

[265] Gregg v. Georgia, 428 US 153, 49 LEd(2d) 859, 96 SCt 2909 (1976).
[266] Id.
[267] Id.
[268] GaCodeAnn §§27-2503(b), 27-2534.1, 27-2537 (Supp 1975).

the crime for hire, whether his acts endangered multiple lives, and similarly pertinent matters. No death penalty may be imposed in Georgia unless the sentencing body makes a written finding as to the existence of at least one of the ten aggravating circumstances stipulated by statute.

As a further check upon arbitrary or erratic exercises of sentencing discretion, the Georgia statute makes provision for expedited appellate review of all cases in which the death penalty has been imposed. The appellate court is authorized to set aside the death sentence if it determines that (1) the sentence was imposed under the influence of passion, prejudice or other arbitrary influences; (2) the finding of a statutory aggravating factor was not supported by the evidence; or (3) the death penalty in this case was excessive or disproportionate to penalties imposed in similar cases.

Georgia's bifurcated capital punishment sentencing scheme is superbly crafted. The division of the trial into two separate phases, the first concerned with guilt and the second with punishment, serves a very practical function. Much of the evidence which is relevant to the defendant's punishment, such as his prior criminal record, is irrelevant to the question of guilt, and its admission into evidence in a unitary proceeding might be highly prejudicial to the accused. (The jury might mistake the purpose for which it was admitted.) By separating the proceedings, the jury does not hear damaging evidence concerning the defendant's criminal record and matters of a like nature until it has determined his guilt or innocence of the immediate crime. Georgia's bifurcated system, when coupled with clear, concise and objective sentencing standards, and appellate review for arbitrary influences, excessiveness and conformity with statutory standards, comes as close to a perfect capital punishment sentencing system as it is legally possible to conceive.

§ 10.21 Summary

Under our criminal justice system, even those charged with the most atrocious crimes are entitled to receive their day in court and to enjoy certain constitutional protections which have for centuries been considered indispensable to a fair and just trial. Included in the more significant procedural rights not discussed in other chapters are the Sixth Amendment right to a "speedy" and "public" trial before an "impartial" jury; the Sixth Amendment right to confront adverse witnesses; and the Eighth Amendment assurance of immunity from cruel and unusual punishments.

1. Speedy trial

The constitutional guarantee of a speedy trial protects three interests of the accused: his interest (1) in being free from lengthy periods of pretrial confinement in the event that bail is unavailable; (2) in avoiding unnecessarily prolonged periods of public suspicion, and personal anxiety and concern; and (3) in having a trial before delay has eroded his capacity to prepare a meaningful defense. The Sixth Amendment says that the "*accused* shall enjoy the right to a speedy . . . trial." The Supreme Court has read this language literally and has ruled that the Sixth Amendment affords no protection against pre-accusatory delays. Even though the pre-accusatory period falls outside the Sixth Amendment's purview, the Supreme Court has implied, and numerous lower federal courts have held, that there is some measure of due process protection against pre-accusatory delays. The precise combination of factors capable of triggering a cognizable due process claim has not been firmly settled, but many lower federal courts have expressed their willingness to dismiss a prosecution if the defendant can show that (1) the government unreasonably delayed in arresting him, and (2) in consequence, he suffered prejudice. The Sixth Amendment right to a speedy trial attaches from the time a suspect becomes an *accused*, either through his arrest, indictment, filing of information, or other method of proferring formal charges. There are four factors which a court will consider in determining whether the delay between accusation and trial has violated the Sixth Amendment: (1) its length, (2) the reasons for it, (3) defendant's assertion of his rights, and (4) whether he has been prejudiced. The length of the delay is important as a triggering mechanism. Once there has been a presumptively pre-judicial delay, the court is obliged to examine the other three factors and to balance them against each other.

2. Public trial

The guarantee of a "public" trial serves as a primary restraint upon government efforts to pervert justice. The openness of the proceedings provides other benefits as well (i.e., improves the quality of testimony, affords the public an opportunity to learn about government, etc.). This right is not absolute and the judge may clear the courtroom, for example, when it is necessary to enable a timid witness to testify.

3. Jury trial

The Sixth Amendment guarantee of the right to a jury trial is available in state, as well as federal, prosecutions. Though the Constitution assures that jury trials will be available in "all criminal prosecutions," the Supreme Court has read the common law "petty offense" exception into the unconditional Sixth Amendment language. An offense is "petty," in the sense of eliminating a constitutional obligation to accord the defendant a jury, if it is punishable by no more than six months' imprisonment. The common-law jury was a body of *twelve* persons selected from the community and charged with the responsibility of listening to evidence developed in open court and reaching a *unanimous* verdict of guilt or innocence. Although this pattern still prevails in the federal courts and in most state jurisdictions, several states have, by statute, reduced the jury's size to under twelve, or have authorized less-than-unanimous criminal verdicts. These modifications of the common-law features of the jury are not offensive to the Sixth Amendment. The Sixth Amendment requires that the jury be drawn from a source fairly representative of a cross section of the community.

4. Fair and impartial trial

The requirement of a fair and impartial trial precludes trying an accused before a judge who has a financial interest in the outcome or before a judge who may harbor personal ill-will against him. The types of irregularities that may prejudice the defendant's right to a fair trial defy meaningful categorization, but two stand out and were given special coverage in this Chapter: (a) prejudicial pretrial publicity, and

(b) the prosecutor's failure to live up to his constitutional disclosure responsibilities.

(a) Prejudicial publicity

The Constitution does not require that the jurors selected be wholly unfamiliar with the case, but it does require that they approach their task with an open mind—i.e., that they be capable of setting aside preconceived notions as to guilt and of rendering a verdict based upon evidence developed in the courtroom. Where there has been massive pretrial publicity, and considering its (1) substance, (2) pervasiveness, (3) recentness and (4) the responses of prospective jurors on their *voir dire* examinations, there is reason to fear an intensely hostile local climate of opinion, and corrective measures must be taken. Trial continuances and changes of venue are the two most commonly employed devices. The Supreme Court has ruled that the solution to the prejudicial publicity problem cannot be sought by a judicially-imposed gag order limiting what the press can print. Police departments should promulgate guidelines regarding departmental press releases. By exercising control over the flow of information reaching the media, police departments can make a significant contribution to protecting the defendant's right to be tried by an impartial judge or jury.

(b) Prosecutor's disclosure obligation

The public prosecutor, as a representative of the government, has a duty to see that no one is unfairly convicted. This obligation includes (1) the duty to correct perjured testimony if the government knows it to be false, and (2) the duty to disclose to the defendant favorable evidence in its possession, which is material to his guilt or innocence. The second obligation arises in all cases where there has been a defense production request, and in some cases, even though defense counsel has made no affirmative request.

5. Confrontation

The Sixth Amendment right of an accused to confront adverse witnesses has been made binding upon the states through the Fourteenth Amendment. By implication, the right to confront adverse witnesses accords the defendant the right to be present in the courtroom at all times when testimony is being taken. The right of personal attendance can, however, be relinquished through fractious conduct or voluntary absentia. The constitutional policy underlying the confrontation clause is concern for testimonial reliability. When a witness testifies in court, he is under oath and subject to cross-examination, and the judge or jury has an opportunity to listen to him, observe his demeanor and form their own opinions as to his truthfulness.

6. Cruel and unusual punishment

The Eighth Amendment provision against cruel and unusual punishment is binding on the states through the Fourteenth Amendment. Cruelty in the constitutional sense is not confined to protection against unnecessarily cruel methods of punishment. The constitutional concept of cruelty is expansive and draws its meaning from contemporary standards and values. The Eighth Amendment has been held to preclude: (1) tortures and other objectionable methods of punishment; (2) excessive punishments or those which are disproportionate to the underlying offense; (3) punishments leveled at human conditions rather than overt behavior; and (4) capital punishment sentencing schemes which are mandatory, on the one hand, or which fail to provide adequate standards, on the other.

Chapter 11

CIVIL RIGHTS AND CIVIL RIGHTS LEGISLATION*

[I]n view of the Constitution, in the eye of the law,
there is in this country no superior, dominant, ruling
class of citizens. There is no caste here. Our Constitution is color-blind, and neither knows nor tolerates
classes among citizens. In respect of civil rights, all
citizens are equal before the law. The humblest is the
peer of the most powerful. The law regards man as
man, and takes no account of his surroundings or of his
color when his civil rights as guaranteed by the supreme law of the land are involved.

Mr. Justice Harlan, dissenting in
Plessy v. Ferguson, 163 U.S. 537, 559 (1896).

Section

§ 11.1   Historical background

In the pre-Civil War era, a Negro slave had no legal status. He was regarded as little more than a chattel or prized
possession. He could not bring suit in a court of law, own

* by Jacqueline R. Kanovitz

property, make contracts, marry or enter into other normal legal relationships.[1] As a precautionary measure against assisting run-away slaves, proprietors of inns and other public accommodations were, in most localities, prohibited by law from receiving persons of African descent.[2]

The institution of slavery found sanction in the Constitution of the United States. The property rights of the master were recognized and protected under article IV, section 2, which guaranteed the return of fugitive slaves. The political consequences of slavery were treated in article I, section 2, which provided that slaves were to be counted as three-fifths of a person for purposes of apportioning representatives to the lower house of Congress. On the eve of the Civil War, the Supreme Court placed its stamp of legitimacy on the institution of slavery. In the famous *Dred Scott* decision,[3] Mr. Chief Justice Taney proclaimed that the dark race as a class was inferior and altogether unfit to associate with the white race, either in social or political relations;[4] and whether enslaved or emancipated, the Negro could not be a citizen of the United States or claim the rights and privileges guaranteed by the Constitution. This, then, was the legal status of the Black man on the eve of the Civil War.

§ 11.2   —Reconstruction amendments and legislation

After the Civil War was brought to a conclusion, Congress turned its attention to the tragic plight of the millions of Black people who had been left homeless and jobless in bitter, war-ravaged communities. Emancipation of the former slaves was accomplished by the Thirteenth Amendment. Ratified in 1865, the Thirteenth Amendment proclaimed that "[n]either slavery nor involuntary servitude . . . shall exist within the United States, or any place subject to their jurisdiction," and authorized Congress to enact appropriate legislation to carry the constitutional purpose into effect.

The blessings of freedom were not immediately realized by

---

[1] Civil Rights Cases, 109 US 3, 27 LEd 835, 3 SCt 18 (1883).
[2] *Id.*

[3] Dred Scott v. Sandford, 60 US(19 How) 393, 15 LEd 691 (1856).
[4] *Id.* at 407, 15 LEd at 701.

the emancipated slaves. Hostile Southern legislatures responded to the Thirteenth Amendment with the enactment of Black Codes which were designed to compel the newly freed slaves to return to the services of their former masters. This purpose was accomplished by prohibiting Black persons from holding, owning or leasing property, entering into contractual relationships, or engaging in any other occupations.[5] A period of racial turbulence and violent unrest followed as terrorist organizations like the Ku Klux Klan and the Knights of the White Camelia sprang up in numerous local communities.

The Congress which met at the close of the Civil War faced some of the most difficult problems which have ever beset any nation. Military governments were set up in the former Confederate states, and traditions of self-government in the South gave way to a period of federal domination. In the decade that followed, two additional constitutional amendments were added, and a host of federal civil rights statutes were enacted.

The Fourteenth Amendment was ratified in 1868. Unlike the Thirteenth, whose mandate was of universal application, the limitations contained in the Fourteenth Amendment were couched in language addressed to the states. The immediate object of the Fourteenth Amendment was to protect the newly freed slaves from arbitrary and unequal treatment at the hands of hostile state legislatures and local government officials. To this end, the Fourteenth Amendment first declared that all persons born within the United States are citizens and then provided:

> No State shall make or enforce any law which shall abridge the privileges or immunities of citizens of the United States; nor shall any State deprive any person of life, liberty, or property, without due process of law; nor deny to any person within its jurisdiction the equal protection of the laws.

By virtue of section 5, Congress was authorized to enact appropriate legislation to implement the Fourteenth Amend-

---

[5] Slaughter-House Cases, 83 US(16 Wall) 36, 21 LEd 394 (1873).

ment. The process of amendment was completed in 1870 with the ratification of the Fifteenth Amendment dealing with suffrage, and providing that the right of a citizen to vote shall not be denied on account of "race, color, or previous condition of servitude."

In the winter of 1865–66, a Joint Congressional Committee on Reconstruction was set up to investigate reports of racial mistreatment and turbulent conditions in the South.[6] The results of this investigation lead to the adoption of the Civil Rights Act of 1866, the first of many federal civil rights laws to come out of the Reconstruction era. Section 1 of the Civil Rights Act of 1866 provided, among other things, that

> citizens, of every race and color, without regard to any previous condition of slavery or involuntary servitude, . . . shall have the same right, in every State and Territory in the United States, to make and enforce contracts, to sue, be parties, and give evidence, to inherit, purchase, lease, sell, hold, and convey real and personal property, and to full and equal benefit of all laws and proceedings for the security of person and property, as is enjoyed by white citizens.[7]

Section 2 of the Civil Rights Act of 1866 has had a more direct impact upon the professional conduct of law enforcement officers. Inspired by reports of racial mistreatment at the hands of local officials, section 2 made it a federal offense, punishable by a $1,000 fine, one year imprisonment, or both, for any person acting "under color of any law, statute, ordinance, regulation, or custom" of any state to deprive any inhabitant of the United States of certain enumerated rights.[8]

---

[6] United States Commission on Civil Rights, LAW ENFORCEMENT: A REPORT OF EQUAL PROTECTION IN THE SOUTH 6-10 (1965).

[7] Act of April 9, 1866, ch 31, §1, 14 Stat 27, re-enacted as 42 USC §§1981 and 1982. As a result of judicial misgivings with regard to the constitutionality of §1, now 42 USC §§1981 and 1982, this statute was allowed to gather dust during the first century of its legal existence. In 1968, the Supreme Court resuscitated the 1866 law in *Jones* v. *Alfred H. Mayer Co.*, 392 US 409, 20 LEd(2d) 1189, 88 SCt 2186 (1968), and it is today a potent civil rights measure. The current interpretation of §§1981 and 1982 is discussed in §11.4, *infra*.

[8] Act of April 9, 1866, ch 31, §2, 14 Stat 27.

Section 2, with a few changes and modifications, survives today as one of the two major federal criminal civil rights statutes. The text of the modern revision is presently codified at 18 U.S.C. §242. Its companion statute, 18 U.S.C. §241, is derived from the Civil Rights Act of 1870,[9] and makes it a federal offense, punishable by fines up to $5,000, imprisonment for as much as 10 years, or both, for conspiring to "injure, oppress, threaten, or intimidate any citizen in the free exercise or enjoyment of any right or privilege secured to him by the Constitution or laws of the United States."[10]

The Ku Klux Klan Act of 1871 was the last significant enactment of the Reconstruction period. Section 1 of the Ku Klux Klan Act,[11] which survives today as 42 U.S.C. §1983, creates a civil cause of action, enforceable in federal courts, against any person, acting under color of state authority, who deprives another of any rights, privileges or immunities secured by the Constitution or laws of the United States. Section 1983 is the civil counterpart of 18 U.S.C. §242. Since all action undertaken by a police officer in an official capacity is "under color of" state authority, a law enforcement officer who abuses his authority may find himself in a federal court defending a section 242 criminal action or a section 1983 damage suit. More will be said about the Reconstruction era laws in the sections which follow.

For the present, it is enough to note that because of conservative early interpretations or judicial misgivings as to their constitutionality, the full legal impact of the Reconstruction laws was not realized until almost a century thereafter. Ironically, their resurrection came after the Congress of the United States had struggled in 1964 with the enactment of the public accommodations law [12] and the equal employment

---

[9] Act of May 31, 1870, ch 114, 16 Stat 140, 144.

[10] Since police abuses are potentially within the ambit of both §§241 and 242, these statutes are treated in fuller detail in §§11.10, 11.11, *infra.*

[11] Act of April 20, 1871, ch 22, §1, 17 Stat 13.

[12] Civil Rights Act of 1964, tit. II, §201, 78 Stat 243, 42 USC §2000(a) *et seq.*, guarantees all persons the right to service in inns, hotels, motels, restaurants, motion picture theatres and other places of public accommodation without regard to race, color, religion or national origin. The remedies provided for are civil.

opportunities act,[13] and in 1968, with the open housing law.[14] In retrospect, the bitterly fought controversies in the 1960's as to whether this nation should have a public accommodations law, an equal employment opportunities act, and a fair housing law were tempests in a teapot. The Black citizens of the nation had virtually all of these rights already and had had them for almost a century. The Reconstruction Congress had taken care of this. It remained only for the Supreme Court to interpret the Reconstruction laws as broadly as they read.[15]

§ 11.3 —Separate but equal

By 1877, the crusading zeal of the Northern liberals and radicals had run its course. The last of the federal troops was withdrawn from the South, and white rule was again restored. In 1883 the Supreme Court formally announced that the period of national wardship for the Black man had come to an end, and the time had arrived for him to take up his own struggle for political equality.[16] The nation turned its attention to industrial expansion and the conquest of the West. For the next seventy years, the South would be left, without substantial interference by the Congress or the Supreme Court, to formulate its own solutions to the race problem. The answers which the South proposed took the form of segregation codes, designed to cut off all social intercourse between the races. By the last decade of the nineteenth century, *Jim-Crow* laws had begun their debut. State legislatures proceeded cautiously

---

[13] Civil Rights Act of 1964, tit.VII, §703, 78 Stat 255, 42 USC §2000(e) *et seq.*, makes it an unlawful employment practice for an employer to fail or refuse to hire or to discharge any individual or otherwise to discriminate against any individual with respect to his compensation, terms, conditions or privileges of employment because of his race, color, religion, sex or national origin. Similar types of restrictions are imposed upon employment agency and labor union practices. Title VII is not a criminal statute. The remedies for enforcement are civil.

[14] Civil Rights Act of 1968, tit. VIII, 82 Stat 81, 42 USC §3601 *et seq.*, makes it unlawful to discriminate against any person in the sale or rental of real estate because of that person's race, color, religion or national origin. As with the other civil rights laws enacted during the 1960's, the remedies provided for the enforcement of the 1968 law are civil rather than criminal.

[15] See §11.4, *infra.*

[16] Civil Rights Cases, 109 US 3, 27 LEd 835, 3 SCt 18 (1883).

at first because doubts existed as to the constitutionality of these measures. The Supreme Court's endorsement came in the 1896 case of *Plessy v. Ferguson*.[17] Plessy, an individual of one-eighth Negro descent, had been criminally prosecuted for violating a state statute requiring racial segregation in public carriers. On appeal, he contended that the statute violated the Thirteenth and Fourteenth Amendments. Eight members of the Supreme Court disagreed, finding no constitutional infirmity in state laws requiring separation of the races provided that equal facilities were available to the members of each. Mr. Justice Harlan alone dissented, sounding what would become the position of the Court in 1945:

> [I]n view of the Constitution, in the eye of the law there is in this country no superior, dominant, ruling class of citizens. There is no caste here. Our Constitution is color-blind, and neither knows nor tolerates classes among citizens. In respect of civil rights, all citizens are equal before the law. The humblest is the peer of the most powerful. The law regards man as man and takes no account of his surroundings or his color when his civil rights as guaranteed by the supreme law of the land are involved.[18]

§ 11.4　—The second Reconstruction

Plessy v. *Ferguson* provided the legal foundation for segregation codes, and they flourished in the South for the next sixty years. In 1954, the Supreme Court handed down the landmark decision of *Brown* v. *Board of Education*,[19] which established that "separate but equal" no longer satisfied the Constitution within the field of public education. It soon became apparent that *Brown* was not limited to the field of public education. The Fourteenth Amendment equal protection clause, as now construed, requires the government to assume a color-blind posture in the field of race relations. This means that state and local governments can not operate *any* public facility on a segregated basis [20] nor compel or assist private

[17] 163 US 537, 41 LEd 256, 16 SCt 1138 (1896).

[18] *Id.* at 559, 41 LEd at 263-64, 16 SCt 1164 (Harlan, J., dissenting).

[19] 347 US 483, 98 LEd 873, 74 SCt 686 (1954).

[20] *See, e.g.*, Holmes v. City of Atlanta, 350 US 879, 100 LEd 776, 76 SCt 141 (1955) (*remanded*); Simkins v. Moses H. Cone Mem'l Hosp., 323 F(2d) 959 (4thCir 1963); Kerr v. Enoch Pratt Free Library, 149 F(2d) 212 (4thCir 1945).

individuals to engage in racially discriminatory practices.[21] The era of government-sponsored obstacles to full racial equity was over.

Simply striking down state laws authorizing or compelling separation of the races and integrating government-operated programs and facilities, by itself, was not sufficient to integrate the Black man into the "Great Society." Private prejudice remained as a formidable barrier to the attainment of full racial equality. So long as private employment opportunities and private housing markets remained closed to the Black man, he was destined to remain a second-class citizen. The focus of the civil rights movement shifted to this new frontier.

The big constitutional issue of the 1960's was whether Congress had the power to direct private individuals—the nation's restaurant and hotel proprietors, employers, and real estate owners—to lay aside their racial prejudice and treat all persons alike in their business and professional dealings. If such a power did exist, it was not to be found in the Fourteenth Amendment. Its directive, "No *State* shall . . . deny to any person within its jurisdiction the equal protection of the laws," had served the civil rights movement well in its drive to eliminate discriminatory government practices, but the focal point now was the private sector; by settled interpretation, the Fourteenth Amendment could not reach or operate upon discriminatory practices engaged in by private citizens.[22] The Thirteenth Amendment's mandate, "Neither slavery nor involuntary servitude . . . shall exist within the United States . . . ," was not similarly restricted, but it was passed over as a source of congressional power to eradicate private barriers to racial equality for an entirely different reason. Discrimination, without more, did not appear to constitute a reestablishment of slavery and, consequently, was thought to fall beyond the reach of Congress's power to implement the Thirteenth Amendment.

Despite this, several important race relations measures

---

[21] Adickes v. S. H. Kress & Co., 398 US 144, 26 LEd(2d) 142, 90 SCt 1598 (1970); Shelley v. Kraemer, 334 US 1, 92 LEd 1161, 68 SCt 836 (1948).

[22] Id.

were enacted by Congress during the 1960's; the primary source of power drawn upon was the Constitution's article I, section 8, Interstate Commerce Clause.[23] With a little imagination, a relationship could be found between discrimination in the operation of places of public accommodation, in the sale and rental of housing, and in employment practices, and the free flow of goods and services across state lines.[24] During the 1960's Congress drafted legislation to the limits of its interstate commerce powers. The first significant enactment came in 1964. Title II of the Civil Rights Act of 1964, known as the Public Accommodations Law,[25] guaranteed all persons the right to equal services in hotels, motels, restaurants, motion picture houses, and other privately-owned places of public accommodation, without regard to race, color, religion, or national origin. Title VII of the same enactment, known as the Equal Employment Opportunities Law,[26] afforded similarly broad protection against discriminatory practices upon the part of employers, employment agencies and labor unions. In 1968, Congress turned its attention to the housing problem and enacted the Fair Housing Law[27] which condemned discrimination in the sale and rental of private housing. The civil rights measures of the 1960's were not criminal statutes; they were and are enforced by means of civil sanctions. Would these utilizations of the commerce power be upheld? The Supreme Court's response was affirmative. In *Katzenback* v. *McClung*,[28] it upheld the constitutionality of the Public Accommodations Law,[29] as applied to a restaurant whose impact upon interstate commerce was almost imperceptible.

In 1968, while the ultimate reach of Congress's power to regulate private discrimination under the Commerce Clause

---

[23] *See, e.g.*, S.REP.NO. 872, 88th Cong, 2d Sess, 12-13.

[24] Heart of Atlanta Motel v. United States, 379 US 241, 13 LEd(2d) 258, 85 SCt 348 (1964); Katzenbach v. McClung, 379 US 294, 13 LEd(2d) 290, 85 SCt 377 (1964).

[25] Civil Rights Act of 1964, tit. II, §201, 78 Stat 243, 42 USC 2000(a) *et seq.*

[26] Civil Rights Act of 1964, tit. VII, §703, 78 Stat 243, 42 USC §2000(e)-2 *et seq.*

[27] Civil Rights Act of 1968, tit. VIII, §801, 82 Stat 81, 42 USC §3601 *et seq.*

[28] 379 US 294, 13 LEd(2d) 290, 85 SCt 377 (1964).

[29] Civil Rights Act of 1964, tit. II, §201, 78 Stat 243, 42 USC §2000(a) *et seq.*

was still a controversial issue, the Supreme Court decided *Jones* v. *Alfred H. Mayer Co.*[30] in which it gave a revolutionary interpretation to the Thirteenth Amendment. Prior to the effective date of the 1968 Fair Housing Law, a housing dispute arose between Jones, a Black man, and the Alfred H. Mayer Co. Jones claimed that Mayer's refusal to sell to him was racially motivated. His attorney found a musty Reconstruction-vintage statute, 42 U.S.C. §1982,[31] dusted it off, and filed suit in a federal court asking for an injunction. The Supreme Court ruled that the Reconstruction Congress intended by this law to prohibit *all* racially motivated refusals to sell or rent housing, private as well as governmental and, what's more important, that Congress had the power to do so. The authority came from the Enabling Clause of the Thirteenth Amendment which, in the words of the Court, empowered Congress *"to pass all laws necessary and proper for abolishing all badges and incidents of slavery in the United States."*[32]

Jones v. *Alfred H. Mayer Co.* is a landmark on several different scores. First, it interpreted the Enabling Clause of the Thirteenth Amendment as a blanket authorization to Congress to "determine what are the badges and incidents of slavery, and . . . to translate that determination into effective legislation"[33] operating upon the acts of private individuals. No longer will it be necessary for Congress to regulate private race relations under the guise of removing "impediments" to the free flow of interstate commerce. Congress has virtually unlimited power under the Thirteenth Amendment to legislate against racial discrimination—private as well as public, federal as well as state. Second, *Jones* stands as precedent for construing civil rights measures to the broadest limits that their language will reach under the Constitution. Finally, *Jones* gave a new lease on life to several Reconstruction civil

---

[30] 392 US 409, 20 LEd(2d) 1189, 88 SCt 2186 (1968).

[31] The text of 42 USC §1982 provides:

All citizens of the United States shall have the same right, in every State and Territory, as is enjoyed by white citizens thereof to inherit, pur-chase, lease, sell, hold, and convey real and personal property.

[32] 392 US at 439, 20 LEd(2d) at 1207, 88 SCt at 2203 (emphasis in original).

[33] *Id.* at 440, 20 LEd(2d) at 1208, 88 SCt at 2203.

rights measures which had lain dormant on the books for a century.

The civil rights laws enacted during the 1960's bear some visible earmarks of political feasibility and compromise. In the Public Accommodations Act of 1964, for instance, Congress exempted the so-called "Mrs. Murphy's boarding houses," which are those owner-occupied establishments having five or fewer rooms.[34] Furthermore, some important fields where racial discrimination is practiced were left untouched by civil rights measures enacted during the 1960's. Discrimination in private school education provides one notable example. The Reconstruction statutes resurrected in *Jones* provide avenues for legal redress in other areas. In *Runyon v. McCray*,[35] the Supreme Court held that the refusal of a private, commercially operated, nonsectarian school to admit Black children because of their race was actionable under 42 U.S.C §1981. (Section 1981[36] is another legacy from the Reconstruction era, enacted by Congress pursuant to its powers to enforce the Thirteenth Amendment by appropriate legislation.) One hundred years after the Civil War was over, this country experienced what will probably be known to our grandchildren as the second Reconstruction, a period of reforms in race relations in which the courts were at least as instrumental as the legislature.

In the remaining sections of this Chapter, we will focus on federal civil and criminal remedies available for redressing unconstitutional conduct upon the part of the police. Like the statutes considered above, most derive from the Reconstruction era. Though mistreatment of racial minorities at the hands of local officials may have provided a primary impetus for the statutes' enactment during the post-War period, their application in modern times has advanced well beyond the evils that inspired their enactment. Thus, 42 U.S.C. §1983, 18 U.S.C §241, and 18 U.S.C. §242 are not merely race-

---

[34] 42 USC §2000(a) (b)(1).

[35] 427 US 160, 49 LEd(2d) 415, 96 SCt 2586 (1976).

[36] 42 USC §1981 provides, in pertinent part, that "[a]ll persons . . . shall have the same right . . . to make and enforce contracts . . . as is enjoyed by white citizens. . . ."

protection statutes. They protect the rights of all the nation's inhabitants.

§ 11.5   Federal civil remedies for official misconduct

Forty-two U.S.C. §1983 [37] creates a federal civil cause of action against any person who "under color of any [state] statute, ordinance, regulation, custom, or usage" deprives another of "rights, privileges, or immunities secured by the Constitution and laws" of the United States. Originally enacted as section 1 of the Ku Klux Klan Act of 1871,[38] section 1983 in recent years has become a widely used vehicle for seeking private redress against law enforcement officers for the violation of basic civil rights. In 1972 alone, some eight thousand section 1983 actions were filed in federal courts.[39] A significant portion of those filed involved suits against law enforcement personnel. The remedy afforded by section 1983 is supplementary to any state law remedy, and an aggrieved individual may resort to either or both.[40]

In order to state an actionable claim under section 1983, the plaintiff must allege that (1) the defendant acted "under color of" state or local law, and (2) that the plaintiff was deprived of some right, privilege or immunity guaranteed under the Constitution or laws of the United States. It is not necessary for the plaintiff to aver that the officer acted with a specific *intent* to deprive him of his civil rights,[41] but, as will be seen shortly, the officer is sometimes permitted to defend on the basis that he acted in good faith and with reasonable grounds to believe that his conduct was lawful.[42]

---

[37] The full text of 42 USC §1983 reads:

Every person who, under color of any statute, ordinance, regulation, custom, or usage, of any State or Territory, subjects, or causes to be subjected, any citizen of the United States or other person within the jurisdiction thereof to the deprivation of any rights, privileges, or immunities secured by the Constitution and laws, shall be liable to the party injured in an action at law, suit in equity, or other proper proceeeding for redress.

[38] Act of April 20, 1871, ch 22, §1, 17 Stat 13.

[39] McCormack, *Federalism and Section 1983: Limitations on Judicial Enforcement of Constitutional Protections*, 60 VaLRev 1 (1974).

[40] Monroe v. Pape, 365 US 167, 5 LEd(2d) 492, 81 SCt 473 (1961).

[41] *Id*.

[42] Pierson v. Ray, 386 US 547, 18 LEd(2d) 288, 87 SCt 1213 (1967).

§ 11.6   —"Under color of" state law

Section 1983 is based upon the Fourteenth Amendment; [43] consequently, it reaches only "state action" or action taken "under color of" state law. Any official conduct engaged in by a law enforcement officer pursuant to some state law authorizing or requiring this action, satisfies the section 1983 "under color of" state law requirement. But state law rarely authorizes, let alone requires, an officer to violate federal constitutional or statutory rights.

1. Officer's section 1983 liability for acts in excess of his state authority

In *Monroe v. Pape,*[44] the Supreme Court faced the issue of whether a police officer could be regarded as acting "under color of" state law and, thus, be suable under section 1983 when he exceeds the lawful authority entrusted him by the state. Monroe brought suit against thirteen members of the Chicago police department, alleging that they had broken into his home without a warrant or probable cause, that they had ransacked the premises, had beaten and arrested him, and that ultimately they released him without charges. The officers defended against section 1983 liability on the grounds that the acts alleged were not authorized by state law and were in fact a violation of it; consequently, they could not be regarded as having been performed "under color of" state law. The Supreme Court disagreed and ruled that section 1983's "under color of" state law requirement did not require actual state legal authorization for the acts complained of; it was sufficient that the state had placed the officers in a position where they were able to assert a "colorable claim" or "pretense" of state authority for their conduct. In the course of its opinion, the Court stated:

> "Misuse of power, possessed by virtue of state law and made possible only because the wrongdoer is clothed with the authority of state law, is action taken 'under color of' state law." [45]

[43] District of Columbia v. Carter, 409 US 418, 34 LEd(2d) 613, 93 SCt 602 (1973).

[44] 365 US 167, 5 LEd(2d) 492, 81 SCt 473 (1961).

[45] *Id.* at 184, 5 LEd(2d) at 503, 81 SCt at 482 *quoting* United States v. Classic, 313 US 299, 326 (1941).

It is significant that the *Monroe* defendants were acting in the line of duty when the unconstitutional behavior occurred. Would the Supreme Court have reached the same result if the Chicago police officers had broken into Monroe's home and ransacked it in the course of attempting a burglary? One can be certain that no action under section 1983 would lie.[46] An officer will not be regarded as acting "under color of" his legal authority when he seeks to advance his private interests in a manner no way connected to his official status or employment responsibilities. The line between "under color of" state law behavior and private acts, however, is not always an easy one to draw. To complicate matters, the courts have consistently ruled that whether the officer is in uniform or out of it, or whether he is on duty or off, are not controlling factors.[47] Where, then, can this line be placed?

Decisions holding an officer's conduct to be "under color of" his legal authority appear to be grouped into two separate categories. In the first category fall excesses committed in the line of duty. When the officer performs acts of a general nature which fall within the scope of his employment duties, such as making an arrest, conducting a search, interrogating a suspect, or quieting disorderly behavior, he will be regarded as acting "under color of" law even though he oversteps his lawful authority. With respect to such acts, it does not matter whether the officer is in uniform or whether he is "on duty" in the strict sense. The reason is, that whenever an officer is engaged in performing the duties of his office, he is asserting at least a "colorable claim" or "pretense" of state legal authority for his conduct. He is thus acting "under color of" state law as *Monroe v. Pape* defines this term.

Even though the officer is not purporting to act in the line of duty when the wrongful behavior occurs, he will still be treated as acting "under color of" his state authority if his status as a police officer materially facilitated his perpetration

---

[46] Russell v. Bodner, 409 F(2d) 280 (3dCir 1973); Rogers v. Fuller, 410 FSupp 187 (MD NC 1976).

[47] Stengel v. Belcher, 522 F(2d) 438 (6thCir 1975); Robinson v. Davis, 447 F(2d) 753 (4thCir 1971), *cert. denied,* 405 US 979, 31 LEd(2d) 254, 92 SCt 1204 (1972); Rogers v. Fuller, 410 FSupp 187, 191 (MD NC 1976); Johnson v. Hackett, 284 FSupp 933, 937 (ED Pa 1968).

of the wrong. In the second category, then, is misbehavior made possible only because the wrongdoer is a police officer. Unless the wrong complained of bears one of these two relationships to the officer's employment status or his duties, it represents private misbehavior and is not actionable under section 1983.

Stengel v. *Belcher* [48] exemplifies the first category. Belcher, a police officer, was off duty and out of uniform when several patrons in a tavern where he was having a drink became involved in a brawl. Without identifying himself as a police officer, Belcher intervened in an effort to restore order; a scuttle followed; Officer Belcher drew his gun and fired several shots. Two men were mortally wounded and a third was injured. Trial testimony established that, under departmental regulations, police officers were required to carry pistols and to halt criminal activity even when they were off duty. On the basis of this, the U.S. Court of Appeals for the Sixth Circuit ruled that Belcher was acting "under color of" his state authority and not as a private citizen. This case is correctly decided since Officer Belcher's excess was committed in the line of duty as defined by state law. Whenever an officer oversteps the Constitution while acting in the line of duty, his conduct is "under color of" his legal authority. [49]

Cases falling in the second category are rarer, but *Catlette* v. *United States* [50] is an example. A group of Jehovah's Witnesses sought legal protection from one Deputy Sheriff Catlette against a band of ruffians who were threatening them with violence. When they reached his office, Catlette detained them, telephoned the gang, and joined with them in forcing the frightened men to drink caster oil and to submit to other indignities. In spite of the fact that Catlette had removed his badge before embarking upon this sadistic course of conduct, the Court of Appeals for the Fourth Circuit ruled that Catlette's misbehavior was "under color of" his legal authority. *Crews* v. *United States* [51] furnishes another illustration. There,

---

[48] 522 F(2d) 438 (6thCir 1975).

[49] See also, United States ex rel. Smith v. Heil, 308 FSupp 1063 (ED Pa 1970).

[50] 132 F(2d) 902 (4thCir 1943).

[51] 160 F(2d) 746 (5thCir 1947).

a town marshal bull-whipped a Black man and then forced him to leap to his death from a bridge. The Fifth Circuit Court of Appeals found these acts to be "under color of" state law, because, minutes before, the marshal had used trumped-up charges to take him into custody.

Catlette and *Crews* cannot be explained as excesses committed in the line of duty; neither man was engaged in performing any duties of his office when these terrible incidents occurred. The explanation for both is that the brutalizations were made possible only because the wrongdoer was a peace officer. Catlette's ability to detain his victims and Crew's to take his into custody depended upon official status. The same connecting link between the officer's status and his misbehavior is found in *Henry* v. *Cagle,*[52] where the Sixth Circuit Court of Appeals ruled that an off-duty constable was suable under section 1983 for assaulting a prisoner, then in custody of another, to settle a private feud. "Under color of" state law was found to be satisfied by the fact that the constable's status afforded him access to the prisoner that would have been unavailable to an ordinary citizen.

Where the police officer is guilty of misbehavior that is neither related to his employment nor made possible by his badge, he acts as a private citizen, and the injured party must look to state law remedies, if any, for redress. Those cases which have dismissed section 1983 actions for failure to establish that the injury was inflicted "under color of" the defendant's authority, appear to fit within this classification scheme. In *Watkins* v. *Oaklawn Jockey Club,*[53] the Eighth Circuit Court of Appeals ruled that a uniformed police officer, working during his off-duty hours as a private guard at a race track, was not suable under section 1983 for ordering the plaintiff to leave where he made it clear that he was issuing this order on instruction of the track owners. Since the officer was neither acting nor purporting to act in the line of duty, nor aided by his office in committing the injury complained of, the case was correctly decided. In rare cases, misconduct committed while on duty may be found to lack "under color

---

[52] 482 F(2d) 137 (6thCir 1973).   [53] 183 F(2d) 440 (8thCir 1950).

of" state authority characteristics. *Johnson v. Hackett,*[54] where a police officer, while on duty, yelled racially disparaging remarks at a pedestrian, who was minding his own business, and then challenged him to fight, furnishes an illustration. In spite of the fact that the officer was on duty, his misbehavior bore no relationship to his employment responsibilities; nor was it facilitated by his badge. The section 1983 action against him was appropriately dismissed.

In summation, an officer will be regarded as acting "under color of" state law for purposes of section 1983 actions if (1) he is acting in the line of duty when the excess occurs, or if (2) his badge assists in perpetrating the wrong.

2. Section 1983 liability of federal law enforcement personnel

Federal law enforcement agents are not suable under section 1983 because they act under color of *federal* rather than *state* law.[55] This does not mean that aggrieved citizens are without avenues of redress against federal agents who invade their constitutional rights. It simply means that no action under section 1983 is available. Until recently, however, the only recourse was a state civil suit under some tort law theory such as false arrest, false imprisonment, assault and battery, or invasion of privacy. While these tort actions parallel some of the constitutional claims assertible under section 1983, state tort law never purported to afford a remedy for all types of constitutional injuries.

An anomalous situation arose. When a citizen was complaining of wrongs committed by a state law enforcement officer, he was assured of a federal forum and an effective remedy under section 1983; but the doors to federal court were closed to him when he suffered a comparable deprivation at the hands of federal enforcement personnel. The federal courts, thus, had broader powers of supervision over state law enforcement officers than over agents of the federal government. In *Bivens v. Six Unknown Named Agents of the Federal Bureau of Narcotics,*[56] the Supreme Court corrected

[54] 284 FSupp 933 (ED Pa 1968).
[55] Bivens v. Six Unknown Named Agents of the Federal Bureau of Nar- cotics, 403 US 388, 29 LEd(2d) 619, 91 SCt 1999 (1971).
[56] *Id.*

this inequity. The Court there announced that federal courts, unaided by statute, could entertain a private action brought against federal agents to recover damages for an unreasonable search and seizure. The action was said to arise directly out of the Fourth Amendment. Although the federal common-law remedy fashioned in *Bivens* dealt with the Fourth Amendment, the lower federal courts have not read *Bivens* as thus limited. The trend is decidedly in favor of permitting private actions against federal law enforcement agents to the same extent and under the same circumstances as have traditionally been available against state officers under section 1983.[57] Indeed, the body of law which has been developed around section 1983 with respect to claims assertible, defenses and immunities is now being applied by analogy in *Bivens* type of actions.[58] No longer will citizens be without a federal remedy for vindicating constitutional injuries inflicted by agents acting "under color of" federal authority.

3. Section 1983 liability of private citizens

Section 1983 is bottomed on the Fourteenth Amendment.[59] Like the amendment on which it is based, it reaches only "state action" or action "under color of" state law, which are alternative ways of expressing the same legal concept.[60] When a private individual acts in his purely private pursuits, he is immune from section 1983 liability no matter how wrongful his conduct may appear. Should a private citizen arbitrarily strike another, it is a simple case of assault and battery, actionable in state court, but not giving rise to a federal section 1983 claim. This stands in sharp contrast to the law enforcement officer's position.[61] The reason inheres, of course, in the Fourteenth Amendment's limited reach.

---

[57] Paton v. La Prade, 524 F(2d) 862 (3dCir 1975) (First Amendment); Wounded Knee Legal Defense/Offense Comm. v. Federal Bureau of Investigation, 507 F(2d) 1281, 1284 (8thCir 1974) (Sixth Amendment); States Marine Lines, Inc. v. Schultz, 498 F(2d) 1146, 1157 (4thCir 1974) (Fifth Amendment).

[58] Mark v. Groff, 521 F(2d) 1376, 1380 (9thCir 1975); Brubaker v. King, 505 F(2d) 534, 537 (7thCir 1974).

[59] District of Columbia v. Carter, 409 US 418, 34 LEd(2d) 613, 93 SCt 602 (1973).

[60] United States v. Price, 383 US 787, 16 LEd(2d) 276, 86 SCt 1152 (1966).

[61] Morgan v. Labiak, 368 F(2d) 338 (10thCir 1966); Basista v. Weir, 340 F(2d) 74 (3dCir 1965).

There are, however, certain instances in which private individuals may become "state actors" suable under section 1983. While a lengthy discourse on "state action" concepts goes well beyond this textbook's practical goals, a limited investigation is desirable. State action has been found to exist in a variety of contexts but two are especially pertinent.

(a) State concert theory

Private parties may be brought within the orbit of section 1983 when they act in concert with, conspire with or participate with state agents in conduct that the agents are constitutionally forbidden to perform.[62] In *Fine v. City of New York*,[63] a private citizen assisted police officers in breaking into and conducting a warrantless search of another man's apartment. Because the illegal search and seizure was a joint endeavor, the Second Circuit Court of Appeals held that the private individual was subject to section 1983 liability along with the government agents. Whether the state concert theory would justify imposing section 1983 liability upon a private individual who makes a groundless complaint leading to a false arrest, is a question for which there are no easy answers.[64] The result should turn upon whether the arresting officer knew that the charges were unfounded. In the absence of such knowledge, there is no conspiracy, and without this, the private citizen is guilty of no more than a private wrong. The better-reasoned cases have declined to find liability where the state's involvement in the arrest was as an innocent tool.

(b) Public function theory

Where the state delegates to a private individual powers which are sovereign or governmental in nature, the "state action" requirement is satisfied, and in exercising these pow-

---

[62] United States v. Price, 383 US 787, 16 LEd(2d) 276, 86 SCt 1152 (1966).

[63] 529 F(2d) 70 (2dCir 1975).

[64] Adickes v. S. H. Kress & Co., 398 US 144, 26 LEd(2d) 142, 90 SCt 1598 (1970) (private party liable if plaintiff can show that defendants reached a common understanding to deprive him of constitutional rights). See also, Smith v. Brookshire Bros., Inc., 519 F(2d) 93 (5thCir 1975); Warner v. Croft, 406 FSupp 717 (WD Okla 1975); Canty v. Richmond, Va., Police Dept., 383 FSupp 1396 (ED Va 1974).

ers, the private individual will be required to measure up to the constitutional responsibilities that are imposed upon the state.[65] It is on the "public function" theory that the Supreme Court, in several cases, has found private detectives to be acting "under color of" state law.[66] Where a private detective is licensed by the state and endowed with powers comparable to police officers, his action is "state action" and his section 1983 liability is commensurate in all respects.[67]

In many jurisdictions there are shoplifting statutes authorizing proprietors to detain those whom they reasonably suspect to be guilty of shoplifting. There have been numerous attempts made by falsely-accused shoppers to hold store owners liable under section 1983 on the theory that state law has delegated to them powers analogous to those of a police officer. These attempts have, for the most part, been unsuccessful.[68] The courts have emphasized that proprietors, unlike police officers, act in their own self-interest and not in the interest of the public; hence, though their acts may resemble those of the police, they are not performing a public function.

It goes without saying that the mere fact that a private individual holds himself out as a police officer or impersonates an officer does not convert his conduct into action "under color of" state law.[69] There must be some actual delegation or vesting of state power to bring private conduct within the ambit of "state action" under the public function theory.

4. Section 1983 liability of government entities and supervisory personnel

In *Monroe v. Pape*,[70] discussed at the beginning of this section, the plaintiff sued the city of Chicago as well as the thirteen police officers who broke into his home. The Supreme

---

[65] Evans v. Newton, 382 US 296, 15 LEd(2d) 373, 86 SCt 486 (1966); Smith v. Allwright, 321 US 649, 88 LEd 987, 64 SCt 757 (1944).

[66] Griffin v. Maryland, 378 US 130, 12 LEd(2d) 754, 84 SCt 1770 (1964); Williams v. United States, 341 US 97, 95 LEd 774, 71 SCt 576 (1951).

[67] See cases cited in note 66, *supra*.

[68] Ouzts v. Maryland Nat'l Ins. Co., 505 F(2d) 547 (9thCir 1974); Battle v. Dayton-Hudson Corp., 399 FSupp 900 (D Minn 1975); Warren v. Cummings, 303 FSupp 803 (D Colo 1969).

[69] *Id.*

[70] 365 US 167, 5 LEd(2d) 492, 81 SCt 473 (1961).

Court ruled that municipalities are not answerable under section 1983 for the unconstitutional conduct of their employees. This municipal immunity has been extended to all municipal agencies. In consequence, a police department is not subject to suit under section 1983 for the wrongful behavior of its employees.[71] A different situation exists, however, with regard to the police chief and other supervisory personnel. Although police department supervisory personnel are not vicariously liable for the unconstitutional acts of subordinates solely because they occupy a supervisory role,[72] they are subject to suit if their own derelictions contribute to the wrong.[73] Section 1983 liability has been imposed upon a superior where he directs the subordinate to take the challenged action;[74] is present at the time and fails to intervene;[75] has prior knowledge of his subordinate's propensities and fails to take corrective measures;[76] or is negligent in supervising or training those under him.[77]

§ 11.7   —Deprivation of federal civil rights

The second element for stating a claim under section 1983 is the deprivation of federal civil rights—rights secured by the Constitution and laws of the United States or by decisions interpreting them. Section 1983 does not purport to create any new rights. It incorporates existing rights secured by the

[71] Canty v. Richmond, Va., Police Dep't, 383 FSupp 1396 (ED Va 1974); Nugent v. Sheppard, 318 FSupp 314 (ND Ind 1970).

[72] Jennings v. Davis, 476 F(2d) 1271 (8thCir 1973); Johnson v. Glick, 481 F(2d) 1028 (2dCir 1973); Manfredonia v. Barry, 401 FSupp 762 (ED NY 1974); Richardson v. Snow, 340 FSupp 1261 (D Md 1972).

[73] Beverly v. Morris, 470 F(2d) 1356 (5thCir 1972); Byrd v. Brishke, 466 F(2d) 6 (7thCir 1972); Wright v. McMann, 460 F(2d) 126 (2dCir 1972); Carter v. Carlson, 447 F(2d) 358 (DC Cir 1971), *rev'd on other grounds sub nom.*, District of Columbia v. Carter,

409 US 418, 34 LEd(2d) 613, 93 SCt 602 (1973); Ford v. Brier, 383 FSupp 505 (ED Wis 1974); Moon v. Winfield, 383 FSupp 31 (ND Ill 1974).

[74] Martinez v. Mancusi, 443 F(2d) 921 (2dCir 1970).

[75] Byrd v. Brishke, 466 F(2d) 6 (7thCir 1972).

[76] Wright v. McMann, 460 F(2d) 126 (2dCir 1972); Moon v. Winfield, 383 FSupp 31 (ND Ill 1974).

[77] Carter v. Carlson, 447 F(2d) 358 (DC Cir 1971) *rev'd on other grounds sub nom.*, District of Columbia v. Carter, 409 US 418, 34 LEd(2d) 613, 93 SCt 602 (1973).

United States Constitution and laws, and provides civil redress for their invasion. In substance, section 1983 is a statute providing a remedy for "constitutional torts"—the tortious invasion of federal civil rights by those acting "under color of" state authority.[78]

Whether an injured party has a claim under section 1983 requires an examination of the rights invaded. Police conduct may be wrongful without, at the same time, violating *federal* civil rights. The failure of a state law enforcement officer to take an arrested person before a magistrate promptly after his arrest furnishes an illustration. The Supreme Court has yet to hold that a state prisoner has a federal constitutional right to be taken before a magistrate without undue delay. A state police officer's failure to conform to the *McNabb-Mallory* rule is, therefore, not actionable under section 1983.[79] Nor has the Court recognized a federal due process right of arrested persons to make a telephone call prior to booking.[80] It is irrelevant that state law may recognize these rights. No redress is available under section 1983 unless the right invaded corresponds to one protected under the United States Constitution or laws. For the invasion of state-protected rights, the aggrieved party must look to the law of his state for a remedy.

It is not the purpose of this Chapter to recanvass the spectrum of rights secured by the United States Constitution. It is, however, no coincidence that the number of civil damage suits filed in federal courts has risen sharply over the past decade, a period parallelling the rapid federalization of numerous specific Bill of Rights guarantees through the medium of the Fourteenth Amendment. Each legal milestone which has expanded the Constitution creates new rights entitled to vindication under section 1983. Police officers have been sued for damages for: infringing upon the First Amendment right of orderly protest,[81] arresting without a warrant or probable

---

[78] Shapo, *Constitutional Tort: Monroe v. Pape and the Frontiers Beyond,* 60 NWULRev 277 (1965).

[79] United States v. O'Dell, 462 F(2d) 224 (6thCir 1972).

[80] *Id*

[81] Glasson v. City of Louisville, 518 F(2d) 899 (6thCir 1975). See Part II for portions of this case.

cause,[82] applying unreasonable force in making arrests,[83] conducting illegal searches and seizures,[84] coercively extracting confessions,[85] denying suspects their *Escobedo* stationhouse counsel rights,[86] and for varied other federal civil rights invasions.[87] Misconduct actionable under section 1983 reaches to the limits of the Constitution and laws of the United States and federal decisions interpreting them.

An examination of section 1983's language yields only two statutory requirements for a civil damage suit. The aggrieved party must establish that (1) the defendant acted "under color of" state authority in committing the conduct complained of, and (2) the aggrieved party's federal civil rights were violated. Unlike its criminal counterpart, section 1983 contains no requirement that the defendant possess a specific intent to inflict a constitutional injury.[88] At first blush, it would appear that section 1983 contemplates strict legal accountability for unconstitutional behavior. Such an impression, however, is not entirely accurate. Many civil rights invasions actionable under section 1983 have parallel causes of action under state tort law. An arrest without a warrant or probable cause, for example, constitutes both the common law tort known as "false arrest," actionable in state courts, and an invasion of Fourth Amendment rights, actionable under section 1983. In *Monroe* v. *Pape*,[89] the Supreme Court instructed that the skeletal federal statute should be read against a tort background. By this, the Court meant that the details for a federal civil rights damage action should be fashioned by reference to state

[82] Monroe v. Pape, 365 US 167, 5 LEd(2d) 492, 81 SCt 473 (1961).

[83] Basista v. Weir, 340 F(2d) 74 (3dCir 1965).

[84] Monroe v. Pape, 365 US 167, 5 LEd(2d) 492, 81 SCt 473 (1961).

[85] Hardwick v. Hurley, 289 F(2d) 529 (7thCir 1961).

[86] Ney v. California, 439 F(2d) 1285 (9thCir 1971).

[87] Philadelphia Yearly Meeting of Friends v. Tate, 519 F(2d) 1335 (3dCir 1975) (disclosure of police dossiers on political activities of citizens to non-law enforcement sources); Jenkins v. Averett, 424 F(2d) 1228 (4thCir 1970) (reckless shooting of youth); Due v. Tallahassee Theatres, Inc., 333 F(2d) 630 (5thCir 1964) (interference with efforts of racial minorities to obtain service in places of public accommodation); York v. Story, 324 F(2d) 450 (9thCir 1963) (invasion of privacy); Huey v. Barloga, 277 FSupp 864 (ND Ill 1967) (failure to provide adequate police protection during period of racial tension).

[88] Monroe v. Pape, 365 US 167, 5 LEd(2d) 492, 81 SCt 473 (1961).

[89] *Id.*

tort law principles in analogous cases. The Court's language, however, was not free of ambiguity and left massive confusion in the lower federal courts.[90]

§ 11.8 —Defenses to section 1983 actions

Section 1983 contains no mention of what defenses, if any, are raisable in a federal damage action. Whether a police officer can absolve himself from liability on the grounds that he acted in a good-faith and reasonable belief that his conduct was lawful is a question of tremendous practical importance. *Pierson v. Ray*[91] provides a partial answer. A racially mixed group of clergymen, who were attempting to integrate the segregated facilities of a bus terminal, were arrested under a state breach-of-the-peace law later declared unconstitutional. They brought suit to recover damages under section 1983. The arresting officers pleaded in their defense that, though the arrest was illegal, they had acted under a good-faith belief in the statute's constitutionality. The lower federal court judge acknowledged that this defense would have been available to the officers had they been sued in a state court for the tort of "false arrest"; but he declined to entertain it under section 1983 because the federal statute did not provide for it.

The Supreme Court took issue with this reading of section 1983 and held that the police officers should have been allowed to raise the defense that they acted under a good-faith belief in the statute's constitutionality. The decision, nevertheless, stops short of holding that a police officer's reasonable, good-faith belief in the lawfulness of his conduct is a defense to section 1983 damages generally. In allowing it here, the Court relied upon the fact that a police officer's good-faith belief in the constitutionality of a statute he enforced was a defense to a common-law tort action charging false arrest. Properly read, *Pierson v. Ray* holds that a police officer's reasonable, good-faith belief in the lawfulness of his conduct is a defense to section 1983 damage claims only where it would

---

[90] *E.g.*, Burton v. Waller, 502 F(2d) 1261 (5thCir 1974); Jenkins v. Averett, 424 F(2d) 1228 (4thCir 1970); Whirl v. Kern, 407 F(2d) 781 (5thCir 1968); Bowens v. Knazze, 237 FSupp 826 (ND Ill 1965).

[91] 386 US 547, 18 LEd(2d) 288, 87 SCt 1213 (1967).

be so in a parallel state tort action. Tort law, however, has been traditionally reluctant to absolve police officers from liability for illegal conduct because they have acted in good faith.[92] The linkage of defenses available in section 1983 actions to those available in analogous state tort actions, therefore, mitigates little. Several lower federal courts have given *Pierson* v. *Ray* a more generous reading, but their precedent value is questionable.[93]

Section 1983 decisions handed down by the Supreme Court since *Pierson* v. *Ray* are not particularly instructive because they have dealt with the liability of state officials other than police officers.[94] There was, however, one bright note in *Pierson* worthy of passing on. The Court volunteered: "A police officer is not charged with predicting the future course of constitutional law."[95] This sounds encouraging. It would be enormously unfair to a police officer to make him pay damages for failure to conform his conduct to constitutional standards as yet unannounced when he acts. But once a constitutional standard has evolved with sufficient clarity that its dictates can be known, the Supreme Court has shown little patience with pleas of ignorance. In *Wood* v. *Strickland*,[96] involving the section 1983 liability of school board members, the Supreme Court asserted:

> [A]n act violating . . . constitutional rights can be no more justified by ignorance or disregard of settled, indisputable law . . . than by the presence of actual malice. To be entitled to a special exemp-

---

[92] Jenkins v. Averett, 424 F(2d) 1228 (4thCir 1970); Whirl v. Kern, 407 F(2d) 781 (5thCir 1968). See also, Theis, *'Good Faith' as a Defense to Suits for Police Deprivations of Individual Rights*, 59 MinnLRev 991 (1975).

[93] Laverne v. Corning, 522 F(2d) 1144 (2dCir 1975); Glasson v. City of Louisville, 518 F(2d) 899 (6thCir 1975); Brubaker v. King, 505 F(2d) 534 (7thCir 1974); Williams v. Gould, 486 F(2d) 547 (9thCir 1973); Bivens v. Six Unknown Named Agents of the Federal Bureau of Narcotics, 456 F(2d) 1339 (2dCir 1972).

[94] Imbler v. Pachtman, 424 US 409, 47 LEd(2d) 128, 96 SCt 984 (1976) (prosecutor); O'Connor v. Donaldson, 422 US 563, 45 LEd(2d) 396, 95 SCt 2486 (1975) (employees of state mental institution); Wood v. Strickland, 420 US 308, 43 LEd(2d) 214, 95 SCt 992 (1975) (school board members); Scheuer v. Rhodes, 416 US 232, 40 LEd(2d) 90, 94 SCt 1683 (1974) (governor and other high-ranking officials).

[95] Pierson v. Ray, 386 US 547, 557, 18 LEd(2d) 288, 296, 87 SCt 1213, 1219 (1967).

[96] 420 US 308, 43 LEd(2d) 214, 95 SCt 992 (1975).

tion from the categorical remedial language of § 1983 [the defendant] must be held to a standard of conduct based not only on permissible intentions, but also on knowledge of basic, constitutional rights. . . . Such a standard imposes neither an unfair burden upon a person assuming a responsible public office requiring a high degree of intelligence and judgment for the proper fulfillment of its duties, nor an unwarranted burden in light of the value which civil rights have in our legal system. . . .[97]

It is doubtful that the Supreme Court would be more tolerant of a policeman's good-faith ignorance of "basic, unquestioned constitutional rights" than a school official's. Consequently, even if the defense that the officer acted under a good-faith belief in the lawfulness of his conduct ultimately gains general acceptance under section 1983, there will always remain the superadded requirement that this belief be reasonable. Ignorance of "basic, unquestioned constitutional rights" is incompatible with reasonableness.

There are some who feel that the Constitution would be better served by constricting rather than expanding the instances under section 1983 where a policeman's reasonable, good-faith belief in the lawfulness of his conduct will absolve him from liability.[98] What is at stake, however, is not simply the rights of the injured citizen and the officer's pocketbook. Policemen are called to make on-the-spot decisions and, indeed, *must* make them. Time pressures preclude research into the intricate constitutional ramifications of their choices. Society cannot expect "principled and fearless decision-making"[99] while, at the same time, hold over the officer the threat of damages if he makes a good-faith and reasonable error.

§ 11.9   Federal criminal remedies for willful police misbehavior

Since the Reconstruction era, the United States Justice Department has been empowered to criminally prosecute public officials for the willful violation of federal civil rights. The

[97] *Id.* at 321-22, 43 LEd(2d) at 225, 95 SCt at 1000-01.

[98] Theis, *'Good Faith' as a Defense to Suits for Police Deprivations of In-*dividual Rights, 59 MINNLREV 991 (1975).

[99] 386 US at 554 18 LEd(2d) at 295, 87 SCt at 1218.

two statutes conferring this power are 18 U.S.C. §§241 and 242.

§ 11.10   —18 U.S.C. §242

Eighteen U.S.C. §242 is the criminal counterpart of 42 U.S.C. §1983. It derives from section 2 of the Civil Rights Act of 1866,[100] and was later incorporated into the Enforcement Act of 1870.[101] Section 242 of the Criminal Code [102] makes it a crime for any person (1) who acts "under color of" legal authority to (2) willfully subject a United States inhabitant to the deprivation of federal constitutional and statutory rights. Its language closely parallels that of section 1983; there are, however, differences. First, and most obvious, section 242 is a criminal statute, whereas section 1983 provides civil remedies. Second, although both statutes employ the phrase "under color of," section 242's reach is broader. It condemns unconstitutional behavior upon the part of those who act "under color of" legal authority without reference to the sovereign source from which their powers derive. While the specific phrase "under color of" carries the same legal meaning under both, [103] the Justice Department's powers of prosecution under section 242 can be brought to bear against federal, as well as state officials, whereas section 1983 civil remedies are available only against the latter.[104] The final and most critical difference between the two statutes resides in the intent requirement. Note has already been taken that a specific intent to deprive the injured party of his federal civil rights need not

[100] Civil Rights Act of 1866, §2, 14 Stat 27.

[101] Enforcement Act of 1870, §17, 16 Stat 144.

[102] The full text of 18 USC §242 reads:

Whoever, under color of any law, statute, ordinance, regulation, or custom, willfully subjects any inhabitant of any State, Territory, or District to the deprivation of any rights, privileges, or immunities secured or protected by the Constitution or laws of the United States, or to different punishments, pains, or penalties, on account of such inhabitant being an alien, or by reason of his color, or race, than are prescribed for the punishment of citizens, shall be fined not more than $1,000 or imprisoned not more than one year, or both; and if death results shall be subject to imprisonment for any term of years or for life.

[103] The legal meaning of "under color of" legal authority is discussed in §11.6, supra.

[104] Screws v. United States, 325 US 91, 89 LEd 1495, 65 SCt 1031 (1945).

be established to recover damages under section 1983.[105] (The defendant's reasonable, good-faith belief in the lawfulness of his conduct may, however, work as a defense and absolve him of liability in some cases.) [106] Obtaining convictions under section 242 is more difficult because the criminal statute adds a *willfulness* requirement. Unconstitutional behavior becomes criminal only when it is accompanied by a willful intent to violate federal civil rights. The latter requirement, long regarded as a thorn in the prosecutor's side, proved in *Screws* v. *United States* [107] to be section 242's salvation.

1. Willful intent under section 242

In *Screws*, three law enforcement officers, prosecuted by the Justice Department for the blackjack murder of a prisoner, attacked section 242's constitutionality under the "void for vagueness" doctrine. Deprivation of due process, they argued, constituted entirely too imprecise a standard to form the core of a criminal statute. The Supreme Court was momentarily taken back by this argument but found the solution to its dilemma in the statutory willfulness requirement. "Willful," Mr. Justice Douglas wrote, imposed upon the prosecutor the burden of establishing that the accused acted with a "specific intent to deprive a person of a federal right *made definite by decision*." [108] Since no due process right could work its way into section 242 or subject its violator to criminal prosecution until fully crystalized and made definite by judicial decisions, the statute, in his opinion, contained a sufficiently clear and ascertainable standard of guilt to save it from constitutional infirmity.

Having salvaged the statute, Mr. Justice Douglas proceeded to elaborate upon what he meant by a "specific intent" to invade federal civil rights. Unless read cautiously, his opinion is confusing. In one breath, he asserts that the defendant must act with a "purpose" to deprive his victim of a clearly-defined

---

[105] See note 88, *supra.*
[106] Wood v. Strickland, 420 US 308, 322, 43 LEd(2d) 214, 225, 95 SCt 992, 1001 (1975).

[107] 325 US 91, 89 LEd 1495, 65 SCt 1031 (1945). See Part II for a reprint of this case.
[108] *Id.* at 104, 89 LEd at 1504, 65 SCt at 1037.

constitutional right, while in the very next breath, he admonishes that the defendant need not be aware of the constitutional character of the right invaded. This apparent inconsistency can be explained by saying that the offender must act with a conscious purpose to bring about a result which, based on well-established precedents, is in violation of the Constitution, though he need not be cognizant of the constitutional derivation of his victim's right. It is his purpose to bring about the result coupled with the fact that the result is constitutionally forbidden, and not his purpose to violate the Constitution or even his knowledge that he is so doing, that makes conduct "willful" in the sense that Mr. Justice Douglas means it.

Thus, if the Justice Department were seeking to prosecute a police officer for making an unconstitutional arrest, it would be required to establish that the officer consciously designed to take his victim into custody, fully aware that probable cause was lacking. If the officer acts with this state of mind, he has a specific intent to violate the arrested person's right to be free from unconstitutional seizures of his person, whether or not the officer is aware that this result is forbidden by the Fourth Amendment.[109]

2. Specific applications

Section 242 makes the willful deprivation of federal civil rights by those acting "under color of" law punishable, without reference to whether the conduct is accompanied by physical abuse, violence or other aggravating circumstances. Nevertheless, the difficulty of establishing the existence of a willful intent has prompted the Justice Department to concentrate its efforts upon blatant misconduct such as torture,[110] brutal beating of prisoners,[111] and extortionate arrests,[112] relying upon state criminal prosecutions and civil claims to redress less serious abuses.

The Kent State incident, in which four students died and

---

[109] Note, *Criminal Law: Criminal Deprivation of Another's Constitutional Rights: The* Mens Rea *Requirement*, 28 OklaLRev 845 (1975).

[110] Williams v. United States, 341 US 97, 95 LEd 774, 71 SCt 756 (1951).

[111] Screws v. United States, 325 US 91, 89 LEd 1495, 65 SCt 1031 (1945).

[112] United States v. Lester, 363 F(2d) 68 (6thCir 1966); United States v. Ramey, 336 F(2d) 512 (4thCir 1964).

nine others were wounded when National Guardsmen opened fire, triggered a section 242 criminal prosecution. At the conclusion of the Justice Department's case, the court directed verdicts of acquittal against all eight defendants because the government's evidence was insufficient to establish a willful intent.[113] While the conduct of the Guardsmen is not to be condoned, the case was correctly decided. The Guardsmen were not motivated by a specific intent to deprive the student victims of any constitutional rights. Their use of force may have been excessive, but it was motivated by an irrational fear of personal safety, exhaustion, confusion, and a mistaken belief that an order had been given. Had the Guardsmen employed excessive force, knowing it to be excessive, and with a specific intent to inflict injury, they could have been convicted for willfully denying the students their constitutional right not to be punished without a trial, because they would have possessed the mental state which *Screws* requires.

In several cases, the Justice Department has been successful in obtaining section 242 convictions where constitutional rights were denied by willful inaction. A prisoner is entitled to protection against angry mobs. If a policeman voluntarily surrenders a prisoner to a violent mob, he may be found by virtue of his deliberate inaction to have become a participant in the denial of federal civil rights. In *Lynch v. United States*,[114] for example, a Georgia sheriff was convicted under section 242 for willful dereliction of duty in voluntarily turning a Black prisoner over to the Ku Klux Klan. And in *Catlette v. United States*,[115] a West Virginia peace officer was convicted for permitting and assisting members of the American Legion to perpetrate vicious acts upon several Jehovah's Witnesses who had come to his office seeking safety. Where the officer joins the mob in the commission of the civil rights invasion, his conduct has the additional consequence of bringing the other participants within the ambit of section 242, though the others are private citizens and their conduct would not otherwise be covered by section 1983.[116]

---

[113] United States v. Shafer, 384 FSupp 496 (ND Ohio 1974).

[114] 189 F(2d) 476 (5thCir 1951).

[115] 132 F(2d) 902 (4thCir 1943).

[116] United States v. Price, 383 US 787, 16 LEd(2d) 276, 86 SCt 1152 (1966).

§ 11.11　—18 U.S.C. §241

Eighteen U.S.C. §241 is a federal criminal conspiracy statute with historical antecedents tracing to the Civil Rights Act of 1870.[117] Its antiquated language reads as follows:

> If two or more persons conspire to injure, oppress, threaten, or intimidate any citizen in the free exercise or enjoyment of any right or privilege secured to him by the Constitution or laws of the United States, or because of his having so exercised the same; or
>
> If two or more persons go in disguise on the highway, or on the premises of another, with intent to prevent or hinder his free exercise or enjoyment of any right or privilege so secured—
>
> They shall be fined not more than $10,000 or imprisoned not more than ten years, or both; and if death results, they shall be subject to imprisonment for any term of years or for life.

1. Conspiracies to violate due process and equal protection rights

Prior to 1966, prosecutions under section 241 were rare because it was thought that this statute reached only *private* conspiratorial behavior designed to interfere with the narrow class of rights which Congress had the power to protect against abridgment by *private individuals*,[118] and did not reach conspiracies implicating *public officials*, which had as their object the denial of due process and equal protection rights.[119] Support for this view was found both in the nature of the conduct condemned—such as going in disguise upon the highway, activity more likely to be associated with private terrorist groups like the Ku Klux Klan than with rational public officials—and in the absence of any explicit requirement that the violator be acting "under color of" law when depriving his victim of his civil rights. This language was utilized by Congress in 42 U.S.C. §1983 and 18 U.S.C. §242 when it had official behavior in mind. Since due process and equal protection rights are, by virtue of their Fourteenth Amendment derivation, capable of being violated only when the invasion is accompanied by "state action" or action "under color of"

---

[117] Civil Rights Act of May 31, 1870, ch 114, 16 Stat 140.

[118] These rights are discussed under the subheading immediately following.

[119] United States v. Williams, 341 US 70, 95 LEd 758, 71 SCt 581 (1951).

state law, the courts reasoned from section 241's omission of any reference to such a requirement, that Congress did not intend to include the conduct of public officials or Fourteenth Amendment rights within the conspiracy statute's coverage. This left within section 241's narrow ambit only a limited category of rights, existing independently of the Fourteenth Amendment, which Congress had the power to secure against invasions by private citizens.[120]

This remained the settled construction until 1966, when the Supreme Court in *United States* v. *Price*[121] took what was, for all practical purposes, a dead statute and restyled it into a respectable civil rights protection law. The *Price* case grew out of the highly-publicized murder of three civil rights workers—James Chaney, Andrew Goodman and Michael Schwerner. A Mississippi deputy sheriff detained the three men and released them late at night in order that he and seventeen others, mostly private citizens, might intercept and murder them on a dark road. All eighteen men were indicted under section 241 for conspiring to "injure, oppress, threaten, and intimidate" the three victims "in the free exercise and enjoyment of the right . . . not to be deprived of life or liberty without due process of law." The district court dismissed the indictments on the ground that section 241 did not embrace conspiracies to deprive an individual of due process of law. The government appealed, and the issue of section 241's breadth was brought squarely before the Supreme Court. The Supreme Court ruled that the trial court had construed section 241 too narrowly and that the section *did* embrace conspiracies to interfere with Fourteenth Amendment rights where public officials are implicated or "state action" is otherwise present.

The significance of *Price* lies not in the fact that the Justice Department now has the power to prosecute conduct formerly unreachable. The identical misbehavior was and is indictable under section 242. Nor will the government's election to proceed under section 241 ease its path to conviction because a requirement of willfulness identical to section 242 has been

---

[120] These rights are discussed under the subheading immediately following.   [121] 383 US 787, 16 LEd(2d) 276, 86 SCt 1152 (1966).

read into the conspiracy law.[122] *Price's* practical impact relates to the punishment that can now be imposed upon conviction for conspiring to deny due process and equal protection rights. Under section 242, the maximum punishment that the Justice Department can secure upon a conviction, unless death has resulted, is a one-year prison sentence; under section 241, however, a ten-year prison sentence is authorized. Through *Price,* the threat of prosecution for denying due process and equal protection rights has a larger punch behind it. *Price* restyled a moribund statute into a serviceable civil rights protection measure.

2. *Private conspiratorial misbehavior*

Section 241 reaches some conspiratorial misconduct participated in by private individuals which is not indictable under section 242. In the years before *Price,* this was believed to be its only coverage. A body of case law developed around section 241, defining a small group of rights which existed independently of the Fourteenth Amendment and which Congress had the power to secure against abridgment by private individuals. These rights, which derived by implication from the Constitution rather than from its express language, were known as the *privileges of national citizenship.*[123] Their common characteristic was that they sprang from the relationship of citizens to their national government. Prosecutions under section 241 were upheld for conspiracies participated in by private individuals to interfere with the rights to vote in a federal election,[124] to inform federal authorities of violations of federal law,[125] to travel from one state to another,[126] to enter upon federal land and to take advantage of benefits offered under federal law,[127] to testify in federal proceedings,[128] to be

---

[122] Anderson v. United States, 417 US 211, 41 LEd(2d) 21, 94 SCt 2253 (1974).

[123] United States v. Classic, 313 US 299, 85 LEd 1368, 61 SCt 1031 (1941); Ex Parte Yarbrough, 110 US 651, 28 LEd 274, 4 SCt 152 (1884).

[124] See cases cited in note 123, *supra.*

[125] In re Quarles, 158 US 532, 39 LEd 1080, 15 SCt 959 (1895).

[126] United States v. Guest, 383 US 745, 16 LEd(2d) 239, 86 SCt 1170 (1966).

[127] United States v. Waddell, 112 US 76, 28 LEd 673, 5 SCt 35 (1884).

[128] United States v. Pacelli, 491 F(2d) 1108 (2dCir 1974).

secure in federal custody,[129] and to assemble for the purpose of discussing national affairs.[130]

Until recently, it was believed that Congress's power to guard the rights of individuals against abridgment by private citizens was narrowly confined. The principal protectors of individual civil rights, under traditional attitudes toward federalism, were the states. This thinking was exploded in *Jones v. Alfred H. Mayer Co.*,[131] where the Supreme Court ruled that Congress was empowered by the Thirteenth Amendment to enact comprehensive laws regulating private race relations. Hints can be found elsewhere which require a rethinking of former conservative assessments of Congress's powers to protect rights. But these cases came too late to make section 241 a useful device for protecting individual civil rights against conspiratorial interference by other private citizens. Section 241 had a century of conservative interpretation impressed upon it. A modern federal law was required.

In 1968 Congress acted. Section 245 of the Criminal Code (18 U.S.C. §245) empowers the Justice Department to institute criminal prosecution against any person who willfully interferes with various enumerated rights, whether he acts "under color of" law or as a private citizen.

§ 11.12   —18 U.S.C. §245

Section 245 enumerates three categories of federal prosecutable civil rights crimes: (1) interference with privileges of national citizenship, (2) racially-motivated crimes of violence, and (3) riot-related looting and vandalism.

1. Interference with privileges of national citizenship

Section 245 makes it a crime for any person, whether acting "under color of" legal authority or as a private citizen, willfully to interfere with the right of another to vote, use federal facilities, seek federal employment, serve on a federal jury, or receive federal assistance. That the rights invasions, here

---

[129] Logan v. United States, 114 US 263, 36 LEd 429, 12 SCt 617 (1892).

[130] United States v. Cruikshank, 92 US (2 Otto) 542, 23 LEd 588 (1876).

[131] 392 US 409, 20 LEd(2d) 1189, 88 SCt 2186 (1968). This case is discussed in detail in §11.4, *supra*.

specified, are remarkably similar to those which the Justice Department formerly prosecuted under section 241 is no coincidence. Litigation under section 241 had established that Congress could protect these civil rights against abridgments by private citizens as well as by public officials. More modern legal equipment for protecting these civil rights was, nevertheless, thought desirable.

2. Racially-motivated crimes of violence

Section 245 further makes it a crime to intimidate or forcibly interfere with the right of any person, because of his race, color, religion, or national origin, to attend public schools, use state facilities, obtain employment, serve on state juries, travel in interstate commerce, or obtain service in places of public accommodations. The primary source of Congressional authority for this part of section 245 is the Thirteenth Amendment, as construed in *Jones* v. *Alfred H. Mayer Co.*[132]

3. Riot-related looting and vandalism

Section 245 authorizes the Justice Department to criminally prosecute any person who, during the course of a riot or civil disorder, engages in looting or vandalism.

§ 11.13   Summary

The Reconstruction era altered the nature of the federal union. The Fourteenth Amendment conferred broad powers on Congress which could be employed to protect individual civil rights against state governments and those acting "under color of" their legal authority. Congress's Thirteenth Amendment powers, operative in the field of race relations, could be brought to bear upon the practices of the nation's citizens. The Congress which met after the Civil War legislated numerous civil rights measures designed to give legal protection to the newly-freed slaves. The first Reconstruction was throttled, however, by conservative judges. A century passed during which the Black citizens of the nation were denied equal rights under the law. A new era was ushered in with *Brown*

---

[132] *Id.*

v. *Board of Education,* handed down in 1954, which integrated the schools. In the decade of the 1960's Congress passed measures prohibiting discrimination in places of public accommodations, in employment, and in housing markets. The second Reconstruction was climaxed by *Jones* v. *Alfred H. Mayer Co.* in which the Supreme Court declared that the Thirteenth Amendment had not exhausted itself in abolishing slavery and that Congress's skepticism concerning its power to regulate private race relations was wholly unfounded.

There are three statutes surviving from the Reconstruction era that have a direct impact upon the professional conduct of law enforcement officers. The first, 42 U.S.C. §1983 creates a civil cause of action against those acting "under color of" state law who invade rights secured by the Constitution and laws of the United States. "Color" means "colorable claim" or "pretense" of state authority. A police officer will be considered as acting "under color of" his authority so as to bring his conduct within section 1983's ambit if (1) his conduct, though excessive, falls within the general category of activities that he is authorized or required by the terms of his employment to perform, or if (2) his official position facilitated his commission of the wrong. With the federalization of numerous specific Bill of Rights protections and the expansion of these rights through judicial interpretation, the officer's potential civil liability under section 1983 has undergone a parallel growth. The existence of section 1983 underscores the need for continuous legal study by law enforcement personnel. Only where the legal standards are themselves uncertain will the officer be permitted to raise his ignorance of the law as a defense. If an officer *willfully* deprives an individual of his federal civil rights, he may incur criminal liability as well. The Justice Department has two statutes at its disposal for prosecuting willful invasions of due process and equal protection rights by those acting under color of law—18 U.S.C. §241 and 18 U.S.C. §242.

PART II:

JUDICIAL DECISIONS RELATING TO PART I

The judicial decisions in this part of the book have been edited and reprinted in order to make the textual discussion in Part I more meaningful. For maximum benefit, they should be read immediately following the chapters they accompany.

Several of the cases cut across chapter lines. For example, *Miranda v. United States*, one of the leading modern cases on self-incrimination, contains some very pertinent and timely comments on the right to counsel as well as on confessions. Consequently, it is mentioned and discussed in all three chapters.

It is not enough to learn the decision or rule of law of a case. To fully appreciate the significance of a rule and to be capable of applying the rule intelligently, the reasoning of the court in reaching the decision must also be considered. Although a court decides only the case which is before it, the decision rendered would be of little use if it did not serve as a guideline for future cases in which similar factual patterns arise. Therefore, the facts are of importance and careful attention must be paid to them in reading the cases.

Cases which follow have been selected primarily for their importance as precedents. Most of the cases interpret constitutional provisions and demonstrate the judicial processes followed when the United States Supreme Court reaches a decision involving a constitutional question. Due to space limitations, some editing has been necessary. However, every effort has been made not to delete those parts of the case which bear directly on the points discussed.

For the reader who desires to acquire the full text of these cases or to research the cases cited in Part I, this material is available in law schools and courthouse libraries. If this book is used as a text, it is recommended that selected cases be assigned to the students and that they be required to report on the cases.

571

Cases relating to **Chapter 1**

HISTORY AND GENERAL APPLICATION OF CONSTITUTIONAL PROVISIONS

M'CULLOCH v. MARYLAND

17 U.S. (4 Wheat.) 316, 4 L.Ed. 579 (1819)

This was an action of debt, brought by the defendant in error, John James, who sued as well for himself as for the State of Maryland, in the county court of Baltimore county, in the said State, against the plaintiff in error, M'Culloch, to recover certain penalties under the act of the legislature of Maryland, hereafter mentioned. Judgment being rendered against the plaintiff in error, upon the following statement of facts, agreed and submitted to the court by the parties, was affirmed by the court of appeals of the State of Maryland, the highest court of law of said State, and the cause was brought, by writ of error, to this court.

It is admitted by the parties in this cause, by their counsel, that there was passed, on the 10th day of April, 1816, by the congress of the United States, an act, entitled, "An act to incorporate the subscribers to the Bank of the United States"; and that there was passed, on the 11th day of February, 1818, by the general assembly of Maryland, an act, entitled, "An act to impose a tax on all banks, or branches thereof, in the State of Maryland, not chartered by the legislature," which said acts are

made part of this statement, and it is agreed may be read from the statute books in which they are respectively printed. It is further admitted, that the president, directors, and company of the bank of the United States, incorporated by the act of congress aforesaid, did organize themselves, and go into full operation in the city of Philadelphia, in the State of Pennsylvania, in pursuance of the said act, and that they did on the . . . day of . . . eighteen hundred and seventeen, establish a branch of the said bank, or an office of discount and deposit, in the city of Baltimore, in the State of Maryland, which has from that time, until the first day of May, eighteen hundred and eighteen, ever since transacted and carried on business as a bank, or office of discount and deposit, and as a branch of the said bank of the United States, by issuing bank notes and discounting promissory notes, and performing other operations usual and customary for banks to do and perform, under the authority and by the direction of the said president, directors, and company of the bank of the United States, established at Philadelphia, as aforesaid. It is further admitted, that the said president, directors, and company of the said bank, had no authority to establish the said branch, or office of discount and deposit, at the city of Baltimore, from the State of Maryland, otherwise than the said State having adopted the constitution of the United States, and composing one of the States of the Union. It is further admitted, that James William M'Culloch, the defendant below, being the cashier of the said branch, or office of discount and deposit, did, on the several days set forth in the declaration in this cause, issue the said respective bank-notes therein described, from the said branch, or office, to a certain George Williams, in the city of Baltimore, in part payment of a promissory note of the said Williams, discounted by the said branch or office, which said respective bank-notes were not, nor was either of them, so issued on stamped paper, in the manner prescribed by the act of assembly aforesaid. It is further admitted, that the said president, directors, and company of the bank of the United States, and the said branch or office of discount and deposit, have not, nor has either of them, paid in advance, or otherwise, the sum of fifteen thousand dollars, to the treasurer of the Western Shore, for the use of the State of Maryland, before the issuing of the said notes, or any of them, nor since those periods. And it is further admitted, that the treasurer of the Western Shore of Maryland, under the direction of the governor and council of the said State, was ready, and offered to deliver to the said president, directors, and company of the said bank, and to the said branch, or office of discount and deposit, stamped paper of the kind and denomination required and described in the said act of assembly.

The question submitted to the court for their decision in this case, is as to the validity of the said act of the general assembly of Maryland, on the ground of its being repugnant to the constitution of the United States, and the act of congress aforesaid, or to one of them.

Upon the foregoing statement of facts, and the pleadings in this cause (all errors in which are hereby agreed to be mutually released), if the court should be of opinion that the plaintiffs are entitled to recover, then judgment, it is agreed, shall be entered for the plaintiffs, for twenty-five hundred dollars, and costs of suit. But if the court should be of opinion that the plaintiffs are not entitled to recover upon the statement and pleadings aforesaid, then judgment of *non pros* shall be entered, with costs, to the defendant.

It is agreed that either party may appeal from the decision of the county court to the court of appeals, and from the decision of the court of appeals to the supreme court of the United States, according to the modes and usages of law, and have the same benefit of this statement of facts, in the same manner as could be had if a jury had been sworn and impanelled in this cause, and a special verdict had been found, or these facts had appeared and been stated in an exception taken to the opinion of the court, and the court's direction to the jury thereon.

. . . .

MARSHALL, C. J., delivered the opinion of the court.

In the case now to be determined, the defendant, a sovereign state, denies the obligation of a law enacted by the legislature of the Union; and the plaintiff, on his part, contests the validity of an act which has been passed by the legislature of that State. The constitution of our country, in its most interesting and vital parts, is to be considered; the conflicting powers of the government of the Union and of its members, as marked in that constitution, are to be discussed; and an opinion given, which may essentially influence the great operations of the government. No tribunal can approach such a question without a deep sense of its importance, and of the awful responsibility involved in its decision. But it must be decided peacefully, or remain a source of hostile legislation, perhaps of hostility of a still more serious nature; and if it is to be so decided, by this tribunal alone can the decision be made. On the supreme court of the United States has the constitution of our country devolved this important duty.

The first question made in the cause is, has congress power to incorporate a bank?

It has been truly said, that this can scarcely be considered as an open question, entirely unpreju-

diced by the former proceedings of the nation respecting it. The principle now contested was introduced at a very early period of our history, has been recognized by many successive legislatures, and has been acted upon by the judicial department, in cases of peculiar delicacy, as a law of undoubted obligation.

It will not be denied that a bold and daring usurpation might be resisted, after an acquiescence still longer and more complete than this. But it is conceived that a doubtful question, one on which human reason may pause, and the human judgment be suspended, in the decision of which the great principles of liberty are not concerned, but the respective powers of those who are equally the representatives of the people, are to be adjusted, if not put at rest by the practice of the government, ought to receive a considerable impression from that practice. An exposition of the constitution, deliberately established by legislative acts, on the faith of which an immense property has been advanced, ought not to be lightly disregarded.

The power now contested was exercised by the first congress elected under the present constitution. The bill for incorporating the Bank of the United States did not steal upon an unsuspecting legislature, and pass unobserved. Its principle was completely understood, and was opposed with equal zeal and ability. After being resisted, first in the fair and open field of debate, and afterwards in the executive cabinet, with as much persevering talent as any measure has ever experienced, and being supported by arguments which convinced minds as pure and as intelligent as this country can boast, it became a law. The original act was permitted to expire; but a short experience of the embarrassments to which the refusal to revive it exposed the government, convinced those who were most prejudiced against the measure of its necessity, and induced the passage of the present law. It would require no ordinary share of intrepidity to assert that a measure adopted under these circumstances was a bold and plain usurpation, to which the constitution gave no countenance.

These observations belong to the cause: but they are not made under the impression that, were the question entirely new, the law would be found irreconcilable with the constitution.

In discussing this question, the counsel for the State of Maryland have deemed it of some importance, in the construction of the constitution, to consider that instrument not as emanating from the people, but as the act of sovereign and independent States. The powers of the general government, it has been said, are delegated by the States, who alone are truly sovereign; and must be exercised in subordination to the States, who alone possess supreme dominion.

It would be difficult to sustain this proposition. The convention which framed the constitution was, indeed, elected by the state legislatures. But the instrument, when it came from their hands, was a mere proposal, without obligation, or pretensions to it. It was reported to the then existing congress of the United States, with a request that it might "be submitted to a convention of delegates, chosen in each State, by the people thereof, under the recommendation of its legislature, for their assent and ratification." This mode of proceeding was adopted; and by the convention, by congress, and by the State legislatures, the instrument was submitted to the people. They acted upon it, in the only manner in which they can act safely, effectively, and wisely, on such a subject, by assembling in convention. It is true, they assembled in their several States; and where else should they have assembled? No political dreamer was ever wild enough to think of breaking down the lines which separate the States, and of compounding the American people into one common mass. Of consequence, when they act, they act in their States. But the measures they adopt do not, on that account, cease to be the measures of the people themselves, or become the measures of the State governments.

From these conventions the constitution derives its whole authority. The government proceeds directly from the people; is "ordained and established" in the name of the people; and is declared to be ordained, "in order to form a more perfect union, establish justice, insure domestic tranquility, and secure the blessings of liberty to themselves and to their posterity."

The assent of the States, in their sovereign capacity, is implied in calling a convention, and thus submitting that instrument to the people. But the people were at perfect liberty to accept or reject it; and their act was final. It required not the affirmance, and could not be negatived, by the State governments. The constitution, when thus adopted, was of complete obligation, and bound the State sovereignties.

It has been said, that the people had already surrendered all their powers to the State sovereignties, and had nothing more to give. But, surely, the question whether they may resume and modify the powers granted to government, does not remain to be settled in this country. Much more might the legitimacy of the general government be doubted, had it been created by the States. The powers delegated to the State sovereignties were to be exercised by themselves, not by a distinct and independent sovereignty, created by themselves. To the formation of a league, such as was the confederation, the State sovereignties were certainly competent. But when, "in order to form a more perfect union," it was deemed necessary to change this alliance into an effective government, possessing great and sovereign powers, and acting directly on the people, the necessity of referring it to the people, and of deriving its powers directly from them, was felt and acknowledged by all.

The government of the Union, then, (whatever may be the influence of this fact on the case,) is, emphatically and truly, a government of the people. In form and in substance it emanates from them. Its powers are granted by them, and are to be exercised directly on them, and for their benefit.

This government is acknowledged by all to be one of enumerated powers. The principle, that it can exercise only the powers granted to it, would seem too apparent to have required to be enforced by all those arguments which its enlightened friends, while it was depending before the people, found it necessary to urge. That principle is now universally admitted. But the question respecting the extent of the powers actually granted, is perpetually arising, and will probably continue to arise, as long as our system shall exist.

In discussing these questions, the conflicting powers of the general and State governments must be brought into view, and the supremacy of their respective laws, when they are in opposition, must be settled.

If any one proposition could command the universal assent of mankind, we might expect it would be this: that the government of the Union, though limited in its powers, is supreme within its sphere of action. This would seem to result necessarily from its nature. It is the government of all; its powers are delegated by all; it represents all and acts for all. Though any one State may be willing to control its operations, no State is willing to allow others to control them. The nation, on those subjects on which it can act, must necessarily bind its component parts. But this question is not left to mere reason: the people have, in express terms, decided it, by saying, "this constitution, and the laws of the United States, which shall be made in pursuance thereof," "shall be the supreme law of the land," and by requiring that the members of the State legislatures, and the officers of the executive and judicial departments of the States, shall take the oath of fidelity to it.

The government of the United States, then, though limited in its powers, is supreme; and its laws, when made in pursuance of the constitution, form the supreme law of the land, "any thing in the constitution or laws of any State, to the contrary notwithstanding."

Among the enumerated powers, we do not find that of establishing a bank or creating a corporation. But there is no phrase in the instrument which, like the articles of confederation, excludes incidental or implied powers; and which requires that every thing granted shall be expressly and minutely described. Even the 10th amendment, which was framed for the purpose of quieting the excessive jealousies which had been excited, omits the word "expressly," and declares only that the powers "not delegated to the United States, nor prohibited to the States, are reserved to the States or to the people"; thus leaving the question, whether the particular power which may become the subject of contest, has been delegated to the one government, or prohibited to the other,

to depend on a fair construction of the whole instrument. The men who drew and adopted this amendment, had experienced the embarrassments resulting from the insertion of this word in the articles of confederation, and probably omitted it to avoid those embarrassments. A constitution, to contain an accurate detail of all the subdivisions of which its great powers will admit, and of all the means by which they may be carried into execution, would partake of the prolixity of a legal code, and could scarcely be embraced by the human mind. It would probably never be understood by the public. Its nature, therefore, requires, that only its great outlines should be marked, its important objects designated, and the minor ingredients which compose those objects be deduced from the nature of the objects themselves. That this idea was entertained by the framers of the American constitution, is not only to be inferred from the nature of the instrument, but from the language. Why else were some of the limitations, found in the 9th section of the 1st article, introduced? It is also, in some degree, warranted by their having omitted to use any restrictive term which might prevent its receiving a fair and just interpretation. In considering this question, then, we must never forget, that it is a constitution we are expounding.

Although, among the enumerated powers of government, we do not find the word "bank" or "incorporation," we find the great powers to lay and collect taxes; to borrow money; to regulate commerce; to declare and conduct a war; and to raise and support armies and navies. The sword and the purse, all the external relations, and no inconsiderable portion of the industry of the nation, are intrusted to its government. It can never be pretended that these vast powers draw after them others of inferior importance, merely because they are inferior. Such an idea can never be advanced. But it may, with great reason, be contended, that a government, intrusted with such ample powers, on the due execution of which the happiness and prosperity of the nation so vitally depends, must also be intrusted with ample means for their execution. The power being given, it is the interest of the nation to facilitate its execution. It can never be their interest, and cannot be presumed to have been their intention, to clog and embarrass its execution by withholding the most appropriate means. Throughout this vast republic, from the St. Croix to the Gulf of Mexico, from the Atlantic to the Pacific, revenue is to be collected and expended, armies are to be marched and supported. The exigencies of the nation may require, that the treasure raised in the North should be transported to the South, that raised in the East conveyed to the West, or that this order should be reversed. Is that construction of the constitution to be preferred which would render these operations difficult, hazardous, and expensive? Can we adopt that construction, (unless the words

imperiously require it,) which would impute to the framers of that instrument, when granting these powers for the public good, the intention of impeding their exercise by withholding a choice of means? If, indeed, such be the mandate of the constitution, we have only to obey; but that instrument does not profess to enumerate the means by which the powers it confers may be executed; nor does it prohibit the creation of a corporation, if the existence of such a being be essential to the beneficial exercise of those powers. It is, then, the subject of fair inquiry, how far such means may be employed.

It is not denied, that the powers given to the government imply the ordinary means of execution. That, for example, of raising revenue, and applying it to national purposes, is admitted to imply the power of conveying money from place to place, as the exigencies of the nation may require, and of employing the usual means of conveyance. But it is denied that the government has its choice of means; or, that it may employ the most convenient means, if, to employ them, it be necessary to erect a corporation.

On what foundation does this argument rest? On this alone: The power of creating a corporation, is one appertaining to sovereignty, and is not expressly conferred on Congress. This is true. But all legislative powers appertain to sovereignty. The original power of giving the law on any subject whatever, is a sovereign power;

and if the government of the Union is restrained from creating a corporation, as a means for performing its functions, on the single reason that the creation of a corporation is an act of sovereignty; if the sufficiency of this reason be acknowledged, there would be some difficulty in sustaining the authority of congress to pass other laws for the accomplishment of the same objects.

The government which has a right to do an act, and has imposed on it the duty of performing that act, must, according to the dictates of reason, be allowed to select the means; and those who contend that it may not select any appropriate means, that one particular mode of effecting the object is excepted, take upon themselves the burden of establishing that exception.

The creation of a corporation, it is said, appertains to sovereignty. This is admitted. But to what portion of sovereignty does it appertain? Does it belong to one more than to another? In America, the powers of sovereignty are divided between the government of the Union, and those of the States. They are each sovereign, with respect to the objects committed to it, and neither sovereign with respect to the objects committed to the other. We cannot comprehend that train of reasoning which would maintain, that the extent of power granted by the people is to be ascertained, not by the nature and terms of the grant, but by its date. Some state constitutions were formed before, some since

that of the United States. We cannot believe that their relation to each other is in any degree dependent upon this circumstance. Their respective powers must, we think, be precisely the same as if they had been formed at the same time. Had they been formed at the same time, and had the people conferred on the general government the power contained in the constitution, and on the States the whole residuum of power, would it have been asserted that the government of the Union was not sovereign with respect to those objects which were intrusted to it, in relation to which its laws were declared to be supreme? If this could not have been asserted, we cannot well comprehend the process of reasoning which maintains, that a power appertaining to sovereignty cannot be connected with that vast portion of it which is granted to the general government, so far as it is calculated to subserve the legitimate objects of that government. The power of creating a corporation, though appertaining to sovereignty, is not like the power of making war, or levying taxes, or of regulating commerce, a great substantive and independent power, which cannot be implied as incidental to other powers, or used as a means of executing them. It is never the end for which other powers are exercised, but a means by which other objects are accomplished. No contributions are made to charity for the sake of an incorporation, but a corporation is created to administer the charity; no seminary of learning is instituted in order to be incorporated, but the corporated character is conferred to subserve the purposes of education. No city was ever built with the sole object of being incorporated, but is incorporated as affording the best means of being well governed. The power of creating a corporation is never used for its own sake, but for the purpose of effecting something else. No sufficient reason is, therefore, perceived, why it may not pass as incidental to those powers which are expressly given, if it be a direct mode of executing them.

But the constitution of the United States has not left the right of congress to employ the necessary means, for the execution of the powers conferred on the government, to general reasoning. To its enumeration of powers is added that of making "all laws which shall be necessary and proper, for carrying into execution the foregoing powers, and all other powers vested by this constitution, in the government of the United States, or in any department thereof."

The counsel for the State of Maryland have urged various arguments, to prove that this clause, though in terms a grant of power, is not so in effect; but is really restrictive of the general right, which might otherwise be implied, of selecting means for executing the enumerated powers.

In support of this proposition, they have found it necessary to contend, that this clause was inserted for the purpose of conferring on congress the power of making laws. That, without it,

doubts might be entertained, whether congress could exercise its powers in the form of legislation.

But could this be the object for which it was inserted? A government is created by the people, having legislative, executive, and judicial powers. Its legislative powers are vested in a congress, which is to consist of a senate and house of representatives. Each house may determine the rule of its proceedings; and it is declared that every bill which shall have passed both houses, shall, before it becomes a law, be presented to the President of the United States. The 7th section describes the course of proceedings, by which a bill shall become a law; and, then, the 8th section enumerates the powers of congress. Could it be necessary to say, that a legislature should exercise legislative powers, in the shape of legislation? After allowing each house to prescribe its own course of proceeding, after describing the manner in which a bill should become a law, would it have entered into the mind of a single member of the convention, that an express power to make laws was necessary to enable the legislature to make them? That a legislature, endowed with legislative powers, can legislate, is a proposition too self-evident to have been questioned.

. . . .

But the argument which most conclusively demonstrates the error of the construction contended for by the counsel for the State of Maryland, is founded on the intention of the convention, as manifested in the whole clause. To waste time and argument in proving that, without it, congress might carry its powers into execution, would be not much less idle than to hold a lighted taper to the sun. As little can it be required to prove, that in the absence of this clause, congress would have some choice of means. That it might employ those which, in its judgment, would most advantageously effect the object to be accomplished. That any means adapted to the end, any means which tended directly to the execution of the constitutional powers of the government, were in themselves constitutional. This clause, as construed by the State of Maryland, would abridge and almost annihilate this useful and necessary right of the legislature to select its means. That this could not be intended, is, we should think, had it not been already controverted, too apparent for controversy. We think so for the following reasons:—

1. The clause is placed among the powers of congress, not among the limitations on those powers.

2. Its terms purport to enlarge, not to diminish the powers vested in the government. It purports to be an additional power, not a restriction on those already granted. No reason has been or can be assigned, for thus concealing an intention to narrow the discretion of the national legislature, under words which purport to enlarge it. The framers of the constitution wished its adoption, and well knew that it would be endangered by its strength, not by its weakness. Had they been capable of using language which would convey to the eye one idea, and after deep reflection, impress on the mind another, they would rather have disguised the grant of power, than its limitation. If then, their intention had been, by this clause, to restrain the free use of means which might otherwise have been implied, that intention would have been inserted in another place, and would have been expressed in terms resembling these: "In carrying into execution the foregoing powers, and all others," &c., "no laws shall be passed but such as are necessary and proper." Had the intention been to make this clause restrictive, it would unquestionably have been so in form as well as in effect.

The result of the most careful and attentive consideration bestowed upon this clause is, that if it does not enlarge, it cannot be construed to restrain the powers of congress, or to impair the right of the legislature to exercise its best judgment in the selection of measures, to carry into execution the constitutional powers of the government. If no other motive for its insertion can be suggested, a sufficient one is found in the desire to remove all doubts respecting the right to legislate on that vast mass of incidental powers which must be involved in the constitution, if that instrument be not a splendid bauble.

. . . .

After the most deliberate consideration, it is the unanimous and decided opinion of this court, that the act to incorporate the Bank of the United States is a law made in pursuance of the constitution, and is a part of the supreme law of the land.

The branches, proceeding from the same stock, and being conducive to the complete accomplishment of the object, are equally constitutional. It would have been unwise to locate them in the charter, and it would be unnecessarily inconvenient to employ the legislative power in making those subordinate arrangements. The great duties of the bank are prescribed; those duties require branches, and the bank itself may, we think, be safely trusted with the selection of places where those branches shall be fixed; reserving always to the government the right to require that a branch shall be located where it may be deemed necessary.

It being the opinion of the court, that the act incorporating the bank is constitutional; and that the power of establishing a branch in the State of Maryland might be properly exercised by the bank itself, we proceed to inquire:—

[The second part of the decision concerned the right of the State of Maryland to tax the Bank of the United States and has been omitted. The Court concluded the opinion with:]

We are unanimously of opinion, that the law passed by the legislature of Maryland, imposing a tax on the Bank of the United States, is unconstitutional and void.

This opinion does not deprive the States of any resources which they originally possessed. It does not extend to a tax paid by the real property of the bank, in common with the other real property within the State, nor to a tax imposed on the interest which the citizens of Maryland may hold in this institution, in common with other property of the same description throughout the State. But this is a tax on the operations of the bank, and is, consequently, a tax on the operation of an instrument employed by the government of the Union to carry its powers into execution. Such a tax must be unconstitutional.

JUDGMENT. This cause came on to be heard on the transcript of the record of the court of appeals of the State of Maryland, and was argued by counsel. On consideration whereof, it is the opinion of this court, that the act of the legislature of Maryland is contrary to the constitution of the United States, and void; and therefore, that the said court of appeals of the State of Maryland erred in affirming the judgment of the Baltimore county court, in which judgment was rendered against James W. M'Culloch, but that the said court of appeals of Maryland ought to have reversed the said judgment of the said Baltimore county court, and ought to have given judgment for the said appellant, M'Culloch. It is therefore adjudged and ordered, that the said judgment of the said court of appeals of the State of Maryland, in this case, be, and the same hereby is, reversed and annulled. And this court, proceeding to render such judgment as the said court of appeals should have rendered, it is further adjudged and ordered, that the judgment of the said Baltimore county court be reversed and annulled, and that judgment be entered in the said Baltimore county court for the said James W. M'Culloch.

OREGON v. HASS

420 U.S. 714, 43 L.Ed.2d 570, 95 S.Ct. 1215 (1975)

Defendant was convicted before the Circuit Court, Klamath County, Oregon, of first-degree burglary, and he appealed. The Court of Appeals of Oregon, 510 P.2d 852, reversed and remanded, and review was granted. The Oregon Supreme Court, 267 Ore. 489, 517 P.2d 671, affirmed the Court of Appeals, and certiorari was granted. The Supreme Court, MR. JUSTICE BLACKMUN, held that State may not impose greater restrictions on police activity as a matter of federal constitutional law than those which the United States Supreme Court holds to be necessary under federal constitutional standards; that for purposes of review, State was aggrieved by holding that, for constitutional reasons, prosecution could not utilize otherwise relevant evidence; and that where defendant, who was in the custody of a state police officer, had been given full *Miranda* warnings and accepted them and later stated that he would like to telephone a lawyer but was told that he could not do so until officer and defendant reached station, and defendant then provided inculpatory information, that information was ad-

missible in evidence solely for impeachment purposes after defendant had taken the stand and testified contrary to the inculpatory information, knowing such information had been ruled inadmissible for the prosecution's case in chief.

Reversed.

MR. JUSTICE BRENNAN, with whom MR. JUSTICE MARSHALL joined, filed a dissenting opinion.

MR. JUSTICE MARSHALL, with whom MR. JUSTICE BRENNAN joined, filed a dissenting opinion.

MR. JUSTICE DOUGLAS took no part in consideration or decision of the case.

MR. JUSTICE BLACKMUN delivered the opinion of the Court.

This case presents a variation of the fact situation encountered by the Court in *Harris v. New York*, 401 U.S. 222 (1971): When a suspect, who is in the custody of a state police officer, has been given full *Miranda* warnings and accepts them, and then later states that he would like to telephone a lawyer but is told that this cannot be done until the officer and the suspect reach the station, and the suspect then provides inculpatory information, is that information admissible in evidence solely for impeachment purposes after the suspect has taken the stand and testified contrarily to the inculpatory information, or is it inadmissible under the Fifth and Fourteenth Amendments?

I

The facts are not in dispute. In August 1972, bicycles were taken from two residential garages in the Moyina Heights area of Klamath Falls, Ore. Respondent Hass, in due course, was indicted for burglary in the first degree, in violation of Ore. Rev. Stat. § 164.225, with respect to the bicycle taken from the garage attached to one of the residences, a house occupied by a family named Lehman. He was not charged with the other burglary.

On the day of the thefts, Officer Osterholme of the Oregon State Police traced an automobile license number to the place where Hass lived. The officer met Hass there and placed him under arrest. At Hass' trial Osterholme testified *in camera* that, after giving Hass the warnings prescribed by *Miranda* v. *Arizona*, 384 U.S. 436, 467–473 (1966), he asked Hass about the theft of the bicycle taken from the Lehman residence. Hass admitted that he had taken two bicycles but stated that he was not sure, at first, which one Osterholme was talking about. He further said that he had returned one of them and that the other was where he had left it.

Osterholme and Hass then departed in a patrol car for the site. On the way Hass opined that he "was in a lot of trouble," and would like to telephone his attorney. Osterholme replied that he could telephone the lawyer "as soon as we got to the office." Thereafter, respondent pointed out a place in the brush where the bicycle was found.

The court ruled that statements made by Hass after he said he wanted to see an attorney, and his identification of the bicycle's location, were not admissible. The prosecution then elicited from Osterholme, in its case in chief before the jury, that Hass had admitted to the witness that he had taken two bicycles that day because he needed money, that he had given one back, and that the other had been recovered.

Later in the trial Hass took the stand. He testified that he and two friends, Walker and Lee, were "just riding around" in his Volkswagen truck; that the other two got out and respondent drove slowly down the street; that Lee suddenly reappeared, tossed a bicycle into the truck, and "ducked down" on the floor of the vehicle; that respondent did not know that Lee "stole it at first"; that it was his own intention to get rid of the bike; that they were overtaken by a jeep occupied by Mr. Lehman and his son; that the son pointed out Lee as "that's the guy"; that Lee then returned the bike to the Lehmans; that respondent drove on and came upon Walker "sitting down there and he had this other bicycle by him," and threw it into the truck; that he, respondent, went "out by Washburn Way and I threw it as far as I could"; that later he told police he had stolen two bicycles; that he had had no idea what Lee and Walker were going to do; and that he did not see any of the bikes being taken and did not know "where those residences were located."

The prosecution then recalled Officer Osterholme in rebuttal. He testified that Hass had pointed out the two houses from which the bicycles were taken. On cross-examination, the officer testified that, prior to so doing, Hass had told Osterholme "that he knew where the bicycles came from, however, he didn't know the exact street address." Osterholme also stated that Lee was along at the time but that Lee "had some difficulty" in identifying the residences "until Mr. Hass actually pointed them" and then "he recognized it."

The trial court, at the request of the defense, then advised the jury that the portion of Officer Osterholme's testimony describing the statement made by Hass to him "may not be used by you as proof of the Defendant's guilt . . . but you may consider that testimony only as it bears on the [credibility] of the Defendant as a witness when he testified on the witness stand."

Respondent again took the stand and said that Osterholme's testimony that he took him out to the residences and that respondent pointed out the houses was "wrong."

The jury returned a verdict of guilty. Hass received a sentence of two years' probation and a $250 fine. The Oregon Court of Appeals, feeling itself bound by the earlier Oregon decision in State v. Brewton, 247 Ore. 241, 422 P.2d 581 (1967), a pre-Harris case, reversed on the ground that Hass' statements were improperly used to impeach his testimony. 13 Ore. App. 368, 374, 510 P.2d 852 (1973). On petition for review, the Supreme Court of Oregon, by a 4-to-3 vote, affirmed. 267 Ore. 489, 517 P.2d 671 (1973). The court reasoned that in a situation of proper Miranda warnings, as here, the police have nothing to lose, and perhaps could gain something, for impeachment purposes, by continuing their interrogation after the warnings; thus, there is no deterrence. In contrast, the court said, where warnings are yet to be given, there is an element of deterrence, for the police "will not take the chance of losing incriminating evidence for their case in chief by not giving adequate warnings." The three dissenters perceived no difference between the two situations. Because the result was in conflict with that reached by the North Carolina court in State v. Bryant, 280 N.C. 551, 554–556, 187 S.E.2d 111 (1972), and because it bore upon the reach of our decision in Harris v. New York, 401 U.S. 222 (1971), we granted certiorari. We reverse.

II

The respondent raises some preliminary arguments. We mention them in passing:

1. Hass suggests that "when state law is more restrictive against the prosecution than federal law," this Court has no power "to compel a state to conform to federal law." Brief for Respondent 1. This, apparently, is proffered as a reference to our expressions that a State is free *as a matter of its own law* to impose greater restrictions on police activity than those this Court holds to be necessary upon federal constitutional standards. See, *e.g., Cooper* v. *California,* 386 U.S. 58, 62 (1967); *Sibron* v. *New York,* 392 U.S. 40, 60–61 (1968). See also *State* v. *Kaluna,* 55 Haw. 361, 368–369, 520 P.2d 51 (1974). But, of course, a State may not impose such greater restrictions as a matter of *federal constitutional law* when this Court specifically refrains from imposing them. See *Smayda* v. *United States,* 352 F.2d 251, 253 (CA9 1965), cert. denied, 382 U.S. 981 (1966); *Aftanase* v. *Economy Baler Co.,* 343 F.2d 187, 193 (CA8 1965).

Although Oregon has a constitutional provision against compulsory self-incrimination in any criminal prosecution, Ore. Const., Art. 1, § 12, the present case was decided by the Oregon courts on Fifth and Fourteenth Amendment grounds. The decision did not rest on the Oregon Constitution or state law; neither was cited. The fact that the Oregon courts found it necessary to attempt to distinguish *Harris* v. *New York, supra,* reveals the federal basis.

2. Hass suggests that a decision by a State's highest court in favor of a criminal defendant is not reviewable here. This, we assume, is a standing argument advanced on the theory that the State is not aggrieved by the Oregon judgment. Surely, a holding that, for constitutional reasons, the prosecution may not utilize otherwise relevant evidence makes the State an aggrieved party for purposes of review. This should be self-evident, but cases such as *California* v. *Green,* 399 U.S. 149 (1970), manifest its validity.

3. *State* v. *Brewton,* 247 Ore. 241, 422 P.2d 581 (1967), by which the Oregon Court of Appeals in the present case felt itself bound, merits comment. There the Oregon court, again by a 4-to-3 vote, held that statements, elicited from a murder defendant, that were inadmissible in the State's case in chief because they had not been preceded by adequate warnings, could not be used to impeach the defendant's own testimony even though the statements had been voluntarily made.

In the present case the Supreme Court of Oregon stated that it took review "for the purpose of deciding whether we wished to overrule *Brewton.*" It found it "not necessary to make that determination" because, in the majority view, *Brewton* and *Harris* were distinguishable. As set forth below, we are unable so to distinguish the two cases. Furthermore, *Brewton* is pre-*Harris.*

III

This takes us to the real issue, namely, that of the bearing of *Harris* v. *New York* upon this case.

In *Harris,* the defendant was charged by the State in a two-count indictment with twice selling heroin to an undercover police officer. The prosecution introduced evidence of the two sales. Harris took the stand in his own defense. He denied the first sale and described the second as one of baking powder utilized as part of a scheme to defraud the purchaser. On cross-examination, Harris was asked whether he had made specified statements to the police immediately following his arrest; the statements partially contradicted Harris' testimony. In response, Harris testified that he could not remember the questions or answers recited by the prosecutor. The trial court instructed the jury that the statements attributed to Harris could be used only in passing on his credibility and not as evidence of guilt. The jury returned a verdict of guilty on the second count of the indictment.

The prosecution had not sought to use the statements in its case in chief, for it conceded that they were inadmissible under *Miranda* because Harris had not been advised of his right to appointed counsel. THE CHIEF JUSTICE, speaking for the Court, observed: "It does not follow from *Miranda* that evidence inadmissible against an accused in the prosecution's case in chief is barred for all purposes, provided of course that the trustworthiness of the evidence satisfies legal standards." Relying on *Walder* v. *United States*, 347 U.S. 62 (1954), a Fourth Amendment case, we ruled that there was no "difference in principle" between *Walder* and *Harris*; that the "impeachment

process here undoubtedly provided valuable aid to the jury in assessing petitioner's credibility"; that the "benefits of this process should not be lost"; that, "[a]ssuming that the exclusionary rule has a deterrent effect on proscribed police conduct, sufficient deterrence flows when the evidence in question is made unavailable to the prosecution in its case in chief," and that the "shield provided by *Miranda* cannot be perverted into a license to use perjury by way of a defense, free from the risk of confrontation with prior inconsistent utterances." It was held, accordingly, that Harris' credibility was appropriately impeached by the use of his earlier conflicting statements.

We see no valid distinction to be made in the application of the principles of *Harris* to that case and to Hass' case. Hass' statements were made after the defendant knew Osterholme's opposing testimony had been ruled inadmissible for the prosecution's case in chief.

As in *Harris*, it does not follow from *Miranda* that evidence inadmissible against Hass in the prosecution's case in chief is barred for all purposes, always provided that "the trustworthiness of the evidence satisfies legal standards." 401 U.S., at 224. Again, the impeaching material would provide valuable aid to the jury in assessing the defendant's credibility; again, "the benefits of this process should not be lost," *id.*, at 225; and, again, making the deterrent-effect assumption, there is sufficient deterrence when the evidence in question is made unavailable to the prosecution in its case in chief. If all this sufficed for the result in *Harris*, it supports and demands a like result in Hass' case. Here, too, the shield provided by *Miranda* is not to be perverted to a license to testify inconsistently, or even perjuriously, free from the risk of confrontation with prior inconsistent utterances.

We are, after all, always engaged in a search for truth in a criminal case so long as the search is surrounded with the safeguards provided by our Constitution. There is no evidence or suggestion that Hass' statements to Officer Osterholme on the way to Moyina Heights were involuntary or coerced. He properly sensed, to be sure, that he was in "trouble"; but the pressure on him was no greater than that on any person in like custody or under inquiry by any investigating officer.

The only possible factual distinction between *Harris* and this case lies in the fact that the *Miranda* warnings given Hass were proper, whereas those given Harris were defective. The deterrence of the exclusionary rule, of course, lies in the necessity to give the warnings. That these warnings, in a given case, may prove to be incomplete, and therefore defective, as in *Harris*, does not mean that they have not served as a deterrent to the officer who is not then aware of their defect; and to the officer who is aware of the defect the full deterrence remains. The effect of inadmissibility in the *Harris* case and in this case is the same: inad-

missibility would pervert the constitutional right into a right to falsify free from the embarrassment of impeachment evidence from the defendant's own mouth.

One might concede that when proper *Miranda* warnings have been given, and the officer then continues his interrogation after the suspect asks for an attorney, the officer may be said to have little to lose and perhaps something to gain by way of possibly uncovering impeachment material. This speculative possibility, however, is even greater where the warnings are defective and the defect is not known to the officer. In any event, the balance was struck in *Harris*, and we are not disposed to change it now. If, in a given case, the officer's conduct amounts to abuse, that case, like those involving coercion or duress, may be taken care of when it arises measured by the traditional standards for evaluating voluntariness and trustworthiness.

We therefore hold that the Oregon appellate courts were in error when they ruled that Officer Osterholme's testimony on rebuttal was inadmissible on Fifth and Fourteenth Amendment grounds for purposes of Hass' impeachment. The judgment of the Supreme Court of Oregon is reversed.

It is so ordered.

MR. JUSTICE DOUGLAS took no part in the consideration or decision of this case.

MR. JUSTICE BRENNAN, with whom MR. JUSTICE MARSHALL joins, dissenting.

. . . .

I adhere to my dissent in *Harris* in which I stated that *Miranda* "completely disposes of any distinction between statements used on direct as opposed to cross-examination. 'An incriminating statement is as incriminating when used to impeach credibility as it is when used as direct proof of guilt and no constitutional distinction can legitimately be drawn.'" *Harris, supra,* at 231. I adhere as well to the view that the judiciary must "avoid even the slightest appearance of sanctioning illegal government conduct." *United States* v. *Calandra,* 414 U.S. 338, 360 (1974) (BRENNAN, J., dissenting). "[I]t is monstrous that courts should aid or abet the law-breaking police officer. It is abiding truth that '[n]othing can destroy a government more quickly than its failure to observe its own laws, or worse, its disregard of the charter of its own existence.'" *Harris, supra,* at 232 (BRENNAN, J., dissenting).

The Court's decision today goes beyond *Harris* in undermining *Miranda.* Even after *Harris,* police had some incentive for following *Miranda* by warning an accused of his right to remain silent and his right to counsel. If the warnings were given, the accused might still make a statement which could be used in the prosecution's case in chief. Under today's holding, however, once the warnings are given, police have almost no incentive for following *Miranda's* requirement that "[i]f the individual states that he wants an attor-

ney, the interrogation must cease until an attorney is present." *Miranda, supra,* at 474. If the requirement is followed there will almost surely be no statement since the attorney will advise the accused to remain silent. If, however, the requirement is disobeyed, the police may obtain a statement which can be used for impeachment if the accused has the temerity to testify in his own defense. Thus, after today's decision, if an individual states that he wants an attorney, police interrogation will doubtless be vigorously pressed to obtain statements before the attorney arrives. I am unwilling to join this fundamental erosion of Fifth and Sixth Amendment rights and therefore dissent. I would affirm or, at least, remand for further proceedings for the reasons given in MR. JUSTICE MARSHALL's dissenting opinion.

MR. JUSTICE MARSHALL, with whom MR. JUSTICE BRENNAN joins, dissenting.

. . . .

In my view, we have too often rushed to correct state courts in their view of federal constitutional questions without sufficiently considering the risk that we will be drawn into rendering a purely advisory opinion. Plainly, if the Oregon Supreme Court had expressly decided that Hass' statement was inadmissible as a matter of state as well as federal law, this Court could not upset that judgment. [Citations omitted.] The sound policy behind this rule was well articulated by Mr. Justice Jackson in *Herb* v. *Pitcairn,* 324 U.S. 117 (1945):

> This Court from the time of its foundation has adhered to the principle that it will not review judgments of state courts that rest on adequate and independent state grounds. The reason is so obvious that it has rarely been thought to warrant statement. It is found in the partitioning of power between the state and federal judicial systems and in the limitations of our own jurisdiction. Our only power over state judgments is to correct them to the extent that they incorrectly adjudge federal rights. And our power is to correct wrong judgments, not to revise opinions. We are not permitted to render an advisory opinion, and if the same judgment would be rendered by the state court after we corrected its views of federal laws, our review could amount to nothing more than an advisory opinion. *Id.,* at 125–126 (citations omitted).

Where we have been unable to say with certainty that the judgment rested solely on federal law grounds, we have refused to rule on the federal issue in the case; the proper course is then either to dismiss the writ as improvidently granted or to remand the case to the state court to clarify the basis of its decision. *California* v. *Krivda,* 409 U.S. 33 (1972); *Mental Hygiene Dept.* v. *Kirchner,* 380 U.S. 194 (1965). Of course, it may often be unclear whether a state court

has relied in part on state law in reaching its decision. As the Court said in *Herb* v. *Pitcairn, supra,* however, where the answer does not appear "of record" and is not "clear and decisive,"

> it seems consistent with the respect due the highest courts of states of the Union that they be asked rather than told what they have intended. If this imposes an unwelcome burden it should be mitigated by the knowledge that it is to protect their jurisdiction from unwitting interference as well as to protect our own from unwitting renunciation. 324 U.S., at 128.

From a perusal of the Oregon Supreme Court's opinion it is evident that these exacting standards were not met in this case. The Constitution of Oregon contains an independent prohibition against compulsory self-incrimination, and there is a distinct possibility that the state court intended to express its view of state as well as federal constitutional law. The majority flatly states that the case was decided below solely on federal constitutional grounds, but I am not so certain. Although the state court did not expressly cite state law in support of its judgment, its opinion suggests that it may well have considered the matter one of state as well as federal law. The court stated that it had initially viewed the issue of the case as whether it should overrule one of its prior precedents in light of this Court's opinion in *Harris* v. *New York,* 401 U.S. 222 (1971). It concluded that it was not required to consider whether to overrule the earlier state case, however, since upon examination it determined that *Harris* did not reach this fact situation. In view of the court's suggestion that the federal constitutional rule in *Harris* would be regarded as merely a persuasive authority even if it were deemed to be squarely in conflict with the state rule, it seems quite possible that the state court intended its decision to rest at least in part on independent state grounds. In any event, I agree with Mr. Justice Jackson that state courts should be "asked rather than told what they have intended."

In addition to the importance of avoiding jurisdictional difficulties, it seems much the better policy to permit the state court the freedom to strike its own balance between individual rights and police practices, at least where the state court's ruling violates no constitutional prohibitions. It is peculiarly within the competence of the highest court of a State to determine that in its jurisdiction the police should be subject to more stringent rules than are required as a federal constitutional minimum.

The Oregon court's decision in this case was not premised on a reluctant adherence to what it deemed federal law to require, but was based on its independent conclusion that admitting evidence such as that held admissible today will encourage police misconduct in violation of the right against compulsory self-incrimination. This is precisely the setting in which it seems most likely that the state court would apply the State's self-incrimination clause to lessen what it perceives as an intolerable risk of abuse. Accordingly, in my view the Court should not review a state-court decision reversing a conviction unless it is quite clear that the state court has resolved all applicable state-law questions adversely to the defendant and that it feels compelled by its view of the federal constitutional issue to reverse the conviction at hand.

Even if the majority is correct that the Oregon Supreme Court did not intend to express a view of state as well as federal law, this Court should, at the very least, remand the case for such further proceedings as the state court deems appropriate. I can see absolutely no reason for departing from the usual course of remanding the case to permit the state court to consider any other claims, including the possible applicability of state law to the issue treated here. [Citation omitted.] Surely the majority does not mean to suggest that the Oregon Supreme Court is foreclosed from considering the respondent's state-law claims or even ruling *sua sponte* that the statement in question is not admissible as a matter of state law. If so, then I should think this unprecedented assumption of authority will be as much a surprise to the Supreme Court of Oregon as it is to me.

I dissent.

FREE SPEECH, PRESS AND ASSEMBLY

HESS v. INDIANA

414 U.S. 105, 38 L.Ed.2d 303, 94 S.Ct. 326 (1973)

PER CURIAM.

Gregory Hess appeals from his conviction in the Indiana courts for violating the State's disorderly conduct statute.[1] Appellant contends that his conviction should be reversed because the statute is unconstitutionally vague, *Connally* v. *General Construction Co.*, 269 U.S. 385 (1926), because the statute is overbroad in that it forbids activity that is protected under the First and Fourteenth Amendments, *Gooding* v. *Wilson*, 405 U.S. 518 (1972), and because the statute, as applied here, abridged his constitutionally protected freedom of speech, *Terminiello* v. *Chicago*, 337 U.S. 1 (1949). These contentions were rejected in the City Court, where Hess was convicted, and in the Superior Court, which reviewed his conviction. The Supreme Court

of Indiana, with one dissent, considered and rejected each of Hess' constitutional contentions, and accordingly affirmed his conviction.

The events leading to Hess' conviction began with an antiwar demonstration on the campus of Indiana University. In the course of the demonstration, approximately 100 to 150 of the demonstrators moved onto a public street and blocked the passage of vehicles. When the demonstrators did not respond to verbal directions from the sheriff to clear the street, the sheriff and his deputies began walking up the street, and the demonstrators in their path moved to the curbs on either side, joining a large number of spectators who had gathered. Hess was standing off the street as the sheriff passed him. The sheriff heard Hess utter the word "fuck" in what he later described as a loud voice and immediately arrested him on the disorderly conduct charge. It was later stipulated that what appellant had said was "We'll take the fucking street later," or "We'll take the fucking street again." Two witnesses who were in the immediate vicinity testified, apparently without contradiction, that they heard Hess' words and witnessed his arrest. They indicated that Hess did not appear to be exhorting the

---

[1] "Whoever shall act in a loud, boisterous or disorderly manner so as to disturb the peace and quiet of any neighborhood or family, by loud or unusual noise, or by tumultuous or offensive behavior, threatening, traducing, quarreling, challenging to fight or fighting, shall be deemed guilty of disorderly conduct, and upon conviction, shall be fined in any sum not exceeding five hundred dollars [$500] to which may be added imprisonment for not to exceed one hundred eighty [180] days." Ind. Code 35–27–2–1 (1971), Ind. Ann. Stat. § 10–1510 (Supp. 1972).

crowd to go back into the street, that he was facing the crowd and not the street when he uttered the statement, that his statement did not appear to be addressed to any particular person or group, and that his tone, although loud, was no louder than that of the other people in the area.

Indiana's disorderly conduct statute was applied in this case to punish only spoken words. It hardly needs repeating that "[t]he constitutional guarantees of freedom of speech forbid the States to punish the use of words or language not within 'narrowly limited classes of speech.'" *Gooding* v. *Wilson, supra*, at 521–522. The words here did not fall within any of these "limited classes." In the first place, it is clear that the Indiana court specifically abjured any suggestion that Hess' words could be punished as obscene under *Roth* v. *United States*, 354 U.S. 476 (1957), and its progeny. Indeed, after *Cohen* v. *California*, 403 U.S. 15 (1971), such a contention with regard to the language at issue would not be tenable. By the same token, any suggestion that Hess' speech amounted to "fighting words," *Chaplinsky* v. *New Hampshire*, 315 U.S. 568 (1942), could not withstand scrutiny. Even if under other circumstances this language could be regarded as a personal insult, the evidence is undisputed that Hess' statement was not directed to any person or group in particular. Although the sheriff testified that he was offended by the language, he also stated that he did not interpret the expression as

being directed personally at him, and the evidence is clear that appellant had his back to the sheriff at the time. Thus, under our decisions, the State could not punish this speech as "fighting words." *Cantwell* v. *Connecticut*, 310 U.S. 296, 309 (1940); *Cohen* v. *California, supra*, at 20.

In addition, there was no evidence to indicate that Hess' speech amounted to a public nuisance in that privacy interests were being invaded. "The ability of government, consonant with the Constitution, to shut off discourse solely to protect others from hearing it is . . . dependent upon a showing that substantial privacy interests are being invaded in an essentially intolerable manner." *Cohen* v. *California, supra*, at 21. The prosecution made no such showing in this case.

The Indiana Supreme Court placed primary reliance on the trial court's finding that Hess' statement "was intended to incite further lawless action on the part of the crowd in the vicinity of appellant and was likely to produce such action." 260 Ind. 427, 297 N.E.2d 413, 415 (1973). At best, however, the statement could be taken as counsel for present moderation; at worst, it amounted to nothing more than advocacy of illegal action at some indefinite future time. This is not sufficient to permit the State to punish Hess' speech. Under our decisions, "the constitutional guarantees of free speech and free press do not permit a State to forbid or proscribe advocacy of the use of force or of law violation except where such advocacy is directed to inciting or producing *imminent* lawless action and is likely to incite or produce such action." *Brandenburg v. Ohio*, 395 U.S. 444, 447 (1969). (Emphasis added.) See also *Terminiello v. Chicago*, 337 U.S., at 4. Since the uncontroverted evidence showed that Hess' statement was not directed to any person or group of persons, it cannot be said that he was advocating, in the normal sense, any action. And since there was no evidence, or rational inference from the import of the language, that his words were intended to produce, and likely to produce, *imminent* disorder, those words could not be punished by the State on the ground that they had "a 'tendency to lead to violence.'" 260 Ind., at 427, 297 N.E.2d, at 415.

Accordingly, the motion to proceed *in forma pauperis* is granted and the judgment of the Supreme Court of Indiana is reversed.

[The opinion of MR. JUSTICE REHNQUIST, with whom THE CHIEF JUSTICE and MR. JUSTICE BLACKMUN join, dissenting, has been omitted.]

GLASSON v. CITY OF LOUISVILLE

518 F.2d 899 (6th Cir. 1975)
cert. denied, 423 U.S. 930

McCree, Circuit Judge.

. . . .

On July 14, 1970, the former President of the United States, Richard M. Nixon, was scheduled to ride in a motorcade in Louisville, Kentucky, before attending the Appalachian Governors' Conference. In anticipation of this procession, appellant Glasson, a young Caucasian woman, had prepared to display to the President a poster on which she had printed, "Lead us to hate and kill poverty, disease and ignorance, not each other." By displaying this poster, she hoped to express to the President and to anyone else who might read it, her concern about the divisive issues of American racism and the Vietnam War, and her wish that the President would channel the energies of his administration to heal the divisions created by these issues, and to eliminate poverty, disease, and ignorance. These problems were on the agenda of the Governors' Conference.

Early that morning, Louisville police officers to whom had been assigned the duty of safeguarding the President during the motorcade by monitoring the crowd and keeping it orderly, were given their general orders of the day by Lt. Colonel Edgar Mulligan, Assistant Chief of Police of Louisville. Appellee Colonel Hyde, the Chief of Police, was also present. Appellees Johnson and Medley, police officers with approximately 25 years of experience, attended the meeting and were instructed to destroy any sign or poster that was "detrimental" or "injurious" to the President of the United States.

. . . .

It is undisputed that on the day in question, appellant Glasson was standing peacefully against a building holding her sign as she awaited the motorcade. Several other persons were also displaying signs and posters, all of which bore salutations like "Welcome to the President." According to Johnson and Medley, a group of persons located across the street from Glasson noticed her poster and were provoked by it into grumbling and muttering threats. Officer Medley testified that this group was "hollering" and that his attention was drawn by this boisterous conduct to appellant's poster on which, he testified, was printed in large letters "Murderer, teach us to hate and kill" and then in smaller letters "Poverty, ignorance and so forth," a message that he determined was detrimental to the President. He then conferred with Officer Johnson and informed him that the poster was "pretty bad because the crowd across the street is going to go over and get her—maybe hurt her." Officer Johnson agreed that the poster was detrimental to the President and directed Medley to follow the general orders given that day—to destroy all signs detrimental to the President. Officer Medley then approached appellant and according to his testimony, asked her

"Would you please take this sign down, Lady; it's detrimental to the United States of America." When Miss Glasson refused, and replied that she had a right to display it, Medley took it from her and tore it up. The hecklers across the street cheered and then immediately quieted down and began to disperse.

At trial, Johnson and Medley testified that the boisterous group that had spurred them into action consisted of twenty-five to thirty persons and that there were approximately seven to twelve police officers stationed on the block where the demonstrators stood. When asked whether the police force at hand was sufficient to handle a possible disorder in a crowd that size, Officer Johnson responded that the answer depended upon the number of people who became involved, but that "if it got so bad that we had to have reinforcements we could have done that also." Moreover, even though Johnson testified that the disturbance "was reaching the stage of a riot," the record shows that not one heckler crossed, or even attempted to cross the street, no reinforcements were ever summoned, and the secret service, the federal agency assigned the duty of safeguarding the President, 18 U.S.C. § 3056, was not alerted. Neither officer told the crowd to quiet down or attempted to calm its members except to assure them that the police would take care of appellant's poster.

. . . .

As a result of this encounter, [Miss Glasson] filed this action in the United States District Court for the Western District of Kentucky under sections 1983 and 1985(3) of the Civil Rights Acts, 42 U.S.C. §§ 1983, 1985(3). Her complaint charged that Officers Johnson and Medley, acting under color of law, deprived her of rights guaranteed by the First and Fourteenth Amendments to the United States Constitution, and that they, acting with appellee Hyde, conspired to deprive her of the equal protection of the laws and of equal privileges and immunities under the laws of the United States. She requested compensatory and punitive damages.

. . . .

On appeal it is contended that the district court erred in holding that the officers acted reasonably and in good faith in seizing and destroying appellant's poster. . . . We agree and reverse. . . . We hold that when Officer Medley destroyed Miss Glasson's poster, she was engaged in activity protected by the First and Fourteenth Amendments; that his action, directed by Officer Johnson and authorized by Chief of Police Hyde, was unreasonable and not taken in good faith; and that it violated her constitutional rights and was actionable under section 1983 of the Civil Rights Acts. . . .

No state may agreeably to the Constitution intercept a message and remove it from the channels of communication or punish its dissemination solely because of its content unless it is obscene, e.g., Miller v. California, 413 U.S. 15 (1973), Roth v. United States, 354 U.S. 476 (1957), defamatory, e.g., New York Times v. Sullivan, 376 U.S. 254 (1964), constitutes "fighting words," e.g., Lewis v. City of New Orleans, 415 U.S. 130 (1974), Chaplinsky v. New Hampshire, 315 U.S. 568 (1942), or substantially and directly imperils national security, see New York Times Co. v. United States, 403 U.S. 713 (1971). Moreover, the Constitution protects not only the substance of an expression but also the use of words selected for their emotive quality even though they may offend the tastes of the community. E.g., Papish v. Board of Curators of the University of Missouri, 410 U.S. 667 (1973), Cohen v. California, 403 U.S. 15 (1971), Thonen v. Jenkins, 491 F.2d 722 (4th Cir. 1973). Inherent in suppressing the use of particular words is the grave risk of inhibiting the expression of ideas, particularly unpopular ones.

The message that Miss Glasson sought to communicate was an expression of her views about important public questions and policies. This kind of expression is entitled to the greatest constitutional protection. As the Supreme Court stated in New York Times Co. v. Sullivan, supra, 376 U.S. at 269:

The general proposition that freedom of expression upon public questions is secured by the First Amendment has long been settled by our decisions. The constitutional safeguard, we have said, "was fashioned to assure unfettered interchange of ideas for the bringing about of political and social changes desired by the people."

Accordingly, even if the appellation "Murderer" appeared on Miss Glasson's placard, and her message was expressly critical of the Nixon administration, it was constitutionally protected. The right of an American citizen to criticize public officials and policies and to advocate peacefully ideas for change is "the central meaning of the First Amendment." 376 U.S. at 273. *See generally* A. Meiklejohn, POLITICAL FREEDOM: THE CONSTITUTIONAL POWERS OF THE PEOPLE (1948), Kalven, *The New York Times Case: A note on "The Central Meaning of the First Amendment,"* 1964 SUP.CT.REV. 191.

Although the content of a communication may be protected, the state may, in some circumstances, regulate the time, place and manner of expressing it. *See, e.g., Grayned v. City of Rockford,* 408 U.S. 104, 115–17 (1972). For example, it may determine not to permit two parades to proceed along the same street at the same time, or two rallies to be held simultaneously in the same part of a public park. Moreover, the state may in appropriate circumstances prohibit rallies in jail yards, *Adderley v. Florida,* 385 U.S. 39 (1966), in public libraries, *see Brown v. Louisiana,* 383 U.S. 131 (1966), and near courthouses, *Cox v. Louisiana,* 379 U.S. 559 (1965). *See generally* Kalven, *The Concept of the Public Forum: Cox v. Louisiana,* 1965 SUP.CT.REV. 1. Yet, at the same time, our public streets and parks have immemorially been held in trust for the use of the public and, time out of mind, have been used for purposes of assembly, communicating thoughts between citizens, and discussing public questions. Such use of the streets and public places has, from ancient times, been a part of the privileges, immunities, rights, and liberties of citizens. The privilege of a citizen of the United States to use the streets and parks for communication of views on national questions may be regulated in the interest of all; it is not absolute, but relative, and must be exercised in subordination to the general comfort and convenience, and in consonance with peace and good order; but it must not, in the guise of regulation, be abridged or denied. *Hague v. CIO,* 307 U.S. 496, 515–16 (1939).

In this case, Miss Glasson was in a place where she had a right to be, at a time that was appropriate, and was conducting herself peacefully and lawfully. She, like many other persons, had taken the opportunity to express her ideas to the President—from a place designated by the state for onlookers and in a manner often used by persons who do not have access to the print or broadcast media.

Moreover, we do not believe that Miss Glasson somehow forfeited the protection afforded her message by the Constitution because it unintentionally evoked a hostile reaction from others. We reach this conclusion after considering this case "against the background of a profound national commitment to the principle that debate on public issues should be uninhibited, robust, and wide-open, and that it may well include vehement, caustic, and sometimes unpleasantly sharp attacks on government and public officials." *New York Times Co.* v. *Sullivan*, 376 U.S. at 270. The purpose of the First Amendment is to encourage discussion, and it is intended to protect the expression of unpopular as well as popular ideas. Accordingly, hostile public reaction does not cause the forfeiture of the constitutional protection afforded a speaker's message so long as the speaker does not go beyond mere persuasion and advocacy of ideas and attempts to incite to riot. *See e.g., Gooding* v. *Wilson*, 405 U.S. 518 (1972); *Brandenburg* v. *Ohio*, 395 U.S. 444 (1969); *Ashton* v. *Kentucky*, 384 U.S. 195 (1966); *Edwards* v. *South Carolina, supra; Feiner* v. *New York*, 340 U.S. 315, 321 (1951).[3]

To permit police officers to prohibit the expression of ideas which they believe to be "detrimental" or "injurious" to the President of the United States or to punish for incitement or breach of the peace the peaceful communication of such messages because other persons are provoked and seek to take violent action against the speaker would subvert the First Amendment, and would incorporate into that constitutional guarantee a "heckler's veto" which would empower an audience to cut off the expression of a speaker with whom it disagreed. The state may not rely on community hostility and threats of violence to justify censorship.

The record before us demonstrates that Miss Glasson, in displaying her placard which contained a constitutionally protected message, in a peaceful manner, from an appropriate place, was engaged in activity protected by the First Amendment and that the destruction of the sign by Louisville police officers Johnson and Medley deprived her of that right. . . .

[The rest of the opinion in this case, dealing with the defendants' civil liability under 42 U.S.C. § 1983, is reproduced under cases relating to Chapter 11.]

---

[3] Feiner used a loudspeaker to address an interracial crowd of seventy-five to eighty persons and urged them to attend a meeting to discuss racial discrimination. During the course of his exhortation, he made derogatory remarks about President Truman, the Marshall Plan, and local officials, and urged the Negroes in the crowd to "rise up in arms" against white people and "fight for equal rights." The crowd blocked sidewalks, forcing pedestrians to walk in the street, and became angry and threatened to attack Feiner if the police failed to act. The police requested Feiner to stop speaking three times before arresting him for disorderly conduct. In upholding the conviction, the Supreme Court determined that the police "in making the arrest were motivated solely by a proper concern for the preservation of order and protection of the general welfare, and that there was no evidence which could lend color to a claim that the acts of the police were a cover for suppression of petitioner's views and opinions." 340 U.S. at 319.

For over twenty years the Supreme Court has confined the rule in *Feiner* to a situation where the speaker in urging his opinion upon an audience intends to incite it to take action that the state has a right to prevent.

Cases relating to **Chapter 3**

AUTHORITY TO DETAIN AND ARREST

HENRY v. UNITED STATES

361 U.S. 98, 4 L.Ed.2d 134, 80 S.Ct. 168 (1959)

Mr. Justice Douglas delivered the opinion of the Court.

Petitioner stands convicted of unlawfully possessing three cartons of radios valued at more than $100 which had been stolen from an interstate shipment. See 18 U.S.C. § 659. The issue in the case is whether there was probable cause for the arrest leading to the search that produced the evidence on which the conviction rests. A timely motion to suppress the evidence was made by petitioner and overruled by the District Court; and the judgment of conviction was affirmed by the Court of Appeals on a divided vote. 259 F.2d 725. The case is here on a petition for a writ of certiorari, 359 U.S. 904.

There was a theft from an interstate shipment of whisky at a terminal in Chicago. The next day two FBI agents were in the neighborhood investigating it. They saw petitioner and one Pierotti walk across a street from a tavern and get into an automobile. The agents had been given, by the employer of Pierotti, information of an undisclosed nature "concerning the implication of the defendant Pierotti with interstate shipments." But, so far as the record shows, he never went so far as to tell

the agents he suspected Pierotti of any such thefts. The agents followed the car and saw it enter an alley and stop. Petitioner got out of the car, entered a gangway leading to residential premises and returned in a few minutes with some cartons. He placed them in the car and he and Picrotti drove off. The agents were unable to follow the car. But later they found it parked at the same place near the tavern. Shortly thereafter they saw petitioner and Pierotti leave the tavern, get into the car, and drive off. The car stopped in the same alley as before; petitioner entered the same gangway and returned with more cartons. The agents observed this transaction from a distance of some 300 feet and could not determine the size, number or contents of the cartons. As the car drove off the agents followed it and finally, when they met it, waved it to a stop. As he got out of the car, petitioner was heard to say, "Hold it; it is the G's." This was followed by, "Tell him he [you] just picked me up." The agents searched the car, placed the cartons (which bore the name "Admiral" and were addressed to an out-of-state company) in their car, took the merchandise and petitioner and Pierotti to their office and held them for about two hours when the agents

600

learned that the cartons contained stolen radios. They then placed the men under formal arrest.

The statutory authority of FBI officers and agents to make felony arrests without a warrant is restricted to offenses committed "in their presence" or to instances where they have "reasonable grounds to believe that the person to be arrested has committed or is committing" a felony. 18 U.S.C. § 3052. The statute states the constitutional standard, for it is the command of the Fourth Amendment that no warrants for either searches or arrests shall issue except "upon probable cause, supported by oath or affirmation, and particularly describing the place to be searched, and the persons or things to be seized."

The requirement of probable cause has roots that are deep in our history. The general warrant, in which the name of the person to be arrested was left blank, and the writs of assistance, against which James Otis inveighed, both perpetuated the oppressive practice of allowing the police to arrest and search on suspicion. Police control took the place of judicial control, since no showing of "probable cause" before a magistrate was required. The Virginia Declaration of Rights, adopted June 12, 1776, rebelled against that practice:

That general warrants, whereby any officer or messenger may be commanded to search suspected places without evidence of a fact committed, or to seize any

person or persons not named, or whose offense is not particularly described and supported by evidence, are grievous and oppressive, and ought not to be granted.

The Maryland Declaration of Rights (1776), Art. XXIII, was equally emphatic:

That all warrants, without oath or affirmation, to search suspected places, or to seize any person or property, are grievous and oppressive; and all general warrants—to search suspected places, or to apprehend suspected persons, without naming or describing the place, or the person in special—are illegal, and ought not to be granted.

And see North Carolina Declaration of Rights (1776), Art. XI; Pennsylvania Constitution (1776), Art. X; Massachusetts Constitution (1780), Pt. I, Art. XIV.

That philosophy later was reflected in the Fourth Amendment. And as the early American decisions both before and immediately after its adoption show, common rumor or report, suspicion, or even "strong reason to suspect" was not adequate to support a warrant for arrest. And that principle has survived to this day. See *United States v. Di Re*, 332 U.S. 581, 593–595; *Johnson v. United States*, 333 U.S. 10, 13–15; *Giordenello v. United States*, 357 U.S. 480, 486. Its high water was *Johnson v. United States, supra*, where the smell of opium coming from a closed room was not enough to support an arrest and search without a warrant. It was against this background that two scholars recently wrote, "Arrest on mere suspicion collides violently with the basic human right of liberty."

Evidence required to establish guilt is not necessary. *Brinegar* v. *United States*, 338 U.S. 160; *Draper* v. *United States*, 358 U.S. 307. On the other hand, good faith on the part of the arresting officers is not enough. Probable cause exists if the facts and circumstances known to the officer warrant a prudent man in believing that the offense has been committed. *Stacey* v. *Emery*, 97 U.S. 642, 645. And see *Director General* v. *Kastenbaum*, 263 U.S. 25, 28; *United States* v. *Di Re, supra*, at 592; *Giordenello* v. *United States, supra*, at 486. It is important, we think, that this requirement be strictly enforced, for the standard set by the Constitution protects both the officer and the citizen. If the officer acts with probable cause, he is protected even though it turns out that the citizen is innocent. *Carroll* v. *United States*, 267 U.S. 132, 156. And while a search without a warrant is, within limits, permissible if incident to a lawful arrest, if an arrest without a warrant is to support an incidental search, it must be made with probable cause. *Carroll* v. *United States, supra*, at 155–156. This immunity of officers cannot fairly be enlarged without jeopardizing the privacy or security of the citizen. We turn then to the question whether prudent men in the shoes of these officers (*Brinegar* v. *United States, supra*, at 175)

would have seen enough to permit them to believe that petitioner was violating or had violated the law. We think not.

The prosecution conceded below, and adheres to the concession here, that the arrest took place when the federal agents stopped the car. That is our view on the facts of this particular case. When the officers interrupted the two men and restricted their liberty of movement, the arrest, for purposes of this case, was complete. It is, therefore, necessary to determine whether at or before that time they had reasonable cause to believe that a crime had been committed. The fact that afterwards contraband was discovered is not enough. An arrest is not justified by what the subsequent search discloses, as *Johnson* v. *United States, supra*, holds.

It is true that a federal crime had been committed at a terminal in the neighborhood, whisky having been stolen from an interstate shipment. Petitioner's friend, Pierotti, had been suspected of some implication in some interstate shipments, as we have said. But as this record stands, what those shipments were and the manner in which he was implicated remain unexplained and undefined. The rumor about him is therefore practically meaningless. On the record there was far from enough evidence against him to justify a magistrate in issuing a warrant. So far as the record shows, petitioner had not even been suspected of criminal activity prior to this time. Riding in the car, stopping in an alley,

picking up packages, driving away
—these were all acts that were out-
wardly innocent. Their movements
in the car had no mark of fleeing
men or men acting furtively. The
case might be different if the packages had been taken from a terminal or from an interstate truck-
ing platform. But they were not.
As we have said, the alley where
the packages were picked up was
in a residential section. The fact
that packages have been stolen
does not make every man who carries a package subject to arrest
nor the package subject to seizure.
The police must have reasonable
grounds to believe that the particular package carried by the citizen is contraband. Its shape and
design might at times be adequate.
The weight of it and the manner
in which it is carried might at times
be enough. But there was nothing
to indicate that the cartons here
in issue probably contained liquor.
The fact that they contained other
contraband appeared only some
hours after the arrest. What transpired at or after the time the car
was stopped by the officers is, as
we have said, irrelevant to the narrow issue before us. To repeat, an
arrest is not justified by what the
subsequent search discloses. Under
our system suspicion is not enough
for an officer to lay hands on a
citizen. It is better, so the Fourth
Amendment teaches, that the guilty
sometimes go free than that citizens be subject to easy arrest.

The fact that the suspects were
in an automobile is not enough.
Carroll v. *United States, supra,* lib-
eralized the rule governing searches
when a moving vehicle is involved.
But that decision merely relaxed
the requirements for a warrant on
grounds of practicality. It did not
dispense with the need for probable cause.

Reversed.

MR. JUSTICE BLACK concurs in
the result.

MR. JUSTICE CLARK, whom THE
CHIEF JUSTICE joins, dissenting.

The Court decides this case on
the narrow ground that the arrest
took place at the moment the Federal Bureau of Investigation agents
stopped the car in which petitioner
was riding and at that time probable cause for it did not exist.
While the Government, unnecessarily it seems to me, conceded
that the arrest was made at the
time the car was stopped, this
Court is not bound by the Government's mistakes.

The record shows beyond dispute that the agents had received
information from co-defendant
Pierotti's employer implicating
Pierotti with interstate shipments.
The agents began a surveillance of
petitioner and Pierotti after recognizing them as they came out of a
bar. Later the agents observed
them loading cartons into an automobile from a gangway up an alley
in Chicago. The agents had been
trailing them, and after it appeared
that they had delivered the first
load of cartons, the suspects returned to the same platform by a
circuitous route through streets
and alleys. The agents then saw

petitioner load another set of cartons into the car and drive off with the same. A few minutes later the agents stopped the car, alighted from their own car, and approached the petitioner. As they did so, petitioner was overheard to say: "Hold it; it is the G's," and "Tell him he [you] just picked me up." Since the agents had actually seen the two suspects together for several hours, it was apparent to them that the statement was untrue. Upon being questioned, the defendants stated that they had borrowed the car from a friend. During the questioning and after petitioner had stepped out of the car one of the agents happened to look through the door of the car which petitioner had left open and saw three cartons stacked up inside which resembled those petitioner had just loaded into the car from the gangway. The agent saw that the cartons bore "Admiral" shipping labels and were addressed to a company in Cincinnati, Ohio. Upon further questioning, the agent was told that the cartons were in the car when the defendants borrowed it. Knowing this to be untrue, the agents then searched the car, arrested petitioner and his companion, and seized the cartons.

The Court seems to say that the mere stopping of the car amounted to an arrest of the petitioner. I cannot agree. The suspicious activities of the petitioner during the somewhat prolonged surveillance by the agents warranted the stopping of the car. The sighting of the cartons with their interstate labels in the car gave the agents reasonable ground to believe that a crime was in the course of its commission in their very presence. The search of the car and the subsequent arrest were therefore lawful and the motion to suppress was properly overruled.

In my view, the time at which the agents were required to have reasonable grounds to believe that petitioner was committing a felony was when they began the search of the automobile, which was after they had seen the cartons with interstate labels in the car. The earlier events certainly disclosed ample grounds to justify the following of the car, the subsequent stopping thereof, and the questioning of petitioner by the agents. This interrogation, together with the sighting of the cartons and the labels, gave the agents indisputable probable cause for the search and arrest.

When an investigation proceeds to the point where an agent has reasonable grounds to believe that an offense is being committed in his presence, he is obligated to proceed to make such searches, seizures, and arrests as the circumstances require. It is only by such alertness that crime is discovered, interrupted, prevented, and punished. We should not place additional burdens on law enforcement agencies.

I would affirm the judgments on the rationale of *Brinegar* v. *United States,* 338 U.S. 160 (1949), and *Carroll* v. *United States,* 267 U.S. 132 (1925).

TERRY v. OHIO

392 U.S. 1, 20 L.Ed.2d 889, 88 S.Ct. 1868 (1968)

MR. CHIEF JUSTICE WARREN delivered the opinion of the Court.

This case presents serious questions concerning the role of the Fourth Amendment in the confrontation on the street between the citizen and the policeman investigating suspicious circumstances.

Petitioner Terry was convicted of carrying a concealed weapon and sentenced to the statutorily prescribed term of one to three years in the penitentiary. Following the denial of a pretrial motion to suppress, the prosecution introduced in evidence two revolvers and a number of bullets seized from Terry and a codefendant, Richard Chilton, by Cleveland Police Detective Martin McFadden. At the hearing on the motion to suppress this evidence, Officer McFadden testified that while he was patrolling in plain clothes in downtown Cleveland at approximately 2:30 in the afternoon of October 31, 1963, his attention was attracted by two men, Chilton and Terry, standing on the corner of Huron Road and Euclid Avenue. He had never seen the two men before, and he was unable to say precisely what first drew his eye to them. However, he testified that he had been a policeman for 39 years and a detective for 35 and that he had been assigned to patrol this vicinity of downtown Cleveland for shoplifters and pickpockets for 30 years. He explained that he had developed routine habits of observation over the years and that he would "stand and watch people or walk and watch people at many intervals of the day." He added: "Now, in this case when I looked over they didn't look right to me at the time."

His interest aroused, Officer McFadden took up a post of observation in the entrance to a store 300 to 400 feet away from the two men. "I get more purpose to watch them when I seen their movements," he testified. He saw one of the men leave the other one and walk southwest on Huron Road, past some stores. The man paused for a moment and looked in a store window, then walked on a short distance, turned around and walked back toward the corner, pausing once again to look in the same store window. He rejoined his companion at the corner, and the two conferred briefly. Then the second man went through the same series of motions, strolling down Huron Road, looking in the same window, walking on a short distance, turning back, peering in the store window again, and returning to confer with the first man at the corner. The two men repeated this ritual alternately between five and six times apiece—in all, roughly a dozen trips. At one point, while the two men were standing together on the corner, a third man approached them and engaged them briefly in conversation. This man then left the two others and walked west on Euclid Avenue. Chilton and Terry resumed their measured pacing, peering, and conferring. After this had gone on for 10 to 12 minutes, the two men walked off together, heading west on Euclid Avenue, following the path taken earlier by the third man.

By this time Officer McFadden had become thoroughly suspicious. He testified that after observing their elaborately casual and oft-repeated reconnaissance of the store window on Huron Road, he suspected the two men of "casing a job, a stick-up," and that he considered it his duty as a police officer to investigate further. He added that he feared "they may have a gun." Thus, Officer McFadden followed Chilton and Terry and saw them stop in front of Zucker's store to talk to the same man who had conferred with them earlier on the street corner. Deciding that the situation was ripe for direct action, Officer McFadden approached the three men, identified himself as a police officer and asked for their names. At this point his knowledge was confined to what he had observed. He was not acquainted with any of the three men by name or by sight, and he had received no information concerning them from any other source. When the men "mumbled something" in response to his inquiries, Officer McFadden grabbed petitioner Terry, spun him around so they were facing the other two, with Terry between McFadden and the others, and patted down the out-side of his clothing. In the left breast pocket of Terry's overcoat Officer McFadden felt a pistol. He reached inside the overcoat pocket, but was unable to remove the gun. At this point, keeping Terry between himself and the others, the officer ordered all three men to enter Zucker's store. As they went in, he removed Terry's overcoat completely, retrieved a .38 caliber revolver from the pocket and ordered all three men to face the wall with their hands raised. Officer McFadden proceeded to pat down the outer clothing of Chilton and the third man, Katz. He discovered another revolver in the outer pocket of Chilton's overcoat, but no weapons were found on Katz. The officer testified that he only patted the men down to see whether they had weapons, and that he did not put his hands beneath the outer garments of either Terry or Chilton until he felt their guns. So far as appears from the record, he never placed his hands beneath Katz's outer garments. Officer McFadden seized Chilton's gun, asked the proprietor of the store to call a police wagon, and took all three men to the station, where Chilton and Terry were formally charged with carrying concealed weapons.

On the motion to suppress the guns the prosecution took the position that they had been seized following a search incident to a lawful arrest. The trial court rejected this theory, stating that it "would be stretching the facts beyond reasonable comprehension" to find that Officer McFadden had

had probable cause to arrest the men before he patted them down for weapons. However, the court denied the defendant's motion on the ground that Officer McFadden, on the basis of his experience, "had reasonable cause to believe . . . that the defendants were conducting themselves suspiciously, and some interrogation should be made of their action." Purely for his own protection, the court held, the officer had the right to pat down the outer clothing of these men, whom he had reasonable cause to believe might be armed. The court distinguished between an investigatory "stop" and an arrest, and between a "frisk" of the outer clothing for weapons and a full-blown search for evidence of crime. The frisk, it held, was essential to the proper performance of the officer's investigatory duties, for without it "the answer to the police officer may be a bullet, and a loaded pistol discovered during the frisk is admissible."

After the court denied their motion to suppress, Chilton and Terry waived jury trial and pleaded not guilty. The court adjudged them guilty, and the Court of Appeals for the Eighth Judicial District, Cuyahoga County, affirmed. *State v. Terry*, 5 OhioApp.2d 122, 214 N.E.2d 114 (1966). The Supreme Court of Ohio dismissed petitioner's appeal on the ground that no "substantial constitutional question" was involved. We granted certiorari, 387 U.S. 929 (1967), to determine whether the admission of the revolvers in evidence violated petitioner's rights under the Fourth Amendment, made applicable to the States by the Fourteenth. *Mapp* v. *Ohio*, 367 U.S. 643 (1961). We affirm the conviction.

I.

The Fourth Amendment provides that "the right of the people to be secure in their persons, houses, papers, and effects, against unreasonable searches and seizures, shall not be violated. . . ." This inestimable right of personal security belongs as much to the citizen on the streets of our cities as to the homeowner closeted in his study to dispose of his secret affairs. For as this Court has always recognized,

No right is held more sacred, or is more carefully guarded, by the common law, than the right of every individual to the possession and control of his own person, free from all restraint or interference, unless by clear and unquestionable authority of law. *Union Pac. R. Co.* v. *Botsford,* 141 U.S. 250, 251 (1891).

. . . .

We would be less than candid if we did not acknowledge that this question thrusts to the fore difficult and troublesome issues regarding a sensitive area of police activity—issues which have never been before squarely presented to this Court. Reflective of the tensions involved are the practical and constitutional arguments pressed with great vigor on both sides of the public debate over the power of the police to "stop and frisk"—as it is sometimes euphemistically termed—suspicious persons.

On the one hand, it is frequently argued that in dealing with the rapidly unfolding and often dangerous situations on city streets the police are in need of an escalating set of flexible responses, graduated in relation to the amount of information they possess. For this purpose it is urged that distinctions should be made between a "stop" and an "arrest" (or a "seizure" of a person), and between a "frisk" and a "search." Thus, it is argued, the police should be allowed to "stop" a person and detain him briefly for questioning upon suspicion that he may be connected with criminal activity. Upon suspicion that the person may be armed, the police should have the power to "frisk" him for weapons. If the "stop" and the "frisk" give rise to probable cause to believe that the suspect has committed a crime, then the police should be empowered to make a formal "arrest," and a full incident "search" of the person. This scheme is justified in part upon the notion that a "stop" and a "frisk" amount to a mere "minor inconvenience and petty indignity," which can be properly imposed upon the citizen in the interest of effective law enforcement on the basis of a police officer's suspicion.

On the other side the argument is made that the authority of the police must be strictly circumscribed by the law of arrest and search as it has developed to date in the traditional jurisprudence of the Fourth Amendment. It is contended with some force that there is not—and cannot be—a variety of police activity which does not depend solely upon the voluntary cooperation of the citizen and yet which stops short of an arrest based upon probable cause to make such an arrest. The heart of the Fourth Amendment, the argument runs, is a severe requirement of specific justification for any intrusion upon protected personal security, coupled with a highly developed system of judicial controls to enforce upon the agents of the State the commands of the Constitution. Acquiescence by the courts in the compulsion inherent in the field interrogation practices at issue here, it is urged, would constitute an abdication of, substantial interference with liberty and personal security by police officers whose judgment is necessarily colored by their primary involvement in "the often competitive enterprise of ferreting out crime." *Johnson* v. *United States*, 333 U.S. 10, 14 (1948). This, it is argued, can only serve to exacerbate police-community tensions in the crowded centers of our Nation's cities.

In this context we approach the issues in this case mindful of the limitations of the judicial function in controlling the myriad daily situations in which policemen and citizens confront each other on the street. The State has characterized the issue here as "the right of a police officer . . . to make an on-the-street stop, interrogate and pat down for weapons (known in the street vernacular as 'stop and frisk')." But this is only partly accurate. For the issue is not the abstract propriety of the police conduct, but the admissibility against petitioner of the evidence uncovered by the search and seizure. Ever since its inception, the rule excluding evidence seized in violation of the Fourth Amendment has been recognized as a principal mode of discouraging lawless police conduct.... Thus its major thrust is a deterrent one, ... and experience has taught that it is the only effective deterrent to police misconduct in the criminal context, and that without it the constitutional guarantee against unreasonable searches and seizures would be a mere "form of words." ... The rule also serves another vital function—"the imperative of judicial integrity." ... Courts which sit under our Constitution cannot and will not be made party to lawless invasions of the constitutional rights of citizens by permitting unhindered governmental use of the fruits of such invasions. Thus in our system evidentiary rulings provide the context in which the judicial process of inclusion and exclusion approves some conduct as comporting with constitutional guarantees and disapproves other actions by state agents. A ruling admitting evidence in a criminal trial, we recognize, has the necessary effect of legitimizing the conduct which produced the evidence, while an application of the exclusionary rule withholds the constitutional imprimatur.

The exclusionary rule has its limitations, however, as a tool of judicial control. It cannot properly be invoked to exclude the products of legitimate police investigative techniques on the ground that much conduct which is closely similar involves unwarranted intrusions upon constitutional protections. Moreover, in some contexts the rule is effective as a deterrent. Street encounters between citizens and police officers are incredibly rich in diversity. They range from wholly friendly exchanges of pleasantries or mutually useful information to hostile confrontations of armed men involving arrests, or injuries, or loss of life. Moreover, hostile confrontations are not all of a piece. Some of them begin in a friendly enough manner, only to take a different turn upon the injection of some unexpected element into the conversation. Encounters are initiated by the police for a wide variety of purposes, some of which are wholly unrelated to a desire to prosecute for crime. Doubtless some police "field interrogation" conduct violates the Fourth Amendment. But a stern refusal by this Court to condone such activity does not necessarily render it responsive to the exclusionary rule. Regardless of how effective the rule may be where obtaining convictions is an important objective of the police, it is powerless to deter invasions of constitutionally guaranteed rights where the police either have no interest in prosecuting or are willing to forego successful prosecution in the interest of serving some other goal.

. . . .

Having thus roughly sketched the perimeters of the constitutional debate over the limits on police investigative conduct in general and the background against which this case presents itself, we turn our attention to the quite narrow question posed by the facts before us: whether it is always unreasonable for a policeman to seize a person and subject him to a limited search for weapons unless there is probable cause for an arrest. Given the narrowness of this question, we have no occasion to canvass in detail the constitutional limitations upon the scope of a policeman's power when he confronts a citizen without probable cause to arrest him.

II.

Our first task is to establish at what point in this encounter the Fourth Amendment becomes relevant. That is, we must decide whether and when Officer McFadden "seized" Terry and whether and when he conducted a "search." There is some suggestion in the use of such terms as "stop" and "frisk" that such police conduct is outside the purview of the Fourth Amendment because neither action rises to the level of a "search" or "seizure" within the meaning of the Constitution. We emphatically reject this notion. It is quite plain that the Fourth Amendment governs "seizures" of the person which do not eventuate in a trip to the station house and prosecution for crime—"arrests" in traditional ter-

minology. It must be recognized that whenever a police officer accosts an individual and restrains his freedom to walk away, he has "seized" that person. And it is nothing less than sheer torture of the English language to suggest that a careful exploration of the outer surfaces of a person's clothing all over his or her body in an attempt to find weapons is not a "search." Moreover, it is simply fantastic to urge that such a procedure performed in public by a policeman while the citizen stands helpless, perhaps facing a wall with his hands raised, is a "petty indignity." It is a serious intrusion upon the sanctity of the person, which may inflict great indignity and arouse strong resentment, and it is not to be undertaken lightly.

The danger in the logic which proceeds upon distinctions between a "stop" and an "arrest," or "seizure" of the person, and between a "frisk" and a "search" is two-fold. It seeks to isolate from constitutional scrutiny the initial stages of the contact between the policeman and the citizen. And by suggesting a rigid all-or-nothing model of justification and regulation under the Amendment, it obscures the utility of limitations upon the scope, as well as the initiation, of police action as a means of constitutional regulation. This Court has held in the past that a search which is reasonable at its inception may violate the Fourth Amendment by virtue of its intolerable intensity and scope. [Citations omitted.] The scope of the search must be "strictly tied to and justified by" the circumstances which rendered its initiation permissible. [Citations omitted.]

The distinctions of classical "stop-and-frisk" theory thus serve to divert attention from the central inquiry under the Fourth Amendment—the reasonableness in all the circumstances of the particular governmental invasion of a citizen's personal security. "Search" and "seizure" are not talismans. We therefore reject the notions that the Fourth Amendment does not come into play at all as a limitation upon police conduct if the officers stop short of something called a "technical arrest" or a "full-blown search."

In this case there can be no question, then, that Officer McFadden "seized" petitioner and subjected him to a "search" when he took hold of him and patted down the outer surfaces of his clothing. We must decide whether at that point it was reasonable for Officer McFadden to have interfered with petitioner's personal security as he did. And in determining whether the seizure and search were "unreasonable" our inquiry is a dual one—whether the officer's action was justified at its inception, and whether it was reasonably related in scope to the circumstances which justified the interference in the first place.

III.

If this case involved police conduct subject to the Warrant Clause of the Fourth Amendment, we would have to ascertain whether "probable cause" existed to justify the search and seizure which took place. However, this is not the case. We do not retreat from our holdings that the police must, whenever practicable, obtain advance judicial approval of searches and seizures through the warrant procedure, [citations omitted], or that in most instances failure to comply with the warrant requirement can only be excused by exigent circumstances, [citations omitted]. But we deal here with an entire rubric of police conduct—necessarily swift action predicated upon the on-the-spot observations of the officer on the beat—which historically has not been, and as a practical matter could not be, subjected to the warrant procedure. Instead, the conduct involved in this case must be tested by the Fourth Amendment's general proscription against unreasonable searches and seizures.

Nonetheless, the notions which underlie both the warrant procedure and the requirement of probable cause remain fully relevant in this context. In order to assess the reasonableness of Officer McFadden's conduct as a general proposition, it is necessary "first to focus upon the governmental interest which allegedly justifies official intrusion upon the constitutionally protected interests of the private citizen," for there is "no ready test for determining reasonableness other than by balancing the need to search [or seize] against the invasion which the search [or seizure] entails." *Camara v. Municipal Court*, 387 U.S. 523–535, 536–537 (1967). And in justifying the particular intrusion the police officer must be able to point to specific and articulable facts which, taken together with rational inferences from those facts, reasonably warrant that intrusion. The scheme of the Fourth Amendment becomes meaningful only when it is assured that at some point the conduct of those charged with enforcing the laws can be subjected to the more detached, general scrutiny of a judge who must evaluate the reasonableness of a particular search or seizure in light of the particular circumstances. And in making that assessment it is imperative that the facts be judged against an objective standard: would the facts available to the officer at the moment of the seizure or the search "warrant a man of reasonable caution in the belief" that the action taken was appropriate? [Citations omitted.] Anything less would invite intrusion upon constitutionally guaranteed rights based on nothing more substantial than inarticulate hunches, a result this Court has consistently refused to sanction. [Citations omitted.] And simple " 'good faith on the part of the arresting officer is not enough.' . . . If subjective good faith alone were the test, the protections of the Fourth Amendment would evaporate, and the people would be 'secure in their persons, houses, papers and effects,' only in the discretion of the police." *Beck* v. *Ohio, supra* at 97.

Applying these principles to this case, we consider first the nature and extent of the governmental interests involved. One general interest is of course that of effective crime prevention and detection; it is this interest which underlies the recognition that a police officer may in appropriate circumstances and in an appropriate manner approach a person for purposes of investigating possibly criminal behavior even though there is no probable cause to make an arrest. It was this legitimate investigative function Officer McFadden was discharging when he decided to approach petitioner and his companions. He had observed Terry, Chilton, and Katz go through a series of acts, each of them perhaps innocent in itself, but which taken together warranted further investigation. There is nothing unusual in two men standing together on a street corner, perhaps waiting for someone. Nor is there anything suspicious about people in such circumstances strolling up and down the street, singly or in pairs. Store windows, moreover, are made to be looked in. But the story is quite different where, as here, two men hover about a street corner for an extended period of time, at the end of which it becomes apparent that they are not waiting for anyone or anything; where these men pace alternately along an identical route, pausing to stare in the same window roughly 24 times; where each completion of this route is followed immediately by a conference between the two men on the corner; where they are joined in one of these conferences by a third man who leaves swiftly and where the two men finally follow the third and rejoin him a couple of blocks away. It would have been poor police work indeed for an officer of 30 years' experience in the detection of thievery from stores in this same neighborhood to have failed to investigate this behavior further.

The crux of the case, however, is not the propriety of Officer McFadden's taking steps to investigate petitioner's suspicious behavior, but rather, whether there was justification for McFadden's invasion of Terry's personal security by searching him for weapons in the course of that investigation. We are now concerned with more than the governmental interest in investigating crime; in addition, there is the more immediate interest of the police officer in taking steps to assure himself that the person with whom he is dealing is not armed with a weapon that could unexpectedly and fatally be used against him. Certainly it would be unreasonable to require that police officers take unnecessary risks in the performance of their duties. American criminals have a long tradition of armed violence, and every year in this country many law enforcement officers are killed in the line of duty, and thousands more are wounded. Virtually all of these deaths and a substantial portion of the injuries are inflicted with guns and knives.

In view of these facts, we cannot blind ourselves to the need for law enforcement officers to protect themselves and other prospective victims of violence in situations where they may lack probable cause for an arrest. When an of-ficer is justified in believing that the individual whose suspicious behavior he is investigating at close range is armed and presently dangerous to the officer or to others, it could appear to be clearly unreasonable to deny the officer the power to take necessary measures to determine whether the person is in fact carrying a weapon and to neutralize the threat of physical harm.

We must still consider, however, the nature and quality of the intrusion on individual rights which must be accepted if police officers are to be conceded the right to search for weapons in situations where probable cause to arrest for crime is lacking. Even a limited search of the outer clothing for weapons constitutes a severe, though brief, intrusion upon cherished personal security, and it must surely be an annoying, frightening, and perhaps humiliating experience. Petitioner contends that such an intrusion is permissible only incident to a lawful arrest, either for a crime involving the possession of weapons or for a crime the commission of which led the officer to investigate in the first place. However, this argument must be closely examined.

Petitioner does not argue that a police officer should refrain from making any investigation of suspicious circumstances until such time as he has probable cause to make an arrest; nor does he deny that police officers in properly discharging their investigative function may find themselves confronting persons who might well be armed and dangerous. Moreover, he does not say that an officer is always unjustified in searching a suspect to discover weapons. Rather, he says it is unreasonable for the policeman to take that step until such time as the situation evolves to a point where there is probable cause to make an arrest. When that point has been reached, petitioner would concede the officer's right to conduct a search of the suspect for weapons, fruits or instrumentalities of the crime, or "mere" evidence, incident to the arrest.

There are two weaknesses in this line of reasoning, however. First, it fails to take account of traditional limitations upon the scope of searches, and thus recognizes no distinction in purpose, character, and extent between a search incident to an arrest and a limited search for weapons. The former, although justified in part by the acknowledged necessity to protect the arresting officer from assault with a concealed weapon, *Preston v. United States,* 376 U.S. 364, 367 (1964), is also justified on other grounds, *ibid.,* and can therefore involve a relatively extensive exploration of the person. A search for weapons in the absence of probable cause to arrest, however, must, like any other search, be strictly circumscribed by the exigencies which justify its initiation. *Warden v. Hayden,* 387 U.S. 294, 310 (1967) (MR. JUSTICE FORTAS, concurring). Thus it must be limited to that which is necessary for the discovery of weapons which might be used to harm the officer or others nearby, and may

realistically be characterized as something less than a "full" search, even though it remains a serious intrusion.

A second, and related, objection to petitioner's argument is that it assumes that the law of arrest has already worked out the balance between the particular interests involved here—the neutralization of danger to the policeman in the investigative circumstance and the sanctity of the individual. But this is not so. An arrest is a wholly different kind of intrusion upon individual freedom from a limited search for weapons, and the interests each is designed to serve are likewise quite different. An arrest is the initial stage of a criminal prosecution. It is intended to vindicate society's interest in having its laws obeyed, and it is inevitably accompanied by future interference with the individual's freedom of movement, whether or not trial or conviction ultimately follows. The protective search for weapons, on the other hand, constitutes a brief, though far from inconsiderable, intrusion upon the sanctity of the person. It does not follow that because an officer may lawfully arrest a person only when he is apprised of facts sufficient to warrant a belief that the person has committed or is committing a crime, the officer is equally unjustified, absent that kind of evidence, in making any intrusions short of an arrest. Moreover, a perfectly reasonable apprehension of danger may arise long before the officer is possessed of adequate information to justify taking a person into custody for the purpose of prosecuting him for a crime. Petitioner's reliance on cases which have worked out standards of reasonableness with regard to "seizures" constituting arrests and searches incident thereto is thus misplaced. It assumes that the interests sought to be vindicated and the invasions of personal security may be equated in the two cases, and thereby ignores a vital aspect of the analysis of the reasonableness of particular type of conduct under the Fourth Amendment. See *Camara* v. *Municipal Court, supra.*

Our evaluation of the proper balance that has to be struck in this type of case leads us to conclude that there must be a narrowly drawn authority to permit a reasonable search for weapons for the protection of the police officer, where he has reason to believe that he is dealing with an armed and dangerous individual, regardless of whether he has probable cause to arrest the individual for a crime. The officer need not be absolutely certain that the individual is armed; the issue is whether a reasonably prudent man in the circumstances would be warranted in the belief that his safety or that of others was in danger. [Citations omitted.] And in determining whether the officer acted reasonably in such circumstances, due weight must be given, not to his inchoate and unparticularized suspicion or "hunch," but to the specific reasonable inferences which he is entitled to draw from the facts in light of his experience. Cf. *Brinegar* v. *United States, supra.*

IV.

We must now examine the conduct of Officer McFadden in this case to determine whether his search and seizure of petitioner were reasonable, both at their inception and as conducted. He had observed Terry, together with Chilton and another man, acting in a manner he took to be preface to a "stick-up." We think on the facts and circumstances Officer McFadden detailed before the trial judge a reasonably prudent man would have been warranted in believing petitioner was armed and thus presented a threat to the officer's safety while he was investigating his suspicious behavior. The actions of Terry and Chilton were consistent with McFadden's hypothesis that these men were contemplating a daylight robbery—which, it is reasonable to assume, would be likely to involve the use of weapons—and nothing in their conduct from the time he first noticed them until the time he confronted them and identified himself as a police officer gave him sufficient reason to negate that hypothesis. Although the trio had departed the original scene, there was nothing to indicate abandonment of an intent to commit a robbery at some point. Thus, when Officer McFadden approached the three men gathered before the display window at Zucker's store he had observed enough to make it quite reasonable to fear that they were armed; and nothing in their response to hailing them, identifying himself as a police officer, and asking their names served to dispel that reasonable belief. We cannot say his decision at that point to seize Terry and pat his clothing for weapons was the product of a volatile or inventive imagination, or was undertaken simply as an act of harassment; the record evidences the tempered act of a policeman who in the course of an investigation had to make a quick decision as to how to protect himself and others from possible danger, and took limited steps to do so.

The manner in which the seizure and search were conducted is, of course, as vital a part of the inquiry as whether they were warranted at all. The Fourth Amendment proceeds as much by limitations upon the scope of governmental action as by imposing preconditions upon its initiation. Compare *Katz* v. *United States*, 389 U.S. 347, 354–356 (1967). The entire deterrent purpose of the rule excluding evidence seized in violation of the Fourth Amendment rest on the assumption that "limitations upon the fruit to be gathered tend to limit the quest itself." [Citations omitted.] Thus, evidence may not be introduced if it was discovered by means of a seizure and search which were not reasonably related in scope to the justification for their initiation. [Citations omitted.]

We need not develop at length in this case, however, the limitations which the Fourth Amendment places upon a protective seizure and search for weapons. These limitations will have to be devel-

oped in the concrete factual circumstances of individual cases. See *Sibron* v. *New York*, 392 U.S. 40, decided today. Suffice it to note that such a search, unlike a search without a warrant incident to a lawful arrest, is not justified by any need to prevent the disappearance or destruction of evidence of crime. See *Preston* v. *United States*, 376 U.S. 364, 367 (1964). The sole justification of the search in the present situation is the protection of the police officer and others nearby, and it must therefore be confined in scope to an intrusion reasonably designed to discover guns, knives, clubs, or other hidden instruments for the assault of the police officer.

The scope of the search in this case presents no serious problem in light of these standards. Officer McFadden patted down the outer clothing of petitioner and his two companions. He did not place his hands in their pockets or under the outer surface of their garments until he had felt weapons, and then he merely reached for and removed the guns. He never did invade Katz's person beyond the outer surfaces of his clothes, since he discovered nothing in his pat-down which might have been a weapon. Officer McFadden confined his search strictly to what was minimally necessary to learn whether the men were armed and to disarm them once he discovered the weapons. He did not conduct a general exploratory search for whatever evidence of criminal activity he might find.

V.

We conclude that the revolver seized from Terry was properly admitted in evidence against him. At the time he seized petitioner and searched him for weapons, Officer McFadden had reasonable grounds to believe that petitioner was armed and dangerous, and it was necessary for the protection of himself and others to take swift measures to discover the true facts and neutralize the threat of harm if it materialized. The policeman carefully restricted his search to what was appropriate to the discovery of the particular items which he sought. Each case of this sort will, of course, have to be decided on its own facts. We merely hold today that where a police officer observed unusual conduct which leads him reasonably to conclude in light of his experience that criminal activity may be afoot and that the persons with whom he is dealing may be armed and presently dangerous, where in the course of investigating this behavior he identifies himself as a policeman and makes reasonable inquiries, and where nothing in the initial stages of the encounter serves to dispel his reasonable fear for his own or others' safety, he is entitled for the protection of himself and others in the area to conduct a carefully limited search of the outer clothing of such persons in an attempt to discover weapons which might be used to assault him. Such a search is a reasonable search under the Fourth Amendment, and any weapons seized may properly be introduced in evidence against the person from whom they were taken.

Affirmed.

[The concurring opinions of MR. JUSTICE BLACK, MR. JUSTICE HARLAN and MR. JUSTICE WHITE, as well as the dissenting opinion of MR. JUSTICE DOUGLAS, have been omitted.]

Cases relating to **Chapter 4**

SEARCH AND SEIZURE

MAPP v. OHIO

367 U.S. 643, 6 L.Ed.2d 1081, 81 S.Ct. 1684 (1961)

Mr. Justice Clark delivered the opinion of the Court.

Appellant stands convicted of knowingly having had in her possession and under her control certain lewd and lascivious books, pictures, and photographs in violation of § 2905.34 of Ohio's Revised Code. As officially stated in the syllabus to its opinion, the Supreme Court of Ohio found that her conviction was valid though "based primarily upon the introduction in evidence of lewd and lascivious books and pictures unlawfully seized during an unlawful search of defendant's home. . . ." 170 Ohio St. 427–428, 166 N.E.2d 387, 388.

On May 23, 1957, three Cleveland police officers arrived at appellant's residence in that city pursuant to information that "a person [was] hiding out in the home, who was wanted for questioning in connection with a recent bombing, and that there was a large amount of policy paraphernalia being hidden in the home." Miss Mapp and her daughter by a former marriage lived on the top floor of the two-family dwelling. Upon their arrival at that house, the officers knocked on the door and demanded entrance but appellant, after telephoning her attorney, refused to admit them without a search warrant. They advised their headquarters of the situation and undertook a surveillance of the house.

The officers again sought entrance some three hours later when four or more additional officers arrived on the scene. When Miss Mapp did not come to the door immediately, at least one of the several doors to the house was forcibly opened and the policemen gained admittance. Meanwhile Miss Mapp's attorney arrived, but the officers, having secured their own entry, and continuing in their defiance of the law, would permit him neither to see Miss Mapp nor to enter the house. It appears that Miss Mapp was halfway down the stairs from the upper floor to the front door when the officers, in this highhanded manner, broke into the hall. She demanded to see the search warrant. A paper, claimed to be a warrant, was held up by one of the officers. She grabbed the "warrant" and placed it in her bosom. A struggle ensued in which the officers recovered the piece of paper and as a result of which they handcuffed appellant because she had been "belligerent" in resisting their official rescue of the "warrant" from her person. Running roughshod over appellant, a policeman "grabbed" her, "twisted [her] hand," and she "yelled [and] pleaded with him" because "it was hurting." Appellant, in handcuffs, was then forcibly taken upstairs to her bedroom where the officers searched a dresser, a chest of drawers, a closet and some suitcases. They also looked into a photo album and through personal papers belonging to the appellant. The search spread to the rest of the second floor including the child's bedroom, the living room, the kitchen and a dinette. The basement of the building and a trunk found therein were also searched. The obscene materials for possession of which she was ultimately convicted were discovered in the course of that widespread search.

At the trial no search warrant was produced by the prosecution, nor was the failure to produce one explained or accounted for. At best, "There is, in the record, considerable doubt as to whether there ever was any warrant for the search of defendant's home." 170 Ohio St., at 430. The Ohio Supreme Court believed a "reasonable argument" could be made that the conviction should be reversed "because the 'methods' employed to obtain the [evidence] . . . were such as to 'offend "a sense of justice," ' " but the court found determinative the fact that the evidence had not been taken "from defendant's person by the use of brutal or offensive physical force against defendant." 170 Ohio St., at 431.

The State says that even if the search were made without authority, or otherwise unreasonably, it is not prevented from using the unconstitutionally seized evidence at trial, citing *Wolf* v. *Colorado*, 338 U.S. 25 (1949), in which this Court did indeed hold "that in a prosecution in a State court for a State crime the Fourteenth Amendment does not forbid the admission of evidence obtained by an unreasonable search and seizure." At p. 33. On this appeal, of which we have noted probable jurisdiction, 364 U.S. 868, it is urged once again that we review that holding.

I.

Seventy-five years ago, in *Boyd* v. *United States*, 116 U.S. 616, 630 (1886), considering the Fourth and Fifth Amendments as running "almost into each other" on the facts before it, this Court held that the doctrines of those Amendments

apply to all invasions on the part of the government and its employés of the sanctity of a man's home and the privacies of life. It is not the breaking of his doors, and the rummaging of his drawers, that constitutes the essence of the offence; but it is the invasion of his indefeasible right of personal security, personal liberty and private property . . . . Breaking into a house and opening boxes and drawers are circumstances of aggravation; but any forcible and compulsory extortion of a man's own testimony or of his private papers to be used as evidence to convict him of crime or to forfeit his goods, is within the condemnation . . . [of those Amendments].

The Court noted that

constitutional provisions for the security of person and property should be liberally construed. . . . It is the duty of courts to be watchful for the constitutional rights of the citizen, and against any stealthy encroachments thereon. At p. 635.

In this jealous regard for maintaining the integrity of individual rights, the Court gave life to Madison's prediction that "independent tribunals of justice . . . will be naturally led to resist every encroachment upon rights expressly stipulated for in the Constitution by the declaration of rights." I Annals of Cong. 439 (1789). Concluding, the Court specifically referred to the use of the evidence there seized as "unconstitutional." At p. 638.

Less than 30 years after *Boyd*, this Court, in *Weeks* v. *United States*, 232 U.S. 383 (1914), stated that

the Fourth Amendment . . . put the courts of the United States and Federal officials, in the exercise of their power and authority, under limitations and restraints [and] . . . forever secure[d] the people, their persons, houses, papers and effects against all unreasonable searches and seizures under the guise of law . . . and the duty of giving to it force and effect is obligatory upon all entrusted under our Federal system with the enforcement of the laws. At pp. 391, 392.

Specifically dealing with the use

of the evidence unconstitutionally seized, the Court concluded:

If letters and private documents can thus be seized and held and used in evidence against a citizen accused of an offense, the protection of the Fourth Amendment declaring his right to be secure against such searches and seizures is of no value, and, so far as those thus placed are concerned, might as well be stricken from the Constitution. The efforts of the courts and their officials to bring the guilty to punishment, praiseworthy as they are, are not to be aided by the sacrifice of those great principles established by years of endeavor and suffering which have resulted in their embodiment in the fundamental law of the land. At p. 393.

Finally, the Court in that case clearly stated that use of the seized evidence involved "a denial of the constitutional rights of the accused." At p. 398. Thus, in the year 1914, in the *Weeks* case, this Court "for the first time" held that "in a federal prosecution the Fourth Amendment barred the use of evidence secured through an illegal search and seizure." *Wolf* v. *Colorado, supra,* at 28. This Court has ever since required of federal law officers a strict adherence to that command which this Court has held to be a clear, specific, and constitutionally required —even if judicially implied—deterrent safeguard without insistence upon which the Fourth Amendment would have been reduced to "a form of words." HOLMES J., *Sil-verthorne Lumber Co. v. United States*, 251 U.S. 385, 392 (1920). It meant, quite simply, that "conviction by means of unlawful seizures and enforced confessions ... should find no sanction in the judgments of the courts ... ," *Weeks* v. *United States, supra,* at 392, and that such evidence "shall not be used at all." *Silverthorne Lumber Co.* v. *United States, supra,* at 392.

There are in the cases of this Court some passing references to the *Weeks* rule as being one of evidence. But the plain and unequivocal language of *Weeks*—and its later paraphrase in *Wolf*—to the effect that the *Weeks* rule is of constitutional origin, remains entirely undisturbed. In *Byars* v. *United States*, 273 U.S. 28 (1927), a unanimous Court declared that "the doctrine [cannot] ... be tolerated *under our constitutional system,* that evidences of crime discovered by a federal officer in making a search without lawful warrant may be used against the victim of the unlawful search where a timely challenge has been interposed." At pp. 29, 30 (emphasis added). The Court, in *Olmstead* v. *United States*, 277 U.S. 438 (1928), in unmistakable language restated the *Weeks* rule:

The striking outcome of the *Weeks* case and those which followed it was the sweeping declaration that the Fourth Amendment, although not referring to or limiting the use of evidence in courts, really for-

bade its introduction if obtained by government officers through a violation of the Amendment. At p. 462.

In *McNabb* v. *United States*, 318 U.S. 332 (1943), we note this statement:

[A] conviction in the federal courts, the foundation of which is evidence obtained in disregard of liberties deemed fundamental by the Constitution, cannot stand. *Boyd* v. *United States* ... *Weeks* v. *United States.* . . . And this Court has, on Constitutional grounds, set aside convictions, both in the federal and state courts, which were based upon confessions "secured by protracted and repeated questioning of ignorant and untutored persons, in whose minds the power of officers was greatly magnified" ... or "who have been unlawfully held incommunicado without advice of friends or counsel". . . . At pp. 339, 340.

Significantly, in *McNabb*, the Court did then pass on to formulate a rule of evidence, saying, "[i]n the view we take of the case, however, it becomes unnecessary to reach the Constitutional issue [for] ... [t]he principles governing the admissibility of evidence in federal criminal trials have not been restricted ... to those derived solely from the Constitution." At pp. 340, 341.

II.

In 1949, 35 years after *Weeks* was announced, this Court, in *Wolf*

v. *Colorado, supra,* again for the first time, discussed the effect of the Fourth Amendment upon the States through the operation of the Due Process Clause of the Fourteenth Amendment. It said:

[W]e have no hesitation in saying that were a State affirmatively to sanction such police incursion into privacy it would run counter to the guaranty of the Fourteenth Amendment. At p. 28.

Nevertheless, after declaring that the "security of one's privacy against arbitrary intrusion by the police" is "implicit in 'the concept of ordered liberty' and as such enforceable against the States through the Due Process Clause," cf. *Palko v. Connecticut,* 302 U.S. 319 (1937), and announcing that it "stoutly adhere[d]" to the *Weeks* decision, the Court decided that the *Weeks* exclusionary rule would not then be imposed upon the States as "an essential ingredient of the right." 338 U.S., at 27–29. The Court's reasons for not considering essential to the right to privacy, as a curb imposed upon the States by the Due Process Clause, that which decades before had been posited as part and parcel of the Fourth Amendment's limitation upon federal encroachment of individual privacy, were bottomed on factual considerations.

While they are not basically relevant to a decision that the exclusionary rule is an essential ingredient of the Fourth Amendment as the right it embodies is vouchsafed against the States by the Due

Process Clause, we will consider the current validity of the factual grounds upon which *Wolf* was based.

The Court in *Wolf* first stated that "[t]he contrariety of views of the States" on the adoption of the exclusionary rule of *Weeks* was "particularly impressive" (at p. 29); and, in this connection, that it could not "brush aside the experience of States which deem the incidence of such conduct by the police too slight to call for a deterrent remedy . . . by overriding the [States'] relevant rules of evidence." At pp. 31, 32. While in 1949, prior to the *Wolf* case, almost two-thirds of the States were opposed to the use of the exclusionary rule, now, despite the *Wolf* case, more than half of those since passing upon it, by their own legislative or judicial decision, have wholly or partly adopted or adhered to the *Weeks* rule. See *Elkins v. United States,* 364 U.S. 206, Appendix, pp. 224–232 (1960). Significantly, among those now following the rule is California, which, according to its highest court, was "compelled to reach that conclusion because other remedies have completely failed to secure compliance with the constitutional provisions . . . ." [Citation omitted.] In connection with this California case, we note that the second basis elaborated in *Wolf* in support of its failure to enforce the exclusionary doctrine against the States was that "other means of protection" have been afforded "the right to privacy." 338 U.S. at 30. The experience of California that such other remedies have been worthless and futile is buttressed by the experience of other States. The obvious futility of relegating the Fourth Amendment to the protection of other remedies has, moreover, been recognized by this Court since *Wolf.* See *Irvine* v. *California,* 347 U.S. 128, 137 (1954).

Likewise, time has set its face against what *Wolf* called the "weighty testimony" of *People* v. *Defore,* 242 N.Y. 13, 150 N.E. 585 (1926). There Justice (then Judge) Cardozo, rejecting adoption of the *Weeks* exclusionary rule in New York, had said that "[t]he Federal rule as it stands is either too strict or too lax." 242 N.Y., at 22. However, the force of that reasoning has been largely vitiated by later decisions of this Court. These include the recent discarding of the "silver platter" doctrine which allowed federal judicial use of evidence seized in violation of the Constitution by state agents, *Elkins* v. *United States, supra;* the relaxation of the formerly strict requirements as to standing to challenge the use of evidence thus seized, so that now the procedure of exclusion, "ultimately referable to constitutional safeguards," is available to anyone even "legitimately on [the] premises" unlawfully searched, *Jones* v. *United States,* 362 U.S. 257, 266, 267 (1960); and, finally, the formulation of a method to prevent state use of evidence unconstitutionally seized by federal agents, *Rea* v. *United States,* 350 U.S. 214 (1956). Because there can be no fixed formula, we are admittedly met with

"recurring questions of the reasonableness of searches," but less is not to be expected when dealing with a Constitution, and, at any rate, "[r]easonableness is in the first instance for the [trial court] ... to determine." *United States* v. *Rabinowitz,* 339 U.S. 56, 63 (1950).

It, therefore, plainly appears that the factual considerations supporting the failure of the *Wolf* Court to include the *Weeks* exclusionary rule when it recognized the enforceability of the right to privacy against the States in 1949, while not basically relevant to the constitutional consideration, could not, in any analysis, now be deemed controlling.

. . . .

V.

. . . .

The ignoble shortcut to conviction left open to the State tends to destroy the entire system of constitutional restraints on which the liberties of the people rest. Having once recognized that the right to privacy embodied in the Fourth Amendment is enforceable against the States, and that the right to be secure against rude invasions of privacy by state officers is, therefore, constitutional in origin, we can no longer permit that right to remain an empty promise. Because it is enforceable in the same manner and to like effect as other basic rights secured by the Due Process Clause, we can no longer permit it to be revocable at the whim of any police officer who, in the name of law enforcement itself, chooses to suspend its enjoyment. Our decision, founded on reason and truth, gives to the individual no more than that which the Constitution guarantees him, to the police officer no less than that to which honest law enforcement is entitled, and, to the courts, that judicial integrity so necessary in the true administration of justice.

The judgment of the Supreme Court of Ohio is reversed and the cause remanded for further proceedings not inconsistent with this opinion.

Reversed and remanded.

[The concurring opinions of MR. JUSTICE BLACK and MR. JUSTICE DOUGLAS have been omitted.]

MR. JUSTICE HARLAN, whom MR. JUSTICE FRANKFURTER and MR. JUSTICE WHITTAKER join, dissenting.

In overruling the *Wolf* case the Court, in my opinion, has forgotten the sense of judicial restraint which, with due regard for *stare decisis*, is one element that should enter into deciding whether a past decision of this Court should be overruled. Apart from that I also believe that the *Wolf* rule represents sounder Constitutional doctrine than the new rule which now replaces it.

I.

From the Court's statement of the case one would gather that the central, if not controlling, issue on this appeal is whether illegally state-seized evidence is Constitutionally admissible in a state prosecution, an issue which would of course face us with the need for re-examining *Wolf*. However, such is not the situation. For, although that question was indeed raised here and below among appellant's subordinate points, the new and pivotal issue brought to the Court by this appeal is whether § 2905.34 of the Ohio Revised Code making criminal the *mere* knowing possession or control of obscence material, and under which appellant has been convicted, is consistent with the rights of free thought and expression assured against state action by the Fourteenth Amendment. That was the principal issue which was decided by the Ohio Supreme Court, which was tendered by appellant's Jurisdictional Statement, and which was briefed and argued in this Court.

In this posture of things, I think it fair to say that five members of this Court have simply "reached out" to overrule *Wolf*. With all respect for the views of the majority, and recognizing that *stare decisis* carries different weight in Constitutional adjudication than it does in nonconstitutional decision, I can perceive no justification for regarding this case as an appropriate occasion for re-examining *Wolf*.

The action of the Court finds no support in the rule that decision of Constitutional issues should be avoided wherever possible. For in overruling *Wolf* the Court, instead of passing upon the validity of Ohio's § 2905.34, has simply chosen between two Constitutional questions. Moreover, I submit that it has chosen the more difficult and less appropriate of the two questions. The Ohio statute which, as construed by the State Supreme Court, punishes knowing possession or control of obscene material, irrespective of the purposes of such possession or control (with exceptions not here applicable) and irrespective of whether the accused had any reasonable opportunity to rid himself of the material after discovering that it was obscene, surely presents a Constitutional question which is both simpler and less far-reaching than the question which the Court decides today. It seems to me that justice might well have been done in this case without overturning a decision on which the administration of criminal law in many of the States has long justifiably relied.

Since the demands of the case before us do not require us to reach the question of the validity of *Wolf*, I think this case furnishes a singularly inappropriate occasion for reconsideration of that decision, if reconsideration is indeed warranted. Even the most cursory examination will reveal that the doctrine of the *Wolf* case has been of continuing importance in the administration of state criminal law. Indeed, certainly as regards its "nonexclusionary" aspect, *Wolf* did no more than articulate the then existing assumption among the States that the federal cases enforcing the exclusionary rule "do not bind [the States], for they construe provisions of the Federal Constitution, the Fourth and Fifth Amendments, not applicable to

the States." [Citation omitted.] Though, of course, not reflecting the full measure of this continuing reliance, I find that during the last three Terms, for instance, the issue of the inadmissibility of illegally state-obtained evidence appears on an average of about fifteen times per Term just in the *in forma pauperis* cases summarily disposed of by us. This would indicate both that the issue which is now being decided may well have untoward practical ramifications respecting state cases long since disposed of in reliance on *Wolf*, and that were we determined to re-examine that doctrine we would not lack future opportunity.

The occasion which the Court has taken here is in the context of a case where the question was briefed not at all and argued only extremely tangentially. The unwisdom of overruling *Wolf* without full-dress argument is aggravated by the circumstance that that decision is a comparatively recent one (1949) to which three members of the present majority have at one time or other expressly subscribed, one to be sure with explicit misgivings. I would think that our obligation to the States, on whom we impose this new rule, as well as the obligation of orderly adherence to our own processes would demand that we seek that aid which adequate briefing and argument lends to the determination of an important issue. It certainly has never been a postulate of judicial power that mere altered disposition, or subsequent membership on the Court, is sufficient warrant for overturning a deliberately decided rule of Constitutional law.

Thus, if the Court were bent on reconsidering *Wolf*, I think that there would soon have presented itself an appropriate opportunity in which we could have had the benefit of full briefing and argument. In any event, at the very least, the present case should have been set down for reargument, in view of the inadequate briefing and argument we have received on the *Wolf* point. To all intents and

purposes the Court's present action amounts to a summary reversal of *Wolf*, without argument.

I am bound to say that what has been done is not likely to promote respect either for the Court's adjudicatory process or for the stability of its decisions. Having been unable, however, to persuade any of the majority to a different procedural course, I now turn to the merits of the present decision.

[Part II of the dissenting opinion is omitted.]

COOLIDGE v. NEW HAMPSHIRE

403 U.S. 443, 29 L.Ed.2d 564, 91 S. Ct. 2022 (1971)

MR. JUSTICE STEWART delivered the opinion of the Court.

We are called upon in this case to decide issues under the Fourth and Fourteenth Amendments arising in the context of a state criminal trial for the commission of a particularly brutal murder. As in every case, our single duty is to determine the issues presented in accord with the Constitution and the law.

Pamela Mason, a 14-year-old girl, left her home in Manchester, New Hampshire on the evening of January 13, 1964, during a heavy snowstorm, apparently in response to a man's telephone call for a babysitter. Eight days later, after a thaw, her body was found by the site of a major north-south highway several miles away. She had been murdered. The event

created great alarm in the area, and the police immediately began a massive investigation.

On January 28, having learned from a neighbor that the petitioner, Edward Coolidge, had been away from home on the evening of the girl's disappearance, the police went to his house to question him. They asked him, among other things, if he owned any guns, and he produced three, two shotguns and a rifle. They also asked whether he would take a lie detector test concerning his account of his activities on the night of the disappearance. He agreed to do so on the following Sunday, his day off. The police later described his attitude on the occasion of this visit as fully "cooperative." His wife was in the house throughout the interview.

On the following Sunday, a policeman called Coolidge early in the morning and asked him to come down to the police station for the trip to Concord, New Hampshire, where the lie-detector test was to be administered. That evening, two plain-clothes policemen arrived at the Coolidge house, where Mrs. Coolidge was waiting with her mother-in-law for her husband's return. These two policemen were not the two who had visited the house earlier in the week, and they apparently did not know that Coolidge had displayed three guns for inspection during the earlier visit. The plain-clothesmen told Mrs. Coolidge that her husband was in "serious trouble" and probably would not be home that night. They asked Coolidge's mother to leave, and proceeded to question Mrs. Coolidge. During the course of the interview they obtained from her four guns belonging to Coolidge, and some clothes that Mrs. Coolidge thought her husband might have been wearing on the evening of Pamela Mason's disappearance.

Coolidge was held in jail on an unrelated charge that night, but he was released the next day. During the ensuing two and a half weeks, the State accumulated a quantity of evidence to support the theory that it was he who had killed Pamela Mason. On February 19, the results of the investigation were presented at a meeting between the police officers working on the case and the State Attorney General, who had personally taken charge of all police activities relating to the murder, and was later to serve as chief prosecutor at the

trial. At this meeting, it was decided that there was enough evidence to justify the arrest of Coolidge on the murder charge and a search of his house and two cars. At the conclusion of the meeting, the Manchester police chief made formal application, under oath, for the arrest and search warrants. The complaint supporting the warrant for a search of Coolidge's Pontiac automobile, the only warrant which concerns us here, stated that the affiant "has probable cause to suspect and believe, and does suspect and believe, and herewith offers satisfactory evidence, that there are certain objects and things used in the commission of said offense, now kept, and concealed in or upon a certain vehicle, to wit: 1951 Pontiac two-door sedan. . . ." The warrants were then signed and issued by the Attorney General himself, acting as a justice of the peace. Under New Hampshire law in force at that time, all justices of the peace were authorized to issue search warrants. N.H. Rev. Stat. Ann. § 595:1 (repealed 1969).

The police arrested Coolidge in his house on the day the warrant issued. Mrs. Coolidge asked whether she might remain in the house with her small child, but was told that she must stay elsewhere, apparently in part because the police believed that she would be harassed by reporters if she were accessible to them. When she asked whether she might take her car, she was told that both cars had been "impounded," and that the police would provide transportation for her. Some time later, the police called a towing company, and about two and a half hours after Coolidge had been taken into custody the cars were towed to the police station. It appears that at the time of the arrest the cars were parked in the Coolidge driveway, and that although dark had fallen they were plainly visible both from the street and from inside the house where Coolidge was actually arrested. The 1951 Pontiac was searched and vacuumed on February 21, two days after it was seized, again a year later, in January 1965, and a third time in April, 1965.

At Coolidge's subsequent jury trial on the charge of murder, vacuum sweepings, including particles of gun powder, taken from the Pontiac were introduced in evidence against him, as part of an attempt by the State to show by microscopic analysis that it was highly probable that Pamela Mason had been in Coolidge's car. Also introduced in evidence was one of the guns taken by the police on their Sunday evening visit to the Coolidge house—a .22-caliber Mossberg rifle, which the prosecution claimed was the murder weapon. Conflicting ballistics testimony was offered on the question whether the bullets found in Pamela Mason's body had been fired from this rifle. Finally, the prosecution introduced vacuum sweepings of the clothes taken from the Coolidge house that same Sunday evening, and attempted to show through microscopic analysis that there was a high probability that the clothes had been in contact with Pamela Mason's body. Pretrial motions to suppress all this evidence were referred by the trial judge to the New Hampshire Supreme Court, which ruled the evidence admissible. 106 N. H. 186, 208 A.2d 322. The jury found Coolidge guilty and he was sentenced to life imprisonment. The New Hampshire Supreme Court affirmed the judgment of conviction, 109 N.H. 403, 260 A.2d 547, and we granted certiorari to consider the constitutional questions raised by the admission of this evidence against Coolidge at his trial.

I.

The petitioner's first claim is that the warrant authorizing the seizure and subsequent search of his 1951 Pontiac automobile was invalid because not issued by a "neutral and detached magistrate." Since we agree with the petitioner that the warrant was invalid for this reason, we need not consider his further argument that the allegations under oath supporting the issuance of the warrant were so conclusory as to violate relevant constitutional standards. [Citations omitted.]

The classic statement of the policy underlying the warrant requirement of the Fourth Amendment is that of MR. JUSTICE JACKSON writing for the Court in *Johnson* v. *United States*, 333 U.S. 10, 13–14:

The point of the Fourth Amendment, which often is not grasped by zealous officers, is not that it denies law enforcement the support of the usual inferences which reasonable men draw from evidence. Its protection consists in requiring that those inferences be drawn by a neutral and detached magistrate instead of being judged by the officer engaged in the often competitive enterprise of ferreting out crime. Any assumption that evidence sufficient to support a magistrate's disinterested determination to issue a search warrant will justify the officers in making a search without a warrant would reduce the Amendment to a nullity and leave the people's homes secure only in the discretion of police officers.

When the right of privacy must reasonably yield to the right of search is, as a rule, to be decided by a judicial officer, not by a policeman or government enforcement agent. [Citations omitted.]

In this case, the determination of probable cause was made by the chief "government enforcement agent" of the State—the Attorney General—who was actively in charge of the investigation and later was to be chief prosecutor at the trial. To be sure, the determination was formalized here by a writing bearing the title "Search Warrant," whereas in *Johnson* there was no piece of paper involved, but the State has not attempted to uphold the warrant on any such artificial basis. Rather, the State argues that the Attorney General, who was unquestionably authorized as a justice of the peace to issue warrants under then-existing state law, did in fact act as a "neutral and detached magistrate." Further, the state claims that *any* magistrate, confronted with the showing of probable cause made by the Manchester chief of police, would have issued the warrant in question. To the first proposition it is enough an answer that there could hardly be a more appropriate setting than this for a *per se* rule of disqualification rather than a case-by-case evaluation of all the circumstances. Without disrespect to the state law enforcement agent here involved, the whole point of the basic rule so well expressed by MR. JUSTICE JACKSON is that prosecutors and policemen simply cannot be asked to maintain the requisite neutrality with regard to their own investigations—the "competitive enterprises" that must rightly engage their single-minded attention.... As for the proposition that the existence of probable cause renders noncompliance with the warrant procedure an irrelevance, it is enough to cite *Agnello* v. *United States,* 269 U.S. 20, 33, decided in 1925:

> Belief, however well founded, that an article sought is concealed in a dwelling house, furnishes no justification for a search of that place without a warrant. And such searches are held unlawful notwithstanding facts unquestionably showing probable cause.

See also *Jones* v. *United States,* 357 U.S. 493, 497, 498; *Silverthorne Lumber Co.* v. *United States,* 251 U.S. 385, 392. ("[T]he rights ...

against unlawful search and seizure are to be protected even if the same result might have been achieved in a lawful way.]

. . . .

We find no escape from the conclusion that the seizure and search of the Pontiac automobile cannot constitutionally rest upon the warrant issued by the state official who was the chief investigator and prosecutor in this case. Since he was not the neutral and detached magistrate required by the Constitution, the search stands on no firmer ground than if there had been no warrant at all. If the seizure and search are to be justified, they must, therefore, be justified on some other theory.

II.

The State proposes three distinct theories to bring the facts of this case within one or another of the exceptions to the warrant requirement.

. . . .

A

The State's first theory is that the seizure on February 19 and subsequent search of Coolidge's Pontiac were "incident" to a valid arrest. We assume that the arrest of Coolidge inside his house was valid, so that the first condition of a warrantless "search incident" is met. . . . And since the events in issue took place in 1964, we assess the State's argument in terms of the law as it existed before *Chimel* v. *California*, 395 U.S. 752, which

substantially restricted the "search incident" exception to the warrant requirement, but did so only prospectively. . . . But even under pre-*Chimel* law, the State's position is untenable.

The leading case in the area before *Chimel* was *United States* v. *Rabinowitz*, 339 U.S. 56, which was taken to stand for the proposition, *inter alia*, that a warrantless search 'incident to a lawful arrest' may generally extend to the area that is considered to be in the 'possession' or under the 'control' of the person arrested." [1] In this case, Coolidge was arrested inside his house, but his car was outside in the driveway. The car was not touched until Coolidge had been removed from the scene. It was then seized and taken to the station, but it was not actually searched until the next day.

First, it is doubtful whether the police could have carried out a contemporaneous search of the car under *Rabinowitz* standards. For this Court has repeatedly held that, even under *Rabinowitz*, "[a] search may be incident to an arrest ' "only if it is substantially contemporaneous with the arrest and is confined to the *immediate* vicinity of the arrest. . . ." ' " [Citations omitted.] These cases make it clear beyond any question that a lawful pre-*Chimel* arrest of a suspect outside his house could never by itself justify a warrantless search inside the house. There is nothing in

_____

[1] See *Chimel* v. *California*, parts of which are printed immediately following this case.

search-incident doctrine (as opposed to the special rules for automobiles and evidence in "plain view," to be considered below) that suggests a different result where the arrest is made inside the house and the search outside and at some distance away.

Even assuming, *arguendo*, that the police might have searched the Pontiac in the driveway when they arrested Coolidge in the house, *Preston v. United States*, 376 U.S. 364, makes plain that they could not legally seize the car, remove it, and search it at their leisure without a warrant. In circumstances virtually identical to those here, MR. JUSTICE BLACK's opinion for a unanimous Court held that "[o]nce an accused is under arrest and in custody, then a search [of his car] made at another place, without a warrant, is simply not incident to the arrest." *Id.*, at 367. . . . Search-incident doctrine, in short, has no applicability to this case.

B

The second theory put forward by the State to justify a warrantless seizure and search of the Pontiac car is that under *Carroll v. United States*, 267 U.S. 132, the police may make a warrantless search of an automobile whenever they have probable cause to do so, and, under our decision last Term in *Chambers v. Maroney*, 399 U.S. 12, whenever the police may make a legal contemporaneous search under *Carroll*, they may also seize the car, take it to the police station and search it there. But even

granting that the police had probable cause to search the car, the application of the *Carroll* case to these facts would extend it far beyond its original rationale.[2]

As we said in *Chambers*, "exigent circumstances" justify the warrantless search of "an automobile *stopped on the highway*," where there is probable cause, because the car is "movable, the occupants are alerted, and the car's contents may never be found again if a warrant must be obtained." "[T]he opportunity to search is fleeting. . . ." (Emphasis supplied.)

In this case, the police had known for some time of the probable role of the Pontiac car in the crime. Coolidge was aware that he was a suspect in the Mason murder, but he had been extremely cooperative throughout the investigation, and there was no indication that he meant to flee. He had already had ample opportunity to destroy any evidence he thought incriminating. There is no suggestion that, on the night in question, the car was being used for any illegal purpose, and it was regularly parked in the driveway of his house. The opportunity for search was thus hardly "fleeting." The objects which the police are assumed to have had probable cause to search for in the car were neither stolen nor contraband nor dangerous.

. . . .

---

[2] See *Chambers v. Maroney* for a discussion of the "search of moving vehicle" doctrine. Parts of case are printed on following pages.

C

The State's third theory in support of the warrantless seizure and search of the Pontiac car is that the car itself was an "instrumentality of the crime," and as such might be seized by the police on Coolidge's property because it was in plain view. Supposing the seizure to be thus lawful, the case of *Cooper v. California*, 386 U.S. 58, is said to support a subsequent warrantless search at the station house, with or without probable cause. Of course, the distinction between an "instrumentality of crime" and "mere evidence" was done away with by *Warden v. Hayden*, 387 U.S. 294, and we may assume that the police had probable cause to seize the automobile. But, for the reasons that follow, we hold that the "plain view" exception to the warrant requirement is inapplicable to this case. Since the seizure was therefore illegal, it is unnecessary to consider the applicability of *Cooper, supra,* to the subsequent search.

It is well established that under certain circumstances the police may seize evidence in plain view without a warrant. But it is important to keep in mind that, in the vast majority of cases, *any* evidence seized by the police will be in plain view, at least at the moment of seizure. The problem with the "plain view" doctrine has been to identify the circumstances in which plain view has legal significance rather than being simply the normal concomitant of any search, legal or illegal.

An example of the applicability of the "plain view" doctrine is the situation in which the police have a warrant to search a given area for specified objects, and in the course of the search come across some other article of incriminating character. [Citations omitted.] Where the initial intrusion which brings the police within plain view of such an article is supported not by a warrant, but by one of the recognized exceptions to the warrant requirement, the seizure is also legitimate. Thus the police may inadvertently come across evidence while in "hot pursuit" of a fleeing suspect. *Warden v. Hayden, supra,* cf. *Hester v. United States*, 265 U.S. 57. And an object which comes into view during a search incident to arrest that is appropriately limited in scope under existing law may be seized without a warrant. *Chimel v. California*, 395 U.S. 752, 762–763. Finally, the "plain view" doctrine has been applied where a police officer is not searching for evidence against the accused, but nonetheless inadvertently comes across an incriminating object. [Citations omitted.]

. . . .

The limits on the doctrine are implicit in the statement of its rationale. The first of these is that plain view *alone* is never enough to justify the warrantless seizure of evidence. This is simply a corollary of the familiar principle discussed above, that no amount of probable cause can justify a warrantless search or seizure absent "exigent circumstances." Incontrovertible testimony of the senses that an incriminating object is on premises belonging to a criminal suspect may establish the fullest possible measure of probable cause. But even where the object is contraband, this Court has repeatedly stated and enforced the basic rule that the police may not enter and make a warrantless seizure [Citations omitted.]

The second limitation is that the discovery of evidence in plain view must be inadvertent. The rationale of the exception to the warrant requirement as just stated, is that a plain view seizure will not turn an initially valid (and therefore limited) search into a "general" one while the inconvenience of procuring a warrant to cover an inadvertent discovery is great. But where the discovery is anticipated, where the police know in advance the location of the evidence and intend to seize it, the situation is altogether different. The requirement of a warrant to seize imposes no inconvenience whatever, or at least none which is constitutionally cognizable in a legal system that regards warrantless searches as "per se unreasonable" in the absence of "exigent circumstances."

. . . .

In the light of what has been said, it is apparent that the "plain view" exception cannot justify the police seizure of the Pontiac car in this case. The police had ample opportunity to obtain a valid warrant; they knew the automobile's exact description and location well in advance; they intended to seize it when they came upon Coolidge's property. And this is not a case involving contraband or stolen goods or objects dangerous in themselves.

The seizure was therefore unconstitutional, and so was the subsequent search at the station house. Since evidence obtained in the course of the search was admitted at Coolidge's trial, the judgment must be reversed and the case remanded to the New Hampshire Supreme Court. *Mapp* v. *Ohio*, 367 U.S. 643.

. . . .

III.

Because of the prospect of a new trial, the efficient administration of justice counsels consideration of the second substantial question under the Fourth and Fourteenth Amendments presented by this case. The petitioner contends that when the police obtained a rifle and articles of his clothing from his home on the night of Sunday, February 2, 1964, while he was being interrogated at the police station, they engaged in a search and seizure violative of the Constitution. . . .

. . . .

The two policemen also asked Mrs. Coolidge what her husband had been wearing on the night of the disappearance. She then produced four pairs of trousers and indicated that her husband had probably worn either of two of them on that evening. She also brought out a hunting jacket. The police gave her a receipt for the guns and the clothing, and after a search of the Coolidge cars not here in issue, took the various articles to the police station.

The first branch of the petitioner's argument is that when Mrs. Coolidge brought out the guns and clothing and then handed them over to the police, she was acting as an "instrument" of the officials, complying with a "demand" made by them. Consequently, it is argued, Coolidge was the victim of a search and seizure within the constitutional meaning of those terms. Since we cannot accept this interpretation of the facts, we need not consider the petitioner's further argument that Mrs. Coolidge could not or did not "waive" her husband's constitutional protection against unreasonable searches and seizures.

Had Mrs. Coolidge, wholly in her own initiative, sought out her husband's guns and clothing and then taken them to the police station to be used as evidence against him, there can be no doubt under existing law that the articles would later have been admissible in evidence.... The question presented here is whether the conduct of the police officers at the Coolidge house was such as to make her actions their actions for purposes of the Fourth and Fourteenth Amendments and their attendant exclusionary rules. The test, as the petitioner's argument suggests, is whether Mrs. Coolidge, in light of all the circumstances of the case, must be regarded as having acted as an "instrument" or agent of

the state when she produced her husband's belongings. [Citations omitted.]

In a situation like the one before us there no doubt always exists forces pushing the spouse to cooperate with the police. Among these are the simple but powerful convention of openness and honesty, the fear that secretive behavior will intensify suspicion, and uncertainty as to what course is most likely to be helpful to the absent spouse. But there is nothing constitutionally suspect in the existence, without more, of these incentives to full disclosure or active cooperation with the police. The exclusionary rules were fashioned "to prevent, not to repair," and their target is official misconduct. They are "to compel respect for the constitutional guaranty in the only effectively available way—by removing the incentive to disregard it." ... But it is not part of the policy underlying the Fourth and Fourteenth Amendments to discourage citizens from aiding to the utmost of their ability in the apprehension of criminals. If, then, the exclusionary rule is properly applicable to the evidence taken from the Coolidge house on the night of February 2, it must be upon the basis that some type of unconstitutional police conduct occurred.

Yet it cannot be said that the police should have obtained a warrant for the guns and clothing before they set out to visit Mrs. Coolidge, since they had no intention of rummaging around among Coolidge's effects or of dispossessing him of any of his property. Nor can it be said that they should have obtained Coolidge's permission for a seizure they did not intend to make. There was nothing to compel them to announce to the suspect that they intended to question his wife about his movements on the night of the disappearance or about the theft from his employer. Once Mrs. Coolidge had admitted them, the policemen were surely acting normally and properly when they asked her, as they had asked those questioned earlier in the investigation, including Coolidge himself; about any guns there might be in the house. The question concerning the clothes Coolidge had been wearing on the night of the disappearance was logical and in no way coercive. Indeed, one might doubt the competence of the officers involved had they not asked exactly the questions they did ask. And surely when Mrs. Coolidge of her own accord produced the guns and clothes for inspection, rather than simply describing them, it was not incumbent on the police to stop her or avert their eyes.

The crux of the petitioner's argument must be that when Mrs. Coolidge asked the policemen whether they wanted the guns, they should have replied that they could not take them, or have first telephoned Coolidge at the police station and asked his permission to take them, or have asked her whether she had been authorized by her husband to release them. Instead, after one policeman had declined the offer, the other turned and said, "We might as well take them," to which Mrs. Coolidge replied, "If you would like them, you may take them."

In assessing the claim that this course of conduct amounted to a search and seizure, it is well to keep in mind that Mrs. Coolidge described her own motive as that of clearing her husband, and that she believed that she had nothing to hide. She had seen her husband himself produce his guns for two other policemen earlier in the week, and there is nothing to indicate that she realized that he had offered only three of them for inspection on that occasion. The two officers who questioned her behaved, as her own testimony shows, with perfect courtesy. There is not the slightest implication of an attempt on their part to coerce or dominate her, or, for that matter, to direct her actions by the more subtle techniques of suggestion that are available to officials in circumstances like these. To hold that the conduct of the police here was a search and seizure would be to hold, in effect, that a criminal suspect has constitutional protection against the adverse consequences of a spontaneous, good-faith effort by his wife to clear him of suspicion.

The judgment is reversed and the case is remanded to the Supreme Court of New Hampshire for further proceedings not inconsistent with this opinion.

It is so ordered.

*Judgment reversed and
case remanded.*

[The complete texts of the following opinions have been omitted.]

MR. JUSTICE HARLAN wrote a concurring opinion stating that the law of search and seizure is due for an overhauling and that *Mapp* v. *Ohio* should be overruled.

MR. CHIEF JUSTICE BURGER dissented in part and concurred in part. He also questioned the exclusionary rule.

MR. JUSTICE BLACK concurred in part and dissented in part stating that the verdict should not have been upset.

MR. JUSTICE BLACKMUN joined Mr. Justice Black in holding that the Fourth Amendment supports no exclusionary rule.

MR. JUSTICE WHITE concurred in part and dissented in part.

CHIMEL v. CALIFORNIA
395 U.S. 752, 23 L.Ed.2d 685, 89 S.Ct. 2034 (1969)

MR. JUSTICE STEWART delivered the opinion of the Court.

This case raises basic questions concerning the permissible scope under the Fourth Amendment of a search incident to a lawful arrest.

The relevant facts are essentially undisputed. Late in the afternoon of September 13, 1965, three police officers arrived at the Santa Ana, California, home of the petitioner with a warrant authorizing his arrest for the burglary of a coin shop. The officers knocked on the door, identified themselves to the petitioner's wife, and asked if they might come inside. She ushered them into the house, where they waited 10 or 15 minutes until the petitioner returned home from work. When the petitioner entered the house, one of the officers handed him the arrest warrant and asked for permission to "look

around." The petitioner objected, but was advised that "on the basis of the lawful arrest," the officers would nonetheless conduct a search. No search warrant had been issued.

Accompanied by the petitioner's wife, the officers then looked through the entire three-bedroom house, including the attic, the garage, and a small workshop. In some rooms the search was relatively cursory. In the master bedroom and sewing room, however, the officers directed the petitioner's wife to open drawers and "to physically move contents of the drawers from side to side so that [they] might view any items that would have come from [the] burglary." After completing the search, they seized numerous items—primarily coins, but also several medals, tokens, and a few other objects. The entire search took between 45 minutes and an hour.

At the petitioner's subsequent state trial on two charges of burglary, the items taken from his house were admitted into evidence against him, over his objection that they had been unconstitutionally seized. He was convicted, and the judgments of conviction were affirmed by both the California District Court of Appeal, 61 Cal.Rptr. 714, and the California Supreme Court, 68 Cal.2d 436, 439 P.2d 333, 67 Cal.Rptr. 421. Both courts accepted the petitioner's contention that the arrest warrant was invalid because the supporting affidavit was set out in conclusory terms, but held that since the arresting officers had procured the warrant "in good faith," and since in any event they had had sufficient information to constitute probable cause for the petitioner's arrest, the arrest had been lawful. From this conclusion the appellate courts went on to hold that the search of the petitioner's home had been justified, despite the absence of a search warrant, on the ground that it had been incident to a valid arrest. We granted certiorari in order to consider the petitioner's substantial constitutional claims.

Without deciding the question, we proceed on the hypothesis that the California courts were correct in holding that the arrest of the petitioner was valid under the Constitution. This brings us directly to the question whether the warrantless search on the petitioner's entire house can be constitutionally justified as incident to that arrest. The decisions of this Court

bearing upon that question have been far from consistent, as even the most cursory review makes evident.

Approval of a warrantless search incident to a lawful arrest seems first to have been articulated by the Court in 1914 as dictum in *Weeks* v. *United States*, 232 U.S. 383, in which the Court stated:

What then is the present case? Before answering that inquiry specifically, it may be well by a process of exclusion to state what it was not. It is not an assertion of the right on the part of the Government, always recognized under English and American law, to search the person of the accused when legally arrested to discover and seize the fruits or evidences of crime. *Id.*, at 392.

That statement made no reference to any right to search the *place* where an arrest occurs, but was limited to a right to search the "person." Eleven years later the case of *Carroll* v. *United States*, 267 U.S. 132, brought the following embellishment of the *Weeks* statement:

When a man is legally arrested for an offense, whatever is found upon his person *or in his control* which it is unlawful for him to have and which may be used to prove the offense may be seized and held as evidence in the prosecution. *Id.*, at 158 (Emphasis added.)

Still, that assertion too was far from a claim that the "place" where one is arrested may be searched so long as the arrest is valid. Without explanation, however, the principle emerged in expanded form a few months later in *Agnello* v. *United States*, 269 U.S. 20—although still by way of dictum:

> The right without a search warrant contemporaneously to search persons lawfully arrested while committing crime and to search the place where the arrest is made in order to find and seize things connected with the crime as its fruits or as the means by which it was committed, as well as weapons and other things to effect an escape from custody, is not to be doubted. [Citations omitted.]

In 1950, two years after *Trupiano*, came *United States* v. *Rabinowitz*, 339 U.S. 56, the decision upon which California primarily relies in the case now before us. In *Rabinowitz*, federal authorities had been informed that the defendant was dealing in stamps bearing forged overprints. On the basis of that information they secured a warrant for his arrest, which they executed at his one-room business office. At the time of the arrest, the officers "searched the desk, safe, and file cabinets in the office for about an hour and a half," *id.*, at 59, and seized 573 stamps with forged overprints. The stamps were admitted into evidence at the defendant's trial, and this Court affirmed his conviction, rejecting the contention that the warrantless search had been unlawful. The Court held that the search in its entirety fell within the principle giving law enforcement authorities "[t]he right 'to search the place where the arrest is made in order to find and seize things connected with the crime. . . .'" *Id.*, at 61. *Harris* was regarded as "ample authority" for that conclusion. *Id.*, at 63. The opinion rejected the rule of *Trupiano* that "in seizing goods and articles, law enforcement agents must secure and use search warrants wherever reasonably practicable." The test, said the Court, "is not whether it is reasonable to procure a search warrant, but whether the search was reasonable." *Id.*, at 66.

Rabinowitz has come to stand for the proposition, *inter alia*, that a warrantless search "incident to a lawful arrest" may generally extend to the area that is considered to be in the "possession" or under the "control" of the person arrested. And it was on the basis of that proposition that the California courts upheld the search of the petitioner's entire house in this case. That doctrine, however, at least in the broad sense in which it was applied by the California courts in this case, can withstand neither historical nor rational analysis.

Even limited to its own facts, the *Rabinowitz* decision was, as we have seen, hardly founded on an unimpeachable line of authority. As Mr. Justice Frankfurter commented in dissent in that case, the "hint" contained in *Weeks* was, without persuasive justification, "loosely turned into dictum and finally elevated to a decision." 339 U.S., at 75. And the approach taken in cases such as *Go-Bart, Lefkowitz,* and *Trupiano* was essentially disregarded by the *Rabinowitz* Court.

Nor is the rationale by which the State seeks here to sustain the search of the petitioner's house supported by a reasoned view of the background and purpose of the Fourth Amendment. Mr. Justice Frankfurter wisely pointed out in his *Rabinowitz* dissent that the Amendment's proscription of "unreasonable searches and seizures" must be read in light of "the history that gave rise to the words"— a history of "abuses so deeply felt by the Colonies as to be one of the potent causes of the Revolution. . . ." 339 U.S., at 69. The Amendment was in large part a reaction to the general warrants and warrantless searches that had so alienated the colonists and had helped speed the movement for independence. In the scheme of the Amendment, therefore, the requirement that "no Warrants shall issue, but upon probable cause," plays a crucial part. As the Court put it in *McDonald* v. *United States,* 335 U.S. 451:

We are not dealing with formalities. The presence of a search warrant serves a high function. Absent some grave emergency, the Fourth Amendment has interposed a magistrate between the citizen and the police. This was done not to shield criminals nor to make the home a safe haven for illegal activities. It

was done so that an objective mind might weigh the need to invade that privacy in order to enforce the law. The right of privacy was deemed too precious to entrust to the discretion of those whose job is the detection of crime and the arrest of criminals. . . . And so the Constitution requires a magistrate to pass on the desires of the police before they violate the privacy of the home. We cannot be true to that constitutional requirement and excuse the absence of a search warrant without a showing by those who seek exemption from the constitutional mandate that the exigencies of the situation made that course imperative.

Even in the *Agnello* case the Court relied upon the rule that "[b]elief, however well founded, that an article sought is concealed in a dwelling house furnishes no justification for a search of that place without a warrant. And such searches are held unlawful notwithstanding facts unquestionably showing probable cause." 269 U.S., at 33. Clearly, the general requirement that a search warrant be obtained is not lightly to be dispensed with, and "the burden is on those seeking [an] exemption [from the requirement] to show the need for it. . . ." *United States* v. *Jeffers,* 342 U.S. 48, 51.

Only last Term in *Terry* v. *Ohio,* 392 U.S. 1, we emphasized that "the police must, whenever practicable, obtain advance judicial approval of searches and seizures through the warrant procedure," *id.,* at 20, and that "[t]he scope of [a] search must be 'strictly tied to and justified by' the circumstances which rendered its initiation permissible." *Id.,* at 19. The search undertaken by the officer in that "stop and frisk" case was sustained under that test, because it was no more than a "protective . . . search for weapons." *Id.,* at 29. But in a companion case, *Sibron* v. *New York,* 392 U.S. 40, we applied the same standard to another set of facts and reached a contrary result, holding that a policeman's action in thrusting his hand into a suspect's pocket had been neither motivated by nor limited to the objective of protection. Rather, the search had been made in order to find narcotics, which were in fact found.

A similar analysis underlies the "search incident to arrest" principle, and marks its proper extent. When an arrest is made, it is reasonable for the arresting officer to search the person arrested in order to remove any weapons that the latter might seek to use in order to resist arrest or effect his escape. Otherwise, the officer's safety might well be endangered, and the arrest itself frustrated. In addition, it is entirely reasonable for the arresting officer to search for and seize any evidence on the arrestee's person in order to prevent its concealment or destruction. And the area into which an arrestee might reach in order to grab a weapon or evidentiary items must, of course, be governed by a like rule. A gun on a table or in a drawer in front of one who is arrested can

be as dangerous to the arresting officer as one concealed in the clothing of the person arrested. There is ample justification, therefore, for a search of the arrestee's person and the area "within his immediate control"—construing that phrase to mean the area from within which he might gain possession of a weapon or destructible evidence.

There is no comparable justification, however, for routinely searching any room other than that in which an arrest occurs—or, for that matter, for searching through all the desk drawers or other closed or concealed areas in that room itself. Such searches, in the absence of well-recognized exceptions, may be made only under the authority of a search warrant. The "adherence to judicial processes" mandated by the Fourth Amendment requires no less.

. . . .

Rabinowitz and *Harris* have been the subject of critical commentary for many years, and have been relied upon less and less in our own decisions. It is time, for the reasons we have stated, to hold that on their own facts, and insofar as the principles they stand for are inconsistent with those that we have endorsed today, they are no longer to be followed.

Application of sound Fourth Amendment principles to the facts of this case produces a clear result. The search here went far beyond the petitioner's person and the area from within which he might have obtained either a weapon or something that could have been used as evidence against him. There was no constitutional justification, in the absence of a search warrant, for extending the search beyond that area. The scope of the search was, therefore, "unreasonable" under the Fourth and Fourteenth Amendments, and the petitioner's conviction cannot stand.

Reversed.

MR. JUSTICE HARLAN, concurring.

I join the Court's opinion with these remarks concerning a factor to which the Court has not alluded. The only thing that has given me pause in voting to overrule *Harris* and *Rabinowitz* is that as a result of *Mapp v. Ohio*, 367 U.S. 643 (1961), and *Ker v. California*, 374 U.S. 23 (1963), every change in Fourth Amendment law must now be obeyed by state officials facing widely different problems of local law enforcement. We simply do not know the extent to which cities and towns across the Nation are prepared to administer the greatly expanded warrant system which will be required by today's decision; nor can we say with assurance that in each and every local situation, the warrant requirement plays an essential role in the protection of those fundamental liberties protected against state infringement by the Fourth Amendment.

Thus, one is now faced with the dilemma, envisioned in my separate opinion in *Ker*, 374 U.S. 23, at 45–46, of choosing between vindicating sound Fourth Amendment

principles at the possible expense of state concerns, long recognized to be consonant with the Fourteenth Amendment before *Mapp* and *Ker* came on the books, or diluting the Federal Bill of Rights in the interest of leaving the States at least some elbow room in their methods of criminal law enforcement. No comparable dilemma exists, of course, with respect to the impact of today's decision within the federal system itself.

This federal-state factor has not been an easy one for me to resolve, but in the last analysis I cannot in good conscience vote to perpetuate bad Fourth Amendment law.

I add only that this case, together with *Benton v. Maryland, Pearce v. North Carolina*, and *Simpson v. Rice*, all decided today, serve to point up, as few other cases have, the profound changes that the "incorporation doctrine" has wrought both in the workings of our federal system and upon the adjudicative processes of this Court.

MR. JUSTICE WHITE, with whom MR. JUSTICE BLACK joins, dissenting.

Few areas of the law have been as subject to shifting constitutional standards over the last 50 years as that of the search "incident to an arrest." There has been a remarkable instability in this whole area, which has seen at least four major shifts in emphasis. Today's opinion makes an untimely fifth. In my view, the Court should not now abandon the old rule.

I.

The modern odyssey of doctrine in this field is detailed in the majority opinion. It began with *Weeks v. United States*, 232 U.S. 383 (1914), where the Court paused to note what the case before it was not. "It is not an assertion of the right on the part of the Government, always recognized under English and American law, to search the person of the accused when legally arrested to discover and seize the fruits or evidences of crime. This right has been uniformly maintained in many cases. ... Nor is it the case of burglar's tools or other proofs of guilt found upon his arrest *within the control of the accused.*" *Id.,* at 392. This scope of search incident to arrest, extending to all items under the suspect's "control," was reaffirmed in a dictum in *Carroll v. United States,* 267 U.S. 132, 158 (1925). Accord, *Agnello v. United States,* 269 U.S. 20, 30 (1925) (holding that "the place where the arrest is made" may be searched "is not to be doubted"). The rule was reaffirmed in *Marron v. United States,* 275 U.S. 192, 199 (1927), where the Court asserted that authority to search incident to an arrest "extended to all parts of the premises used for the unlawful purpose."

Within four years, this rule was qualified by two Prohibition Act cases, *Go-Bart Importing Co. v. United States,* 282 U.S. 344, 356–358 (1931), and *United States v. Lefkowitz,* 285 U.S. 452, 463–467 (1932).

If *Go-Bart* and *Lefkowitz* represented a retreat from the rule of *Weeks, Carroll, Agnello,* and *Marron,* the vigor of the earlier rule was reaffirmed in *Harris v. United States,* 331 U.S. 145 (1947) which has, but for one brief interlude, clearly been the law until today. The very next Term after *Harris,* in *Trupiano v. United States,* 334 U.S. 699 (1948), the Court held unjustifiable the seizure of a still incident to the arrest of a man at the still site, even though the still was contraband, had been visible through an open door before entering the premises to be "searched," and although a crime was being committed in the officers' presence. Accord, that year, *McDonald v. United States,* 335 U.S. 451 (1948) (gambling game seen through transom before entry). Two years later, however, the Court returned to the *Harris* rule in *United States v. Rabinowitz,* 339 U.S. 56 (1950), where the Court held that the reasonableness of a search does not depend upon the practicability of obtaining a search warrant, and that the fact of a valid arrest is relevant to reasonableness. *Trupiano* was *pro tanto* overruled.

Such rapid reversals had occurred before, but they are rare. Here there had been two about-faces, one following hard upon the other. JUSTICE FRANKFURTER objected in this language: "Especially ought the Court not reenforce needlessly the instabilities of our day by giving fair ground for the belief that Law is the expression of chance—for instance, of unexpected changes in the Court's composition and the contingencies in the choice of successors." 339 U.S., at 86. Since that time, the rule of *Weeks, Marron, Harris,* and *Rabinowitz* has clearly been the law. [Citations omitted.]

II.

The rule which has prevailed, but for very brief or doubtful periods of aberration, is that a search incident to an arrest may extend to those areas under the control of the defendant and where items subject to constitutional seizure may be found. The justification for this rule must, under the language of the Fourth Amendment, lie in the reasonableness of the rule. [Citations omitted.] The Amendment provides:

> The right of the people to be secure in their persons, houses, papers, and effects, against unreasonable searches and seizures, shall not be violated, and no Warrants shall issue, but upon probable cause, supported by Oath or affirmation, and particularly describing the place to be searched, and the persons or things to be seized.

In terms, then, the Court must decide whether a given search is reasonable. The Amendment does not proscribe "warrantless searches" but instead it proscribes "unreasonable searches" and this Court has never held nor does the majority today assert that warrantless searches are necessarily unreasonable.

Applying this reasonableness test to the area of searches incident to arrests, one thing is clear at the outset. Search of an arrested man and of the items within his immediate reach must in almost every case be reasonable. There is always a danger that the suspect will try to escape, seizing concealed weapons with which to overpower and injure the arresting officers, and there is a danger that he may destroy evidence vital to the prosecution. Circumstances in which these justifications would not apply are sufficiently rare that inquiry is not made into searches of this scope, which have been considered reasonable throughout.

. . . .

IV.

. . . .

An arrested man, by definition conscious of the police interest in him, and provided almost immediately with a lawyer and a judge, is in an excellent position to dispute the reasonableness of his arrest and contemporaneous search in a full adversary proceeding. I would uphold the constitutionality of this search contemporaneous with an arrest since there was probable cause both for the search and for the arrest, exigent circumstances involving the removal or destruction of evidence, and a satisfactory opportunity to dispute the issues of probable cause shortly thereafter. In this case, the search was reasonable.

CHAMBERS v. MARONEY

399 U.S. 42, 26 L.Ed.2d 419, 90 S.Ct. 1975 (1970)

MR. JUSTICE WHITE delivered the opinion of the Court.

The principal question in this case concerns the admissibility of evidence seized from an automobile, in which petitioner was riding at the time of his arrest, after the automobile was taken to a police station and was there thoroughly searched without a warrant. The Court of Appeals for the Third Circuit found no violation of petitioner's Fourth Amendment rights. We affirm.

I.

During the night of May 20, 1963, a Gulf service station in North Braddock, Pennsylvania, was robbed by two men each of whom carried and displayed a gun. The robbers took the currency from the cash register; the service station attendant, one Stephen Kovacich, was directed to place the coins in his right-hand glove, which was then taken by the robbers. Two teen-agers, who had earlier noticed a blue compact station wagon circling the block in the vicinity of the Gulf station, then saw the station wagon speed away from a parking lot close to the Gulf station. At the same time, they learned that the Gulf station had been robbed. They reported to police, who arrived immediately, that four men were in the station wagon and one was wearing a green sweater. Kovacich told the police that one of the men who robbed him was wearing a green sweater and the other was wearing a trench coat. A description of the car and the two robbers was broadcast over the police radio. Within an hour, a light blue compact station wagon answering the description and carrying four men was stopped by the police about two miles from the Gulf station. Petitioner was one of the men in the station wagon. He was wearing a green sweater and there was a trench coat in the car. The occupants were arrested and the car was driven to the police station. In the course of a thorough search of the car at the station, the police found concealed in a compartment under the dashboard two .38-caliber revolvers (one loaded with dumdum bullets), a right hand glove containing small change, and certain cards bearing the name of Raymond Havicon, the attendant at a Boron service station in McKeesport, Pennsylvania, who had been robbed at gun point on May 13, 1963. In the course of a warrant-authorized search of petitioner's home the day after petitioner's arrest, police found and seized certain .38-caliber ammunition, including some dumdum bullets similar to those found in one of the guns taken from the station wagon.

Petitioner was indicted for both robberies. His first trial ended in a mistrial but he was convicted of both robberies at the second trial. Both Kovacich and Havicon identified petitioner as one of the robbers. The materials taken from the station wagon were introduced into evidence, Kovacich identifying his glove and Havicon the cards taken in the May 13 robbery. The bullets seized at petitioner's house were also introduced over objections of petitioner's counsel. Petitioner was sentenced to a term of four to eight years' imprisonment for the May 13 robbery and to a term of two to seven years' imprisonment for the May 20 robbery, the sentences to run consecutively. Petitioner did not take a direct appeal from these convictions. In 1965, petitioner sought a writ of habeas corpus in the state court, which denied the writ after a brief evidentiary hearing; the denial of the writ was affirmed on appeal in the Pennsylvania appellate courts. Habeas corpus proceedings were then commenced in the United States District Court for the Western District of Pennsylvania. An order to show cause was issued. Based on the State's response and the state court record, the petition for habeas corpus was denied without a hearing. The Court of Appeals for the Third Circuit affirmed, . . . and we granted certiorari.

II.

We pass quickly the claim that the search of the automobile was the fruit of an unlawful arrest. Both the courts below thought the arresting officers had probable cause to make the arrest. We agree. Having talked to the teen-age observers and to the victim Kovacich, the police had ample cause to stop a light blue compact station wagon

carrying four men and to arrest the occupants, one of whom was wearing a green sweater and one of whom had a trench coat with him in the car.[6]

Even so, the search which produced the incriminating evidence was made at the police station some time after the arrest and cannot be justified as a search incident to an arrest: "Once an accused is under arrest and in custody, then a search made at another place, without a warrant, is simply not incident to the arrest." . . . [T]he reasons which have been thought sufficient to justify warrantless searches carried out in connection with an arrest no longer obtain when the accused is safely in custody at the station house.

There are, however, alternative grounds arguably justifying the search of the car in this case. In *Preston, supra,* the arrest was for vagrancy; it was apparent that the officers had no cause to believe that evidence of crime was concealed in the auto. In *Dyke, supra,* the Court expressly rejected the suggestion that there was probable cause to search the car, 391 U.S., at 221–222. Here the situation is different, for the police had probable cause to believe that the robbers, carrying guns and the fruits of the

_____

[6] In any event, as we point out below, the validity of an arrest is not necessarily determinative of the right to search a car if there is probable cause to make the search. Here, as will be true in many cases, the circumstances justifying the arrest are also those furnishing probable cause for the search.

crime, had fled the scene in a light blue compact station wagon which would be carrying four men, one wearing a green sweater and another wearing a trench coat. As the state courts correctly held, there was probable cause to arrest the occupants of the station wagon that the officers stopped; just as obviously was there probable cause to search the car for guns and stolen money.

In terms of the circumstances justifying a warrantless search, the Court has long distinguished between an automobile and a home or office. In *Carroll* v. *United States*, 267 U.S. 132 (1925), the issue was the admissibility in evidence of contraband liquor seized in a warrantless search of a car on the highway. After surveying the law from the time of the adoption of the Fourth Amendment onward, the Court held that automobiles and other conveyances may be searched without a warrant in circumstances which would not justify the search without a warrant of a house or an office, provided that there is probable cause to believe that the car contains articles that the officers are entitled to seize. The Court expressed its holding as follows:

We have made a somewhat extended reference to these statutes to show that the guaranty of freedom from unreasonable searches and seizures by the Fourth Amendment has been construed, practically since the beginning of the government, as recognizing a necessary differ-

ence between a search of a store, dwelling house, or other structure in respect of which a proper official warrant readily may be obtained and a search of a ship, motor boat, wagon, or automobile for contraband goods, where it is not practicable to secure a warrant because the vehicle can be quickly moved out of the locality or jurisdiction in which the warrant must be sought.

Having thus established that contraband goods concealed and illegally transported in an automobile or other vehicle may be searched for without a warrant, we come now to consider under what circumstances such search may be made.... [T]hose lawfully within the country, entitled to use the public highways, have a right to free passage without interruption or search unless there is known to a competent official authorized to search, probable cause for believing that their vehicles are carrying contraband or illegal merchandise....

The measure of legality of such a seizure is, therefore, that the seizing officer shall have reasonable or probable cause for believing that the automobile which he stops and seizes has contraband liquor therein which is being illegally transported. 267 U.S., at 153–156.

The Court also noted that the search of an auto on probable cause proceeds on the theory wholly different from that justifying the search incident to an arrest:

The right to search and the validity of the seizure are not dependent on the right to arrest. They are dependent on the reasonable cause the seizing officer has for belief that the contents of the automobile offend against the law. 267 U.S., at 158–159.

Finding that there was probable cause for the search and seizure at issue before it, the Court affirmed the convictions.

. . . .

Neither *Carroll, supra,* nor other cases in this Court require or suggest that in every conceivable circumstance the search of an auto even with probable cause may be made without the extra protection for privacy which a warrant affords. But the circumstances that furnish probable cause to search a particular auto for particular articles are most often unforeseeable; moreover, the opportunity to search is fleeting since a car is readily movable. Where this is true, as in *Carroll* and the case before us now, if an effective search is to be made at any time, either the search must be made immediately without a warrant or the car itself must be seized and held without a warrant for whatever period is necessary to obtain a warrant for the search.

In enforcing the Fourth Amendment's prohibition against unreasonable searches and seizures, the Court has insisted upon probable cause as a minimum requirement for a reasonable search permitted by the Constitution. As a general rule, it has also required the judg-

ment of a magistrate on the probable cause issue and the issuance of a warrant before a search is made. Only in exigent circumstances will the judgment of the police as to probable cause serve as a sufficient authorization for a search. *Carroll, supra,* holds a search warrant unnecessary where there is probable cause to search an automobile stopped on the highway; the car is movable, the occupants are alerted, and the car's contents may never be found again if a warrant must be obtained. Hence an immediate search is constitutionally permissible.

Arguably, because of the preference for a magistrate's judgment, only the immobilization of the car should be permitted until a search warrant is obtained; arguably, only the "lesser" intrusion is permissible until the magistrate authorizes the "greater." But which is the "greater" and which the "lesser" intrusion is itself a debatable question and the answer may depend on a variety of circumstances. For constitutional purposes, we see no difference between on the one hand seizing and holding a car before presenting the probable cause issue to a magistrate and on the other hand carrying out an immediate search without a warrant. Given probable cause to search, either course is reasonable under the Fourth Amendment.

On the facts before us, the blue station wagon could have been searched on the spot when it was stopped since there was probable cause to search and it was a fleeting target for a search. The probable cause factor still obtained at the station house and so did the mobility of the car unless the Fourth Amendment permits a warrantless seizure of the car and the denial of its use to anyone until a warrant is secured. In that event there is little to choose in terms of practical consequences between an immediate search without a warrant and the car's immobilization until a warrant is obtained. The same consequences may not follow where there is unforseeable cause to search a house. Compare *Vale* v. *Louisiana*, 399 U.S. 30. But as *Carroll, supra*, held, for the purposes of the Fourth Amendment there is a constitutional difference between houses and cars.

. . . .

Affirmed.

MR. JUSTICE BLACKMUN took no part in the consideration or decision of this case.

MR. JUSTICE STEWART, concurring.

I adhere to the view that the admission at trial of evidence acquired in alleged violation of Fourth Amendment standards is not of itself sufficient ground for a collateral attack upon an otherwise valid criminal conviction, state or federal. [Citations omitted.] But until the Court adopts that view, I regard myself as obligated to consider the merits of the Fourth and Fourteenth Amendment claims in a case of this kind. Upon that premise I join the opinion and judgment of the Court.

MR. JUSTICE HARLAN, concurring in part and dissenting in part.

I find myself in disagreement with the Court's disposition of this case in two respects.

. . . .

In sustaining the search of the automobile I believe the Court ignores the framework of our past decisions circumscribing the scope of permissible search without a warrant. The Court has long read the Fourth Amendment's proscription of "unreasonable" searches as imposing a general principle that a search without a search warrant is not justified by the mere knowledge by the searching officers of facts showing probable cause. The "general requirement that a warrant be obtained" is basic to the Amendment's protection of privacy, and " 'the burden is on those seeking [an] exemption. . . .' " [Citations omitted.]

Fidelity to this established principle requires that, where exceptions are made to accommodate the exigencies of particular situations, those exceptions be no broader than necessitated by the circumstances presented. For example, the Court has recognized that an arrest creates an emergency situation justifying a warrantless search of the arrestee's person and of "the area from within which he might gain possession of a weapon or destructible evidence": however, because the exigency giving rise to this exception extends only that far, the search may go no further.

[Citations omitted.] Similarly we held in *Terry* v. *Ohio* that a warrantless search in a "stop and frisk" situation must "be strictly circumscribed by the exigencies which justify its initiation." Any intrusion beyond what it necessary for the personal safety of the officer or others nearby is forbidden.

Where officers have probable cause to search a vehicle on a public way, a further limited exception to the warrant requirement is reasonable because "the vehicle can be quickly moved out of the locality or jurisdiction in which the warrant must be sought." . . . Because the officers might be deprived of valuable evidence if required to obtain a warrant before effecting any search or seizure, I agree with the Court that they should be permitted to take the steps necessary to preserve evidence and to make a search possible. . . . The Court holds that those steps include making a warrantless search of the entire vehicle on the highway—a conclusion reached by the Court in *Carroll* without discussion—and indeed appears to go further and to condone the removal of the car to the police station for a warrantless search there at the convenience of the police. I cannot agree that this result is consistent with our insistence in other areas that departures from the warrant requirement strictly conform to the exigency presented.

. . . .

Cases relating to **Chapter 5**

WIRETAPPING AND EAVESDROPPING

BERGER v. NEW YORK

388 U.S. 41, 18 L.Ed.2d 1040, 87 S.Ct. 1873 (1967)

Defendant was convicted in the Supreme Court, Special and Trial Term, New York County, on two counts of conspiracy to bribe public officer attached to New York State Liquor Authority and the Supreme Court, Appellate Division, First Department, 25 A.D.2d 718, 269 N.Y.S.2d 368 affirmed and on appeal the Court of Appeals, 18 N.Y.2d 638, 272 N.Y.S.2d 782, 219 N.E.2d 295 affirmed, and certiorari was granted. The Supreme Court, Mr. Justice Clark, held that statute authorizing any justice of Supreme Court or judge of county court or of court of general sessions of New York county to issue *ex parte* order for eavesdropping upon oath or affirmation of district attorney or of attorney general or officer above rank of sergeant of any police department or political subdivision thereof that there is reasonable ground to believe that evidence of crime may be thus obtained, containing no requirement for particularity as to what specific crime has been or is being committed or place to be searched or conversations sought as required by Fourth Amendment, and requiring no showing of exigent circumstances, is too broad in its sweep, resulting in trespassory intrusion into con-

stitutionally protected area and is violative of Fourth and Fourteenth Amendments.

Reversed.

Mr. Justice Black, Mr. Justice Harlan and Mr. Justice White dissented.

Mr. Justice Clark delivered the opinion of the Court.

This writ tests the validity of New York's permissive eavesdrop statute, N.Y. Code Crim.Proc. § 813–a, under the Fourth, Fifth, Ninth, and Fourteenth Amendments. The claim is that the statute sets up a system of surveillance which involves trespassory intrusions into private, constitutionally protected premises, authorizes "general searches" for "mere evidence," and is an invasion of the privilege against self-incrimination. The trial court upheld the statute, the Appellate Division affirmed without opinion, and the Court of Appeals did likewise by a divided vote. We granted certiorari. We have concluded that the language of New York's statute is too broad in its sweep resulting in a trespassory intrusion into a constitutionally protected area and is, therefore, violative of the Fourth and Fourteenth Amendments. This disposition obviates the necessity for any discussion of the other points raised.

I.

Berger, the petitioner, was convicted on two counts of conspiracy to bribe the Chairman of the New York State Liquor Authority. The case arose out of the complaint of one Ralph Pansini to the District Attorney's office that agents of the State Liquor Authority had entered his bar and grill and without cause seized his books and records. Pansini asserted that the raid was in reprisal for his failure to pay a bribe for a liquor license. Numerous complaints had been filed with the District Attorney's office charging the payment of bribes by applicants for liquor licenses. On the direction of that office, Pansini, while equipped with a "minifon" recording device, interviewed an employee of the Authority. The employee advised Pansini that the price for a license was $10,000 and suggested that he contact attorney Harry Neyer. Neyer subsequently told Pansini that he worked with the Authority employee before and that the latter was aware of the going rate on liquor licenses downtown.

On the basis of this evidence an eavesdrop order was obtained from a Justice of the State Supreme Court, as provided by § 813–a. The order permitted the installation, for a period of 60 days, of a recording device in Neyer's office. On the basis of leads obtained from this eavesdrop a second order per-

mitting the installation, for a like period, of a recording device in the office of one Harry Steinman was obtained. After some two weeks of eavesdropping a conspiracy was uncovered involving the issuance of liquor licenses for the Playboy and Tenement Clubs, both of New York City. Petitioner was indicted as "a go-between" for the principal conspirators, who though not named in the indictment were disclosed in a bill of particulars. Relevant portions of the recordings were received in evidence at the trial and were played to the jury, all over the objection of the petitioner. The parties have stipulated that the District Attorney "had no information upon which to proceed to present a case to the Grand Jury, or on the basis of which to prosecute" the petitioner except by the use of the eavesdrop evidence.

II.

Eavesdropping is an ancient practice which at common law was condemned as a nuisance. 4 Blackstone, COMMENTARIES 168. At one time the eavesdropper listened by naked ear under the eaves of houses or their windows, or beyond their walls seeking out private discourse. The awkwardness and undignified manner of this method as well as its susceptibility to abuse was immediately recognized. Electricity, however, provided a better vehicle and with the advent of the telegraph surreptitious interception of messages began. As early as 1862 California found it necessary to prohibit the practice by statute. Statutes of

California 1862, p. 288, CCLX II. During the Civil War General J. E. B. Stuart is reputed to have had his own eavesdropper along with him in the field whose job it was to intercept military communications of the opposing forces. Subsequently newspapers reportedly raided one another's news gathering lines to save energy, time, and money. Racing news was likewise intercepted and flashed to bettors before the official result arrived.

The telephone brought on a new and more modern eavesdropper known as the "wiretapper." Interception was made by a connection with a telephone line. This activity has been with us for three-quarters of a century. Like its cousins, wiretapping proved to be a commercial as well as a police technique. Illinois outlawed it in 1895 and in 1905 California extended its telegraph interception prohibition to the telephone. Some 50 years ago a New York legislative committee found that police, in cooperation with the telephone company, had been tapping telephone lines in New York despite an Act passed in 1895 prohibiting it. During prohibition days wiretaps were the principal source of information relied upon by the police as the basis for prosecutions. In 1934 the Congress outlawed the interception without authorization, and the divulging or publishing of the contents of wiretaps by passing § 605 of the Communications Act of 1934. New York, in 1938, declared by constitutional amendment that "[t]he right of the people to be secured against unreasonable interception of telephone and telegraph communications shall not be violated," but permitted by *ex parte* order of the Supreme Court of the State the interception of communications on a showing of "reasonable ground to believe that evidence of crime" might be obtained. N.Y.Const. Art. I, § 12.

Sophisticated electronic devices have now been developed (commonly known as "bugs") which are capable of eavesdropping on anyone in most any given situation. They are to be distinguished from "wiretaps" which are confined to the interception of telegraphic and telephonic communications. Miniature in size (3/8" x 3/8" x 1/8")—no larger than a postage stamp—these gadgets pick up whispers within a room and broadcast them half a block away to a receiver. It is said that certain types of electronic rays beamed at walls or glass windows are capable of catching voice vibrations as they are bounced off the surfaces. Since 1940 eavesdropping has become a big business. Manufacturing concerns offer complete detection systems which automatically record voices under almost any conditions by remote control. A microphone concealed in a book, a lamp, or other unsuspected place in a room, or made into a fountain pen, tie clasp, lapel button, or cuff link increases the range of these powerful wireless transmitters to a half mile. Receivers pick up the transmission with interference-free reception on a special wave frequency. And, of late, a combination mirror transmitter has been developed which permits not only sight but voice transmission up to 300 feet. Likewise, parabolic microphones, which can overhear conversations without being placed within the premises monitored, have been developed. See Westin, *Science, Privacy, and Freedom: Issues and Proposals for the 1970's*, 66 Col.L.Rev. 1003, 1005–1010.

As science developed these detection techniques, law makers, sensing the resulting invasion of individual privacy, have provided some statutory protection for the public. Seven states, California, Illinois, Maryland, Massachusetts, Nevada, New York, and Oregon, prohibit surreptitious eavesdropping by mechanical or electronic device. However, all save Illinois permit official court-ordered eavesdropping. Some 36 states prohibit wiretapping. But of these, 27 permit "authorized" interception of some type. Federal law, as we have seen, prohibits interception and divulging or publishing of the content of wiretaps without exception. In sum, it is fair to say that wiretapping on the whole is outlawed, except for permissive use by law enforcement officials in some states; while electronic eavesdropping is —same for seven states—permitted both officially and privately. And, in six of the seven states, electronic eavesdropping ("bugging") is permissible on court order.

III.

The law, though jealous of individual privacy, has not kept pace with these advances in scientific knowledge. This is not to say that individual privacy has been relegated to a second-class position for it has been held since Lord Camden's day that intrusions into it are "subversive of all the comforts of society." *Entick* v. *Carrington*, 19 How.St.Tr. 1029, 1066 (1765). And the Founders so decided a quarter of a century later when they declared in the Fourth Amendment that the people had a right "to be secure in their persons, houses, papers, and effects, against unreasonable searches and seizures. . . ." Indeed, that right, they wrote, "shall not be violated, and no Warrants shall issue, but upon probable cause, supported by Oath or affirmation, and particularly describing the place to be searched, and the persons or things to be seized." Almost a century thereafter this Court took specific and lengthy notice of *Entick* v. *Carrington, supra*, finding that its holding was undoubtedly familiar in the minds of those who framed the fourth amendment. . . ." *Boyd* v. *United States*, 116 U.S. 616, 626–627, (1886). And after quoting from Lord Camden's opinion at some length, Mr. Justice Bradley characterized it thus:

The principles laid down in this opinion affect the very essence of constitutional liberty and security. They reach farther than the concrete form of the case . . . they apply to all invasions on the part of the government and its employés of the sanctity of a man's home and the privacies of life.

Boyd held unconstitutional an Act of the Congress authorizing a court of the United States to require a defendant in a revenue case to produce in court his private books, invoices, and papers or else the allegations of the Government were to be taken as confessed. The Court found that "the essence of the offense . . . [was] the invasion of this sacred right which underlies and constitutes the essence of Lord Camden's judgment." *Ibid.* The Act—the Court found—violated the Fourth Amendment in that it authorized a general search contrary to the Amendment's guarantee.

The Amendment, however, carried no criminal sanction, and the federal statutes not affording one, the Court in 1914 formulated and pronounced the federal exclusionary rule in *Weeks* v. *United States,* 232 U.S. 383. Prohibiting the use in federal courts of any evidence seized in violation of the Amendment, the Court held:

> The effect of the 4th Amendment is to put the courts of the United States . . . under limitations and restraints as to the exercise of such power . . . and to forever secure the people . . . against all unreasonable searches and seizures under the guise of law. This protection reaches all alike, whether accused of crime or not, and the duty of giving to it force and effect is obligatory upon all. . . . The tendency of those who execute the criminal laws of the country to obtain conviction by means of unlawful

seizures . . . should find no sanction in the judgments of the courts, which are charged at all times with the support of the Constitution, and to which people of all conditions have a right to appeal for the maintenance of such fundamental rights.

IV.

The Court was faced with its first wiretap case in 1928, *Olmstead* v. *United States,* 277 U.S. 438. There the interception of Olmstead's telephone line was accomplished without entry upon his premises and was, therefore, found not to be proscribed by the Fourth Amendment. The basis of the decision was that the Constitution did not forbid the obtaining of evidence by wiretapping unless it involved actual unlawful entry into the house. Statements in the opinion that a conversation passing over a telephone wire cannot be said to come within the Fourth Amendment's enumeration of "persons, houses, papers, and effects" have been negated by our subsequent cases as hereinafter noted. They found "conversation" was within the Fourth Amendment's protections, and that the use of electronic devices to capture it was a "search" within the meaning of the Amendment, and we so hold. In any event, Congress soon thereafter, and some say in answer to *Olmstead,* specifically prohibited the interception without authorization and the divulging or publishing of the contents of telephonic communications. And the *Nardone* cases (*Nardone* v. *United States*),

302 U.S. 379, (1937) and 308 U.S. 338 (1939), extended the exclusionary rule to wiretap evidence offered in federal prosecutions.

The first "bugging" case reached the Court in 1942 in *Goldman* v. *United States*, 316 U.S. 129. There the Court found that the use of a detectaphone placed against an office wall in order to hear private conversations in the office next door did not violate the Fourth Amendment because there was no physical trespass in connection with the relevant interception. And in *On Lee* v. *United States*, 343 U.S. 747 (1952), we found that since "no trespass was committed" a conversation between Lee and a federal agent, occurring in the former's laundry and electronically recorded, was not condemned by the Fourth Amendment. Thereafter in *Silverman* v. *United States*, 365 U.S. 505 (1961), the Court found "that the eavesdropping was accomplished by means of an unauthorized physical penetration into the premises occupied by the petitioners." A spike a foot long with a microphone attached to it was inserted under a baseboard into a party wall until it made contact with the heating duct that ran through the entire house occupied by Silverman, making a perfect sounding board through which the conversations in question were overheard. Significantly, the Court held that its decision did "not turn upon the technicality of a trespass upon a party wall as a matter of local law. It is based upon the reality of an actual intrusion into a constitutionally protected area."

In *Wong Sun* v. *United States*, 371 U.S. 471 (1963), the Court for the first time specifically held that verbal evidence may be the fruit of official illegality under the Fourth Amendment along with the more common tangible fruits of unwarranted intrusion. It used these words:

> The exclusionary rule has traditionally barred from trial physical, tangible materials obtained either during or as a direct result of an unlawful invasion. It follows from our holding in *Silverman* v. *United States*, 365 U.S. 505, that the Fourth Amendment may protect against the overhearing of verbal statements as well as against the more traditional seizure of "papers and effects."

And in *Lopez* v. *United States*, 373 U.S. 427 (1963), the Court confirmed that it had "in the past sustained instances of 'electronic eavesdropping' against constitutional challenge, when devices have been used to enable government agents to overhear conversations which would have been beyond the reach of the human ear. . . . It has been insisted only that the electronic device not be planted by an unlawful physical invasion of a constitutionally protected area." In this case a recording of a conversation between a federal agent and the petitioner in which the latter offered the agent a bribe was admitted in evidence. Rather than constituting "eavesdropping" the Court found that the recording "was used only to obtain the most reliable evidence possible of a conversation in which the Government's own agent was a participant and which that agent was fully entitled to disclose."

V.

It is now well settled that "the Fourth Amendment's right of privacy has been declared enforceable against the States through the Due Process Clause of the Fourteenth" Amendment. *Mapp* v. *Ohio*, 367 U.S. 643, 655 (1961). "The security of one's privacy against arbitrary intrusion by the police—which is at the core of the Fourth Amendment—is basic to a free society." *Wolf* v. *Colorado*, 338 U.S. 25, 27 (1949). And its "fundamental protections . . . are guaranteed . . . against invasion by the States." *Stanford* v. *Texas*, 379 U.S. 476, 481 (1965). This right has most recently received enunciation in *Camara* v. *Municipal Court*, 387 U.S. 523 (1967). "The basic purpose of this Amendment, as recognized in countless decisions of this Court, is to safeguard the privacy and security of individuals against arbitrary invasions by governmental officials." Likewise the Court has decided that while the "standards of reasonableness" required under the Fourth Amendment are the same under the Fourteenth, they "are not susceptible of Procrustean application. . . ." *Ker* v. *California*, 374 U.S. 23, 33 (1963). We said there that "the reasonableness of a search is . . . [to be determined] by the trial court from the facts and circumstances of the case and in the light of the

'fundamental criteria' laid down by the Fourth Amendment and in opinions of this Court applying that Amendment." *Ibid.*

We, therefore, turn to New York's statute to determine the basis of the search and seizure authorized by it upon the order of a state supreme court justice, a county judge or general sessions judge of New York County. Section 813–a authorizes the issuance of an "ex parte order for eavesdropping" upon "oath or affirmation of a district attorney, or of the attorney-general or of an officer above the rank of sergeant of any police department of the state or of any political subdivision thereof. . . ." The oath must state "that there is reasonable ground to believe that evidence of crime may be thus obtained, and particularly describing the person or persons whose communications, conversations or discussions are to be overheard or recorded and the purpose thereof, and . . . identifying the particular telephone number or telegraph line involved." The judge "may examine on oath the applicant and any other witness he may produce and shall satisfy himself of the existence of reasonable grounds for the granting of such application." The order must specify the duration of the eavesdrop—not exceeding two months unless extended—and "[a]ny such order together with the papers upon which the application was based, shall be delivered to and retained by the applicant as authority for the eavesdropping authorized therein."

While New York's statute satisfies the Fourth Amendment's requirement that a neutral and detached authority be interposed between the police and the public, or *Johnson* v. *United States,* 333 U.S. 10, 14 (1948), the broad sweep of the statute is immediately observable. It permits the issuance of the order, or warrant for eavesdropping, upon the oath of the attorney general, the district attorney or any police officer above the rank of sergeant stating that "there is reasonable ground to believe that evidence of crime may be thus obtained. . . ." Such a requirement raises a serious probable-cause question under the Fourth Amendment. Under it warrants may only issue "but upon probable cause, supported by Oath or affirmation, and particularly describing the place to be searched, and the persons or things to be seized." Probable cause under the Fourth Amendment exists where the facts and circumstances within the affiant's knowledge, and of which he has reasonably trustworthy information, are sufficient unto themselves to warrant a man of reasonable caution to believe that an offense has been or is being committed. *Carroll* v. *United States,* 267 U.S. 132, 162 (1925); *Husty* v. *United States,* 282 U.S. 694, 700–701 (1931); *Brinegar* v. *United States,* 338 U.S. 160, 175–176 (1949).

It is said, however, by the petitioner, and the State agrees, that the "reasonable ground" requirement of § 813-a "is undisputedly equivalent to the probable cause requirement of the Fourth Amendment." This is indicated by *People* v. *Grossman,* 45 Misc.2d 557, 257 N.Y.S.2d 266, reversed on other grounds, 27 A.D.2d 572, 276 N.Y.S.2d 168 Also see *People* v. *Beshany,* 43 Misc.2d 521, 252 N.Y.S.2d 110. While we have found no case on the point by New York's highest court, we need not pursue the question further because we have concluded that the statute is deficient on its face in other respects. Since petition clearly has standing to challenge the statute, being indisputably affected by it, we need not consider either the sufficiency of the affidavits upon which the eavesdrop orders were based, or the standing of petitioner to attack the search and seizure made thereunder.

The Fourth Amendment commands that a warrant issue not only upon probable cause supported by oath or affirmation, but also "particularly describing the place to be searched, and the persons or things to be seized." New York's statute lacks this particularization. It merely says that a warrant may issue on reasonable ground to believe that evidence of crime may be obtained by the eavesdrop. It lays down no requirement for particularity in the warrant as to what specific crime has been or is being committed, nor "the place to be searched," or "the persons or things to be seized" as specifically required by the Fourth Amendment. The need for particularity and evidence of reliability in the showing required when judicial authorization of a search is sought is especially great in the case of eavesdropping. By its very nature eavesdropping involves an intrusion on privacy that is broad in scope. As was said in *Osborn* v. *United States*, 385 U.S. 323 (1966), the "indiscriminate use of such devices in law enforcement raises grave constitutional questions under the Fourth and Fifth Amendments," and imposes "a heavier responsibility on this Court in its supervision of the fairness of procedures. . . ." There, two judges acting jointly authorized the installation of a device on the person of a prospective witness to record conversations between him and an attorney for a defendant then on trial in the United States District Court. The judicial authorization was based on an affidavit of the witness setting out in detail previous conversations between the witness and the attorney concerning the bribery of jurors in the case. The recording device was, as the Court said, authorized "under the most precise and discriminate circumstances, circumstances which fully met the 'requirement of particularity' " of the Fourth Amendment. The Court was asked to exclude the evidence of the recording of the conversations seized pursuant to the order on constitutional grounds, *Weeks* v. *United States*, *supra*, or in the exercise of supervisory power, *McNabb* v. *United States*, 318 U.S. 332 (1943). The Court refused to do so finding that the recording, although an invasion of the privacy protected by the Fourth Amendment, was admissible because of the authorization

of the judges, based upon "a detailed factual affidavit alleging the commission of a specific criminal offense directly and immediately affecting the administration of justice . . . for the narrow and particularized purpose of ascertaining the truth of the affidavit's allegations." The invasion was lawful because there was sufficient proof to obtain a search warrant to make the search for the limited purpose outlined in the order of the judges. Through these "precise and discriminate" procedures the order authorizing the use of the electronic device afforded similar protections to those that are present in the use of conventional warrants authorizing the seizure of tangible evidence. Among other safeguards, the order described the type of conversation sought with particularity, thus indicating the specific objective of the Government in entering the constitutionally protected area and the limitations placed upon the officer executing the warrant. Under it the officer could not search unauthorized areas; likewise, once the property sought, and for which the order was issued, was found the officer could not use the order as a passkey to further search. In addition, the order authorized one limited intrusion rather than a series or a continuous surveillance. And, we note that a new order was issued when the officer sought to resume the search and probable cause was shown for the succeeding one. Moreover, the order was executed by the officer with dispatch, not over a prolonged and extended period. In this manner no greater invasion of privacy was permitted than was necessary under the circumstances. Finally the officer was required to and did make a return on the order showing how it was executed and what was seized. Through these strict precautions the danger of an unlawful search and seizure was minimized.

By contrast, New York's statute lays down no such "precise and discriminate" requirements. Indeed, it authorizes the "indiscriminate use" of electronic devices as specifically condemned in Osborn. "The proceeding by search warrant is a drastic one," Sgro v. United States, 287 U.S. 206, 210 (1932), and must be carefully circumscribed so as to prevent unauthorized invasions of "the sanctity of a man's home and the privacies of life." Boyd v. United States, 116 U.S. 616, 630. New York's broadside authorization rather than being "carefully circumscribed" so as to prevent unauthorized invasions of privacy actually permits general searches by electronic devices, the truly offensive character of which was first condemned in Entick v. Carrington, 19 How.St.Tr. 1029, and which were then known as "general warrants." The use of the latter was a motivating factor behind the Declaration of Independence. In view of the many cases commenting on the practice it is sufficient here to point out that under these "general warrants" customs officials were given blanket authority to conduct general searches for goods imported to the Colonies in violation of the tax laws of the Crown. The Fourth Amendment's requirement that a warrant "particularly describ[e] the place to be searched, and the persons or things to be seized," repudiated these general warrants and "makes general searches ... impossible and prevents the seizure of one thing under a warrant describing another. As to what is to be taken, nothing is left to the discretion of the officer executing the warrant." Marron v. United States, 275 U.S. 192, 196 (1927); Stanford v. Texas, supra.

We believe the statute here is equally offensive. First, as we have mentioned, eavesdropping is authorized without requiring belief that any particular offense has been or is being committed; nor that the "property" sought, the conversations, be particularly described. The purpose of the probable-cause requirement of the Fourth Amendment, to keep the state out of constitutionally protected areas until it has reason to believe that a specific crime has been or is being committed, is thereby wholly aborted. Likewise the statute's failure to describe with particularity the conversations sought gives the officer a roving commission to "seize" any and all conversations. It is true that the statute requires the naming of "the person or persons whose communications, conversations or discussions are to be overheard or recorded...." But this does no more than identify the person whose constitutionally protected area is to be invaded rather than "particularly describing" the communications, conversations, or discussions to be seized. As with general warrants this leaves too much to the discretion of the officer executing the order. Secondly, authorization of eavesdropping for a two-month period is the equivalent of a series of intrusions, searches, and seizures pursuant to a single showing of probable cause. Prompt execution is also avoided. During such a long and continuous (24 hours a day) period the conversations of any and all persons coming into the area covered by the device will be seized indiscriminately and without regard to their connection with the crime under investigation. Moreover, the statute permits, and there were authorized here, extensions of the original two-month period — presumably for two months each—on a mere showing that such extension is "in the public interest." Apparently the original grounds on which the eavesdrop order was initially issued also form the basis of the renewal. This we believe insufficient without a showing of present probable cause for the continuance of the eavesdrop. Third, the statute places no termination date on the eavesdrop once the conversation sought is seized. This is left entirely in the discretion of the officer. Finally, the statute's procedure, necessarily because its success depends on secrecy, has no requirement for notice as do conventional warrants, nor does it overcome this defect by requiring some showing of special facts. On the contrary, it permits uncontested entry without any showing of exigent circumstances.

Such a showing of exigency, in order to avoid notice would appear more important in eavesdropping, with its inherent dangers, than that required when conventional procedures of search and seizure are utilized. Nor does the statute provide for a return on the warrant thereby leaving full discretion in the officer as to the use of seized conversations of innocent as well as guilty parties. In short, the statute's blanket grant of permission to eavesdrop is without adequate judicial supervision or protective procedures.

VI.

It is said with fervor that electronic eavesdropping is a most important technique of law enforcement and that outlawing it will severely cripple crime detection. The monumental report of the President's Commission on Law Enforcement and Administration of Justice entitled "The Challenge of Crime in a Free Society" informs us that the majority of law enforcement officials say that this is especially true in the detection of organized crime. As the Commission reports, there can be no question about the serious proportions of professional criminal activity in this country. However, we have found no empirical statistics on the use of electronic devices (bugging) in the fight against organized crime. Indeed, there are even figures available in the wiretap category which indicate to the contrary. See District Attorney Silver's Poll of New York Prosecutors, in

Dash, Schwartz & Knowlton, THE EAVESDROPPERS 105, 117–119 (1959). Also see Semerjian, *Proposals on Wiretapping in Light of Recent Senate Hearings*, 45 B.U.L. Rev 217, 229. As the Commission points out, "[w]iretapping was the mainstay of the New York attack against organized crime until Federal court decisions intervened. Recently chief reliance in some offices has been placed on bugging, where the information is to be used in court. Law enforcement officials believe that the successes achieved in some parts of the State are attributable primarily to a combination of dedicated and competent personnel and adequate legal tools; and that the failure to do more in New York has resulted primarily from the failure to commit additional resources of time and men," rather than electronic devices. Moreover, Brooklyn's District Attorney Silver's poll of the State of New York indicates that during the 12-year period (1942–1954) duly authorized wiretaps in bribery and corruption cases constituted only a small percentage of the whole. It indicates that this category involved only 10% of the total wiretaps. The overwhelming majority were in the categories of larceny, extortion, coercion, and blackmail, accounting for almost 50%. Organized gambling was about 11%. Statistics are not available on subsequent years. Dash, Schwartz & Knowlton, *supra*, at 40.

An often repeated statement of District Attorney Hogan of New York County was made at a hearing before the Senate Judiciary Committee at which he advocated the amendment of the Communications Act of 1934, supra, so as to permit "telephonic interception" of conversations. As he testified, "Federal statutory law [the 1934 Act] has been interpreted in such a way as to bar us from divulging wiretap evidence, even in the courtroom in the course of criminal prosecution." Mr. Hogan then said that "[w]ithout it [wiretaps] my own office could not have convicted" "top figures in the underworld." He then named nine persons his office had convicted and one on whom he had furnished "leads" secured from wiretaps to the authorities of New Jersey. Evidence secured from wiretaps, as Mr. Hogan said, was not admissible in "criminal prosecutions." He was advocating that the Congress adopt a measure that would make it admissible; Hearings on S. 2813 and S. 1495, before the Senate Committee on the Judiciary, 87 Cong., 2d Sess., pp. 173, 174 (1962). The President's Commission also emphasizes in its report the need for wiretapping in the investigation of organized crime because of the telephone's "relatively free use" by those engaged in the business and the difficulty of infiltrating their organizations. P. 201. The Congress, though long importuned, has not amended the 1934 Act to permit it.

We are also advised by the Solicitor General of the United States that the Federal Government has abandoned the use of electronic eavesdropping for "prosecutorial purposes." [Citations omitted.] Despite these actions of the Federal Government there has been no failure of law enforcement in that field.

As The Chief Justice said in concurring in the result in *Lopez* v. *United States*, 373 U.S. 427, "the fantastic advances in the field of electronic communications constitute a great danger to the privacy of the individual; . . . indiscriminate use of such devices in law enforcement raises grave constitutional questions under the Fourth and Fifth Amendments. . . ."

In any event we cannot forgive the requirements of the Fourth Amendment in the name of law enforcement. This is no formality that we require today but a fundamental rule that has long been recognized as basic to the privacy of every home in America. While "[t]he requirements of the Fourth Amendment are not inflexible, or obtusely unyielding to the legitimate needs of law enforcement," *Lopez* v. *United States, supra,* at 464, 83 S.Ct. at 1404 (dissenting opinion of BRENNAN, J.), it is not asking too much that officers be required to comply with the basic command of the Fourth Amendment before the innermost secrets of one's home or office are invaded. Few threats to liberty exist which are greater than that posed by the use of eavesdropping devices. Some may claim that without the use of such devices crime detection in certain areas may suffer some delays since eavesdropping is quicker, easier, and more certain. However, techniques and practices may well be developed that will operate just as speedily and certainly and—what is more important—without attending illegality.

It is said that neither a warrant nor a statute authorizing eavesdropping can be drawn so as to meet the Fourth Amendment's requirements. If that be true then the "fruits" of eavesdropping devices are barred under the Amendment. On the other hand this Court has in the past, under specific conditions and circumstances, sustained the use of eavesdropping devices. See *Goldman* v. *United States*, 316 U.S. 129; *On Lee* v. *United States*, 343 U.S. 747; *Lopez* v. *United States, supra*; and *Osborn* v. *United States, supra*. In the latter case the eavesdropping device was permitted where the "commission of a specific offense" was charged, its use was "under the most precise and discriminate circumstances" and the effective administration of justice in a federal court was at stake. The States are under no greater restrictions. The Fourth Amendment does not make the "precincts of the home or the office . . . sanctuaries where the law can never reach," DOUGLAS, J., dissenting in *Warden, Maryland Penitentiary* v. *Hayden,* 387 U.S. 294, 321, but it does prescribe a constitutional standard that must be met before official invasion is permissible. Our concern with the statute here is whether its language permits a trespassory invasion of the home or office, by general warrant, contrary to the command of the Fourth Amendment. As it is written, we believe that it does.

Reversed.

MR. JUSTICE DOUGLAS, concurring.

I join the opinion of the Court because at long last it overrules *sub silentio Olmstead* v. *United States*, 277 U.S. 438, and its offspring and brings wiretapping and other electronic eavesdropping fully within the purview of the Fourth Amendment. I also join the opinion because it condemns electronic surveillance, for its similarity to the general warrants out of which our Revolution sprang and allows a discreet surveillance only on a showing of "probable cause." These safeguards are minimal if we are to live under a regime of wiretapping and other electronic surveillance.

. . . .

That is the essence of my dissent in *Hayden*. In short, I do not see how any electronic surveillance that collects evidence or provides leads to evidence is or can be constitutional under the Fourth and Fifth Amendments. We could amend the Constitution and so provide—a step that would take us closer to the ideological group we profess to despise. Until the amending process ushers us into that kind of totalitarian regime, I would adhere to the protection of privacy with the Fourth Amendment, fashioned in Congress and submitted to the people, was designed to afford the individual. And unlike my BROTHER BLACK, I would adhere to *Mapp* v. *Ohio*, 367 U.S. 643, 81 S.Ct. 1684, 6 L.Ed.2d 1081, and apply the exclusionary rule in state as well as federal trials

—a rule fashioned out of the Fourth Amendment and constituting a high constitutional barricade against the intrusion of Big Brother into the lives of all of us.

MR. JUSTICE STEWART, concurring in the result.

I fully agree with MR. JUSTICE BLACK, MR. JUSTICE HARLAN, and MR. JUSTICE WHITE that this New York law is entirely constitutional. In short, I think that "electronic eavesdropping, as *such* or as it is permitted by this statute, is not an unreasonable search and seizure." The statute contains many provisions more stringent than the Fourth Amendment generally requires, as MR. JUSTICE BLACK has so forcefully pointed out. And the petitioner himself has told us that the law's "reasonable grounds" requirement "is undisputedly equivalent to the probable cause requirement of the Fourth Amendment." This is confirmed by decisions of the New York courts. *People* v. *Cohen*, 42 Misc.2d 403, 248 N.Y.S. 2d 339; *People* v. *Beshany*, 43 Misc.2d 521, 252 N.Y.S.2d 110; *People* v. *Grossman*, 45 Misc.2d 557, 257 N.Y.S.2d 266. Of course, a state court's construction of a state statute is binding upon us.

In order to hold this statute unconstitutional, therefore, we would have to either rewrite the statute or rewrite the Constitution. I can only conclude that the Court today seems to have rewritten both.

The issue before us, as MR. JUSTICE WHITE says, is "whether *this* search complied with Fourth Amendment standards." For me that issue is an extremely close one in the circumstances of this case. It certainly cannot be resolved by incantation of ritual phrases like "general warrant." Its resolution involves "the unavoidable task in any search and seizure case: was the particular search and seizure reasonable or not?"

I would hold that the affidavits on which the judicial order issued in this case did not constitute a showing of probable cause adequate to justify the authorizing order. The need for particularity and evidence of reliability in the showing required when judicial authorization is sought for the kind of electronic eavesdropping involved in this case is especially great. The standard of reasonableness embodied in the Fourth Amendment demands that the showing of justification match the degree of intrusion. By its very nature electronic eavesdropping for a 60-day period, even of a specified office, involves a broad invasion of a constitutionally protected area. Only the most precise and rigorous standard of probable cause should justify an intrusion of this sort. I think the affidavits presented to the judge who authorized the electronic surveillance of the Steinman office failed to meet such a standard.

So far as the record shows, the only basis for the Steinman order consisted of two affidavits. One of them contained factual allegations supported only by bare, unexplained references to "evidence" in the district attorney's office and "evidence" obtained by the Neyer eavesdrop. No underlying facts were presented on the basis of which the judge could evaluate these general allegations. The second affidavit was no more than a statement of another assistant district attorney that he had read his associate's affidavit and was satisfied on that basis alone that proper grounds were presented for the issuance of an authorizing order.

This might be enough to satisfy the standards of the Fourth Amendment for a conventional search or arrest. Cf. *Aguilar* v. *Texas*, 378 U.S. 108, 116 (dissenting opinion). But I think it was constitutionally insufficient to constitute probable cause to justify an intrusion of the scope and duration that was permitted in this case.

Accordingly, I would reverse the judgment.

MR. JUSTICE BLACK, dissenting.

New York has an eavesdropping statute which permits its judges to authorize state officers to place on other people's premises electronic devices that will overhear and record telephonic and other conversations for the purpose of detecting secret crimes and conspiracies and obtaining evidence to convict criminals in court. Judges cannot issue such eavesdropping permits except upon oath or affirmation of certain state officers that "there is reasonable ground to believe that evidence of crime may be thus obtained, and particularly describing the person or persons whose communications, conversations or discussions are to be overheard or recorded and the purpose thereof. . . ." N.Y.Code Crim. Proc.

§ 813-a. Evidence obtained by such electronic eavesdropping was used to convict the petitioner here of conspiracy to bribe the chairman of the State Liquor Authority which controls the issuance of liquor licenses in New York. It is stipulated that without this evidence a conviction could not have been obtained and it seems apparent that use of that evidence showed petitioner to be a briber beyond all reasonable doubt. Notwithstanding petitioner's obvious guilt, however, the Court now strikes down his conviction in a way that plainly makes it impossible ever to convict him again. This is true because the Court not only holds that the judicial orders which were the basis of the authority to eavesdrop were insufficient, but also holds that the New York eavesdropping statute is *on its face* violative of the Fourth Amendment. And while the Court faintly intimates to the contrary, it seems obvious to me that its holding, by creating obstacles that cannot be overcome, makes it completely impossible for the State or the Federal Government ever to have a valid eavesdropping statute. All of this is done, it seems to me, in part because of the Court's hostility to eavesdropping as "ignoble" and "dirty business" and in part because of fear that rapidly advancing science and technology is making eavesdropping more and more effective. Cf. *Lopez* v. *United States*, 373 U.S. 427, 446 (dissenting opinion of BRENNAN, J.). Neither these, nor any other grounds that I can think of, are sufficient in my

judgment to justify a holding that the use of evidence secured by eavesdropping is barred by the Constitution.

. . . .

IV.

While the electronic eavesdropping here bears some analogy to the problems with which the Fourth Amendment is concerned, I am by no means satisfied that the Amendment controls the constitutionality of such eavesdropping. As pointed out, the Amendment only bans searches and seizures of "persons, houses, papers, and effects." This literal language imports tangible things, and it would require an expansion of the language used by the framers, in the interest of "privacy" or some equally vague judge-made goal, to hold that it applies to the spoken word. It simply requires an imaginative transformation of the English language to say that conversations can be searched and words seized. Referring to wiretapping, this Court in *Olmstead* v. *United States*, 277 U.S. 438, 465, refused to make that transformation:

> Justice Bradley in the *Boyd* case, and Justice Clarke in the *Gouled* case, said that the Fifth Amendment and the Fourth Amendment were to be liberally construed. . . . But that cannot justify enlargement of the language employed beyond the possible practical meaning of houses, persons, papers, and effects, or so to apply the words search and seizure as to forbid hearing or sight.

Though *Olmstead* has been severely criticized by various individual members of this Court, and though the Court stated an alternative ground for holding the Amendment inapplicable in that case, the *Olmstead* holding that the Fourth Amendment does not apply to efforts to hear and obtain oral conversations has never been overruled by this Court. The Court today, however, suggests that this holding has been "negated" by subsequent congressional action and by four decisions of this Court. First, the Court intimates, though it does not exactly state, that Congress "in answer to *Olmstead*," passed an Act to prohibit "the interception without authorization and the divulging or publishing of the contents of telephonic communications." The Court cites no authority for this strange surmise, and I assert with confidence that none can be recited. And even if it could, Congress' action would not have the slightest relevance to the scope of the Fourth Amendment. Second, the Court cites *Goldman* v. *United States*, 316 U.S. 129, and *On Lee* v. *United States*, 343 U.S. 747, in an effort to explain away *Olmstead*. But neither of those cases purported to repudiate the *Olmstead* case or any part of it. In fact, in both of those cases the Court refused to exclude the challenged eavesdrop evidence. Finally, the Court relies on *Silverman* v. *United States*, 365 U.S. 505, and *Wong Sun* v. *United States*, 371 U.S. 471. In both of these cases the Court did imply that the "Fourth Amendment *may* protect

against the overhearing of verbal statements as well as against the more traditional seizure of 'papers and effects,' " 371 U.S., at 485 (emphasis added), but in neither did the Court find it necessary to overrule *Olmstead*, an action that would have been required had the Court based its exclusion of the oral conversations solely on the ground of the Fourth Amendment. The fact is that both *Silverman* and *Wong Sun* were federal cases dealing with the use of verbal evidence in federal courts, and the Court held the evidence should be excluded by virtue of the exclusionary rule of the *Weeks* case. As I have previously pointed out, that rule rested on the Court's supervisory power over federal courts, not on the Fourth Amendment: it is not required by the Amendment, nor is a violation of the Amendment a prerequisite to its application. I would not have agreed with the Court's opinion in *Silverman*, which, by the way, cited *Olmstead* with approval, had I thought that the result depended on finding a violation of the Fourth Amendment or had I any inkling that the Court's general statements about the scope of the Amendment were intended to negate the clear holding of *Olmstead*. And again in *Wong Sun*, which did not even mention *Olmstead*, let alone overrule it, the Court clearly based its exclusion of oral statements made to federal agents during an illegal arrest on its supervisory power to deter lawless conduct by federal officers and on the alternative ground that the incriminating statements were made under compulsive circumstances and were not the product of a free will. It is impossible for me to read into that noneavesdropping federal case an intent to overrule *Olmstead* implicitly. In short, the only way this Court can escape *Olmstead* here is to overrule it. Without expressly saying so, the Court's opinion, as my BROTHER DOUGLAS acknowledges, does just that. And that overruling is accomplished by the simple expedient of substituting for the Amendment's words, "The right of the people to be secure in their persons, houses, papers, and effects," the words "The right of the people to be secure in their privacy," words the Court believes the Framers should have used, but did not. I have frequently stated my opposition to such judicial substitution. Although here the Court uses it to expand the scope of the Fourth Amendment to include words, the Court has been applying the same process to contract the Fifth Amendment's privilege against self-incrimination so as to exclude all types of incriminating evidence but words, or what the Court prefers to call "testimonial evidence." See *United States* v. *Wade*, 388 U.S. 218; *Gilbert* v. *California*, 388 U.S. 263.

There is yet another reason why I would adhere to the holding of *Olmstead* that the Fourth Amendment does not apply to eavesdropping. Since the Framers in the first clause of the Amendment specified that only persons, houses, and things were to be protected, they obviously wrote the second clause, regulating search warrants, in reference only to such tangible things. To hold, as the Court does, that the first clause protects words, necessitates either a virtual rewriting of the particularity requirements of the Warrant Clause or a literal application of that clause's requirements and our cases construing them to situations they were never designed to cover. I am convinced that the Framers of the Amendment never intended this Court to do either, and yet it seems to me clear that the Court here does a little of both.

V.

Both the States and the National Government are at present confronted with a crime problem that threatens the peace, order, and tranquility of the people. There are, as I have pointed out, some constitutional commands that leave no room for doubt—certain procedures must be followed by courts regardless of how much more difficult they make it to convict and punish for crime. These commands we should enforce firmly and to the letter. But my objection to what the Court does today is the picking out of a broad general provision against unreasonable searches and seizures and the erecting out of it a constitutional obstacle against electronic eavesdropping that makes it impossible for lawmakers to overcome. Honest men may rightly differ on the potential dangers or benefits inherent in electronic eavesdropping and wiretapping. See *Lopez* v. *United States, supra*. But that is the very reason that legislatures, like New York's should be left free to pass laws about the subject, rather than be told that the Constitution forbids it on grounds no more forceful than the Court has been able to muster in this case.

MR. JUSTICE HARLAN, dissenting.

The Court in recent years has more and more taken to itself sole responsibility for setting the pattern of criminal law enforcement throughout the country. Time-honored distinctions between the constitutional protections afforded against federal authority by the Bill of Rights and those provided against state action by the Fourteenth Amendment have been obliterated, thus increasingly subjecting state criminal law enforcement policies to oversight by this Court. See, e.g., *Mapp* v. *Ohio*, 367 U.S. 643; *Ker* v. *California*, 374 U.S. 23; *Malloy* v. *Hogan*, 378 U.S. 1; *Murphy* v. *Waterfront Commission*, 378 U.S. 52. Newly contrived constitutional rights have been established without any apparent concern for the empirical process that goes with legislative reform. See, e.g., *Miranda* v. *Arizona*, 384 U.S. 436. And overlying the particular decisions to which this course has given rise is the fact that, short of future action by this Court, their impact can only be undone or modified by the slow and uncertain process of constitutional amendment.

Today's decision is in this mold. Despite the fact that the use of electronic eavesdropping devices as instruments of criminal law enforcement is currently being comprehensively addressed by the Congress and various other bodies in the country, the Court has chosen, quite unnecessarily, to decide this case in a manner which will seriously restrict, if not entirely thwart, such efforts, and will freeze further progress in this field, except as the Court may itself act or a constitutional amendment may set things right.

In my opinion what the Court is doing is very wrong, and I must respectfully dissent.

. . . .

MR. JUSTICE WHITE, dissenting.

With all due respect, I dissent from the majority's decision which unjustifiably strikes down "on its face" a 1938 New York statute applied by state officials in securing petitioner's conviction. In addition, I find no violation of petitioner's constitutional rights and I would affirm.

. . . .

[MR. JUSTICE WHITE's opinion includes a complete discussion of previous cases and a reprint of the President's Commission report.]

OMNIBUS CRIME CONTROL AND SAFE STREETS ACT OF 1968

Public Law 90–351, Title III, §§ 801–803, enacted June 19, 1968. Section 802 (82 Stat. 112, 213 *et seq.*) appears as codified and amended at 18 United States Code §§ 2510–2520 (1970).

TITLE III—WIRETAPPING AND ELECTRONIC SURVEILLANCE

FINDINGS

SEC. 801. On the basis of its own investigations and of published studies, the Congress makes the following findings:

(a) Wire communications are normally conducted through the use of facilities which form part of an interstate network. The same facilities are used for interstate and intrastate communications. There has been extensive wiretapping carried on without legal sanctions, and without the consent of any of the parties to the conversation. Electronic, mechanical, and other intercepting devices are being used to overhear oral conversations made in private, without the consent of any of the parties to such communications. The contents of these communications and evidence derived therefrom are being used by public and private parties as evidence in court and administrative proceedings, and by persons whose activities affect interstate commerce. The possession, manufacture, distribution, advertising, and use of these devices are facilitated by interstate commerce.

(b) In order to protect effectively the privacy of wire and oral communications, to protect the integrity of court and administrative proceedings, and to prevent the obstruction of interstate commerce, it is necessary for Congress to define on a uniform basis the circumstances and conditions under which the interception of wire and oral communications may be authorized, to prohibit any unauthorized interception of such communications, and the use of the contents thereof in evidence in courts and administrative proceedings.

(c) Organized criminals make extensive use of wire and oral communications in their criminal activities. The interception of such communications to obtain evidence of the commission of crimes or to prevent their commission is an indispensable aid to law enforcement and the administration of justice.

(d) To safeguard the privacy of innocent persons, the interception of wire or oral communications where none of the parties to the communication has consented to the interception should be allowed only when authorized by a court of competent jurisdiction and should remain under the control and supervision of the authorizing court. Interception of wire and oral communications should further be limited to certain major types of offenses and specific categories of crime with assurances that the interception is justified and that the information obtained thereby will not be misused.

SEC. 802. Part I of title 18, United States Code, is amended by adding at the end the following new chapter:

CHAPTER 119. WIRE INTERCEPTION AND INTERCEPTION OF ORAL COMMUNICATIONS

Section

§ 2510. Definitions

As used in this chapter—

(1) "wire communication" means any communication made in whole or in part through the use of facilities for the transmission of communications by the aid of wire, cable, or other like connection between the point of origin and the point of reception furnished or operated by any person engaged as a common carrier in providing or operating such facilities for the transmission of interstate or foreign communications;

(2) "oral communication" means any oral communication uttered by a person exhibiting an expectation that such communication is not subject to interception under circumstances justifying such expectation;

(3) "State" means any State of the United States, the District of Columbia, the Commonwealth of Puerto Rico, and any territory or possession of the United States;

(4) "intercept" means the aural acquisition of the contents of any wire or oral communication through the use of any electronic, mechanical, or other device.

(5) "electronic, mechanical, or other device" means any device or apparatus which can be used to in-

tercept a wire or oral communication other than—

(a) any telephone or telegraph instrument, equipment or facility, or any component thereof, (i) furnished to the subscriber or user by a communications common carrier in the ordinary course of its business and being used by the subscriber or user in the ordinary course of its business; or (ii) being used by a communications common carrier in the ordinary course of its business, or by an investigative or law enforcement officer in the ordinary course of his duties;

(b) a hearing aid or similar device being used to correct subnormal hearing to not better than normal;

(6) "person" means any employee, or agent of the United States or any State or political subdivision thereof, and any individual, partnership, association, joint stock company, trust, or corporation;

(7) "Investigative or law enforcement officer" means any officer of the United States or of a State or political subdivision thereof, who is empowered by law to conduct investigations of or to make arrests for offenses enumerated in this chapter, and any attorney authorized by law to prosecute or participate in the prosecution of such offenses;

(8) "contents," when used with respect to any wire or oral communication, includes any information concerning the identity of the parties to such communication or the existence, substance, purport,

or meaning of that communication;

(9) "Judge of competent jurisdiction" means—

(a) a judge of a United States district court or a United States court of appeals; and

(b) a judge of any court of general criminal jurisdiction of a State who is authorized by a statute of that State to enter orders authorizing interceptions of wire or oral communications;

(10) "communication common carrier" shall have the same meaning which is given the term "common carrier" by section 153(h) of title 47 of the United States Code; and

(11) "aggrieved person" means a person who was a party to any intercepted wire or oral communication or a person against whom the interception was directed.

§ 2511. Interception and disclosure of wire or oral communications prohibited

(1) Except as otherwise specifically provided in this chapter any person who—

(a) willfully intercepts, endeavors to intercept, or procures any other person to intercept or endeavor to intercept, any wire or oral communication;

(b) willfully uses, endeavors to use, or procures any other person to use or endeavor to use any electronic, mechanical, or other device to intercept any oral communication when—

(i) such device is affixed to, or otherwise transmits a signal through, a wire, cable, or other like connection used in wire communication; or

(ii) such device transmits communications by radio, or interferes with transmission of such communication; or

(iii) such person knows, or has reason to know, that such device or any component thereof has been sent through the mail or transported in interstate or foreign commerce; or

(iv) such use or endeavor to use (A) takes place on the premises of any business or other commercial establish-. ment the operations of which affect interstate or foreign commerce; or (B) obtains or is for the purpose of obtaining information relating to the operations of any business or other commercial establishment the operations of which affect interstate or foreign commerce; or

(v) such person acts in the District of Columbia, the Commonwealth of Puerto Rico, or any territory or possession of the United States;

(c) willfully discloses, or endeavors to disclose, to any other person the contents of any wire or oral communication, knowing or having reason to know that the information was obtained through the interception of a wire or oral communication in violation of this subsection; or

(d) willfully uses, or endeavors to use, the contents of any wire or oral communication, knowing or having reason to know that the information was obtained through the interception of a wire or oral communication in violation of this subsection;

shall be fined not more than $10,000 or imprisoned not more than five years, or both.

(2) (a) (i) It shall not be unlawful under this chapter for an operator of a switchboard, or an officer, employee, or agent of any communication common carrier, whose facilities are used in the transmission of a wire communication, to intercept, disclose, or use that communication in the normal course of his employment while engaged in any activity which is a necessary incident to the rendition of his service or to the protection of the rights or property of the carrier of such communication: *Provided,* That said communication common carriers shall not utilize service observing or random monitoring except for mechanical or service quality control checks.

(ii) It shall not be unlawful under this chapter for an officer, employee, or agent of any communication common carrier to provide information, facilities, or technical assistance to an investigative or law enforcement officer who, pursuant to this chapter, is authorized to intercept a wire or oral communication. [1]

(b) It shall not be unlawful under this chapter for an officer, employee, or agent of the Federal

[1] Subsections (2)(a)(i) and (ii) appear as amended by Pub.L. 91–358, Title II, § 211(a), July 29, 1970, 84 Stat. 654.

Communications Commission, in the normal course of his employment and in discharge of the monitoring responsibilities exercised by the Commission in the enforcement of chapter 5 of title 47 of the United States Code, to intercept a wire communication, or oral communication transmitted by radio, or to disclose or use the information thereby obtained.

(c) It shall not be unlawful under this chapter for a person acting under color of law to intercept a wire or oral communication, where such person is a party to the communication or one of the parties to the communication has given prior consent to such interception.

(d) It shall not be unlawful under this chapter for a person not acting under color of law to intercept a wire or oral communication where such person is a party to the communication or where one of the parties to the communication has given prior consent to such interception unless such communication is intercepted for the purpose of committing any criminal or tortious act in violation of the Constitution of laws of the United States or of any State or for the purpose of committing any other injurious act.

(3) Nothing contained in this chapter or in section 605 of the Communications Act of 1934 (48 Stat. 1143; 47 U.S.C. § 605) shall limit the constitutional power of the President to take such measures as he deems necessary to protect the Nation against actual or potential attack or other hostile acts of a foreign power, to obtain foreign intelligence information deemed essential to the security of the United States, or to protect national security information against foreign intelligence activities. Nor shall anything contained in this chapter be deemed to limit the constitutional power of the President to take such measures as he deems necessary to protect the United States against the overthrow of the Government by force or other unlawful means, or against any other clear and present danger to the structure or existence of the Government. The contents of any wire or oral communication intercepted by authority of the President in the exercise of the foregoing powers may be received in evidence in any trial hearing, or other proceeding only where such interception was reasonable, and shall not be otherwise used or disclosed except as is necessary to implement that power.

§ 2512. Manufacture, distribution, possession, and advertising of wire or oral communication intercepting devices prohibited

(1) Except as otherwise specifically provided in this chapter, any person who willfully—

(a) sends through the mail, or sends or carries in interstate or foreign commerce, any electronic, mechanical, or other device, knowing or having reason to know that the design of such device renders it primarily useful for the purpose of the surreptitious interception of wire or oral communications;

(b) manufactures, assembles, possesses, or sells any electronic, mechanical, or other device, knowing or having reason to know that the design of such device renders it primarily useful for the purpose of the surreptitious interception of wire or oral communications, and that such device or any component thereof has been or will be sent through the mail or transported in interstate or foreign commerce; or

(c) places in any newspaper, magazine, handbill, or other publication any advertisement of—

(i) any electronic, mechanical, or other device knowing or having reason to know that the design of such device renders it primarily useful for the purpose of the surreptitious interception of wire or oral communications; or

(ii) any other electronic, mechanical, or other device, where such advertisement promotes the use of such device for the purpose of the surreptitious interception of wire or oral communications, knowing or having reason to know that such advertisement will be sent through the mail or transported in interstate or foreign commerce,

shall be fined not more than $10,000 or imprisoned not more than five years, or both.

(2) It shall not be unlawful under this section for—

(a) a communications common carrier or an officer, agent, or employee of, or a person under contract with, a communications common carrier, in the normal course of the communications common carrier's business, or

(b) an officer, agent, or employee of, or a person under contract with, the United States, a State, or a political subdivision thereof, in the normal course of the activities of the United States, a State, or a political subdivision thereof, to send through the mail, send or carry in interstate or foreign commerce, or manufacture, assemble, possess, or sell any electronic, mechanical, or other device knowing or having reason to know that the design of such device renders it primarily useful for the purpose of the surreptitious interception of wire or oral communications.

§ 2513. Confiscation of wire or oral communication intercepting devices

Any electronic, mechanical, or other device used, sent, carried, manufactured, assembled, possessed, sold, or advertised in violation of section 2511 or section 2512 of this chapter may be seized and forfeited to the United States. All provisions of law relating to (1) the seizure, summary and judicial forfeiture, and condemnation of vessels, vehicles, merchandise, and baggage for violations of the customs laws contained in title 19 of the United States Code, (2) the disposition of such vessels, vehicles, merchandise, and baggage or the proceeds from the sale thereof, (3) the remission or mitigation of such forfeiture, (4) the compromise of claims, and (5) the award of compensation to informers in respect of such forfeitures, shall apply to seizures and forfeitures incurred, or alleged to have been incurred, under the provisions of this section, insofar as applicable and not inconsistent with the provisions of this section; except that such duties as are imposed upon the collector of customs or any other person with respect to the seizure and forfeiture of vessels, vehicles, merchandise, and baggage under the provisions of the customs laws contained in title 19 of the United States Code shall be performed with respect to seizure and forfeiture of electronic, mechanical, or other intercepting devices under this section by such officers, agents, or other persons as may be authorized or designated for that purpose by the Attorney General.

§ 2514.   Immunity of witnesses

Repealed. Pub.L. 91–452, Title II, § 227(a), Oct. 15, 1970, 84 Stat. 930. [²]

[²] Section 2514 of the 1968 Crime Control Act providing for immunity of witnesses who give testimony in grand jury or court proceedings was repealed in 1970 by Pub.L. 91–452, Title II, § 227(a), Oct. 15, 1970 (84 Stat. 930). Repeal of this section effective four years following sixtieth day after date of enactment of Pub.L. 91–152, which was approved Oct. 15, 1970, such repeal not affecting any immunity to which any individual was entitled under this section by reason of any testimony or other information given before such date. Subject matter now covered under 18 U.S.C. §§ 6002, 6003.

§ 2515.   Prohibition of use as evidence of intercepted wire or oral communications

Whenever any wire or oral communication has been intercepted, no part of the contents of such communication and no evidence derived therefrom may be received in evidence in any trial, hearing, or other proceeding in or before any court, grand jury, department, officer, agency, regulatory body, legislative committee, or other authority of the United States, a State, or a political subdivision thereof if the disclosure of that information would be in violation of this chapter.

§ 2516.   Authorization for interception of wire or oral communications

(1) The Attorney General, or any Assistant Attorney General specially designated by the Attorney General, may authorize an application to a Federal judge of competent jurisdiction for, and such judge may grant in conformity with section 2518 of this chapter an order authorizing or approving the interception of wire or oral communications by the Federal Bureau of Investigation, or a Federal agency having responsibility for the investigation of the offense as to which the application is made, when such interception may provide or has provided evidence of—

(a) any offense punishable by death or by imprisonment for more than one year under sections 2274 through 2277 of title 42 of the United States Code (relating to the enforcement of the Atomic Energy Act of 1954), or under the following chapters of this title: chapter 37 (relating to espionage), chapter 105 (relating to sabotage), chapter 115 (relating to treason), or chapter 102 (relating to riots);

(b) a violation of section 186 or section 501(c) of title 29, United States Code (dealing with restrictions on payments and loans to labor organizations), or any offense which involves murder, kidnapping, robbery, or extortion, and which is punishable under this title:

(c) any offense which is punishable under the following sections of this title: section 201 (bribery of public officials and witnesses), section 224 (bribery in sporting contests), subsection (d), (e), (f), (g), (h) or (i) of section 844 (unlawful use of explosives), section 1084 (transmission of wagering information), section 1503 (influencing or injuring an officer, juror, or witness generally), section 1510 (obstruction of criminal investigations), section 1511 (obstruction of State or local law enforcement), section 1751 (Presidential assassinations, kidnapping, and assault), section 1951 (interference with commerce by threats or violence), section 1952 (interstate and foreign travel or transportation in aid of racketeering enterprises), section 1954 (offer, acceptance, or solicitation to influence operations of employee benefit plan), section 1955 (prohibition of business enterprises of gambling),

section 659 (theft from interstate shipment), section 664 (embezzlement from pension and welfare funds), sections 2314 and 2315 (interstate transportation of stolen property), section 1963 (violations with respect to racketeer influenced and corrupt organizations) or section 351 violations with respect to congressional assassination, kidnapping and assault); [3]

(d) any offense involving counterfeiting punishable under section 471, 472, or 473 of this title;

(e) any offense involving bankruptcy fraud or the manufacture, importation, receiving, concealment, buying, selling, or otherwise dealing in narcotic drugs, marihuana, or other dangerous drugs, punishable under any law of the United States;

(f) any offense including extortionate credit transactions under sections 892, 893, or 894 of this title; or

(g) any conspiracy to commit any of the foregoing offenses.

(2) The principal prosecuting attorney of any State, or the principal prosecuting attorney of any political subdivision thereof, if such attorney is authorized by a statute of that State to make application to a State court judge of competent jurisdiction for an order authorizing or approving the in-

---

[3] Subsection (c) appears as amended by Pub.L. 91–452, Title VIII, § 810, Title IX, § 902(a), Title XI, § 1103, Oct. 15, 1970, 84 Stat. 940, 947, 959; Pub.L. 91–644, Title IV, § 16, Jan. 2, 1971, 84 Stat. 1891.

terception of wire or oral communications, may apply to such judge for, and such judge may grant in conformity with section 2518 of this chapter and with the applicable State statute an order authorizing, or approving the interception of wire or oral communications by investigative or law enforcement officers having responsibility for the investigation of the offense as to which the application is made, when such interception may provide or has provided evidence of the commission of the offense of murder, kidnapping, gambling, robbery, bribery, extortion, or dealing in narcotic drugs, marihuana or other dangerous drugs, or other crime dangerous to life, limb, or property, and punishable by imprisonment for more than one year, designated in any applicable State statute authorizing such interception, or any conspiracy to commit any of the foregoing offenses.

§ 2517. Authorization for disclosure and use of intercepted wire or oral communications

(1) Any investigative or law enforcement officer who, by any means authorized by this chapter, has obtained knowledge of the contents of any wire or oral communication, or evidence derived therefrom, may disclose such contents to another investigative or law enforcement officer to the extent that such disclosure is appropriate to the proper performance of the official duties of the

officer making or receiving the disclosure.

(2) Any investigative or law enforcement officer who, by any means authorized by this chapter, has obtained knowledge of the contents of any wire or oral communication or evidence derived therefrom may use such contents to the extent such use is appropriate to the proper performance of his official duties.

(3) Any person who has received, by any means authorized by this chapter, any information concerning a wire or oral communication, or evidence derived therefrom intercepted in accordance with the provisions of this chapter may disclose the contents of that communication or such derivative evidence while giving testimony under oath or affirmation in any proceeding held under the authority of the United States or of any State or political subdivision thereof.[¹]

(4) No otherwise privileged wire or oral communication intercepted in accordance with, or in violation of, the provisions of this chapter shall lose its privileged character.

(5) When an investigative or law enforcement officer, while engaged in intercepting wire or oral communications in the manner authorized herein, intercepts wire or oral communications relating to offenses other than those specified in the order of authorization or ap-

---

[¹] Subsection (3) appears as amended by Pub.L. 91–452, Title IX, § 902(b), Oct. 15, 1970, 84 Stat. 947.

proval, the contents thereof, and evidence derived therefrom, may be disclosed or used as provided in subsection (1) and (2) of this section. Such contents and any evidence derived therefrom may be used under subsection (3) of this section when authorized or approved by a judge of competent jurisdiction where such judge finds on subsequent application that the contents were otherwise intercepted in accordance with the provisions of this chapter. Such application shall be made as soon as practicable.

§ 2518. Procedure for interception of wire or oral communications

(1) Each application for an order authorizing or approving the interception of a wire or oral communication shall be made in writing upon oath or affirmation to a judge of competent jurisdiction and shall state the applicant's authority to make such application. Each application shall include the following information:

(a) the identity of the investigative or law enforcement officer making the application, and the officer authorizing the application;

(b) a full and complete statement of the facts and circumstances relied upon by the applicant, to justify his belief that an order should be issued, including (i) details as to the particular offense that has been, is being, or is about to be committed, (ii) a particular descrip-

tion of the nature and location of the facilities from which or the place where the communication is to be intercepted, (iii) a particular description of the type of communications sought to be intercepted, (iv) the identity of the person, if known, committing the offense and whose communications are to be intercepted;

(c) a full and complete statement as to whether or not other investigative procedures have been tried and failed or why they reasonably appear to be unlikely to succeed if tried or to be too dangerous;

(d) a statement of the period of time for which the interception is required to be maintained. If the nature of the investigation is such that the authorization for interception should not automatically terminate when the described type of communication has been first obtained, a particular description of facts establishing probable cause to believe that additional communications of the same type will occur thereafter;

(e) a full and complete statement of the facts concerning all previous applications known to the individual authorizing and making the application, made to any judge for authorization to intercept, or for approval of interceptions of, wire or oral communications involving any of the same persons, facilities or places specified in the application, and the action taken by the judge on each such application; and

(f) where the application is for the extension of an order, a statement setting forth the results thus far obtained from the interception, or a reasonable explanation of the failure to obtain such results.

(2) The judge may require the applicant to furnish additional testimony or documentary evidence in support of the application.

(3) Upon such application the judge may enter an ex parte order, as requested or as modified, authorizing or approving interception of wire or oral communications within the territorial jurisdiction of the court in which the judge is sitting, if the judge determines on the basis of the facts submitted by the applicant that—

(a) there is probable cause for belief that an individual is committing, has committed, or is about to commit a particular offense enumerated in section 2516 of this chapter;

(b) there is probable cause for belief that particular communications concerning that offense will be obtained through such interception;

(c) normal investigative procedures have been tried and have failed or reasonably appear to be unlikely to succeed if tried or to be too dangerous;

(d) there is probable cause for belief that the facilities from which, or the place where, the wire or oral communications are to be intercepted are being used, or are about to be used, in connection with the commission of such offense, or are leased to, listed in the name of, or commonly used by such person.

(4) Each order authorizing or approving the interception of any wire or oral communication shall specify—

(a) the identity of the person, if known, whose communications are to be intercepted;

(b) the nature and location of the communications facilities as to which, or the place where, authority to intercept is granted;

(c) a particular description of the type of communication sought to be intercepted, and a statement of the particular offense to which it relates;

(d) the identity of the agency authorized to intercept the communications, and of the person authorizing the application; and

(e) the period of time during which such interception is authorized, including a statement as to whether or not the interception shall automatically terminate when the described communication has been first obtained.

An order authorizing the interception of a wire or oral communication shall, upon request of the applicant, direct that a communication common carrier, landlord, custodian or other person shall furnish the applicant forthwith all information, facilities, and technical assistance necessary to accomplish the interception unobtrusively and with a minimum of interference with the services that such carrier, landlord, custodian, or person is according the person whose communications are to be intercepted.

Any communication common carrier, landlord, custodian or other person furnishing such facilities or technical assistance shall be compensated therefor by the applicant at the prevailing rates.[5]

(5) No order entered under this section may authorize or approve the interception of any wire or oral communication for any period longer than is necessary to achieve the objective of the authorization, nor in any event longer than thirty days. Extensions of an order may be granted, but only upon application for an extension made in accordance with subsection (1) of this section and the court making the findings required by subsection (3) of this section. The period of extension shall be no longer than the authorizing judge deems necessary to achieve the purposes for which it was granted and in no event for longer than thirty days. Every order and extension thereof shall contain a provision that the authorization to intercept shall be executed as soon as practicable, shall be conducted in such a way as to minimize the interception of communications not otherwise subject to interception under this chapter, and must terminate upon attainment of the authorized objective, or in any event in thirty days.

(6) Whenever an order authorizing interception is entered pursuant to this chapter, the order may require reports to be made to the judge who issued the order showing what progress has been made toward achievement of the authorized objective and the need for continued interception. Such reports shall be made at such intervals as the judge may require.

(7) Notwithstanding any other provision of this chapter, any investigative or law enforcement officer, specially designated by the Attorney General or by the principal prosecuting attorney of any State or subdivision thereof acting pursuant to a statute of that State, who reasonably determines that—

(a) an emergency situation exists with respect to conspiratorial activities threatening the national security interest or to conspiratorial activities characteristic of organized crime that requires a wire or oral communication to be intercepted before an order authorizing such interception can with due diligence be obtained, and

(b) there are grounds upon which an order could be entered under this chapter to authorize such interception, may intercept such wire or oral communication if an application for an order approving the interception is made in accordance with this section within forty-eight hours after the interception has occurred, or begins to occur. In the absence of an order, such interception shall immediately terminate when the communication sought is obtained or when the application for the order is denied, whichever is earlier. In the event such application for ap-

[5] This paragraph added by Pub.L. 91-358, Title II, § 211(b), July 29, 1970, 84 Stat. 654.

proval is denied, or in any other case where the interception is terminated without an order having been issued, the contents of any wire or oral communication intercepted shall be treated as having been obtained in violation of this chapter, and an inventory shall be served as provided for in subsection (d) of this section on the person named in the application.

(8)(a) The contents of any wire or oral communication intercepted by any means authorized by this chapter shall, if possible, be recorded on tape or wire or other comparable device. The recording of the contents of any wire or oral communication under this subsection shall be done in such way as will protect the recording from editing or other alterations. Immediately upon the expiration of the period of the order, or extensions thereof, such recordings shall be made available to the judge issuing such order and sealed under his directions. Custody of the recordings shall be wherever the judge orders. They shall not be destroyed except upon an order of the issuing or denying judge and in any event shall be kept for ten years. Duplicate recordings may be made for use or disclosure pursuant to the provisions of subsections (1) and (2) of section 2517 of this chapter for investigations The presence of the seal provided for by this subsection, or a satisfactory explanation for the absence thereof, shall be a prerequisite for the use or disclosure of the contents of any wire or oral communication or evidence derived therefrom under subsection (3) of section 2517.

(b) Applications made and orders granted under this chapter shall be sealed by the judge. Custody of the applications and orders shall be wherever the judge directs. Such applications and orders shall be disclosed only upon a showing of good cause before a judge of competent jurisdiction and shall not be destroyed except on order of the issuing or denying judge, and in any event shall be kept for ten years.

(c) Any violation of the provisions of this subsection may be punished as contempt of the issuing or denying judge.

(d) Within a reasonable time but not later than ninety days after the filing of an application for an order of approval under section 2518(7) (b) which is denied or the termination of the period of an order or extensions thereof, the issuing or denying judge shall cause to be served, on the persons named in the order or the application, and such other parties to intercepted communications as the judge may determine in his discretion that is in the interest of justice, an inventory which shall include notice of—

(1) the fact of the entry of the order or the application;

(2) the date of the entry and the period of authorized, approved or disapproved interception, or the denial of the application; and

(3) the fact that during the period wire or oral communications were or were not intercepted.

The judge, upon the filing of a motion, may in his discretion make available to such person or his counsel for inspection such portions of the intercepted communications, applications and orders as the judge determines to be in the interest of justice. On an ex parte showing of good cause to a judge of competent jurisdiction the serving of the inventory required by this subsection may be postponed.

(9) The contents of any intercepted wire or oral communication or evidence derived therefrom shall not be received in evidence or otherwise disclosed in any trial, hearing, or other proceeding in a Federal or State court unless each party, not less than ten days before the trial, hearing, or proceeding, has been furnished with a copy of the court order, and accompanying application, under which the interception was authorized or approved. This ten-day period may be waived by the judge if he finds that it was not possible to furnish the party with the above information ten days before the trial, hearing, or proceeding and that the party will not be prejudiced by the delay in receiving such information.

(10)(a) Any aggrieved person in any trial, hearing, or proceeding in or before any court, department, officer, agency, regulatory body, or other authority of the United States, a State, or a political subdivision thereof, may move to suppress the contents of any intercepted wire or oral communication, or evidence derived therefrom, on the grounds that—

(i) the communication was unlawfully intercepted;

(ii) the order of authorization or approval under which it was intercepted is insufficient on its face; or

(iii) the interception was not made in conformity with the order of authorization or approval.

Such motion shall be made before the trial, hearing, or proceeding unless there was no opportunity to make such motion or the person was not aware of the grounds of the motion. If the motion is granted, the contents of the intercepted wire or oral communication, or evidence derived therefrom, shall be treated as having been obtained in violation of this chapter. The judge, upon the filing of such motion by the aggrieved person, may in his discretion make available to the aggrieved person or his counsel for inspection such portions of the intercepted communication or evidence derived therefrom as the judge determines to be in the interests of justice.

(b) In addition to any other right to appeal, the United States shall have the right to appeal from an order granting a motion to suppress made under paragraph (a) of this subsection, or the denial of an application for an order of approval, if the United States attorney shall certify to the judge or other official granting such motion or denying such application that the appeal is not taken for purposes of delay. Such appeal shall be taken within thirty days after the date the order was entered and shall be diligently prosecuted.

§ 2519. Reports concerning intercepted wire or oral communications

(1) Within thirty days after the expiration of an order (or each extension thereof) entered under section 2518, or the denial of an order approving an interception, the issuing or denying judge shall report to the Administrative Office of the United States Courts—

(a) the fact that an order or extension was applied for;

(b) the kind of order or extension applied for;

(c) the fact that the order or extension was granted as applied for, was modified, or was denied;

(d) the period of interceptions authorized by the order, and the number and duration of any extensions of the order;

(e) the offense specified in the order or application, or extension of an order;

(f) the identity of the applying investigative or law enforcement officer and agency making the application and the person authorizing the application; and

(g) the nature of the facilities from which or the place where communications were to be intercepted.

(2) In January of each year the Attorney General, an Assistant Attorney General specially designated by the Attorney General, or the principal prosecuting attorney of a State, or the principal prosecuting attorney for any political subdivision of a State, shall report to the Administrative Office of the United States Courts—

(a) the information required by paragraphs (a) through (g) of subsection (1) of this section with respect to each application for an order or extension made during the preceding calendar year;

(b) a general description of the interceptions made under such order or extension, including (i) the approximate nature and frequency of incriminating communications intercepted, (ii) the approximate nature and frequency of other communications intercepted, (iii) the approximate number of persons whose communications were intercepted, and (iv) the approximate nature, amount, and cost of the manpower and other resources used in the interceptions;

(c) the number of arrests resulting from interceptions made under such order or extension, and the offenses for which arrests were made;

(d) the number of trials resulting from such interceptions;

(e) the number of motions to suppress made with respect to such interceptions, and the number granted or denied;

(f) the number of convictions resulting from such interceptions and the offenses for which the convictions were obtained and a general assessment of the importance of the interceptions; and

(g) the information required by paragraphs (b) through (f)

of this subsection with respect to orders or extensions obtained in a preceding calendar year.

(3) In April of each year the Director of the Administrative Office of the United States Courts shall transmit to the Congress a full and complete report concerning the number of applications for orders authorizing or approving the interception of wire or oral communications and the number of orders and extensions granted or denied during the preceding calendar year. Such report shall include a summary and analysis of the data required to be filed with the Administrative Office by subsections (1) and (2) of this section. The Director of the Administrative Office of the United States Courts is authorized to issue binding regulations dealing with the content and form of the reports required to be filed by subsections (1) and (2) of this section.

§ 2520. Recovery of civil damages authorized

Any person whose wire or oral communications is intercepted, disclosed, or used in violation of this chapter shall (1) have a civil cause of action against any person who intercepts, discloses, or uses, or procures any other person to intercept, disclose, or use such communications, and (2) be entitled to recover from any such person—

(a) actual damages but not less than liquidated damages computed at the rate of $100 a day for each day of violation or $1,000, whichever is higher;

(b) punitive damages; and

(c) a reasonable attorney's fee and other litigation costs reasonably incurred.

A good faith reliance on a court order or legislative authorization shall constitute a complete defense to any civil or criminal action brought under this chapter or under any other law.[6]

Sec. 803. Section 605 of the Communications Act of 1934 (48 Stat. 1103), codified at 47 U.S.C. § 605, is amended to read as follows:

UNAUTHORIZED PUBLICATION OF COMMUNICATIONS

Sec. 605. Except as authorized by chapter 119, title 18, United States Code, no person receiving, assisting in receiving, transmitting, or assisting in transmitting, any interstate or foreign communication by wire or radio shall divulge or publish the existence, contents, substance, purport, effect, or meaning thereof, except through authorized channels of transmission or reception, (1) to any person other than the addressee, his agent, or attorney, (2) to a person employed or authorized to forward such communication to its destination, (3) to proper accounting or distributing officers of the various communicating centers over which the communication may be passed, (4) to the master of a ship under

[6] This paragraph amended by Pub.L. 91–358, Title II, § 211(c), July 29, 1970, 84 Stat. 654.

whom he is serving, (5) in response to a subpoena issued by a court of competent jurisdiction, or (6) on demand of other lawful authority. No person not being authorized by the sender shall intercept any radio communication and divulge or publish the existence, contents, substance, purport, effect, or meaning of such intercepted communication to any person. No person not being entitled thereto shall receive or assist in receiving any interstate or foreign communication by radio and use such communication (or any information therein contained) for his own benefit or for the benefit of another not entitled thereto. No person having received any intercepted radio communication or having become acquainted with the contents, substance, purport, effect, or meaning of such communication (or any part thereof) knowing that such communication was intercepted, shall divulge or publish the existence, contents, substance, purport, effect, or meaning of such communication (or any part thereof) or use such communication (or any information therein contained) for his own benefit or for the benefit of another not entitled thereto. This section shall not apply to the receiving, divulging, publishing, or utilizing the contents of any radio communication which is broadcast or transmitted by amateurs or others for the use of the general public, or which relates to ships in distress.

UNITED STATES v. WHITE

401 U.S. 745, 28 L.Ed.2d 453, 91 S.Ct. 1122 (1971)

Defendant was convicted in the United States District Court for the Northern District of Illinois, Eastern Division, of narcotics violations and he appealed. The United States Court of Appeals for the Seventh Circuit, 405 F.2d 838, reversed and remanded, and certiorari was granted. MR. JUSTICE WHITE announced the judgment of the Supreme Court and delivered an opinion in which it was held that where radio transmitter was concealed on the person of an informant with knowledge of the informant, and where conversations between the informant and defendant at various locations, including defendant's home, were overheard when the frequency of the transmitter was monitored, without warrant, by government agents, who testified as to the conversations at defendant's trial, there was no violation of defendant's Fourth Amendment right to be secure against unreasonable searches and seizures.

Judgment of Court of Appeals reversed.

MR. JUSTICE BLACK filed statement concurring in judgment; MR. JUSTICE BRENNAN filed opinion concurring in result; MR. JUSTICE DOUGLAS, MR. JUSTICE HARLAN, and MR. JUSTICE MARSHALL dissented and filed opinions.

MR. JUSTICE WHITE announced the judgment of the Court and an opinion in which THE CHIEF JUSTICE, MR. JUSTICE STEWART, and MR. JUSTICE BLACKMUN join.

In 1966, respondent James A. White was tried and convicted under two consolidated indictments charging various illegal transactions in narcotics violative of 26 U.S.C. § 4705(a) and 21 U.S.C. § 174. He was fined and sentenced as a second offender to 25-year concurrent sentences. The issue before us is whether the Fourth Amendment bars from evidence the testimony of governmental agents who related certain conversations which had occurred between defendant White and a government informant, Harvey Jackson, and which the agents overheard by monitoring the frequency of a radio transmitter carried by Jackson and concealed on his person. On four occasions the conversations took place in Jackson's home; each of these conversations was overheard by an agent concealed in a kitchen closet with Jackson's consent and by a second agent outside the house using a radio receiver. Four other conversations—one in respondent's home, one in a restaurant, and two in Jackson's car—were overheard by the use of radio equipment. The prosecution was unable to locate and produce Jackson at the trial and the trial court overruled objections to the testimony of the agents who conducted the electronic surveillance. The jury returned a guilty verdict and defendant appealed.

The Court of Appeals read *Katz* v. *United States*, 389 U.S. 347 (1967), as overruling *On Lee* v. *United States*, 343 U.S. 747 (1952), and interpreting the Fourth Amendment to forbid the introduction of the agents' testimony in the circumstances of this case. Accordingly, the court reversed but without adverting to the fact that the transactions at issue here had occurred before *Katz* was decided in this Court. In our view, the Court of Appeals misinterpreted both the *Katz* case and the Fourth Amendment and in any event erred in applying the *Katz* case to events which occurred before that decision was rendered by this Court.

I.

Until *Katz* v. *United States*, neither wiretapping nor electronic eavesdropping violated a defendant's Fourth Amendment rights "unless there has been an official search and seizure of his person, or such a seizure of his papers or his tangible material effects, or an actual physical invasion of his house 'or curtilage' for the purpose of making a seizure." *Olmstead* v. *United States*, 277 U.S. 438, 466 (1928); *Goldman* v. *United States*, 316 U.S. 129, 135–136 (1942). But where "eavesdropping was accomplished by means of an unauthorized physical penetration into the premises occupied" by the defendant, although falling short of a "technical trespass under the local property law," the Fourth Amendment was violated and any evidence of what was seen and heard, as well as tangible objects seized, were considered inadmissible fruits of an unlawful invasion. *Silverman v. United States*, 365 U.S. 505, 509, 511 (1961); see also *Wong Sun v. United States*, 371 U.S. 471 (1963); *Berger v. New York*, 388 U.S. 41, 52 (1967); *Alderman v. United States*, 394 U.S. 165, 177–178 (1969).

Katz v. United States, however, finally swept away doctrines that electronic eavesdropping is permissible under the Fourth Amendment unless physical invasion of a constitutionally protected area produced the challenged evidence. In that case government agents, without petitioner's consent or knowledge, attached a listening device to the outside of a public telephone booth and recorded the defendant's end of his telephone conversations. In declaring the recordings inadmissible in evidence in the absence of a warrant authorizing the surveillance, the Court overruled *Olmstead* and *Goldman* and held that the absence of physical intrusion into the telephone booth did not justify using electronic devices in listening to and recording Katz's words, thereby violating the privacy on which he justifiably relied while using the telephone in those circumstances.

The Court of Appeals understood *Katz* to render inadmissible against White the agents' testimony concerning conversations which Jackson broadcast to them. We cannot agree. *Katz* involved no revelation to the Government by a party to conversations with the defendant nor did the Court indicate in any way that a defendant has a justifiable and constitutionally protected expectation that a person with whom he is conversing will not then or later reveal the conversation to the police.

Hoffa v. United States, 385 U.S. 293 (1966), which was left undisturbed by *Katz*, held that however strongly a defendant may trust an apparent colleague, his expectations in this respect are not protected by the Fourth Amendment when it turns out that the colleague is a government agent regularly communicating with the authorities. In these circumstances, "no interest legitimately protected by the Fourth Amendment is involved," for that amendment affords no protection to "a wrongdoer's misplaced belief that a person to whom he voluntarily confides his wrongdoing will not reveal it." [*Id.* at 302.] No warrant to "search and seize" is required in such circumstances, nor is it when the Government sends to defendant's home a secret agent who conceals his identity and makes a purchase of narcotics from the accused, *Lewis v. United States*, 385 U.S. 206 (1966), or when the same agent, unbeknown to the defendant, carries electronic equipment to record the defendant's words and the evidence so gathered is later offered in evidence. *Lopez v. United States*, 373 U.S. 427 (1963).

Conceding that *Hoffa*, *Lewis*, and *Lopez* remained unaffected by *Katz*, the Court of Appeals nevertheless read both *Katz* and the Fourth Amendment to require a different result if the agent not only records his conversations with the defendant but instantaneously transmits them electronically to other agents equipped with radio receivers. Where this occurs, the Court of Appeals held, the Fourth Amendment is violated and the testimony of the listening agents must be excluded from evidence.

To reach this result it was necessary for the Court of Appeals to hold that *On Lee* v. *United States* was no longer good law. In that case, which involved facts very similar to the case before us, the Court first rejected claims of a Fourth Amendment violation because the informer had not trespassed when he entered the defendant's premises and conversed with him. To this extent the Court's rationale cannot survive *Katz*. But the Court announced a second and independent ground for its decision; for it went on to say that overruling *Olmstead* and *Goldman* would be of no aid to On Lee since he "was talking confidentially and indiscreetly with one he trusted, and he was overheard. . . . It would be a dubious service to the genuine liberties protected by the Fourth Amendment to make them bedfellows with spurious liberties improvised by farfetched analogies which would liken eavesdropping on a conversation, with the connivance of one of the parties, to an unreasonable search or seizure. We find no violation of the Fourth Amendment here." 343 U.S., at 753–754. We see no indication in *Katz* that the Court meant to disturb that understanding of the Fourth

Amendment or to disturb the result reached in the *On Lee* case, nor are we now inclined to overturn this view of the Fourth Amendment.

Concededly a police agent who conceals his police connections may write down for official use his conversations with a defendant and testify concerning them, without a warrant authorizing his encounters with the defendant and without otherwise violating the latter's Fourth Amendment rights. [Citation omitted.] For constitutional purposes, no different result is required if the agent instead of immediately reporting and transcribing his conversations with defendant, either (1) simultaneously records them with electronic equipment which he is carrying on his person, *Lopez* v. *United States, supra;* (2) or carries radio equipment which simultaneously transmits the conversations either to recording equipment located elsewhere or to other agents monitoring the transmitting frequency. *On Lee* v. *United States, supra.* If the conduct and revelations of an agent operating without electronic equipment do not invade the defendant's constitutionally justifiable expectations of privacy, neither does a simultaneous recording of the same conversations made by the agent or by others from transmissions received from the agent to whom the defendant is talking and whose trustworthiness the defendant necessarily risks.

Our problem is not what the privacy expectations of particular defendants in particular situations may be or the extent to which they may in fact have relied on the discretion of their companions. Very probably, individual defendants neither know nor suspect that their colleagues have gone or will go to the police or are carrying recorders or transmitters. Otherwise, conversation would cease and our problem with these encounters would be nonexistent or far different from those now before us. Our problem, in terms of the principles announced in *Katz*, is what expectations of privacy are constitutionally "justifiable"—what expectations the Fourth Amendment will protect in the absence of a warrant. So far, the law permits the frustration of actual expectations of privacy by permitting authorities to use the testimony of those associates who for one reason or another have determined to turn to the police, as well as by authorizing the use of informants in the manner exemplified by *Hoffa* and *Lewis*. If the law gives no protection to the wrongdoer whose trusted accomplice is or becomes a police agent, neither should it protect him when that same agent has recorded or transmitted the conversations which are later offered in evidence to prove the State's case. See *Lopez v. United States*, 373 U.S. 427 (1963).

Inescapably, one contemplating illegal activities must realize and risk that his companions may be reporting to the police. If he sufficiently doubts their trustworthiness, the association will very probably end or never materialize. But if he has no doubts, or allays

them, or risks what doubt he has, the risk is his. In terms of what his course will be, what he will or will not do or say, we are unpersuaded that he would distinguish between probable informers on the one hand and probable informers with transmitters on the other. Given the possibility or probability that one of his colleagues is cooperating with the police, it is only speculation to assert that the defendant's utterances would be substantially different or his sense of security any less if he also thought it possible that the suspected colleague is wired for sound. At least there is no persuasive evidence that the difference in this respect between the electronically equipped and the unequipped agent is substantial enough to require discrete constitutional recognition, particularly under the Fourth Amendment which is ruled by fluid concepts of "reasonableness."

Nor should we be too ready to erect constitutional barriers to relevant and probative evidence which is also accurate and reliable. An electronic recording will many times produce a more reliable rendition of what a defendant has said than will the unaided memory of a police agent. It may also be that with the recording in existence it is less likely that the informant will change his mind, less chance that threat or injury will suppress unfavorable evidence and less chance that cross-examination will confound the testimony. Considerations like these obviously do not favor the defendant, but we are not prepared to hold that a defendant who has no constitutional right to exclude the informer's unaided testimony nevertheless has a Fourth Amendment privilege against a more accurate version of the events in question.

It is thus untenable to consider the activities and reports of the police agent himself, though acting without a warrant, to be a "reasonable" investigative effort and lawful under the Fourth Amendment but to view the same agent with a recorder or transmitter as conducting an "unreasonable" and unconstitutional search and seizure. Our opinion is currently shared by Congress and the Executive Branch, Title III, Omnibus Crime Control and Safe Streets Act of 1968, 82 Stat. 212 et seq., 18 U.S.C. §§ 2510 et seq. (1964 ed., Supp. V) and the American Bar Association. ABA Project on Minimum Standards for Criminal Justice, Standards Relating to Electronic Surveillance § 4.1 (Final Draft 1971). It is also the result reached by prior cases in this Court. On Lee, supra; Lopez v. United States, supra.

No different result should obtain where, as in On Lee and the instant case, the informer disappears and is unavailable at trial; for the issue of whether specified events on a certain day violate the Fourth Amendment should not be determined by what later happens to the informer. His unavailability at trial and proffering the testimony of other agents may raise evidentiary problems or pose issues of prosecutorial misconduct with respect to the informer's disappearance, but they do not appear critical to deciding whether prior events invaded the defendant's Fourth Amendment rights.

II.

The Court of Appeals was in error for another reason. In Desist v. United States, 394 U.S. 244 (1969), we held that our decision in Katz v. United States applied only to those electronic surveillances which occurred subsequent to the date of that decision. Here the events in question took place in late 1965 and early 1966, long prior to Katz. We adhere to the rationale of Desist, see Williams v. United States, 401 U.S. 646. It was error for the Court of Appeals to dispose of this case based on its understanding of the principles announced in the Katz case. The court should have judged this case by the pre-Katz law and under that law, as On Lee clearly holds, the electronic surveillance here involved did not violate White's rights to be free from unreasonable searches and seizures.

The judgment of the Court of Appeals is reversed.

It is so ordered.

MR. JUSTICE BLACK, while adhering to his views expressed in Linkletter v. Walker, 381 U.S. 618, 640 (1965), concurs in the judgment of the Court for the reasons set forth in his dissent in Katz v. United States, 389 U.S. 347, 364 (1967).

MR. JUSTICE BRENNAN, concurring in the result. [That opinion is not included.]

MR. JUSTICE DOUGLAS, dissenting.

I.

The issue in this case is clouded and concealed by the very discussion of it in legalistic terms. What the ancients knew as "eavesdropping," we now call "electronic surveillance"; but to equate the two is to treat man's first gunpowder on the same level as the nuclear bomb. Electronic surveillance is the greatest leveler of human privacy ever known. How most forms of it can be held "reasonable" within the meaning of the Fourth Amendment is a mystery. To be sure the Constitution and Bill of Rights are not to be read as covering only the technology known in the 18th century. Otherwise its concept of "commerce" would be hopeless when it comes to the management of modern affairs. At the same time the concepts of privacy which the Founders enshrined in the Fourth Amendment vanish completely when we slavishly allow an all-powerful government, proclaiming law and order, efficiency, and other benign purposes, to penetrate all the walls and doors which men need to shield them from the pressures of a turbulent life around them and give them the health and strength to carry on.

That is why a "strict construction" of the Fourth Amendment is necessary if every man's liberty and privacy are to be constitutionally honored

. . . .

MR. JUSTICE HARLAN, dissenting.

. . . .

I.

. . . We deal here with the constitutional validity of instantaneous third-party electronic eavesdropping, conducted by federal law enforcement officers, without any prior judicial approval of the technique utilized, but with the consent and cooperation of a participant in the conversation, and where the substance of the matter electronically overheard is related in a federal criminal trial by those who eavesdropped as direct, not merely corroborative, evidence of the guilt of the nonconsenting party. The magnitude of the issue at hand is evidenced not simply by the obvious doctrinal difficulty of weighing such activity in the Fourth Amendment balance, but also, and more importantly, by the prevalence of police utilization of this technique. . . .

. . . .

III.

B

. . . .

Finally, it is too easy to forget—and, hence, too often forgotten—that the issue here is whether to interpose a search warrant procedure between law enforcement agencies engaging in electronic eavesdropping and the public generally. By casting its "risk analysis" solely in terms of the expectations and risks that "wrongdoers" or "one contemplating illegal activities" ought to bear, the plurality opinion, I think, misses the mark entirely. On Lee does not simply mandate that criminals must daily run the risk of unknown eavesdroppers prying into their private affairs; it subjects each and every law-abiding member of society to that risk. The very purpose of interposing the Fourth Amendment warrant requirement is to redistribute the privacy risks throughout society in a way that produces the results the plurality opinion ascribes to the On Lee rule. Abolition of On Lee would not end electronic eavesdropping. It would prevent public officials from engaging in that practice unless they first had probable cause to suspect an individual of involvement in illegal activities and had tested their version of the facts before a detached judicial officer. The interest On Lee fails to protect is the expectation of the ordinary citizen, who has never engaged in illegal conduct in his life, that he may carry on his private discourse freely, openly, and spontaneously without measuring his every word against the connotations it might carry when instantaneously heard by others unknown to him and unfamiliar with his situation or analyzed in a cold, formal record played days, months, or years after the conversation. Interposition of a warrant requirement is designed not to shield "wrongdoers," but to secure a measure of privacy and a sense of personal security throughout our society.

The Fourth Amendment does, of course, leave room for the employment of modern technology in criminal law enforcement, but in the stream of current developments in Fourth Amendment law I think it must be held that third-party electronic monitoring, subject only to the self-restraint of law enforcement officials, has no place in our society.

. . . .

V.

. . . .

I would hold that On Lee is no longer good law and affirm the judgment below.

MR. JUSTICE MARSHALL, dissenting.

I am convinced that the correct view of the Fourth Amendment in the area of electronic surveillance is one that brings the safeguards of the warrant requirement to bear on the investigatory activity involved in this case. In this regard I agree with the dissents of MR. JUSTICE DOUGLAS and MR. JUSTICE HARLAN. In short, I believe that On Lee v. United States, 343 U.S. 747 (1952), cannot be considered viable in light of the constitutional principles articulated in Katz v. United States, 389 U.S. 347 (1967), and other cases. And for reasons expressed by MR. JUSTICE FORTAS in dissent in Desist v. United States, 394 U.S. 244 (1969), I do not think we should feel constrained to employ a discarded theory of the Fourth Amendment in evaluating the governmental intrusions challenged here.

Cases relating to **Chapter 6**

INTERROGATIONS AND CONFESSIONS

CULOMBE v. CONNECTICUT

367 U.S. 568, 6 L.Ed.2d 1037, 81 S.Ct. 1860 (1961)

MR. JUSTICE FRANKFURTER announced the judgment of the Court and an opinion in which MR. JUSTICE STEWART joins.

Once again the Court is confronted with the painful duty of sitting in judgment on a State's conviction for murder, after a jury's verdict was found flawless by the State's highest court, in order to determine whether the defendant's confessions, decisive for the conviction, were admitted into evidence in accordance with the standards for admissibility demanded by the Due Process Clause of the Fourteenth Amendment. This recurring problem touching the administration of criminal justice by the States presents in an aggravated form in this case the anxious task of reconciling the responsibility of the police for ferreting out crime with the right of the criminal defendant, however guilty, to be tried according to constitutional requirements.

On December 15, 1956, the dead bodies of two men where found in Kurp's Gasoline Station in New Britain, Connecticut. Edward J. Kurpiewski, the proprietor, was found in the boiler room with a bullet in his head. Daniel J. Janowski, a customer, was found in the men's toilet room shot twice in the head. Parked at the pumps in front of the station was Janowski's car. In it was Janowski's daughter, physically unharmed. She was the only surviving eyewitness of what had happened at the station. She was eighteen months old.

The Kurp's affair was one in a series of holdups and holdup killings that terrified the operators of gasoline stations, package stores and small shops throughout the environing Connecticut area. Newspapers and radio and television broadcasters reported each fresh depredation of the "mad killers." At Hartford, the State Police were at work investigating the crimes, apparently with little evidence to go on. At the scene of the killings of Kurpiewski and Janowski no physical clues were discovered. The bullet slugs removed from the brains of the two victims were split and damaged.

In the last week of February 1957, for reasons which do not appear in this record, suspicion in connection with at least two of the holdups under investigation, holdups of a country store in Coventry and of a package store in Rocky Hill, focused on two friends, Arthur Culombe and Joseph Taborsky. On the afternoon of February 23, the two were accosted by teams of officers and asked to come to

State Police Headquarters. They were never again out of police custody. In the Headquarters interrogation room and elsewhere, they were questioned about the Coventry and Rocky Hill holdups, Kurp's, and other matters. Within ten days Culombe had five times confessed orally to participation in the Kurp's Gasoline Station affair—once reenacting the holdup for the police—and had signed three typed statements incriminating himself and Taborsky in the Kurp's killings. Taborsky also confessed.

The two were indicted and tried jointly for murder in the first degree before a jury in the Superior Court at Hartford. Certain of their oral and written statements were permitted to go to the jury over their timely objections that these had been extracted from them by police methods which made the confessions inadmissible consistently with the Fourteenth Amendment. Both men were convicted of first-degree murder and their convictions affirmed by the Supreme Court of Errors. 147 Conn. 194, 158 A.2d 239. Only Culombe sought review by this Court. Because his petition for certiorari presented serious questions concerning the limitations imposed by the Federal Due Process Clause upon the investigative activities of state criminal law enforcement officials, we issued the writ. 363 U.S. 826.

The occasion which in December 1956 confronted the Connecticut State Police with two corpses and an infant as their sole informants to a crime of community-disturbing violence is not a rare one. Despite modern advances in the technology of crime detection, offenses frequently occur about which things cannot be made to speak. And where there cannot be found innocent human witnesses to such offenses, nothing remains—if police investigation is not to be balked before it has fairly begun—but to seek out possibly guilty witnesses and ask them questions, witnesses, that is, who are suspected of knowing something about the offense precisely because they are suspected of implication in it.

The questions which these suspected witnesses are asked may serve to clear them. They may serve, directly or indirectly, to lead the police to other suspects than the persons questioned. Or they may become the means by which the persons questioned are themselves made to furnish proofs which will eventually send them to prison or death. In any event, whatever its outcome, such questioning is often indispensable to crime detection. Its compelling necessity has been judicially recognized as its sufficient justification, even in a society which, like ours, stands strongly and constitutionally committed to the principle that persons accused of crime cannot be made to convict themselves out of their own mouths.

But persons who are suspected of crime will not always be unreluctant to answer questions put by the police. Since under the procedures of Anglo-American criminal justice they cannot be constrained by legal process to give answers which incriminate them, the police have resorted to other means to unbend their reluctance, lest criminal investigation founder. Kindness, cajolery, entreaty, deception, persistent cross-questioning, even physical brutality have been used to this end. In the United States, "interrogation" has become a police technique, and detention for purposes of interrogation a common, although generally unlawful, practice. Crime detection officials, finding that if their suspects are kept under tight police control during questioning they are less likely to be distracted, less likely to be recalcitrant and, of course, less likely to make off and escape entirely, not infrequently take such suspects into custody for "investigation."

This practice has its manifest evils and dangers. Persons subjected to it are torn from the reliances of their daily existence and held at the mercy of those whose job it is—if such persons have committed crimes, as it is supposed they have—to prosecute them. They are deprived of freedom without a proper judicial tribunal having found them guilty, without a proper judicial tribunal having found even that there is probable cause to believe that they may be guilty. What actually happens to them behind the closed door of the interrogation room is difficult if not impossible to ascertain. Certainly, if through excess of zeal or aggressive impatience or flaring up of temper in the face of obstinate silence a prisoner is abused, he is faced with the task of overcoming,

by his lone testimony, solemn official denials. The prisoner knows this—knows that no friendly or disinterested witness is present—and the knowledge may itself induce fear. But, in any case, the risk is great that the police will accomplish behind their closed door precisely what the demands of our legal order forbid: make a suspect the unwilling collaborator in establishing his guilt. This they may accomplish not only with ropes and a rubber hose, not only by relay questioning persistently, insistently subjugating a tired mind, but by subtler devices.

In the police station a prisoner is surrounded by known hostile forces. He is disoriented from the world he knows and in which he finds support. He is subject to coercing impingements, undermining even if not obvious pressures of every variety. In such an atmosphere, questioning that is long continued—even if it is only repeated at intervals, never protracted to the point of physical exhaustion—inevitably suggests that the questioner has a right to, and expects, an answer. This is so, certainly, when the prisoner has never been told that he need not answer and when, because his commitment to custody seems to be at the will of his questioners, he has every reason to believe that he will be held and interrogated until he speaks.

However, a confession made by a person in custody is not always the result of an overborne will. The police may be midwife to a declaration naturally born of remorse, or relief, or desperation, or calculation. If that is so, if the "suction process" has not been at the prisoner and drained his capacity for freedom of choice, does not the awful responsibility of the police for maintaining the peaceful order of society justify the means which they have employed? It will not do to forget, as Sir Patrick (now Lord Justice) Devlin has put it, that "The least criticism of police methods of interrogation deserves to be most carefully weighed because the evidence which such interrogation produces is often decisive; the high degree of proof which the English law requires—proof beyond reasonable doubt—often could not be achieved by the prosecution without the assistance of the accused's own statement." Yet even if one cannot adopt "an undiscriminating hostility to mere interrogation . . . without unduly fettering the States in protecting society from the criminal," there remain the questions: When, applied to what practices, is a judgment of impermissibility drawn from the fundamental conceptions of Anglo-American accusatorial process "undiscriminating"? What are the characteristics of the "mere interrogation" which is allowable consistently with those conceptions?

. . . . [Parts of this case have been omitted. These parts should be read for a history of the rules concerning confessions.]

Each of these factors, in company with all of the surrounding circumstances—the duration and conditions of detention (if the confessor has been detained), the manifest attitude of the police toward him, his physical and mental state, the diverse pressures which sap or sustain his powers of resistance and self-control—is relevant. The ultimate test remains that which has been the only clearly established test in Anglo-American courts for two hundred years: the test of voluntariness. Is the confession the product of an essentially free and unconstrained choice by its maker? If it is, if he has willed to confess, it may be used against him. If it is not, if his will has been overborne and his capacity for self-determination critically impaired, the use of his confession offends due process. *Rogers* v. *Richmond*, 365 U.S. 534. The line of distinction is that at which governing self-direction is lost and compulsion, of whatever nature or however infused, propels or helps to propel the confession.

IV.

The inquiry whether, in a particular case, a confession was voluntarily or involuntarily made involves, at the least, a three-phased process. First, there is the business of finding the crude historical facts, the external, "phenomenological" occurrences and events surrounding the confession. Second, because the concept of "voluntariness" is one which concerns a mental state, there is the imaginative re[-]creation, largely inferential, of internal, "psychological" fact. Third, there is the application to this psychological fact of standards for judgment informed by the larger legal

conceptions ordinarily characterized as rules of law but which, also,
comprehend both induction from,
and anticipation of, factual circumstances.

. . . .

VI.

In the view we take of this case,
only the Wednesday confessions
need be discussed. If these were
coerced, Culombe's conviction,
however convincingly supported
by other evidence, cannot stand.
Malinski v. New York, 324 U.S.
401; *Stroble v. California*, 343 U.S.
181; *Payne v. Arkansas*, 356 U.S.
560. On all the circumstances of
this record we are compelled to
conclude that these confessions
were not voluntary. By their use
petitioner was deprived of due
process of law.

Consideration of the body of this
Court's prior decisions which have
found confessions coerced informs
this conclusion. For although the
question whether a particular criminal defendant's will has been overborne and broken is one, it deserves repetition, that must be
decided on the peculiar, individual
set of facts of his case, it is only
by a close, relevant comparison of
situations that standards which are
solid and effectively enforceable—
not doctrinaire or abstract—can be
evolved. In approaching these decisions, we may put aside at the
outset cases involving physical brutality, threats of physical brutality,
and such convincingly terror-
arousing, and otherwise unexplain-
able, incidents of interrogation as

the removal of prisoners from jail
at night for questioning in secluded
places, the shuttling of prisoners
from jail to jail, at distances from
their homes, for questioning, the
keeping of prisoners unclothed or
standing on their feet for long periods during questioning. No such
obvious, crude devices appear in
this record. We may put aside also
cases where deprivation of sleep
has been used to sap a prisoner's
strength and drug him or where
bald disregard of his rudimentary
need for food is a factor that adds
to enfeeblement. Culombe was not
subjected to wakes or starvation.
We may put aside cases stamped
with the overhanging threat of the
lynch mob, for although it is true
that Culombe saw crowds of people gathered to witness his booking
and presentation in New Britain,
this circumstance must be accounted of small significance here.
There were no mobs at Hartford
where he was held securely imprisoned at State Police Headquarters. Finally, we may put aside
cases of gruelling, intensely unre-
laxing questioning over protracted
periods. Culombe's most extended
session prior to his first confession
ran three and a half hours with
substantial respites. Because all of
his questioning concerned not one
but several offenses, it does not
present an aspect of relentless, constantly repeated probing designed
to break concentrated resistance.
Particularly, the sustained four-
and-a-half-hour interview that preceded the Wednesday-midnight
confession was almost wholly
taken up with matters other than

Kurp's, and at that time, far from resisting, Culombe was wholly co-operating with the police.

. . . .

What appears in this case, then, is this. Culombe was taken by the police and held in the carefully controlled environment of police custody for more than four days before he confessed. During that time he was questioned—questioned every day about the Kurp's affair—and with the avowed intention, not merely to check his story to ascertain whether there was cause to charge him, but to obtain a confession if a confession was obtainable.

All means found fit were employed to this end. Culombe was not told that he had a right to remain silent. Although he said that he wanted a lawyer, the police made no attempt to give him the help he needed to get one. Instead of bringing him before a magistrate with reasonable promptness, as Connecticut law requires, to be duly presented for the grave crimes of which he was in fact suspected (and for which he had been arrested under the felony-arrest statute), he was taken before the New Britain Police Court on the palpable ruse of a breach-of-the-peace charge concocted to give the police time to pursue their investigation. This device is admitted. It had a two-fold effect. First, it kept Culombe in police hands without any of the protections that a proper magistrate's hearing would have assured him. Certainly, had he been brought before it charged

with murder instead of an insignificant misdemeanor, no court would have failed to warn Culombe of his rights and arrange for appointment of counsel. Second, every circumstance of the Police Court's procedure was, in itself, potentially intimidating. Culombe had been told that morning that he would be presented in a court of law and would be able to consult counsel. Instead, he was led into a crowded room, penned in a corner, and, without ever being brought before the bench or given a chance to participate in any way, his case was disposed of. Culombe had been convicted of crimes before and presumably was not ignorant of the way in which justice is regularly done. It would deny the impact of experience to believe that the impression which even his limited mind drew from this appearance before a court which did not even hear him, a court which may well have appeared a mere tool in the hands of the police, was not intimidating.

That same evening, by arrangement of the State Police, Culombe's wife and daughter appeared at Headquarters for the interview that left him sobbing in his cell. The next morning, although the mittimus of the New Britain Police Court had committed Culombe to the Hartford Jail until released by due course of law, the police "borrowed" him, and later the questioning resumed. There can be no doubt of its purpose at this time. For Paige then "knew"—if he was ever to know—that Culombe was guilty. Paige opened by telling Culombe to stop lying and to say instead that he did not want to answer. But when Culombe said that he did not want to answer, Detective Murphy took over and repeated the same questions that Paige had asked.

It is clear that this man's will was broken Wednesday afternoon. It is no less clear that his will was broken Wednesday night when, after several hours in a car with four policemen, two interviews with his wife and his apparently ill child, further inquiries made of him in the presence of the Police Commissioner, and a four-and-a-half-hour session which left him (by police testimony) "tired," he agreed to the composition of a statement that was not even cast in his own words. We do not overlook the fact that Culombe told his wife at their apartment that he wanted to cleanse his conscience and make a clean breast of things. This item, in the total context, does not overbalance the significance of all else, particularly since it was his wife who the day before, at the request of Lieutenant Rome, had asked him to confess. Neither the Wednesday-afternoon nor the Wednesday-midnight statement may be proved against Culombe, and [nor] he [be] convicted by their use, consistently with the Constitution.

VII.

Regardful as one must be of the problems of crime detection confronting the States, one does not reach the result here as an easy decision. In the case of such unwitnessed crimes as the Kurp's killings, the trials of detection challenge the most imaginative capacities of law enforcement officers. Often there is little else the police can do than interrogate suspects as an indispensable part of criminal investigation. But when interrogation of a prisoner is so long continued, with such a purpose, and under such circumstances, as to make the whole proceeding an effective instrument for extorting an unwilling admission of guilt, due process precludes the use of the confession thus obtained. Under our accusatorial system, such an exploitation of interrogation, whatever its usefulness, is not a permissible substitute for judicial trial.

Reversed.

. . . . [Additional concurring opinions have been omitted.]

Mr. Justice Harlan, whom Mr. Justice Clark and Mr. Justice Whittaker join, dissenting.

I agree to what my Brother Frankfurter has written in delineation of the general principles governing police interrogation of those suspected of, or under investigation in connection with, the commission of crime, and as to the factors which should guide federal judicial review of state action in this field. I think, however, that upon this record, which contains few of the hallmarks usually found in "coerced confession" cases, such considerations find their proper reflection in affirmance of this judgment.

With due regard to the medical and other evidence as to petitioner's history and subnormal mentality, I am unable to consider that it was constitutionally impermissible for the State to conclude that petitioner's "Wednesday" confessions were the product of a deliberate choice on his part to try to ameliorate his fate by making a clean breast of things, and not the consequence of improper police activity. To me, petitioner's supplemental confession on the following Saturday night, which as depicted by the record bears all the *indicia* of spontaneity, is especially persuasive against this Court's contrary view.

I should also add that I find no constitutional infirmity in the standards used by the Connecticut courts in evaluating the voluntariness of petitioner's confessions. Cf. *Rogers* v. *Richmond*, 365 U.S. 534.

I would affirm.

MALLORY v. UNITED STATES

354 U.S. 449, 1 L.Ed.2d 1479, 77 S.Ct. 1356 (1957)

MR. JUSTICE FRANKFURTER delivered the opinion of the Court.

Petitioner was convicted of rape in the United States District Court for the District of Columbia, and, as authorized by the District Code, the jury imposed a death sentence. The Court of Appeals affirmed, one judge dissenting. 98 U.S.App.D.C. 406, 236 F.2d 701. Since an important question involving the interpretation of the Federal Rules of Criminal Procedure was involved in this capital case, we granted the petition for certiorari. 352 U.S. 877.

The rape occurred at six p.m. on April 7, 1954, in the basement of the apartment house inhabited by the victim. She had descended to the basement a few minutes previous to wash some laundry. Experiencing some difficulty in detaching a hose in the sink, she sought help from the janitor, who lived in a basement apartment with his wife, two grown sons, a younger son and the petitioner, his nineteen-year-old half-brother. Petitioner was alone in the apartment at the time. He detached the hose and returned to his quarters. Very shortly thereafter, a masked man, whose general features were identified to resemble those of petitioner and his two grown nephews, attacked the woman. She had heard no one descend the wooden steps that furnished the only means of entering the basement from above.

Petitioner and one of his grown nephews disappeared from the apartment house shortly after the crime was committed. The former was apprehended the following afternoon between two and two-thirty p.m. and was taken, along with his older nephews, also suspects, to police headquarters. At least four officers questioned him there in the presence of other officers for thirty to forty-five minutes, beginning the examination by telling him, according to his testimony, that his brother had said that he was the assailant. Petitioner strenuously denied his guilt. He spent the rest of the afternoon at headquarters, in the company of the other two suspects and his brother a good part of the time. About four p.m. the three suspects were asked to submit to "lie detector" tests, and they agreed. The officer in charge of the polygraph machine was not located for almost two hours, during which time the suspects received food and drink. The nephews were then examined first. Questioning of petitioner began just after eight p.m. Only he and the polygraph operator were present in a small room, the door to which was closed.

Following almost an hour and one-half of steady interrogation, he "first stated that he could have done this crime, or that he might have done it. He finally stated that he was responsible. . . ." (Testimony of polygraph operator, R. 70.) Not until ten p.m., after petitioner had repeated his confession to other officers, did the police attempt to reach a United States Commissioner for the purpose of arraignment. Failing in this, they obtained petitioner's consent to examination by the deputy coroner, who noted no *indicia* of physical or psychological coercion. Petitioner was then confronted by the complaining witness and "[p]ractically every man in the Sex Squad," and in response to questioning by three officers, he repeated the confession. Between eleven-thirty p.m. and twelve-thirty a.m. he dictated the confession to a typist. The next morning he was brought before a Commissioner. At the trial, which was delayed for a year because of doubt about petitioner's capacity to understand the proceedings against him, the signed confession was introduced in evidence.

The case calls for the proper application of Rule 5(a) of the Federal Rules of Criminal Procedure, promulgated in 1946, 327 U.S. 821. That Rule provides:

(a) APPEARANCE BEFORE THE COMMISSIONER. An officer making an arrest under a warrant issued upon a complaint or any person making an arrest without a warrant shall take the arrested person without unnecessary delay before the nearest available commissioner or before any other nearby officer empowered to commit persons charged with offenses against the laws of the United States. When a person arrested without a warrant is brought before a commissioner or other officer, a complaint shall be filed forthwith.

This provision has both statutory and judicial antecedents for guidance in applying it. The requirement that arraignment be "without unnecessary delay" is a compendious restatement, without substantive change, of several prior specific federal statutory provisions. [Citations omitted.] Nearly all the States have similar enactments.

In *McNabb* v. *United States,* 318 U.S. 332, 343–344, we spelled out the important reasons of policy behind this body of legislation:

> The purpose of this impressively pervasive requirement of criminal procedure is plain. . . . The awful instruments of the criminal law cannot be entrusted to a single functionary. The complicated process of criminal justice is therefore divided into different parts, responsibility for which is separately vested in the various participants upon whom the criminal law relies for its vindication. Legislation such as this, requiring that the police must with reasonable promptness show legal cause for detaining arrested persons, constitutes an important safeguard —not only in assuring protection for the innocent but also in securing conviction of the guilty by methods that commend themselves to a progressive and self-confident society. For this procedural requirement checks resort to those reprehensible practices known as the 'third degree' which, though universally rejected as indefensible, still find their way into use. It aims to avoid all the evil implications of secret interrogation of persons accused of crime.

Since such unwarranted detention led to tempting utilization of intensive interrogation, easily gliding into the evils of "the third degree," the Court held that police detention of defendants beyond the time when a committing magistrate was readily accessible constituted "willful disobedience of law." In order adequately to enforce the congressional requirement of prompt arraignment, it was deemed necessary to render inadmissible incriminating statements elicited from defendants during a period of unlawful detention.

In *Upshaw* v. *United States,* 335 U.S. 410, which came here after the Federal Rules of Criminal Procedure had been in operation, the Court made it clear that Rule 5(a)'s standard of "without unnecessary delay" implied no relaxation of the *McNabb* doctrine.

The requirement of Rule 5(a) is part of the procedure devised by Congress for safeguarding individual rights without hampering effective and intelligent law enforcement. Provisions related to Rule 5(a) contemplate a procedure that allows arresting officers little more leeway than the interval between arrest and the ordinary administrative steps required to bring a suspect before the nearest available magistrate. Rule 4(a) provides: "If it appears from the complaint that there is probable cause to believe that an offense has been committed and that the defendant has committed it, a warrant for the arrest of the defendant shall issue. . . ." Rule 4(b) requires that the warrant "shall command that the defendant be arrested and brought before the nearest available commissioner." And Rules 5(b) and (c) reveal the function of the requirement of prompt arraignment:

> (b) STATEMENT BY THE COMMISSIONER. The commissioner shall inform the defendant of the

complaint against him, of his right to retain counsel and of his right to have a preliminary examination. He shall also inform the defendant that he is not required to make a statement and that any statement made by him may be used against him. The commissioner shall allow the defendant reasonable time and opportunity to consult counsel and shall admit the defendant to bail as provided in these rules.

(c) Preliminary Examination. The defendant shall not be called upon to plead. If the defendant waives preliminary examination, the commissioner shall forthwith hold him to answer in the district court. If the defendant does not waive examination, the commissioner shall hear the evidence within a reasonable time. The defendant may cross-examine witnesses against him and may introduce evidence in his own behalf. If from the evidence it appears to the commissioner that there is probable cause to believe that an offense has been committed and that the defendant has committed it, the commissioner shall forthwith hold him to answer in the district court; otherwise the commissioner shall discharge him. The commissioner shall admit the defendant to bail as provided in these rules.

The scheme for initiating a federal prosecution is plainly defined. The police may not arrest upon mere suspicion but only on "probable cause." The next step in the proceeding is to arraign the arrested person before a judicial officer as quickly as possible so that he may be advised of his rights and so that the issue of probable cause may be promptly determined. The arrested person may, of course, be "booked" by the police. But he is not to be taken to police headquarters in order to carry out a process of inquiry that lends itself, even if not so designed, to eliciting damaging statements to support the arrest and ultimately his guilt.

The duty enjoined upon arresting officers to arraign "without unnecessary delay" indicates that the command does not call for mechanical or automatic obedience. Circumstances may justify a brief delay between arrest and arraignment, as for instance, where the story volunteered by the accused is susceptible of quick verification through third parties. But the delay must not be of a nature to give opportunity for the extraction of a confession.

The circumstances of this case preclude a holding that arraignment was "without unnecessary delay." Petitioner was arrested in the early afternoon and was detained at headquarters within the vicinity of numerous committing magistrates. Even though the police had ample evidence from other sources than the petitioner for regarding the petitioner as the chief suspect, they first questioned him for approximately a half hour. When this inquiry of a nineteen-year-old lad of limited intelligence produced no confession, the police asked him to submit to a "lie-detector" test. He was not told of his rights to counsel or to a preliminary examination before a magistrate, nor was he warned that he might keep silent and "that any statement made by him may be used against him." After four hours of further detention at headquarters, during which arraignment could easily have been made in the same building in which the police headquarters were housed, petitioner was examined by the lie-detector operator for another hour and a half before his story began to waiver. Not until he had confessed, when any judicial caution had lost its purpose, did the police arraign him.

We cannot sanction this extended delay, resulting in confession, without subordinating the general rule of prompt arraignment to the discretion of arresting officers in finding exceptional circumstances for its disregard. In every case where the police resort to interrogation of an arrested person and secure a confession, they may well claim, and quite sincerely, that they were merely trying to check on the information given by him. Against such a claim and the evil potentialities of the practice for which it is urged stands Rule 5(a) as a barrier. Nor is there an escape from the constraint laid upon the police by that Rule in that two other suspects were involved for the same crime. Presumably, whomever the police arrest they must arrest on "probable cause." It is not the function of the police to arrest, as it were, at large and to use an interrogating process at police headquarters in order to determine whom they should charge before a committing magistrate on "probable cause."

Reversed and remanded.

MIRANDA v. ARIZONA
384 U.S. 436, 16 L.Ed.2d 694, 86 S.Ct. 1602 (1966)

MR. CHIEF JUSTICE WARREN delivered the opinion of the Court.

The cases before us raise questions which go to the roots of our concepts of American criminal jurisprudence: the restraints society must observe consistent with the Federal Constitution in prosecuting individuals for crime. More specifically, we deal with the admissibility of statements obtained from an individual who is subjected to custodial police interrogation and the necessity for procedures which assure that the individual is accorded his privilege under the Fifth Amendment to the Constitution not to be compelled to incriminate himself.

We dealt with certain phases of this problem recently in *Escobedo v. Illinois*, 378 U.S. 478 (1964). There, as in the four cases before us, the law enforcement officials took the defendant into custody and interrogated him in a police station for the purpose of obtaining a confession. The police did not effectively advise him of his right to remain silent or of his right to consult with his attorney. Rather, they confronted him with an alleged accomplice who accused him of having perpetrated a murder. When the defendant denied the accusation and said "I didn't shoot Manuel, you did it," they handcuffed him and took him to an interrogation room. There, while handcuffed and standing, he was questioned for four hours until he confessed. During this interrogation, the police denied his request to speak to his attorney, and they prevented his retained attorney, who had come to the police station, from consulting with him. At his trial, the State, over his objection, introduced the confession against him. We held that the statements thus made were constitutionally inadmissible.

This case has been the subject of judicial interpretation and spirited legal debate since it was decided two years ago. Both state and federal courts, in assessing its implications, have arrived at varying conclusions. A wealth of scholarly material has been written tracing its ramifications and underpinnings. Police and prosecutor have speculated on its range and desirability. We granted certiorari in these cases [discussed *infra*] in order further to explore some facets of the problems, thus exposed, of applying the privilege against self-incrimination to in-custody interrogation, and to give concrete constitutional guidelines for law enforcement agencies and courts to follow.

We start here, as we did in *Es-*

cobedo, with the premise that our holding is not an innovation in our jurisprudence, but is an application of principles long recognized and applied in other settings. We have undertaken a thorough re-examination of the *Escobedo* decision and the principles it announced, and we reaffirm it. That case was but an explication of basic rights that are enshrined in our Constitution—that "No person . . . shall be compelled in any criminal case to be a witness against himself," and that "the accused shall . . . have the Assistance of Counsel"—rights which were put in jeopardy in that case through official overbearing. These precious rights were fixed in our Constitution only after centuries of persecution and struggle. And in the words of CHIEF JUSTICE MARSHALL, they were secured "for ages to come, and . . . designed to approach immortality as nearly as human institutions can approach it," *Cohens v. Virginia,* 19 U.S. (6 Wheat.) 264, 387 (1821).

Over 70 years ago, our predecessors on this Court eloquently stated:

The maxim 'Nemo tenetur seipsum accusare,' had its origin in a protest against the inquisitorial and manifestly unjust methods of interrogating accused persons, which [have] long obtained in the continental system, and, until the expulsion of the Stuarts from the British throne in 1688, and the erection of additional barriers for the protection of the people against the exercise of arbitrary power,

[were] not uncommon even in England. While the admissions or confessions of the prisoner, when voluntarily and freely made, have always ranked high in the scale of incriminating evidence, if an accused person be asked to explain his apparent connection with a crime under investigation, the ease with which the questions put to him may assume an inquisitorial character, the temptation to press the witness unduly, to browbeat him if he be timid or reluctant, to push him into a corner, and to entrap him into fatal contradictions, which is so painfully evident in many of these earlier state trials, notably in those of Sir Nicholas Throckmorton, and Udal, the Puritan minister, made the system so odious as to give rise to a demand for its total abolition. The change in the English criminal procedure in that particular seems to be founded upon no statute and no judicial opinion, but upon a general and silent acquiescence of the courts in a popular demand. But, however adopted, it has become firmly embedded in English, as well as in American jurisprudence. So deeply did the iniquities of the ancient system impress themselves upon the minds of the American colonists that the States, with one accord, made a denial of the right to question an accused person a part of their fundamental law, so that a maxim, which in England was a mere rule of evidence, became clothed in this country with the impregnability of a constitutional enactment. *Brown* v. *Walker*, 161 U.S. 591, 596–597 (1896).

. . . .

Our holding will be spelled out with some specificity in the pages which follow but briefly stated it is this: the prosecution may not use statements, whether exculpatory or inculpatory, stemming from custodial interrogation of the defendant unless it demonstrates the use of procedural safeguards effective to secure the privilege against self-incrimination. By custodial interrogation, we mean questioning initiated by law enforcement officers after a person has been taken into custody or otherwise deprived of his freedom of action in any significant way. As for the procedural safeguards to be employed, unless other fully effective means are devised to inform accused persons of their right of silence and to assure a continuous opportunity to exercise it, the following measures are required. Prior to any questioning, the person must be warned that he has a right to remain silent, that any statement he does make may be used as evidence against him, and that he has a right to the presence of an attorney, either retained or appointed. The defendant may waive effectuation of these rights, provided the waiver is made voluntarily, knowingly and intelligently. If, however, he indicates in any manner, and at any stage of the process, that he wishes to consult with an attorney before speaking there can be no questioning. Likewise, if the individual is alone and indicates in any manner that he does not wish to be interrogated, the police may not question him. The mere fact that he may have answered some questions or volunteered some statements on his own does not deprive him of the right to refrain from answering any further inquiries until he has consulted with an attorney and thereafter consents to be questioned.

I.

The constitutional issue we decide in each of these cases is the admissibility of statements obtained from a defendant questioned while in custody or otherwise deprived of his freedom of action in any significant way. In each, the defendant was questioned by police officers, detectives, or a prosecuting attorney in a room in which he was cut off from the outside world. In none of these cases was the defendant given a full and effective warning of his rights at the outset of the interrogation process. In all the cases, the questioning elicited oral admissions, and in three of them, signed statements as well which were admitted at their trials. They all thus share salient features—incommunicado interrogation of individuals in a police-dominated atmosphere, resulting in self-incriminating statements without full warnings of constitutional rights.

An understanding of the nature and setting of this in-custody interrogation is essential to our decision today. The difficulty in depicting what transpires at such interrogations stems from the fact that in this country they have largely taken place incommunicado. From extensive factual studies undertaken in the early 1930's, including the famous Wickersham Report to Congress by a Presidential Commission, it is clear that police violence and the "third degree" flourished at that time. In a series of cases decided by this Court long after these studies, the police resorted to physical brutality —beatings, hanging, whipping— and to sustained and protracted questioning incommunicado in order to extort confessions. The Commission on Civil Rights in 1961 found much evidence to indicate that "some policemen still resort to physical force to obtain confessions," 1961 Comm'n on Civil Rights Rep., Justice, pt. 5, 17. The use of physical brutality and violence is not, unfortunately, relegated to the past or to any part of the country. Only recently in Kings County, New York, the police brutally beat, kicked and placed lighted cigarette butts on the back of a potential witness under interrogation for the purpose of securing a statement incriminating a third party. *People v. Portelli*, 15 N.Y.2d 235, 257 N.Y.S.2d 931, 205 N.E.2d 857 (1965).

The examples given above are undoubtedly the exception now, but they are sufficiently widespread to be the object of concern. Unless a proper limitation upon custodial interrogation is achieved—such as these decisions will advance—there can be no assurance that practices of this nature will be eradicated in the foreseeable future. . . .

Again we stress that the modern practice of in-custody interrogation is psychologically rather than physically oriented. As we have stated before, "Since *Chambers* v. *Florida,* 309 U.S. 227, this Court has recognized that coercion can be mental as well as physical, and that the blood of the accused is not the only hallmark of an unconstitutional inquisition." *Blackburn* v. *Alabama,* 361 U.S. 199, 206 (1960). Interrogation still takes place in privacy. Privacy results in secrecy and this in turn results in a gap in our knowledge as to what in fact goes on in the interrogation rooms. A valuable source of information about present police practices, however, may be found in various police manuals and texts which document procedures employed with success in the past, and which recommend various other effective tactics. These texts are used by law enforcement agencies themselves as guides. It should be noted that these texts professedly present the most enlightened and effective means presently used to obtain statements through custodial interrogation. By considering these texts and other data, it is possible to describe procedures observed and noted around the country.

. . . . [Here the court includes a detailed description of techniques and procedures advocated in texts and manuals. This description should be read to understand the Court's conception of police investigation techniques.]

From these representative samples of interrogation techniques, the setting prescribed by the manuals and observed in practice becomes clear. In essence, it is this: To be alone with the subject is essential to prevent distraction and to deprive him of any outside support. The aura of confidence in his guilt undermines his will to resist. He merely confirms the preconceived story the police seek to have him describe. Patience and persistence, at times relentless questioning, are employed. To obtain a confession, the interrogator must "patiently maneuver himself or his quarry into a position from which the desired object may be obtained." When normal procedures fail to produce the needed result, the police may resort to deceptive stratagems such as giving false legal advice. It is important to keep the subject off balance, for example, by trading on his insecurity about himself or his surroundings. The police then persuade, trick, or cajole him out of exercising his constitutional rights.

. . . .

In the cases before us today, given this background, we concern ourselves primarily with this interrogation atmosphere and the evils it can bring. In *Miranda* v. *Arizona*, the police arrested the defendant and took him to a special interrogation room where they secured a confession. In *Vignera* v. *New York*, the defendant made oral admissions to the police after interrogation in the afternoon, and then signed an inculpatory statement upon being questioned by an assistant district attorney later the same evening. In *Westover v. United States*, the defendant was handed over to the Federal Bureau of Investigation by local authorities after they had detained and interrogated him for a lengthy period, both at night and the following morning. After some two hours of questioning, the federal officers had obtained signed statements from the defendant. Lastly, in *California v. Stewart*, the local police held the defendant five days in the station and interrogated him on nine separate occasions before they secured his inculpatory statement.

In these cases, we might find the defendants' statements to have been involuntary in traditional terms. Our concern for adequate safeguards to protect precious Fifth Amendment rights is, of course, not lessened in the slightest. In each of the cases, the defendant was thrust into an unfamiliar atmosphere and run through menacing police interrogation procedures. The potentiality for compulsion is forcefully apparent, for example in *Miranda*, where the indigent Mexican defendant was a seriously disturbed individual with pronounced sexual fantasies, and in *Stewart*, in which the defendant was an indigent Los Angeles Negro who had dropped out of school in the sixth grade. To be sure, the records do not evince overt physical coercion or patent psychological ploys. The fact remains that in

none of these cases did the officers undertake to afford appropriate safeguards at the outset of the interrogation to insure that the statements were truly the product of free choice.

It is obvious that such an interrogation environment is created for no purpose other than to subjugate the individual to the will of his examiner. This atmosphere carries its own badge of intimidation. To be sure, this is not physical intimidation, but it is equally destructive of human dignity. The current practice of incommunicado interrogation is at odds with one of our Nation's most cherished principles —that the individual may not be compelled to incriminate himself. Unless adequate protective devices are employed to dispel the compulsion inherent in custodial surroundings, no statement obtained from the defendant can truly be the product of his free choice.

From the foregoing, we can readily perceive an intimate connection between the privilege against self-incrimination and police custodial questioning. It is fitting to turn to history and precedent underlying the Self-Incrimination Clause to determine its applicability in this situation.

. . . .

II.

The question in these cases is whether the privilege is fully applicable during a period of custodial interrogation. In this Court, the privilege has consistently been accorded a liberal construction. [Citations omitted.] We are satisfied that all the principles embodied in the privilege apply to informal compulsion exerted by law-enforcement officers during in-custody questioning. An individual swept from familiar surroundings into police custody, surrounded by antagonistic forces, and subjected to the techniques of persuasion described above cannot be otherwise than under compulsion to speak. As a practical matter, the compulsion to speak in the isolated setting of the police station may well be greater than in courts or other official investigations, where there are often impartial observers to guard against intimidation or trickery.

. . . .

In addition to the expansive historical development of the privilege and the sound policies which have nurtured its evolution, judicial precedent thus clearly establishes its application to incommunicado interrogation. In fact, the Government concedes this point as well established in *Westover* v. *United States*, stating: "We have no doubt . . . that it is possible for a suspect's Fifth Amendment right to be violated during in-custody questioning by a law-enforcement officer."

Because of the adoption by Congress of Rule 5(a) of the Federal Rules of Criminal Procedure, and this Court's effectuation of that Rule in *McNabb* v. *United States*, 318 U.S. 332 (1943), and *Mallory* v. *United States*, 354 U.S. 449 (1957), we have had little occasion in the past quarter century to reach the constitutional issues in dealing with federal interrogations. These supervisory rules, requiring production of an arrested person before a commissioner "without unnecessary delay" and excluding evidence obtained in default of that statutory obligation, were nonetheless responsive to the same considerations of Fifth Amendment policy that unavoidably face us now as to the States. In *McNabb*, 318 U.S., at 343–344, and in *Mallory*, 354 U.S., at 455–456, we recognized both the dangers of interrogation and the appropriateness of prophylaxis stemming from the very fact of interrogation itself.

Our decision in *Malloy* v. *Hogan*, 378 U.S. 1 (1964), necessitates an examination of the scope of the privilege in state cases as well. In *Malloy*, we squarely held the privilege applicable to the States, and held that the substantive standards underlying the privilege applied with full force to state court proceedings. There, as in *Murphy* v. *Waterfront Comm'n* and *Griffin* v. *California*, we applied the existing Fifth Amendment standards to the case before us. Aside from the holding itself, the reasoning in *Malloy* made clear what had already became apparent—that the substantive and procedural safeguards surrounding admissibility of confessions in state cases had become exceedingly exacting, reflecting all the policies embedded in the privilege. The voluntariness doctrine in the state cases, as *Malloy* indicates, encompasses all interrogation practices which are likely to exert such pressure upon an individual as to disable him from making a free and rational choice. The implications of this proposition were elaborated in our decision in *Escobedo* v. *Illinois*, decided one week after *Malloy* applied the privilege to the States.

. . . .

III.

Today, then, there can be no doubt that the Fifth Amendment privilege is available outside of criminal court proceedings and serves to protect persons in all settings in which their freedom of action is curtailed in any significant way from being compelled to incriminate themselves. We have concluded that without proper safeguards the process of in-custody interrogation of persons suspected or accused of crime contains inherently compelling pressures which work to undermine the individual's will to resist and to compel him to speak where he would not otherwise do so freely. In order to combat these pressures and to permit a full opportunity to exercise the privilege against self-incrimination, the accused must be adequately and effectively apprised of his rights and the exercise of those rights must be fully honored.

It is impossible for us to foresee the potential alternatives for protecting the privilege which might be devised by Congress or the States in the exercise of their creative rule-making capacities. Therefore we cannot say that the constitution necessarily requires adherence to any particular solution for the inherent compulsions of the interrogation process as it is presently conducted. Our decision in no way creates a constitutional strait-jacket which will handicap sound efforts at reform, nor is it intended to have this effect. We encourage Congress and the States to continue their laudable search for increasingly effective ways of protecting the rights of the individual while promoting efficient enforcement of our criminal laws. However, unless we are shown other procedures which are at least as effective in apprising accused persons of their right of silence and in assuring a continuous opportunity to exercise it, the following safeguards must be observed.

At the outset, if a person in custody is to be subjected to interrogation, he must first be informed in clear and unequivocal terms that he has the right to remain silent. For those unaware of the privilege, the warning is needed simply to make them aware of it—the threshold requirement for an intelligent decision as to its exercise. More important, such a warning is an absolute prerequisite in overcoming the inherent pressures of the interrogation atmosphere. It is not just the subnormal or woefully ignorant who succumb to an interrogator's imprecations, whether implied or expressly stated, that the interrogation will continue until a confession is obtained or that silence in the face of accusation is itself damning and will bode ill when presented to a jury. Further, the warning will show the individual that his interrogators are prepared to recognize his privilege should he choose to exercise it.

The Fifth Amendment privilege is so fundamental to our system of constitutional rule and the expedient of giving an adequate warning as to the availability of the privilege so simple, we will not pause to inquire in individual cases whether the defendant was aware of his rights without a warning being given. Assessments of the knowledge the defendant possessed, based on information as to his age, education, intelligence, or prior contact with authorities, can never be more than speculation; a warning is a clearcut fact. More important, whatever the background of the person interrogated, a warning at the time of the interrogation is indispensable to overcome its pressures and to insure that the individual knows he is free to exercise the privilege at that point in time.

The warning of the right to remain silent must be accompanied by the explanation that anything said can and will be used against the individual in court. This warning is needed in order to make him aware not only of the privilege, but also of the consequences of foregoing it. It is only through an awareness of these consequences that there can be any assurance of real understanding and intelligent exercise of the privilege. Moreover, this warning may serve to make the individual more acutely aware that he is faced with a phase of the adversary system—that he is not in the presence of persons acting solely in his interest.

The circumstances surrounding in-custody interrogation can operate very quickly to overbear the will of one merely made aware of his privilege by his interrogators. Therefore, the right to have counsel present at the interrogation is indispensable to the protection of the Fifth Amendment privilege under the system we delineate today. Our aim is to assure that the individual's right to choose between silence and speech remains unfettered throughout the interrogation process. A once-stated warning, delivered by those who will conduct the interrogation, cannot itself suffice to that end among those who most require knowledge of their rights. A mere warning given by the interrogators is not alone sufficient to accomplish that end. Prosecutors themselves claim that the admonishment of the right to remain silent without more "will benefit only the recidivist and the professional." . . . Even preliminary advice given to the accused by his own attorney can be swifty overcome by the secret interrogation process. . . . Thus, the need for counsel to protect the Fifth Amendment privilege comprehends not merely a right to consult with counsel prior to questioning, but also to have counsel present during any questioning if the defendant so desires.

The presence of counsel at the interrogation may serve several significant subsidiary functions as well. If the accused decides to talk to his interrogators, the assistance of counsel can mitigate the dangers of untrustworthiness. With a lawyer present the likelihood that the police will practice coercion is reduced, and if coercion is nevertheless exercised the lawyer can testify to it in court. The presence of a lawyer can also help to guarantee that the accused gives a fully accurate statement to the police and that the statement is rightly reported by the prosecution at trial. [Citation omitted.]

An individual need not make a pre-interrogation request for a lawyer. While such request affirmatively secures his right to have one, his failure to ask for a lawyer does not constitute a waiver. No effective waiver of the right to counsel during interrogation can be recognized unless specifically made after the warnings we here delineate have been given. The accused who does not know his rights and therefore does not make a request may be the person who most needs counsel. . . .

In *Carnley* v. *Cochran*, 369 U.S. 506, 513 (1962), we stated: "[I]t is settled that where, the assistance of counsel is a constitutional requisite, the right to be furnished counsel does not depend on a request." This proposition applies with equal force in the context of providing counsel to protect an accused's Fifth Amendment privilege in the face of interrogation. Although the role of counsel at trial differs from the role during interrogation, the differences are not relevant to the question whether a request is a prerequisite.

Accordingly, we hold that an individual held for interrogation must be clearly informed that he has the right to consult with a lawyer and to have the lawyer with him during interrogation under the system for protecting the privilege we delineate today. As with the warnings of the right to remain silent and that anything stated can be used in evidence against him, this warning is an absolute prerequisite to interrogation. No amount of circumstantial evidence that the person may have been aware of this right will suffice to stand in its stead. Only through such a warning is there ascertainable assurance that the accused was aware of this right.

If an individual indicates that he wishes the assistance of counsel before any interrogation occurs, the authorities cannot rationally ignore or deny his request on the basis that the individual does not have or cannot afford a retained attorney. The financial ability of the individual has no relationship to the scope of the rights involved here. The privilege against self-incrimination secured by the Constitution applies to all individuals. The need for counsel in order to protect the privilege exists for the indigent as well as the affluent. In fact, were we to limit these constitutional rights to those who can retain an attorney, our decisions today would be of little significance. The cases before us as well as the vast majority of confession cases with which we have dealt in the past involve those unable to retain counsel. While authorities are not required to relieve the accused of his poverty, they have the obligation not to take advantage of indigence in the administration of justice. Denial of counsel to the indigent at the time of interrogation while allowing an attorney to those who can afford one would be no more supportable by reason or logic than the similar situation at trial and on appeal struck down in *Gideon* v. *Wainwright* and *Douglas* v. *California*.

In order to fully apprise a person interrogated of the extent of his rights under this system then, it is necessary to warn him not only that he has the right to consult with an attorney, but also that if he is indigent a lawyer will be appointed to represent him. Without this additional warning, the admonition of the right to consult with counsel would often be understood as meaning only that he can consult with a lawyer if he has one or has the funds to obtain one. The warning of a right to counsel would be hollow if not couched in terms that would convey to the indigent—the person most often subjected to interrogation—the knowledge that he too has a right to have counsel present. As with the warnings of the right to remain silent and of the general right to counsel, only by effective and express explanation to the indigent of this right can there be assurance that he was truly in a position to exercise it.

Once warnings have been given, the subsequent procedure is clear. If the individual indicates in any manner, at any time prior to or during questioning, that he wishes to remain silent, the interrogation must cease. At this point he has

shown that he intends to exercise his Fifth Amendment privilege; any statement taken after the person invokes his privilege cannot be other than the product of compulsion, subtle or otherwise. Without the right to cut off questioning, the setting of in-custody interrogation operates on the individual to overcome free choice in producing a statement after the privilege has been once invoked. If the individual states that he wants an attorney, the interrogation must cease until an attorney is present. At that time, the individual must have an opportunity to confer with the attorney and to have him present during any subsequent questioning. If the individual cannot obtain an attorney and he indicates that he wants one before speaking to police, they must respect his decision to remain silent.

This does not mean, as some have suggested, that each police station must have a "station house lawyer" present at all times to advise prisoners. It does mean, however, that if police propose to interrogate a person they must make known to him that he is entitled to a lawyer and that if he cannot afford one, a lawyer will be provided for him prior to any interrogation. If authorities conclude that they will not provide counsel during a reasonable period of time in which investigation in the field is carried out, they may do so without violating the person's Fifth Amendment privilege so long as they do not question him during that time.

If the interrogation continues

without the presence of an attorney and a statement is taken, a heavy burden rests on the government to demonstrate that the defendant knowingly and intelligently waived his privilege against self-incrimination and his right to retained or appointed counsel. . . . This Court has always set high standards of proof for the waiver of constitutional rights, . . . and we reassert these standards as applied to in-custody interrogation. Since the State is responsible for establishing the isolated circumstances under which the interrogation takes place and has the only means of making available corroborated evidence of warnings given during incommunicado interrogation, the burden is rightly on its shoulders.

An express statement that the individual is willing to make a statement and does not want an attorney followed closely by a statement could constitute a waiver. But a valid waiver will not be presumed simply from the silence of the accused after warnings are given or simply from the fact that a confession was in fact eventually obtained. A statement we made in *Carnley v. Cochran*, 369 U.S. 506, 516 (1962), is applicable here:

Presuming waiver from a silent record is impermissible. The record must show, or there must be an allegation and evidence which show, that an accused was offered counsel but intelligently and understandingly rejected the offer. Anything less is not waiver.

. . . Moreover, where in-custody interrogation is involved, there is no room for the contention that the privilege is waived if the individual answers some questions or gives some information on his own prior to invoking his right to remain silent when interrogated.

Whatever the testimony of the authorities as to waiver of rights by an accused, the fact of lengthy interrogation or incommunicado incarceration before a statement is made is strong evidence that the accused did not validly waive his rights. In these circumstances the fact that the individual eventually made a statement is consistent with the conclusion that the compelling influence of the interrogation finally forced him to do so. It is inconsistent with any notion of a voluntary relinquishment of the privilege. Moreover, any evidence that the accused was threatened, tricked, or cajoled into a waiver will, of course, show that the defendant did not voluntarily waive his privilege. The requirement of warnings and waiver of rights is a fundamental with respect to the Fifth Amendment privilege and not simply a preliminary ritual to existing methods of interrogation.

The warnings required and the waiver necessary in accordance with our opinion today are, in the absence of a fully effective equivalent, prerequisites to the admissibility of any statement made by a defendant. No distinction can be drawn between statements which are direct confessions and statements which amount to "admissions" of part or all of an offense.

The privilege against self-incrimination protects the individual from being compelled to incriminate himself in any manner; it does not distinguish degrees of incrimination. Similarly, for precisely the same reason, no distinction may be drawn between inculpatory statements and statements alleged to be merely "exculpatory." If a statement made were in fact truly exculpatory it would, of course, never be used by the prosecution. In fact, statements merely intended to be exculpatory by the defendant are often used to impeach his testimony at trial or to demonstrate untruths in the statement given under interrogation and thus to prove guilt by implication. These statements are incriminating in any meaningful sense of the word and may not be used without the full warnings and effective waiver required for any other statement. In *Escobedo* itself, the defendant fully intended his accusation of another as the slayer to be exculpatory as to himself.

The principles announced today deal with the protection which must be given to the privilege against self-incrimination when the individual is first subjected to police interrogation while in custody at the station or otherwise deprived of his freedom of action in any way. It is at this point that our adversary system of criminal proceedings commences, distinguishing itself at the outset from the inquisitorial system recognized in some countries. Under the system of warnings we delineate today or under any other system which may be devised and found effective, the safeguards to be erected about the privilege must come into play at this point.

Our decision is not intended to hamper the traditional function of police officers in investigating crime.... When an individual is in custody on probable cause, the police may, of course, seek out evidence in the field to be used at trial against him. Such investigation may include inquiry of persons not under restraint. General on-the-scene questioning as to facts surrounding a crime or other general questioning of citizens in the fact-finding process is not affected by our holding. It is an act of responsible citizenship for individuals to give whatever information they may have to aid in law enforcement. In such situations the compelling atmosphere inherent in the process of in-custody interrogation is not necessarily present.

In dealing with statements obtained through interrogation, we do not purport to find all confessions inadmissible. Confessions remain a proper element in law enforcement. Any statement given freely and voluntarily without any compelling influences is, of course, admissible in evidence. The fundamental import of the privilege while an individual is in custody is not whether he is allowed to talk to the police without the benefit of warnings and counsel, but whether he can be interrogated. There is no requirement that police stop a person who enters a police station and states that he wishes to confess to a crime, or a person who calls the police to offer a confession or any other statement he desires to make. Volunteered statements of any kind are not barred by the Fifth Amendment and their admissibility is not affected by our holding today.

To summarize, we hold that when an individual is taken into custody or otherwise deprived of his freedom by the authorities and is subjected to questioning, the privilege against self-incrimination is jeopardized. Procedural safeguards must be employed to protect the privilege, and unless other fully effective means are adopted to notify the person of his right of silence and to assure that the exercise of the right will be scrupulously honored, the following measures are required. He must be warned prior to any questioning that he has the right to remain silent, that anything he says can be used against him in a court of law, that he has the right to the presence of an attorney, and that if he cannot afford an attorney one will be appointed for him prior to any questioning if he so desires. Opportunity to exercise these rights must be afforded to him throughout the interrogation. After such warnings have been given, and such opportunity afforded him, the individual may knowingly and intelligently waive these rights and agree to answer questions or make a statement. But unless and until such warnings and waiver are demonstrated by the prosecution at trial, no evidence obtained as a result of interrogation can be used against him.

IV.

A recurrent argument made in these cases is that society's need for interrogation outweighs the privilege. This argument is not unfamiliar to this Court. [Citation omitted.] The whole thrust of our foregoing discussion demonstrates that the Constitution has prescribed the rights of the individual when confronted with the power of government when it provided in the Fifth Amendment that an individual cannot be compelled to be a witness against himself. That right cannot be abridged. As Mr. Justice Brandeis once observed:

Decency, security, and liberty alike demand that government officials shall be subjected to the same rules of conduct that are commands to the citizen. In a government of laws, existence of the government will be imperilled if it fails to observe the law scrupulously. Our government is the potent, the omnipresent teacher. For good or for ill, it teaches the whole people by its example. Crime is contagious. If the government becomes a lawbreaker, it breeds contempt for law; it invites every man to become a law unto himself; it invites anarchy. To declare that in the administration of the criminal law the end justifies the means ... would bring terrible retribution. Against that pernicious doctrine this court should resolutely set its face. *Olmstead v. United States*, 277 U.S. 438, 485 (1928) (dissenting opinion).

In this connection, one of our

country's distinguished jurists has pointed out: "The quality of a nation's civilization can be largely measured by the methods it uses in the enforcement of its criminal law."

If the individual desires to exercise his privilege, he has the right to do so. This is not for the authorities to decide. An attorney may advise his client not to talk to police until he has had an opportunity to investigate the case, or he may wish to be present with his client during any police questioning. In doing so an attorney is merely exercising the good professional judgment he has been taught. This is not cause for considering the attorney a menace to law enforcement. He is merely carrying out what he is sworn to do under oath—to protect to the extent of his ability the rights of his client. In fulfilling this responsibility the attorney plays a vital role in the administration of criminal justice under our Constitution.

In announcing these principles, we are not unmindful of the burdens which law enforcement officials must bear, often under trying circumstances. We also fully recognize the obligation of all citizens to aid in enforcing the criminal laws. This Court, while protecting individual rights, has always given ample latitude to law enforcement agencies in the legitimate exercise of their duties. The limits we have placed on the interrogation process should not constitute an undue interference with a proper system of law enforcement. As we have noted, our decision does not in any way preclude police from carrying our their traditional investigatory functions. Although confessions may play an important role in some convictions, the cases before us present graphic examples of the overstatement of the "need" for confessions. In each case authorities conducted interrogations ranging up to five days in duration despite the presence, through standard investigating practices, of considerable evidence against each defendant. [Citations omitted.]

It is also urged that an unfettered right to detention for interrogation should be allowed because it will often redound to the benefit of the person questioned. When police inquiry determines that there is no reason to believe that the person has committed any crime, it is said, he will be released without need for further formal procedures. The person who has committed no offense, however, will be better able to clear himself after warnings with counsel present than without. It can be assumed that in such circumstances a lawyer would advise his client to talk freely to police in order to clear himself.

Custodial interrogation, by contrast, does not necessarily afford the innocent an opportunity to clear themselves. A serious consequence of the present practice of the interrogation alleged to be beneficial for the innocent is that many arrests "for investigation" subject large numbers of innocent persons to detention and interrogation. In one of the cases before us, *California* v. *Stewart*, police held four persons, who were in the defendant's house at the time of the arrest, in jail for five days until defendant confessed. At that time they were finally released. Police stated that there was "no evidence to connect them with any crime." Available statistics on the extent of this practice where it is condoned indicate that these four are far from alone in being subjected to arrest, prolonged detention, and interrogation without the requisite probable cause.

. . . .

It is also urged upon us that we withhold decision on this issue until state legislative bodies and advisory groups have had an opportunity to deal with these problems by rule making. We have already pointed out that the Constitution does not require any specific code of procedures for protecting the privilege against self-incrimination during custodial interrogation. Congress and the States are free to develop their own safeguards for the privilege, so long as they are fully as effective as those described above in informing accused persons of their right of silence and in affording a continuous opportunity to exercise it. In any event, however, the issues presented are of constitutional dimensions and must be determined by the courts. The admissibility of a statement in the face of a claim that it was obtained in violation of the defendant's constitutional rights is an issue the resolution of which has long since been undertaken by this Court. . . . Judicial solutions to problems of

constitutional dimension have evolved decade by decade. As courts have been presented with the need to enforce constitutional rights, they have found means of doing so. That was our responsibility when *Escobedo* was before us and it is our responsibility today. Where rights secured by the Constitution are involved, there can be no rule making or legislation which would abrogate them.

V.

Because of the nature of the problem and because of its recurrent significance in numerous cases, we have to this point discussed the relationship of the Fifth Amendment privilege to police interrogation without specific concentration on the facts of the cases before us. We turn now to these facts to consider the application to these cases of the constitutional principles discussed above. In each instance, we have concluded that statements were obtained from the defendant under circumstances that did not meet constitutional standards for protection of the privilege.

No. 759. *Miranda v. Arizona*

On March 13, 1963, petitioner, Ernesto Miranda, was arrested at his home and taken in custody to a Phoenix police station. He was there identified by the complaining witness. The police then took him to "Interrogation Room No. 2" of the detective bureau. There he was questioned by two police officers The officers admitted at trial that Miranda was not advised that he had a right to have an attorney present. Two hours later, the officers emerged from the interrogation room with a written confession signed by Miranda. At the top of the statement was a typed paragraph stating that the confession was made voluntarily, without threats or promises of immunity and "with full knowledge of my legal rights, understanding any statement I make may be used against me."

At his trial before a jury, the written confession was admitted into evidence over the objection of defense counsel, and the officers testified to the prior oral confession made by Miranda during the interrogation. Miranda was found guilty of kidnapping and rape. He was sentenced to 20 to 30 years' imprisonment on each count, the sentences to run concurrently. On appeal, the Supreme Court of Arizona held that Miranda's constitutional rights were not violated in obtaining the confession and affirmed the conviction. In reaching its decision, the court emphasized heavily the fact that Miranda did not specifically request counsel.

We reverse. From the testimony of the officers and by the admission of respondent, it is clear that Miranda was not in any way apprised of his right to consult with an attorney and to have one present during the interrogation, nor was his right not to be compelled to incriminate himself effectively protected in any other manner. Without these warnings the statements were inadmissible. The mere fact that he signed a statement which contained a typed-in clause stating that he had "full knowledge" of his "legal rights" does not approach the knowing and intelligent waiver required to relinquish constitutional rights. [Citations omitted.]

No. 760. *Vignera v. New York.*

Petitioner, Michael Vignera, was picked up by New York police on October 14, 1960, in connection with the robbery three days earlier of a Brooklyn dress shop. They took him to the 17th Detective Squad headquarters in Manhattan. Sometime thereafter he was taken to the 66th Detective Squad. There a detective questioned Vignera with respect to the robbery. Vignera orally admitted the robbery to the detective. The detective was asked on cross-examination at trial by defense counsel whether Vignera was warned of his right to counsel before being interrogated. The prosecution objected to the question and the trial judge sustained the objection. Thus, the defense was precluded from making any showing that warnings had not been given. While at the 66th Detective Squad, Vignera was identified by the store owner and a saleslady as the man who robbed the dress shop. At about 3:00 p.m. he was formally arrested. The police then transported him to still another station, the 70th Precinct in Brooklyn, "for detention." At 11:00 p.m. Vignera was questioned by an assistant district attorney in the presence of a hearing reporter who transcribed the questions and Vignera's answers. This verbatim account of these proceedings contains no statement of any warnings given by the assistant district attorney. At Vignera's trial on a charge of first degree robbery, the detective testified as to the oral confession. The transcription of the statement taken was also introduced in evidence. At the conclusion of the testimony, the trial judge charged the jury in part as follows:

> The law doesn't say that the confession is void or invalidated because the police officer didn't advise the defendant as to his rights. Did you hear what I said? I am telling you what the law of the State of New York is.

Vignera was found guilty of first degree robbery. He was subsequently adjudged a third-felony offender and sentenced to 30 to 60 years' imprisonment. The conviction was affirmed without opinion by the Appellate Division, Second Department, and by the Court of Appeals, also without opinion. In argument to the Court of Appeals, the State contended that Vignera had no constitutional right to be advised of his right to counsel or his privilege against self-incrimination.

We reverse. The foregoing indicates that Vignera was not warned of any of his rights before the questioning by the detective and by the assistant district attorney. No other steps were taken to protect these rights. Thus he was not effectively apprised of his Fifth Amendment privilege or of his right to have counsel present and his statements are inadmissible.

No. 761. *Westover v. United States.*

At approximately 9:45 p.m. on March 20, 1963, petitioner, Carl Calvin Westover, was arrested by local police in Kansas City as a suspect in two Kansas City robberies. A report was also received from the FBI that he was wanted on a felony charge in California. The local authorities took him to a police station and placed him in a line-up on the local charges, and at about 11:45 p.m. he was booked. Kansas City police interrogated Westover on the night of his arrest. He denied any knowledge of criminal activities. The next day local officers interrogated him again throughout the morning. Shortly before noon they informed the FBI that they were through interrogating Westover and that the FBI could proceed to interrogate him. There is nothing in the record to indicate that Westover was ever given any warning as to his rights by local police. At noon, three special agents of the FBI continued the interrogation in a private interview room of the Kansas City Police Department, this time with respect to the robbery of a savings and loan association and a bank in Sacramento, California. After two or two and one-half hours, Westover signed separate confessions to each of these two robberies which had been prepared by one of the agents during the interrogation. At trial one of the agents testified, and a paragraph on each of the statements states, that the agents advised Westover that he did not have to make a statement, that any statement he made could be used against him, and that he had the right to see an attorney.

Westover was tried by a jury in federal court and convicted of the California robberies. His statements were introduced at trial. He was sentenced to 15 years' imprisonment on each count, the sentences to run consecutively. On appeal, the conviction was affirmed by the Court of Appeals for the Ninth Circuit. 342 F.2d 684.

We reverse. On the facts of this case we cannot find that Westover knowingly and intelligently waived his right to remain silent and his right to consult with counsel prior to the time he made the statement. At the time the FBI agents began questioning Westover, he had been in custody for over 14 hours and had been interrogated at length during that period. The FBI interrogation began immediately upon the conclusion of the interrogation by Kansas City police and was conducted in local police headquarters. Although the two law enforcement authorities are legally distinct and the crimes for which they interrogated Westover were different, the impact on him was that of a continuous period of questioning. There is no evidence of any warning given prior to the FBI interrogation nor is there any evidence of an articulated waiver of rights after the FBI commenced its interrogation. The record simply shows that the defendant did in fact confess a short time after being turned over to the FBI following interrogation by local police. Despite the fact that the FBI agents gave warnings at the outset of their interview, from Westover's point of view the warnings came at the end of the interrogation process. In these circumstances an intelligent waiver of constitutional rights cannot be assumed.

We do not suggest that law enforcement authorities are precluded from questioning any individual who has been held for a period of time by other authorities and interrogated by them without appropriate warnings. A different case would be presented if an accused were taken into custody by the second authority, removed both in time and place from his original surroundings, and then adequately advised of his rights and given an opportunity to exercise them. But here the FBI interrogation was conducted immediately following the state interrogation in the same police station—in the same compelling surroundings. Thus, in obtaining a confession from Westover the federal authorities were the beneficiaries of the pressure applied by the local in-custody interrogation. In these circumstances the giving of warnings alone was not sufficient to protect the privilege.

No. 584. *California v. Stewart*

In the course of investigating a series of purse-snatch robberies in which one of the victims had died of injuries inflicted by her assailant, respondent, Roy Allen Stewart, was pointed out to Los Angeles police as the endorser of dividend checks taken in one of the robberies. At about 7:15 p.m.,

January 31, 1963, police officers went to Stewart's house and arrested him. One of the officers asked Stewart if they could search the house to which he replied, "Go ahead." The search turned up various items taken from the five robbery victims. At the time of Stewart's arrest police also arrested Stewart's wife and three other persons who were visiting him. These four were jailed along with Stewart and were interrogated. Stewart was taken to the University Station of the Los Angeles Police Department where he was placed in a cell. During the next five days, police interrogated Stewart on nine different occasions. Except during the first interrogation session, when he was confronted with an accusing witness, Stewart was isolated with his interrogators.

During the ninth interrogation session, Stewart admitted that he had robbed the deceased and stated that he had not meant to hurt her. Police then brought Stewart before a magistrate for the first time. Since there was no evidence to connect them with any crime, the police then released the other four persons arrested with him.

Nothing in the record specifically indicates whether Stewart was or was not advised of his right to remain silent or his right to counsel. In a number of instances, however, the interrogating officers were asked to recount everything that was said during the interrogations. None indicated that Stewart was ever advised of his rights.

Stewart was charged with kidnapping to commit robbery, rape, and murder. At his trial, transcripts of the first interrogation and the confession at the last interrogation were introduced in evidence. The jury found Stewart guilty of robbery and first degree murder and fixed the penalty at death. On appeal, the Supreme Court of California reversed. 62 Cal.2d 571, 43 Cal.Reptr. 201, 400 P.2d 97. It held that under this Court's decision in *Escobedo*, Stewart should have been advised of his right to remain silent and of his right to counsel and that it would not presume, in the face of a silent record, that the police advised Stewart of his rights.

We affirm. In dealing with custodial interrogation, we will not presume that a defendant has been effectively apprised of his rights and that his privilege against self-incrimination has been adequately safeguarded on a record that does not show that any warnings have been given or that any effective alternative has been employed. Nor can a knowing and intelligent waiver of these rights be assumed on a silent record. Furthermore, Stewart's steadfast denial of the alleged offenses through eight of the nine interrogations over a period of five days is subject to no other construction than that he was compelled by persistent interrogation to forego his Fifth Amendment privilege.

Therefore, in accordance with the foregoing, the judgments of the Supreme Court of Arizona in No. 759 of the New York Court of Appeals in No. 760, and of the Court of Appeals for the Ninth

Circuit in No. 761 are reversed. The judgment of the Supreme Court of California in No. 584 is affirmed.

It is so ordered.

MR. JUSTICE CLARK, dissenting in Nos. 759, 760, and 761 and concurring in the result in No. 584.

It is with regret that I find it necessary to write in these cases. However, I am unable to join the majority because its opinion goes too far on too little, while my dissenting brethren do not go quite far enough. Nor can I join in the Court's criticism of the present practices of police and investigatory agencies as to custodial interrogation. The materials it refers to as "police manuals" are, as I read them, merely writings in this field by professors and some police officers. Not one is shown by the record here to be the official manual of any police department, much less in universal use in crime detection. Moreover, the examples of police brutality mentioned by the Court are rare exceptions to the thousands of cases that appear every year in the law reports. The police agencies—all the way from municipal and state forces to the federal bureaus—are responsible for law enforcement and public safety in this country. I am proud of their efforts, which in my view are not fairly characterized by the Court's opinion.

I.

The *ipse dixit* of the majority has no support in our cases. Indeed, the Court admits that "we might not find the defendants'

statements [here] to have been involuntary in traditional terms." *Ante.* In short, the Court has added more to the requirements that the accused is entitled to consult with his lawyer and that he must be given the traditional warning that he may remain silent and that anything that he says may be used against him. [Citation omitted.] Now, the Court fashions a constitutional rule that the police may engage in no custodial interrogation without additionally advising the accused that he has a right under the Fifth Amendment to the presence of counsel during interrogation and that, if he is without funds, that counsel will be furnished him. When at any point during an interrogation the accused seeks affirmatively or impliedly to invoke his rights to silence or counsel, interrogation must be foregone or postponed. The Court further holds that failure to follow the new procedures requires inexorably the exclusion of any statement by the accused, as well as the fruits thereof. Such a strict constitutional specific inserted at the nerve center of crime detection may well kill the patient. Since there is at this time a paucity of information and an almost total lack of empirical knowledge on the practical operations of requirements truly comparable to those announced by the majority, I would be more restrained lest we go too far too fast.

II.

Custodial interrogation has long been recognized as "undoubtedly an essential tool in effective law enforcement." [Citation omitted.]

Recognition of this fact should put us on guard against the promulgation of doctrinaire rules. Especially is this true where the Court finds that "the Constitution has prescribed" its holding and where the light of our past cases, from *Hopt* v. *Utah*, 110 U.S. 574 (1884), down to *Haynes* v. *Washington*, *supra*, are to the contrary. Indeed, even in *Escobedo* the Court never hinted that an affirmative "waiver" was a prerequisite to questioning; that the burden of proof as to waiver was on the prosecution; that the presence of counsel—absent a waiver—during interrogation was required; that a waiver can be withdrawn at the will of the accused; that counsel must be furnished during an accusatory stage to those unable to pay; nor that admissions and exculpatory statements are "confessions." To require all those things at one gulp should cause the Court to choke over more cases than *Crooker* v. *California* and *Cicenia* v. *La Gay*, which it expressly overrules today.

The rule prior to today—as MR. JUSTICE GOLDBERG, the author of the Court's opinion in *Escobedo*, stated it in *Haynes* v. *Washington* —depended upon "a totality of circumstances evidencing an involuntary . . . admission of guilt." And he concluded:

Of course, detection and solution of crime is, at best, a difficult and arduous task requiring determination and persistence on the part of all responsible officers charged with the duty of law enforcement. And, certainly, we do not mean to suggest that all interrogation of witnesses and suspects is impermissible. Such questioning is undoubtedly an essential tool in effective law enforcement. The line between proper and permissible police conduct and techniques and methods offensive to due process is, at best, a difficult one to draw, particularly in cases such as this where it is necessary to make fine judgments as to the effect of psychologically coercive pressures and inducements on the mind and will of an accused. . . . We are here impelled to the conclusion, from all of the facts presented, that the bounds of due process have been exceeded." *Id.*, at 515.

III.

I would continue to follow that rule. Under the "totality of circumstances" rule of which my BROTHER GOLDBERG spoke in *Haynes*, I would consider in each case whether the police officer prior to custodial interrogation added the warning that the suspect might have counsel present at the interrogation and, further, that a court would appoint one at his request if he was too poor to employ counsel. In the absence of warnings, the burden would be on the State to prove that counsel was knowingly and intelligently waived or that in the totality of the circumstances, including the failure to give the necessary warnings, the confession was clearly voluntary.

Rather than employing the arbitrary Fifth Amendment rule which the Court lays down I would follow the more pliable dictates of Due Process Clauses of the Fifth and Fourteenth Amendments which we are accustomed to administering and which we know from our cases are effective instruments in protecting persons in police custody. In this way we would not be acting in the dark nor in one full sweep changing the traditional rules of custodial interrogation which this Court has for so long recognized as a justifiable and proper tool in balancing individual rights against the rights of society. It will be soon enough to go further when we are able to appraise with somewhat better accuracy the effect of such a holding.

I would affirm the convictions in *Miranda* v. *Arizona*, No. 759; *Vignera* v. *New York*, No. 760; and *Westover* v. *United States*, No. 761. In each of those cases I find from the circumstances no warrant for reversal. In *California* v. *Stewart*, No. 584, I would dismiss the writ of certiorari for want of a final judgment, 28 U.S.C. § 1257(3) (1964); but if the merits are to be reached I would affirm on the ground that the State failed to fulfill its burden, in the absence of a showing that appropriate warnings were given, of proving a waiver or a totality of circumstances showing voluntariness. Should there be a retrial, I would leave the State free to attempt to prove these elements.

[MR. JUSTICE HARLAN also wrote a dissenting opinion in which JUSTICES STEWART and WHITE joined, and MR. JUSTICE WHITE wrote a dissenting opinion in which JUSTICES HARLAN and STEWART joined. These have been omitted. However, the opinion of MR. JUSTICE WHITE is especially good as it traces the history of the confession rules and the self-incrimination clause.]

SELF-INCRIMINATION AND RELATED ISSUES*

SCHMERBER v. CALIFORNIA

384 U.S. 757, 16 L.Ed.2d 908, 86 S.Ct. 1826 (1966)

Mr. Justice Brennan delivered the opinion of the Court.

Petitioner was convicted in Los Angeles Municipal Court of the criminal offense of driving an automobile while under the influence of intoxicating liquor. He had been arrested at a hospital while receiving treatment for injuries suffered in an accident involving the automobile that he had apparently been driving. At the direction of a police officer, a blood sample was then withdrawn from petitioner's body by a physician at the hospital. The chemical analysis of this sample revealed a percent by weight of alcohol in his blood at the time of the offense which indicated intoxication, and the report of this analysis was admitted in evidence at the trial. Petitioner objected to receipt of this evidence of the analysis on the ground that the blood had been withdrawn despite his refusal, on the advice of his counsel, to consent to the test. He contended that in that circumstance the withdrawal of the blood and the admission of the analysis in evidence denied him due process of law under the Fourteenth Amendment, as well as specific guarantees of the Bill of Rights secured against the States by that

Amendment: his privilege against self-incrimination under the Fifth Amendment; his right to counsel under the Sixth Amendment; and his right not to be subjected to unreasonable searches and seizures in violation of the Fourth Amendment. The Appellate Department of the California Superior Court rejected these contentions and affirmed the conviction. In view of constitutional decisions since we last considered these issues in *Breithaupt* v. *Abram*, [citations omitted] we granted certiorari. We affirm.

I.

The Due Process Clause Claim

Breithaupt was also a case in which police officers caused blood to be withdrawn from the driver of an automobile involved in an accident, and in which there was ample justification for the officer's conclusion that the driver was under the influence of alcohol. There, as here, the extraction was made by a physician in a simple, medically acceptable manner in a hospital environment. There, however, the driver was unconscious at the time the blood was withdrawn and hence had no opportunity to object to the procedure. We affirmed the conviction there resulting from the use of the test in evidence, holding

---

* See also *Miranda* v. *Arizona, supra.*

that under such circumstances the withdrawal did not offend "that 'sense of justice' of which we spoke in *Rochin* v. *California*, 342 U.S. 165." 352 U.S., at 435. *Breithaupt* thus requires the rejection of petitioner's due process argument, and nothing in the circumstances of this case or in supervening events persuades us that this aspect of *Breithaupt* should be overruled.

II.

THE PRIVILEGE AGAINST SELF-INCRIMINATION CLAIM

Breithaupt summarily rejected an argument that the withdrawal of blood and the admission of the analysis report involved in that state case violated the Fifth Amendment privilege of any person not to "be compelled in any criminal case to be a witness against himself," citing *Twining* v. *New Jersey*, 211 U.S. 78. But that case, holding that the protections of the Fourteenth Amendment do not embrace this Fifth Amendment privilege, has been succeeded by *Malloy* v. *Hogan*, 378 U.S. 1. We there held that "[t]he Fourteenth Amendment secures against state invasion the same privilege that the Fifth Amendment guarantees against federal infringement—the right of a person to remain silent unless he chooses to speak in the unfettered exercise of his own will, and to suffer no penalty . . . for such silence." We therefore must now decide whether the withdrawal of the blood and admission in evidence of the analysis involved in this case violated petitioner's

privilege. We hold that the privilege protects an accused only from being compelled to testify against himself, or otherwise provide the State with evidence of a testimonial or communicative nature, and that the withdrawal of blood and use of the analysis in question in this case did not involve compulsion to these ends.

It could not be denied that in requiring petitioner to submit to the withdrawal and chemical analysis of his blood the State compelled him to submit to an attempt to discover evidence that might be used to prosecute him for a criminal offense. He submitted only after the police officer rejected his objection and directed the physician to proceed. The officer's direction to the physician to administer the test over petitioner's objection constituted compulsion for the purposes of the privilege. The critical question, then, is whether petitioner was thus compelled "to be a witness against himself."

If the scope of the privilege coincided with the complex of values it helps to protect, we might be obliged to conclude that the privilege was violated. In *Miranda* v. *Arizona*, the Court said of the interests protected by the privilege: "All these policies point to one overriding thought: the constitutional foundation underlying the privilege is the respect a government—state or federal—must accord to the dignity and integrity of its citizens. To maintain a 'fair state-individual balance,' to require the government 'to shoulder the entire load,' . . . to respect the inviolability of the human personality, our accusatory system of criminal justice demands that the government seeking to punish an individual produce the evidence against him by its own independent labors, rather than by the cruel, simple expedient of compelling it from his own mouth." The withdrawal of blood necessarily involves puncturing the skin for extraction, and the percent by weight of alcohol in that blood, as established by chemical analysis, is evidence of criminal guilt. Compelled submission fails on one view to respect the "inviolability of the human personality." Moreover, since it enables the State to rely on evidence forced from the accused, the compulsion violates at least one meaning of the requirement that the State procure the evidence against an accused "by its own independent labors."

As the passage in *Miranda* implicitly recognizes, however, the privilege has never been given the full scope which the values it helps to protect suggest. History and a long line of authorities in lower courts have consistently limited its protection to situations in which the State seeks to submerge those values by obtaining the evidence against an accused through "the cruel, simple expedient of compelling it from his own mouth. . . . In sum, the privilege is fulfilled only when the person is guaranteed the right 'to remain silent unless he chooses to speak in the unfettered exercise of his own will.' " *Ibid.* The leading case in this Court is *Holt* v. *United States*, 218 U.S. 245.

There the question was whether evidence was admissible that the accused, prior to trial and over his protest, put on a blouse that fitted him. It was contended that compelling the accused to submit to the demand that he model the blouse violated the privilege. MR. JUSTICE HOLMES, speaking for the Court, rejected the argument as "based upon an extravagant extension of the Fifth Amendment," and went on to say:

> [T]he prohibition of compelling a man in a criminal court to be witness against himself is a prohibition of the use of physical or moral compulsion to extort communications from him, not an exclusion of his body as evidence when it may be material. The objection in principle would forbid a jury to look at a prisoner and compare his features with a photograph in proof. 218 U.S., at 252–253.

It is clear that the protection of the privilege reaches an accused's communications, whatever form they might take, and the compulsion of responses which are also communications, for example, compliance with a subpoena to produce one's papers. *Boyd* v. *United States*, 116 U.S. 616. On the other hand, both federal and state courts have usually held that it offers no protection against compulsion to submit to fingerprinting, photographing, or measurements, to write or speak for identification, to appear in court, to stand, to assume a stance, to walk, or to make a particular gesture. The distinction which has emerged, often expressed in different ways, is that the privilege is a bar against compelling "communications" or "testimony," but that compulsion which makes a suspect or accused the source of "real or physical evidence" does not violate it.

Although we agree that this distinction is a helpful framework for analysis, we are not to be understood to agree with past applications in all instances. There will be many cases in which such a distinction is not readily drawn. Some tests seemingly directed to obtain "physical evidence," for example, lie detector tests measuring changes in body function during interrogation, may actually be directed to eliciting responses which are essentially testimonial. To compel a person to submit to testing in which an effort will be made to determine his guilt or innocence on the basis of physiological responses, whether willed or not, is to evoke the spirit and history of the Fifth Amendment. Such situations call to mind the principle that the protection of the privilege "is as broad as the mischief against which it seeks to guard." [Citation omitted.]

In the present case, however, no such problem of application is presented. Not even a shadow of testimonial compulsion upon or enforced communication by the accused was involved either in the extraction or in the chemical analysis. Petitioner's testimonial capacities were in no way implicated; indeed, his participation, except as a donor, was irrelevant to the results of the test, which depend on chemical analysis and on that alone. Since the blood test evidence, although an incriminating product of compulsion, was neither petitioner's testimony nor evidence relating to some communicative act or writing by the petitioner, it was not inadmissable on privilege grounds.

III.

THE RIGHT TO COUNSEL CLAIM

This conclusion also answers petitioner's claim that in compelling him to submit to the test in face of the fact that his objection was made on the advice of counsel, he was denied his Sixth Amendment right to the assistance of counsel. Since petitioner was not entitled to assert the privilege, he has no greater right because counsel erroneously advised him that he could assert it. His claim is strictly limited to the failure of the police to respect his wish, reinforced by counsel's advice, to be left inviolate. No issue of counsel's ability to assist petitioner in respect of any rights he did possess is presented. The limited claim thus made must be rejected.

IV.

THE SEARCH AND SEIZURE CLAIM

In *Breithaupt*, as here, it was also contended that the chemical analysis should be excluded from evidence as the product of an unlawful search and seizure in violation of the Fourth and Fourteenth Amendments. The Court did not decide whether the extraction of blood in that case was unlawful, but rejected the claim on the basis of *Wolf* v. *Colorado*, 338 U.S. 25. That case had held that the Constitution did not require, in state prosecutions for state crimes, the exclusion of evidence obtained in violation of the Fourth Amendment's provisions. We have since overruled *Wolf* in that respect, holding in *Mapp* v. *Ohio* that the exclusionary rule adopted for federal prosecutions in *Weeks* v. *United States* must also be applied in criminal prosecutions in state courts. The question is squarely presented therefore, whether the chemical analysis introduced in evidence in this case should have been excluded as the product of an unconstitutional search and seizure.

. . . .

Because we are dealing with intrusions into the human body rather than with state interferences with property relationships or private papers—"houses, papers, and effects"—we write on a clean slate. Limitations on the kinds of property which may be seized under warrant, as distinct from the procedures for search and the permissible scope of search, are not instructive in this context. We begin with the assumption that once the privilege against self-incrimination has been found not to bar compelled intrusions into the body for blood to be analyzed for alcohol content, the Fourth Amendment's proper function is to constrain, not against all intrusions as such, but against intrusions which are not justified in the cir-

cumstances, or which are made in an improper manner. In other words, the questions we must decide in this case are whether the police were justified in requiring petitioner to submit to the blood test, and whether the means and procedures employed in taking his blood respected relevant Fourth Amendment standards of reasonableness.

In this case, as will often be true when charges of driving under the influence of alcohol are pressed, these questions arise in the context of an arrest made by an officer without a warrant. Here, there was plainly probable cause for the officer to arrest petitioner and charge him with driving an automobile while under the influence of intoxicating liquor. The police officer who arrived at the scene shortly after the accident smelled liquor on petitioner's breath, and testified that petitioner's eyes were "bloodshot, watery, sort of a glassy appearance." The officer saw petitioner again at the hospital, within two hours of the accident. There he noticed similar symptoms of drunkenness. He thereupon informed petitioner "that he was under arrest and that he was entitled to the services of an attorney, and that he could remain silent and that anything that he told me would be used against him in evidence."

While early cases suggest that there is an unrestricted "right on the part of the government always recognized under English and American law, to search the person of the accused when legally arrested to discover and seize the fruits or evidences of crime," . . . the mere fact of a lawful arrest does not end our inquiry. The suggestion of these cases apparently rests on two factors—first, there may be more immediate danger of concealed weapons or of destruction of evidence under the direct control of the accused, [citation omitted]; second, once a search of the arrested person for weapons is permitted, it would be both impractical and unnecessary to enforcement of the Fourth Amendment's purpose to attempt to confine the search to those objects alone [citation omitted]. Whatever the validity of these considerations in general, they have little applicability with respect to searches involving intrusions beyond the body's surface. The interests in human dignity and privacy which the Fourth Amendment protects forbid any such intrusions on the mere chance that desired evidence might be obtained. In the absence of a clear indication that in fact such evidence will be found, these fundamental human interests require law officers to suffer the risk that such evidence may disappear unless there is an immediate search.

Although the facts which established probable cause to arrest in this case also suggested the required relevance and likely success of a test of petitioner's blood for alcohol, the question remains whether the arresting officer was permitted to draw these inferences himself, or was required instead to procure a warrant before proceeding with the test. Search warrants are ordinarily required for searches of dwellings, and absent an emergency, no less could be required where intrusions into the human body are concerned. The requirement that a warrant be obtained is a requirement that inferences to support the search "be drawn by a neutral and detached magistrate instead of being judged by an officer engaged in the often competitive enterprise of ferreting out crime." [Citations omitted.] The importance of informed, detached and deliberate determinations of the issue whether or not to invade another's body in search of evidence of guilt is indisputable and great.

The officer in the present case, however, might reasonably have believed that he was confronted with an emergency, in which the delay necessary to obtain a warrant, under the circumstances, threatened "the destruction of evidence." . . . We are told that the percentage of alcohol in the blood begins to diminish shortly after drinking stops, as the body functions to eliminate it from the system. Particularly in a case such as this, where time had to be taken to bring the accused to a hospital and to investigate the scene of the accident, there was no time to seek out a magistrate and secure a warrant. Given these special facts, we conclude that the attempt to secure evidence of blood-alcohol content in this case was an appropriate incident to petitioner's arrest.

Similarly, we are satisfied that the test chosen to measure petitioner's blood-alcohol level was a reasonable one. Extraction of blood samples for testing is a highly effective means of determining the degree to which a person is under the influence of alcohol. . . . Such tests are commonplace in these days of periodic physical examinations and experience with them teaches that the quantity of blood extracted is minimal, and that for most people the procedure involves virtually no risk, trauma, or pain. Petitioner is not one of the few who on grounds of fear, concern for health, or religious scruple might prefer some other means of testing, such as the "breathalyzer" test petitioner refused. We need not decide whether such wishes would have to be respected.

Finally, the record shows that the test was performed in a reasonable manner. Petitioner's blood was taken by a physician in a hospital environment according to accepted medical practices. We are thus not presented with the serious questions which would arise if a search involving use of medical technique, even of the most rudimentary sort, were made by other than medical personnel or in other than a medical environment—for example, if it were administered by police in the privacy of the stationhouse. To tolerate searches under these conditions might be to invite an unjustified element of personal risk of infection and pain.

We thus conclude that the present record shows no violation of petitioner's right under the Fourth and Fourteenth Amendments to be free of unreasonable searches and seizures. It bears repeating, however, that we reach this judgment only on the facts of the present record. The integrity of an individual's person is a cherished value of our society. That we today hold that the Constitution does not forbid the States minor intrusions into an individual's body under stringently limited conditions in no way indicates that it permits more substantial intrusions, or intrusions under other conditions.

Affirmed.

MR. JUSTICE HARLAN, whom MR. JUSTICE STEWART joins, concurring.

In joining the Court's opinion I desire to add the following comment. While agreeing with the Court that the taking of this blood test involved no testimonial compulsion, I would go further and hold that apart from this consideration the case in no way implicates the Fifth Amendment. Cf. my dissenting opinion and that of MR. JUSTICE WHITE in *Miranda* v. *Arizona*, 384 U.S. 436, 526.

MR. CHIEF JUSTICE WARREN, dissenting.

While there are other important constitutional issues in this case, I believe it is sufficient for me to reiterate my dissenting opinion in *Breithaupt* v. *Abram*, 352 U.S. 432, 440, as the basis on which to reverse this conviction.

MR. JUSTICE BLACK with whom MR. JUSTICE DOUGLAS joins, dissenting.

I would reverse petitioner's conviction. I agree with the Court that the Fourteenth Amendment made applicable to the States the Fifth Amendment's provision that "No person . . . shall be compelled in any criminal case to be a witness against himself. . . ." But I disagree with the Court's holding that California did not violate petitioner's constitutional right against self-incrimination when it compelled him, against his will, to allow a doctor to puncture his blood vessels in order to extract a sample of blood and analyze it for alcoholic content, and then used that analysis as evidence to convict petitioner of a crime.

The Court admits that "the State compelled [petitioner] to submit to an attempt to discover evidence [in his blood] that might be [and was] used to prosecute him for a criminal offense." To reach the conclusion that compelling a person to give his blood to help the State convict him is not equivalent to compelling him to be a witness against himself strikes me as quite an extraordinary feat. The Court, however, overcomes what had seemed to me to be an insuperable obstacle to its conclusion by holding that

> . . . the privilege protects an accused only from being compelled to testify against himself, or otherwise provide the State with evidence of a testimonial or communicative nature, and that the withdrawal of blood and use of the analysis in question in this case did not involve compulsion to these ends. (Footnote omitted.)

I cannot agree that this distinction and reasoning of the Court justify denying petitioner his Bill of Rights' guarantee that he must not be compelled to be a witness against himself.

In the first place it seems to me that the compulsory extraction of petitioner's blood for analysis so that the person who analyzed it could give evidence to convict him had both a "testimonial" and a "communicative nature." The sole purpose of this project which proved to be successful was to obtain "testimony" from some person to prove that petitioner had alcohol in his blood at the time he was arrested. And the purpose of the project was certainly "communicative" in that the analysis of the blood was to supply information to enable a witness to communicate to the court and jury that petitioner was more or less drunk.

I think it unfortunate that the Court rests so heavily for its very restrictive reading of the Fifth Amendment's privilege against self-incrimination on the words "testimonial" and "communicative." These words are not models of clarity and precision as the Court's rather labored explication shows. Nor can the Court, so far as I know, find precedent in the former opinions of this Court for using these particular words to limit the scope of the Fifth Amendment's protection. . . .

. . . .

How can it reasonably be doubted that the blood test evidence was not in all respects the actual equivalent of "testimony" taken from petitioner when the result of the test was offered as testimony, was considered by the jury as testimony, and the jury's verdict of guilt rests in part on that testimony? The refined, subtle reasoning and balancing process used here to narrow the scope of the Bill of Rights' safeguard against self-incrimination provides a handy instrument for further narrowing of that constitutional protection, as well as others, in the future. Believing with the Framers that these constitutional safeguards broadly construed by independent tribunals of justice provide our best hope for keeping our people free from governmental oppression, I deeply regret the Court's holding. For the foregoing reasons as well as those set out in concurring opinions of BLACK and DOUGLAS, JJ., in *Rochin* v. *California*, and my concurring opinion in *Mapp* v. *Ohio*, and the dissenting opinions in *Breithaupt* v. *Abram*, I dissent from the Court's holding and opinion in this case.

MR. JUSTICE DOUGLAS, dissenting.

I adhere to the views of THE CHIEF JUSTICE in his dissent in *Breithaupt* v. *Abrams*, and to the views I stated in my dissent in that case and add only a word.

We are dealing with the right of privacy which, since the *Breithaupt* case, we have held to be within the penumbra of some specific guarantees of the Bill of Rights. *Griswold* v. *Connecticut*, 381 U.S. 479. Thus, the Fifth Amendment marks "a zone of privacy" which the Government may not force a person to surrender. Likewise the Fourth Amendment recognizes that right when it guarantees the right of the people to be secure "in their persons." *Ibid*. No clearer invasion of this right of privacy can be imagined than forcible blood-letting of the kind involved here.

MR. JUSTICE FORTAS, dissenting.

I would reverse. In my view, petitioner's privilege against self-incrimination applies. I would add that, under the Due Process Clause, the State, in its role as prosecutor, has no right to extract blood from an accused or anyone else, over his protest. As prosecutor, the State has no right to commit any kind of violence upon the person, or to utilize the results of such a tort, and the extraction of blood, over protest, is an act of violence. [Citation omitted.]

NEIL v. BIGGERS

409 U.S. 188, 34 L.Ed.2d 401, 93 S.Ct. 375 (1972)

Habeas corpus proceeding by state prisoner. The United States District Court for the Middle District of Tennessee, Nashville Division, entered judgment granting writ, and the state appealed. The

Court of Appeals, 448 F.2d 91, affirmed, and certiorari was granted. The Supreme Court, MR. JUSTICE POWELL, held that United States Supreme Court's equally divided affirmance of petitioner's state court conviction was not an "actual adjudication" barring subsequent consideration on habeas corpus. The Court further held that even though station house showup may have been suggestive, and notwithstanding lapse of seven months between crime and the confrontation, there was no substantial likelihood of misidentification and evidence concerning the out-of-court identification by victim was admissible, where victim spent up to half an hour with her assailant, victim was with assailant under adequate artificial light in her house and under a full moon outdoors and at least twice faced him directly and intimately, victim's description to police included her assailant's approximate age, height, weight, complexion, skin texture, build, and voice, victim had "no doubt" that defendant was person who raped her, and victim made no previous identification at any of the showups, lineups, or photographic showings.

Affirmed in part, reversed in part, and remanded.

MR. JUSTICE MARSHALL took no part in consideration or decision of case.

MR. JUSTICE BRENNAN concurred in part and dissented in part and filed opinion in which MR. JUSTICE DOUGLAS and MR. JUSTICE STEWART concurred.

MR. JUSTICE POWELL delivered the opinion of the Court.

In 1965, after a jury trial in a Tennessee court, respondent was convicted of rape and was sentenced to 20 years' imprisonment. The State's evidence consisted in part of testimony concerning a station-house identification of respondent by the victim. The Tennessee Supreme Court affirmed. *Biggers* v. *State*, 219 Tenn. 553, 411 S.W.2d 696 (1967). On certiorari, the judgment of the Tennessee Supreme Court was affirmed by an equally divided Court. *Biggers* v. *Tennessee*, 390 U.S. 404, 88 S.Ct. 979, 19 L.Ed.2d 1267 (1968) (MARSHALL, J., not participating). Respondent then brought a federal habeas corpus action raising several claims. . . .

[That part of the decision dealing with the question of whether an affirmance by an equally divided court is an actual adjudication barring subsequent consideration on habeas corpus is not included.]

II.

We proceed, then, to consider respondent's due process claim. As the claim turns upon the facts, we must first review the relevant testimony at the jury trial and at the habeas corpus hearing regarding the rape and the identification. The victim testified at trial that on the evening of January 22, 1965, a youth with a butcher knife grabbed her in the doorway to her kitchen:

A. [H]e grabbed me from behind, and grappled—twisted me

on the floor. Threw me down on the floor.

Q. And there was no light in that kitchen?

A. Not in the kitchen.

Q. So you couldn't have seen him then?

A. Yes, I could see him, when I looked up in his face.

Q. In the dark?

A. He was right in the door-way—it was enough light from the bedroom shining through. Yes, I could see who he was.

Q. You could see? No light? And you could see him and know him then?

A. Yes.

When the victim screamed, her 12-year-old daughter came out of her bedroom and also began to scream. The assailant directed the victim to "tell her [the daughter] to shut up, or I'll kill you both." She did so, and was then walked at knifepoint about two blocks along a railroad track, taken into a woods, and raped there. She testified that "the moon was shining brightly, full moon." After the rape, the assailant ran off, and she returned home, the whole incident having taken between 15 minutes and half an hour.

She then gave the police what the Federal District Court characterized as "only a very general description," describing him as "being fat and flabby with smooth skin, bushy hair and a youthful voice." Additionally, though not mentioned by the District Court, she testified at the habeas corpus hearing that she had described her

assailant as being between 16 and 18 years old and between five feet ten inches and six feet tall, as weighing between 180 and 200 pounds, and as having a dark brown complexion. This testimony was substantially corroborated by that of a police officer who was testifying from his notes.

On several occasions over the course of the next seven months, she viewed suspects in her home or at the police station, some in lineups and others in showups, and was shown between 30 and 40 photographs. She told the police that a man pictured in one of the photographs had features similar to those of her assailant, but identified none of the suspects. On August 17, the police called her to the station to view respondent, who was being detained on another charge. In an effort to construct a suitable lineup, the police checked the city jail and the city juvenile home. Finding no one at either place fitting respondent's unusual physical description, they conducted a showup instead.

The showup itself consisted of two detectives walking respondent past the victim. At the victim's request, the police directed respondent to say "shut up or I'll kill you." The testimony at trial was not altogether clear as to whether the victim first identified him and then asked that he repeat the words or made her identification after he had spoken. In any event, the victim testified that she had "no doubt" about her identification. At the habeas corpus hearing, she elaborated in response to questioning.

A. That I have no doubt, I mean that I am sure that when I—see, when I first laid eyes on him, I knew that it was the individual, because his face—well, there was just something that I don't think I could ever forget. I believe—

Q. You say when you first laid eyes on him, which time are you referring to?

A. When I identified him—when I seen him in the courthouse when I was took up to view the suspect.

We must decide whether, as the courts below held, this identification and the circumstances surrounding it failed to comport with due process requirements.

III.

We have considered on four occasions the scope of due process protection against the admission of evidence deriving from suggestive identification procedures. In *Stovall* v. *Denno*, 388 U.S. 293 (1967), the Court held that the defendant could claim that "the confrontation conducted . . . was so unnecessarily suggestive and conducive to irreparable mistaken identification that he was denied due process of law." This we held, must be determined "on the totality of the circumstances." We went on to find that on the facts of the case then before us, due process was not violated, emphasizing that the critical condition of the injured witness justified a showup in her hospital room. At trial, the witness, whose view of the suspect at the

time of the crime was brief, testified to the out-of-court identification, as did several police officers present in her hospital room, and also made an in-court identification.

Subsequently, in a case where the witnesses made in-court identifications arguably stemming from previous exposure to a suggestive photographic array, the Court restated the governing test:

> [W]e hold that each case must be considered on its own facts, and that convictions based on eye-witness identification at trial following a pretrial identification by photograph will be set aside on that ground only if the photographic identification procedure was so impermissibly suggestive as to give rise to a very substantial likelihood of irreparable misidentification. *Simmons* v. *United States*, 390 U.S. 377, 384 (1968).

Again we found the identification procedure to be supportable, relying both on the need for prompt utilization of other investigative leads and on the likelihood that the photographic identifications were reliable, the witnesses having viewed the bank robbers for periods of up to five minutes under good lighting conditions at the time of the robbery.

The only case to date in which this Court has found identification procedures to be violative of due process is *Foster* v. *California*, 394 U.S. 440, 442 (1969). There, the witness failed to identify Foster the first time he confronted him, despite a suggestive lineup. The police then arranged a showup, at which the witness could make only a tentative identification. Ultimately, at yet another confrontation, this time a lineup, the witness was able to muster a definite identification. We held all of the identifications inadmissible, observing that the identifications were "all but inevitable" under the circumstances. *Id.*, at 443.

In the most recent case of *Coleman v. Alabama,* 399 U.S. 1 (1970), we held admissible an in-court identification by a witness who had a fleeting but "real good look" at his assailant in the headlights of a passing car. The witness testified at a pretrial suppression hearing that he identified one of the petitioners among the participants in the lineup before the police placed the participants in a formal line. MR. JUSTICE BRENNAN for four members of the Court stated that this evidence could support a finding that the in-court identification was "entirely based upon observations at the time of the assault and not at all induced by the conduct of the lineup."

Some general guidelines emerge from these cases as to the relationship between suggestiveness and misidentification. It is, first of all, apparent that the primary evil to be avoided is "a very substantial likelihood of irreparable misidentification." *Simmons v. United States,* 390 U.S., at 384. While the phrase was coined as a standard for determining whether an in-court identification would be ad-

missible in the wake of a suggestive out-of-court identification, with the deletion of "irreparable" it serves equally well as a standard for the admissibility of testimony concerning the out-of-court identification itself. It is the likelihood of misidentification which violates a defendant's right to due process, and it is this which was the basis of the exclusion of evidence in *Foster.* Suggestive confrontations are disapproved because they increase the likelihood of misidentification, and unnecessarily suggestive ones are condemned for the further reason that the increased chance of misidentification is gratuitous. But as *Stovall* makes clear, the admission of evidence of a showup without more does not violate due process.

What is less clear from our cases is whether, as intimated by the District Court, unnecessary suggestiveness alone requires the exclusion of evidence. While we are inclined to agree with the courts below that the police did not exhaust all possibilities in seeking persons physically comparable to respondent, we do not think that the evidence must therefore be excluded. The purpose of a strict rule barring evidence of unnecessarily suggestive confrontations would be to deter the police from using a less reliable procedure where a more reliable one may be available, and would not be based on the assumption that in every instance the admission of evidence of such a confrontation offends due process. *Clemons v. United States,* 133 U.S.App.D.C. 27, 48, 408 F.2d 1230,

1251 (1968) (Leventhal, J., concurring); cf. *Gilbert* v. *California*, 388 U.S. 263, 273 (1967); *Mapp* v. *Ohio*, 367 U.S. 643 (1961). Such a rule would have no place in the present case, since both the confrontation and the trial preceded *Stovall* v. *Denno, supra,* when we first gave notice that the suggestiveness of confrontation procedures was anything other than a matter to be argued to the jury.

We turn, then, to the central question, whether under the "totality of circumstances" the identification was reliable even though the confrontation procedure was suggestive. As indicated by our cases, the factors to be considered in evaluating the likelihood of misidentification include the opportunity of the witness to view the criminal at the time of the crime, the witness' degree of attention, the accuracy of the witness' prior description of the criminal, the level of certainty demonstrated by the witness at the confrontation, and the length of time between the crime and the confrontation. Applying these factors, we disagree with the District Court's conclusion.

In part, as discussed above, we think the District Court focused unduly on the relative reliability of a lineup as opposed to a showup, the issue on which expert testimony was taken at the evidentiary hearing. It must be kept in mind also that the trial was conducted before *Stovall* and that therefore the incentive was lacking for the parties to make a record at trial of facts corroborating or undermin-

ing the identification. The testimony was addressed to the jury, and the jury apparently found the identification reliable. Some of the State's testimony at the federal evidentiary hearing may well have been self-serving in that it too neatly fit the case law, but it surely does nothing to undermine the state record, which itself fully corroborated the identification.

We find that the District Court's conclusions on the critical facts are unsupported by the record and clearly erroneous. The victim spent a considerable period of time with her assailant, up to half an hour. She was with him under adequate artificial light in her house and under a full moon outdoors, and at least twice, once in the house and later in the woods, faced him directly and intimately. She was no casual observer, but rather the victim of one of the most personally humiliating of all crimes. Her description to the police, which included the assailant's approximate age, height, weight, complexion, skin texture, build, and voice, might not have satisfied Proust but was more than ordinarily thorough. She had "no doubt" that respondent was the person who raped her. In the nature of the crime, there are rarely witnesses to a rape other than the victim, who often has a limited opportunity of observation. The victim here, a practical nurse by profession, had an unusual opportunity to observe and identify her assailant. She testified at the habeas corpus hearing that there was something about his face "I don't think I could ever forget." App. 127.

There was, to be sure, a lapse of seven months between the rape and the confrontation. This would be a seriously negative factor in most cases. Here, however, the testimony is undisputed that the victim made no previous identification at any of the showups, lineups, or photographic showings. Her record for reliability was thus a good one, as she had previously resisted whatever suggestiveness inheres in a showup. Weighing all the factors, we find no substantial likelihood of misidentification. The evidence was properly allowed to go to the jury.

Affirmed in part, reversed in part, and remanded.

MR. JUSTICE MARSHALL took no part in the consideration or decision of this case.

MR. JUSTICE BRENNAN, with whom MR. JUSTICE DOUGLAS and MR. JUSTICE STEWART concur, concurring in part and dissenting in part. [That opinion has been omitted.]

ASSISTANCE OF COUNSEL*

ESCOBEDO v. ILLINOIS

378 U.S. 478, 12 L.Ed.2d 977, 84 S.Ct. 1758 (1964)

MR. JUSTICE GOLDBERG delivered the opinion of the Court.

The critical question in this case is whether, under the circumstances, the refusal by the police to honor petitioner's request to consult with his lawyer during the course of an interrogation constitutes a denial of "the Assistance of Counsel" in violation of the Sixth Amendment to the Constitution as "made obligatory upon the States by the Fourteenth Amendment," . . . and thereby renders inadmissible in a state criminal trial any incriminating statement elicited by the police during the interrogation.

On the night of January 19, 1960, petitioner's brother-in-law was fatally shot. In the early hours of the next morning, at 2:30 a.m., petitioner was arrested without a warrant and interrogated. Petitioner made no statement to the police and was released at 5 that afternoon pursuant to a state court writ of habeas corpus obtained by Mr. Warren Wolfson, a lawyer who had been retained by petitioner.

On January 30, Benedict DiGerlando, who was then in police custody and who was later indicted

for the murder along with petitioner, told the police that petitioner had fired the fatal shots. Between 8 and 9 that evening, petitioner and his sister, the widow of the deceased, were arrested and taken to police headquarters. En route to the police station, the police "had handcuffed the defendant behind his back," and "one of the arresting officers told defendant that DiGerlando had named him as the one who shot" the deceased. Petitioner testified, without contradiction, that the "detectives said they had us pretty well, up pretty tight, and we might as well admit to this crime," and that he replied, "I am sorry but I would like to have advice from my lawyer." A police officer testified that although petitioner was not formally charged "he was in custody" and "couldn't walk out the door."

Shortly after petitioner reached police headquarters, his retained lawyer arrived. The lawyer described the ensuing events in the following terms:

On that day I received a phone call [from "the mother of another defendant"] and pursuant to that phone call I went to the Detective Bureau at 11th and State. The first person I talked to was the Sergeant on duty at

---

* Also see *Miranda* v. *Arizona* for further comments on assistance of counsel.

the Bureau Desk, Sergeant Pidgeon. I asked Sergeant Pidgeon for permission to speak to my client, Danny Escobedo. . . . Sergeant Pidgeon made a call to the Bureau lockup and informed me that the boy had been taken from the lockup to the Homicide Bureau. This was between 9:30 and 10:00 in the evening. Before I went anywhere, he called the Homicide Bureau and told them there was an attorney waiting to see Escobedo. He told me I could not see him. Then I went upstairs to the Homicide Bureau. There were several Homicide Detectives around and I talked to them. I identified myself as Escobedo's attorney and asked permission to see him. They said I could not. . . . The police officer told me to see Chief Flynn who was on duty. I identified myself to Chief Flynn and asked permission to see my client. He said I could not. . . . I think it was approximately 11:00 o'clock. He said I couldn't see him because they hadn't completed questioning. . . . [F]or a second or two I spotted him in an office in the Homicide Bureau. The door was open and I could see through the office. . . . I waved to him and he waved back and then the door was closed, by one of the officers at Homicide. There were four or five officers milling around the Homicide Detail that night. As to whether I talked to Captain Flynn any later that day, I waited around for another hour or two and went back again and renewed

by [sic] request to see my client. He again told me I could not. . . . I filed an official complaint with Commissioner Phelan of the Chicago Police Department. I had a conversation with every police officer I could find. I was told at Homicide that I couldn't see him and I would have to get a writ of habeas corpus. I left the Homicide Bureau and from the Detective Bureau at 11th and State at approximately 1:00 a.m. [Sunday morning] I had no opportunity to talk to my client that night. I quoted to Captain Flynn the Section of the Criminal Code which allows an attorney the right to see his client.

Petitioner testified that during the course of the interrogation he repeatedly asked to speak to his lawyer and that the police said that his lawyer "didn't want to see" him. The testimony of the police officers confirmed these accounts in substantial detail.

Nothwithstanding repeated requests by each, petitioner and his retained lawyer were afforded no opportunity to consult during the course of the entire interrogation. At one point, as previously noted, petitioner and his attorney came into each other's view for a few moments but the attorney was quickly ushered away. Petitioner testified "that he heard a detective telling the attorney the latter would not be allowed to talk to [him] 'until they were done'" and that he heard the attorney being refused permission to remain in the adjoining room. A police officer testified that he had told the lawyer that he could not see petitioner until "we were through interrogating" him.

There is testimony by the police that during the interrogation, petitioner, a 22-year-old of Mexican extraction with no record of previous experience with the police, "was handcuffed" in a standing position and that he "was nervous, he had circles under his eyes and he was upset" and was "agitated" because "he had not slept well in over a week."

It is undisputed that during the course of the interrogation Officer Montejano, who "grew up" in petitioner's neighborhood, who knew his family, and who uses "Spanish language in [his] police work," conferred alone with petitioner "for about a quarter of an hour. . . ." Petitioner testified that the officer said to him "in Spanish that my sister and I could go home if I pinned it on Benedict DiGerlando," that "he would see to it that we would go home and be held only as witnesses, if anything, if we had made a statement against DiGerlando . . . , that we would be able to go home that night." Petitioner testified that he made the statement in issue because of his assurance. Officer Montejano denied offering any such assurance.

A police officer testified that during the interrogation the following occurred:

I informed him of what DiGerlando told me and when I did, he told me that DiGerlando was [lying] and I said, "Would you care to tell DiGerlando

that?" and he said, "Yes, I will." So, I brought . . . Escobedo in and he confronted DiGerlando and he told him that he was lying and said, "I didn't shoot Manuel, you did it."

In this way, petitioner, for the first time, admitted to some knowledge of the crime. After that he made additional statements further implicating himself in the murder plot. At this point an Assistant State's Attorney, Theodore J. Cooper, was summoned "to take" a statement. Mr. Cooper, an experienced lawyer who was assigned to the Homicide Division to take "statements from some defendants and some prisoners that they had in custody," "took" petitioner's statement by asking carefully framed questions apparently designed to assure the admissibility into evidence of the resulting answers. Mr. Cooper testified that he did not advise petitioner of his constitutional rights, and it is undisputed that no one during the course of the interrogation so advised him.

Petitioner moved both before and during trial to suppress the incriminating statement, but the motions were denied. Petitioner was convicted of murder and he appealed the conviction.

The Supreme Court of Illinois, in its original opinion of February 1, 1963, held the statement inadmissible and reversed the conviction. The court said:

[I]t seems manifest to us, from the undisputed evidence and the circumstances surrounding defendant at the time of his statement and shortly prior thereto, that the defendant understood he would be permitted to go home if he gave the statement and would be granted an immunity from prosecution. Compare *Lynumn v. Illinois*, 372 U.S. 528.

The State petitioned for, and the court granted, rehearing. The court then affirmed the conviction. It said: "[T]he officer denied making the promise and the trier of fact believed him. We find no reason for disturbing the trial court's finding that the confession was voluntary." The court also held, on the authority of this Court's decisions in *Crooker v. California*, 357 U.S. 433, and *Cicenia v. La Gay*, 357 U.S. 504, that the confession was admissible even though "it was obtained after he had requested the assistance of counsel, which request was denied." We granted a writ of certiorari to consider whether the petitioner's statement was constitutionally admissible at his trial. We conclude, for the reasons stated below, that it was not and, accordingly, we reverse the judgment of conviction.

In *Massiah v. United States*, 377 U.S. 201, this Court observed that "a Constitution which guarantees a defendant the aid of counsel at ... trial could surely vouchsafe no less to an indicted defendant under interrogation by the police in a completely extrajudicial proceeding. Anything less ... might deny a defendant 'effective representation by counsel at the only stage

when legal aid and advice would help him.' " [Citation omitted.]

The interrogation here was conducted before petitioner was formally indicted. But in the context of this case, that fact should make no difference. When petitioner requested, and was denied, an opportunity to consult with his lawyer, the investigation had ceased to be a general investigation of "an unsolved crime." . . . Petitioner had become the accused, and the purpose of the interrogation was to "get him" to confess his guilt despite his constitutional right not to do so. At the time of his arrest and throughout the course of the interrogation, the police told petitioner that they had convincing evidence that he had fired the fatal shots. Without informing him of his absolute right to remain silent in the face of this accusation, the police urged him to make a statement. As this Court observed many years ago:

It cannot be doubted that, placed in the position in which the accused was when the statement was made to him that the other suspected person · had charged him with crime, the result was to produce upon his mind the fear that if he remained silent it would be considered an admission of guilt, and therefore render certain his being committed for trial as the guilty person, and it cannot be conceived that the converse impression would not also have naturally arisen, that by denying there was hope of removing the suspicion from himself." *Bram* v. *United States*, 168 U.S. 532, 562.

Petitioner, a layman, was undoubtedly unaware that under Illinois law an admission of "mere" complicity in the murder plot was legally as damaging as an admission of firing of the fatal shots. . . . The "guiding hand of counsel" was essential to advise petitioner of his rights in this delicate situation. *Powell* v. *Alabama*, 287 U.S. 45, 69. This was the "stage when legal aid and advice" were most critical to petitioner. . . . It was a stage surely as critical as was the arraignment in *Hamilton* v. *Alabama*, 368 U.S. 52, and the preliminary hearing in *White* v. *Maryland*, 373 U.S. 59. What happened at this interrogation could certainly "affect the whole trial," since rights "may be as irretrievably lost, if not then and there asserted, as they are when an accused represented by counsel waives a right for strategic purposes." *Hamilton* v. *Alabama, supra.* It would exalt form over substance to make the right to counsel, under these circumstances, depend on whether at the time of the interrogation, the authorities had secured a formal indictment. Petitioner had, for all practical purposes, already been charged with murder.

The New York Court of Appeals, whose decisions this Court cited with approval in *Massiah*, 377 U.S. 201, at 205, has recently recognized that, under circumstances such as those here, no meaningful distinction can be drawn between interrogation of an accused before and after formal indictment. In *People* v. *Donovan*, 13 N.Y.2d 148, 243 N.Y.S.2d 841, 193 N.E.2d 628, that court, in an opinion by Judge Fuld, held that a "confession taken from a defendant, during a period of detention [prior to indictment], after his attorney had requested and been denied access to him" could not be used against him in a criminal trial. The court observed that it "would be highly incongruous if our system of justice permitted the district attorney, the lawyer representing the State, to extract a confession from the accused while his own lawyer, seeking to speak with him was kept from him by the police." *Id.*, at 151, 152.

In *Gideon* v. *Wainwright*, 372 U.S. 335, we held that every person accused of a crime, whether state or federal, is entitled to a lawyer at trial. The rule sought by the State here, however, would make the trial no more than an appeal from the interrogation; and the "right to use counsel at the formal trial [would be] a very hollow thing [if], for all practical purposes, the conviction is already assured by pretrial examination." *In re Groban*, 352 U.S. 330, 344 (BLACK, J., dissenting). "One can imagine a cynical prosecutor saying: 'Let them have the most illustrious counsel, now. They can't escape the noose. There is nothing that counsel can do for them at the trial.' " *Ex parte Sullivan*, 107 F.Supp. 514, 517–518.

It is argued that if the right to counsel is afforded prior to indictment, the number of confessions obtained by the police will diminish significantly, because most confessions are obtained during the period between arrest and indictment, and "any lawyer worth his salt will tell the suspect in no uncertain terms to make no statement to police under any circumstances." *Watts* v. *Indiana,* 338 U.S. 49, 59. This argument, of course, cuts two ways. The fact that many confessions are obtained during this period points up its critical nature as a "stage when legal aid and advice" are surely needed. [Citations omitted.] The right to counsel would indeed be hollow if it began at a period when few confessions were obtained. There is necessarily a direct relationship between the importance of a stage to the police in their quest for a confession and the criticalness of that stage to the accused in his need for legal advice. Our Constitution, unlike some others, strikes the balance in favor of the right of the accused to be advised by his lawyer of his privilege against self-incrimination.

We have learned the lesson of history, ancient and modern, that a system of criminal law enforcement which comes to depend on the "confession" will, in the long run, be less reliable and more subject to abuses than a system which depends on extrinsic evidence independently secured through skillful investigation. As Dean Wigmore so wisely said:

[A]*ny system of administration which permits the prosecution to trust habitually to compul-*sory self-disclosure as a source of proof must itself suffer morally thereby.* The inclination develops to rely mainly upon such evidence, and to be satisfied with an incomplete investigation of the other sources. The exercise of the power to extract answers begets a forgetfulness of the just limitations of that power. The simple and peaceful process of questioning breeds a readiness to resort to bullying and to physical force and torture. If there is a right to an answer, there soon seems to be a right to the expected answer,—that is, to a confession of guilt. Thus the legitimate use grows into the unjust abuse; ultimately, the innocent are jeopardized by the encroachments of a bad system. Such seems to have been the course of experience in those legal systems where the privilege was not recognized. 8 Wigmore, EVIDENCE (3d ed. 1940), 309. (Emphasis in original.)

This Court also has recognized that "history amply shows that confessions have often been extorted to save law enforcement officials the trouble and effort of obtaining valid and independent evidence. . . ." *Haynes* v. *Washington,* 373 U.S. 503, 519.

We have also learned the companion lesson of history that no system of criminal justice can, or should, survive if it comes to depend for its continued effectiveness on the citizens' abdication through unawareness of their constitutional rights. No system worth preserving should have to *fear* that if an accused is permitted to consult with a lawyer, he will become aware of, and exercise, these rights. If the exercise of constitutional rights will thwart the effectiveness of a system of law enforcement, then there is something very wrong with that system.

We hold, therefore, that where, as here, the investigation is no longer a general inquiry into an unsolved crime but has begun to focus on a particular suspect, the suspect has been taken into police custody, the police carry out a process of interrogations that lends itself to eliciting incriminating statements, the suspect has requested and been denied an opportunity to consult with his lawyer, and the police have not effectively warned him of his absolute constitutional right to remain silent, the accused has been denied "the Assistance of Counsel" in violation of the Sixth Amendment to the Constitution as "made obligatory upon the States by the Fourteenth Amendment," *Gideon* v. *Wainwright*, 372 U.S., at 342, and that no statement elicited by the police during the interrogation may be used against him at a criminal trial.

. . . .

Nothing we have said today affects the powers of the police to investigate "an unsolved crime" by gathering information from witnesses and by other "proper investigative efforts." [Citations omitted.] We hold only that when the process shifts from investigatory to accusatory—when its focus is on the accused and its purpose is to elicit a confession—our adversary system begins to operate, and, under the circumstances here, the accused must be permitted to consult with his lawyer.

The judgment of the Illinois Supreme Court is reversed and the case remanded for proceedings not inconsistent with this opinion.

Reversed and remanded.

MR. JUSTICE HARLAN, dissenting.

I would affirm the judgment of the Supreme Court of Illinois on the basis of *Cicenia* v. *La Gay*, decided by this Court only six years ago. Like my Brother WHITE, [*infra*] I think the rule announced today is most ill-conceived and that it seriously and unjustifiably fetters perfectly legitimate methods of criminal law enforcement.

MR. JUSTICE STEWART, dissenting.

I think this case is directly controlled by *Cicenia* v. *La Gay*, and I would therefore affirm the judgment.

Massiah v. *United States*, is not in point here. In that case a federal grand jury had indicted Massiah. He had retained a lawyer and entered a formal plea of not guilty.

. . . .

The confession which the Court today holds inadmissible was a voluntary one. It was given during the course of a perfectly legitimate police investigation of an unsolved murder. The Court says that what happened during this investigation "affected" the trial. I had always supposed that the whole purpose of a police investigation of a murder was to "affect" the trial of the murderer, and that it would be only an incompetent, unsuccessful, or corrupt investigation which would not do so. The Court further says that the Illinois police officers did not advise the petitioner of his "constitutional rights" before he confessed to the murder. This Court has never held that the Constitution requires the police to give any "advice" under circumstances such as these.

Supported by no stronger authority than its own rhetoric, the Court today converts a routine police investigation of an unsolved murder into a distorted analogue of a judicial trial. It imports into this investigation constitutional concepts historically applicable only after the onset of formal prosecutorial proceedings. By doing so, I think the Court perverts those precious constitutional guarantees, and frustrates the vital interests of society in preserving the legitimate and proper function of honest and purposeful police investigation.

Like my Brother CLARK, I cannot escape the logic of my Brother WHITE's conclusions as to the extraordinary implications which emanate from the Court's opinion in this case, and I share their views as to the untold and highly unfortunate impact today's decision may have upon the fair administration of criminal justice. I can only hope we have completely misunderstood what the Court has said.

MR. JUSTICE WHITE, with whom MR. JUSTICE CLARK and MR. JUSTICE STEWART join, dissenting.

In *Massiah* v. *United States*, the Court held that as of the date of the indictment the prosecution is disentitled to secure admissions from the accused. The Court now moves that date back to the time when the prosecution begins to "focus" on the accused. Although the opinion purports to be limited to the facts of this case, it would be naive to think that the new constitutional rights announced will depend upon whether the accused has retained his own counsel [citations omitted], or has asked to consult with counsel in the course of interrogation. . . . At the very least the Court holds that once the accused becomes a suspect and, presumably, is arrested, any admission made to the police thereafter is inadmissible in evidence unless the accused has waived his right to counsel. The decision is thus another major step in the direction of the goal which the Court seemingly has in mind— to bar from evidence all admissions obtained from an individual suspected of crime, whether involuntarily made or not. It does of course put us one step "ahead" of the English judges who have had the good sense to leave the matter a discretionary one with the trial court. I reject this step and the invitation to go farther which the Court has now issued.

By abandoning the voluntary-involuntary test for admissibility of confessions, the Court seems driven by the notion that it is un-civilized law enforcement to use an accused's own admissions against him at his trial. It attempts to find a home for this new and nebulous rule of due process by attaching it to the right to counsel guaranteed in the federal system by the Sixth Amendment and binding upon the States by virtue of the due process guarantee of the Fourteenth Amendment. *Gideon v. Wainwright, supra.* The right to counsel now not only entitles the accused to counsel's advice and aid in preparing for trial but stands as an impenetrable barrier to any interrogation once the accused has become a suspect. From that very moment apparently his right to counsel attaches, a rule wholly unworkable and impossible to administer unless police cars are equipped with public defenders and undercover agents and police informants have defense counsel at their side. I would not abandon the Court's prior cases defining with some care and analysis the circumstances requiring the presence or aid of counsel and substitute the amorphous

and wholly unworkable principle that counsel is constitutionally required whenever he would or could be helpful.... Under this new approach one might just as well argue that a potential defendant is constitutionally entitled to a lawyer before, not after, he commits a crime, since it is then that crucial incriminating evidence is put within the reach of the Government by the would-be accused. Until now there simply has been no right guaranteed by the Federal Constitution to be free from the use at trial of a voluntary admission made prior to indictment.

. . . .

I do not suggest for a moment that law enforcement will be destroyed by the rule announced today. The need for peace and order is too insistent for that. But it will be crippled and its task made a great deal more difficult, all in my opinion, for unsound, unstated reasons, which can find no home in any of the provisions of the Constitution.

ARGERSINGER v. HAMLIN

407 U.S. 25, 32 L.Ed.2d 530, 92 S.Ct. 2006 (1972)

A state prisoner brought an original habeas corpus proceeding in the Florida Supreme Court, which discharged the writ, 236 So.2d 442. Certiorari was granted. The Supreme Court, MR. JUSTICE DOUGLAS, held that absent knowing and intelligent waiver, no person may be imprisoned for any offense, whether

classified as petty, misdemeanor or felony, unless he was represented by counsel at his trial.

Reversed.

MR. CHIEF JUSTICE BURGER concurred in result and filed opinion.

MR. JUSTICE BRENNAN filed a concurring opinion in which MR. JUS-

TICE DOUGLAS and MR. JUSTICE STEWART joined.

MR. JUSTICE POWELL concurred in result and filed opinion in which MR. JUSTICE REHNQUIST joined.

MR. JUSTICE DOUGLAS delivered the opinion of the Court.

Petitioner, an indigent, was charged in Florida with carrying a concealed weapon, an offense punishable by imprisonment up to six months, a $1,000 fine, or both. The trial was to [before] a judge, and petitioner was unrepresented by counsel. He was sentenced to serve 90 days in jail, and brought this habeas corpus action in the Florida Supreme Court, alleging that, being deprived of his right to counsel, he was unable as an indigent layman properly to raise and present to the trial court good and sufficient defenses to the charge for which he stands convicted. The Florida Supreme Court by a four-to-three decision, in ruling on the right to counsel, followed the line we marked out in *Duncan v. Louisiana*, 391 U.S. 145, 159, as respects the right to trial by jury and held that the right to court-appointed counsel extends only to trials "for non-petty offenses punishable by more than six months imprisonment." 236 So.2d 442, 443.

The case is here on a petition for certiorari, which we granted. We reverse.

The Sixth Amendment, which in enumerated situations has been made applicable to the States by reason of the Fourteenth Amend-ment (see *Duncan v. Louisiana*, *supra*; *Washington v. Texas*, 388 U.S. 14; *Klopfer v. North Carolina*, 386 U.S. 213; *Pointer v. Texas*, 380 U.S. 400; *Gideon v. Wainwright*, 372 U.S. 335; and *In re Oliver*, 333 U.S. 257), provides specified standards for "all criminal prosecutions."

One is the requirement of a "public trial." *In re Oliver*, *supra*, held that the right to a "public trial" was applicable to a state proceeding even though only a 60-day sentence was involved.

Another guarantee is the right to be informed of the nature and cause of the accusation. Still another, the right of confrontation. *Pointer v. Texas*, *supra*. And another, compulsory process for obtaining witnesses in one's favor. *Washington v. Texas*, *supra*. We have never limited these rights to felonies or to lesser but serious offenses.

In *Washington v. Texas*, we said, "We have held that due process requires that the accused have the assistance of counsel for his defense, that he be confronted with the witnesses against him, and that he have the right to a speedy and public trial." Respecting the right to a speedy and public trial, the right to be informed of the nature and cause of the accusation, the right to confront and cross-examine witnesses, the right to compulsory process for obtaining witnesses, it was recently stated, "It is simply not arguable, nor has any court ever held, that the trial of a petty offense may be held in secret, or without notice to the accused of the charges, or that in such cases the defendant has no right to confront his accusers or to compel the attendance of witnesses in his own behalf." [Citation omitted.]

District of Columbia v. *Clawans*, 300 U.S. 617, illustrates the point. There, the offense was engaging without a license in the business of dealing in second-hand property, an offense punishable by a fine of $300 or imprisonment for not more than 90 days. The Court held that the offense was a "petty" one and could be tried without a jury. But the conviction was reversed and a new trial ordered, because the trial court had prejudicially restricted the right of cross-examination, a right guaranteed by the Sixth Amendment.

The right to trial by jury, also guaranteed by the Sixth Amendment by reason of the Fourteenth, was limited by *Duncan* v. *Louisiana*, *supra*, to trials where the potential punishment was imprisonment for six months or more. But, as the various opinions in *Baldwin* v. *New York*, 399 U.S. 66, make plain, the right to trial by jury has a different genealogy and is brigaded with a system of trial to a judge alone. As stated in *Duncan*:

Providing an accused with the right to be tried by a jury of his peers gave him an inestimable safeguard against the corrupt or overzealous prosecutor and against the complaint [complaint], biased, or eccentric judge. If the defendant preferred the

common-sense judgment of a jury to the more tutored but perhaps less sympathetic reaction of the single judge, he was to have it. Beyond this, the jury trial provisions in the Federal and State Constitutions reflect a fundamental decision about the exercise of official power—a reluctance to entrust plenary powers over the life and liberty of the citizen to one judge or to a group of judges. Fear of unchecked power, so typical of our State and Federal Governments in other respects, found expression in the criminal law in this insistence upon community participation in the determination of guilt or innocence. The deep commitment of the Nation to the right of jury trial in serious criminal cases as a defense against arbitrary law enforcement qualifies for protection under the Due Process Clause of the Fourteenth Amendment, and must therefore be respected by the States.

While there is historical support for limiting the "deep commitment" to trial by jury to "serious criminal cases," there is no such support for a similar limitation on the right to assistance of counsel:

Originally, in England, a person charged with treason or felony was denied the aid of counsel, except in respect of legal questions which the accused himself might suggest. At the same time parties in civil cases and persons accused of misdemeanors were entitled to the full assistance of counsel. . . .

. . . .

[It] appears that in at least twelve of the thirteen colonies the rule of the English common law, in the respect now under consideration, had been definitely rejected and the right to counsel fully recognized in all criminal prosecutions, save that in one or two instances the right was limited to capital offenses or to the more serious crimes . . . *Powell* v. *Alabama*, 287 U.S. 45, 60, 64–65.

The Sixth Amendment thus extended the right to counsel beyond its common-law dimensions. But there is nothing in the language of the Amendment, its history, or in the decisions of this Court, to indicate that it was intended to embody a retraction of the right in petty offenses wherein the common law previously did require that counsel be provided.

We reject, therefore, the premise that since prosecutions for crimes punishable by imprisonment for less than six months may be tried without a jury, they may also be tried without a lawyer.

The assistance of counsel is often a requisite to the very existence of a fair trial. The Court in *Powell* v. *Alabama, supra*—a capital case—said:

The right to be heard would be, in many cases, of little avail if it did not comprehend the right to be heard by counsel. Even the intelligent and educated layman has small and sometimes no skill in the science of law. If charged with crime, he is incapable, generally, of determining for himself whether the indictment is good or bad. He is unfamiliar with the rules of evidence. Left without the aid of counsel he may be put on trial without a proper charge, and convicted upon incompetent evidence, or evidence irrelevant to the issue or otherwise inadmissible. He lacks both the skill and knowledge adequately to prepare his defense, even though he have a perfect one. He requires the guiding hand of counsel at every step in the proceedings against him. Without it, though he be not guilty, he faces the danger of conviction because he does not know how to establish his innocence. If that be true of men of intelligence, how much more true is it of the ignorant and illiterate, or those of feeble intellect.

In *Gideon* v. *Wainwright, supra* (overruling *Betts* v. *Brady*, 316 U.S. 455), we dealt with a felony trial. But we did not so limit the need of the accused for a lawyer. We said:

[I]n our adversary system of criminal justice, any person haled into court, who is too poor to hire a lawyer, cannot be assured a fair trial unless counsel is provided for him. This seems to us to be an obvious truth. Governments, both state and federal, quite properly spend vast sums of money to establish machinery to try defendants accused of crime. Lawyers to prosecute are everywhere deemed essential to protect the public's interest in an orderly society. Similarly, there are few defendants charged with crime, few indeed, who fail to hire the best lawyers they can get to prepare and present their defenses. That government hires lawyers to prosecute and defendants who have the money hire lawyers to defend are the strongest indications of the widespread belief that lawyers in criminal courts are necessities, not luxuries. The right of one charged with crime to counsel may not be deemed fundamental and essential to fair trials in some countries, but it is in ours. From the very beginning, our state and national constitutions and laws have laid great emphasis on procedural and substantive safeguards designed to assure fair trials before impartial tribunals in which every defendant stands equal before the law. This noble ideal cannot be realized if the poor man charged with crime has to face his accusers without a lawyer to assist him.

Both *Powell* and *Gideon* involved felonies. But their rationale has relevance to any criminal trial, where an accused is deprived of his liberty. *Powell* and *Gideon* suggest that there are certain fundamental rights applicable to all such criminal prosecutions, even those, such as *In re Oliver, supra,* where

the penalty is 60 days' imprisonment:

A person's right to reasonable notice of a charge against him, and an opportunity to be heard in his defense—a right to his day in court—are basic in our system of jurisprudence; and these rights include, as a minimum, a right to examine the witnesses against him, to offer testimony, *and to be represented by counsel.* (Emphasis supplied.)

The requirement of counsel may well be necessary for a fair trial even in a petty-offense prosecution. We are by no means convinced that legal and constitutional questions involved in a case that actually leads to imprisonment even for a brief period are any less complex than when a person can be sent off for six months or more. See, *e.g., Powell v. Texas,* 392 U.S. 514; *Thompson v. Louisville,* 362 U.S. 199; *Shuttlesworth v. Birmingham,* 382 U.S. 87.

The trial of vagrancy cases is illustrative. While only brief sentences of imprisonment may be imposed, the cases often bristle with thorny constitutional questions. See *Papachristou v. Jacksonville,* 405 U.S. 156.

In re Gault, 387 U.S. 1, dealt with juvenile delinquency and an offense, which, if committed by an adult, would have carried a fine of $5 to $50 or imprisonment in jail for not more than two months, but which when committed by a juvenile might lead to his detention in a state institution until he reached the age of 21. We said that "[t]he juvenile needs the assistance of counsel to cope with problems of law, to make skilled inquiry into the facts, to insist upon regularity of the proceedings, and to ascertain whether he has a defense and to prepare and submit it. The child 'requires the guiding hand of counsel at every step in the proceedings against him,' " citing *Powell* v. *Alabama, supra.* The premise of *Gault* is that even in prosecutions for offenses less serious than felonies, a fair trial may require the presence of a lawyer.

Beyond the problem of trials and appeals is that of the guilty plea, a problem which looms large in misdemeanor as well as in felony cases. Counsel is needed so that the accused may know precisely what he is doing, so that he is fully aware of the prospect of going to jail or prison, and so that he is treated fairly by the prosecution.

. . . .

We must conclude, therefore, that the problems associated with misdemeanor and petty offenses often require the presence of counsel to insure the accused a fair trial. MR. JUSTICE POWELL suggests that these problems are raised even in situations where there is no prospect of imprisonment. We need not consider the requirements of the Sixth Amendment as regards the right to counsel where loss of liberty is not involved, however, for here petitioner was in fact sentenced to jail. And, as we said in *Baldwin* v. *New York, supra,* "the prospect of imprisonment for however short a time will seldom be viewed by the accused as a trivial or 'petty' matter and may well result in quite serious repercussions affecting his career and his reputation."

We hold, therefore, that absent a knowing and intelligent waiver, no person may be imprisoned for any offense, whether classified as petty, misdemeanor, or felony, unless he was represented by counsel at his trial.

That is the view of the Supreme Court of Oregon, with which we agree. It said in *Stevenson* v. *Holzman*, 254 Or. 94, 102, 458 P.2d 414, 418:

We hold that no person may be deprived of his liberty who has been denied the assistance of counsel as guaranteed by the Sixth Amendment. This holding is applicable to all criminal prosecutions, including prosecutions for violations of municipal ordinances. The denial of the assistance of counsel will preclude the imposition of a jail sentence.

We do not sit as an ombudsman to direct state courts how to manage their affairs but only to make clear the federal constitutional requirement. How crimes should be classified is largely a state matter. The fact that traffic charges technically fall within the category of "criminal prosecutions" does not necessarily mean that many of them will be brought into the class where imprisonment actually occurs.

. . . .

Under the rule we announce

today, every judge will know when the trial of a misdemeanor starts that no imprisonment may be imposed, even though local law permits it, unless the accused is represented by counsel. He will have a measure of the seriousness and gravity of the offense and therefore know when to name a lawyer to represent the accused before the trial starts.

The run of misdemeanors will not be affected by today's ruling. But in those that end up in the actual deprivation of a person's liberty, the accused will receive the benefit of "the guiding hand of counsel" so necessary when one's liberty is in jeopardy.

Reversed.

MR. CHIEF JUSTICE BURGER, concurring in the result.

I agree with much of the analysis in the opinion of the Court and with MR. JUSTICE POWELL's appraisal of the problems. Were I able to confine my focus solely to the burden that the States will have to bear in providing counsel, I would be inclined, at this stage of the development of the constitutional right to counsel, to conclude that there is much to commend drawing the line at penalties in excess of six months' confinement. Yet several cogent factors suggest the infirmities in any approach that allows confinement for any period without the aid of counsel at trial; any deprivation of liberty is a serious matter. The issues that must be dealt with in a trial for a petty offense or a misdemeanor may often be simpler than

those involved in a felony trial and yet be beyond the capability of a layman, especially when he is opposed by a law-trained prosecutor. There is little ground, therefore, to assume that a defendant, unaided by counsel, will be any more able adequately to defend himself against the lesser charges that may involve confinement than more serious charges. Appeal from a conviction after an uncounseled trial is not likely to be of much help to a defendant since the die is usually cast when judgment is entered on an uncounseled trial record.

. . . .

MR. JUSTICE BRENNAN, with whom MR. JUSTICE DOUGLAS and MR. JUSTICE STEWART join, concurring.

I join the opinion of the Court and add only an observation upon its discussion of legal resources *ante* at n. 7 [omitted]. Law students as well as practicing attorneys may provide an important source of legal representation for the indigent. The Council on Legal Education for Professional Responsibility (CLEPR) informs us that more than 125 of the country's 147 accredited law schools have established clinical programs in which faculty-supervised students aid clients in a variety of civil and criminal matters. CLEPR Newsletter, May 1972, p. 2. These programs supplement practice rules enacted in 38 States authorizing students to practice law under prescribed conditions. *Ibid.* Like the American Bar Association's Model Student Practice Rule (1969), most of these regulations permit students to make supervised court appearances as defense counsel in criminal cases. CLEPR, State Rules Permitting the Student Practice of Law: Comparisons and Comments 13 (1971). Given the huge increase in law school enrollments over the past few years, see Ruud, *That Burgeoning Law School Enrollment*, 58 A.B.A.J. 146 (1972), I think it plain that law students can be expected to make a significant contribution, quantitatively and qualitatively, to the representation of the poor in many areas, including cases reached by today's decision.

MR. JUSTICE POWELL, with whom MR. JUSTICE REHNQUIST joins, concurring in the result.

Gideon v. *Wainwright*, 372 U.S. 335 (1963), held that the States were required by the Due Process Clause of the Fourteenth Amendment to furnish counsel to all indigent defendants charged with felonies. The question before us today is whether an indigent defendant convicted of an offense carrying a maximum punishment of six months' imprisonment, a fine of $1,000, or both, and sentenced to 90 days in jail, is entitled as a matter of constitutional right to the assistance of appointed counsel. The broader question is whether the Due Process Clause requires that an indigent charged with a state petty offense be afforded the right to appointed counsel.

. . . .

I am unable to agree with the Supreme Court of Florida that an indigent defendant, charged with a petty offense, may in every case be afforded a fair trial without the assistance of counsel. Nor can I agree with the new rule of due process, today enunciated by the Court, that "absent a knowing and intelligent waiver, no person may be imprisoned . . . unless he was represented by counsel at his trial." *Ante.* It seems to me that the line should not be drawn with such rigidity.

There is a middle course, between the extremes of Florida's six-month rule and the Court's rule, which comports with the requirements of the Fourteenth Amendment. I would adhere to the principle of due process that requires fundamental fairness in criminal trials, a principle which I believe encompasses the right to counsel in petty cases whenever the assistance of counsel is necessary to assure a fair trial.

I.

. . . .

. . . Where the possibility of a jail sentence is remote and the probable fine seems small, or where the evidence of guilt is overwhelming, the costs of assistance of counsel may exceed the benefits. It is anomalous that the Court's opinion today will extend the right of appointed counsel to indigent defendants in cases where the right to counsel would rarely be exercised by nonindigent defendants.

Indeed, one of the effects of this ruling will be to favor defendants classified as indigents over those not so classified, yet who are in low-income groups where engaging counsel in a minor petty-offense case would be a luxury the family could not afford. The line between indigency and assumed capacity to pay for counsel is necessarily somewhat arbitrary, drawn differently from State to State and often resulting in serious inequities to accused persons. The Court's new rule will accent the disadvantage of being barely self-sufficient economically.

. . . .

The Fifth and Fourteenth Amendments guarantee that property, as well as life and liberty, may not be taken from a person without affording him due process of law. The majority opinion suggests no constitutional basis for distinguishing between deprivations of liberty and property. In fact, the majority suggests no reason at all for drawing this distinction. The logic it advances for extending the right to counsel to all cases in which the penalty of any imprisonment is imposed applies equally well to cases in which other penalties may be imposed. Nor does the majority deny that some "non-jail" penalties are more serious than brief jail sentences.

Thus, although the new rule is extended today only to the imprisonment category of cases, the Court's opinion foreshadows the adoption of a broad prophylactic rule applicable to all petty offenses. No one can foresee the consequences of such a drastic enlargement of the constitutional right to free counsel. But even today's decision could have a seriously adverse impact upon the day-to-day functioning of the criminal justice system. We should be slow to fashion a new constitutional rule with consequences of such unknown dimensions, especially since it is supported neither by history nor precedent.

. . . .

III.

I would hold that the right to counsel in petty-offense cases is not absolute but is one to be determined by the trial courts exercising a judicial discretion on a case-by-case basis. The determination should be made before the accused formally pleads; many petty cases are resolved by guilty pleas in which the assistance of counsel may be required. If the trial court should conclude that the assistance of counsel is not required in any case, it should state its reasons so that the issue could be preserved for review. The trial court would then become obligated to scrutinize carefully the subsequent proceedings for the protection of the defendant. If an unrepresented defendant sought to enter a plea of guilty, the Court should examine the case against him to insure that there is admissible evidence tending to support the elements of the offense. If a case went to trial without defense counsel, the court should intervene, when necessary, to insure that the defendant adequately brings out the facts in his favor and to prevent legal issues from being overlooked. Formal trial rules should not be applied strictly against unrepresented defendants. Finally, appellate courts should carefully scrutinize all decisions not to appoint counsel and the proceedings which follow.

It is impossible, as well as unwise, to create a precise and detailed set of guidelines for judges to follow in determining whether the appointment of counsel is necessary to assure a fair trial. Certainly three general factors should be weighed. First, the court should consider the complexity of the offense charged. For example, charges of traffic law infractions would rarely present complex legal or factual questions, but charges that contain difficult intent elements or which raise collateral legal questions, such as search-and-seizure problems, would usually be too complex for an unassisted layman. If the offense were one where the State is represented by counsel and where most defendants who can afford to do so obtain counsel there would be a strong indication that the indigent also needs the assistance of counsel.

Second, the court should consider the probable sentence that will follow if a conviction is obtained. The more serious the likely consequences, the greater is the probability that a lawyer should be appointed. As noted in Part I above [omitted], imprisonment is not the only serious consequence the court should consider.

Third, the court should consider the individual factors peculiar to each case. These, of course, would be the most difficult to anticipate. One relevant factor would be the competency of the individual defendant to present his own case. The attitude of the community toward a particular defendant or particular incident would be another consideration. But there might be other reasons why a defendant would have a peculiar need for a lawyer which would compel the appointment of counsel in a case where the court would normally think this unnecessary. Obviously, the sensitivity and diligence of individual judges would be crucial to the operation of a rule of fundamental fairness requiring the consideration of the varying factors in each case.

Such a rule is similar in certain respects to the special-circumstances rule applied to felony cases in *Betts* v. *Brady*, 316 U.S. 455 (1942), and *Bute* v. *Illinois*, 333 U.S. 640 (1948), which this Court overruled in *Gideon*. One of the reasons for seeking a more definitive standard in felony cases was the failure of many state courts to live up to their responsibilities in determining on a case-by-case basis whether counsel should be appointed. See the concurring opinion of MR. JUSTICE HARLAN in *Gideon*, 372 U.S., at 350–351, 83 S.Ct., at 800–801. But this Court should not assume that the past insensitivity of some state courts to the rights of defendants will continue. Certainly if the Court follows the course of reading rigid rules into the Constitution, so that the state courts will be unable to exercise judicial discretion within the limits of fundamental fairness, there is little reason to think that insensitivity will abate.

In concluding, I emphasize my long-held conviction that the adversary system functions best and most fairly only when all parties are represented by competent counsel. Before becoming a member of this Court, I participated in efforts to enlarge and extend the availability of counsel. The correct disposition of this case, therefore, has been a matter of considerable concern to me—as it has to the other members of the Court. We are all strongly drawn to the ideal of extending the right to counsel, but I differ as to two fundamentals: (i) what the Constitution *requires*, and (ii) the effect upon the criminal justice system, especially in the smaller cities and the thousands of police, municipal, and justice of the peace courts across the country.

The view I have expressed in this opinion would accord considerable discretion to the courts, and would allow the flexibility and opportunity for adjustment which seems so necessary when we are imposing new doctrine on the lowest level of courts of 50 States. Although this view would not precipitate the "chaos" predicted by the Solicitor General as the probable result of the Court's absolutist rule, there would still remain serious practical problems resulting from the expansion of indigents' rights to counsel in petty-offense cases. But the according of reviewable discretion to the courts in determining when counsel is necessary for a fair trial, rather than mandating a completely inflexible rule, would facilitate an orderly transition to a far wider availability and use of defense counsel.

In this process, the courts of first instance which decide these cases would have to recognize a duty to consider the need for counsel in every case where the defendant faces a significant penalty. The factors mentioned above, and such standards or guidelines to assure fairness as might be prescribed in each jurisdiction by legislation or rule of court, should be considered where relevant. The goal should be, in accord with the essence of the adversary system, to expand as rapidly as practicable the availability of counsel so that no person accused of crime must stand alone if counsel is needed.

As the proceedings in the courts below were not in accord with the views expressed above, I concur in the result of the decision in this case.

KIRBY v. ILLINOIS

406 U.S. 682, 32 L.E.2d 411, 92 S.Ct. 1877 (1972)

Petitioner was convicted in the Circuit Court, Cook County, Illinois, of robbery and he appealed. The Appellate Court of Illinois, First District, 121 Ill. App.2d 323, 257 N.E.2d 589, affirmed, and certiorari was granted. MR. JUSTICE STEWART announced the judgment of the Supreme Court and delivered an opinion that police station showup that took place after petitioner's arrest but before he had been indicted or otherwise formally charged with any criminal offense was not a "criminal prosecution" at which he had constitutional right to be represented by counsel; thus robbery victim's testimony at trial describing his showup identification of petitioner, when he was not represented by counsel, was admissible.

Judgment affirmed.

MR. CHIEF JUSTICE BURGER filed a concurring statement.

MR. JUSTICE POWELL filed statement concurring in the result.

MR. JUSTICE BRENNAN filed a dissenting opinion in which MR. JUSTICE DOUGLAS and MR. JUSTICE MARSHALL joined.

MR. JUSTICE WHITE filed a dissenting statement.

MR. JUSTICE STEWART announced the judgment of the Court and an opinion in which THE CHIEF JUSTICE, MR. JUSTICE BLACKMUN, and MR. JUSTICE REHNQUIST join.

In *United States* v. *Wade,* 388 U.S. 218, and *Gilbert* v. *California,* 388 U.S. 263, this Court held "that a post indictment pretrial lineup at which the accused is exhibited to identifying witnesses is a critical stage of the criminal prosecution; that police conduct of such a lineup without notice to and in the absence of his counsel denies the ac-

cused his Sixth [and Fourteenth] Amendment right to counsel and calls in question the admissibility at trial of the in-court identifications of the accused by witnesses who attended the lineup." Those cases further held that no "in-court identifications" are admissible in evidence if their "source" is a lineup conducted in violation of this constitutional standard. "Only a *per se* exclusionary rule as to such testimony can be an effective sanction," the Court said, "to assure that law enforcement authorities will respect the accused's constitutional right to the presence of his counsel at the critical lineup." *Id.* In the present case we are asked to extend the *Wade-Gilbert per se* exclusionary rule to identification testimony based upon a police station showup that took place *before* the defendant had been indicted or otherwise formally charged with any criminal offense.

On February 21, 1968, a man named Willie Shard reported to the Chicago police that the previous day two men had robbed him on a Chicago street of a wallet containing, among other things, traveler's checks and a Social Security card. On February 22, two police officers stopped the petitioner and a companion, Ralph Bean, on West Madison Street in Chicago. When asked for identification, the petitioner produced a wallet that contained three traveler's checks and a Social Security card, all bearing the name of Willie Shard. Papers with Shard's name on them were also found in Bean's possession. When asked to explain his possession of

Shard's property, the petitioner first said that the traveler's checks were "play money," and then told the officers that he had won them in a crap game. The officers then arrested the petitioner and Bean and took them to a police station.

Only after arriving at the police station, and checking the records there, did the arresting officers learn of the Shard robbery. A police car was then dispatched to Shard's place of employment, where it picked up Shard and brought him to the police station. Immediately upon entering the room in the police station where the petitioner and Bean were seated at a table, Shard positively identified them as the men who had robbed him two days earlier. No lawyer was present in the room, and neither the petitioner nor Bean had asked for legal assistance, or been advised of any right to the presence of counsel.

More than six weeks later, the petitioner and Bean were indicted for the robbery of Willie Shard. Upon arraignment, counsel was appointed to represent them, and they pleaded not guilty. A pretrial motion to suppress Shard's identification testimony was denied, and at the trial Shard testified as a witness for the prosecution. In his testimony he described his identification of the two men at the police station on February 22, and identified them again in the courtroom as the men who had robbed him on February 20. He was cross-examined at length regarding the circumstances of his identification of the two defendants. Cf. *Pointer*

v. *Texas*, 380 U.S. 400. The jury found both defendants guilty, and the petitioner's conviction was affirmed on appeal. The Illinois appellate court held that the admission of Shard's testimony was not error, relying upon an earlier decision of the Illinois Supreme Court, *People* v. *Palmer*, 41 Ill.2d 571, 244 N.E.2d 173, holding that the *Wade-Gilbert per se* exclusionary rule is not applicable to preindictment confrontations. We granted certiorari, limited to this question.

I.

We note at the outset that the constitutional privilege against compulsory self-incrimination is in no way implicated here. The Court emphatically rejected the claimed applicability of that constitutional guarantee in *Wade* itself:

Neither the lineup itself nor anything shown by this record that Wade was required to do in the lineup violated his privilege against self-incrimination. We have only recently reaffirmed that the privilege "protects an accused only from being compelled to testify against himself, or otherwise provide the State with evidence of a testimonial or communicative nature...." *Schmerber* v. *California*. ...

. . . .

We have no doubt that compelling the accused merely to exhibit his person for observation by a prosecution witness prior to trial involves no compulsion of the accused to give evidence having testimonial significance. It is compulsion of the accused to exhibit his physical characteristics, not compulsion to disclose to any knowledge he might have. . . .

It follows that the doctrine of *Miranda* v. *Arizona*, 384 U.S. 436, has no applicability whatever to the issue before us; for the *Miranda* decision was based exclusively upon the Fifth and Fourteenth Amendment privilege against compulsory self-incrimination, upon the theory that custodial *interrogation* is inherently coercive.

The *Wade-Gilbert* exclusionary rule, by contrast, stems from a quite different constitutional guarantee—the guarantee of the right to counsel contained in the Sixth and Fourteenth Amendments. Unless all semblance of principled constitutional adjudication is to be abandoned, therefore, it is to the decisions construing that guarantee that we must look in determining the present controversy.

In a line of constitutional cases in this Court stemming back to the Court's landmark opinion in *Powell* v. *Alabama*, 287 U.S. 45, it has been firmly established that a person's Sixth and Fourteenth Amendment right to counsel attaches only at or after the time that adversary judicial proceedings have been initiated against him. See *Powell* v. *Alabama, supra; Johnson* v. *Zerbst,* 304 U.S. 458; *Hamilton* v. *Alabama,* 368 U.S. 52; *Gideon* v. *Wainwright,* 372 U.S. 335; *White* v. *Maryland,* 373 U.S. 59; *Massiah*

v. *United States,* 377 U.S. 201; *United States* v. *Wade,* 388 U.S. 218; *Gilbert* v. *California,* 388 U.S. 263; *Coleman* v. *Alabama,* 399 U.S. 1.

This is not to say that a defendant in a criminal case has a constitutional right to counsel only at the trial itself. The *Powell* case makes clear that the right attaches at the time of arraignment, and the Court has recently held that it exists also at the time of a preliminary hearing. *Coleman* v. *Alabama, supra.* But the point is that, while members of the Court have differed as to existence of the right to counsel in the contexts of some of the above cases, *all* of those cases have involved points of time at or after the initiation of adversary judicial criminal proceedings —whether by way of formal charge, preliminary hearing, indictment, information, or arraignment.

The only seeming deviation from this long line of constitutional decisions was *Escobedo* v. *Illinois,* 378 U.S. 478. But *Escobedo* is not apposite here for two distinct reasons. First, the Court in retrospect perceived that the "prime purpose" of *Escobedo* was not to vindicate the constitutional right to counsel as such, but, like *Miranda,* "to guarantee full effectuation of the privilege against self-incrimination. . . ." *Johnson* v. *New Jersey,* 384 U.S. 719, 729. Secondly, and perhaps even more important for purely practical purposes, the Court has limited the holding of *Escobedo* to its own facts, and those facts are not remotely akin to the facts of the case before us.

The initiation of judicial criminal proceedings is far from a mere formalism. It is the starting point of our whole system of adversary criminal justice. For it is only then that the government has committed itself to prosecute, and only then that the adverse positions of government and defendant have solidified. It is then that a defendant finds himself faced with the prosecutorial forces of organized society, and immersed in the intricacies of substantive and procedural criminal law. It is this point, therefore, that marks the commencement of the "criminal prosecutions" to which alone the explicit guarantees of the Sixth Amendment are applicable. [Citations omitted.]

In this case we are asked to import into a routine police investigation an absolute constitutional guarantee historically and rationally applicable only after the onset of formal prosecutorial proceedings. We decline to do so. Less than a year after *Wade* and *Gilbert* were decided, the Court explained the rule of those decisions as follows: "The rationale of those cases was that an accused is entitled to counsel at any 'critical stage of the *prosecution*,' and that a post-indictment lineup is such a 'critical stage.' " (Emphasis supplied.) *Simmons* v. *United States*, 390 U.S. 377. We decline to depart from that rationale today by imposing a *per se* exclusionary rule upon testimony concerning an identification that took place long before the commencement of any prosecution whatever.

II.

What has been said is not to suggest that there may not be occasions during the course of a criminal investigation when the police do abuse identification procedures. Such abuses are not beyond the reach of the Constitution. As the Court pointed out in *Wade* itself, it is always necessary to "scrutinize *any* pretrial confrontation. . . ." The Due Process Clause of the Fifth and Fourteenth Amendments forbids a lineup that is unnecessarily suggestive and conducive to irreparable mistaken identification. *Stovall* v. *Denno*, 388 U.S. 293; *Foster* v. *California*, 394 U.S. 440. When a person has not been formally charged with a criminal offense, *Stovall* strikes the appropriate constitutional balance between the right of a suspect to be protected from prejudicial procedures and the interest of society in the prompt and purposeful investigation of an unsolved crime.

The judgment is affirmed.

MR. CHIEF JUSTICE BURGER, concurring.

I agree that the right to counsel attaches as soon as criminal charges are formally made against an accused and he becomes the subject of a "criminal prosecution." Therefore, I join in the plurality opinion and in the judgment. Cf. *Coleman* v. *Alabama*, 399 U.S. 1, 21 (dissenting opinion).

MR. JUSTICE POWELL, concurring in the result.

As I would not extend the *Wade-*

Gilbert per se exclusionary rule, I concur in the result reached by the Court.

MR. JUSTICE BRENNAN, with whom MR. JUSTICE DOUGLAS and MR. JUSTICE MARSHALL join, dissenting.

After petitioner and Ralph Bean were arrested, police officers brought Willie Shard, the robbery victim, to a room in a police station where petitioner and Bean were seated at a table with two other police officers. Shard testified at trial that the officers who brought him to the room asked him if petitioner and Bean were the robbers and that he indicated they were. The prosecutor asked him, "And you positively identified them at the police station, is that correct?" Shard answered, "Yes." Consequently, the question in this case is whether, under *Gilbert v. California*, 388 U.S. 263 (1967), it was constitutional error to admit Shard's testimony that he identified petitioner at the pretrial station-house showup when that showup was conducted by the police without advising petitioner that he might have counsel present. *Gilbert* held, in the context of a post-indictment lineup, that "[o]nly a *per se* exclusionary rule as to such testimony can be effective sanction to assure that law enforcement authorities will respect the

accused's constitutional right to the presence of his counsel at the critical lineup." I would apply *Gilbert* and the principles of its companion case, *United States v. Wade*, 388 U.S. 218 (1967), and reverse.

. . . .

Wade and *Gilbert*, of course, happened to involve post-indictment confrontations. Yet even a cursory perusal of the opinions in those cases reveals that nothing at all turned upon that particular circumstance. In short, it is fair to conclude that rather than "declin[ing] to depart from [the] rationale" of *Wade* and *Gilbert*, the plurality today, albeit purporting to be engaged in "principled constitutional adjudication," refuses even to recognize that "rationale." For my part, I do not agree that we "extend" *Wade* and *Gilbert* by holding that the principles of those cases apply to confrontations for identification conducted after arrest. Because Shard testified at trial about his identification of petitioner at the police station showup, the exclusionary rule of *Gilbert* requires reversal.

MR. JUSTICE WHITE, dissenting.

United States v. Wade and *Gilbert v. California* govern this case and compel reversal of the judgment below.

Case relating to **Chapter 9**

DOUBLE JEOPARDY

ASHE v. SWENSON

397 U.S. 436, 25 L.Ed.2d 469, 90 S.Ct. 1189 (1970)

Mr. Justice Stewart delivered the opinion of the Court.

In *Benton v. Maryland,* 395 U.S. 784, the Court held that the Fifth Amendment guarantee against double jeopardy is enforceable against the States through the Fourteenth Amendment. The question in this case is whether the State of Missouri violated that guarantee when it prosecuted the petitioner a second time for armed robbery in the circumstances here presented.

Sometime in the early hours of the morning of January 10, 1960, six men were engaged in a poker game in the basement of the home of John Gladson at Lee's Summit, Missouri. Suddenly three or four masked men, armed with a shotgun and pistols, broke into the basement and robbed each of the poker players of money and various articles of personal property. The robbers—and it has never been clear whether there were three or four of them—then fled in a car belonging to one of the victims of the robbery. Shortly thereafter the stolen car was discovered in a field, and later that morning three men were arrested by a state trooper while they were walking on a highway not far from where the abandoned car had been found. The petitioner was arrested by another officer some distance away.

The four were subsequently charged with seven separate offenses—the armed robbery of each of the six poker players and the theft of the car. In May 1960 the petitioner went to trial on the charge of robbing Donald Knight, one of the participants in the poker game. At the trial the State called Knight and three of his fellow poker players as prosecution witnesses. Each of them described the circumstances of the holdup and itemized his own individual losses. The proof that an armed robbery had occurred and that personal property had been taken from Knight as well as from each of the others was unassailable. The testimony of the four victims in this regard was consistent both internally and with that of the others. But the State's evidence that the petitioner had been one of the robbers was weak. Two of the witnesses thought that there had been only three robbers altogether, and could not identify the petitioner as one of them. Another of the victims, who was the petitioner's uncle by marriage, said that at the "patrol station" he had positively identified each of the other three men accused of the holdup, but could say only the petitioner's voice "sounded very much like" that of one of the robbers. The fourth participant in the poker game did identify the petitioner, but only by his "size and height, and his actions."

The cross-examination of these witnesses was brief, and it was aimed primarily at exposing the weakness of their identification testimony. Defense counsel made no attempt to question their testimony regarding the holdup itself or their claims as to their losses. Knight testified without contradiction that the robbers had stolen from him his watch, $250 in cash, and about $500 in checks. His billfold, which had been found by the police in the possession of one of the three other men accused of the robbery, was admitted in evidence. The defense offered no testimony and waived final argument.

The trial judge instructed the jury that if it found that the petitioner was one of the participants in the armed robbery, the theft of "any money" from Knight would sustain a conviction. He also instructed the jury that if the petitioner was one of the robbers, he was guilty under the law even if he had not personally robbed Knight. The jury—though not instructed to elaborate upon its verdict—found the petitioner "not guilty due to insufficient evidence."

Six weeks later the petitioner was brought to trial again, this time for the robbery of another participant in the poker game, a man named Roberts. The petitioner filed a motion to dismiss, based on his previous acquittal. The motion was overruled, and the second

trial began. The witnesses were for the most part the same, though this time their testimony was substantially stronger on the issue of the petitioner's identity. For example, two witnesses who at the first trial had been wholly unable to identify the petitioner as one of the robbers, now testified that his features, size, and mannerisms matched those of one of their assailants. Another witness who before had identified the petitioner only by his size and actions now also remembered him by the unusual sound of his voice. The State further refined its case at the second trial by declining to call one of the participants in the poker game whose identification testimony at the first trial had been conspicuously negative. The case went to the jury on instructions virtually identical to those given at the first trial. This time the jury found the petitioner guilty, and he was sentenced to a 35-year term in the state penitentiary.

The Supreme Court of Missouri affirmed the conviction, holding that the "plea of former jeopardy must be denied." *State v. Ashe*, 350 S.W.2d 768, at 771. . . .

. . . .

The doctrine of *Benton v. Maryland*, 395 U.S. 784, puts the issues in the present case in a perspective quite different from that in which the issues were perceived in *Hoag v. New Jersey*, [356 U.S. 464]. The question is no longer whether collateral estoppel is a requirement of due process, but whether it is a part of the Fifth Amendment's guarantee against double jeopardy. And if collateral estoppel is embodied in that guarantee, then its applicability in a particular case is no longer a matter to be left for state court determination within the broad bounds of "fundamental fairness," but a matter of constitutional fact we must decide through an examination of the entire record. Cf. *New York Times Co. v. Sullivan*, 376 U.S. 254, 285; *Niemotko v. Maryland*, 340 U.S. 268, 271; *Watts v. Indiana*, 338 U.S. 49, 51; *Chambers v. Florida*, 309 U.S. 227, 229; *Norris v. Alabama*, 294 U.S. 587, 590.

"Collateral estoppel" is an awkward phrase, but it stands for an extremely important principle in our adversary system of justice. It means simply that when an issue of ultimate fact has once been determined by a valid and final judgment, that issue cannot again be litigated between the same parties in any future lawsuit. Although first developed in civil litigation, collateral estoppel has been an established rule of federal criminal law at least since this Court's decision more than 50 years ago in *United States v. Oppenheimer*, 242 U.S. 85. As Mr. JUSTICE HOLMES put the matter in that case, "It cannot be that the safeguards of the person, so often and so rightly mentioned with solemn reverence, are less than those that protect from a liability in debt." 242 U.S., at 87. As a rule of federal law, therefore, "[i]t is much too late to suggest that this principle is not fully applicable to a former judgment in a criminal case, either be-cause of lack of 'mutuality' or because the judgment may reflect only a belief that the Government had not met the higher burden of proof exacted in such cases for the Government's evidence as a whole although not necessarily as to every link in the chain." *United States v. Kramer*, 289 F.2d 909, at 913.

The federal decisions have made clear that the rule of collateral estoppel in criminal cases is not to be applied with the hypertechnical and archaic approach of a 19th century pleading book, but with realism and rationality. Where a previous judgment of acquittal was based upon a general verdict, as is usually the case, this approach requires a court to "examine the record of a prior proceeding, taking into account the pleadings, evidence, charge, and other relevant matter, and conclude whether a rational jury could have grounded its verdict upon an issue other than that which the defendant seeks to foreclose from consideration." The inquiry "must be set in a practical frame, and viewed with an eye to all the circumstances of the proceedings." *Sealfon v. United States*, 332 U.S. 575, 579. Any test more technically restrictive would, of course, simply amount to a rejection of the rule of collateral estoppel in criminal proceedings, at least in every case where the first judgment was based upon a general verdict of acquittal.

Straightforward application of the federal rule to the present case can lead to but one conclusion. For the record is utterly devoid of any indication that the first jury could rationally have found that an armed robbery had not occurred, or that Knight had not been a victim of that robbery. The single rationally conceivable issue in dispute before the jury was whether the petitioner had been one of the robbers. And the jury by its verdict found that he had not. The federal rule of law, therefore, would make a second prosecution for the robbery of Roberts wholly impermissible.

The ultimate question to be determined, then, in the light of *Benton v. Maryland, supra,* is whether this established rule of federal law is embodied in the Fifth Amendment guarantee against double jeopardy. We do not hesitate to hold that it is. For whatever else that constitutional guarantee may embrace, *North Carolina v. Pearce,* 395 U.S. 711, 717, it surely protects a man who has been acquitted from having to "run the gantlet" a second time. *Green v. United States,* 355 U.S. 184, 190.

The question is not whether Missouri could validly charge the petitioner with six separate offenses for the robbery of the six poker players. It is not whether he could have received a total of six punishments if he had been convicted in a single trial of robbing the six victims. It is simply whether, after a jury determined by its verdict that the petitioner was not one of the robbers, the State could constitutionally hale him before a new jury to litigate that issue again.

After the first jury had acquitted the petitioner of robbing Knight, Missouri could certainly not have brought him to trial again upon that charge. Once a jury had determined upon conflicting testimony that there was at least a reasonable doubt that the petitioner was one of the robbers, the State could not present the same or different identification evidence in a second prosecution for the robbery of Knight in the hope that a different jury might find that evidence more convincing. The situation is constitutionally no different here, even though the second trial related to another victim of the same robbery. For the name of the victim, in the circumstances of this case, had no bearing whatever upon the issue of whether the petitioner was one of the robbers.

In this case the State in its brief has frankly conceded that following the petitioner's acquittal, it treated the first trial as no more than a dry run for the second prosecution: "No doubt the prosecutor felt the state had a provable case on the first charge, and, when he lost, he did what every good attorney would do—he refined his presentation in light of the turn of events at the first trial." But this is precisely what the constitutional guarantee forbids.

The judgment is reversed, and the case is remanded to the Court of Appeals for the Eighth Circuit for further proceedings consistent with this opinion.

It is so ordered.

[The concurring opinions of MR. JUSTICE BLACK and of MR. JUSTICE HARLAN are not included.]

MR. JUSTICE BRENNAN, whom MR. JUSTICE DOUGLAS and MR. JUSTICE MARSHALL join, concurring.

I agree that the Double Jeopardy Clause incorporates collateral estoppel as a constitutional requirement and therefore join the Court's opinion. However, even if the rule of collateral estoppel had been inapplicable to the facts of this case, it is my view that the Double Jeopardy Clause nevertheless bars the prosecution of petitioner a second time for armed robbery. The two prosecutions, the first for the robbery of Knight and the second for the robbery of Roberts, grew out of one criminal episode, and therefore I think it clear on the facts of this case that the Double Jeopardy Clause prohibited Missouri from prosecuting petitioner for each robbery at a different trial. *Abbate* v. *United States*, 359 U.S. 187, 196–201 (1959) (separate opinion).

. . . .

The Double Jeopardy Clause is a guarantee "that the State with all its resources and power [shall] not be allowed to make repeated attempts to convict an individual for an alleged offense, thereby subjecting him to embarrassment, expense and ordeal and compelling him to live in a continuing state of anxiety and insecurity. . . ." *Green* v. *United States*, 355 U.S. 184, 187 (1957). This guarantee is expressed as a prohibition against multiple prosecutions for the "same offence." Although the phrase "same offence" appeared in most

of the early common-law articulations of the double-jeopardy principle, questions of its precise meaning rarely arose prior to the 18th century, and by the time the Bill of Rights was adopted it had not been authoritatively defined.

When the common law did finally attempt a definition, in *Rex* v. *Vandercomb & Abbott*, 2 Leach 708, 720, 168 Eng. Rep. 455, 461 (Crown 1796), it adopted the "same evidence" test, which provided little protection from multiple prosecution:

> [U]nless the first indictment were such as the prisoner might have been convicted upon by proof of the facts contained in the second indictment, an acquittal on the first indictment can be no bar to the second.

The "same evidence" test of "same offence" was soon followed by a majority of American jurisdictions, but its deficiencies are obvious. It does not enforce but virtually annuls the constitutional guarantee. For example, where a single criminal episode involves several victims, under the "same evidence" test a separate prosecution may be brought as to each. E.g., *State* v. *Hoag*, 21 N.J. 496, 122 A.2d 628, (1956), aff'd, 356 U.S. 464 (1958). The "same evidence" test permits multiple prosecutions where a single transaction is divisible into chronologically discrete crimes. E.g., *Johnson* v. *Commonwealth*, 201 Ky. 314, 256 S.W. 388 (1923) (each of 75 poker hands a separate "offense"). Even a single criminal act may lead to multiple prosecutions if it is viewed from the perspectives of different statutes. E.g., *State* v. *Elder*, 65 Ind. 282 (1879). Given the tendency of modern criminal legislation to divide the phases of criminal transaction into numerous separate crimes, the opportunities for multiple prosecutions for an essentially unitary criminal episode are frightening. And given our tradition of virtually unreviewable prosecutorial discretion concerning the initiation and scope of a criminal prosecution, the potentialities for abuse inherent in the "same evidence" test are simply intolerable.

. . . .

In my view, the Double Jeopardy Clause requires the prosecution, except in most limited circumstances, to join at one trial all the charges against a defendant which grow out of a single criminal act, occurrence, episode, or transaction. This "same transaction" test of "same offence" not only enforces the ancient prohibition against vexatious multiple prosecutions embodied in the Double Jeopardy Clause, but responds as well to the increasingly widespread recognition that the consolidation in one lawsuit of all issues arising out of a single transaction or occurrence best promotes justice, economy, and convenience. Modern rules of criminal and civil procedure reflect this recognition. See *UMW* v. *Gibbs*, 383 U.S. 715, 724–726 (1966). Although in 1935 the American Law Institute adopted the "same evidence" test, it has since replaced it with the "same

transaction" test. England, too, has abandoned its surviving rules against joinder of charges and has adopted the "same transaction" test. . . .

. . . .

The present case highlights the hazards of abuse of the criminal process inherent in the "same evidence" test and demonstrates the necessity for the "same transaction" test. The robbery of the poker game involved six players— Gladson, Knight, Freeman, Goodwin, McClendon, and Roberts. The robbers also stole a car. Seven separate informations were filed against the petitioner, one covering each of the robbery victims, and the seventh covering the theft of the car. Petitioner's first trial was under the information charging the robbery of Knight. Since Missouri has offered no justification for not trying the other informations at that trial, it is reasonable to infer that the other informations were held in reserve to be tried if the State failed to obtain a conviction on the charge of robbing Knight. Indeed, the State virtually concedes as much since it argues that the "same evidence" test is consistent with such an exercise of prosecutorial discretion.

Four of the robbery victims testified at the trial. Their testimony conflicted as to whether there were three or four robbers. Gladson testified that he saw four robbers, but could identify only one, a man named Brown. McClendon testified that he saw only three men at any one time during the course of the robbery, and he positively identified Brown, Larson, and Johnson; he also thought he heard petitioner's voice during the robbery, but said he was not sure. Knight thought only three men participated in the robbery, and he could not identify anyone. Roberts said he saw four different men and he identified them as Brown, Larson, Johnson, and petitioner. Under cross-examination, he conceded that he did not recognize petitioner's voice, and that he did not see his face or his hands. He maintained that he could identify him by his "size and height" even though all the robbers had worn outsized clothing, and even though he could not connect petitioner with the actions of any of the robbers. On this evidence the jury acquitted petitioner.

At the second trial, for the robbery of Roberts, McClendon was not called as a witness. Gladson, who previously had been able to identify only one man—Brown—now was able to identify three—Brown, Larson, and petitioner. On a number of details his memory was much more vivid than it had been at the first trial. Knight's testimony was substantially the same as at the first trial—he still was unable to identify any of the robbers. Roberts, who previously had identified petitioner only by his size and height, now identified him by his size, actions, voice, and a peculiar movement of his mouth. As might be expected, this far

stronger identification evidence brought a virtually inevitable conviction.

The prosecution plainly organized its case for the second trial to provide the links missing in the chain of identification evidence that was offered at the first trial. McClendon, who was an unhelpful witness at the first trial was not called at the second trial. The hesitant and uncertain evidence of Gladson and Roberts at the first trial became detailed, positive, and expansive at the second trial. One must experience a sense of uneasiness with any double jeopardy standard that would allow the State this second chance to plug up the holes in its case. The constitutional protection against double jeopardy is empty of meaning if the State may make "repeated attempts" to touch up its case by forcing the accused to "run the gantlet" as many times as there are victims of a single episode.

Fortunately for petitioner, the conviction at the second trial can be reversed under the doctrine of collateral estoppel, since the jury at the first trial clearly resolved in his favor the only contested issue at that trial, which was the identification of him as one of the robbers. There is at least doubt whether collateral estoppel would have aided him had the jury been required to resolve additional contested issues on conflicting evidence. But correction of the abuse of criminal process should not in any event be made to depend on the availability of collateral estoppel. Abuse of the criminal process is foremost among the feared evils which led to the inclusion of the Double Jeopardy Clause in the Bill of Rights. That evil will be most effectively avoided, and the Clause can thus best serve its worthy ends, if "same offence" is construed to embody the "same transaction" standard. Then both federal and state prosecutors will be prohibited from mounting successive prosecutions for offenses growing out of the same criminal episode, at least in the absence of a showing of unavoidable necessity for successive prosecutions in the particular case.

MR. CHIEF JUSTICE BURGER, dissenting.

. . . .

III.

The essence of MR. JUSTICE BRENNAN's concurrence is that this was all one transaction, one episode, or, if I may so characterize it, one frolic, and, hence, only one crime. His approach, like that taken by the Court, totally overlooks the significance of there being *six entirely separate charges of robbery* against six individuals.

This "single transaction" concept is not a novel notion; it has been urged in various courts including this Court. One of the theses underlying the "single transaction" notion is that the criminal episode is "indivisible." The short answer to that is that to the victims, the criminal conduct is readily divisible and intensely personal; each offense is an offense against

a person. For me it demeans the dignity of the human personality and individuality to talk of "a single transaction" in the context of six separate assaults on six individuals.

No court which elevates the individual rights and human dignity of the accused to a high place—as we should—ought to be so casual as to treat the victims as a single homogenized lump of human clay. I would grant the dignity of individual status to the victims as much as to those accused, not more but surely no less.

If it be suggested that multiple crimes can be separately punished but must be collectively tried, one can point to the firm trend in the law to allow severance of defendants and offenses into separate trials so as to avoid possible prejudice of one criminal act or of the conduct of one defendant to "spill over" on another.

What the Court holds today must be related to its impact on crimes more serious than ordinary housebreaking, followed by physical assault on six men and robbery of all of them. To understand its full impact we must view the holding in the context of four men who break and enter, rob and then kill six victims. The concurrence tells us that unless all the crimes are joined in one trial the alleged killers cannot be tried for more than one of the killings even if the evidence is that they personally killed two, three or more of the victims. Or alter the crime to four men breaking into a college dormitory and assaulting six girls. What the Court is holding is, in effect, that the second and third and fourth criminal acts are "free," unless the accused is tried for the multiple crimes in a single trial— something defendants frantically use every legal device to avoid, and often succeed in avoiding. This is the reality of what the Court holds today; it does not make good sense and it cannot make good law.

I therefore join with the four courts which have found no double jeopardy in this case.

To borrow some wise words from Mr. Justice Black in his [separate opinion] in *Jackson* v. *Denno*, 378 U.S. 368, 401, 407–408 (1964), the conviction struck down in this case "is in full accord with all the guarantees of the Federal Constitution and . . . should not be held invalid by this Court because of a belief that the Court can improve on the Constitution."

Case relating to **Chapter 10**

FAIR TRIAL AND HUMANE PUNISHMENT

UNITED STATES v. JONES

524 F.2d 834 (D.C.Cir. 1975)

Tamm, Circuit Judge.

Appellant John E. Jones was convicted on three counts of violating the Federal Narcotics Laws, 21 U.S.C. § 174, repealed, Pub.L. 91–513, 84 Stat. 1291 (October 27, 1970); 26 U.S.C. §§ 4704(a), 4705(a), repealed, Pub.L. 91–513, 84 Stat. 1292 (October 27, 1970). Appellant sold narcotics to an undercover narcotics agent on October 21, 1970, but he was not arrested until December 15, 1971, after agents were able to identify him from a photograph fortuitously discovered during an unrelated search. . . .

. . . .

II. Pre-Arrest Delay

A. *The Legal Framework:* Ross *and Its Progeny*

Appellant contends that the charges against him should be dismissed because the delay of more than 13 months between the date of the narcotics sale and the date of his arrest was unreasonable, prejudiced his ability to put on a defense and increased the likelihood of misidentification. Appellant relies on a line of cases in this circuit beginning with *Ross* v. *United States,* 349 F.2d 210 (D.C.Cir. 1965). Generally speaking, the *Ross* line of cases establishes the proposition that any unreasonable or unnecessary pre-arrest delay which results in prejudice to the accused may necessitate dismissal of the charges against him. See, *e. g., Robinson* v. *United States,* 459 F.2d 847 (D.C.Cir. 1972); *Woody* v. *United States,* 370 F.2d 214 (D.C.Cir. 1966). We noted in these cases that the increased use of undercover police methods had necessitated a reconciliation between the competing interests of effective enforcement of the narcotics laws and early notice to the accused-to-be of the impending accusation. *Robinson* v. *United States, supra,* 459 F.2d at 850. See, *e. g., Godfrey* v. *United States,* 358 F.2d 850, 851 (D.C.Cir. 1966); *Powell* v. *United States,* 352 F.2d 705, 708 (D.C.Cir. 1965). A general pattern emerges from these cases: in each case, the police knew the whereabouts of the accused-to-be but postponed arresting him, despite his availability, in order to protect an informer or avoid revealing the identity of an undercover agent who had not yet "surfaced." Mindful of the fact that such undercover investigations often continue for many months while alleged violators remain unaware that they will be charged, the *Ross* court cautioned that:

[i]t is always to be remembered that the [delay] is a conscious act on the part of the police. That alone does not condemn it, because the Department is motivated solely by a purpose to enhance its effectiveness in the public interest. But the Constitution contemplates a separate interest in fair procedures for the citizen faced with the loss of his liberty by reason of criminal charges. When interests of this nature impinge on each other, as they have a way of doing, they must be accommodated. A balance must be struck, if one or the other is not to be sacrificed completely.

Ross v. *United States*, 349 F.2d at 213, quoted in *Robinson* v. *United States*, 459 F.2d at 851.

On the basis of our supervisory power over criminal trials in this circuit, but mindful of the due process overtones of the problem, we thus held that narcotics charges must be dismissed where the delay between the undercover agent's detection of the crime and notice to the accused of criminal charges is unreasonable and prejudicial to him. *Robinson* v. *United States*, 459 F.2d at 851, citing *Ross* v. *United States*, 349 F.2d at 213. The *Ross* rule assumes that the accused is available for arrest and would be arrested were it not for the need to protect an informer or to keep an undercover agent underground; its purpose is to limit the extent to which the police may consciously trade off the interests of the accused-to-be in receiving early no-

tice of the accusations against him in favor of the societal interest in discovering and apprehending narcotics offenders. The fundamental concern underlying the rule is that the delay necessitated by this choice of police methods significantly increases "the risk of conviction of an innocent person." *Daniels* v. *United States*, 357 F.2d 587, 590 (D.C.Cir. 1966) (dissenting opinion) (rehearing denied 1966) (footnote omitted). See also *Woody* v. *United States*, 370 F.2d at 216 (D.C.Cir. 1966). Some delay is, of course, inevitable, and therefore legally permissible, due to the requirements of effective police work. Courts, nevertheless, must consider the adverse impact on the accused. Accordingly, a two-pronged test has evolved under which the court must examine the reasonableness of the delay and the resulting harm, if any, to the accused. *Robinson* v. *United States*, 459 F.2d at 852. See, *e. g.*, *Lee* v. *United States*, 368 F.2d 834, 835 n. 2 (D.C.Cir. 1966).

. . . .

B. *The* Ross *Analysis Applied*

1. The Requirement of Purposefulness.

Turning now to the facts before us, we confront the initial question: whether this case fits within the *Ross* line at all. The Government argues with some force that this case is distinguishable from the *Ross*-type cases because the delay was not purposeful and because Jones was not continuously available for arrest; he merely successfully evaded all efforts to apprehend him. The Government further contends that, because Agent Logan was undercover for only a single transaction, there was absolutely nothing to gain from further delay and, therefore, the agents attempted diligently, if unsuccessfully, to identify and locate appellant. When, finally, their luck changed and Agent Logan stumbled across a photograph of appellant during the course of an entirely unrelated search, the Government contends that Agent Logan acted with reasonable promptness to identify appellant and bring about his arrest.

Appellant argues in response that the delay was in fact purposeful because the agents unjustifiably allowed appellant to drive away following the illegal transaction when there was surely probable cause and sufficient manpower to arrest him. . . .

The facts before us to some extent differentiate this case from more typical *Ross* situations. It does appear that the agents initially acted purposefully in not arresting appellant at the time of the illegal sale, whatever their reasons. Nevertheless, there is no indication whatsoever that the great bulk of the delay was purposeful or that the Government secured or attempted to secure any tactical advantage in delaying appellant's arrest. Indeed, the facts show that Agents Logan and Jackson made a number of genuine, if unsuccessful, attempts to identify and locate appellant. In short, the bulk of the substantial delay in appellant's ar-

rest is attributable not to any conscious decision to postpone his arrest, but to the inability of the agents to identify or locate him. Because of the initial decision not to make an arrest at the time of the illegal sale, and because of the undercover police methods used, however, we conclude that the facts before us must be analyzed against the background of the *Ross* line of cases. . . .

. . . .

3. The Requirement of Prejudice

Under the test articulated in *Robinson, supra,* perhaps the most important recent case in the *Ross* line, even if we were to conclude that the delay in appellant's arrest was unreasonable and that the agents' conduct was less than diligent, "[it] would not end the matter; it would simply chalk up one mark against the Government." *United States* v. *Mills,* 463 F.2d at 301 (D.C.Cir. 1972). Under the test enunciated in *Ross* and refined in cases like *Robinson,* appellant still has the burden of demonstrating some "special circumstances," or some prejudice to his case. Such a showing requires more than a general assertion that the accused has difficulty remembering the day of the illegal transaction.

In *Robinson* v. *United States, supra,* the accused denied having committed the alleged offense, but testified that he could not recall his whereabouts during the relevant period. He also testified as to his employment during the period, although he failed to call his employer as a witness, and further claimed that his then-deceased sister, with whom he had been living at the time of the offense, could have established an alibi. On these facts, the court held that the appellant had failed to demonstrate that his ability to present a defense had been prejudiced by the pre-arrest delay, and stated, "Any inference that harm did result is negated when the accused testifies in detail or brings forward an alibi witness, or perhaps even when he holds a steady job." 459 F.2d at 852–53. Thus, after *Robinson*, the *Ross* requirement that the accused present a "plausible claim" of prejudice is not satisfied by the mere assertion that the accused cannot remember his whereabouts on the day of the offense or by the "slender hope" that a witness, now unavailable, might have been able to come forth with testimony favorable to the defense. *Id.*, 459 F.2d at 854. In brief, without a more definite showing of prejudice, "the probability of damage to appellant's ability to defend himself [is] not significant enough to warrant upsetting his conviction." *Id.* Also relevant to the issue of prejudice is the quality of the Government's proof in the particular case. *Id.* The principal concern of the *Ross* line of undercover narcotics cases is, again, the "lurking danger of misidentification" where the Government's case consists solely of testimony by a single eyewitness recollecting an event that occurred over a very short time, often in the very distant past.

Applying these principles to the instant case, we begin by noting that appellant relied at trial upon two defenses, alibi and misidentification. The Government presented three witnesses to support the identification of appellant as the seller of the illegal drugs. At the first trial, appellant attempted to establish an alibi, relying upon his mother's testimony (II Tr. I 91–93). At the second trial, appellant subpoenaed his employer to support his alibi defense (Tr. II 16, 296, 299). Moreover, appellant testified in detail about his employment and specifically denied being present on October 21, 1970, at each location mentioned by the three Government witnesses. Appellant called Fleming and Nicks, who confirmed that the illegal transaction took place but denied that appellant was a participant. Under these circumstances, appellant's claim of prejudice does not warrant upsetting his conviction. The record demonstrates that the failure of appellant's defense turned not on the expressed inability of appellant's witnesses to remember his whereabouts on October 21, 1970, but on the credibility of their statements that appellant was not present during the narcotics sale. As such, the matter was properly left to the jury.

Finally, this case is distinguished from "typical" *Ross*-type cases by another factor: the nature and strength of the undercover agents' identification. The general pattern of the *Ross* cases is that of an agent, often relatively inexperienced, who goes undercover for an extended period of time in order to participate in as many narcotics transactions as possible. When he surfaces, a flood of warrants may issue and a large number of suspected narcotics offenders may be arrested and charged solely on the basis of the undercover agent's testimony. Often the agent has had but a single brief encounter with each individual among the many. In *Ross*, for example, the agent had been involved in 125 transactions —so many, in fact, that he required a notebook to refresh his memory before testifying as to a single transaction. 349 F.2d at 212. It is the danger of misidentification inherent in this kind of mass-production law enforcement which underlies much of this court's concern for pre-arrest delay as expressed in *Ross* and its progeny.

We find that the danger of misidentification is minimized in this case by several factors. First, Agent Logan went undercover for but a single transaction. Moreover, although Agent Logan participated with appellant in only a single narcotics transaction, his identification appears to have been made, insofar as possible, in adherence with the factors set forth in *Woody* v. *United States*, 370 F.2d at 217 n. 6: he took fairly detailed notes, gave a detailed description of appellant and his dress, elicited a written corroborative statement from the in-

formant, and personally confronted the accused at the time of the arrest. Secondly, Agent Logan's testimony was substantially corroborated by the testimony of Agents Jackson and Marshall, assigned to observe his activities with informant Fleming. Third, Agent Logan identified appellant from a group of approximately 350 photographs, and even appellant's clothing in the photograph partially matched the description Logan had given immediately following the transaction. Neither Jackson nor Marshall was present during Logan's identification, and neither saw the photograph, yet their observations both tended to corroborate Logan's identification.

In conclusion, we hold on these facts that appellant has failed to demonstrate that the delay between the offense and his arrest was reasonably avoidable or that it prejudiced his ability to present a defense. We find that the "lurking danger of misidentification" in this case is substantially less than in more typical *Ross* mass-production arrest situations. We therefore conclude that the trial judge properly refused to dismiss the indictment.

. . . .

CIVIL RIGHTS AND CIVIL RIGHTS LEGISLATION

GLASSON v. CITY OF LOUISVILLE

518 F.2d 899 (6thCir. 1975)
cert. denied, 423 U.S. 930

[The facts and first part of this opinion are reproduced with cases relating to Chapter 2, *supra*. The court there determined that the defendants' conduct had infringed upon the plaintiff's First Amendment rights. In the portion of the opinion below, the court considers whether the defendants should be required to respond in damages under 42 U.S.C. § 1983.]

McCree, Circuit Judge.

. . . .

The record before us demonstrates that Miss Glasson, in displaying her placard which contained a constitutionally protected message, in a peaceful manner, from an appropriate place, was engaged in activity protected by the First Amendment and that the destruction of the sign by Louisville police officers Johnson and Medley deprived her of that right. She thus made out a prima facie case for damages under section 1983. This section of the Civil Rights Act provides, in relevant part:

Every person who, under color of any statute, regulation, custom or usage of any State . . . subjects, or causes to be subjected, any citizen of the United States . . . to the deprivation of any rights, privileges, or immunities secured by the Constitution and the laws shall be liable to the party injured in an action at law, suit in equity, or other proper proceeding for redress.

This statute imposes on the states and their agents certain obligations and responsibilities. A police officer has the duty not to ratify and effectuate a heckler's veto nor may he join a moiling mob intent on suppressing ideas. Instead, he must take reasonable action to protect from violence persons exercising their constitutional rights. E.g., *Sellers* v. *Johnson*, 163 F.2d 877 (8th Cir. 1947), *Cottonreader* v. *Johnson*, 252 F.Supp. 492 (M.D.Ala. 1966). And, in the absence of a speaker's exhortation to violence, in carefully defined circumstances, "state officials are not entitled to rely on community hostility as an excuse not to protect, by inaction or affirmative conduct, the exercise of fundamental rights." *Smith* v. *Ross*, 482 F.2d 33, 37 (6th Cir. 1973). Accord, *e.g.*, *Gregory* v. *Chicago*, 394 U.S. 111, 119 (1969) (BLACK, J., concurring) and cases cited therein.

. . . .

If this were a case requiring us to review a criminal conviction of Miss Glasson for displaying her sign or to review the denial of an injunction prohibiting appellees from engaging in activity like that challenged here (assuming that the other prerequisites for injunctive relief were satisfied), our inquiry would be ended. See, *e.g., Gregory v. Chicago, supra.* In this appeal, however, we review not a criminal conviction nor a denial of injunctive relief, but a civil action for damages based upon state deprivation of constitutional rights by means short of an arrest.

In determining the circumstances under which a police officer must respond in damages for the tortious interference with a person's right to express ideas, we do not write upon a blank slate. In *Pierson v. Ray*, 386 U.S. 547 (1967), the Supreme Court announced that reasonableness and good faith was an affirmative defense to an action brought under 42 U.S.C. § 1983. The Court recognized that police officers acting in good faith should be accorded an area of discretion when their actions are the subject of a suit for damages for unlawful or wrongful conduct ostensibly within the scope of their duties. And, when a police officer is accused of false arrest, "good faith and probable cause" affords a defense to a section 1983 action brought against him. *Id.* at 557, 87 S.Ct. 1213. See *also Scheuer v. Rhodes*, 416 U.S. 232 (1974).

This affirmative defense was re-cently reconsidered by the Supreme Court in *Wood v. Strickland*, 420 U.S. 308 (1975), an action brought by high school students who claimed that they had been suspended from school in violation of their constitutional rights and sought appropriate damages. In its discussion of the affirmative defense available to the school board members who had ordered the suspension, the Court stated:

The official must himself be acting sincerely and with a belief that he is doing right but *an act violating a student's constitutional rights can be no more justified by ignorance or disregard of settled, indisputable law* on the part of one entrusted with supervision of students' daily lives than by the presence of actual malice. To be entitled to a special exemption from the categorical remedial language of § 1983 in a case in which his action violated a student's constitutional rights, a school board member, who has voluntarily undertaken the task of supervising the operation of the school and the activities of the students, must be held to *a standard of conduct based not only on permissible intentions, but also on knowledge of the basic, unquestioned constitutional rights of his charges.* Such a standard neither imposes an unfair burden upon a person assuming a responsible public office requiring a high degree of intelligence and judgment for the proper fulfillment of its duties, nor an unwarranted burden in light of the value which civil rights have in our legal system. Any lesser standard would deny much of the promise of § 1983. Therefore, in the specific context of school discipline, we hold that a school board member is not immune from liability for damages under § 1983 if he knew or reasonably should have known that the action he took within his sphere of official responsibility would violate the constitutional rights of the student affected, or if he took the action with the malicious intention to cause a deprivation of constitutional rights or other injury to the student. (Emphasis supplied.) *Id.* at 321.

Although only *Pierson* specifically concerns the liability of police officers for invasion of constitutional rights, both *Scheuer* v. *Rhodes* and *Wood* v. *Strickland* are helpful in determining the conditions under which an affirmative defense of reasonableness and good faith has been established. From an examination of all three cases, we conclude that the factors to be considered in determining whether the defense has been established are whether the police officers knew or should have known that the complainant was engaged in the exercise of constitutionally protected activity, and if they knew (or should have known), whether they acted out of an honest and reasonable belief that their interference with the exercise of those rights was required to avoid imminent and serious injury to persons or property. Every asserted justification must be considered carefully on a case by case basis, and due regard must be given to the fact that the officers may be acting in the urgency of a street confrontation and not in the contemplative atmosphere of judicial chambers.

. . . .

Ideally, police officers will always protect to the extent of their ability the rights of persons to engage in First Amendment activity. Yet, the law does not expect or require them to defend the right of a speaker to address a hostile audience, however large and intemperate, when to do so would unreasonably subject them to violent retaliation and physical injury. In such circumstances, they may discharge their duty of preserving the peace by intercepting his message or by removing the speaker for his own protection without having to respond in damages. Accordingly, whether a police officer must respond in damages for his actions is judged by whether his conduct was reasonable, considering all the circumstances, and by whether he acted in good faith. A police officer's stated good faith belief in the necessity or wisdom of his action is not dispositive of that element of the defense, but must be supported by objective evidence. See, *e.g., Pierson* v. *Ray, supra; Monroe* v. *Pape*, 365 U.S. 167 (1961); *Scott* v. *Vandiver*, 476 F.2d 238 (4th Cir. 1973); *Rodriguez* v. *Jones*, 473 F.2d 599 (5th Cir. 1973); *Dowsey* v. *Wilkins*, 467 F.2d 1022 (5th Cir. 1972). To hold that a police officer is exonerated from liability if he merely acts in subjective good faith might foster ignorance of the law or, at least, encourage feigned ignorance of the law. This we are unwilling to do. The law does not expect police officers to be sophisticated constitutional or criminal lawyers, but because they are charged with the responsibility of enforcing the law, it is not unreasonable to expect them to have some knowledge of it. We cannot permit a police officer to avoid liability for damages by pleading ignorance of the law when he unreasonably or in bad faith oversteps the bounds of his authority and invades the constitutional rights of others. At the same time, courts should not "second guess" police officers who are often required to assess a potentially dangerous situation and respond to it without studied reflection. Thus, even though a police officer may not have chosen the wisest or most reasonable course of action, he will not be civilly liable if his conduct is based on a reasonable and good faith belief that it was necessary under the circumstances. See, *e.g.*, *Smith* v. *Ross*, 482 F.2d 33, 37 (6th Cir. 1973), where this court stated, in affirming the dismissal of a complaint in a section 1983 action after trial, "We do not condone the actions of the deputy, who would have served his office more honorably by unequivocally protecting appellants regardless of the local unpopularity his actions might have evoked."

In examining whether appellees

Johnson and Medley acted in good faith and whether their asserted belief that their actions were necessary to protect the President was reasonable under the circumstances, it is "our duty . . . to make an independent examination of the whole record." *Edwards* v. *South Carolina*, 372 U.S. at 235. There is no evidence that Miss Glasson's placard posed any threat to the safety of the President, to his motorcade, or to onlookers. If any danger to public order existed, it was posed by the persons who were offended by her message. Yet, these persons were located across the street from appellant, were only twenty-five to thirty in number, and never even stepped off the curb on their side of the street in the direction of Miss Glasson. In addition, there were approximately eight to twelve police officers on duty in close proximity to this moderately sized crowd and, although Johnson testified that he was not sure whether this force would have been adequate to maintain order, he also testified that reinforcements could have been obtained rapidly had that been necessary. Although Officers Medley and Johnson characterized the hecklers as "near to riot," at no time did they admonish the crowd, call for reinforcements, or even alert the Secret Service despite the claimed danger to the President. Moreover, the disturbance did not attract the attention of any other police officers stationed nearby. These circumstances, taken together, demonstrate that their asserted belief that the destruction of appellant's poster was necessary to presidential security and to public order was not reasonable.

Our examination of the record also convinces us that the destruction of appellant's poster was not done in good faith. The general order of the day was to destroy all posters "detrimental" or "injurious" to the President. When Officer Medley first noticed Miss Glasson's poster he determined that it was detrimental to the President, a judgment in which Officer Johnson concurred before ordering its destruction. When Officer Medley took the poster from Miss Glasson he informed her that the reason for his action was that the poster was "detrimental to the United States," not that she, the President, or any other person was endangered by it. Both officers testified that only posters favorable to the President were permissible. Moreover, Officer Johnson unequivocally testified that had this same crowd under the same circumstances been outraged by a poster favorable to the President he would not have ordered its destruction. Although he later qualified his answer, his testimony still demonstrates that a different standard would have been applied had the crowd been provoked by a poster favorable to the President. The actions of Officers Medley and Johnson were the result of an official determination not to permit dissent and of their failure to accord to appellant the right to engage in activity protected by the First Amendment. Also, they failed to recognize her right to be protected from criminal

assault and battery. They testified that they had no obligation to protect appellant, and that had any member of the crowd proceeded against her they would not have arrested the aggressor because in their judgment appellant's poster was "inflammatory." The actions and attitudes of appellees Medley and Johnson thus bespeak a callous disregard of Miss Glasson's right to express and to advocate peacefully her ideas and exhibit shocking disregard of her right to have her person and property protected by the state from violence at the hands of persons in disagreement with her ideas. Compare *Gregory* v. *Chicago, supra.*

Accordingly, we hold that these police officers are required to respond in damages under section 1983 of the Civil Rights Act because they suppressed appellant's peaceful communication of ideas protected by the First Amendment. When other persons became hostile because of disagreement with the content of her communication, the police officers were not authorized to suppress the offending speech. They may not defend against a section 1983 action on the ground that her message "could impede the progress of the motorcade and jeopardize the safety of the President, other members of the motorcade and the onlookers in the crowd," when they made no attempt to calm the crowd whose unruliness was limited to muttering threats unaccompanied by action; when they admit that they, either alone or with available reinforcements, could have handled a potential disturbance; when they did not contact the Secret Service or call for reinforcements; and when they admit that had the same crowd been provoked by a poster favorable to the President, they would not have destroyed it.

. . . .

We hold that the district court erred in entering a judgment for appellees in the section 1983 action on the grounds that Officers Johnson and Medley acted reasonably and in good faith in destroying appellant's poster. . . . Accordingly, we reverse and remand for further proceedings consistent with this opinion and for a determination of the damages Miss Glasson sustained. In so doing, we observe that appellant may recover not only for out-of-pocket expenses but also for emotional and mental distress. *Donovan* v. *Reinbold*, 433 F.2d 738 (9th Cir. 1970).

Reversed and remanded.

SCREWS v. UNITED STATES
325 U.S. 91, 89 L.Ed. 1495, 65 S.Ct. 1031 (1945)

MR. JUSTICE DOUGLAS announced the judgment of the Court and delivered the following opinion, in which the CHIEF JUSTICE, MR. JUSTICE BLACK and MR. JUSTICE REED concur.

This case involves a shocking and revolting episode in law enforcement. Petitioner Screws was sheriff of Baker County, Georgia. He enlisted the assistance of petitioner Jones, a policeman, and petitioner Kelley, a special deputy, in arresting Robert Hall, a citizen of the United States and of Georgia. The arrest was made late at night at Hall's home on a warrant charging Hall with theft of a tire. Hall, a young negro about thirty years of age, was handcuffed and taken by car to the court house. As Hall alighted from the car at the court house square, the three petitioners began beating him with their fists and with a solid-bar blackjack about eight inches long and weighing two pounds. They claimed Hall had reached for a gun and had used insulting language as he alighted from the car. But after Hall, still handcuffed, had been knocked to the ground they continued to beat him from fifteen to thirty minutes until he was unconscious. Hall was then dragged feet first through the court house yard into the jail and thrown upon the floor dying. An ambulance was called and Hall was removed to a hospital where he died within the hour and without regaining consciousness. There was evidence that Screws held a grudge against Hall and had threatened to "get" him.

An indictment was returned against petitioners—one count charging a violation of § 20 of the Criminal Code, 18 U.S.C. § 52,*

* This statute has been re-codified as 18 U.S.C. § 242

and another charging a conspiracy to violate § 20 contrary to § 37 of the Criminal Code, 18 U.S.C. § 88. Sec. 20 provides:

Whoever, under color of any law, statute, ordinance, regulation, or custom, willfully subjects, or causes to be subjected, any inhabitant of any State, Territory, or District to the deprivation of any rights, privileges, or immunities secured or protected by the Constitution and laws of the United States, or to different punishments, pains, or penalties, on account of such inhabitant being an alien, or by reason of his color, or race, than are prescribed for the punishment of citizens, shall be fined not more than $1,000, or imprisoned not more than one year, or both.

The indictment charged that petitioners, acting under color of the laws of Georgia, "willfully" caused Hall to be deprived of "rights, privileges, or immunities secured or protected" to him by the Fourteenth Amendment—the right not to be deprived of life without due process of law; the right to be tried, upon the charge on which he was arrested, by due process of law and if found guilty to be punished in accordance with the laws of Georgia; that is to say that petitioners "unlawfully and wrongfully did assault, strike and beat the said Robert Hall about the head with human fists and a blackjack causing injuries" to Hall "which were the proximate and immediate cause of his death." A

like charge was made in the conspiracy count.

The case was tried to a jury. The court charged the jury that due process of law gave one charged with a crime the right to be tried by a jury and sentenced by a court. On the question of intent it charged that

... if these defendants, without its being necessary to make the arrest effectual or necessary to their own personal protection, beat this man, assaulted him or killed him while he was under arrest, then they would be acting illegally under color of law, as stated by this statute, and would be depriving the prisoner of certain constitutional rights guaranteed to him by the Constitution of the United States and consented to by the State of Georgia.

The jury returned a verdict of guilty and a fine and imprisonment on each count was imposed. The Circuit Court of Appeals affirmed the judgment of conviction, one judge dissenting. 140 F.2d 662. The case is here on a petition for a writ of certiorari which we granted because of the importance in the administration of the criminal laws of the questions presented.

I.

We are met at the outset with the claim that § 20 is unconstitutional, in so far as it makes criminal acts in violation of the due process clause of the Fourteenth Amendment. . . .

It is said that the Act must be read as if it contained . . . broad and fluid definitions of due process and that if it is so read it provides no ascertainable standard of guilt. It is pointed out that in *United States* v. *Cohen Grocery Co.*, 255 U.S. 81, 89, an Act of Congress was struck down, the enforcement of which would have been "the exact equivalent of an effort to carry out a statute which in terms merely penalized and punished all acts detrimental to the public interest when unjust and unreasonable in the estimation of the court and jury." In that case the act declared criminal was the making of "any unjust or unreasonable rate or charge in handling or dealing in or with any necessaries." 255 U.S. at 86. The Act contained no definition of an "unjust or unreasonable rate" nor did it refer to any source where the measure of "unjust or unreasonable" could be ascertained. In the instant case the decisions of the courts are, to be sure, a source of reference for ascertaining the specific content of the concept of due process. But even so the Act would incorporate by reference a large body of changing and uncertain law. That law is not always reducible to specific rules, is expressible only in general terms, and turns many times on the facts of a particular case. Accordingly, it is argued that such a body of legal principles lacks the basic specificity necessary for criminal statutes under our system of government. Congress did not define what it desired to punish but referred the citizen to a comprehen-

sive law library in order to ascertain what acts were prohibited. To enforce such a statute would be like sanctioning the practice of Caligula who "published the law, but it was written in a very small hand, and posted up in a corner, so that no one could make a copy of it." Suetonius, LIVES OF THE TWELVE CAESARS, p. 278.

The serious character of that challenge to the constitutionality of the Act is emphasized if the customary standard of guilt for statutory crimes is taken. As we shall see, specific intent is at times required. Holmes, THE COMMON LAW, pp. 66 *et seq.* But the general rule was stated in *Ellis* v. *United States*, 206 U.S. 246, 257, as follows: "If a man intentionally adopts certain conduct in certain circumstances known to him, and that conduct is forbidden by the law under those circumstances, he intentionally breaks the law in the only sense in which the law ever considers intent." And see *Horning* v. *District of Columbia*, 254 U.S. 135, 137; *Nash* v. *United States*, 229 U.S. 373, 377. Under that test a local law enforcement officer violates § 20 and commits a federal offense for which he can be sent to the penitentiary if he does an act which some court later holds deprives a person of due process of law. And he is a criminal though his motive was pure and though his purpose was unrelated to the disregard of any constitutional guarantee. The treacherous ground on which state officials—police, prosecutors, legislators, and judges —would walk is indicated by the character and closeness of decisions of this Court interpreting the due process clause of the Fourteenth Amendment. A confession obtained by too long questioning (*Ashcraft* v. *Tennessee*, 322 U.S. 143); the enforcement of an ordinance requiring a license for the distribution of religious literature (*Murdock* v. *Pennsylvania*, 319 U.S. 105); the denial of the assistance of counsel in certain types of cases (Cf. *Powell* v. *Alabama*, 287 U.S. 45 with *Betts* v. *Brady*, supra); the enforcement of certain types of anti-picketing statutes (*Thornhill* v. *Alabama*, 310 U.S. 88); the enforcement of state price control laws (*Olsen* v. *Nebraska*, 313 U.S. 236); the requirement that public school children salute the flag (*Board of Education* v. *Barnette*, 319 U.S. 624)—these are illustrative of the kind of state action which might or might not be caught in the broad reaches of § 20 dependent on the prevailing view of the Court as constituted when the case arose. Those who enforced local law today might not know for many months (and meanwhile could not find out) whether what they did deprived some one of due process of law. The enforcement of a criminal statute so construed would indeed cast law enforcement agencies loose at their own risk on a vast uncharted sea.

. . . .

We hesitate to say that when Congress sought to enforce the Fourteenth Amendment in this fashion it did a vain thing. We hesitate to conclude that for 80 years this effort of Congress, renewed several times, to protect the important rights of the individual guaranteed by the Fourteenth Amendment has been an idle gesture. Yet if the Act falls by reason of vagueness so far as due process of law is concerned, there would seem to be a similar lack of specificity when the privileges and immunities clause (*Madden* v. *Kentucky*, 309 U.S. 83) and the equal protection clause (*Smith* v. *Texas*, 311 U.S. 128; *Hill* v. *Texas*, 316 U.S. 400) of the Fourteenth Amendment are involved. Only if no construction can save the Act from this claim of unconstitutionality are we willing to reach that result. We do not reach it, for we are of the view that if § 20 is confined more narrowly than the lower courts confined it, it can be preserved as one of the sanctions to the great rights which the Fourteenth Amendment was designed to secure.

II.

. . . .

[I]f we construe "willfully" in § 20 as connoting a purpose to deprive a person of a specific constitutional right, we would introduce no innovation. The Court, indeed, has recognized that the requirement of a specific intent to do a prohibited act may avoid those consequences to the accused which may otherwise render a vague or indefinite statute invalid. The constitutional vice in such a statute is the essential injustice to the accused of placing him on trial for an offense, the nature of which the statute does not define and hence of which it gives no warning. . . .

. . . .

[A] requirement of a specific intent to deprive a person of a federal right made definite by decision or other rule of law saves the Act from any charge of unconstitutionality on the grounds of vagueness.

Once the section is given that construction, we think that the claim that the section lacks an ascertainable standard of guilt must fail. The constitutional requirement that a criminal statute be definite serves a high function. It gives a person acting with reference to the statute fair warning that his conduct is within its prohibition. This requirement is met when a statute prohibits only "willful" acts in the sense we have explained. One who does act with such specific intent is aware that what he does is precisely that which the statute forbids. He is under no necessity of guessing whether the statute applies to him (see *Connally* v. *General Construction Co.*, 269 U.S. 385) for he either knows or acts in reckless disregard of its prohibition of the deprivation of a defined constitutional or other federal right. See *Gorin* v. *United States*, 312 U.S. 19, 27, 28. Nor is such an act beyond the understanding and comprehension of juries summoned to pass on them. The Act would then not become a trap for law enforcement agencies acting in good faith.

"A mind intent upon willful evasion is inconsistent with surprised innocence." *United States* v. *Ragen, supra*, 314 U.S. at 524.

It is said, however, that this construction of the Act will not save it from the infirmity of vagueness since neither a law enforcement official nor a trial judge can know with sufficient definiteness the range of rights that are constitutional. But that criticism is wide of the mark. For the specific intent required by the Act is an intent to deprive a person of a right which has been made specific either by the express terms of the Constitution or laws of the United States or by decisions interpreting them. Take the case of a local officer who persists in enforcing a type of ordinance which the Court has held invalid as violative of the guarantee of free speech or freedom of worship. Or a local official continues to select juries in a manner which flies in the teeth of decisions of the Court. If those acts are done willfully, how can the officer possibly claim that he had no fair warning that his acts were prohibited by the statute? He violates the statute not merely because he has a bad purpose but because he acts in defiance of announced rules of law. He who defies a decision interpreting the Constitution knows precisely what he is doing. If sane, he hardly may be heard to say that he knew not what he did. Of course, willful conduct cannot make definite that which is undefined. But willful violators of constitutional requirements, which have been defined, certainly are in no position to say that they had no adequate advance notice that they would be visited with punishment. When they act willfully in the sense in which we use the word, they act in open defiance or in reckless disregard of a constitutional requirement which has been made specific and definite. When they are convicted for so acting, they are not punished for violating an unknowable something.

The Act so construed has a narrower range in all its applications than if it were interpreted in the manner urged by the government. But the only other alternative, if we are to avoid grave constitutional questions, is to construe it as applicable only to those acts which are clearly marked by the specific provisions of the Constitution as deprivations of constitutional rights, privileges, or immunities, and which are knowingly done within the rule of *Ellis* v. *United States, supra.* But as we have said, that course would mean that all protection for violations of due process of law would drop out of the Act. We take the course which makes it possible to preserve the entire Act and save all parts of it from constitutional challenge. If Congress desires to give the Act wider scope, it may find ways of doing so. Moreover, here as in *Apex Hosiery Co.* v. *Leader,* 310 U.S. 469, we are dealing with a situation where the interpretation of the Act which we adopt does not preclude any state from punishing any act made criminal by its own laws. Indeed, the narrow

construction which we have adopted more nearly preserves the traditional balance between the States and the national government in law enforcement than that which is urged upon us.

United States v. *Classic, supra,* met the test we suggest. In that case we were dealing merely with the validity of an indictment, not with instructions to the jury. The indictment was sufficient since it charged a willful failure and refusal of the defendant election officials to count the votes cast, by their alteration of the ballots and by their false certification of the number of votes cast for the respective candidates. 313 U.S. at 308, 309. The right so to vote is guaranteed by art. I, § 2 and § 4 of the Constitution. Such a charge is adequate since he who alters ballots or without legal justification destroys them would be acting willfully in the sense in which § 20 uses the term. The fact that the defendants may not have been thinking in constitutional terms is not material where their aim was not to enforce local law but to deprive a citizen of a right and that right was protected by the Constitution. When they so act they at least act in reckless disregard of constitutional prohibitions or guarantees. Likewise, it is plain that basic to the concept of due process of law in a criminal case is a trial—a trial in a court of law, not a "trial by ordeal." *Brown* v. *Mississippi,* 297 U.S. 278, 285. It could hardly be doubted that they who "under color of any law, statute, ordinance, regulation, or custom" act with that evil motive violate § 20. Those who decide to take the law into their own hands and act as prosecutor, jury, judge, and executioner plainly act to deprive a prisoner of the trial which due process of law guarantees him. And such a purpose need not be expressed; it may at times be reasonably inferred from all the circumstances attendant on the act. See *Tot v. United States*, 319 U.S. 463.

The difficulty here is that this question of intent was not submitted to the jury with the proper instructions. . . .

. . . .

Since there must be a new trial, the judgment below is reversed.

Reversed.

[The concurring opinion of MR. JUSTICE RUTLEDGE, the dissenting opinions of MR. JUSTICE MURPHY and of MR. JUSTICE ROBERTS, joined by MR. JUSTICE FRANKFURTER and MR. JUSTICE JACKSON, have been omitted.]

PART III: APPENDIX

THE CONSTITUTION OF THE UNITED STATES OF AMERICA

WE THE PEOPLE of the United States, in Order to form a more perfect Union, establish Justice, insure domestic Tranquility, provide for the common defence, promote the general Welfare, and secure the Blessings of Liberty to ourselves and our Posterity, do ordain and establish this CONSTITUTION for the United States of America.

ARTICLE I.

SECTION 1. All legislative Powers herein granted shall be vested in a Congress of the United States, which shall consist of a Senate and House of Representatives.

SECTION 2. The House of Representatives shall be composed of Members chosen every second Year by the People of the several States, and the Electors in each State shall have the Qualifications requisite for Electors of the most numerous Branch of the State Legislature.

No Person shall be a Representative who shall not have attained to the Age of twenty-five Years, and been seven Years a Citizen of the United States, and who shall not, when elected, be an Inhabitant of that State in which he shall be chosen.

[1] Representatives and direct Taxes shall be apportioned among the several States which may be included within this Union, according to their respective Numbers, which shall be determined by adding to the whole Number of free Persons, including those bound to Service for a Term of Years, and excluding Indians not taxed, three fifths of all other Persons. The actual Enumeration shall be made within three Years after the first Meeting of the Congress of the United States, and within every subsequent Term of ten Years, in such Manner as they shall by Law direct. The Number of Rep-

---

[1] This clause has been affected by the Fourteenth and Sixteenth Amendments.

resentatives shall not exceed one for every thirty Thousand, but each State shall have at Least one Representative; and until such enumeration shall be made, the State of New Hampshire shall be entitled to chuse three, Massachusetts eight, Rhode-Island and Providence Plantations one, Connecticut five, New-York six, New Jersey four, Pennsylvania eight, Delaware one, Maryland six, Virginia ten, North Carolina five, South Carolina five, and Georgia three.

When vacancies happen in the Representation from any State, the Executive Authority thereof shall issue Writs of Election to fill such Vacancies.

The House of Representatives shall chuse their Speaker and other Officers; and shall have the sole Power of Impeachment.

[2] SECTION 3. The Senate of the United States shall be composed of two Senators from each State, chosen by the Legislature thereof for six Years; and each Senator shall have one Vote.

Immediately after they shall be assembled in Consequence of the first Election, they shall be divided as equally as may be into three Classes. The Seats of the Senators of the first Class shall be vacated at the Expiration of the second Year, of the second Class at the Expiration of the fourth Year, and of the third Class at the Expiration of the sixth Year, so that one third may be chosen every second Year; and if Vacancies happen by Resignation, or otherwise, during the Recess of the Legislature of any State, the Executive thereof may make temporary Appointments until the next Meeting of the Legislature, which shall then fill such Vacancies.

No Person shall be a Senator who shall not have attained to the Age of thirty Years, and been nine Years a Citizen of the United States, and who shall not, when elected, be an Inhabitant of that State for which he shall be chosen.

The Vice President of the United States shall be President of the Senate, but shall have no Vote, unless they be equally divided.

The Senate shall chuse their other Officers, and also a

[2] This section has been affected by the Seventeenth Amendment.

President pro tempore, in the absence of the Vice President, or when he shall exercise the Office of President of the United States.

The Senate shall have the sole Power to try all Impeachments. When sitting for that Purpose, they shall be on Oath or Affirmation. When the President of the United States is tried, the Chief Justice shall preside: And no Person shall be convicted without the Concurrence of two thirds of the Members present.

Judgment in Cases of Impeachment shall not extend further than to removal from Office, and disqualification to hold and enjoy any Office of honor, Trust or Profit under the United States: but the Party convicted shall nevertheless be liable and subject to Indictment, Trial, Judgment and Punishment, according to Law.

[3] SECTION 4. The Times, Places and Manner of holding Elections for Senators and Representatives, shall be prescribed in each State by the Legislature thereof; but the Congress may at any time by Law make or alter such Regulations, except as to the Place of chusing Senators.

The Congress shall assemble at least once in every Year, and such Meeting shall be on the first Monday in December, unless they shall by Law appoint a different Day.

SECTION 5. Each House shall be the Judge of the Elections, Returns and Qualifications of its own Members, and a Majority of each shall constitute a Quorum to do Business; but a smaller Number may adjourn from day to day, and may be authorized to compel the Attendance of absent Members, in such Manner, and under such Penalties as each House may provide.

Each House may determine the Rules of its Proceedings, punish its Members for disorderly Behaviour, and, with the Concurrence of two thirds, expel a Member.

Each House shall keep a Journal of its Proceedings, and from time to time publish the same, excepting such Parts as may in their Judgment require Secrecy; and the Yeas and Nays

[3] This section has been affected by the Twentieth Amendment.

of the Members of either House on any question shall, at the Desire of one fifth of those Present, be entered on the Journal.

Neither House, during the Session of Congress, shall, without the Consent of the other, adjourn for more than three days, nor to any other Place than that in which the two Houses shall be sitting.

SECTION 6. The Senators and Representatives shall receive a Compensation for their Services, to be ascertained by Law, and paid out of the Treasury of the United States. They shall in all Cases, except Treason, Felony and Breach of the Peace, be privileged from Arrest during their Attendance at the Session of their respective Houses, and in going to and returning from the same; and for any Speech or Debate in either House, they shall not be questioned in any other Place.

No Senator or Representative shall, during the Time for which he was elected, be appointed to any civil Office under the Authority of the United States, which shall have been created, or the Emoluments whereof shall have been encreased during such time; and no Person holding any Office under the United States, shall be a Member of either House during his Continuance in Office.

SECTION 7. All Bills for raising Revenue shall originate in the House of Representatives; but the Senate may propose or concur with Amendments as on other Bills.

Every Bill which shall have passed the House of Representatives and the Senate, shall, before it become a Law, be presented to the President of the United States; If he approve he shall sign it, but if not he shall return it, with his Objections to that House in which it shall have originated, who shall enter the Objections at large on their Journal, and proceed to reconsider it. If after such Reconsideration two thirds of that House shall agree to pass the Bill, it shall be sent, together with the Objections, to the other House, by which it shall likewise be reconsidered, and if approved by two thirds of that House, it shall become a Law. But in all such Cases the Votes of both Houses shall be determined by Yeas and Nays, and the Names of the Persons voting for and against the Bill shall be entered on the Journal of each House respectively. If any

Bill shall not be returned by the President within ten Days (Sundays excepted) after it shall have been presented to him, the Same shall be a Law, in like Manner as if he had signed it, unless the Congress by their Adjournment prevent its Return, in which Case it shall not be a Law.

Every Order, Resolution, or Vote to which the Concurrence of the Senate and House of Representatives may be necessary (except on a question of Adjournment) shall be presented to the President of the United States; and before the Same shall take Effect, shall be approved by him, or being disapproved by him, shall be repassed by two thirds of the Senate and House of Representatives, according to the Rules and Limitations prescribed in the Case of a Bill.

SECTION 8. The Congress shall have Power To lay and collect Taxes, Duties, Imposts and Excises, to pay the Debts and provide for the common Defence and general Welfare of the United States; but all Duties, Imposts and Excises shall be uniform throughout the United States;

To borrow Money on the credit of the United States;

To regulate Commerce with foreign Nations, and among the several States, and with the Indian Tribes;

To establish an uniform Rule of Naturalization, and uniform Laws on the subject of Bankruptcies throughout the United States;

To coin Money, regulate the Value thereof, and of foreign Coin, and fix the Standard of Weights and Measures;

To provide for the Punishment of counterfeiting the Securities and current Coin of the United States;

To establish Post Offices and post Roads;

To promote the Progress of Science and useful Arts, by securing for limited Times to Authors and Inventors the exclusive Right to their respective Writings and Discoveries;

To constitute Tribunals inferior to the supreme Court;

To define and punish Piracies and Felonies committed on the high Seas, and Offences against the Law of Nations;

To declare War, grant Letters of Marque and Reprisal, and make Rules concerning Captures on Land and Water;

To raise and support Armies, but no Appropriation of

Money to that Use shall be for a longer Term than two Years;

To provide and maintain a Navy;

To make Rules for the Government and Regulation of the land and naval Forces;

To provide for calling forth the Militia to execute the Laws of the Union, suppress Insurrections and repel Invasions;

To provide for organizing, arming, and disciplining the Militia, and for governing such Part of them as may be employed in the Service of the United States, reserving to the States respectively, the Appointment of the Officers, and the Authority of training the Militia according to the discipline prescribed by Congress;

To exercise exclusive Legislation in all Cases whatsoever, over such District (not exceeding ten Miles square) as may, by Cession of particular States, and the Acceptance of Congress, become the Seat of the Government of the United States, and to exercise like Authority over all Places purchased by the Consent of the Legislature of the State in which the Same shall be, for the Erection of Forts, Magazines, Arsenals, dock-Yards, and other needful Buildings;—And

To make all Laws which shall be necessary and proper for carrying into Execution the foregoing Powers, and all other Powers vested by this Constitution in the Government of the United States, or in any Department or Officer thereof.

SECTION 9. The Migration or Importation of such Persons as any of the States now existing shall think proper to admit, shall not be prohibited by the Congress prior to the Year one thousand eight hundred and eight, but a Tax or duty may be imposed on such Importation, not exceeding ten dollars for each Person.

The privilege of the Writ of Habeas Corpus shall not be suspended, unless when in Cases of Rebellion or Invasion the public Safety may require it.

No Bill of Attainder or ex post facto Law shall be passed.

[4] No Capitation, or other direct, Tax shall be laid, unless in Proportion to the Census or Enumeration herein before directed to be taken.

[4] This clause has been affected by the Sixteenth Amendment.

No Tax or Duty shall be laid on Articles exported from any State.

No Preference shall be given by any Regulation of Commerce or Revenue to the Ports of one State over those of another: nor shall Vessels bound to, or from, one State, be obliged to enter, clear, or pay Duties in another.

No Money shall be drawn from the Treasury, but in Consequence of Appropriations made by Law; and a regular Statement and Account of the Receipts and Expenditures of all public Money shall be published from time to time.

No Title of Nobility shall be granted by the United States: And no Person holding any Office of Profit or Trust under them, shall, without the Consent of the Congress, accept of any present, Emolument, Office, or Title, of any kind whatever, from any King, Prince, or foreign State.

SECTION 10. No State shall enter into any Treaty, Alliance, or Confederation; grant Letters of Marque and Reprisal; coin Money; emit Bills of Credit; make any Thing but gold and silver Coin a Tender in Payment of Debts; pass any Bill of Attainder, ex post facto Law, or Law impairing the Obligation of Contracts, or grant any Title of Nobility.

No State shall, without the Consent of the Congress, lay any Imposts or Duties on Imports or Exports, except what may be absolutely necessary for executing it's inspection Laws: and the net Produce of all Duties and Imposts, laid by any State on Imports or Exports, shall be for the Use of the Treasury of the United States; and all such Laws shall be subject to the Revision and Controul of the Congress.

No State shall, without the Consent of Congress, lay any Duty of Tonnage, keep Troops, or Ships of War in time of Peace, enter into any Agreement or Compact with another State, or with a foreign Power, or engage in War, unless actually invaded, or in such imminent Danger as will not admit of delay.

ARTICLE II.

SECTION 1. The executive Power shall be vested in a President of the United States of America. He shall hold his Office during the Term of four Years, and, together with the Vice President, chosen for the same Term, be elected, as follows

Each State shall appoint, in such Manner as the Legislature thereof may direct, a Number of Electors, equal to the whole Number of Senators and Representatives to which the State may be entitled in the Congress: but no Senator or Representative, or Person holding an Office of Trust or Profit under the United States, shall be appointed an Elector.

[5] The Electors shall meet in their respective States, and vote by Ballot for two persons, of whom one at least shall not be an Inhabitant of the same State with themselves. And they shall make a List of all the Persons voted for, and of the Number of Votes for each; which List they shall sign and certify, and transmit sealed to the Seat of the Government of the United States, directed to the President of the Senate. The President of the Senate shall, in the Presence of the Senate and House of Representatives, open all the Certificates, and the Votes shall then be counted. The Person having the greatest Number of Votes shall be the President, if such Number be a Majority of the whole Number of Electors appointed; and if there be more than one who have such Majority, and have an equal Number of Votes, then the House of Representatives shall immediately chuse by Ballot one of them for President; and if no Person have a Majority, then from the five highest on the List the said House shall in like Manner chuse the President. But in chusing the President, the Votes shall be taken by States, the Representation from each State having one Vote; A quorum for this Purpose shall consist of a Member or Members from two thirds of the States, and a Majority of all the States shall be necessary to a Choice. In every Case, after the Choice of the President, the Person having the greatest Number of Votes of the Electors shall be the Vice President. But if there should remain two or more who have equal Votes, the Senate shall chuse from them by Ballot the Vice President.

The Congress may determine the Time of chusing the

[5] This clause has been affected by the Twelfth Amendment.

Electors, and the Day on which they shall give their Votes; which Day shall be the same throughout the United States.

No person except a natural born Citizen, or a Citizen of the United States, at the time of the Adoption of this Constitution, shall be eligible to the Office of President; neither shall any Person be eligible to that Office who shall not have attained to the Age of thirty five Years, and been fourteen Years a Resident within the United States.

In Case of the Removal of the President from Office, or of his Death, Resignation, or Inability to discharge the Powers and Duties of the said Office, the same shall devolve on the Vice President, and the Congress may by Law provide for the Case of Removal, Death, Resignation or Inability, both of the President and Vice President, declaring what Officer shall then act as President, and such Officer shall act accordingly, until the Disability be removed, or a President shall be elected.

The President shall, at stated Times, receive for his Services, a Compensation, which shall neither be encreased nor diminished during the Period for which he shall have been elected, and he shall not receive within that Period any other Emolument from the United States, or any of them.

Before he enter on the Execution of his Office, he shall take the following Oath or Affirmation:—"I do solemnly swear (or affirm) that I will faithfully execute the Office of President of the United States, and will to the best of my Ability, preserve, protect and defend the Constitution of the United States."

SECTION 2. The President shall be Commander in Chief of the Army and Navy of the United States, and of the Militia of the several States, when called into the actual Service of the United States; he may require the Opinion in writing, of the principal Officer in each of the executive Departments, upon any subject relating to the Duties of their respective Offices, and he shall have Power to grant Reprieves and Pardons for Offenses against the United States, except in Cases of Impeachment.

He shall have Power, by and with the Advice and Consent of the Senate, to make Treaties, provided two thirds of the

Senators present concur; and he shall nominate, and by and with the Advice and Consent of the Senate, shall appoint Ambassadors, other public Ministers and Consuls, Judges of the supreme Court, and all other Officers of the United States, whose Appointments are not herein otherwise provided for, and which shall be established by Law: but the Congress may by Law vest the Appointment of such inferior Officers, as they think proper, in the President alone, in the Courts of Law, or in the Heads of Departments.

The President shall have Power to fill up all Vacancies that may happen during the Recess of the Senate, by granting Commissions which shall expire at the End of their next Session.

SECTION 3. He shall from time to time give to the Congress Information of the State of the Union, and recommend to their Consideration such Measures as he shall judge necessary and expedient; he may, on extraordinary Occasions, convene both Houses, or either of them, and in Case of Disagreement between them, with Respect to the Time of Adjournment, he may adjourn them to such Time as he shall think proper; he shall receive Ambassadors and other public Ministers; he shall take Care that the Laws be faithfully executed, and Shall Commission all the Officers of the United States.

SECTION 4. The President, Vice President and all civil Officers of the United States, shall be removed from Office on Impeachment for, and Conviction of, Treason, Bribery, or other high Crimes and Misdemeanors.

ARTICLE III.

SECTION 1. The judicial Power of the United States, shall be vested in one supreme Court, and in such inferior Courts as the Congress may from time to time ordain and establish. The Judges, both of the supreme and inferior Courts, shall hold their Offices during good Behaviour, and shall, at stated Times, receive for their Services, a Compensation, which shall not be diminished during their Continuance in Office.

[6] SECTION 2. The judicial Power shall extend to all Cases, in Law and Equity, arising under this Constitution, the Laws of the United States, and Treaties made, or which shall be made, under their Authority;—to all Cases affecting Ambassadors, other public Ministers and Consuls;—to all Cases of admiralty and maritime Jurisdiction;—to Controversies to which the United States shall be a Party;—to Controversies between two or more States;—between a State and Citizens of another State;—between citizens of different States;—between Citizens of the same State claiming Lands under Grants of different States, and between a State, or the Citizens thereof, and foreign States, Citizens or Subjects.

In all Cases affecting Ambassadors, other public Ministers and Consuls, and those in which a State shall be Party, the supreme Court shall have original Jurisdiction. In all the other Cases before mentioned, the supreme Court shall have appellate Jurisdiction, both as to Law and Fact, with such Exceptions, and under such Regulations as the Congress shall make.

The Trial of all Crimes, except in Cases of Impeachment, shall be by Jury; and such Trial shall be held in the State where the said Crimes shall have been committed; but when not committed within any State, the Trial shall be at such Place or Places as the Congress may by Law have directed.

SECTION 3. Treason against the United States, shall consist only in levying War against them, or in adhering to their Enemies, giving them Aid and Comfort. No Person shall be convicted of Treason unless on the Testimony of two Witnesses to the same overt Act, or on Confession in open Court.

The Congress shall have Power to declare the Punishment of Treason, but no Attainder of Treason shall work Corruption of Blood, or Forfeiture except during the Life of the Person attainted.

ARTICLE IV.

SECTION 1. Full Faith and Credit shall be given in each State to the public Acts, Records, and judicial Proceedings of every

[6] This section has been affected by the Eleventh Amendment.

other State. And the Congress may by general Laws prescribe the Manner in which such Acts, Records and Proceedings shall be proved, and the Effect thereof.

SECTION 2. The Citizens of each State shall be entitled to all Privileges and Immunities of Citizens in the several States.

A Person charged in any State with Treason, Felony, or other Crime, who shall flee from Justice, and be found in another State, shall on Demand of the executive Authority of the State from which he fled, be delivered up, to be removed to the State having Jurisdiction of the Crime.

[7] No Person held to Service or Labour in one State, under the Laws thereof, escaping into another, shall, in Consequence of any Law or Regulation therein, be discharged from such Service or Labour, but shall be delivered up on Claim of the Party to whom such Service or Labour may be due.

SECTION 3. New States may be admitted by the Congress into this Union; but no new State shall be formed or erected within the Jurisdiction of any other State; nor any State be formed by the Junction of two or more States, or parts of States, without the Consent of the Legislatures of the States concerned as well as of the Congress.

The Congress shall have Power to dispose of and make all needful Rules and Regulations respecting the Territory or other Property belonging to the United States; and nothing in this Constitution shall be so construed as to Prejudice any Claims of the United States, or of any particular State.

SECTION 4. The United States shall guarantee to every State in this Union a Republican Form of Government, and shall protect each of them against Invasion; and on Application of the Legislature, or of the Executive (when the Legislature cannot be convened) against domestic Violence.

ARTICLE V.

The Congress, whenever two thirds of both Houses shall deem it necessary, shall propose Amendments to this Constitution, or, on the Application of the Legislatures of two

[7] This clause was affected by the Thirteenth Amendment.

thirds of the several States, shall call a Convention for proposing Amendments, which, in either Case, shall be valid to all Intents and Purposes, as Part of this Constitution, when ratified by the Legislatures of three fourths of the several States, or by Conventions in three fourths thereof, as the one or the other Mode of Ratification may be proposed by the Congress; Provided that no Amendment which may be made prior to the Year One thousand eight hundred and eight shall in any Manner affect the first and fourth Clauses in the Ninth Section of the first Article; and that no State, without its Consent, shall be deprived of its equal Suffrage in the Senate.

ARTICLE VI.

All Debts contracted and Engagements entered into, before the Adoption of this Constitution, shall be as valid against the United States under this Constitution, as under the Confederation.

This Constitution, and the Laws of the United States which shall be made in Pursuance thereof; and all Treaties made, or which shall be made, under the Authority of the United States, shall be the supreme Law of the Land; and the Judges in every State shall be bound thereby; any Thing in the Constitution or Laws of any State to the Contrary notwithstanding.

The Senators and Representatives before mentioned, and the Members of the several State Legislatures, and all executive and judicial Officers, both of the United States and of the several States, shall be bound by Oath or Affirmation, to support this Constitution; but no religious Test shall ever be required as a Qualification to any Office or public Trust under the United States.

ARTICLE VII.

The Ratification of the Conventions of nine States shall be sufficient for the Establishment of this Constitution between the States so ratifying the Same.

DONE in Convention by the Unanimous Consent of the States present the Seventeenth Day of September in the Year of our Lord one thousand seven hundred and Eighty seven and of

the Independence of the United States of America the Twelfth.
IN WITNESS whereof We have hereunto subscribed our Names,

Go. WASHINGTON—*Presidt.*
and deputy from Virginia

New Hampshire

JOHN LANGDON   NICHOLAS GILMAN

Massachusetts

NATHANIEL GORHAM   RUFUS KING

Connecticut

WM. SAML. JOHNSON   ROGER SHERMAN

New York

ALEXANDER HAMILTON

New Jersey

WIL: LIVINGSTON   WM. PATERSON
DAVID BREARLEY   JONA: DAYTON

Pennsylvania

B. FRANKLIN   THOS. FITZSIMONS
THOMAS MIFFLIN   JARED INGERSOLL
ROBT. MORRIS   JAMES WILSON
GEO. CLYMER   GOUV MORRIS

Delaware

GEO: READ   RICHARD BASSETT
GUNNING BEDFORD jun   JACO: BROOM
JOHN DICKINSON

Maryland

JAMES McHENRY   DANL. CARROLL
DAN OF ST THOS JENIFER

Virginia

JOHN BLAIR   JAMES MADISON, JR.

North Carolina

WM. BLOUNT   HU WILLIAMSON
RICHD. DOBBS SPAIGHT

South Carolina

J. RUTLEDGE   CHARLES PINCKNEY
CHARLES COTESWORTH PINCKNEY   PIERCE BUTLER

Georgia

WILLIAM FEW   ABR BALDWIN

Attest   WILLIAM JACKSON
                                      Secretary

Articles in Addition To, and Amendment Of, the Constitution of the United States of America, Proposed by Congress, and Ratified by the Legislatures of the Several States, Pursuant to the Fifth Article of the Original Constitution.

AMENDMENT I. (1791)

Congress shall make no law respecting an establishment of religion, or prohibiting the free exercise thereof; or abridging the freedom of speech, or of the press; or the right of the people peaceably to assemble, and to petition the Government for a redress of grievances.

AMENDMENT II. (1791)

A well regulated Militia, being necessary to the security of a free State, the right of the people to keep and bear Arms, shall not be infringed.

AMENDMENT III. (1791)

No Soldier shall, in time of peace be quartered in any house, without the consent of the Owner, nor in time of war, but in a manner to be prescribed by law.

AMENDMENT IV. (1791)

The right of the people to be secure in their persons, houses, papers, and effects, against unreasonable searches and seizures, shall not be violated, and no Warrants shall issue, but upon probable cause, supported by Oath or affirmation, and particularly describing the place to be searched, and the persons or things to be seized.

AMENDMENT V. (1791)

No person shall be held to answer for a capital, or otherwise infamous crime, unless on a presentment or indictment of a Grand Jury, except in cases arising in the land or naval forces, or in the Militia, when in actual service in time of War or public danger; nor shall any person be subject for the same offence to be twice put in jeopardy of life or limb; nor shall be compelled in any criminal case to be a witness against himself, nor be deprived of life, liberty, or property, without due process of law; nor shall private property be taken for public use, without just compensation.

AMENDMENT VI. (1791)

In all criminal prosecutions, the accused shall enjoy the right to a speedy and public trial, by an impartial jury of the State and district wherein the crime shall have been committed, which district shall have been previously ascertained by law, and to be informed of the nature and cause of the accusation; to be confronted with the witnesses against him; to have compulsory process for obtaining Witnesses in his favor, and to have the Assistance of Counsel for his defence.

AMENDMENT VII. (1791)

In Suits at common law, where the value in controversy shall exceed twenty dollars, the right of trial by jury shall be preserved, and no fact tried by a jury, shall be otherwise reexamined in any Court of the United States, than according to the rules of the common law.

AMENDMENT VIII. (1791)

Excessive bail shall not be required, nor excessive fines imposed, nor cruel and unusual punishments inflicted.

AMENDMENT IX. (1791)

The enumeration of the Constitution, of certain rights, shall not be construed to deny or deparage others retained by the people.

AMENDMENT X. (1791)

The powers not delegated to the United States by the Constitution, nor prohibited by it to the States, are reserved to the States respectively, or to the people.

AMENDMENT XI. (1798)

The Judicial power of the United States shall not be construed to extend to any suit in law or equity, commenced or prosecuted against one of the United States by Citizens of another State, or by Citizens or Subjects of any Foreign State.

AMENDMENT XII.[8] (1804)

The Electors shall meet in their respective states and vote by ballot for President and Vice-President, one of whom, at least, shall not be an inhabitant of the same state with themselves; they shall name in their ballots the person voted for as President, and in distinct ballots the person voted for as Vice-President, and they shall make distinct lists of all persons voted for as President, and of all persons voted for as Vice-President, and of the number of votes for each, which lists they shall sign and certify, and transmit sealed to the seat of the government of the United States, directed to the President of the Senate;—The President of the Senate shall, in the presence of the Senate and House of Representatives, open all the certificates and the votes shall then be counted; —The person having the greatest number of votes for President, shall be the President, if such number be a majority of the whole number of Electors appointed; and if no person have such majority, then from the persons having the highest numbers not exceeding three on the list of those voted for as President, the House of Representatives shall choose immediately, by ballot, the President. But in choosing the President, the votes shall be taken by states, the representation from each state having one vote; a quorum for this purpose shall consist of a member or members from two-thirds of the states, and a majority of all the states shall be necessary to a choice.

[8] This amendment was affected by the Twentieth Amendment, section 3.

And if the House of Representatives shall not choose a President whenever the right of choice shall devolve upon them, before the fourth day of March next following, then the Vice-President shall act as President, as in the case of the death or other constitutional disability of the President. The person having the greatest number of votes as Vice-President, shall be the Vice-President, if such number be a majority of the whole number of Electors appointed, and if no person have a majority, then from the two highest numbers on the list, the Senate shall choose the Vice-President; a quorum for the purpose shall consist of two-thirds of the whole number of Senators, and a majority of the whole number shall be necessary to a choice. But no person constitutionally ineligible to the office of President shall be eligible to that of Vice-President of the United States.

AMENDMENT XIII. (1865)

SECTION 1. Neither slavery nor involuntary servitude, except as a punishment for crime whereof the party shall have been duly convicted, shall exist within the United States, or any place subject to their jurisdiction.

SECTION 2. Congress shall have power to enforce this article by appropriate legislation.

AMENDMENT XIV. (1868)

SECTION 1. All persons born or naturalized in the United States, and subject to the jurisdiction thereof, are citizens of the United States and of the State wherein they reside. No State shall make or enforce any law which shall abridge the privileges or immunities of citizens of the United States; nor shall any State deprive any person of life, liberty, or property, without due process of law; nor deny to any person within its jurisdiction the equal protection of the laws.

SECTION 2. Representatives shall be apportioned among the several States according to their respective numbers, counting the whole number of persons in each State, excluding Indians not taxed. But when the right to vote at any election for the choice of electors for President and Vice-President of the

United States, Representatives in Congress, the Executive and Judicial officers of a State, or the members of the Legislature thereof, is denied to any of the male inhabitants of such State, being twenty-one years of age, and citizens of the United States, or in any way abridged, except for participation in rebellion, or other crime, the basis of representation therein shall be reduced in the proportion which the number of such male citizens shall bear to the whole number of male citizens twenty-one years of age in such State.

SECTION 3. No person shall be a Senator or Representative in Congress, or elector of President and Vice-President, or hold any office, civil or military, under the United States, or under any State, who, having previously taken an oath, as a member of Congress, or as an officer of the United States, or as a member of any State legislature, or as an executive or judicial officer of any State, to support the Constitution of the United States, shall have engaged in insurrection or rebellion against the same, or given aid or comfort to the enemies thereof. But Congress may by a vote of two-thirds of each House, remove such disability.

SECTION 4. The validity of the public debt of the United States, authorized by law, including debts incurred for payment of pensions and bounties for services in suppressing insurrection or rebellion, shall not be questioned. But neither the United States nor any State shall assume or pay any debt or obligation incurred in aid of insurrection or rebellion against the United States, or any claim for the loss or emancipation of any slave; but all such debts, obligations and claims shall be held illegal and void.

SECTION 5. The Congress shall have power to enforce, by appropriate legislation, the provisions of this article.

AMENDMENT XV. (1870)

SECTION 1. The right of citizens of the United States to vote shall not be denied or abridged by the United States or by any State on account of race, color, or previous condition of servitude.

SECTION 2. The Congress shall have power to enforce this article by appropriate legislation.

AMENDMENT XVI. (1913)

The Congress shall have power to lay and collect taxes on incomes, from whatever source derived, without apportionment among the several States, and without regard to any census or enumeration.

AMENDMENT XVII. (1913)

The Senate of the United States shall be composed of two Senators from each State, elected by the people thereof, for six years; and each Senator shall have one vote. The electors in each State shall have the qualifications requisite for electors of the most numerous branch of the State legislatures.

When vacancies happen in the representation of any State in the Senate, the executive authority of such State shall issue writs of election to fill such vacancies: *Provided*, That the legislature of any State may empower the executive thereof to make temporary appointments until the people fill the vacancies by election as the legislature may direct.

This amendment shall not be so construed as to affect the election or term of any Senator chosen before it becomes valid as part of the Constitution.

AMENDMENT XVIII.[9] (1919)

SECTION 1. After one year from the ratification of this article the manufacture, sale, or transportation of intoxicating liquors within, the importation thereof into, or the exportation thereof from the United States and all territory subject to the jurisdiction thereof for beverage purposes is hereby prohibited.

SECTION 2. The Congress and the several States shall have concurrent power to enforce this article by appropriate legislation.

SECTION 3. This article shall be inoperative unless it shall have been ratified as an amendment to the Constitution by the legislatures of the several States, as provided in the Constitution, within seven years from the date of the submission hereof to the States by the Congress.

[9] Repealed. See the Twenty-first Amendment.

AMENDMENT XIX. (1920)

The right of citizens of the United States to vote shall not be denied or abridged by the United States or by any State on account of sex.

Congress shall have power to enforce this article by appropriate legislation.

AMENDMENT XX. (1933)

SECTION 1. The terms of the President and Vice President shall end at noon on the 20th day of January, and the terms of Senators and Representatives at noon on the 3d day of January, of the years in which such terms would have ended if this article had not been ratified; and the terms of their successors shall then begin.

SECTION 2. The Congress shall assemble at least once in every year, and such meeting shall begin at noon on the 3d day of January, unless they shall by law appoint a different day.

SECTION 3. If, at the time fixed for the beginning of the term of the President, the President elect shall have died, the Vice President elect shall become President. If a President shall not have been chosen before the time fixed for the beginning of his term, or if the President elect shall have failed to qualify, then the Vice President elect shall act as President until a President shall have qualified; and the Congress may by law provide for the case wherein neither a President elect nor a Vice President elect shall have qualified, declaring who shall then act as President, or the manner in which one who is to act shall be selected, and such person shall act accordingly until a President or Vice President shall have qualified.

SECTION 4. The Congress may by law provide for the case of the death of any of the persons from whom the House of Representatives may choose a President whenever the right of choice shall have devolved upon them, and for the case of the death of any of the persons from whom the Senate may choose a Vice President whenever the right of choice shall have devolved upon them.

SECTION 5. Sections 1 and 2 shall take effect on the 15th day of October following the ratification of this article.

SECTION 6. This article shall be inoperative unless it shall have been ratified as an amendment to the Constitution by the legislatures of three-fourths of the several States within seven years from the date of its submission.

AMENDMENT XXI. (1933)

SECTION 1. The eighteenth article of amendment to the Constitution of the United States is hereby repealed.

SECTION 2. The transportation or importation into any State, Territory, or possession of the United States for delivery or use therein of intoxicating liquors, in violation of the laws thereof, is hereby prohibited.

SECTION 3. This article shall be inoperative unless it shall have been ratified as an amendment to the Constitution by conventions in the several States, as provided in the Constitution, within seven years from the date of the submission hereof to the States by the Congress.

AMENDMENT XXII. (1951)

SECTION 1. No person shall be elected to the office of the President more than twice, and no person who has held the office of President, or acted as President, for more than two years of a term to which some other person was elected President shall be elected to the office of the President more than once. But this Article shall not apply to any person holding the office of President when this Article was proposed by the Congress, and shall not prevent any person who may be holding the office of President, or acting as President, during the term within which this Article becomes operative from holding the office of President or acting as President during the remainder of such term.

SECTION 2. This article shall be inoperative unless it shall have been ratified as an amendment to the Constitution by the legislatures of three-fourths of the several States within seven years from the date of its submission to the States by the Congress.

AMENDMENT XXIII. (1961)

SECTION 1. The District constituting the seat of Government of the United States shall appoint in such manner as the Congress may direct:

A number of electors of President and Vice President equal to the whole number of Senators and Representatives in Congress to which the District would be entitled if it were a State, but in no event more than the least populous State; they shall be in addition to those appointed by the States, but they shall be considered, for the purposes of the election of President and Vice President, to be electors appointed by a State; and they shall meet in the District and perform such duties as provided by the twelfth article of amendment.

SECTION 2. The Congress shall have power to enforce this article by appropriate legislation.

AMENDMENT XXIV. (1964)

SECTION 1. The right of citizens of the United States to vote in any primary or other election for President or Vice President, for electors for President or Vice President, or for Senator or Representative in Congress, shall not be denied or abridged by the United States or any State by reason of failure to pay any poll tax or other tax.

SECTION 2. The Congress shall have power to enforce this article by appropriate legislation.

AMENDMENT XXV. (1967)

SECTION 1. In case of the removal of the President from office or of his death or resignation, the Vice President shall become President.

SECTION 2. Whenever there is a vacancy in the office of the Vice President, the President shall nominate a Vice President who shall take office upon confirmation by a majority vote of both Houses of Congress.

SECTION 3. Whenever the President transmits to the President pro tempore of the Senate and the Speaker of the House of Representatives his written declaration that he is unable to discharge the powers and duties of his office, and until he transmits to them a written declaration to the contrary, such powers and duties shall be discharged by the Vice President as Acting President.

SECTION 4. Whenever the Vice President and a majority of either the principal officers of the executive departments or of such other body as Congress may by law provide, transmit to the President pro tempore of the Senate and the Speaker of the House of Representatives their written declaration that the President is unable to discharge the powers and duties of his office, the Vice President shall immediately assume the powers and duties of the office as Acting President.

Thereafter, when the President transmits to the President pro tempore of the Senate and the Speaker of the House of Representatives his written declaration that no inability exists, he shall resume the powers and duties of his office unless the Vice President and a majority of either the principal officers of the executive department or of such other body as Congress may by law provide, transmit within four days to the President pro tempore of the Senate and the Speaker of the House of Representatives their written declaration that the President is unable to discharge the powers and duties of his office. Thereupon Congress shall decide the issue, assembling within forty-eight hours for that purpose if not in session. If the Congress, within twenty-one days after receipt of the latter written declaration, or, if Congress is not in session, within twenty-one days after Congress is required to assemble, determines by two-thirds vote of both Houses that the President is unable to discharge the powers and duties of his office, the Vice President shall continue to discharge the same as Acting President; otherwise, the President shall resume the powers and duties of his office.

AMENDMENT XXVI. (1971)

SECTION 1. The right of citizens of the United States, who are eighteen years of age or older, to vote shall not be denied or abridged by the United States or by any State on account of age.

SECTION 2. The Congress shall have power to enforce this article by appropriate legislation.

TABLE OF CASES

This listing includes all cases cited in the textual material in Part I. Those cases which appear in **bold face type** are also reprinted in Part II. For those select cases, see the Table of Cases for Part II which appears on p. 571.

INDEX

References are to section numbers and subheadings.

CARROLL-CHAMBERS DOCTRINE, 4.10

CITATION
Arrest, as alternative, 3.12

CIVIL RIGHTS, 11.1 *et seq.*
Civil remedies for violation of, 11.5 *et seq.*
Criminal remedies for violation of federal, 11.10–11.12
Federal, deprivation of, 11.7
Integration, racial, 11.4
  (*See also, same heading, this index*)
Legislation, 11.1 *et seq.*
  (*See also Civil Rights Legislation*)
Separate but equal doctrine, 11.3
Violation of, 11.5 *et seq.*
  Conspiracy, 11.11
  Intent, willful, 11.10(1)
  Liability for—
    Federal agents, 11.6(2)
    Government and supervisors, 11.6(4)
    Police, 11.6(1)
    Private citizens, 11.6(3), 11.11, 11.12
  Public function theory, 11.6(3)(b)
  State concert theory, 11.6(3)(a)

CIVIL RIGHTS LEGISLATION
Act of 1866, 11.2
Act of 1870, 11.2, 11.11
Act of 1964, Equal Employment Opportunities Law, 11.4
Act of 1964, Public Accommodations Law, 11.4
Fair Housing Law, 11.4
Ku Klux Klan Act (42 USC §1983), 11.2 *et seq.*

CLEAR AND PRESENT DANGER DOCTRINE, 2.5

COLLATERAL ESTOPPEL, 9.11

COMMERCE CLAUSE, 1.8(a)(c)

COMMERCIAL SPEECH, 2.4

CONFESSIONS, 6.1 *et seq.*
(*See also Interrogations*)
Co-defendants, statements of, 6.6
Corroboration, 6.6
Delay in arraignment rule, 6.3
Due process of law, improperly obtained confession as violative of, 6.2(3)(d)
Evidence derived from, invalid, 6.7
Exclusion of, 6.5

EAVESDROPPING—*Continued*
History of, 5.8
National Commission for Review, 5.25
State legislation, 5.10
Warrantless listening, 5.24

ELECTRONIC LISTENING DEVICES
Bumper beepers, 5.24(4)
Concealed use by informers, 5.11
Confiscation of, 5.15
Pen registers, 5.24(2)
Public radio frequencies, 5.24(3)
Regulated by legislation, 5.14

ELECTRONIC SURVEILLANCE, 5.1 *et seq.*
(See also Eavesdropping, Wiretapping)

ENTRY
Warrant, without, 3.11

EQUAL OPPORTUNITIES LAW, 11.4

ESCOBEDO, 8.9

EVIDENCE
Arrest based on, 3.9(3)(e)
Confession, invalid, evidence derived from, 6.7
Disclosure of—
    Materiality, 10.15(4)
    Prosecutor's obligation, 10.15
    Request for, 10.15(3)
Electronic surveillance—
    Authorization for disclosure, 5.19
    Exclusion of, 5.17
    Pre-use notice to parties involved, 5.20(7)
    Recording of communication, 5.20(6)
    Use of derivative, 5.19
Exclusionary Rule, 4.3
    Adoption of, by federal courts, 4.4
    Extension to all courts, 4.5
    Modification of, 4.6
Mere Evidence Rule, 4.7(2)(b)
Wiretap, exclusion of—
    In federal courts, 5.6
    In state courts, 5.7

FAIR AND IMPARTIAL TRIAL *(See Trial)*

FAIR HOUSING LAW, 11.4